Asian / American

Historical Crossings of a Racial Frontier

Asian /

American

Historical Crossings of a Racial Frontier

David Palumbo-Liu

Stanford University Press / Stanford, California 1999

Stanford University Press

Stanford, California

© 1999 by the Board of Trustees of the

Leland Stanford Junior University

Printed in the United States of America

CIP data appear at the end of the book

Acknowledgments

A BOOK SO LONG IN THE MAKING owes much to many. I benefited from discussions with Homi K. Bhabha, King-kok Cheung, Eileen Chow, Chris Connery, Regenia Gagnier, Henry Giroux, Estella Habal, Marilyn Ivy, Abdul JanMohamed, Elaine Kim, Mary Louise Pratt, Vince Rafael, Rosane Rocher, Steve Sumida, E. San Juan, Jr., Naomi Schor, and Ronald Takaki. Several friends and colleagues offered cogent and careful readings of various chapters and made invaluable suggestions that have enriched the book considerably: Tani Barlow, Scott Bukatman, Arif Dirlik, Lisa Lowe, Colleen Lye, Michael Omi, Aihwa Ong, Saskia Sassen, Priscilla Wald, Rob Wilson, and Sau-ling Wong.

Moral and intellectual support from the Asian American Studies group at Stanford has often kept me going: I thank Rudy Busto, Gordon Chang, Akhil Gupta, Bill Ong Hing, Purnima Mankekar, and Sylvia Yanagisako, as well as Rick Yuen and Cindy Ng, and my colleagues in the Program in Comparative Studies in Race and Ethnicity, especially Al Camarillo and Ramón Saldívar. The research assistance provided by Davina Chen, Eileen Chow, Sheba Hosley, Edna Tow, and sponsored by the Center for East Asian Studies, deserves special acknowledgment—I would still be writing this book were it not for their indispensable assistance. I am also grateful to the Center for grant support and to the Stanford Humanities Center for a year's stay and the fellowship of my colleagues there. I also wish to thank Helen Tartar, my editor at the Press, for guiding this project into print; Pamela Holway and Stacey Lynn for bringing a bulky manuscript through production; and Ann Klefstad for her meticulous copyediting.

I dedicate this book to those without whom this study could never even have been begun, much less been written: I am profoundly grateful to L. Ling-chi

Wang for bringing me into the field at Berkeley more years (indeed, now decades) ago than either of us would want to admit, and for continuing to be a model, mentor, and inspiration; to Sau-ling C. Wong, for being an exemplary reader, critic, colleague, friend, and moral compass; to Sucheng Chan, for her personal support and for her unending sacrifices for and commitment to a field she helped inaugurate; to all those colleagues, students, staff, and community members who have tirelessly worked to further the cause of Asian American studies despite unending frustration; and, finally, to Sylvie and Fabrice for weathering many of these storms with me. It is in the hope that this book might be a guidepost to a historical formation that deeply shaped his father's life that I write it for my son.

D. P.-L.

Contents

Figures

Asian / American

Historical Crossings of a Racial Frontier

Introduction

As soon as possible he [the white man] will tell me that it is not enough to try to be white, but that a white totality must be achieved. —FRANTZ FANON, *Black Skin, White Masks*

LIKE THE WHITE TOTALITY OF which Fanon speaks, the persistent deferral of the status of "American" to "hyphenated" Americans (a group whose membership has changed through the years, but whose most conspicuous and constant members to this date have been those differentiated by race) begs the question of the precise constitution of the totality presumed to inhere beneath the signifier "American." In this study, I argue that the proximity of Asian Americans to that ideal should be read as a history of persistent reconfigurations and transgressions of the Asian/American "split," designated here by a solidus that signals those instances in which a liaison between "Asian" and "American," a *sliding over* between two seemingly separate terms, is constituted. As in the construction "and/or," where the solidus at once instantiates a choice between two terms, their simultaneous and equal status, and an element of indecidability, that is, as it at once implies both exclusion and inclusion, "Asian/American" marks *both* the distinction installed between "Asian" and "American" *and* a dynamic, unsettled, and inclusive movement.

This dynamic motion could not be possible without recognizing the unsettledness as well of "America." Similar to my construction of "Asian/American," I use "Asian America" to designate certain historical reformulations of modern America, both as it has modified itself with regard to Asia and as Asians in America have variously affected its refiguration. The goal of this book is not to inventory the "failures" of Asians in America to become Americans, nor to assume a pristine and transcendent notion of "America." Rather than couch the problem in the familiar parlance of assimilation, we will ask, not whether Asians have become assimilated, but, "to *what*, exactly, are they to be assimilated?"; "how does the history of Asian America demonstrate the centrality of Asia to the imagining of modern America?"; and "what have been the various historical incarnations and precise contents of the Asian/American dynamic?"

The very shape and character of the United States in the twentieth century — specifically, in the imaginings of modern American development in the global system — is inseparable from historical occasions of real contact between and interpenetrations of Asia and America, in and across the Pacific Ocean. The defining mythos of America, its "manifest destiny," was, after all, to form a bridge westward from the Old World, *not just* to the western coast of the North American continent, but from there to the trans-Pacific regions of Asia. This "lure" toward and across the Pacific expanse was complemented by anxiety regarding what the eminent Chicago sociologist Robert E. Park designated as America's "racial frontier." For him, the Pacific represented a formidable challenge to modern America in terms of both race and culture. Crucially, at the same time that many Americans retreated from that challenge and held firmly to a particular narrative of nation that stopped at such frontiers in order to preserve a certain definition of the nation (as a narrative that would still cling to the old world of Europe), Park and others sketched out possible modalities in which that "frontier," perhaps marked more by race than geography, might be transsected.

This was not an idle intellectual conjecture; the possible consequences of such a transgression were not in the least slight. While crossing over would advance the geopolitical and economic interests of modern America, it would also test the social and cultural fabric of the nation and its ability to accommodate a race heretofore deemed to be radically different. If successful, this (selective) melding would be a central part of the defining character of modern America: history had placed America at the limit of the west coast and challenged it to cross over the Pacific in order to fulfill its national destiny, away from the old world of Europe and into Asia and modernity. Crucially, we must note that these crossings, both physical and mental, were not only undertaken in a westerly direction by America: as America crossed over to Asia, Asians came to the United States.

As conceptual entities with which (and against which) America measured itself, *and also* as active agents, Asians in America have historically participated in the constitution of what "America" was and is at any given moment. The very revision of modern American time and space was enabled by Chinese labor on the transcontinental railroad, that concrete, modern technological link that, in a particular enactment of time/space compression, shrank the distance between the Atlantic seaboard and the Pacific coast and allowed America to imagine more precisely its particularly modern dream of an American Pacific "lake." [1] While I am firmly aware of America's persistent history of institutional racism and its effect of marginalizing many Asian populations politically, economically, socially, and culturally (indeed, a large part of this study details and analyzes how and why this has been the case), the tendency to situate too strictly the minor only at the margins of the dominant downplays the uneven, complex, and multiple imbrications of Asians in America. Here I will suggest that Asian America is a complicated and particularly contradictory concept that cannot be so easily reduced and objectified.

This approach demands that we reconceptualize the nature of national identity as at once less stable and more dynamic. In such an enterprise, I understand the notion of "identity" as not solely the burden of minority groups in the United States, though certainly it is that as well. Rather, I wrestle with the idea that the various modes of naming Asian Americans and the different functions of that designation in American discourse are indices to specific points of articulation: to name Asian America is to assume a particular, exterior vantage point. I suggest that the distinctions installed between "Asian" and "American" might be best read within specific historical moments in which such a "great wall" was constructed precisely because modern history had presented the occasion wherein these two entities threatened to merge (in however brief and delimited a manner). This wall, in fact, has proven to be porous and unevenly constructed. There is no doubt that "Asia" and "America" have merged and continue to merge in different ways on different terrains of the imagination, as well as in real political, ideological, and economic arenas.

Nevertheless, this crossing over is constantly compromised by the essential, racial separation of Asians from "Americans," a distinction buttressed by a belief system deeply ingrained in the American imaginary which insists on the essential difference of racialized peoples. To give one example: since the 1970s, Asian Americans have been depicted as "overachievers," and thus successful in certain ways. Yet that achievement (in both domestic and international economies) can be (and has been) recoded variously as unfair competition or as success gained by subjects unfit for authentic social integration because of one sort of "flaw" or another—lack of "broad interests" or "people skills." Economic success and class ascension do not necessarily erase racial distinctions that leave Asian Americans susceptible to being redefined as "foreign" at specific historical moments.

"Difference" is thus understood and deployed in various manners—some benign, or even conciliatory, others emphatically brutal. Each instantiation has its own particular historical context.

My central thesis is certainly informed by my own particular historical situation, which can be most fully and usefully understood as a specifically sedimented one. It is in these years at the waning of the twentieth century that the term "Asian" in the United States has achieved a certain highly productive invisibility (or at least opacity). Just a few years ago, in the inventorying of racial groups in the United States, "Asian American" was normally part of the cluster "Afro-American," "Native American," "Hispanic American," popularly evoked and presented as the essential markers of race and ethnicity in the United States. Now, however, one increasingly finds that "Asian American" is omitted. To question why this is so is motivated neither by resentment at not being "included" nor by a desire to find a rationale for celebrating this negatively articulated equivalence with "white"; rather, I am interested in understanding, precisely, what has allowed this "benign neglect" if not for the assumption that Asians are no longer "minorities" in the sense that they are economically disadvantaged, and therefore the sensitivities of the American political economy are excused from laboring to "include" Asian Americans—we have already made it "inside." This economic acsension brings with it then an assumption of full social, cultural, and political integration. Part of the task of this study is to track, explain, and query that internalization.

Indeed, in the late twentieth century it would be difficult to argue that Asian Americans (as an invented designation) are "disadvantaged" in the same sense that blacks, Latino/as, and indigenous peoples are still the objects of a virulent strain of American racism. The "model minority myth" has in large part done its work in separating out Asians as particularly viable objects for admiration (this is of course a specific mode of containment). There are certainly good arguments that various dynamics of class distinction both allow for ethnic mobility into the "mainstream" and fissure ethnic solidarities. Recent public discussions of illegal immigrants smuggled into the United States from China and other Asian states and debates over affirmative action and bilingual education have polarized Asian American communities. Some renounce any notion of Asian solidarity, aligning themselves instead with an anti-immigrant, antirefugee stance on the basis of either conservative positions against immigrants or liberal positions against overtaxing welfare monies that should be spent on the American poor; others, either those conservatively anti-Communist or those liberal and sympathetic to refugees, support efforts of Chinese to leave China.

On affirmative action, some hold to a historical sense of how anti-Asian racism conjoins with racism toward African Americans, Latinos, and Native

Americans, and support the continuation of affirmative action policies; others, convinced of the validity of the American system and seeing themselves as evidence of the rightness of the model minority thesis, reject such policies. In such debates and others, the privilege of indifference afforded to the well-to-do loosens or directly negates racial identification. For some, it may simply be a matter of their time in the United States or political ideologies carried over from the country of origin that play a greater role in differentiating Asian American identity. However, race continues to intrude upon this picture to belie the notion that class distinction permanently erases all others.

The focus on class supports the conservative notion that what best characterizes America is the promise of upward mobility, to which all may aspire. Pointing to instances of such mobility among different racial groups, it suggests that race has been elided as a significant category. But that elision is incomplete and uneven; race does not "disappear" as much as it is muted. It is still available for activation and mobilization, as the recent scandal over Asian contributions to the 1996 presidential campaign attests. Here, successful, well-to-do Asian Americans found themselves "foreignized" and investigated for contributing to the Democractic National Committee. Was this "American" money, or "Asian" money? Another example is the recently reported concern that the proportion of Asian Americans at the various campuses of the University of California are significantly exceeding that of all other groups. Is academic success now a cause for concern and resentment? Are Asian Americans *too* assimilated? What happens when success is not simply intuited vaguely in imputed "behavior," but witnessed in concrete ways that disturb the complacency of the state?

The nature of Asian American social subjectivity now vacillates between whiteness and color. Its visibility is of a particular texture and density; its function is always to trace a racial minority's possibilities for assimilation. The occasional absence of "Asian American" from racial categories in America reflects the undecidability of the term. Asia/America resides *in transit*, as a point of reference on the horizon that is part of *both* a "minority" identity and a "majority" identity. This constant transitivity evinces precisely the malleability and resistance of "America" with regard to racial reformation.

"Asian/American" of course collects together an unwieldy set of points of "origin" traceable to different Asian states (and often enough that "origin" is visible only after tracking complex and heterogeneous diasporic movements). There are significant differences between the histories of these various groups, which become blurred when they are forced together under that single rubric.

I remain attentive to those differences, even as I will continue to speak of "Asian Americans," because the *de jure* and *de facto* discourses of America (those institutionalized in the state and those performed in the public arena) have tended to collapse such distinctions. Also, such blurrings are themselves instructive.

The reader will notice that this study does not attempt to evenly treat all groups gathered under that term. Indeed, conspicuously absent is a treatment of South Asians. There is a historical rationale for this: the definition of modern Asian America allows me to understand how the nature of Asian America partakes of historical phenomena and cultural concepts that arose in the 1920s and 1930s, as the more "established" Asians in America (largely Chinese) were to be incorporated into the nation. I have been intrigued by how the discourse on the modernizing of America has been deeply linked to East Asia and how the development of the global economy has focused on the specific expansion of East and Southeast Asian regions as variously the "Pacific Frontier," the "Pacific Rim," and "Asia Pacific." Nevertheless, in the conclusion I will argue that the deconstruction of this Asia Pacific paradigm is a crucial task for Asian American studies, one that might be facilitated by an analysis of alternate modernities in South Asia, especially as the momentum toward the Pacific has been modified by the recent instabilities of Asian economies and new waves of South Asian populations have refigured America in critical ways.

In delineating the contours and contents of Asian America, I track the interplay of three concepts. To gain a sense of the appearance and function of Asian America historically and in the national imaginary of race, I follow the formation of the *Body*, the *Psyche*, and *Space*. By "Body," I mean both the material, corporeal forms of Asian American peoples and the semiotics of those forms—that is, both the objective body, with its particular inscriptions in material history, and the way that body is semiotically deployed in social and cultural discourse. The Body, as a somatic entity that exists within the contingencies of time and space, desire, need, gratification and denial, thus helps us maintain a sense of Asian America as imbricated in material history—specifically, immigration, economic, gender, and racial history. For instance, Asian America is deeply rooted in the histories of both willed and forced migrations, of both national and global economic change, of wars of colonization, decolonization, and global strife, in which the general category of "Asian/American" is predicated upon the placement, the labor, and the sexual, economic, and social interactions of Asian American bodies.

The presence and function of Asian bodies in America necessitated the invention of a way to understand the implication of that presence as both productive and reproductive force. Here is where the Psyche comes into play—how to understand Asians if not to plumb the psychic content of the body, to see the possible affinities and points of alienation? This in turn suggests the possibilities for harmonizing this particularly construed being within the social fabric of the modern American state: to turn Asians into Americans required a particular transformation of mental habits and psychic dispositions and necessitated the installation of particular intuitions that approximated the American psyche. None of this was believed to be entirely achievable—the goal rather was to reach a point of tolerable proximity. The narrative of the late twentieth century has also included, however, a strong suggestion that that abstract "Asian" psyche might well be better equipped for an age of "postindustrial," transnational economies, and that "America" might do well to learn from Asia. It is in this grey and shifting area of compromise, between an idealized Asian psyche and an equally idealized American mentality, that "Asian America" has been and continues to be produced. That "understanding" served to situate more exactly the Asian body in American space, both figuratively and literally.

By "Space" I designate both the real, physical environment and the symbolic logics that attach themselves to physical place. I will ask how Asian Americans have "taken place" in the United States and how the United States itself bears the imprint of new spatializations. The history of Asian America is indeed legible in a history of spatialization and respatialization, of different deterritorializations and reterritorializations, disenfranchisements, reclamations and (re)constructions, from the long histories of America's twentieth-century wars in Asia and their effects on migration and domestic policy, to the restructuring of Asian American space as Pacific Rim space and the transnationalizing of the local. Again, like my approach to the Body, I read Space not only symbolically but also literally.

The key instruments that have been deployed in the historical construction of Asian America—immigration law, scientific racism, economic and social policies, and cultural practices—all drew on particular understandings and imaginings of the racialized Asian/American body and psyche, and the ways Asian Americans might occupy, or should occupy, a particular place in America. Nevertheless, throughout I want to insist upon the fact that the point of discursive articulation is always set within a complex historical situation wherein it is not exempt from the forces that work to produce Asian America: to understand the subject positions of "white" as absolutely apart from those of "Asian" in the discursive interplay of nation formation is to play into the very alibi that serves to fortify racism. Similarly, to deny the effect of Asians on "America" is to render "America" invulnerable and Asians without agency; neither is true historically.

This book is divided into five sections of two chapters each. In the first section, "Modernity, Asia, America," I argue that the specific character of the modern formulation of Asian America moves away from the particular view of Asia as Yellow Peril that began in the late nineteenth century and reached a high point of dogmatism in the early 1930s, and toward a more nuanced and complex notion of how Asia would be part of America in an age marked by the arrival of new immigrant groups and new foreign policies. These topics cannot be fully appreciated without addressing America's redefinition of itself in the modern age as a nation (unique among many in the modern age) faced toward the Pacific. In Chapter 1, "Pacific America: Projection, Introjection, and the Beginnings of Modern Asian America," I address the particular efforts to redefine the state as excluding certain groups and accommodating variously those already present in the United States: after excluding Asians, how was the nation to integrate those now locked within its borders? This crisis management had to be flexible enough to allow America to pursue the new definition of its national interests in the Pacific. The notion of the Pacific as a particular locus for American development as a global power sets in motion a complex history of strategizing the precise nature of that contact and incorporation, and of reading the effects of increased contact upon the national body.

At the same moment that political, journalistic, sociological, and academic discourses grappled with an unpredictable and unstable set of issues regarding the introjection and projection of Asian America, literary narratives written by Asian Americans and by other Americans attempted to invent within their specific discursive spaces images of Asian America that both delineate the boundaries of Asian America and envision particular modes of crossing them. This is the subject of Chapter 2, "Rescripting the Imaginary," which analyzes a number of literary narratives as well as one very important cinematic imagining of Asian America. These narratives each manifest in different ways a shift in the literary representations of and by Asians in America, located in a new world of modern foreign relations, technologies, nationalisms, and a newly valorized cosmopolitan hybridity. They strain to stage Asian American realities that can only be set in future time or disclosed inadvertently from the repressed sociopolitical unconscious. It is precisely the invention of such realities that points up the disjuncture between what the imagination proffers and the limits of narration as historical act. Nevertheless, at the same time that the American imaginary projected these images of an Asian American liaison into the fantastic, there began as well serious speculation on the actual manifestation of Asian American intercourse. The Asian American liaison threatened to exceed the borders of the fantastic and manifest itself in concrete terms, and this called for particular modes of conceiving and understanding this new modernity brought about by America's increased engagement with East Asia.

In the second section, "Bodies and Souls," I examine two particular sites of Asian/American predication as scripted on the bodies of Asian Americans. In Chapter 3, "Written on the Face: Race, Nation, Migrancy, and Sex," I extend my discussion of the embodiment of hybridity and examine the racialized and deracialized body, framed within a somatic aesthetic. This aesthetic is read within various historical occasions of migrancy, from mid-century to the present day. Here the body is seen as a *reproductive* entity whose decisions and actions sexually reflect the specific character of Asian migration and assimilation, and dramatize the cultural tension of modern migrancy in racial terms, specifically as these new negotiations impact upon the "face" of the nation. I pay particular attention to the new techniques of plastic and reconstructive surgery developed in the mid-twentieth century, as they are deployed to hasten the slow physical transformation of immigrants into Americans. I then place these practices of body fashioning within the context of the contemporary age, with its own particular anxieties with regard to "diversity," and examine the instantiation of a new aesthetic of symmetry. Rather than similitude, "symmetry" seeks to entirely bypass the imaging of race. Within this cluster of terms—migrancy, similitude, diversity, symmetry—one finds the changing scripts for domesticating the foreign body.

In Chapter 4, "Transacting Culture: Bodies at the Seam of the Social," I analyze the representation of the Asian/American body and its social inscriptions in literary narrative. Despite their shared assimilationist themes, these Asian/American narratives refuse to jettison the corporeal in order to set forth a story of a purely disembodied psychic adjustment to modern America; each remains attached to the materiality of the body and its inscription in the worldly. Herein, "Asian culture" becomes a particular kind of cross-cultural capital, which is used to materially sustain the physical body as well as secure a particular psychic equilibrium. Discovering the system of exchange and value in which these transactions take place requires analysis of the nation's sense of itself regarding this new entity. The "bildung" discovered at the center of these narratives links the general formula of self-fashioning to the national political economy of race, while underwriting the construction of a particular social subject. The question that arises out of these formulas is how, exactly, to integrate this new Asian/American subject into the nation. How are we to understand this newly constructed presence, and "our" relationship to it?

The ratio of otherness, as distributed through and across the images of the Asian American body and psyche, is measured within a problematic of identification and disidentification that engages a particular vision of the American nation and the social discourse of race. In the third section, "Modeling the Nation," I argue that the introjection of Asians into America has always taken place within a complex *multi*-racial dynamic—the Asian presence has historically prompted a reassessment of not only the general ideological specificity of white America but also the presence of other racial minorities within American ideology. From the 1920s, the understanding of any one racial group in America has been either explicitly or implicitly linked to a reassessment of *each* of America's racial groups. This "local" analysis is complemented by a global one: Asian/American subjectivity also has been produced by referencing Asia, and comparing Asia to America and other nations.

Were this always a simple matter of constant degradation and marginalization, the nature of Asian/American would be relatively straightforward. Yet it is the specific nature of Asians in America *and* in Asia to be held up as models at various points in history, not only for other racial minorities to emulate but for whites to do so as well. I place particular attention to how these phenomena were, and continue to be, connected to America's sense of its domestic ethnic and racial affairs as well as to a reassessment of U.S. national identity in relation to Asia. This process has involved both identifying and disidentifying "Americans" with a particularly constructed image of Asians. Chapter 5, "Citizens and Subnations," focuses on the emergence of the "model minority" thesis as a sociological explanation of Asian American success and the failures of blacks in America, and reads this thesis in the contexts of both Civil Rights policies and the ascension of the Japanese economy.

Chapter 6, "Disintegrations and Reconsolidations," reads race and ethnicity in the United States according to global identifications of "culture" and "civilization." In each case I am particularly interested in the correlation of the raced body and the national psyche. What does the impulse to emulate Asians disclose? And what is the particular nature of Asian/American that elicits this impulse? And, perhaps most significantly, how can Asian Americans be emulated without radically rescripting the contents of America? In each case, we find a particular value placed on social and economic performativity, on both the local and global levels (which, indeed, interpenetrate to a great degree). And yet, no matter how flawless that performance, we find in each case as well an attempt (but not necessarily a successful one) to recontain Asian as apart from American. This variegation of the psyche is not simply an abstract mode of speculation: it is found as well in the textures of the physical environment.

The fourth section, "Placing Asian America," reads Asian America as eminently situated in the politics of space. How have Asians been located psychically and physically in what is deemed "American" space? How have they variously taken possession and been dispossessed of a place in the nation? How have such negotiations evinced the historical formations and reformations of Asian America? How have race and ethnicity, those markers of difference, entered into the negotiations over "common ground"? And, finally, how have imagined claims to space and place clashed or coincided with juristic ones, and how is the imagination of space linked to political and racial ideologies of the nation? This section examines two major forces in Asian American history and their impact upon the constitution of Asian American space.

Chapter 7, "War, the Homeland, and the Traces of Memory," focuses primarily on agricultural and rural areas and is aimed toward understanding the effects of America's twentieth-century wars. How did the wars in Asia mark a specific set of engagements, and how did they affect the formation of Asia/America? I read the relocation of Asian populations in/to the United States as particular acts of redefining and rehistoricizing the nation, and consider Asian Americans' role in such reformations. How do these national places bear the specifying marks of race and ethnicity, and how is place inflected by different identificatory desires? How is it possessed differently? Chapter 8, "Demarcations and Fissures: Reconstructing Space," looks at the restructuring of urban and suburban space in the postwar years, specifically as new transnational economies penetrate the local and give rise to a set of anxieties regarding this particularly visible appearance of Asian America. This notion takes as its evidence the more pronounced presence of ethnic populations in assumed "American" spaces—their storefronts, products, commodities, and bodies are all taken as signs of America's inability to maintain its borders and to sustain itself. Basic questions of the nation-state, such as who belongs here and who controls "here," become all the more pressing and more difficult to resolve.

The final section, "Mind Readings," gathers together the analyses of Body, Psyche, and Space. I examine how the key tropes used to identify the Asian/American subject in the late twentieth century are related to the redefinition of national psychic identities, and how this redefinition has taken place in political, social, and cultural discourses. Specifically, I am interested in the *tropology* of the psychic, which posits in the Asian/American subject a particular set of mental and spiritual capabilities and weaknesses, dispositions, encumberances, and values. This mode of social analysis is arrived at by means of psychological attempts to gauge the "fit" between Asian and American. These modes of apprehending the liaisons between Asia and America take place in the seam between modernity and postmodernity—I will show how new psychologies are mobilized to explain the Asian/American crossing in late capitalism, as bodies and spaces are revised and recontextualized in this new mode of production. In Chapter 9, "Double Trouble: The Pathology of Ethnicity Meets White Schizophrenia," I examine the use of "schizophrenia" to describe the "dual personalities" of "hyphenated Americans," depicted as unable to engage unproblematically in an invented hegemonic memory. I discuss the various debates surrounding the notion "dual personality" and read it in terms of the discourse of the nation-state and its particular fissuring in late modernity. I conclude that this pathology, if read critically and historically, describes a more global case of "schizophrenia" in transnational postmodernity. Rather than marking ethnic and racial minorities alone, "schizophrenia" might be an even better descriptor for a postmodern *white* malaise.

In the 1980s and 1990s, the reading of Asian America according to a pathology of schizophrenia encounters a series of different discourses that seek to rationalize and accommodate new perspectives of Asian America as taking form within increasingly complex spatio-temporalities. At the same time that Asian Americans are imbricated within more and more complex understandings of both the local and the transnational, this age has witnessed the flourishing of electronic technologies that assert a new "borderless world" in cyberspace. In Chapter 10, "Asia Pacific: A Transnational Imaginary," I address these new points of identification, which try to accommodate more and more diverse Asian American identities as diasporic ones and test the boundedness of the nation and of culture. We follow a progressive loosening of national ties as we are launched into a world of cybernetic ports that link Asia and America in the fiction of such writers as William Gibson. Yet I conclude that Gibson's innovative and imaginative construction of cyberspace turns out to be predicated upon reinstalling the boundary between Asia and America, East and West. What does it mean that this seemingly daring author could imagine such cybernetic borderlessness (between the real and the hallucinatory, between Asia and America), and yet retreat from the consummation of that vision?

The project set forth in the early twentieth century to "manifest" the *modern* destiny of America in the Pacific continues well into this postmodern age. The transitions in various analytic terms, from monopoly capitalism to late capitalism, from "dual personalities" to "hybrid" subjects, and so on, has merely complicated our notions of Asian/American, rather than resolved them. Yet there is reason to believe that, perhaps more now than ever, the Asian/American predication may be completed, somewhere on the horizon. That formulation, however, would have to take into account the historical reconstitution of both terms, which makes Asian/American a constantly shifting designation. We cannot clearly see what that formation will look like. Another, perhaps more worthwhile task might be to ascertain at each historical moment the nature of that subjectivity, the way it is embedded within the complex matrix of race, ethnicity, and nation, and what that might teach us about our own historical situation.

Part I / Modernity, Asia, America

1 / Pacific America: Projection, Introjection, and the Beginnings of Modern Asian America

IT IS NEVER AN EASY TASK to decide when a "modernity" begins; such a question brings with it the question of why is it important to name that particular point of rupture. "Asian America" could be said to have existed long before what I am designating as its modern incarnation—from the very beginnings of Asian-American "contact" any number of discursive efforts were made to map out the nature and significance of such contact. But what I am most intrigued by is how the formation of "modern America" in the early twentieth century is so deeply and particularly attached to the Pacific region. In a very essential manner, America's "modernization" called for its penetration into the Pacific region, and that action could not but foreground the effects of such crossing over on both Asia and America. America's forays into the Pacific region and East Asia (and later, of course, Southeast Asia) defined a particular strategy of expansion and "development." Yet such "forward movements" necessitated a particular set of negotiations with the inhabitants of those areas. The movement of America into Asia was complemented by the reverse. Although obviously this did not occur proportionately in any sense, the symbolic and ideological maneuvering that sought to tame and accommodate this mutual penetration looked closely at the precise nature of American modernization and its unintended and undesired consequences. Managing the modern was inseparable from managing Asian America.

The 1930s are a particularly appropriate site in which to locate the modern introjection of Asia into the American imaginary. During this period, the "Yellow Peril," the term popularly used in the imaging of an Asian-American connection, begins to designate a more complex phenomenon, drawing from both deep-seated orientalist discourse and anxiety regarding the newly modern world of the late nineteenth and early twentieth centuries. During the late 1930s, conceptualizations of Asia and its relation to and appearance in America are modified and rearticulated. These changes evince specific, historicized political economies whose complexities appear in a revised notion of hybridity driven by modernity. The very integrity of America is now seen as open to a particularly modern kind of penetration, one that broke up apparent purities and mixed them with foreign elements. The result, in American bodies, psyches, and spaces, constitutes a particular facet of Asian America. "Hybridity" here designates a specific, temporalized dialectic, viewed not so much as America "absorbing" the foreign (in the usual model of assimilation), as it is at once an integrative and *reformulative* model, in which both the "domestic" and "foreign" are constantly revised.

From this period onward, Asia presents to America a particular test of its self-conception, domestically and internationally. This conception begins as determinedly self-protective. Beginning in 1882 with the passage of the first Chinese exclusion act, and culminating in the period between the 1924 National Origins Act and the Tydings-McDuffie Act of 1934, we find the consolidation of anti-Asian sentiment. Yet it is precisely during this period, when it would seem that the Yellow Peril would have been neutralized, that one finds the appearance and intensification of another, cognate set of problems. First, how to account for and accommodate those Asians *already in* the United States? The focus shifts from exclusion to the management of a newly defined interiority. It is this set of psychosocial problems that I refer to as "introjection." But it would be wrong to assume that America's eyes now only turned inward, for in the late 1930s events in East Asia required the United States to engage in a new set of negotiations of its national destiny in a new global political economy. The U.S. had anticipated this state of affairs in its annexations of Pacific territories in the late nineteenth century. In 1937, E. H. Norman, writing in the first issue of the journal *Amerasia* (a neologism that itself signifies a conjoining of America and Asia and, in fact, the invention of a unity of sorts), articulates a new project to identify specifically the seam of Asia and America at the Pacific:

> We are . . . united in striving to attain the ultimate objective of promoting among all peoples inhabiting the periphery of the Pacific Ocean a harmony of relationships which transcend the merely legalistic concepts of justice with its emphasis on property over human rights or upon specious national honor or sovereignty over the economic welfare and the spiritual needs of the 700 million people who live on the islands or in the countries bordering the Pacific.[1]

The interest in exploring the modern liaisons between Asia and America grew considerably at the turn of the century. For instance, a series of world's fairs and exhibitions concentrated on the Pacific as the focal point of American development and modernization. Every major Pacific coast city in the United States (except Los Angeles) had staged such an exhibition before World War One: the Lewis and Clark Centennial Expositions (1905); Seattle's Alaska-Yukon Exposition (1909); San Francisco's Panama-Pacific International Exposition (1915), San Diego's Panama-California Exposition (1915–16). All these fairs "contained elaborate exhibits on the nation's new Pacific possessions, particularly Hawai'i and the Philippines, as well as exhibits from Japan and/or China."[2] The particular role that the United States imagined Asia Pacific to play was (and, as we will see at the end of this study, still continues to be) to be a market for the overaccumulation of goods and capital. In 1900, Senator Albert Beveridge, speaking of the invasion of the Philippines, notes: "The Philippines are ours forever. . . . And just beyond the Philippines are China's illimitable markets. We will not retreat from either. . . . The Pacific is our ocean. . . . Where shall we turn for customers of our surplus? Geography answers the question. China is our natural customer."[3] History (and economic interest) pushed the United States to cross the Pacific. This liaison brought with it, however, the necessity to negotiate the connection on multiple fronts. Just as America would "grow" westward, so its *interior*, its deep psychic spaces, as well as its material ones, would be affected by that contact. This point would be elaborated and driven home, deeper and more urgently, over the next decades.

Thus we have a double movement: imagining a set of possible modes of introjecting Asians into America, and projecting onto East Asia a set of possible rearticulations of "western presence." The particular nexus of these issues is well illustrated in this rather ironic citation from the late 1920s by the enormously influential sociologist Robert Ezra Park:

> We have the program of the Pacific coast as stated succinctly and accurately by George Wheeler Hinman, one of the trumpets through which Mr. Hearst, of the Examiners, has essayed to proclaim the voice of the people all over our broad land:
>
> > First, no more Japanese immigration, because "Americans do not intend to be disinherited from their own country."
> > Second, fair treatment to the Japanese already here.
> > Third, equal rights and privileges in the business and commercial development of East Asia.[4]

Exclusion to protect national identity in the face of possible dispossession, a "fair" mode of accommodating an already present Asian population, an "open door" policy of trade guaranteeing U.S. access to East Asian countries (preserving the interiority of the state while vouchsafing its economic and political prerogatives abroad so as to assure its growth) are all neatly encapsulated here.[5]

One of the most interesting aspects of early twentieth-century redefinitions of the American state was the particular blend of exclusionist practices coupled with liberal ideology, the latter used to distinguish the United States as the modern nation above all. Specifically, after the Treaty of Versailles, America held itself up as the nation that would lead in the reformation of the modern world, and such reformation had a particular connection to the modern state's ability to assimilate migrant populations. America was to be "a living exemplar of pluralistic assimilation."[6] It is significant that the Pacific was a particular site for such assimilationist experimentation—the interior of the modern United States now included a consideration of its Pacific territories. Park's students, most notably Romanzo Adams, traveled to Hawai'i to plumb what he called a "racial laboratory," wherein the limits of racial hybridity and the parameters for an engagement with Asia would be tested.[7]

Yet the ideology of assimilation was mired in the contradiction posed by the politics of race and nation set against the imperatives of capitalist enterprise. This contradiction formed a particular context both for mapping the new relations between countries and, by implication, for negotiating ethnicity within America:

> The Japanese, the Chinese, . . . would be all right in their place, no doubt. That place, if they find it, will be one in which they do not greatly intensify and so embitter the struggle for existence of the white man. The difficulty is that the Japanese is still less disposed than the Negro or the Chinese to submit to the regulations of a caste system and stay in his place. The Japanese are an organized and morally efficient nation. They have the national pride and the national egotism which rest on the consciousness of this efficiency. In fact it is not too much to say that national egotism, if one pleases to call it such, is essential to national efficiency, just as a certain irascibility of temper seems to be essential to a good fighter.
>
> Another difficulty is that caste and the limitation of free competition is economically unsound, even though it be politically desirable.[8]

As we will see below, this particular estimation of the Japanese is derived in large part from Japan's rising success as an imperialist power—in 1917, Japan had already defeated Russia in war and colonized Korea. Park's difficulty in "placing" Asians runs up against what he calls a "racial frontier," a limit of otherness, and the necessity to think through the logic of a new political economy which would sweep aside that boundary.

The phenomena of introjection and projection are not absolutely mutually determined nor commensurate; indeed, what has most deeply informed, and continues to inform, attitudes and actions toward Asians in America has been an image of Asians located *not* "in" Asia *nor* in the United States, but of shifting and often contradictory *predications* of "Asia" onto and into the U.S. imaginary. These predications have been and continue to be caught up in a process of transition and transformation, drawing on images of a highly reified "traditional Asia," a vacillating and often contradictory set of images of "America," and incipient forms of an Asian American ontology. For example, early waves of "cheap" Asian labor and exclusionist reaction would seem to have pitted the interests of capitalists who needed an Asian workforce against those of workers who fought against being displaced. Yet exclusion came about precisely because the working class, the middle class, and the ruling class found that the Yellow Peril—an image generated in the racist imagining of a particular *transposition* of Asians to and within America, and its *multivalent* effects—superseded class interests. Exclusion in turn profoundly influenced U.S. policy in East Asia. As Michael Hunt notes: "In the first years of the twentieth century the immigration question once again assumed a central position in Chinese-American relations."[9]

Another example of the transitory nature of Asian America is the contemporary notion of the "model minority," founded upon the supposed persistence and rearticulation of "*traditional* Confucian values" in Asian Americans, whose success lies in their ability to adapt Asia to America as well as to transform America through the application of a "Confucian" ethos. The incommensurability of introjection and projection, however—the gaps between both in the American imaginary—becomes evident as one traces both the intended and unintended functions of these various narrations of Asian America; indeed, they signal the dominant ideological crises of Asian America. Ultimately, both the domestic and foreign relations facets of this Asian American problematic may be linked to a general project of national redefinition.

In this section I argue that the specific character of the reformulation of Asian America moves away from the particular, closely delineated view of Asia as Yellow Peril that began in the late nineteenth century and reached a high point of dogmatism in the early 1930s, and toward a more nuanced and complex notion of how Asia would be part of America in an age marked by the arrival of new immigrant groups, a highly developed world economy, increased U.S. neo-colonial activities and military action in the foreign sphere, the rise of fascism, the development and proliferation of mass technologies and communications, labor activism, and the inklings of a "coming of age" of Asians already in the United States. These topics cannot be fully appreciated without addressing America's redefinition of itself in the modern age. To understand this reformulation, which both incorporated and rearticulated residual elements from earlier brands of Yellow Perilism and produced new discursive strategies to narrate Asian America, it is first necessary to outline the point of transition.

During the first third of the twentieth century, faced with the increased visibility of new immigrants, a perception of decay in the mental and spiritual life of America that paralleled its economic crisis, and collective and radical attempts for sociopolitical reform, the United States embarked on a vast and multifaceted project to reconsolidate its national body with an eye toward a new world order: specifically germane here is America's engagement with East Asia. First, I discuss its general modalities; then I address the specific case of Asians.

(Re)Building the National Body

As early as 1907, Congress established an Immigration Commission (also known as the Dillingham Commission) to investigate the impact of immigration on the United States. This was no small project: Congress provided it with a staff of three hundred, and a million dollars for two years' work. The result was a series of forty-two volumes.[10]

> The Commission, which investigated chiefly the social and economic effects of immigration, filled most of its volumes with impressive and detailed figures showing the impact of new immigrants upon wages, working conditions, sanitation, housing, crime, and mental illness. Often by ignoring the factor of recent arrival in the economic and social status of new immigrants and comparing them with a somewhat idealized picture of previous immigrants, the Commission demonstrated what most of its members assumed: that the new immigration exerted a generally unsatisfactory influence upon American society. As a result of its investigations, the Commission, with but one dissent, duly recommended a literacy test for adult immigrants, but on economic rather than racial grounds: to alleviate an oversupply of unskilled labor. The principal result of the Commission's

report, however, was to fix the stereotyped distinction between the desirable, easily assimilated old immigrants and an undesirable, inassimilable new.[11]

This new immigrant population consisted of those conspicuously marked as "other" by race, those deemed inferior because of class and poverty, and those in what came to form a catch-all category, the "feebleminded," a particular group that was to be placed under surveillance and separated out during the project of defining the modern U.S. nation.[12]

The United States rushed to establish and legitimize its powers to exclude and expel. While such powers were not explicitly provided for in the Constitution, it was argued that the federal government's power to exclude other peoples was implicit in its status as a sovereign nation. Beginning in 1871, Justice Bradley had asserted that "the national government had jurisdiction over all subjects of legislation and sovereignty which affected the interests of the whole people equally and which required uniformity of laws and regulations." In 1889, Field used this as an argument for the rightness of Chinese exclusion. Such decisions became particularly powerful modes of enacting the definition of "America" that came about after 1907. Konvitz notes that "in 1936, Mr. Justice Sutherland, speaking for the court in *United States v. Curtiss-Wright Corporation*, stated that the investment of the federal government with the powers of 'external sovereignty' did not depend upon the affirmative grants of the Constitution. The incidents of this sovereignty are vested in the federal government 'as a necessary concomitant of nationality'": [13]

> In short, the power of the National Government in the field of international relationship is not a complexus of particular enumerated powers, but it is an *inherent power, one which is attributed to the National Government on the ground solely of its belonging to the American People as a sovereign political entity at International Law. It follows that silence on the part of the Constitution as to the power of the National Government to adopt any particular measure in relation to other nations is not a denial of such power, as it would be if the doctrine on Enumerated Powers applied, but is, on the contrary, an affirmation of power* [italics in the original].[14]

Increasingly, exclusionists plumbed the "silences" of constitutional documents to ventriloquize and legitimate their arguments, taking advantage of what the Constitution could not anticipate in the way of increased immigration in the modern age. In short, the argument for the state's right to exclude established the very *constitution* of the state, and hence begged the question of its positive definition.

The argument for the government's sovereign power to exclude went hand-in-hand with the justification for deporting aliens. In 1913 (*Tiaco v. Forbes, 228 U.S. 549*), Justice Holmes held that "sovereign states have the inherent power to deport aliens." The United States immediately and forcefully exercised this newly established power in order to redefine its state: between 1921 and 1925, 26,427 persons were deported; in the next five years the number rose to 64,123 (Konvitz, 55). The power to argue against deportation was nil: in *Li Sing v. U.S., 180 U.S. 486* (1901), the court held that in the process of deportation hearings the alien was not protected against unreasonable search and seizures, nor could he claim the right of trial by jury; Chinese could only call on white witnesses for support. In the same year (*Chin Bak Kan v. U.S., 186 U.S. 193*), the court held that a Chinese resident of the United States, claiming citizenship, was faced with the burden of proof (55). In 1924, the court maintained that *ex post facto* laws did not apply in deportation cases: if an alien committed an act that was legal at the time it was performed, but which later was outlawed, he or she could be deported for it (56).

Psychological and other scientific discourses reached into a newly objectified "American mind" to validate a prophylactic mentality of isolation and exclusion. Such a mentality required, of course, a wholesale, explicit revision of American democratic ideology. William McDougall, who came from England to direct Harvard's department of psychology, became a popular advocate for such social and political restructuring, underwriting his argument with psychological data. In his 1921 book, *Is America Safe for Democracy?*, he answered negatively: history, he held, was strewn with dead civilizations because the inherited capacities of the citizens could no longer cope with the complexities of civilization. Since the poorer stocks in a democracy were likely to have freedom to reproduce, democracy was incompatible with the maintenance of a stable civilization, and he foresaw America's impending degeneration. He suggested that democracy be replaced by a caste system based on biological worth, in which political rights would depend on caste and in which laws would prevent marriages between castes and restrict breeding by inferior castes.[15]

The eugenics movement provided a "scientific" argument for exclusion, deportation, imprisonment, commitment to insane asylums, anti-miscegenation laws, and forced sterilization. Those intent on a particular reformation of America used eugenics to argue that "a large proportion of the nation's population was of low intelligence, although not actually feebleminded, and that such persons—tramps, poor farmers, slum dwellers, unskilled laborers, Negroes, and immigrants—were breeding and swamping those relatively few families that still carried the light of intelligence and initiative in their genes. Thus the earlier myth of the menace of the feebleminded was transformed into a larger myth: the menace of mass man." A particular discursive formation evolved that blended science with politics, economics with sociology, national and international interests, within which the nation was imagined as a body that must, through fastidious hygienic measures, guard against what passes from the exterior, excise the cancerous cells that have already penetrated it, and prevent any reproductive act that would compromise the regeneration of its species in an increasingly massified and mobile world. This list of suspect populations collects the urban and rural poor, the legacy of slavery, and new immigrants from Eastern Europe and Asia. American and world history seems to militate against an ever-shrinking American core.[16]

The critical element to note in the most extreme efforts to exclude those deemed "other" and prohibit their reproduction is that this argument assumed that, contrary to the myth of the melting pot, nature won over nurture. No matter what environmental conditions might be, no matter what progressive social reform, health habits, educational programs, not to mention long-term passive exposure to "America," might be experienced by a member of this group, nothing could erase his or her basic genetic disposition. Especially targeted were those moving across national boundaries. Even acquired American traits could not be passed on to one's children: "Racists denied that American institutions could mold the immigrant or his children to the American pattern. Hence the exclusion of 'inferior' races had the same justification as other eugenics programs. 'The same arguments which induce us to segregate criminals and feebleminded and thus prevent their breeding,' Prescott Hall explained in 1910, 'apply to excluding from our borders individuals whose multiplying here is likely to lower the average of our people.'"[17]

Madison Grant, one of the most prominent eugenicists of the age, asserted that race was determined by physical and psychological traits that were ignorant of geography and culture. They simply were carried within by the individual.[18] In this formulation, immigrants were thus marked by both physical and psychic "disease." Charles Benedict Davenport, another famous eugenicist, became secretary of the Committee on Eugenics of the American Breeders' Association and helped establish within it a committee on immigration. Nearly every anti-immigrant policy from that point on anchored its argument on this science. Especially noteworthy is the fact that the disposition to *change location* came under suspicion:

As data poured in to the Eugenics Record Office [a bureau created to keep data on genetic traits from all over the United States and to serve the purpose of advising individuals on desirable and undesirable mates, among other things] he studied in some detail personality traits involved in antisocial and criminal behavior. Nomadism (the wandering impulse) was clearly a hereditary trait, Davenport felt, because such racial groups as Comanches, Gypsies, and Huns were nomadic. He searched pedigrees for examples of nomadism: tramps and vagabonds, traveling salesmen, railroad workers, and boys who played truant or ran away.[19]

Such beliefs reflect a deep fear of movement, of contact, indeed, of any change at all in one's location outside specific parameters; hence, the targets of these attacks were not only racial minorities, the poor, and immigrants—it was the modern world of increased flows of people from the rural to the urban, and from the foreign to the domestic, acting under the demands of a new world economy, which unsettled the national body.

One of the most commonly articulated fears during these times was that of miscegenation. It was feared that miscegenation would bring about the dilution of the American blood and lead to the eventual demise of the nation. Coupled with a declining birthrate among the elite stock, "interbreeding" with the lower social and racial orders would lead to "race suicide": "Unless a radical change is effected very soon . . . the stock that founded this nation and which nurtured it through the grave perils and trials of the formative period, will soon have vanished from the face of the earth."[20] Eugenicists like Davenport made clear that miscegenation would result in the decline of the American state: "miscegenation commonly spells disharmony—disharmony of physical, mental, and temperamental qualities. . . . A hybridized people are a badly put together people and a dissatisfied, restless, ineffective people."[21] The connection between such beliefs and political discourse, between the local and the national, the domestic and public spaces, is made explicit in Calvin Coolidge's essay "Whose Country Is This?" published fittingly enough in that primer for managing domestic space, *Good Housekeeping*, in February 1921. In it, the then vice president maintained the integrity of American space by carefully distinguishing between the "right kind" of immigration and the wrong kind, between that which was needed to meet the national interests and that which would only destroy the State:

Our country must cease to be regarded as a dumping ground. Which does not mean that it must deny the value of rich accretions drawn from the right kind of immigration.

Any such restriction, except as a necessary and momentary expediency, would assuredly paralyze our national vitality. But measured practically, it would be suicidal for us to let down the bars for the inflowing of cheap manhood, just as, commercially, it would be unsound for this country to allow her markets to be overflooded with cheap goods, the product of cheap labor. There is no room either for cheap man or the cheap goods. . . . We might avoid this danger were we insistent that the immigrant, before he leaves foreign soil, is temperamentally keyed for our national background. There are racial considerations too grave to be brushed aside for any sentimental reasons. Biological laws tell us that certain divergent people will not mix or blend. The Nordics propagate themselves successfully. With other races, the outcome shows deterioration on both sides. Quality of mind and body suggests that observance of ethnic law is as great a necessity to a nation as immigration law.[22]

While we see an attempt to shrewdly leave the door open for future economic contingencies, ultimately this text declares that immigration law simply articulates a primordial "natural" law. The hybrid is clearly both a diseased entity that could only perpetuate and intensify that illness, and a sign of a monstrous union. One finds a tension between the melting pot ideology and a rejection of it on the basis of both economics and biology, joined in the overall discourse of the highly rationalized project of American modernity. This tension is dramatically illustrated in Henry Ford's lavish staging of the melting pot:

For a festival sponsored by Henry Ford during the early 1920s a giant pot was built outside the gates of his factory. Into this pot danced groups of gaily dressed immigrants dancing and singing their native songs. From the other side of the pot emerged a single stream of Americans dressed alike in the contemporary standard dress and singing the national anthem. As the tarantellas and the polkas at last faded away only the rising strains of the national anthem could be heard as all the immigrants finally emerged. The enormous pressures which created this vast transformation amounted almost to forced conversion.[23]

This catalyst had a more concrete manifestation. In 1914, Ford set up a team of over a hundred "inspectors" to go into workers' homes and investigate their living quarters and habits. Workers were advised on issues such as hygiene, thrift, and gambling. If they were reported as deficient in any of these areas, they were declared ineligible for full pay.[24] Obviously, this program can be seen for its positive benefits, but we should not take Ford to be an enlightened philanthropist; after all, he was guarding his bottom line and assuring the productivity of his workers. Here and elsewhere we find the intimate link between the national body, the immigrant body, labor, and "hygiene," and, crucially, the psychic identifications that allowed these notions to have traffic with one another.

The real tension between the need for "cheap labor" seen in Coolidge's essay and the cultural and ideological displacements seen to accompany the arrival of new immigrants is described by Edmond Cros:

> At the beginning of the twentieth century, with the return of prosperity and despite the efforts of the Immigration Restriction League, [restrictive immigration policy] was fought by chambers of commerce and by the National Association of Manufacturers because economic expansion and the simplification of industrial techniques required an unskilled labor force. . . . [With the war with Germany], Americans discovered all at once that they could not remain apart from world conflicts and that inside the country were millions of unassimilated people. This emotional climate affected mental structures; patriotic loyalty was confused with conforming; marginality was suspected of potential treachery.[25]

The effort to place the bodies of new immigrants under surveillance and regulation is thus intimately linked to anxiety regarding their psychic dispositions. It is precisely at this moment that the American "mind" is negatively defined against a particular backdrop.

The rate of sterilization practiced in the United States in the first decades of the twentieth century is astounding and is explicitly connected to immigration and reproduction. Chapter headings for the Immigration Commission's reports included titles such as "Immigration and Insanity," and "Report on the Fecundity of Immigrant Women." By the end of the 1920s, sterilization laws existed in twenty-four states (as late as 1985, twenty-two states still had such laws). By the mid-1930s, some twelve thousand sterilizations had been legally performed in the United States.[26] Besides attempting to root out "criminal behavior" (which could be defined in any number of ways), sterilization was practiced to discipline those prone to "sexual excitement."[27] One of the most disturbing cases to be brought before the court was that of *Buck v. Bell*. It involved a seventeen-year-old Virginia girl named Carrie Buck, who was deemed a "moral imbecile" and committed to the Virginia Colony for Epileptics and Feebleminded. Her mother, Emma, had also been diagnosed as feebleminded. When Carrie became pregnant, she was given the Stanford revision of the Binet-Simon I.Q. test (since the First World War intelligence tests were commonly deployed to "sort out" blacks and other suspect populations). She was found to have the mental age of nine years.

Virginia officials asked Harry Laughlin of the Eugenics Records Office to advise them. Without even seeing Carrie or her mother, he proclaimed that they and their forbears "belong to the shiftless, ignorant, and worthless class of anti-social whites of the South."[28] The case was heard before a number of courts as a test case on sterilization. The Supreme Court's opinion was voiced by Oliver Wendell Holmes: "We have seen more than once that the public welfare may call upon the best citizens for their lives. It would be strange if it could not call upon those who already sap the strength of the State for these lesser sacrifices . . . in order to prevent our being swamped with incompetence. . . . The principle that sustains compulsory vaccination is broad enough to cover cutting the Fallopian tubes."[29]

Holmes's choice of analogy confirms that the general discourse of protecting the body had tremendous elasticity, linking the individual to the State by way of the commonly shared property of the body; one deemed to be a drain on the State was thus called on to patriotically submit to sterilization. The obverse of this is that if he or she did not, the State would suffer the slow but sure demise of its own body. Crucially, the correlation of the mental and the physical, the psychic and somatic, signals a powerful coalition that had to be brought under control by precisely the same, mutually legitimizing tools: a physical science that would excise and prevent reproduction (and underwrite legislative actions to do the same), and a mentality that placed difference under surveillance. Kevles notes: "A 1937 *Fortune* magazine poll revealed that 63 percent of Americans endorsed the compulsory sterilization of habitual criminals and that 61 percent were in favor of sterilizing mental defectives. The country, said E. A. Hooton, professor of physical anthropology at Harvard University, had to do some 'biological housecleaning'. . . . H. L. Mencken . . . suggested that the federal government pay a thousand dollars to every 'adult American' who volunteered to be sterilized" (114). Again, such metaphors are revealing, for the cleaning of the domestic space found that the "social problem group" conveniently defined the social Other. In an increasingly complex world, with the threat of further and more frequent contact with other types of peoples, miscegenation then was precisely the wrong sort of assimilation. Sterilization was proposed to permanently alter the bodies of those whose genes would contaminate the national body; similarly, anti-miscegenation laws were written to prevent the intermingling and weakening of American "stock." The immigration, naturalization, and exclusionary laws, and those limiting or prohibiting aliens from owning land or engaging in work, which became codified in the 1920s, effectively represent the nature of America's obsession with redefining its national body.

The relation between such acts and the specific case of Asian Americans is clear. The Cable Act of 1922 declared that any woman citizen of the United States would be stripped of her citizenship if she married an alien ineligible for naturalization. Under U.S. law, the only other act for which one could have one's citizenship revoked was treason. This act was one of the first and most significant laws addressing precisely the introjection of Asians in America—an attempt to legislate the nature of the Americanization of Asians. This, of course, would affect the composition of the Asian American community. As Osumi explains, "The aim . . . was to discourage *Nisei* women and women of other races from marrying *Issei* men."[30] This prohibition took place precisely at the time that laws prohibiting aliens from owning land (the first of which was passed in California in 1913) became widespread, and particularly intervened in the trade between aliens and U.S. citizens. Sucheng Chan notes:

> California's voters supported an initiative on the 1920 state ballot that ended the ability of Asian aliens to lease farm land altogether. It also forbade them to purchase land through corporations in which they held more than 50 percent of the stocks or in the names of their American-born (hence citizen) minor children. A 1923 amendment made cropping contracts—agreements between landowners and alien farmers under which the latter planted and harvested crops for wages —illegal, even though such arrangements technically conferred no legal interest in the land itself.
>
> Following California's example, Arizona enacted a similar law in 1917, Washington and Louisiana in 1921, New Mexico in 1922, Idaho, Montana, and Oregon in 1923, and Kansas in 1925.[31]

Hence we may note in the 1920s an intensification in the segregation and partitioning of Asia from America, which is entirely in keeping with a general and increased anxiety over what modernity had brought to America. The chances of any liaison between Asia and America that might produce a racial hybrid, and the chance of an Asian American being a propertied citizen (i.e., the dual threat of merged bodies and economies) were considered correlate. We come up against a willed barrier, and yet at this time there is as well a historical imperative to shrewdly finesse this barrier.

Asians in the Modern American State

It is if we had said: Europe, of which after all America is a mere
western projection, ends here. The Pacific Coast is our racial frontier.

In the long run it is difficult if not impossible to maintain, in
America or elsewhere, racial frontiers. All the currents of modern life
run counter to a policy of racial or national isolation.

—Robert Ezra Park, "Our Racial Frontier on the Pacific"

We have seen that notions of modernity are intimately linked to the notion of migrancy. One of the fundamental questions for the modern state has been how to address dramatically increased flows of people, moving across borders and inserted into national spaces in ever more informal, chaotic, and uneven ways, how to exploit these flows and at the same time neutralize their threat. This tension between the national and the migrant is most visible, for example, in debates over immigration policy, citizenship, labor laws, and human rights, which attempt to track, legislate, and codify the movements of people, and yet leave open, however briefly and unevenly, certain avenues for certain bodies.

The above citations from Robert Park attest to the centrality of East Asia in the imagining of American modernity. The American state, "after all," is relegated to the status of mere extension of Europe; American exceptionalism is collapsed and triumphant "manifest destiny" erased in the process, and another imperative instantiated. Within this logic, the historical, nation-defining westward movement of the modern United States is re-identified as simply part of a project of extending European racial continuity from the old world. The "racial frontier" presented at the edge of the Pacific marks the limit of America's ability to extend the European *race* (and, by implication, European culture and civilization) beyond its own geographic limits.

Yet Park, having raised this "frontier" as an object of scrutiny, then proceeds to erode its fortifications—modern life is, after all, slowly making *all* frontiers problematic. He specifies the root of this new, more far-reaching problematic, setting forth a prescient portrayal of the global economy:

The effect of the steady expansion of international commerce has been to create over the whole earth a vast unconscious cooperation of races and peoples, such that a wheat corner in Chicago a few years ago caused a bread riot in Liverpool, and the price of rubber on the London market has been at times a matter of life and death to the native of Central Africa. This world-wide division of labor, which every new device of transportation and communication has progressively made possible, and every new application of science to industry has made increasingly desirable, has not been effected without some costs and some disorganization of industrial and social life.[32]

This general "disorganization," manifesting a dramatic contraction of space, deeply informs the specific events that surround the "new racial frontier" of the Pacific in the late 1920s. For example, Japan's victory over Russia in 1905 had catapulted Japan into the role of East Asian hegemon. Japan was now seen through the optics of a new, technologically sophisticated and capitalist-oriented imperialism. While China lacked any real military or political credibility, and hence its protests over the the U.S. exclusion acts fell on deaf ears, Japan's victory over Russia and its progressive annexation of parts of East Asia made it a formidable foe, especially as regards the United States' own interests in East Asia. Under these circumstances, the issue of whether the Japanese should even be considered as Asians arose. The boundaries of a "racial frontier" not marked exclusively by race but now correlated with imperialistic and economic power came to the foreground. Imperialist expansion was read into Japanese migrancy as well.

As early as 1914, Kiyoshi Kawakami notes the suspicion with which some in the United States viewed the immigration of Japanese into Mexico and South America. He felt that the alarmist evocation of the Monroe Doctrine to stem this Japanese migration was uncalled for: in his view, this migration was simply attributed to the fact that the Japanese were merely following the "universal" trend toward modernity along with the rest of the western world: "Japan clearly realizes the impossibility of casting her lot with the huge, inert mass of humanity that inhabits the Asian continent. She believes that her interest is more closely interwoven with that of the Occident than with that of the Oriental races, that in temperament and inclination she has much more in common with the Western peoples that with those of Asia."[33] This passage clearly distinguishes the enterprising, modernizing Japanese state from the "mass" of Asia, and articulates a new geopolitical imaginary that refuses to contain nations within racial categories. Fed by a strong sense of self-confidence derived from its economic, political, and military victories, Japan came to feel itself on a par with the West in all respects.

Hence its particularly vehement outcry at the San Francisco School Board's decision to group Japanese children in with Chinese and other non-white children, a decision into which President Theodore Roosevelt had to intervene and which was a strong factor in bringing about the Gentlemen's Agreement in 1907, which set certain parameters regarding the immigration of Japanese to America. Rebuffed in its attempt to be treated as "western," Japan declared itself leader of Asia and champion of equal rights for all Asian countries. This conjoined neatly with its imperialist project—its incursions into other Asian countries were now represented as acts of protection against "foreign" invasion by western powers.[34] Therefore, the "racial frontier" of which Park speaks is put under pressure by Japanese insistence that they had earned the right to be "white" (that is, considered a world power), and American resistance to such an audacious notion.

While above we noted Park's reduction of America to mere extension of Europe, he also posited America's unique destiny as a Pacific state. Indeed, that is what distinguishes modern America. In particular, the link between U.S. domestic and foreign policy with regard to Asia is noted by Park as joined in a common definitive moment: "The present ferment in Asia and the racial conflict on the Pacific Coast of America are but different manifestations of what is, broadly speaking, a single process; a process which we may expect to continue until some sort of permanent equilibrium has been established between the races and peoples on both sides of the oceans."[35] Any attempt to legislate away the steady advance of Asia into America is futile: "It is vain to underestimate the character and force of the tendencies that are drawing the races and peoples about the Pacific into the ever narrowing circle of common life. Rising tides of color and oriental exclusion laws are merely incidental evidences of these diminishing distances."[36] The effects of this "diminished distance," brought about by the "tendencies" of modernity (the global political economy), are to be read precisely on American terrain, which is now reconfigured by the presence of Asians. This line of demarcation is read as a *racial* frontier in the midst of a global economy that demanded free trade. The interplay between racial ideology and economic interests drives the formation of Asian America. While economic relations were a necessary part of America's modern dream, the uncertainty of racial relations was its nightmare.

The Tydings-McDuffie Act of 1934 was the culmination of anti-Asian legislation that can be traced at least as far back as the 1882 Chinese Exclusion Act, the Gentlemen's Agreement of 1908, and the 1917 and 1924 Immigration Acts.[37] The Asian presence in America prompted the first federal law ever designed to exclude a racial group. Bill Ong Hing argues that "their very presence fostered a fundamental rethinking of the role that immigration law might play in the construction of the United States as a national community."[38] Tydings-McDuffie excluded Chinese, Japanese, Korean, Asian Indian, and Filipino immigration. The latter two groups, for reasons we will address below, were particularly difficult to exclude; hence, the 1934 act marks a significant attempt to uniformly bar Asian immigration, and redefines America's notion of "Asian."

As noted above, the thing most guarded against was the production of any hybrid, any sign of producing something other than a perceived "norm." The racial hybrid was, to be precise, the sign of America's malleability. To manage that disruption of the American peace of mind, the hybrid had to be disavowed. Any such product was graphically depicted as monstrous and dangerous at worst, pathological and pathetic at best. In these fears, the biological and the psychological, the somatic and the psychic, became inextricably linked. The actual hybrid was only the most concrete form of the fear of difference. To neutralize this "monster," it had to be made self-destructive. Eugene F. Wong describes a 1936 serial:

> Shadow of Chinatown . . . used the figure of an insane Eurasian chemist, Victor Poten [portrayed by Bela Lugosi], not only to propagandize on the undesirability of interracial marriages between whites and Chinese, but also more importantly to emphasize the enfeebled and socially unacceptable character traits allegedly inherent to the offspring of such unions. Although Poten's own devilry was superlative, he nevertheless remained a subtly pathetic creature whose personal dilemma was rejection by whites and Chinese alike, and whose personal and social degeneracy lurked in his hatred for "both the Chinese and the white race."[39]

The language used to describe such abominations is often clearly marked as Asian. The term "mongoloid," first used in 1866 by a doctor to describe certain "mentally retarded" infants because he thought he saw "oriental" characteristics in their faces, became entrenched in popular speech as designating a particularly deformed entity.[40]

One of the key charges against Asians, and especially Filipinos, was that they were "breeders." One of the most outspoken exclusionists, C. M. Goethe, wrote in 1931, "The Filipino tends to interbreed with near-moron white girls. The resulting hybrid is almost invariably undesirable. The ever increasing brood of children of Filipino coolie fathers and low-grade white mothers may in time constitute a serious social burden."[41] Filipinos, themselves "products" of native, Hispanic, Asian, and white blood, are now seen as amplifying their hybridity on American soil. The result of layers of imperialist occupation comes to America in the form of the Filipino, and these bodies were attributed a particularly malicious sexuality. In 1933, California Attorney General Webb stated that biologically inassimilable races like the Pilipinos [sic] should no longer be allowed to mingle with the "dominant race in this country." Yet this statement against Filipinos is only the latest and most hysterical in the general movement against miscegenation with Asians.[42] Here we have compacted the issue of sex, class, and racial prejudice; most striking is the effect of such upon the white male middle-class figure. The production of these "others" (which can be expanded to include other racial and ethnic groups) can overwhelm the socioeconomic body and its psychic faculty. It is in this light that the particular articulation of "Yellow Peril" ideology in the 1920s and 1930s must be viewed in its specific historical relation to the modern U.S. state. The fear of racial otherness was not a mere abstraction, but connected to specific material histories.

For example, some have wondered why the Yellow Peril was associated with the Chinese, whose nation was in a generally weakened state throughout the early twentieth century, when the rising imperialist power, Japan, would seem a more logical choice (this situation changed, of course, most markedly after the beginning of the Sino-Japanese war in 1937). The long association of "Chinese" with "mass" helps explain this incongruity; for if China lacked military and political strength, it had more people than any other nation. In a survey of American attitudes toward Asia, Howard Isaacs found that the sheer brute imagery of the mass is what most associated with Asia: "From by far the largest number (139), a first response to a geographic term, Asia, was a geographic image, starting with the map itself, all the great expanse of it carried in outline on some mental screen first exposed in the early grades of school. . . . The places of Asia are first of all and overwhelmingly filled with people."[43] The 1929–34 edition of *Ripley's Believe It or Not* carries a cartoon entitled: "The Marching Chinese." Pictured is a mass of Chinese peasants, faces pointed to the ground and hidden under the shadows of their coolie hats, in a long line stretching off into the horizon. The text explains, "If all the Chinese in the world were to march—4 abreast—past a given point they would *never* finish passing though they marched forever and ever (based on U.S. Army marching regulations)."[44]

The "authority" of the source signals the seriousness of this "fact": the idea of innumerable, indeed infinite, "marching" Chinese was certainly not arrived at casually. The implied military purposes to which this uniform, seemingly mindless mass could be put for an infinite amount of time crossing infinite space drives the image. Is not this overwhelming faculty exactly the most horrific vision imaginable in an age that held onto a notion of the sanctity of the localization of the nation against all empirical evidence to the contrary? Indeed, the logic of the 1924 National Origins Act reflects the desire to control the effects of massification: immigrants were to be admitted in proportion to their numbers already in the United States, and the symmetry of the nation was to be retained even in conceding the inevitability of new numbers of arrivals. The contradiction such a phenomenon presented to those racists who subscribed to a distorted notion of "social Darwinism" is clear: if only the "fittest" survived, how could the white race falter? The contradiction was finessed by claiming that inferior races matured earlier and reproduced more quickly.[45] Nevertheless, between the Chinese "masses" and Japanese military and technological success, we have the instantiation of a fear that Asians might actually hold some superiority over whites.[46]

Certainly with the attack of the Japanese on China (not to mention Japan's earlier defeat of China over Manchuria), the notion of China's military might was at least partially neutralized. But the exportation of modern sanitation methods coupled with technology made China a particularly potent threat in terms of both an increased and more long-lived population, and in terms of their being harnessed to both new technologies as producers of commodities and to new global economics as consumers (although along with this ran the counter-argument that Chinese were hoarders who would produce for the west but not buy back its goods, thus destroying the west through a trade imbalance, a theme redeployed in the Japan-bashing of the 1970s and 1980s). The Chinese "mass" takes on a particular set of implications. Thompson notes: "In 1920 T. Lothrop Stoddard warned that even the Japanese could not compete against Chinese coolies. White world supremacy resulted from the Industrial Revolution but should that revolution sweep Asia, he warned, the white world would lose its prosperity as well as its economic and political power. . . . Stoddard saw social stagnation as the end for whites faced with Asiatic industrialization."[47]

The longstanding notion that Chinese lacked nerves and had special powers of resisting disease and physical strain only intensified the characterization of the Yellow Peril as a distinctly modern phenomenon of the mass. In 1894 Arthur H. Smith, a missionary in China, published a book, *Chinese Characteristics*, which had a chapter entitled "The Absence of Nerves." Later, in 1911, sociologist E. A. Ross wrote of the incredible recuperative powers of the Chinese, who had "a special race vitality" with "special resistance to infection and tolerance of unwholesome conditions of living." And in 1929, Bruno Lasker cited a contemporary detective story that told of a certain midget who could drink enormous quantities of alcohol without effect, explaining: "In the case of a white man, such indulgence might have caused sensational results. The midget, though, was Chinese, which means that his nerves were not highly organized — that he was virtually immune to stimulants." Lasker also noted a popular camping manual for boys that noted: "And there is the Chinaman, who being of a breed that has been crowded and coerced for thousands of years, seems to have done away with nerves. He will stand all day in one place without seeming in the least distressed; he thrives amidst the most unsanitary surroundings; overcrowding and bad air are as nothing to him."[48]

Although this may appear to be simply another version of the fear of the "Mongol horde," it is crucial to see the specifically historical character of this articulation of the Yellow Peril. We need to discern its particular ideological function. In this period, such a racial product fits into the mode of Fordist production especially well; we have in effect the perfect "laboring machine." Balibar notes that mechanized physical work requires a process that "modifies the status of the human body (the human status of the body): it creates *body-men*, men whose body is a machine-body, that is fragmented and dominated, and used to perform one isolable function or gesture, being both destroyed in its integrity *and* fetishized, atrophied *and* hypertropied in its 'useful' organs."[49]

We find in the late 1930s that the factory and the body (and by extension, the national body) become imaginatively condensed: "The human body is a machine, amenable to the same chemical and physical laws as most of the machines man makes himself for his own ends." The cells of the body are "disciplines" that now are imaginatively linked to a new urban economy: "like the City during working hours, the organs and limbs of the body are nourished by the body's blood just as the workers in a busy factory depend on the surrounding community for their nourishment".[50] The specific nature of the "Yellow Peril" as referring to Chinese thus is driven by a particular convergence of racist stereotyping with the new economics of labor and production in the 1930s—again and again we find the correlation of the racialized Asian body and the psyche in a discourse of new American and global space.

Certainly, anti-Asianists had long ago deployed such images to exclude Asians. Takaki notes that in the late nineteenth century, Chinese were recruited as an "'industrial reserve army' . . . migrant laborers forced to be foreigners forever, aliens ineligible for citizenship."[51] At this time, two visions of Asiatic labor had come into focus: first, that it would provide the raw mechanical labor for the industrial economy and thus free whites to be foremen and managers. A second view, popularized by Henry George, held that the ability of Asian cheap labor to perform as if it were a machine would actually set back industrialization. He reasoned that cheap Asian labor would serve as a substitute for mechanical invention and production; as the remnants of a bygone age, Chinese labor would retard technological advances.[52] Yet these views underwent significant modification in the 1930s.

First, the "migrant" status of Chinese became complicated by the development of entrenched communities after the Exclusion Act; this forced a revision of the notion that Chinese were merely sojourners in the United States and the realization that the problem now was to situate "Asia" within America. The comfortable notion that Asians were confined to specific geographic regions and ethnic ghettoes was counterbalanced, if only subliminally, by persistent questions as to the solidity of those borders. At the same time that the specter of masses of Chinese entering the United States was forestalled by exclusionary acts, there had been injected into the American imagination an entire set of other possibilities facilitated and even driven by new arrangements of global politics. On one hand, the ability of the United States to contain Asia was challenged by the nationalist upheavals in East Asia that engaged the West in new negotiations of Pacific neocolonialism. And on the other hand, as we will see in greater detail in Chapter 5, the view of Asians as confined to the laboring class changes to a more flexible one of Asians occupying the median space between white owners and black laborers. This, I believe, can be at least partially attributed to the recognition of Asia as a potential capitalist competitor (and hence the need for greater neocolonial control) and the fact that Henry George was proven wrong—Asian labor had not deterred technological advance. Instead, technological advance had contributed powerfully to the reinvention of social space and political economies, particularly with increased urbanization. So much so that the rough distinctions between classes were modified and nuanced, as was the geography of the American city, and this included a modification in the location of Asians within the American imaginary.

As the Chinese were seen as a particular manifestation of the Yellow Peril, closely linked with the general trope of "the mass" that was now particularly named within a discourse of global economic and technological change, as discussed above, Japan was largely seen through the optics of a new, technologically sophisticated and capitalist-oriented imperialism. Invasion from Japan was viewed in a way qualitatively different from the fear of mass Chinese immigration to the United States—it called into question the ability of the United States to monopolize the prerogatives of modernity. The "Yellow Peril" has to be read within particular historical specificities which show that the various mutations of the "peril" stem from particular economic and political phenomena in the United States itself. If the "peril" was Chinese, it can be linked closely to the particular mode of mass life that demanded a revision of American life around Fordist manufacturing. If it were Japanese, it has to be seen as the mirror image of recently developed American neocolonialism in East Asia, a project deeply attached to the imagining of a modern state.

The case of antipathy toward South Asian immigration into the United States was differentiated in terms of a perception of class; this projection is a direct outgrowth of colonization. On one hand, anti–South Asian exclusionists de-

cried their presence in much the same manner that the Chinese had been described: "From every part of the Coast complaints are made of the undesirabil-
ity of the Hindoos, their lack of cleanliness, disregard of sanitary laws, petty pil-
fering." There was the fear of a "Hindoo Invasion."[53] On the other hand, many
Americans, "postcolonials" themselves, felt a special annoyance at the appearance of Indian immigrants whose British manners and accents seemed to indicate that they thought better of themselves than of the Americans. One person
interviewed by Isaacs remarks: "The Indians are Anglicized in dress, manners,
and speech to a degree that is sometimes irritating. . . . They are consciously
imitating the British manner."[54]

The Thind case of 1923 illustrates well the dilemma American racists faced
in trying to exclude South Asians, and the elasticity with which they imbued the
legal fabric of the United States.[55] Several cases were brought before the courts
arguing that Indians should be eligible for naturalization because, in the triadic
categorization of race—Caucasian/Mongolian/Negro—they should, because
of geographic and ethnographic reasons, be considered Caucasians. In 1917,
Oliver B. Dickinson, a Pennsylvania federal judge, ruled that the geographic argument was invalid: "Congress had a vision of what the United States has since
become . . . the melting pot of almost all the nations of the world."[56] This judgment thus remaps the world according to the inner logic of American racism—
what counts is not the world "as is," but the world as it might appear relative to
the internal, highly historicized, interests of the United States. It becomes clear
that what will determine eligibility is no longer belonging to a group that was
now shown to include portions of the world thought to be Other, but rather a
more nebulous, malleable term—"white." "Whiteness" became the signified of
the *will* of Congress. That is, whatever Congress had in mind when it decided
on whom to accept as naturalizable, a necessary component was "whiteness." In
1923, the Supreme Court heard the case of Bhagat Singh Thind. He argued that
he, as a Caucasian, should be eligible for naturalization, since just the previous
year the Court had thrown out the case of Takao Ozawa based solely on the fact
that Ozawa was *not* Caucasian. However, as Jensen explains, "The government
had a different theory. It simply refused to accept the arguments of social scientists that Indians were Aryans, and hence Caucasians. The government argued
that *white* should be interpreted according to the usage of the common man, and
in that usage Indians were not white. . . . The supreme court had rejected science, history, legal precedent, and logic to put the Constitution at the disposal
of a legal fiction called 'the common man'."[57]

As Indians were thus relegated to the status of "non-white" along with Chinese, Japanese, and Koreans (who were colonized subjects of Japan and there-fore treated as Japanese), one group remained marginal—the Filipinos. Until 1934, Filipinos were considered American nationals, and hence their move-ment into the United States was relatively free. If Indians were disdained be-cause of their supposedly filthy "Hindoo" lifestyles, and distrusted for their An-glicized behavior, which elevated them above Americans, Filipinos, hybridized as they were with Indian, Asian, and Spanish blood, presented another complex set of reasons for exclusion. As noted above, what seems most conspicuous in anti-Filipino tirades is a fear of Filipino sexuality. In the late 1920s, Judge Rohrback of Monterey described the Filipino: "little brown men attired like 'Solomon in all his glory,' strutting like peacocks and endeavoring to attract the eyes of young American and Mexican girls."[58] Under such conditions, the deci-sion in 1932 to grant Philippine independence (after a ten-year interim period) must be seen as a result of great ambivalence. On the one hand, the United States seemed to be giving up its control of the Philippines as a "mother colony" for its new Pacific enterprise; on the other hand, it could now drastically limit Filipino immigration, which was what the Tydings-McDuffie Act of 1934 did, setting an annual quota of fifty. With this act, the United States completed the program to stifle immigration from Asia.

Yet at this precise moment, the introjection of minorities within the United States evinced a new complexity: the mixture of the foreign with the domestic and the various possibilities of interracial and interethnic connections presented a new set of concerns. For example, the particular fear of labor agitation was founded in part on the possibility of foreign radicalism coupled with interethnic solidarity. In 1925, the Pullman Company hired Filipino workers to break a strike by the Brotherhood of Sleeping Car Porters. In 1930, the union opened its doors to the Filipinos (in contradistinction to the American Federation of Labor, which excluded Asians): "We wish it understood that the Brotherhood has nothing against the Filipinos. They have been used against the unionization of Pullman porters just as Negroes have been used against the unionization of white workers."[59] In the same year, between January 19 and January 23, anti-Filipino agitation reached a peak in the Watsonville (California) riot.[60] Although this riot was fed in large part by the belief that Filipinos were committed to the communist cause, DeWitt argues that this portrayal is largely exaggerated.[61] Nevertheless, he also notes the union formed across ethnic lines by Mexican and Filipino farm workers. Catapusan's 1940 study of the relationship between Fili-pino workers and the labor unions during this period comments on the shift in AFL policies toward Filipinos: "the American Federation of Labor took advan-

tage of this situation [the organizing by Filipinos of separate union groups] to in-
vite these loosely organized minority labor groups to come into their organization with the idea that [it was] only through the unions that unnecessary cut-
throat competition could be properly eliminated."[62]

Thus while the fear of a mass, multiethnic socialist movement was not entirely well founded, it reveals the particular contours of the social imagination:
what could strike more fear into the hearts of "Americans" than the image of immigrants, whose movement into the country had been contained, gathering together in such a way as to offset that containment? (This, of course, can be linked
to the depiction of newer immigrants from Eastern Europe as "anarchists.") The
most dramatic example of this fear was perhaps manifested in the "Hilo Massacre." On August 1, 1938, several hundred people marched in support of an
I.L.W.U. strike. The protest was highly organized as a passive demonstration in
support of the workers. Demonstrators and workers were whites, blacks, and
Asians of various ethnicities. The demonstration was broken up by police who
used buckshot and bayonets against the men, women, and children.[63] These acts
of solidarity certainly do not overshadow the fact that American labor provided
the greatest momentum for anti-Asian legislation in the years leading up to the
1930s. But what is most significant is that the particular fear of the American
state regarding the *interpenetrability* of groups from different races and ethnicities is now defined in these specific terms.

In this period new strategies had to be evolved to address the problem of Asians
in a modern, multi-ethnic state. William Carlson Smith's *Americans In Process: A
Study of Our Citizens of Oriental Ancestry* (1937) takes up this question in its very
title: these orientals are claimed as "ours," and properly recognized as citizens
of the United States. Yet they are still, at once, *in process*. Although legally American, they have yet to achieve the full ontological status of American. In his introduction to Smith's book, Romanzo Adams makes several significant points.
First, he notes the shift from the country to the city: "We are faced by the necessity of redefining America. Formerly America was predominantly agricultural and rural, but it is becoming industrial and urban. Those American traits
that represent the old pioneer life are undergoing modification and new urban
traits, ultimately to be regarded as American, are in the process of development." But in the meanwhile, there is a vacuum: "There seems to be no well-
defined tendency among these newer immigrant peoples in the direction of
Americanism—the Americanism of tradition."[64] Hence, in the introjection of
Asians into America, a movement intimately linked to the emergence of moder-

nity, there is a substantial and troubling question as to not only their predication into full "Americanism," but what, exactly, that America is to be.

Part of the strategy to address this indecidability was to exploit a flexible ideology to meet these new contingencies in the domestic and international arenas. There is a specific variability in the articulations of the "Yellow Peril" in the 1920s and 1930s that evinces a mixture of fear, anxiety, and necessity, fueled by the formation of an eminently *modern* America, focused now on the precise nature of the new relationship between Asia and America. The copresence of a residual ideology of general anti-Asian Yellow Perilism, and an emergent ideology of difference that discriminates between different Asian groups according to their new national identities, can be tracked to both a gradual shift in notions of migrant identity in the 1920s and 1930s and the dramatic events in East Asia in the late 1930s.

This relocating was produced within both emergent and residual discourses; I would not claim that modern America simply "evolved" into a more enlightened stage of apprehending Asia and Asian Americans. While the discourse of exclusion anticipated the full development of anti-Asian imagery in the early 1930s, this discourse discloses as well a recognition that what were formerly regarded as well-defined domestic and global spaces were now crosshatched by new contests over national interests under the imperatives of monopoly capitalism and neocolonialism. And it was this instability that gave the images of Asians in America their particular texture. In the next chapter, I will examine how this retexturing, if repressed in the political consciousness of the American state, was articulated (however subliminally) in imaginative fictions.

2 / Rescripting the Imaginary

AT THE SAME MOMENT THAT political, journalistic, sociological, and academic discourses grappled with an unpredictable and unstable set of issues regarding the introjection and projection of Asian America, literary narratives written by both Asian Americans and non-Asian Americans attempted to invent within their specific discursive spaces images of Asian America that both delineate its boundaries and envision particular modes of crossing them. The very desire to do so discloses the heightened interest in that possibility, and perhaps even an acknowledgment of its historical necessity. Just as, in 1939, the editor of the journal *Philosophy East and West* convened the first East-West Philosophers' Conference to "explore the significance of eastern ways of thinking for the development of a global consciousness, a sort of 'synthesis' of the ideas and ideals of East and West," so too did literary narratives attempt to imagine how the "East" and the "West" might meet in modern American consciousness.[1]

The narratives treated below each manifest in different ways a shift in the literary representations of Asians, now located in a new world of modern foreign relations, technologies, and nationalisms. While political, sociological, journalistic, and academic (to name but a few) discourses share a certain ideological relationship synchronically, it is important to attend to the specific manners in which particular sorts of imaging are allowed and enabled by each discursive regime. Literature and film, as codified systems of imaginative representation, share a particular trait. Here, both strain to create a particular staging of realities that can only be anticipated in future time. This postponement discloses a repressed sociopolitical unconscious. It is precisely the invention of such realities that points up the disjuncture between what the imagination proffers and the limits of narration as historical act. The narratives I address in this study attempt to map out and make visible an Asian America that cannot but lapse back into contradiction under the weight of history. In their very unevenness, these attempts to create a unified portrait, conforming to narrative conventions and under pressure to "make sense," productively raise central questions as to the precise nature of Asian America in the American imaginary.

Literary narratives touching upon the projection and introjection of Asia into America in the 1930s evince a common set of complications of Yellow Peril discourse: the long-anticipated Asiatic "invasion" becomes highly verbal and mental, disclosing a particular apprehension of the possibilities of discursive intercourse in a new global space that references the rise of fascism, imperialism, and monopoly capitalism, as well as the production of particular nationalistic discourses in Asia and in America. Asian America is confronted with a specific set of issues regarding its imbrication in the national, the diasporic, and the global. The *modus operandi* of Asian "invasions" shows a concrete awareness of the specific historical moment, and in particular it acknowledges a different sort of political economy at work. For example, Sax Rohmer's 1936 novel, *President Fu Manchu*, shows a marked contrast to earlier Fu Manchu tales, which centered on Fu Manchu's grandiose attempts to conquer the world via a potent blend of modern technology and ancient "oriental" methods of assassination. While *President Fu Manchu* draws on such devices (notably a rare breed of poison spiders), the main tool for the conquest of America this time is the democratic process itself. Fu Manchu sets up a populist candidate, Harvey Bragg, a blustering, crude politician capitalizing on working-class and middle-class discontent in the aftermath of the Depression. His campaign slogan is "America for every man— every man for America." The one person who seems to understand the particular threat Bragg poses is a Father Donegal. He, and Rohmer's hero, Sir Denis Nayland Smith (representing, respectively, the vestiges of Catholic mysticism and Anglo-Saxon pragmatism), discuss Bragg:

> Then the priest, whose burning rhetoric, like that of Peter the Hermit, had roused a nation, found voice; he spoke in very low tones:
> "Why do you say he will certainly be Dictator?"
> "I said *almost* certainly. His war cry, 'America for every man—every man for America' is flashing like a fiery cross through the country. Do you realize that in office Harvey Bragg has made remarkable promises?"
> "He has carried them out! He controls enormous funds."
> "He does! Have you any suspicion, Father, of the source of those funds?"
> For a fleeting moment a haunted look came into the abbot's eyes. A furtive memory had presented itself, only to elude him.

"None," he replied wearily; "but his following today is greater than mine. Just as a priest and with no personal pretensions, I have tried—God knows I have tried—to keep the people sane, and clean. Machinery has made men mad. As machines reach nearer and nearer the province of miracles, as Science mounts higher and higher—so Man sinks lower and lower. On the day that Machinery reaches up to the stars, Man, spiritually, will have sunk back to the primeval jungle."

He dropped into his chair.

Smith, resting a lean, nervous hand upon his desk, leaned across it, staring into the speaker's face.

"Harvey Bragg is a true product of his age," he said tensely—"and he is backed by *one man*! . . . In the political disruption of this country he sees his supreme opportunity."[2]

Donegal touches upon the prominent themes of the 1920s—the mental and physical health of the masses has been corrupted by the rise of technology; any spirituality is now but an outmoded source of healing. But in the 1930s, it is crucial to note that it is precisely on the *rhetorical* that victory will be based, not on physical or technological aggression: Fu Manchu has infiltrated and mastered the very political discourse that controls the democratic process.[3]

This conquest differs significantly from earlier articulations of Asian infiltration of American politics, such as Pierton W. Dooner's *The Last Days of the Republic* (1880). In this novel, Dooner predicates an invasion of America on a modification of its naturalization laws, which makes Asians eligible for citizenship. Masses of Asiatics arrive, become naturalized, and take over U.S. politics.[4] In contradistinction, in Rohmer's narrative the weak spot of America is class antagonism and a spiritually deprived, technologically obsessed populace. It is not brought about by simple ignorance of the threat posed by the Yellow Peril. Rather than Dooner's crude conquest by sheer numbers (which is used to argue for exclusion and the permanent status of "alien" for all Asians in the United States, and is published two years before the Chinese Exclusion Act), Rohmer's narrative focuses on the ability of his Asiatic "genius" to infiltrate the political machinery and read the political landscape of the U.S. so masterfully that he is able to script a presidential campaign based precisely upon the present economic conditions of the country and to deliver that script in the "voice of America."

But this infiltration has a surprising twist. At the moment of his greatest popularity, Bragg is assassinated by Fu Manchu. His second in command, the person behind Bragg's speeches, is put in his place. This character is Paul Salvaletti, who now takes over Bragg's "League of Good Americans": "Could anything, short of the destruction of that apparently indestructible life [Fu's], prevent the triumph of Paul Salvaletti? The puzzle was maddeningly insoluble. The League of Good Americans began frankly to assume the dimensions of a Fascisti movement."[5]

Social and political popular reform is transformed into a fascism, distanced from the possibility that it could be an *American* product by attributing it to an Italian, backed by a Chinese. These "aliens" represent new and unassimilable waves of immigration from the Mediterranean and Asia. The specific mechanism that affects this conquest of the American vote is both technologically managed and discursively produced—Bragg's and Salvaletti's words are broadcast via radio to all the country. Yellow Perilism here must be understood then in terms of Rohmer's perception of the greatest fears of the American public— old-style emplotments of sinister agents of the orient are cast in the context of contemporary problems affecting the nation-state. These problems disclose the ideological contradictions of democratic capitalism in a time of increased fascist activity abroad.

A second example of how the Yellow Peril is rearticulated in a more complex frame in order to comment on contemporary political issues is Solomon Cruso's *The Last of the Japs and the Jews* (1933), a sweeping revision of utopian/ dystopian narratives. Certainly, other novels had speculated on the possibilities of global war made possible by new technologies, for example, H. G. Wells's *War in the Air* (published in 1907 and reprinted in 1922). In Wells's novel, Germany attacks the U.S. in retaliation for American interference in German imperialist activities in Latin America. A "complex system of alliances and ententes quickly drew every Western nation into the conflict. . . . Just as the Western nations were locked in their titanic air struggle, China and Japan leaped into the fray with thousands of aircraft which no one so much as dreamed they possessed. The Orientals assaulted both sides without favor or discrimination and embarked upon an orgy of fearful destruction."[6] In contrast to this rather easily delineated world war, Cruso's text is animated by a peculiarly "multicultural" progressive agenda, which articulates a convoluted but compelling set of meditations on a dysfunctional world of monopoly capitalism, masculinism, and racial and ethnic oppression and separatism.

Cruso begins by dedicating his narrative to the "proud Aryan brotherhood" that vainly battled the incursions of the orient. Yet even though he tries to maintain the voice of a persecuted WASP racist minority, it soon becomes clear that this narrative is motivated by an agenda quite different from that of white supremacism. The tale begins in 2390, with Native Americans roaming the land on horseback; they have repopulated the entire North American continent. The narrator then sets out to provide the lost history of how this came to be. First, he narrates the demise of world socialism during the 1930s, which was brought about by the corruption of the communist/socialist regime. During this time a young man named "Chang Kochubey" comes of age. His father is a Russian prince, his mother a Manchu princess; his father is the son of a Russian prince and the daughter of the chief rabbi of the "Jewish community of Plevna." His great grandfather was a general in the Russian calvary who was married to a Swedish countess.

This eminently hybridized individual takes on a mission given him by his Jewish grandmother—to avenge the Jews killed in the pogroms. Only the Turks, who gave shelter to the Jews, will be spared. Chang falls in love with a beautiful Mexican aristocrat, Arabella, but their marriage is forbidden by her father, who curses Chang as a "Chinaman and a half-breed."[7] Chang then goes off alone to pursue his mission. En route, he is lost at sea. But this turns out to be fortuitous, for he lands on a lost island—which happens to be Japan. In 1960, Japan had been drowned under a huge tidal wave, and all its advanced technology and accumulated capital was lost.[8] Chang inherits all this, and when his father finally discovers him, they agree to keep the island a secret and use it as a base of operations. Chang recruits masses of Americans, mostly Jews, to sail to a "foreign country" and participate in the building of a new nation. A decade later, he addresses the League of Nations, seeking compensation for the "historical injustices and crimes, committed by the European nations in the past, and . . . still being committed by them against the weaker races, weaker nations" (153). He demands universal decolonization and compensation for all colonized or historically persecuted peoples, including Native Americans and blacks. The League scoffs at his demands. In a show of force, Chang begins an air attack on the west, deploying super airships based on the recovered Japanese technologies. This sets off a devastating global war, which leaves the world nearly depopulated and the Jews victims of a horrible backlash. The victors turn out to be China, India, and Turkey, under whose rule the world is reconsolidated:

> India and China have both shown that they were worthy of leadership; that they were destined and fit to rule the world, though in a different manner; in a different way; in real Asiatic fashion; because they have different conceptions of ruling—socially, politically, and economically.
>
> For instance, China and India, right after the war, were of the opinion, that the peace of the world would always be threatened, due to racial disturbances.
>
> They also understood that not all evils were due to the capitalistic structure and the greed for power.

They believed that even if the entire human race ever acquired economic and political equality, there still would be hatred, the chauvinistic, the racial hatred. . . .

They decided to intermingle all races of the world, except the red, into one race, thus delivering a crushing blow to the racial abcess. (323)

The three Asian countries then embark upon a program of setting all peoples into a global diaspora, thereby accelerating cosmopolitanism and hybridization. Alongside this racial equalizing, they do away with capitalism:

Through a very simple manner, in real Asiatic, barbaric fashion, [they] cut the abcess, squeezed out the poison, and healed it to the satisfaction and admiration of the entire world.

The abcess was the beginning of a dangerous cancer, which commenced to grow very fast, in the form of big capitalistic trusts; the big capitalistic mergers; the centralization of big capital in the hands of a few ravenous individuals and groups, which caused misery to the middle class and the workers. (328)

This utopian plan is attempted by nationalizing all transportation, utilities, mining, and so on. The words "socialism, communism, anarchism, bolshevism" are "not to be found in the dictionaries of China, India and Turkey, for they became words of the past" (329). Nevertheless, the narrator withholds Utopia—capitalism still exists; Utopia will not be completely attained until "all races will have melted into one race" (330).

This heady admixture of socialist utopian fantasy rewrites the Yellow Peril within a progressive agenda that works against the grain of former Yellow Peril literature. To begin with, "yellow" here is dispersed and reconfigured as a particular Asiatic regime which, because of its "barbaric" heritage, is ironically the sole agent capable of neutralizing equally barbaric capitalism and imperialism by nationalization and decolonization. But concomitant with that excision is the eradication of that other "abcess," racism, which is programmatically to be erased by hybridization.[9] Now, obviously, this text cannot be held to be "representative" of a new trend; however, it does hint at a new flexibility in the imagining of Asia within the new global and domestic worlds. Most significantly, racial hybridity takes on a specific pragmatic function within this historical specificity, and is attached to a specific address to global history: the threat posed by Japan's rise as a technological and military power is neutralized (if only by an act of God) and, in fact, put in the service of socialist utopianism, as is the authoritarian "tradition" of China. This potent combination accesses real anxieties and contrives out of them a particular picture of the post-apocalyptic world.

The domestic space of the United States is also narrated within a frame of increased cultural hybridity, and with reference to particular modes of introjection and projection that refer both to new understandings of Asia and its relation to the United States and to the particular dynamics of incorporating Asians into America. Within the domestic, one finds a particular attention paid to notions of cultural mixedness within the specific themes of the diasporic. Sandra Hawley's "The Importance of Being Charlie Chan" demonstrates how this popular figure becomes staged precisely as the representation of the anxiety over the process of hybridization and assimilation in the middle of that "Pacific Racial Frontier."[10] She notes:

> Part of Charlie Chan's ambivalence toward the Americanization of his children derives from the fact that he himself is part of the process of Americanization. He constantly tests himself to see how much he has become American and how much that has changed him. . . .
>
> Trying to explain his inability to interrogate an elderly Chinese servant, Chan admits that "a gulf like the heaving Pacific lies between us. Because he, although among Caucasians for many more years than I, still remains Chinese. . . . While I—I bear the brand—the label—Americanized."[11]

Located in the liminal space of Hawai'i, Chan's mental prowess represents the utility of the "Asian mind," yet devotes its imaginative potential to the service of American law. Caught in the role of serving the legal prerogatives of the United States, Chan is rewarded with the dubious distinction of being more sophisticated than the simple, monocultural whites he encounters. And yet this "sophistication" is haunted by a sense of loss; its celebration of a "good" Chinese portrait is compromised by the character's own awareness of the disappearance of China itself. This romantic eulogy, this portrayal of cultural loss from the pen of a European, stands in contrast to another narrative, which embeds its representation in a particular material history.

H. T. Tsiang's *And China Has Hands* (1937), one of the earliest fictional narratives by a modern Chinese American author, similarly raises the question of mixedness (in this case, both racial and cultural) and the disappearance of "China" as an idealized point of national identification, with particular reference to a political as well as cultural attachment to an Asia undergoing profound political and cultural change.[12] The protagonist, Wong Wan-Lee, saves his earnings as a waiter in a Chinese restaurant and buys a laundry, hoping some day to return to the restaurant and buy it. The novel describes his attempts at eco-nomic self-determination, at fulfilling the promise of American democratic capi-talism. Throughout he is faced with anti-Chinese racism, but Tsiang's treatment of race becomes more complicated with the introduction of the character of Pearl Chang, who arrives in New York from the south, and in fact "rescues" him from the racist taunts of a group of young white boys. It turns out that she is biracial—half Chinese and half black, born and raised in a white supremacist southern state. The novel thus presents the problems of the shifting signifi-cances of race, as Chinese in the south are perceived (and perceive themselves) as better than blacks, yet are prevented from ascending to the status of white. Pearl comes north to pass for Chinese; her relation with Wan-Lee articulates their respective uses of "China" as a nodal point of identification. Wan-Lee and Pearl become engaged in a disjointed romance that evinces their differing per-ceptions of being "raced" in America. The interactions between the two mark off the assumptions of ethnic authenticity, that is, the behavior necessary to "qualify" as Chinese, as well as the value of such identification. Such negotiations are carried out in a number of ideological crises: sexual, economic, political, nationalistic, but all deeply inscribed historically.

For instance, the interconnection of these elements is found in the first en-counter between Wan-Lee and Pearl: unable either verbally or physically to ward off the white boys who are harassing him with racist slurs, Wan-Lee at-tempts to win their favor by throwing lichee nuts at them. He hopes that they will eat the nuts and stop taunting him. Throughout the novel, Tsiang allegori-cally links the action of the characters to the respective national situations of the United States and China. Here he clearly is alluding to the weakened state of China struggling with civil strife, foreign capital, and Japanese imperialism. One strategy adopted by Chinese leaders was, indeed, to curry favor with the powerful by bribing them. In this scene, Pearl heroically appears and banishes the boys with her sharp American slang, which catches them unawares. Pearl's motives for helping Wan-Lee are not primarily romantic, but rather founded upon her desire to "know a Chinaman" and thus understand that part of her racial and cultural background, which was inaccessible to her in the South, the site of her maternal legacy. Similarly, Wan-Lee is forced to work in a Chinese cafete-ria after he loses his laundry to a loan shark, and there he organizes restaurant workers against the big bosses of Chinatown. At the same time as he attains a sense of class struggle—which crosses over racial and national boundaries— Wan-Lee becomes more and more involved in arguing for Chinese unity. He sets aside his partisanship with the Chinese Communist Party and argues that it must work together with the nationalist Kuomintang (KMT) in order to defeat their common foe: the Japanese.

The issue of how "Asian America" is constituted in this novel of the late 1930s thus evinces a careful attention to the issues of both internal and foreign subjectivities; to the constitution of Asian/American identity according to issues of gender, race, ethnicity, and class; and to the relationship of Asians in America to their country of origin. Indeed, it suggests that "Asian America" be read precisely within a shifting relationship of rearticulations of race, gender, and class within the United States, and of the vision of "Asia" as the site of increasingly complex geopolitical negotiations. Most significantly, in the process of negotiating its identifications of and with "China," the novel ends up maintaining a dual focus on socialist utopias in Asia and America.[13]

The narrative sets up Wan-Lee's laundry as a specific chronotope. Wan-Lee is confronted by a series of scams, beginning with a forced payoff to an immigration official and followed by encounters with traveling salesmen, prostitutes, extortionists, and city inspectors. He attempts to fend off such attacks from within the space of his laundry, which he regards as a "temple" (34). This appellation obviously is founded on his nostalgic identification with China, which he has transported in small form to America, and yet the laundry is also a space wherein Wan-Lee can exercise the prerogatives of modern American private enterprise: "He thought he could move freely, breathe freely, and there would be no boss to tell him how to move, how to breathe, or when he should and when he should not" (12). He jealously protects his identity as owner, and his private life, carefully delineating the nature and space of his relationship with the outside: "This counter told customers, 'Outside you stay; inside there is a kingdom and there is an emperor, His Majesty, Wong Wan-Lee!'" (14). Economic necessity requires a point of contact and intercourse with America, but Wan-Lee's ownership of his laundry provides him the (limited) right to negotiate that contact. In the course of the narrative, however, that control becomes more and more contingent and tenuous.

Pearl's situation also is deeply linked to the relationship between China and America. We first see her working as an artist's model. Initially she is reluctant to take the job: "Not only was her own reputation but that of her race involved" (29). This statement implies Pearl's assumption of her sexual attraction and the debased motives of the artists; she seems almost disappointed when the artists turn out to be genuine: "The artists seemed more interested in what was going on on the canvas than in looking at her" (30). Her pride in being Chinese (rather than black), her certainty that as a Chinese woman she bears both the burden of maintaining the dignity of "her race" and the desirability of the feminine and the orient, is short-circuited. The Americans who employ her show no special interest in these facts—what matters to them is the way they can manipulate and fashion the real object into a mimetic one, "on their canvas."

Pearl maintains a proud identification with China precisely because her ability to "pass" rescues her from the onus of her racial hybridity. Her interest in Wan-Lee is prompted by her desire to work in the opposite direction the artists do; that is, from representation to reality. She is trying to obtain a "genuine" sense of China and claim her right to identify herself with that and that alone (and to jettison the black part of her identity):

> She had seen things about China in the movies and read things about China in novels. She had heard things about China from her white teachers and white schoolmates. She had a general idea of how a Chinaman looked. But she felt she would learn more if she could have a chance to see a Chinaman herself, with her own eyes, and to feel one with her own hands. (35)

But, crucially, Tsiang is careful to link this desire for racial authentication with Pearl's desire for assimilation in America, specifically targeted to the middle class. She and her female roommate decorate their apartment:

> The bookshelves in both rooms were filled with books which they had picked up in second-hand book stores. The cover of each book was attractive and the price was not more than ten or fifteen cents a copy. With all the books lined up and various colors mixed, these bookshelves were certainly good decorations—economical and highbrow. (54)

As their relationship develops, Wan-Lee uses his Chineseness as a token of his superiority over the American-born Pearl, specifically to neutralize her power over him as both an American and a strong woman whom he desires: "Wong Wan-Lee sneered at Pearl Chang and was proud of himself—how well he could handle his chopsticks! . . . Wong Wan-Lee thought that Pearl Chang was an angel, but now he thought she was just a 'Mo No,' a term which China-born Chinese use to make fun of an American-born Chinese. In Cantonese, 'Mo' means 'no' and 'no' means 'brain'" (61). This appellation becomes especially fitting in Wan-Lee's eyes when Pearl "innocently" uses the term "Chinky" as one of endearment. She cannot see the connection between her using this term and the initial instance of the boys taunting Wan-Lee with the term "Chinaman"; she cannot glimpse her own complicity in American racism:

> Pearl Chang, in the midst of looking everywhere, looked at the baby, and touched her cheek and called: 'You little Chinky!' The baby stared at her and cried.
>
> Wong Wan-Lee thought she was "Mo No"—had no brain. How could she call the baby Chinky! The baby did not like it; that was why she was crying. And Pearl Chang was a Chinese herself! (66)

Nevertheless, Pearl's difference holds a certain attraction for Wan-Lee because it maintains his superiority ("But because she was a little bit 'Mo No' he liked her more" [78]). The two characters seem to work at cross purposes: as Wan-Lee is fascinated by Pearl's Americanization, Pearl wishes to achieve full knowledge of Wan-Lee's "China." Wan-Lee indulges her, identifying himself as indeed the embodiment of China: "I; Wong Wan-Lee—the descendant of the first Emperor, the great Huang Ti, the great-great grandson of the T'ang Dynasty, the grandson of the Sung Dynasty and the son of the Ming Dynasty—was exiled to a savage land, first as a waiter and then as a laundryman" (83ff; 87). It is important to note how he elides the Yuan and the Qing dynasties, those periods of foreign rule, as well as the post-imperial period, to adapt the persona of the idealized exile seen in traditional Chinese literature. This recitation and identification has a particular effect on Pearl. Immediately after this litany, "Pearl Chang took the small mirror out of her pocketbook. She had a look at herself and she was glad she was a Chinese, and quietly she threw away a small picture of a white movie actress" (85f). At this moment her racial hybridity disappears and in its stead is a "pure" Asian image.

But if Wan-Lee effects this racial and cultural transformation, in their subsequent quasi-sexual encounter it is Pearl who dominates. Once again, Tsiang embeds this event within the context of race, gender, and nation: what begins as a discussion of Chinese cuisine turns into an interrogation of national strength. Pearl asserts that perhaps Chinese vegetarianism has produced weak citizens, perhaps they should be more like the Japanese meat-eaters. Wan-Lee then fears Pearl will think he's a vegetarian, that is, weak, and he keeps wondering if this is the case as she attempts to seduce him. His recourse is to transform her body into metonymic pieces and metaphorize them, that is, to reduce Pearl to a series of figural elements. In so doing, he transforms her as he himself is changed. Wan-Lee names Pearl as object even as she calls him her Chinese "prince" and he becomes a symbol of China.

When he squeezes her nipple too tightly, the mystification and figuration of both Wan-Lee and Pearl is broken:

> "What a beautiful tennis ball and what a nice Lee-Chee nut you have, my dear Angel!" commented Wong Wan-Lee.
>
> "Thanks very much for your compliment, my dear Prince!" returned Pearl Chang.
>
> Pearl Chang rested herself comfortably on the sofa.
>
> For the sake of curiosity, Wong Wan-Lee squeezed Pearl Chang's Lee-Chee nut to find out whether there was a pit in it.
>
> Suddenly Pearl Chang stood up, put on her coat, grabbed her pocket-book and yelled:
>
> "This is not a tennis ball; this is my breast! This is not a Lee-Chee nut; this is my nipple! You hurt me! I thought you were born in China, the land of Confucius, Lao-Tze, and Buddha. But you are as tough as any white brat I ever met when I was South!"
>
> Pearl Chang opened the door and left. (93f)

Wan-Lee's ardent figuration of life and Pearl's idealization of Wan-Lee as her "Chinese prince," an idealization that she uses to leverage her own identity as "Chinese," cannot withstand intersubjective testing beyond a certain point. No matter how much the illusion is desired by both Wan-Lee and Pearl, it is broken by the somatic realities of material life. From this point on, the novel narrates the coming-into-consciousness of Wan-Lee and Pearl.

Wan-Lee is portrayed at the beginning of the narrative as a simpleton, a naive "Chinaman" who believes he can exploit his time in the United States to return to China rich. This "sojourner" mentality helps him to maintain a sense of superiority and hope until he becomes politicized by, at once, class consciousness and a new brand of Chinese nationalism. This takes place during the same period that Pearl is also made conscious of her mixedness. Pearl finds work at a Chinatown restaurant (she can speak, but not write, Chinese). In time, the owner finds out she's mixed: "We Chinese are dark enough and don't want to become any darker. As I am a member of the Chinese Nationalist Party, I have to respect the national race-purity. You fooled me! You have spoiled my business on account of it. You have scorned my racial theory! Get out!" (127). The very "purity" of her idealized image of China cannot accept her; this rejection is set within the context of 1930s nationalism and race theory.

Linked to this aspect of the modern is the mechanization of life, which is portrayed at the nexus of national and ethnic identity and the economic:

There were more Chinese cafeterias springing up in the city and the old fashioned Chinese restaurant gradually died out.

According to some, the Chinese restaurant was the result of American curiosity. When the curiosity was satisfied, Americans gradually forgot about Chop Suey and Chow Mein.

According to others, the Chinese restaurant was largely the result of American prohibition. . . . According to still others, the Chinese restaurant was the result of American prosperity. (128f)

Thus the demise of "traditional China" is connected to historical change in America—"China" exists in a particular dialectical relationship to American taste (specifically, the novelty of the orient and its appearance in American urban space), to American law and morality, and to American economics.

While Pearl is disqualified as a waitress in a "traditional" Chinese restaurant, she finds work in a new-style Chinese cafeteria. In this modern Chinese American topos, Chinese "reality" is but an effect: "Pearl Chang lost her job in the Chinese restaurant in Chinatown because she was not a pure Chinese, but she got her job in this cafeteria because the owner thought that so long as Pearl Chang looked like a Chinese, the Americans would not know whether she was genuine or not" (130). Complementing this rise in mechanization and loss of authenticity in the commodification of China is the mechanization of laundry: "Even in the laundry business, where hand-work was supposedly preferred, machines also tended eventually to eat up men" (137).

Under these conditions of economic depression and the rise of mechanical culture, racial, social, and familial ties are broken; the Chinese turn against each other: "Fat Wong began to feel sorry that he had paid Skinny Wong so much and he decided to economize: to fire Skinny Wong and to engage a new man at less pay" (140). Skinny warns that he will seek protection under state labor law:

Skinny Wong begged and Skinny Wong reasoned with Fat Wong, but Fat Wong didn't want to hear these things and he definitely warned Skinny Wong that if he said more he was going to inform the immigration office.

Skinny Wong had come to this country through Cuba and he had no papers. He was scared, yet he was angered.

He shot Fat Wong and turned the gun on his own temple.

Both were dead.

They were cousins. (140)

Wan-Lee eventually loses all his money to a loan shark, and has to take work as a busboy, not in a restaurant, but in its modern, degraded form, the cafeteria.

The cafeteria becomes the place where both Wan-Lee and Pearl discover class politics. As ever, Tsiang is careful to connect the issue of class with that of race, specifically addressing the exploitation of both within the frame of contemporary politics:

> There were two white bus-boys besides Wong Wan-Lee. When white men worked in the place, the boss thought, the white customers would behave better.
>
> When the boss talked to the Chinese workers, he would say the whites were no good. The whites were jealous of the Chinese—a yellow race. When the boss talked to the white workers, he would say that "Chinks" were no good—easygoing, weeping too much. He was an Internationalist and was doing his best to create jobs for poor men.
>
> He advertised in a radical paper and he advertised in Hearst papers that he was a true American and a friend of Hitler.
>
> He sold an established Chinese cafeteria to an American and he bought a bankrupt American cafeteria and opened a new Chinese one. (156)

Within these manipulations, the nation loses all power as a point of reference outside its commodification. For Tsiang, the ultimate evidence of the owner's moral bankruptcy is the fact that, despite his wealth, "when Chinatown raised money to defend China against the Japanese, he contributed nothing" (157).

For Pearl, political consciousness displaces her dream of identifying with an idealized China: "Because of the unpleasant experience Pearl Chang had had in the restaurant in Chinatown, now she laughed little, talked little and moved her hands little; but she thought more. All these thoughts passed thru her mind. And now her youth had passed away and she had reached her maturity" (131). The cafeteria, then, replaces the laundry as a chronotope—in the place of a privately owned, sequestered ethnic enterprise we find a space of alienated labor and mechanized life. Yet this is also the locus for the solidarity of a multiracial laboring class, wherein the identification with both the native land and the American dream are elided:

> One day Wong Wan-Lee, "the descendant of the great Huang Ti, the great-great-great grandson of the Han Dynasty, the great-great-grandson of the T'ang Dynasty, the grandson of the Sung Dynasty and the son of the Ming Dynasty," and Pearl Chang, "the future movie star," and many other workers quit their jobs and paraded in front of the Chinese cafeteria in which they worked. (157f)

Tsiang describes the solidarity among not only different racial groups, but among those whose racial identifications fall within the interstices:

All the workers in this cafeteria paraded.
The workers in the other cafeterias joined:
The white, the yellow and the black,
The ones between yellow and black,
The ones between yellow and white,
And the ones between white and black.
They were marching on, singing their song:
The song of the white,
The song of the yellow,
The song of the black,
The song of the ones who were neither yellow nor white,
The song of the ones who were neither yellow nor black,
The song of the ones who were neither black nor white,
And the song that knows nothing of white, yellow or black. (158)

Yet in this final scene, Tsiang also rehabilitates nationalism, but with a difference. While he has demystified "China" as a nodal point of identification characterized by its primordial purity, its seamless "tradition" extending from the mythical past to the present, he places in its stead a China in which the rival factions of capitalism and socialism (the KMT and CCP) are reunited against a common foe: the Japanese.[14] When he is shot, Wan-Lee's first thought is that he's been shot by a Chinese Tong member, hired by the owner to suppress the strike, but it is later discovered that the murderer is in fact a Japanese agent, who shoots Wan-Lee because of his demonstration in front of the Japanese embassy. The battle between classes is superseded by nationalist politics. Wan-Lee dies in Pearl's arms, predicting a Communist victory in China and a utopian socialist reign.

Like Tsiang's two other books, China Red and Hanging on Union Square, And China Has Hands is written in the rather crude prose style of a social realist fable, making all the gestures of political critique proper to the genre. What is important about this novel for the introjection of Asia into America in the early twentieth century is the way Tsiang sets the novel within a global scenario. He defines the function of China in the diasporic and hybrid imagination, and extracts the image of "China" and the Chinese from the indistinct, massified conglomerate of popular America media. Tsiang makes specific the complex interweaving of national, racial, and diasporic subjectivity in historical terms, and links that discussion to a particular political and cultural economy. The figure of Wan-Lee represents the Chinese sojourner who retains an identification with "China"; Pearl is the racially and culturally hybrid Asian-African American who is equally, but differently, drawn to identify with the idealization of one part of her racial identity. At same time that Tsiang evokes class solidarity across racial lines within an industrialized and newly mechanized United States, he retains a utopian vision of a reunified China as his main focal point. Tsiang has not entirely given up on the socialist utopian possibilities of a class-solidified hybrid, but the historical contingencies of 1937 pressed him to more immediate and concrete imaginings of a communist China and foreign invasion.

In the 1930s, one thus witnesses a revision of the ardent segregation of Asia from America in the American imaginary—if the Tydings-McDuffie act closed off Asian immigration, it left America to ponder how it would manage those Asians already in the United States under the conditions of economic crisis within the nation and growing U.S. involvement in neocolonial operations in Asia. Part of that response was, as we have seen, to try to suppress the liaison between Asia and America both within and outside the nation. Yet that suppression caused the ambivalent images of self and other to be displaced in specific ways within the American imaginary, ways that evinced the anxiety of modernity. For early Asian American writers such as Tsiang, these tensions were particularly palpable and could be read in material history. In Hollywood as well, we discover these complications of the Asian America imaginary, but invented in a different modality.

The "Bitter Tea" of Frank Capra

Frank Capra's film *The Bitter Tea of General Yen* signals an audacious attempt to articulate the possibility of a liaison between Asia and America under specific historical circumstances. On the evening of January 11, 1933, *The Bitter Tea of General Yen* became the first film to play Radio City Music Hall. Capra had been drawn to the project of adapting the 1930 novel of Grace Zaring Stone to the screen: "Representatives of two cultures as far apart as the poles, clash and fall in love. To me it was Art with a capital A."[15] Reputed to have been the most ambitious and expensive film Columbia studios had ever made, costing $1 million to produce, the film was intended to be "the nucleus around which the whole Columbia program [of 1933] will be sold."[16]

The main plot revolves around a young American woman, Megan Davis, and a Chinese warlord, General Yen.[17] Capra updates the novel's time frame, beginning his narrative with the bombing of Chapei (on January 29, 1932; the novel's action would seem to take place in 1927).[18] Davis arrives in Shanghai to marry her childhood sweetheart, Bob Striker, a missionary. However, immediately upon their reunion, Bob tells Megan that he must postpone their wedding while he goes out to rescue some orphans who are endangered by the rapidly escalating "civil war." Davis refuses to be left behind, insisting that she wants to help her future husband in his work. He agrees to this, and they both set out, leaving behind the sanctuary of the missionaries' drawing room and entering the realm of the "teeming masses" of China. While trying to evacuate the children, Davis and Striker are caught up in a mob; after Bob is knocked unconscious, Megan places him in a rickshaw, and then is herself struck down. She awakes to find herself in General Yen's private car, on his military train. Yen tells her that he found her unconscious and, wishing to rescue her from the crowd, placed her on board his train. She asks to be sent back to Shanghai; he tells her that would be unsafe, and that instead he is taking her to his estate and military headquarters until things quiet down. At Yen's villa, Davis vacillates between feeling herself a prisoner and a protected guest, between wanting to escape from Yen and wishing to convert him to Christianity. Along with these ambivalent feelings is her own growing sexual interest in Yen. Two crises arise in the course of the film. First, a developing romantic relationship between Davis and Yen; second, Davis's attempt to dramatically embody Christian principles so as to persuade Yen of God's greatness—two different, yet linked types of seduction.

The issue of "romance" is distributed differently in Davis's psyche and in Yen's. From their first encounter, which occurs at the opening of the film and before they know each other's identity, the film suggests a mutual curiosity, if not attraction—Yen's car has run over a rickshaw driver; Davis tries to aid the victim, while Yen remains cool and aloof. While she pleads with Yen for help and chastises him for his callousness, she notices that he is bleeding from a cut on the forehead. She offers him her handkerchief; he responds that he has one of his own. This scene sets up a number of key elements: Davis's Christian charity and sympathy; Yen's aristocratic detachment and bearing and the message that the west has nothing of value to offer China that it does not already have. Importantly, Yen is depicted both as "Chinese" in his disregard for life (a common racist stereotype of Asians reiterated throughout the film) and as eminently "western": his first words are uttered in French as he negotiates with the French sentry in the foreign quarter of Shanghai. In contrast to the images we have received thus far in the film of the Chinese "masses," Yen stands out as self-confident, able to articulate his power and authority in both western and Chinese spheres. When Yen offers Davis a cigarette, he offers her a choice between Virginia and English tobacco; Yen dresses in both western and Chinese clothes throughout the film. Even the introduction of the theme of death is instantiated in a confrontation between the general's automobile and the coolie's rickshaw. The vehicle of the modern world, the auto-mobile, delivers Yen and crushes the rickshaw (literally "man-powered cart"), the vestige of the premodern world of old China. The elite retains its power, but this power has increased exponentially in new modes of production even as it has supposedly rationalized its brutality in modern terms. It is precisely this power to cross over that makes Yen a specifically viable object of desire for Davis.

Within this problematic we find the second crisis. Mah-li, Yen's concubine whom Davis has befriended, is discovered to have passed vital information to his enemies concerning the whereabouts of Yen's treasure and armaments, and his plans. She does so by way of a Captain Li, with whom she is having an affair. Yen suspects the loyalty of Li's father, another powerful warlord. To insure his loyalty, Yen recruits Li's son and keeps him as, in effect, a hostage. Jones, Yen's financial advisor and self-proclaimed "renegade" American, discovers Mah-li's treason and exposes her. Yen then sentences Mah-li to die; Davis intervenes, and pleads for Mah-li's life on the basis of Christian principles. Yen, bemused by Davis's spirit and what he takes to be her naivete, agrees to spare Mah-li on the condition that Davis agree to "take her place" should Mah-li betray him again. Davis accepts Yen's bargain; Mah-li professes her deep gratitude and promises not to betray Davis's trust. Yet in the next scene, we find Mah-li passing more crucial information on to Yen's enemies, and Yen is thereupon destroyed as the enemy captures his gold and armaments and his troops desert him.

Davis then goes to Yen. Against her expectations, he refuses to accept her gesture of defeat. She expects that he will exact his punishment in the form of a sexual attack (as she must now fulfil Mah-li's role as concubine); he counters, "Do you think General Yen would accept anything not freely given?" As we will see, this issue of freely fulfilling sexual desire is for Davis a vexed one, caught as she is between her profession of Christianity's insistence on equality of all human beings and her recognition of the significance of racial difference in the sexual sphere, the latter despite her own barely unacknowledged desire for Yen. With the knowledge of Yen's inherent nobility and wisdom, Davis then retreats to her room and dons the shimmering evening gown (borrowed from Mah-li) that she wore on the occasion of her first dinner with Yen. She makes her face up with Mah-li's cosmetics, thus in effect superimposing Mah-li upon her own visage and body. Capra's filming of Davis at this point makes the dress appear intensely luminous — indeed the entire scene in Yen's chamber is the most fantastically lit segment of the film. But while Davis has been transforming herself,

Yen has brewed himself a cup of tea, into which he has dropped a fatal dose of poison.[19] This narrative element is Capra's invention, and ironically plays on the title of Stone's novel. Davis cries out that she will never leave Yen; as he dies, Yen gazes on her affectionately and pathetically, giving the impression of a kindness born of a superior wisdom: having become fluent in the languages, manners, and protocols of the west, he knows that east is east and west is west when it comes to sexuality. The film's ending has Davis and Jones aboard a steamer to Shanghai. Davis is mute; Jones engages in a long address to Davis and the audience.

One might expect that such an exotic and adventurous film would fulfil Columbia's and Capra's expectations. Gina Marchetti claims that "*The Bitter Tea of General Yen* testifies to Hollywood's genius for turning controversy into cash and orchestrating textual ambivalence in such a way that a potentially scandalous theme would titillate rather than repulse the average viewer."[20] Rather than reaping profits for Columbia, however, *The Bitter Tea of General Yen* proved disastrous. Scheduled for at least a two-week run at Radio City and other major movie theaters around the country, it was pulled after only eight days. Radio City Music Hall alone lost $20,000. It was one of only two of Capra's films ever to lose money.[21]

Critics have asserted that the interracial love theme sank the movie. Others were disappointed in the lack of "action." Still others simply found the narrative incredible. *Variety* called it "a queer story of a romance in China between a Chinese and a white woman. That kind of stuff has still to be decided upon by screen patrons. . . . After the Chinese general goes on the make for the white girl the picture goes blah. Seeing a Chinaman attempting to romance a pretty and supposedly decent young American white woman is bound to evoke adverse reaction." But the case is much more complex than that. In the following analysis, I argue that the film's failure may be attributed in part to the fact that it is unable to establish a stable identificatory position. The instability of identification is intimately linked to the adumbration of a different and tenuous notion of the Asian/American hybrid. Ultimately, Capra's film attempts to finesse these interpellative contradictions by recourse to a retrenched notion of nationalism, a move made possible only by a conspicuous elision of history. Nevertheless, I will argue that the articulation of the hybrid signals a general complication of the notion of Asia and America's different relations to it, both externally and within its domestic space.

In her essay "Visual Pleasure and Narrative Cinema," Laura Mulvey stresses the interpellation of the spectator's subjectivity. The spectator's identification is split: as voyeur, as one who locates the female character as object of desire and thereby solidifies his subject position within the patriarchal order; and as one who sees in the male protagonist an ego ideal, and forms a bond of identification with him: "The cinema offers a number of possible pleasures. One is scopophilia. There are circumstances in which looking itself is a source of pleasure, just as, in the reverse formation, there is pleasure in being looked at."[22] Critics have taken Mulvey to task for many simplifications—for instance, for assuming the gender position of the spectator and for not taking into account the classic films that have women as their protagonists. Jane Gaines points out that one must factor in the question of race, as well.[23] In *The Bitter Tea of General Yen*, the element of race creates a particular, triangulated scene of desire, most vividly conveyed in the relationship between Davis, Mah-li, and Yen. I would add that identifications based on class and nationality also complicate the spectator's position. *The Bitter Tea of General Yen*'s failure can thus be understood as the result of the failure to establish a stable looking position that would satisfy the moviegoing public in the 1930s. On one hand, its experimental character dislodged the stereotypes to which the American public was accustomed; on the other hand, even though it reestablished conventional premises of difference, it did not provide a compelling narrative as a vehicle for such closure. Understanding this interdependence of the complex set of identifications necessary to suture the subject into the symbolic order reveals not only how "daring" and "filmic" *Bitter Tea* was in its challenge to those conventions, but how necessary those conventions were to the audience's being able to understand the film at the time. My analysis of the film thus involves the kind of inquiry remarked upon by Staiger: "What we are interested in, then, is not a so-called correct reading of a particular film but the range of possible readings and reading processes at historical moments and their relation or lack of relation to groups of historical spectators."[24]

There are a number of ways that Capra obstructs and confuses identification. If we begin by accepting that the female character in this film is the object of the male gaze, then we have to adapt the position of the Asian male figure in the film, that is, identify with him across the conventional racial lines of Hollywood protagonists; if we accept the position of the female protagonist, who is the orienting point of view, then we have to accept the Asian male as an object of desire. Yet race is not always the predominate point of identification. Early in the film, as Bob goes to Yen to get a safe-conduct pass to save the orphans, he finds him with Jones. As Yen expresses his surprise that Bob would rather rescue orphans than be with his lover, he glances over to Jones, whose smirk confirms the

Figure 1. Scene from *The Bitter Tea of General Yen*. Courtesy George Eastman House.

bond between men of different races with regard to heterosexual desire. Later in the film, Davis arrives at this conclusion: "East or west, men are all the same." Class can also cut across race. Davis, visited by Yen near the beginning of her stay, suspects that as he lingers in her bedroom he intends to rape her. She curses him ("You yellow swine"), then realizes from his shocked and disappointed reaction that she has insulted him, and that in turn makes her aware of his class distinction. Yen's moral bearing is rearticulated in his famous rejection of Davis: "Do you think General Yen would accept anything that the heart does not freely give?" Finally, when Yen confers with Jones after interviewing Davis, Jones warns him, "This is a white woman!" Yen ironically replies, "I have no prejudice against the color" (this, of course, a parody of missionary moralizing). Yen says this as he straightens Jones's tie and makes a face of disgust as he brushes the dirt off Jones's hat. We realize that Yen is, after all, always immaculate, whether in western or Chinese garb. This again sets up a class allegiance: Yen and Davis, different in race and gender but of similar "class," against Jones, the petty bourgeois materialist (the term "class" is problematic here, but I want to specifically signal the class linkages between a western-educated, cosmopolitan Chinese and a college-educated, middle-class New Englander; even though there are appreciable differences between the two, those differences may be bracketed when confronted with an "other" such as Jones).

Nevertheless, it is Jones who becomes the sole remaining voice of the film; it is he who reconsolidates the fragments of identification dispersed in *Bitter Tea*. Even though Capra wants to move beyond a simplistic reading of the east/west binarism, he ultimately reinscribes not gender, nor class, nor race, but the nation as a point of suture. One of the most conspicuous and localized changes Capra and his screenwriter (Edward Paramore) made in adapting the novel to the screen was to change the name of the American "advisor" from Schultz to Jones. This change has to be read in the context of America's perception of Germany in the 1930s; the switch makes more credible the rehabilitation of the figure as American. Initially drawn to Jones as a "fellow American" in China, Davis is rebuffed; Jones tells her that he doubts she would really want to know him—he declares himself "a renegade." In the novel, Davis is repulsed by Schultz, so much so that she feels sorry for Yen, under the sway of such a crude opportunist. Yet in both narratives Davis comes to find Schultz/Jones more sympathetic, especially during his moments of kindness toward her after Mah-li betrays her. It is after this betrayal that Yen is ruined—his fortunes are depleted, his army deserts; he pays the price of gambling between his instincts and his desire for Megan Davis. It is also at this moment that Schultz/Jones, rather than destroying Davis for ruining Yen (and consequently himself), decides that, after all, Davis is an American: "I was going to make Yen the biggest man in China—you sure queered that deal. But you're an American, and we have to stick together now."

In so doing, he reveals that his own nationalistic impulses were merely dormant, not dead. Indeed, this revival rehabilitates Jones—he sloughs off his degraded materialist garb for the uniform of an American. This revival of nationalistic identity is even more dramatically narrated in the novel. Whereas in Capra's treatment, Yen dies at his own hand, in Stone's novel the three (Schultz, Yen, Davis) try to escape. They are cornered while trying to board a boat. Schultz instinctively first saves Davis. Their boat takes off, and when he turns to look for Yen, Yen has been shot to death. America is thus reconsolidated across boundaries of class and gender (it is crucial to note that in neither the film nor the novel is there even the implication that Schultz/Jones desires Davis; his primary goal is always wealth, and he in fact avoids Davis if anything, as she presents an unwelcome complication). Yet if we believe that the figure of Jones is the one with whom audiences are supposed to identify—if national identity is the anchor of the film — then it is a problematic one, to say the least. To begin with, although white and male, Jones's class status remains an obstacle. He is an unstable character, not presented as having "learned" from his encounter with the orient. One cannot imagine him completely converting from his basically materialistic, egotistic bent. His moment of national "solidarity" comes at a time of duress; and after all, Yen is no longer of any use to him. But most tellingly, the last line of the film, which is his, ironically undercuts his subject position: "I'm drunk; this is all a lot of hooey." This is not a total deconstruction of his prior disquisition, by any means, for if he is unreliable now how are we to tell that anything he says can be trusted, even his own denial? Rather, the statement poses us on the edge of uncertainty and contributes all the more to the ambiguities of the film.

The most interesting and sweeping modification Capra and Paramore made to the novel in order to extract this narrative of interracial love is the excision of the novel's criticism of capitalism and imperialism and the foregrounding instead of the theme of romance, present but not so dominant in the novel. In the novel, in fact, the romance is subordinated to the ideological tension not only between Yen's "pagan" philosophy and Davis's Christianity, but the ambivalence within Megan Davis's own psyche with regard to her commitment to Christian work. Stone goes to some lengths to portray Davis as having mixed motives for being in China in the first place. In the film, her hypocrisy is severely downplayed — near the beginning, Capra draws the distinction between Davis's innocence and the ugly bigotry of the missionary wives. The film centers upon the notion of romance as a more "real," more genuine and immediate motive for human interaction. For example, Davis naively reads the love affair between Mah-li and Captain Li as being entirely motivated by "romance," thereby erasing the political issues that motivate both to ruin Yen. This reduction of desire into romance (note the culmination of her dream sequence in its stereotypical representation of romantic love before sexual consummation) replicates her own attempt to "love" Yen while ignoring race. In short, in order to change Stone's novel in this direction, Capra, like his protagonist Megan, had to write out the historical while burying in "romance" a particular set of ideological contradictions. To understand the specific effects of this elision one must restore certain key elements.

U.S. investment in China between 1914, 1930, and 1936 grew enormously. In 1914, U.S. investments amounted to about $49 million (3 percent of total foreign investment); by 1931 the United States had almost quadrupled its holdings in China, to $197 million (6.1 percent of foreign investments). In five years, that figure had increased by nearly 50 percent—in 1936 U.S. investments amounted to $298 million (7 percent). Obviously, this was still far short of other countries' holdings; the big investors remained Britain (by far), then Russia and Germany, then Japan.[25] Nevertheless, this increase does reflect a growing interest in China on the part of the United States, as it developed its neocolonial policies in Asia.[26]

U.S. foreign policy in Asia had become driven by the notion of "common security," which basically meant the legitimation of U.S. involvement in the affairs of foreign governments based on what the U.S. deemed their "common" interests. Griswold traces the modern East Asian policy of the United States to its invasion and colonization of the Philippines:

> Had the War with Spain gone no further than the crusade to liberate Cuba the change would not have been so momentous. But it did go further. It was carried beyond those continental boundaries envisioned in Washington's Farewell Address, beyond the popular conception of the Monroe Doctrine and Manifest Destiny; beyond, even, the seemingly inevitable assertion of American supremacy in the Caribbean, and the long-pending annexation of Hawaii. Amid the clash of arms the Philippine Archipelago became an American colony. These islands, lying some six hundred miles off the Chinese coast, bore no conceivable relation to American supremacy in the Caribbean, much less to the continental security of the United States. With their annexation the United States emerged from its habitual, self-sufficient abode in the Western Hemisphere and entered the limitless realm of world politics, naval rivalry, and imperial domination.[27]

He then draws the connection between this turning point and its elaboration in the U.S. policies of the 1920s and 1930s: "The impact of this imperialism on the Far Eastern policy of the United States caused a change of emphasis that placed political interests on a par with commercial. Thereafter, the principle of the territorial integrity of China, introduced by Hay as a means to equal opportunity for American commerce in that country, became to all intents and purposes an end in itself."[28]

What most likely provided background for the novel were the violent events of March and April of 1927. First, on March 21, the General Labor Union in Shanghai, under the direction of the Chinese Communist Party, "launched a general strike and an armed insurrection against the warlords and in support of the approaching Guomindang [Kuomintang] forces."[29] In this general strike, police stations were seized, railways occupied, power and telephone lines cut. Five hundred unions, 820,000 workers, and a worker's militia of 3,000 were involved. A few days later, on March 24, "Victorious Kuomintang troops entered the city of Nanking and proceeded to carry out a systematic attack on the foreign community. British, French, Italian, Japanese and American consulates were raided, and much foreign property was looted and destroyed. Foreign refugees hastily sought shelter in the buildings of the University of Nanking, at the British consulate and on the grounds of the Standard Oil Company. To protect the last group from the onslaughts of Kuomintang soldiers, British and American gunboats anchored on the Yangtse River dropped a barrage between the Standard Oil [building] and its attackers." [30] At this time there were 22,000 foreign troops and police in Shanghai and 42 foreign warships, backed by 129 additional warships in other Chinese waters. [31]

But the most climactic of these events were the actions taken by Chiang Kai-shek to consolidate his power. After securing the backing of foreign and domestic elites, Chiang led a wholesale slaughter of labor unionists and CCP sympathizers: "When Shanghai townspeople, workers, and students staged a protest rally the next day, they were fired upon by Guomindang troops with machine guns and almost 100 were killed. Arrests and executions continued over the next several weeks, the General Labor Union organizations declared illegal, and all strike activity in the city ceased. . . . In Shanghai, Chiang had shown his true colors: he had emerged as a representative of the 'national bourgeoisie'." [32] Thus, the turmoil in China was emphatically not simply internal fighting among "warlords," as suggested in Capra's film, but a complex war involving foreign capital and a Chinese nationalist movement that was in the process of defining its differences in terms of both domestic and foreign retrenching capitalist elites, and socialist revolution. The events that shaped Stone's narrative were particularly critical in delineating the positions of the CCP and the KMT and, concomitantly, foreign understanding of the nature of the Chinese nationalistic project. [33] The film also conspicuously brackets out Japanese imperialism. The beginning sequence takes place as a text reading the "Burning of Chapei" is flashed before the screen. The burning of Chapei on September 18, 1931, was a recent event that occurred after Stone's novel was written. Capra cites the event to capture a "contemporary" flavor, but doesn't mention that Chapei was bombed by the Japanese during a series of attempts to consolidate its hold on Manchuria. Thus, Capra's film tries to exploit contemporary history while deleting actuality; we find instead an insistence on the issue being a "civil war." In Capra's work the struggle is simply one of internal wrestling over primitive acquisition, rather than an international fight over nationalism, capitalism, and imperialism.

On the other hand, Stone's novel calls attention to precisely the histories that Capra and Paramore had to deliberately ignore. In one episode, Davis sees an etching:

> In the midst of all this, the Jesuit church lifted its flat facade, broken half-way by two orderly volutes, with half-dimensional, twisted pillars on either side of its doors. The suggestion of the grandiose and the gigantic was discreetly tempered by reflections of logic, of Aristotle and the sciences, and the inappropriateness of the whole to its surroundings lent it a delicious perversity and charm. A Jesuit facade in China. The first small wedge in the breach which was to grow wider and wider till all Europe poured in, no longer, alas, the Europe of amiable sophistries and the art of making clocks, but a vast and terrible lava flow of artillery, transportation, oil, steel-girded buildings, sanitation, jazz, democracy, equality of the sexes, business efficiency and the true word of God. (55)

Indeed, Stone's novel has Yen himself address the particular mode of America's entry into China: "And perhaps you are even wondering if you will be able to do more for us than the others did, yes, even with all that you are willing to give away with it in the way of kerosene and munitions and a thousand like commodities, tucked in like a coupon in a package of cigarettes, entitling one after so many to six plated silver spoons" (249). The journalist Carl Crow, who produced such books as *I Speak for the Chinese* and *400 Million Customers*, and who later became an advertising agent in China, commented favorably on the global infusion of western, specifically U.S., commodities in the late 1930s:

> During the past few years I have visited more than twenty different countries and was never far away from a shop which stocked one or more American products. In a mud-walled village I found a can of Del Monte fruit salad. In a single shop I saw on the shelves Chiclets, Sloan's Liniment and Kodak films and bought an ice cold bottle of Coca-Cola. One may travel all over the world and never get far away from a supply of Gillette blades, Palmolive Soap, Pond's Cold Cream, Kolynos Toothpaste and dozens of other well-known American products.[34]

Crow notes, "[In 1937] we foreign devils were making money."[35]

Not only was the infusion of western commodities into China a continual reminder of the Open Door policies forced upon the Chinese in the late nineteenth century, but as the above pronouncement by Yen implies, the U.S. missionary project in China was closely associated with this invasion—economic and ideological hegemonies were linked inextricably. Again, this aspect of the novel is conspicuously untouched in the film. The vast majority of U.S. investment in China was, in fact, in missionary buildings and hospitals. Christianity was a powerful signifier: Yuan Shikai pled for Americans to pray to God for the Chinese republic (newspapers described him "subjecting pagan nations to the yoke of Christ"), and Chiang Kai-shek's very public Christian marriage (even though it was polygamous) to a "Wellesley girl" and his public "conversion" to Christianity attracted worldwide attention. By 1922, there were fifty-four thousand members of the YMCA in thirty-six Chinese cities. In light of this, Chinese nationalists declared, "[The YMCA] is a device to cheat laborers so that they will be contented and will regard the capitalists as their benefactors. . . . [Missionaries] are doing evangelical work so as to smother the political thought of youth—they are a detriment to the patriotic movement."[36] This sentiment conforms in general to a Chinese response to American reformist activities in China at the beginning of the twentieth century: "The unprecedented appeal of reform thought on the American side after 1900 extended beyond the mission movement and the foreign service to policy makers in Washington and tied all to a conception of the United States as guide and patron of 'modernizing' China. These pretensions were, however, to run up against a Chinese conception of reform heavily tinctured with nationalist preoccupations."[37] In fact, the Guomindang government declared that missionary schools were not to propagate religion, and instead insisted that a strong national patriotism should be promoted.[38]

While the film stresses Davis's inner conflict as to whether her Christian principles of equality will accommodate sexual relations with an Asiatic, the novel focuses on the moral power that Davis attempts to use to her own aggrandizement—thus Capra's critique becomes located in Davis's personal dilemma and away from a focus on her participation in a larger social formation. In the film, Megan pleads with Yen to spare Mah-li. He asks how she can be interested in the welfare of someone whom she hardly knows, a Chinese at that. She replies: "We're all of the same flesh and blood." Yen asks, "Do you really mean that?", placing his hand over hers. At this she recoils and quickly draws her hand back. She then says, with a somewhat sickly expression on her face, "Of course I do." While her words would affirm her faith, her physical instincts betray her. But in the novel, the dilemma is not over the way that race compromises idealism, but rather how the aspiring missionary's hypocrisy might be located in her self-interest and egoism. In Stone's novel, Yen asks of Davis: "Is it really understanding that you want? I have an idea that understanding doesn't enter very largely into your program. I have an idea that what you really want, certainly where I am concerned, is to change me, to make me over into some new image; the image of God, but also, slightly, the image of Miss Davis, His creation and at the same time hers" (281). Donald C. Willis comes close to the mark when he writes: "Why Paramore and Capra would take a perfectly decent novel, ignore its strengths, and fashion almost incidental material into a perfectly decent movie which hardly even resembles the book, I don't know, unless they assumed that the movie-going public was not ready for a pointed examination of the motivations of the Christian missionary, but was ready for miscegenation."[39] The *London Times* noted: "A climax showing Megan in front of a firing squad would have been the logical development, but *The Bitter Tea of General Yen*, which breaks conventions bravely for three-quarters of the time, repents of its rashness at the last" (March 13, 1933).

Yet the issue was not only the mild critique of Davis, but the inability of the film to make a positive and decisive moral statement that could neutralize the liberalization of desire Capra suggests: if Yen "does the right thing" by killing himself and allowing the status quo to be reinstated, at the same moment Megan realizes that her love for him supersedes racial difference. But most important, the omission of material history—which seems to allow the "nation" to triumph as a nodal point of identification—conspicuously signals the way that the American director can displace the critique of the mission of the west in China onto a meditation on the possibilities of another kind of connection—interracial love—and retain an aggressive blindness to imperialism and nationalism. In fact, it is precisely because Capra has bracketed these issues that he is able to set forward his "progressive" message. While he focuses our attention on the contradictions of a Christian universalism that retains racial distinctions and a romantic sentiment that, although failed, at least signals the possibility of an Asian-American connection, he elides the contradiction between the promulgation of a U.S. presence in Asia that was to foster democratic ideals and the infusion of western capitalistic practices that preempted democracy in China by maintaining the ruling elites. But, critically, the figure of Jones is both invested with identification *and* debunked. The question becomes whether or not the humbling of Jones is simply a covert way to have the audience accept him and allow Capra to evade further the question of this particular nationalism. Thus the film's erasure of history and its displacement onto a radically reified Chinese civil war evinces precisely the repression of the *international* "political," and especially the emergence of an international scenario that was far removed from prior political economies, which deepened American contact with Asia just when Asian exclusion laws in the United States had reached their zenith.

To conclude this treatment of *The Bitter Tea of General Yen*, I return to the representation of interracial relations in the film, the area into which Capra poured all the narrative logic of Stone's novel and for which he sacrificed history. This portrayal of interracial love signals a liminal moment in the history of the projection of American ideology onto the nexus of Asia and America. It indicates change in the modes of introjecting Asians into the U.S. national body, suggesting a different inflection to the term "hybrid," which deeply informs the modern period. The notion of liminality derived from Victor Turner's usage is useful in understanding Capra's fantasy (not only in Megan's dream, but in the entire fantastic portrayal of China and Megan's adventure there) as presenting the occasion for reinstating norms of social behavior. Turner argues that rites of passage are liminal moments that take place between two conditions, the latter of which is marked by socially recognized and demanded maturation. In this passage, the neophyte is confronted with a series of fantastic monsters that force him or her to entertain the way they gesture beyond, and yet recircumscribe, the norm:

> Monsters are manufactured precisely to teach neophytes to distinguish clearly between the different factors of reality, as it is conceived of in their culture. . . . Much of the grotesqueness and monstrosity of liminal *sacra* may be seen to be aimed not so much at terrorizing or bemusing neophytes into submission or out of their wits as at making them vividly and rapidly aware of what may be called the "factors" of their culture. . . . During the liminal period, neophytes are alternately forced and encouraged to think about their society, their cosmos, and the powers that generate and sustain them.[40]

Monsters are therefore the combination of previously dissociated elements which force the neophyte to realign these elements in their proper bodies. The ritual existence of these monsters points to the possibility of their togetherness in the realm of fantasy, yet it is precisely that realm which must be relinquished so that social sense can be reinscribed and a particular social subjectivity constructed. In Capra's film, the viewer is indulged in the fantastic possibilities of a "normal" liaison between Davis and Yen, but the fantasy must be broken in order that the dominant ideological barriers be reinstated, and indeed, fortified.

Yet Turner's conception of the liminal is not precisely appropriate for the phenomena I wish to describe. In the case of *The Bitter Tea of General Yen*, what is instantiated after the liminal period is not simply a prior social norm, but a new construction that bears not only the residual ideological elements of what came before, but emergent forms as well. What I wish to draw from Turner is his analysis of how the liminal period stages fantasy as a moment of socialization which is made effective precisely because it isolates the subject from prior constraints and contingencies and unleashes repressed psychic energies (the work of Raymond Bellour, for instance, is concerned with seeing the film-viewing experience as like the hypnotic trance).[41] But Capra's film contains a certain "semiotic excess" that inadvertently allows a set of other readings to disrupt that closure, the reinscription of social normalcy after that brief indulgence in fantasy. As Fiske notes: "The theory of semiotic excess proposes that once the ideological, hegemonic work has been performed, there is still excess meaning that escapes the control of the dominant."[42] I would suggest that that excess is precisely the residue of critique that Capra sets forth. After representing the union of Megan and Yen (for the purpose of critiquing Christian hypocrisy), he cannot remove the image from the audience's memory: it remains fixed, albeit in the realm of an uncertain fantasy. Once the particular figure of Yen is invented, its specific cosmopolitan hybridity lifts Yen above the indefinite "mass" of China to present a subjectivity that might possibly merge with the west. And it was precisely the moment for a meditation on the possibilities of such a liaison, for the late 1930s represented a watershed in the history of America's understanding of and relation to Asia.

Harold Isaacs's study of the images of Asia retained by Americans in the mid-twentieth century found that, of 135 interviewees, 48 said that the beginning of the Sino-Japanese War (1937) made them most aware of Asia.[43] This represented the largest number of responses on a single event, followed in kind only by the bombing of Pearl Harbor. There was simply no way to ignore Asia: "No matter how peripheral or incidental their interest in Asia might be, serious people interested enough in affairs to read the press with earnest care could hardly help being reached by the news, passions, controversies, and fears aroused by Japan's invasion of China."[44] While there may have been appreciable "relief" on the part of anti-Asian racists after the solidification of exclusionary legislation, this did not tame the general anxiety regarding the definition of the U.S. nation-state with regard to Asia. Changes in technology and means of production, communications, the dramatic revision of national and global economics during and after the Great Depression, increased Japanese imperialism, and struggles for national independence and sovereignty in Asia (Korea, India, China, the Philippines) had made intercourse with Asia—political, economic, social, and cultural—increasingly unavoidable and unpredictable. In this context the staging of the figure of Yen is crucially important as an *allegorical* instance.

The film's most famous scene takes place shortly after Davis has arrived at Yen's villa; I argue that it presents a particular image of the specific conditions under which an Asian-American liaison could be imagined during that period. Smoking a cigarette languorously on her balcony one evening under a full moon, Davis watches the arrival of a truckload of prostitutes and the rush of soldiers to meet them. These two groups couple up and dash off to indulge themselves in the bushes; Davis witnesses a few embracing and fondling each other under the light of a full moon. The scene is set up as a vivid tableau, reminiscent of neo-classical representations of Greek bacchanals, of satyrs and nymphs. This explicit and deliberately obvious coding is critically important, for it represents Davis's perceptual orientations, that is, how she understands the activity, as well as how the filmmaker wishes the audience to identify the scene. Its importance lies in its contrast with the next scene—Davis's dream fantasy of her own erotic encounter with the orient.

Davis falls asleep on the balcony and begins to dream. What she has just witnessed prompts a fantasy of what she has repressed: her own desire for Yen. But what I wish to stress is not the fantasy itself, but rather the specific conditions upon which it is produced. In Davis's dream, she is lying on a bed in Yen's villa. She is startled by someone smashing in her door; it splinters apart, and a sinister Asian figure wearing a Chinese robe and cap enters. He is made up as a caricature of a caricature: an exaggerated Fu Manchu (a cinematic image itself beholden to Murnau's Nosferatu), rubbing his hands together evilly.[45] The camera angles create a skewed, diagonally framed and slightly out of focus image as he circles around toward the cowering Davis. Upon this figure Capra briefly superimposes that of Yen, making the link explicit. The figure's hands linger dramatically just over Davis's breasts. At that moment, the double glass doors that open out onto the balcony spring open and a man enters, dressed in a dark collegiate blazer and white trousers, and sporting a white panama hat. He is also wearing a white mask. He knocks the villain down. Marchetti describes the scene:

> [The villain] falls back surrealistically in a process shot and disappears on impact with the wall.
>
> Gleefully, the masked figure throws off his hat, and Davis draws close to take off the hero's mask. Without a hint of surprise, she sees that the masked man is also Yen. They look deeply into each other's eyes, and Megan falls back onto the bed. A swirling effect created by another process shot denotes her ecstasy. Yen sits on the bed next to her; he caresses her face and hair; she pulls back her head, revealing her neck in a gesture of both passion and submission; finally, they kiss. Slowly, the shot dissolves back to the sleeping Megan's face as Yen lowers her onto the bed.[46]

The dream is abruptly broken as Megan is startled to consciousness and finds Yen beside her on the balcony. She tries to distract attention from her obviously disturbed state, protesting: "Even a common soldier would have knocked," to which Yen smoothly replies, "I did, I nearly broke down your door." Thus it is in fulfilling his gentlemanly obligations (obviously playing off the two "entrances" of the villain/hero in the fantasy and drawing on a rather crude sexual metaphor) that Yen then breaks Megan's reverie and rebuffs her attempt to foist her transgression onto him.

Just as the liaison between the soldiers and the prostitutes is coded in a cross-cultural travesty of the Greek bacchanal, so Capra parodies Hollywood's coding of both the sinister Asiatic and the collegiate hero. When Davis removes Yen's mask, and Yen throws off his white hat, the camera moves in for a close-up. All the props Capra has deployed for his parody are off-screen; all that is left are the faces of Yen and Davis as they embrace and kiss. Capra's message seems to be that "true romance" can only exist when the vestiges of both crude racial stereotypes and equally simplistic counterimages of whiteness are sloughed off.

Yet Capra's filming of Davis's near swoon, just before their kiss, is encumbered by dramatic excess as well: the music swells, Davis seems to gaze wondrously at the heavens, her face bathed in light, her eyes slowly close before the moment of bliss. At this point it becomes clear that *Davis* is the director of this scene; it is she, or at least what Capra represents as her unconscious, that has set up the proper conditions for her liaison with Yen. That Davis "controls" the fantasy becomes clear as we watch her objectify "Yen," cupping his face, manipulating him, drawing him to bed. At this point, the villain having been destroyed and the otherness of the "hero" domesticated, Davis is no longer the passive object of desire—*Yen* is. It is precisely because of this pre-scription that Davis shows no surprise over the fact that it is Yen behind the mask. That she would be rescued from the orient by an oriental who is not, as was usually the case, a subaltern figure, but rather a potent and desirable one, is perhaps the most telling element in the scene.

Nevertheless, this "climax" remains anchored in irreality (in no small part due to the Hollywood code that included a prohibition against miscegenation). The rest of the film narrates the impossibility of realizing such fantasies and puts Yen ahead of the curve: he knows, despite his desire to believe in the possibility of "equality" under the eyes of God, that interracial love is not to be consummated. His is the superior point of view, but while the two Americans, Jones and Davis, remain alive at the end of the film, Yen is relegated to the realm of the incorporeal. Yet as such he is also stubbornly transcendent. In this regard the casting and staging of Yen is of special significance. The problematic status of Yen is linked to the signifiers of racial and cultural complexity: how to make a white man Asian, and, in particular, an Asian who is westernized.

Capra explained that he was unable to get an Asian actor to play the part: "General Yen was the big casting problem. . . . I looked for a tall, overpowering, real Chinese. But there were no tall Chinese in the casting directories, or even in laundries; most Chinese-Americans were short Cantonese. After many interviews we settled on a not-too-well-known Swedish actor, Nils Asther. He was tall, blue-eyed, handsome; spoke with the slightly pedantic 'book' accent; his impassive face promised the serenity and mystery of a centuries-old culture."[47] To make his foreigner into another kind of foreigner, the following measures were taken:

> The make-up man covered Nils Asther's upper eyelids with smooth, round, false "skins," and clipped his eyelashes to one-third their natural length. Without adding any other make-up we made photographic tests of Asther's face. On the screen he looked strange—unfathomable. The stiff, upper eyelids kept his eyes in a permanent half-closed position. Of a certain he was *not* a Caucasian—and his face looked natural, uncontorted! Bedecked in rich Mandarin costumes, and a fez-like, black, tall skullcap for added height, Asther could pass for an awe-inspiring warlord. I added one final touch: an eccentric walk—long slow strides with both his long arms moving back and forth together—in parallel—with each stride. By keeping the camera low to accentuate height, Nils Asther became General Yen—ruthless, cultured, mysterious, and devastatingly attractive. (141)[48]

Some argue that such substitutions helped directors skirt the anti-miscegenation clause in the Hollywood code, but I would comment on another aspect of this "yellow-face." I see it as projecting the specter of a racial hybrid that evinced the liaison of west and east in a particular fashion. Most Hollywood films used whites to play Asians. Films such as *Shanghai* (1935) explicitly cast whites as Asian hybrids, in that case staging Charles Boyer as Russian-Chinese, and condemned the mixture ("It is not how noble the strains. If they have been crossed, as yours have been, a man becomes an outcast"). But the unintended hybridity created in staging Yen not as a *racial* hybrid but a *cultural* one produced the specter of something different. How to explain that, even without the "genetic" advantage of a biracial, a "pure" Asian could be biculturally fluent enough to be a viable object of desire? Yen was, as noted before, eminently "westernized," and yet able to function as Chinese as well. One reviewer found it hard to believe that such a man as Yen could even exist: "The Chinese warlord around whom the plot is built is a curious and rather questionable human composition of a poet, philosopher, and bandit. He speaks rather fluent English and essays somewhat dainty American mannerisms. . . . Customers may wonder about such a conglomerous combination of a man."[49] The casting of Asther as an Asian produces inadvertently an image of the hybrid which reinforces the diegesis. Most important, it adumbrates a subject no longer wholly under the rule of the west precisely because it has *assimilated* the west. Cultural hybridity rehabilitates the stigma of racial hybridity. This empowered image of the hybrid stands in stark contrast to the conventional image of the hybrid as a diseased pariah.[50]

Capra was looking for an "overpowering" figure to play Yen, which seemed to run counter to the "actual" Chinese he could see around him (or whom he imagined to populate the laundries of Los Angeles). Instead, he manufactured one to fit his mind's eye from non-Asian material. The elements that were essential to the characterization of Yen must be seen as derived from a particular formula that merged the western and the Asian. Crucially, Capra did not want a well-known American actor to play the role. In casting the Swedish actor Asther, Capra created a particular kind of foreign hybrid. Asther's "pedantic 'book' accent" signals specifically European breeding, and worked well to underline the notion that Yen had received such an education. Nevertheless, this Swede possessed a "passivity" that could be decoded as "oriental." (All this is especially remarkable since the great "pure stock" which formed the base of American blood was seen to be Nordic; it is heavily ironic and significant, then, that a Swede would be so transformed into the image of a Chinese.) The "eccentricity" of Yen's movements as directed by Capra serve thus to embody emphatically the "conglomerous" nature of Yen: "ruthless" (in the mode of Asiatic villains), yet "cultured" (as a modernized, viz. westernized, Chinese); "mysterious" in his ability to move between the cultural spheres of east and west, and "devastatingly attractive" not only because of his strength and bearing so untypical of Chinese, but also because of his eccentricity, his difference, which is both exotic and yet somehow accessible to understanding and desire, oriental and western. Yet it is crucial to recognize that this "hybrid" figure—the westernized Asiatic male—must die, whereas the *sinicized* Anglo-American female is allowed, and called upon, to witness and validate this death: Yen's last vision of life, after all, is of a westerner made up as a Chinese. *Two* hybrid figures thus vie for dominance in the imaginary construct: the physically neutralized and absented yet immortal Yen, and the surviving, yet mute Megan. The irresolvability of this struggle for significance (and moral guidance) reflects the end point of Capra's ability to cognitively map the Asian/American liaison.

The foregrounding of such a complex figure and the contradictory subtexts that drive *Bitter Tea* thus help explain the unpopularity of the film, especially if we contrast it to the enormous success of Pearl Buck's *The Good Earth*, published in 1931. "It sold 1.5 million copies, received the Pulitzer prize, and was translated into thirty languages. It became a Broadway play in 1933, and four years later a movie that was seen in the United States by an estimated 23 million people."[51] Its popularity is usually attributed to its "realistic" depiction of China — that is, because it departed from the stereotypical representations of China as exotic, evil, mystical. I would add that the American public, still retaining the image of the Dust Bowl, could find a positive image of rural persistence in the saga of *The Good Earth* (especially as it preserved an image of an agrarian economy sequestered from incipient agribusiness and monopoly capitalism — if anything, the protagonist in the novel becomes a successful member of the small-scale gentry). But even more significant is the fact that the novel is about the *non*westernized Chinese *in China*, that is, there is no hint of the west in Buck's text. Rather, China is contained within particular ideological and geopolitical parameters.[52] If Capra's film attempts to bracket the historical within romance, Buck's narrative opts for representing a particularized and distanciated (albeit "authentic") material history.

C. L. R. James's essay "Popular Arts and Modern Society" addresses the issue of American films' deleting the historical during this period:

> It is one of the most astonishing things about the modern American film which as many as 95 million people per week look at in the United States, that it does not treat of the Great Depression, the pervading fear of another economic collapse, the birth and development of the union movement, the fear of war, the fundamental social and political questions of the day. In novels and plays, yes. . . . Whenever possible a piece of direct propaganda is injected, but the C.I.O., the great strikes, capital and labor, war and peace, these are left out by mutual understanding, a sort of armed neutrality.[53]

Films of this period instead place a premium on iconoclastic individuality: "In such a society [post-Depression era], the individual demands an esthetic compensation [for the effects of economic crises that delimit individual surety within the political economy] in the contemplation of free individuals who go out into the world and settle their problems by free activity and individualistic methods."[54] Under such an analysis, *The Bitter Tea of General Yen* presents both the suppression or deletion of material history *and* the "compensation" of Davis's adventure. Certainly, this adventure fails, but it is in understanding the terms of its failure that we see, in a narrative of double suppression, that the denial of the historical parallels the limiting of the imaginary. Capra's refusal of the historical, which would have referenced at least partially the operations of neocolonialism (casting the violence instead in terms of primitive acquisition, which may have signaled a linkage with the devastation visited by monopoly capitalism in the domestic) parallels the blockage of Davis's fantasy. She is reduced to silence at the end of the film. This silence refuses to disclose *either* its failure or its success (for all we know, Davis's psyche may be all the more incited to the imagining of the unorthodox). To end the film so decidedly in the *indecidable* points to the particular quandary Capra is placed within: having intimations of another kind of liaison between Asia and America, but unable to find any way of articulating it.

In reading Capra's film, it is crucial to attend to what Althusser calls the "symptomatics of the narrative."[55] Jameson explains: "The interpretive mission of a properly structural causality will . . . find its privileged content in rifts and discontinuities within the work, and ultimately in a conception of the former 'work of art' as a heterogeneous and schizophrenic text. In the case of Althusserian literary criticism proper, then, the appropriate object of study emerges only when the appearance of formal unification is unmasked as a failure or an ideological mirage."[56] Under such a critique, the *non*appearance of certain elements points to that which the narrative cannot accommodate without disclosing its contradictory underpinnings. Nevertheless, Capra's film presents the suggestion of a liaison between Asia and America that entails a more complex and nuanced notion of hybridity produced within the specific history of the projections and introjections of the 1930s. On the road to modernity, Asia and America were to have a set of defining encounters. The next section will develop this notion of hybridity as an essential term in modern and contemporary imaginings of Asian America, specifically on the terrains of culture and the body, of mimesis and reproduction, and the invention of a new subjectivity in modern migration.

Part II / Bodies and Souls

3 / Written on the Face: Race, Nation, Migrancy, and Sex

IN THE 1930S, UNDER CONDITIONS of increased migration and urbanization, a new sociocultural "hybrid" subjectivity is discursively produced. This new subjectivity is interpolated into a new set of possible frameworks and alignments that complicate our sense of identity as produced dialectically in an encounter between the "self" and the "other." In this complication, Asian/ American identity is set within a particular notion of the modern which wrestles with the precise nature of "becoming" American, as America itself is inflected by modernity. In this section I examine two particular sites of Asian/American predication. In this chapter, I extend my preceding discussion of the embodiment of hybridity and examine the racialized and deracialized body, framed within a somatic aesthetic. This aesthetic is read within various historical occasions of migrancy, from the midcentury to the present day. Here the body is seen as a *reproductive* entity whose decisions and actions sexually reflect the specific character of migration and assimilation, and dramatize the cultural tension of modern migrancy in racial terms, specifically as these new negotiations impact upon the "face" of the nation. In Chapter 4, I analyze representation of the Asian/American body and its social inscriptions in literary narrative. Despite their shared assimilationist themes, these narratives refuse to jettison the corporeal in order to set forth a story of a purely disembodied psychic adjustment to modern America. While each seeks to join up with a "universal" aesthetic (which becomes synonymous with a certain type of cultural assimilation), each remains attached to the materiality of the body and its inscription in the worldly.

In both chapters, my study of the body accords with Bryan Turner's general observation that "the body is a site of enormous symbolic work and symbolic production. Its deformities are stigmatic and stigmatizing, while at the same time its perfections, culturally defined, are objects of praise and admiration. . . . The body is both an environment we practice on and also practice with. We labour on, in and with bodies."[1] In particular, the issue of the racialized body provides a specific site of cultural mapping that inquires as to the body's manifestation of a psychic and spiritual content. This manifestation is read as a litmus test of sociability, its gradations evidence as to the precise calibration of the Asian/American ratio.[2] But along with an attention to the symbolic, I maintain a focus on the material densities of bodies placed in the circuits of labor and consumption. Without such a focus, the body threatens to become disembodied, a free-floating signifier released from historical materialism, disjoined from the very productive forces that have given us Asian America.

In an essay written in 1928, Robert E. Park argues that modern civilization must be understood as a quantitative change in a process that began with the Greeks: "What took place in Greece first has since taken place in the rest of Europe and is now going on in America. The movement and migration of peoples, the expansion of trade and commerce, and particularly the growth, in modern times, of these vast melting-pots of races and cultures, the metropolitan cities."[3] He emplots this process entirely along the lines of contact between formerly heterogeneous peoples: "If it is true that races are the products of isolation and interbreeding, it is just as certain that civilization, on the other hand, is a consequence of contact and communication."[4] Park carefully differentiates race from civilization, yet it is clear that his axiomatic argument favors the process of civilizing the world in terms of the prerogatives of modernity. For Park, race is a problem carried over from the premodern age, still anchored in the local and tribal. The modern resides precisely in the metropolis, the site of modern technologies and political economies. The tension between the loss of the premodern and the shock of the modern produces what he calls the "marginal man," a hybrid of different cultures, who is "an effect of imperialism, economic, political and cultural; an incident of the process by which civilization, as Spengler has said, grows at the expense of earlier and simpler cultures."[5] But it produces as well a particular crisis for the modern nation, which must now negotiate not only cultural complications brought on by migrancy but racial ones as well. It is no accident that the focus tends to stay upon the cultural, as it is a more easily negotiated terrain. The racial will nonetheless stubbornly abide to remind the sociologist of the residual and persistent elements of the "premodern."

In this world, the cultural hybrid becomes valorized as the subject most able to live in the modern age:

The fate which condemns him to live, at the same time, in two worlds is the same which compels him to assume, in relation to the worlds in which he lives, the rôle of a cosmopolitan and a stranger. Inevitably he becomes, relatively to his cultural milieu, the individual with the wider horizon, the keener intelligence, the more detached and rational viewpoint. The marginal man is always relatively the more civilized human being. He occupies the position which has been, historically, that of the Jew in the Diaspora. The Jew, particularly the Jew who has emerged from the provincialism of the ghetto, has everywhere and always been the most civilized of human creatures.[6]

Here Park writes a decade after his pioneering essay on the marginal man to introduce a book by his student, E. V. Stonequist. Stonequist's understanding of the marginal man shows the effect of a historically produced skepticism; his study centers upon the psychologistic effects of marginality and argues a much less sanguine attitude toward the production of modern subjects in migration: "The modern world of economic competition and shifting social relations places the individual in a situation where change and uncertainty are the keynotes. Fixed or permanent adjustments become impossible. The world moves and the individual must continually readjust himself. The possibility that he will not do this with complete success is greater than ever before. Social maladjustment, whether slight or great, then becomes characteristic of modern man."[7] Nevertheless, by the end of his study, Stonequist decides, "The marginal man is the key-personality in the contacts of cultures. It is in his mind that the cultures come together, conflict, and eventually work out some kind of mutual adjustment and interpenetration. He is the crucible of cultural fusion."[8] Thus, rather than "confusion," we find an adjustment that becomes synonymous with the altogether necessary act of adopting to the terms of modernity. Indeed, the mentality of modern life is characterized by such negotiations; the marginal individual reads his or her own life according to such prescribed problematics and is read as well accordingly.

Crucially, we find in these writings an uneasy slippage between cultural and racial hybridity. At times they are synonymous, but at others race persists in being much more visible and problematic—sometimes racial others are read as synonymous with the general exotica of modern forms; at other times, they are markers of a "racial frontier" that cannot be crossed without cost. As modern man is "confused" by both the disorientation that comes with moving between two cultures and the disappearance of premodern sureties, the "unfamiliar" is found everywhere. But like movement itself, which we saw regarded as a suspect condition in the 1920s but valorized as the very sign of the progress of civilization in

Park's conceptualization, the unfamiliar is endowed with particular erotic and sensual value. Park cites W. I. Thomas's *Sex and Society*:

> It is psychologically true that only the unfamiliar and not completely controlled is interesting. This is the secret of modern scientific pursuit and of games. States of high emotional tension are due to the presentation of the unfamiliar—i.e., the unanalyzed, the uncontrolled—to the attention. And although the intimate association and daily familiarity of family life produce affection, they are not favorable to the genesis of romantic love. Cognition is so complete that no place is left for emotional appreciation. Our common expressions, "falling in love" and "love at first sight" imply, in fact, unfamiliarity; and there can be no question that men and women would prefer at present to get mates away from home.[9]

Park makes explicit the connection between "romantic" attraction, sexual reproduction, and social effect. He cites this passage to confirm his assertions regarding intermarriage: "sexual interest, which is still one of the most powerful motives in human contact, operates independently and often counter to the interests represented by the organization of society. Romantic love, which is proverbially interested in the exotic and unfamiliar, not infrequently crosses racial barriers, and is never completely inhibited by class and caste taboos."[10]

This notion of the attraction of the exotic and the consequences of such for society have to be historicized within the context of modernity. It is no longer a matter of seeking the foreign *out there*—during this period, like no time before, the foreign has moved into the familiar, and has been endowed with a particular erotic charge that is linked obviously to the notion of sexual reproduction. It is precisely the fantasy of the interpenetration of Asia and America that we saw operating doubly in Capra's film: Megan's liaison with Yen is complemented by the figure of the westernized Asian, who occupies now an idealized space of both the familiar and the exotic. It is that doubleness that is contained within the figure of General Yen as he appears in Davis's fantasy and in the subtextual interstices of *The Bitter Tea of General Yen*. Simultaneously, then, we have both the rehabilitation of the cultural hybrid as the modern cosmopolitan subject and the argument that environment and culture can indeed affect racial difference. In both we find a conceptualization that allows for the rapprochement (at least culturally) of heretofore mutually exclusive terms: Asian American. Yet it is crucial to note that this cannot be regarded as a unidirectional, evolutionary moment; rather, there persists a racism that will be rearticulated variously in modified discursive forms and will repudiate or at least rebuff the "cultural" connection of Asia and America.

For instance, the notion that the sign of race itself is being gradually effaced to good effect betrays a skepticism regarding both the actual possibilities of socially sanctioned intermarriage, which would biologically produce a hybridized *race*, and thereby a sign of harmony between races and of a more enlightened, less racist America. Instead we have increased meditations on the workings of America upon the foreign body, which will wear away the marks of difference and mold Asia. The point may not be so much the malleability of Asia as the shaping power of America. Previously, we noted how the Immigration Commission was set the task of determining the precise nature and effects of modern migration to the United States. One of its key points of interest was the work of Franz Boas entitled "Changes in Bodily Form of Descendants of Immigrants."[11] The Commission was excited about his findings (laid out over dozens of graphs and charts) that immigrants' bodies were actually being transformed the longer they stayed in America.

Assimilation, then, was both a psychic *and* a somatic phenomenon, the latter now presenting in concrete form the actuality of Americanization (and, conversely, if certain bodies *won't* change, or do so only recalcitrantly, then it is taken as an index to their resistance or inability to assimilate). The summary introduction to the report begins: "The Immigration's anthropological investigation had for its object an inquiry into the assimilation of the immigrants with the American people as far as the form of the body is concerned."[12] One typical finding is found in the following statement, which reveals the issues of greatest concern to the Commission—the capability of immigrants to change and the "natural" conditions that would inevitably transform them in America: "In most of the European types that have been investigated the head form, which has always been considered one of the most stable and permanent characteristics of human races, undergoes far-reaching changes due to the transfer of the people from European to American soil. For instance, the east European Hebrew, who has a very round head, becomes more long-headed; the south Italian, who in Italy has an exceedingly long head, becomes more short headed; so that in this country both approach a uniform type, as far as the roundness of the head is concerned."[13] Such evidence seemed irrefutable proof of the effect of America upon the bodies of immigrants, which now metamorphized into American bodies. And correlated to this was a psychic change: "This fact [of bodily transformation] . . . shows that not even those characteristics of a race which have proved to be the most permanent in their old home remain the same under the new surroundings; and we are compelled to conclude that when these features of the body change, the whole bodily *and mental make-up* of the immigrants may change. . . . The influence of American environment makes itself felt with in-creasing intensity, according to the time elapsed between the arrival of the mother and the birth of the child [emphasis added]."[14]

Nevertheless, despite this new hope of transforming immigrants naturally by prolonged exposure to America, the notion of America as a catalytic space runs up against the Racial Frontier—such bodily transformations are considered only in terms of eastern European and Mediterrean immigrants; it seemed to go without saying that "orientals," whom the Commission agreed should be ex-cluded from the nation, were not susceptible to such transformation, no mat-ter how intense or lengthy their exposure—both the physiognomic and the psy-chic gaps to be crossed were too great.

The abstraction of "race" is the logical outcome of such absolute difference: "The Japanese, like the Negro, is condemned to remain among us as an abstrac-tion, a symbol—and a symbol not merely of his own race but of the Orient and of that vague, ill-defined menace we sometimes refer to as the 'yellow peril.'"[15] Park insists that racial difference is determined not by mental nature, but by a *physical* sign. It is because of the persistence of this physical sign that racial oth-ers are so "condemned" to "abstraction." Their physical difference renders them inaccessible *except* as a mental construct; racial phenotypology casts Asians into the realm of ideology. Until the face of race changes, there is no hope for any manifest understanding. Yet there is a tremendous gap between Park's recogni-tion that race is merely physical difference and the recourse he ultimately makes to the abstract mental prejudices of modern "Americans." He completely by-passes the socioeconomic apparatuses that perpetuate and manage racism.

The abandonment of material history for the abstract, to which Park seems to acquiesce, allows the notion of the marginal man to take two directions. First, it consolidates modern dilemmas into a universal psychological space that it is the duty of each individual to negotiate as he or she will, given the absence in the modern world of anything like traditional, nation-bound belief systems: we are all, in a sense, "marginal" in our existence at the cusp of modern cos-mopolitan industrial life in a "world economy." Second, it particularizes the racial other as the most problematic manifestation of marginality and relegates it to the margins until such time as it completes its phenotypical transformation (into a likely image of assimilation), or, until (much more fatalistically) "soci-ety" is willing and able to recognize it as one of its own. In Chapter 9 I discuss the "mental" facet of this displacement of marginality exclusively into the psy-ches of racialized peoples; here I will concentrate on its mapping of the somatic. Park and Stonequist literalize the "margin" within and upon the body of the racial other, and in so doing create an abject sign of negativity, a sign that is consigned to the exterior as a perpetual reminder not of our shared "marginality," but of the outcast "we" all fear ourselves to be, yet do not *have* to be to such an extent. It is for time, not social action, to redeem this outcast figure; it is only time that will gradually efface the sign of racial difference and welcome the racial other into the fold.

It is of particular interest that Park's analysis stays within the abstract, as if a critique of the actual material histories of American racism would disrupt his mental mapping of race relations. This general tendency toward the abstract (here, toward a vaguely defined notion of modern "psychology") allows for the consolidation of the modern as marginal, and its valorization as the cosmopolitan, while leaving the issue of race abstracted and bracketed. It is important to stress the number of ways that the presence, real and anticipated, of Asians in America is regarded through the ambivalent optics of marginality and tracked along an uncertain telos of social assimilation, uncertain precisely because of the abiding mystery of the "abstraction" of Asians as racial others. And I would suggest that (*contra* Park) this ability to abstract Asians should be read against the inability to do so with African Americans. The "exotic" east lends itself to certain mystifications, whereas the history of slavery in America, while certainly secured in part by ideological imaginings, has nonetheless embedded blacks more concretely and determinedly in the material.

The issue of the "Asian race" should be read as a fantasy in itself—modern discourse on race and hybridity is doubly haunted by an ideologically driven desire to see America as the exemplary modern state wherein difference is accommodated by the discourses of democracy and cosmopolitanism, and by a recognition that the utopian social age was still, always, on the horizon, when it came to those on the other side of the racial frontier. The element of race presents the particular impediment to modernizing the racial Other. The psychologistic and the somatic therefore become intimately attached in the discourse on race and migrancy, nationhood and cosmopolitanism. And that sign of race can best be seen on the face.

In fact, Park's fascination with the Pacific racial frontier (see Section I of this book) is elaborated in an essay that focuses precisely on the face, "Behind Our Masks." Here the face is elaborated as the site of racial negotiations and the transformation of racial identity.[16] Park's general thesis is found in this passage: "Racial traits and racial differences that constitute the racial type and conceal the individual man are not always or altogether physical. Physical differences are emphasized and reenforced by differences of dress, of manner, of deportment, and by characteristic expressions of the face."[17] Park's usage of the term "face" designates a universal connection between the physical, the psychosocial, and the national:

> It is probably no mere historical accident that the word *person*, in its first mean-
> ing, is a mask. It is rather a recognition of the fact that everyone is always and
> everywhere, more or less consciously, playing a role. . . . Our very faces are liv-
> ing masks, which reflect, to be sure, the changing emotions of our inner lives, but
> tend more and more to conform to the type we are seeking to impersonate. Not
> only every race, but every nationality, has its characteristic "face," its conven-
> tional mask. . . . In the end, our conception of our role becomes second nature
> and an integral part of our personality.[18]

Thus, each individual's face expresses that person's internalization of certain social codes and conventions. The face carries the traces of specific historical conditions that exert particular pressure upon the body and its comportment, the
face and its expressions. He quotes Fishberg with regard to Jews: "centuries of
confinement in the ghetto, ceaseless sufferings under the ban of abuse and persecution have been instrumental in producing a characteristic, psychic type,
which manifests itself in his cast of countenance, which is considered particularly Jewish."[19]

It is this "face," then, not (only) in its phenotypology but (also) in animation,
that demarcates essential differences between groups. The racial frontier of the
Pacific finds expression in the behavior of the oriental, which is manifested on
their visages, real and symbolic: "Present differences between the Orient and
the Occident are largely concerned with what the Chinese call 'face'."[20] He
continues: "one striking difference between Oriental and Occidental people is
that the former are more conscious, more conventional, in their behavior than
we. . . . That is the reason why the Chinese go to such elaborate lengths to save
their face. 'To save your face' is to preserve an attitude, and to maintain self-
control."[21] This leads to certain cultural misunderstandings: "Orientals live
more completely behind the mask than the rest of us. Naturally enough we mis-
interpret them, and attribute to disingenuousness and craft what is actually conformity to an ingrained convention."[22] It becomes clear that the opposition Park
is drawing lines up squarely behind the binarism of "oriental" conformity and
"western" individual freedom, between the premodern and the modern world.
It is up to the second generation, then, to bear witness to the unshackling of
Asians in America: "All this changes, however, in the second generation. . . .

With this change in residence and ideals, there has been an abrupt mutation in racial characteristics."[23] Thus race itself is "mutated," faces change, as the psychic content of the second generation has been transformed. Harking back to our earlier discussion, Asians are rescued *then* from the realm of abstraction, and concretized, finally. They may then be admitted to America's imagined sociality, recognized particularly, as their faces have changed, and thus given evidence of their psychic change.

This transformation seems so complete that it produces an eerie, *unheimlich* effect on those who observe the "new" oriental face. Although Park wants to delink the inert physicality of the face from its expression of the psychosocial (the liberal notion that racial markings are less significant than the individual interiority—the former being permanent but insignificant, the latter being essential but changeable), this neat compartmentalization breaks down in the following account, in which Park tells of meeting a young Japanese American woman: "I found myself watching her expectantly for some slight accent, some gesture, or intonation that would *betray* her racial origin. When I was not able, by the slightest expression, to *detect* the oriental mentality behind the oriental mask, I was still not able to escape the impression that I was listening to an American woman in a Japanese *disguise* [my emphasis]."[24] The language here is emphatically that of inspection and detection, attempting to locate the seeming contradiction held within the term "Japanese American." Nevertheless, this all but complete Americanization ultimately fails, since, as Park himself attests, the uneradicable sign of race cannot be ignored, even by people of goodwill:

> Physical traits, however, do not change. The Oriental in America experiences a profound transfiguration in sentiment and attitude, but he cannot change his physical characteristics. He is still constrained to wear his racial uniform; he cannot, much as he may sometimes like to do so, cast aside the racial mask.
>
> The physical marks of race, in so far as they increase the racial visibility, inevitably segregate the races, set them apart, and so prolong and intensify the racial conflict. (252)

It is here that Park's double use of "face"—as comportment and as phenotype—becomes disaggregated and specified. The form may change, but never the latter. And in this passage, Park implies that it is that *fact* that accounts for racism.

His student, E. V. Stonequist, who popularized Park's notion of "marginality," reaches the conclusion that the pathological psychic state of marginality can only be resolved by erasing the outward sign of racial difference through intermarriage: "In the final analysis the adjustment of immigrants and their descendants is conditioned by the possibility of interracial marriage. Where this is permitted by law and public sentiment, assimilation proceeds swiftly and with minor difficulties. Where sentiment is adverse, race problems are prolonged, or even accentuated."[25] Racism will always exist as long as there is discernible racial difference. The only way to lessen the distinctiveness of racial difference is to gradually erase it by biological means—the very means that were so particularly feared by anti-miscegenationists.

We find in this passage from Albert Palmer's 1934 text, *The Oriental in American Life*, however, the notion that the physical might be affected by means other than interbreeding. Palmer, a clergyman, found for Asians what the Dillingham Commission found true for European immigrants: that American life had a particular effect on the body. Palmer argued that the physical environment of the United States was relentlessly changing (even) the appearance and bodily habits of "Orientals," gradually giving them bodies and deportment that approximated those of the dominant. The following remarks share with Park's notion of "face" an attention to the ethnically and socially expressive aspects of the countenance, but suggest a more amorphous mode of physical transformation:

> It is very interesting to note how the physical bearing and even the facial expression of Orientals born in this country are shifting in the American direction. . . . For example, twelve-year-old American-Japanese boys average over an inch and a half taller and five and four-tenths pounds heavier than the Japan-born. Japanese are notably short-legged, but their children tend to have longer legs in this country. Changes in eyelids and eyelashes are also evident, but the most noteworthy adjustment is in the shape of the mouth and the general openness and responsiveness of the countenance. Whether these changes are due to using American furniture, food habits, better dentistry, general freedom of life, or subconscious imitation of the dominant type, no one knows. The important thing is that they are taking place. . . .
>
> Is it too much to believe and hope that, sooner or later, an enlightened and intelligent American public opinion will discover that these Oriental young people, born and reared among us, are not just replicas of the old type foreign-born Chinese or Japanese, but a new type? When that day dawns and we come to see that the Oriental masks are looking more and more like American faces and that behind them are personalities that think and feel as we do and cherish similar dreams and ideals, then the barriers will crumble away.[26]

Following the trajectory of this passage, we witness an attention specifically to American-born Asians, who, reared in the American environment, seem to exhibit the inevitable outcomes of inhabiting America. In heliotropic fashion, the bodies and minds of these Asians bear mute witness to the dominant traits of American life. Palmer's particular attention to the "shape of the mouth and the general openness and responsiveness of the countenance" reflects a focus on merely the most outward representations of an inner change: the production of an "American" social subject, whether it be produced by furniture that molds the body to its contours, food that nourishes a particular growth spurt, dentistry that intervenes in unhealthy orthodontics, a "freedom of life" that signals a distinct departure and liberation from Asian authoritarian "tradition," *or*, possibly, the subconscious but nonetheless willed "imitation" of the dominant type. Nevertheless, Palmer is not interested in what, exactly, produces these changes; "the important thing is that they are taking place." This marks the essential difference between "these Oriental young people" and "old type foreign-born" Asians. These young people do not reproduce their parents' sociality, but represent an as yet unclassifiable "new type."

Most significant is Palmer's evocation of Park's distinction between Oriental "masks" and actual faces. The former are seen as the unwelcome residue of foreign social habits that are deemed here to be eminently unreal—insincere, merely the blind repetition of traditional conventions—while American faces are taken as eminently "real" in their unabashed individualistic freedom of expression. It is that necessary transformation that must be worked for "us" to ever imagine that "they" are like us, and that would be the first step toward a nonracist society. But, unlike Park, Palmer suggests that something much more subtle and mysterious is at work. While he, too, comes to suggest intermarriage as a possible way to accelerate the disappearance of race, as a clergyman he is only too familiar with the psychic damage that might bring about, given the still unenlightened nature of the general public.

What I want to draw out from this discussion is the formation of a particular discourse on the migrant and second-generation Asian body, its "face," and how its difference from the dominant notion of "face" is addressed by hybridization, whether it be biologically or environmentally induced. This discourse finds particular rearticulation in the second half of the twentieth century, as the new field of plastic reconstructive surgery provides the technical means to accelerate and make more precise the slow environmental phenomena remarked upon by Palmer. But before I turn to a consideration of that newly discovered "plasticity" we should note that the correlation between Asian/American material and psychic interpenetrations is noted as well in the reconstructed landscape of

Asia. Consider these passages from a young Chinese college student returning to China:

> With regard to material traits I saw and enjoyed many things in Tsing Hua, which are similar to those I have seen and am enjoying at Stanford. For instance, tub baths, ice cream, milk, "drinking fountains," aerated water, electric light, steampipe, phonograph, radio, and some other kinds of modern conveniences. Whenever I wished to go to the city, for Tsing Hua College is situated a few miles away from Peking, I could go there by bus. Whenever I was sick, I went to see a Western doctor and took Western medicine. Moreover, the fountain pen I possessed was manufactured in America; the suit of foreign dress I used to put on was made in Western style; and the shoes I used to wear were just like what I am wearing in America. For amusement, I used to see moving pictures. The movie, I think, is one of the most powerful cultural influences, for good or for evil, that America has brought to China. . . . From the moving pictures they are learning the Western way of making love, of committing suicide, of saying this or that. . . . However, my contact with the Western material traits is nothing compared to my contact with the Western ideal and spiritual traits. In fact, it is not the wearing of a collar and necktie but the study of Western subjects that has changed me into a "cultural hybrid."[27]

Chieng Fu Lung here carefully inventories the new material environment of China—the college seems to replicate Stanford, the transport of the body to and from the city, the clothes it wears, the very fountain pen that scripts the essay, are all echoes of America in China. The comportments for sexuality and death are carried over from American celluloid. And even when he asserts that "studying" does more to hybridize him than those materialities, it is difficult not to see the two realms of the spirit and the body working in tandem, each one confirming the other. If Palmer sees Asians in America changing their bodies and minds, here we find the exportability of such transformation in modern Asia.

The postwar years presented a historically distinct context for meditations on the Asian/American body. If the 1930s anticipated the intensification of Asian/American formation in the context of absorbing and domesticating already present Asians in America, and inventing neocolonial strategies of American/Asian geopolitics, the Second World War and the Immigration Act of 1965 drove home the point that Asia's and America's destinities were indeed intimately connected in the journey into the second half of the twentieth century and beyond. We witness the foregrounding of the body in particular as a sign, whose signifying power is complicated by both a new technologically driven malleability and by a historically driven re-imaging of the "face of America."

After the Second World War there developed a concrete manner of representing the Asian body for American socialization, one that has increased in practice as its technology has improved parallel to the intensification of the circulation of western images of beauty and the power seen to be attached to it. Reporting from Bangkok, Sheila McNulty chronicles the rising popularity of plastic surgery upon the Asian eyelid: "As Thailand embraces fast-food restaurants, blue jeans and Hollywood movies in its zeal to Westernize, its women are having their faces nipped and tucked to fit in. . . . From South Korea to the Philippines to Malaysia, women who can afford it are going under the knife in hopes of achieving the now-popular European concept of beauty." [28] The title of her article, "Asians Bear the Knife for Western Look," along with this quotation, draws together the key elements of this reportage: "western" notions of beauty have solidified a hegemonic hold as commodities have delocalized Asian customs and tastes. So great is that hegemony that it has produced a masochistic, self-sacrificial mentality among the natives who are willing to endure physical and economic discomfort. The benefits are, ostensibly, psychic, but that psychic gain is always transacted intersubjectively. Ronald Matsunaga, a Beverly Hills plastic surgeon, promotes his technique of eyelid surgery as resulting in "a marked improvement of the narrow, puffy Asian eye and greater patient satisfaction. . . . The goal of each author performing this operation is to surgically create a supratarsal fold, commonly referred to as a 'double eyelid' changing the eyelid of the typical Asian to a more esthetic and cosmetically larger eyelid characteristic of the occidental. The newly created eyelids can be further enhanced by proper cosmetic application, resulting in greater self image and confidence" (149). [29]

Here, I draw attention to two issues. First, that the shaping of the exterior is taken to effect a modification of the interior: as appearances change, the projection of the psychic interiority is assumed to be altered by dint of the fact that a different "spirit" is seen to lie beneath that surface. This projection is *imagined* by the patient to take place upon the Asian face in the mind of a white observer. So secure is the patient in this assumption that it is supposed to have the effect of endowing the patient with a new spirit, that is, *reconstituting* that subjectivity. [30] In this regard, it is not enough to remark only on the internalization of aesthetic judgments and values; it is crucial to place that observation in the wider context of social being that extends "beauty" into morality, social engagement, and mental structures. The display of the Asian face suggests a particular zone of contact, which in turn implies the contact of certain contents and elements. Appearances are not everything, but they are assumed to correlate with that which they are not. If the "narrow" eyelid betrays "dullness," "stupidity," "passivity," it is futile to try to posit a causality (are they read such because they belong to an Asian face?). Rather, the key point is the correlation of the exterior with the interior, which signals a set of behaviors readable on the face and permanently ensconced in the psyche.[31] The modification of the sign of race will thus affect what liberal rational thinking cannot (that is, skin color doesn't matter). If Park was impatient about the pace of racial "enlightenment" in the United States during the thirties, if Stonequist could only see intermarriage as performing that necessary modification of racial markings, and if Palmer could rely only on the slow change brought about by furniture and diet, after the Second World War technology stepped in with something more immediate. It will allow race to change because the individual has been allowed to change cosmetically.

But it is crucial to note that the alteration of the Asian eyelid is not absolute, but rather, measured. McCurdy advises his colleagues, "Many patients . . . simply desire a small 'double eyelid' while maintaining the Oriental look" (4). Similarly, a press release from the American Academy of Cosmetic Surgery notes, "The procedures they [minorities, including Asian Americans] seek are not so much to look 'western' but to refine their features to attain facial harmony."[32] While such qualifications might be motivated by a desire to mute the racist undertones of this surgery (though they certainly seep through in phrases such as "facial harmony"), this also suggests that the desire to alter the eyelid is not undertaken necessarily to "be white," but to partake of whiteness in a selective fashion. And that whiteness exists precisely in the discourse of social power. Ann duCille makes this point with regard to a black child's imaging of self in relation to whiteness: "A child's dreaming in the color scheme privileged by the world around her is not necessarily the same was wanting *to be* that color. . . . What guided my fantasy life, I believe, was less a wish to flee my own black flesh than a desire to escape the limitations that went with such bodies."[33] Similarly, Asian Americans interviewed as to why they wanted to change their appearance pointed to economic benefits as much as "self-image" benefits.[34]

This leads us back to Matsunaga's notion that the "revised surface" is now suitable to further cosmetic (nonpermanent) application: "The newly created eyelids can be further enhanced by proper cosmetic application, resulting in greater self image and confidence." That is, the scalpel of the surgeon discretely steps back after a limited but critical intervention—the subject is now endowed not just with a newly "created" eyelid, but with a surface that is able to be individually modified at will. True American individualism is allowed to flourish and adjust itself according to the specific contours and reshapings of body and social life. Why is this important? Again, such a liberal add-on is advertised not only as another incentive, but to map out a much more potent site of malleability, one that we can call the ideation of the adjustable, temporalized modernization of Asian America. Things are not simply yellow or white, but are now eminently flexible given the proper surface, the proper contact zone. Nonetheless, the functionality of this is predicated on a blind faith in the interpretive correctness of the patient, who must wonder, "If I do this will I be seen as 'other' than what I am now *in the way* I anticipate and expect to be seen?" This links the body to the psyche. The morphing of physical form anticipates the revision of the psyche within, and the way that transformed body will be viewed by others. Such projection into an other's point of view ("I can see how others see me") is linked to notions of racial "schizophrenia."

The contemporary practice of plastic surgery on the Asian eyelid should not be understood as a recent phenomenon, solely concerned with self-image. It is more fully appreciated as participating in the general discourse of migrancy and national identity established in this study. Surgery on the Asian eyelid flourished after the Second World War, specifically in Japan, as many Japanese women, especially "war brides," anticipated having to "fit into" their adoptive countries. But no attention has been paid to the fact that the high point of such surgery began as a public relations program of United States occupational forces in Korea. To get such an account, we need to examine D. R. Millard's 1955 essay, "Oriental Peregrinations," his narrative of his service in Korea as an army surgeon. Here I connect this specifically Asian American topic to the general topic of modern hybridity.

Millard is initially sent to Korea to help reconstruct war-damaged bodies. He begins his essay by outlining the connection between "rehabilitating" the state of Korea and rehabilitating Korean bodies:

> One of the purposes of the U.S. Marines remaining in Korea after the ceasefire was to assist the war-ravaged people in their rehabilitation. It seemed that plastic surgery should be a part of this project and through it would be constructed visible evidence of American goodwill in Asia. This is a land where anomalies and deformities must be borne through life without relief. What, to us, is no more than a pedicle flap or a skin graft, to them is little less than a miracle. Thus it proved to be a direct type of aid that people could see and appreciate.

Figure 2. Illustration from D. Ralph Millard, "Oriental Pereginations," *Plastic and Reconstructive Surgery* 16 (1955). Used with permission.

Pouring unearned money into a country often causes more chaos and waste than goodwill. . . .

We Americans are naive babes in the Asian wood never knowing whether we are feeding the mouths of friends or loading the guns of communists. Yet we can be relatively certain that after each deformity was corrected or improved and the Korean returned home, America had won the heart of the patient, his family and possibly even part of his village. (319)

In other words, where ideology is uncertain, the rehabilitated body bears irrefutable witness to goodwill. The American diplomat/soldier, lost in the unknown territory of Asia, cannot be sure how any of his acts will be interpreted. The reconstituting of bodies, however, is a certain sign of intent and goodwill; it is not open to misinterpretation. And it is hard to miss the corollary to such acts of reconstituting the Korean body—a map of Korea drawn by Millard, showing the areas where plastic surgery was performed, marks as well the segmentation of north and south, and we can extrapolate the hidden desire to make "Korea" whole again, under U.S. sponsorship.[35]

And one could, indeed, link this to the general crisis in postwar East Asian policy, and the crisis of the Cold War. It relates not only to the division of Korea

ORIENTAL PEREGRINATIONS

LEGEND: ◼ Hospitals Where Korean Plastic Surgery Was Performed

Figure 3. From Millard, "Oriental Pereginations." Used with permission.

but also to the division of Germany. In both cases, we have a crisis of accommodation by division, a compromise acceptable to none of the players. "To make whole again" forms the common discursive link, but the question still remains, what would this new whole look like, given the impossibility of effacing the scars of the sutures, which attest to the body's prior fragmentation?

What needs to be secured before any such surgery is a sense of how, exactly, to reconstitute the Korean body—specifically the face—in a form not only as good as but superior to its prior, unviolated form. To do this requires a particularly contrived investigation. Millard gives this account of the procedure:

Before venturing into Plastic on Orientals, however, it seemed wise to become adjusted to their standard of beauty. On every Saturday night at a certain Officer's Club there is "moose call" in the form of a dinner dance. A buffet supper baited with ham, chicken, sausage, and pickles is served and bak-san [many] . . . attractive young ladies of Seoul line up outside the gate. The more exotic *baby-sans* are soon escorted into the party and by candlelight with a background of soft music it is possible to study the facial contour of the Oriental. Occasionally an American or English girl is allowed into the party, and with a round-eyed control at a table of slant-eyes the social gathering becomes a veritable laboratory for scientific comparison. (322)

It is hard to leave such a loaded passage behind without commenting on the particular issues of "baiting" a war-ravaged female population, of the necessity to have a "control" against which to measure the difference (and hence identity) of the "oriental," nor the transformation of a bar into a candle-lit laboratory. Specifically noteworthy is Millard's fondness for metonymy, signaling his attachment to reducing the human being to the medical case, and also to the parceling up of bodies, so as to allow for his recombinatory poetics. This "seduction" works in two directions, for the Korean landscape is transformed into an irresistible operating theater for Millard:

In a country so ravaged by war and so lacking in medical care there is little wonder that in the hidden corners of each village lurked the devastating results of untreated raw contracture. Evidence of this was seen in toes drawn back on the dorsum of the foot, eyelids pulled off the eye and chins soldered down with keloid to the chest. Orphanages were combed for children with deformities. In any of the numerous leper colonies alone, there is a lifetime of reconstruction. This is indeed a plastic surgeon's paradise. (323)

Yet this "paradise" takes on a particular allure when Millard shifts his mission from rehabilitating Korea to advancing the range and nature of the technical. The rehabilitative is given over to a delight in the purely aesthetic, an aesthetic, as we saw above, informed by *transformation*, not reconstruction. Witness how the language of desire, imagination, and bounty gives way to that of fascination with this particular case of transformation that captures Millard's attention:

Every night during my first week in the Orient I dreamed of "Z" plasties on thousands of mongoloid faces but by the time a month had passed I seldom gave them another thought. When the inevitable did occur, it took me by surprise. A slant-eyed Korean intepreter, speaking excellent English, came in requesting to be made into a "round-eye." His future lies in his relation with the west and he felt

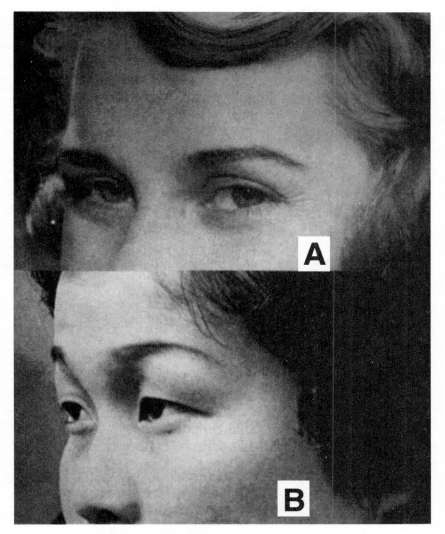

FIG. 12A. The Occidental look.
FIG. 12B. The Oriental look.

Figure 4. From Millard, "Oriental Pereginations." Used with permission.

that because of the squint in his slant eyes, Americans could not tell what he was thinking and consequently did not trust him. As this was partly true, I consented to do what I could. (331)

This quotation takes us firmly from the realm of the reconstruction of a past form (a project Millard soon tires of, its novelty exhausted) to that of transformation for *future* applications: the invention of a hybrid that is produced by "correcting" a "defect" inherent in the Asian face. This defect must "inevitably" be modified if the east is to have any authentic contact with the west: "Due to the droop of the upper lid only the lower half of the iris is exposed. This gives the effect of an expressionless eye sneaking a peep through a slit, a characteristic which through fact and fiction has become associated with mystery and intrigue" (333).

What is most important is the particular relation that this interpreter has with the west — that of acting at the seam of Asia and America, as cementing their communication in translation. And that individual, being Asian, cannot be trusted without being physically transformed to approximate a particular social subjectivity. This new, hybrid figure must be able to vacillate unimpeded between self and other. Contrary to Park's belief that the countenance of each individual was an expression of his or her cultural conventions, Millard believes the opposite: the social does not determine the physical — the physical determines the social.[36] Millard is at once more absolutely and biologically racist, but, given the advance in techniques that allowed the transformation of facial characteristics, also more progressive in a weird way. For surgical technique can intervene in the process of hybridization and accelerate the more slowly produced effects of interbreeding.[37] According to this logic, which is the obverse of Park's notion of "face," the transformation of the physical should bring about a change in the psychic. This is indeed what we find in the caption that accompanies the "before and after" photos of the interpreter.

We see in Millard's description of this patient's outcome an attention to a *deep* transformation worked by the adjustment of the surface: "Note the flat nose and hooded eyes of the Korean interpreter. After cartilage to nose and plastic to eyelids the interpreter was mistaken for Mexican or Italian. He became a Christian and hopes to travel to the United States to study for the ministry" (334). This surgically produced image of the hybrid reaches into the interior to work a psychic change. And with any appearance of untrustworthiness erased, the soul itself is adequately westernized and rectified, and a new "person" emerges. One notes how the interpreter is not transformed into an "American" — that would be too immodest and impossible a task. Rather, he is situated in the terrain of a

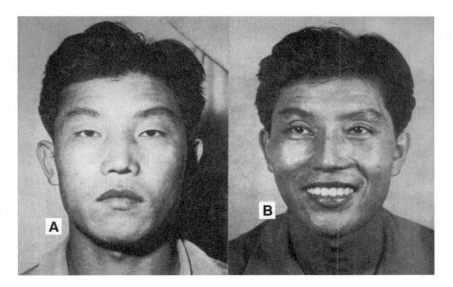

Figure 5. From Millard, "Oriental Pereginations." Used with permission.

positive indecideability, a flexible, albeit still ethnic, identity, that benefits from
its potential confusion with other, presumably more "assimilable" ethnic types
still in that liminal space of pre-Americanization, yet closer than the racially
marked Oriental.

Millard, encouraged by these results, embarks upon a program of "deorien-
talizing." Although there is a marked difference between the rationale for "de-
orientalizing" Asian males and females ("professional" reasons for men, to make
them appear more trustworthy; "aesthetic" for women, to make them closer to
the American "norm" of beauty), in both cases this procedure removes an essential semiotic element and thereby enables a particular set of social relations
between east and west:

> Many ask why the Oriental wants to change his face. Of course the majority do
> not, but those who do give reasons which range from religious or economic to
> the universal desire to appear more beautiful. It is felt that this deorientalizing
> problem may well come home to the American plastic surgeon, for there have
> been well over 10,000 Japanese war brides as well as many post-war marriages
> with Korean girls. These numbers are continually mounting, for when a lone-
> some G.I. comes face to face with the gentle humility, artistic grace and myste-
> rious charm of feminine *baby-san*, he brings her back alive. Alas, folds that were
> exotic in Pusan or Kyoto will become strangely foreign to Main Street of a mid-

west town or under the columns of a southern mansion. Especially in the products of the second generation, the plastic surgeon may be called upon to help them blend with their surroundings.

The oriental must not disturb the placid landscape of the United States. This is not just an aesthetic consideration, for the "overtly Asian" face is brought "back alive" as American plunder from Asia. On a less dramatic but more compelling level, the Asian face, unmodified, recalls the ungovernability of the Asian/American encounter. The folded eyelid is to be a sign of its containment. But especially telling is Millard's focus on the "products of the second generation," who need particular attention. How do we reconcile the fact that they, as half-white, should carry within and upon themselves already the beginnings of "deorientalization," and yet need particular help in "blending in"? Are we not confronted with the contradictions of this aesthetic, that at once celebrates the hybrid and recoils before its concretization when it is produced not by controlled surgical technique but by sexual reproduction?

If Millard worries about how "slant eyes" will be viewed by the "American" spectator, not as a distant, abstract image, but as a concrete presence on Main Street U.S.A., then the issue of beauty, the aesthetic of the body, becomes part of an anxious and fragmented social discourse of race. Asian bodies are present precisely as representing the impeachability of domestic space in a sexualized, potentially reproductive, fashion. The anxiety over the hybrid returns and must be tamed, as "contact" with Asia under the imperatives of Cold War policies has intensified and made itself a permanent part of the American landscape, not only as labor, but as sexualized and reproductive force. The discovery and promotion of cosmetic surgery provided an opportunity for the Asian body to demonstrate its acquiescence to American aesthetics, social codings, and racist assumptions of behavioralism. At the same time, though, this artificially produced image of a hybrid form seemed to offer both the conditions for intermarriage and socialization in the United States and a preview of an actual state of hybridity that could and would be produced by intermarriage. This operation thus contains a contradiction: the epicanthal fold is at once a sign of acquiescence and an occasion for subversion. The racial economies of faciality are thus to be located not in absolutely territorialized otherness, but in a calibration of similitude. What we witness above is the surgical erosion of the Asian face, so as to allow a certain situatedness with regard to America. Deleuze and Guattari note:

If the face is in fact Christ, in other words, your average ordinary White Man, then the first deviances, the first divergence-types, are racial: yellow man, black man, men in the second or third category. . . . They must be Christianized, in other words, facialized. European racism as the white man's claim has never operated by exclusion, or by the designation of someone as Other. . . . Racism operates by the determination of degrees of deviance in relation to the White Man face, which endeavors to integrate nonconforming traits into increasingly eccentric and backward waves, sometimes tolerating them at given places under given conditions. . . . From the viewpoint of racism, there is no exterior, there are no people on the outside. There are only people who should be like us and whose crime it is not to be.[38]

But a discussion of Millard's essay would be incomplete without noting that the transformation of the face is not performed solely upon Asians. Millard notes: "We all know the U.S. Marines are the world's greatest fighting force but it never occurred to me that they would turn out to be the ugliest. Headquarters approved a 'new look' program—ears were pinned, noses straightened, chins bolstered and faces lifted" (320). In particular he reports requests by soldiers to have stronger chins and less hooked noses. The Anglo-Saxon norm thus affects other "Americans" as well. What we have then is a much more complicated set of negotiations, enabled and prompted by developments in surgical technique, and which, I will argue here and in the study generally, evinces a complex set of flexible racial identifications in the modern and postmodern ages.

Having traced the development of the aesthetic of the hybrid in the period following the Second World War, I want to turn to its development in a direction that will ultimately seek to erase all signs of raciality: in the late twentieth century we find the displacement of the hybridity onto the terrain of the "symmetrical." We note a persistent attention to migrancy as we move from the Cold War spirit of containment (that nonetheless had to accommodate migration to the United States produced within the logic of its postwar involvements in East Asia) to the contemporary age of transnational capital.

D. R. Millard's work did not end in Korea. His major work was published thirty years after "Oriental Pereginations." In it, we witness the development of the notion of hybridity, but also the ascension of another concept with which to address the effects of migrancy—the symmetrical. Millard's *Principalization of Plastic Surgery* (1986) is a long treatise on the essentials guiding the practice of plastic surgery. In particular, Millard addresses what he calls "*aesthetic* plastic surgery." The title of his eighth principle is particularly instructive: "Know the

Ideal Beautiful Normal." Millard explains: "Since the normal is our goal, any reconstructive surgeon must know the normal, be sensitive to it and use it as a
guide and challenge. Still the true plastic surgeon will go further to know the
ideal beautiful normal" (78). First, the norm for the body's appearance must be
ascertained, but the surgeon as true artist cannot rest there—he must discover
a norm that is endowed with the aura of an ideal beauty. Millard calls to his
aid Plato, Aquinas, and Umberto Eco. But he rests his case on the words of
Dr. M. Gonzalez-Ulloa:

> It is not possible to establish a universal canon of beauty because of the different
> ethnic types, but in every face, notwithstanding the ethnic origin, is found pro-
> portion and harmony between the segments and a good architectural frame. . . .
>
> Then too, the morphology of the human body has begun to change so that it
> becomes similar to that of the community's dominant group. It could be said that
> the use of aesthetic plastic surgery corresponds to the great Jewish migration to-
> wards the western world. . . .
>
> Now we come to an era that has no classic type of beauty, no dominating type
> to influence the concept of "prototype of beauty." Cross-breeding, due to mass
> migration between continents, to wars, to constant traveling or to mass com-
> merce has resulted in races with mixed traits. (93f)

We see a rationalization that becomes entirely familiar in modern discourses on
physical beauty and race: races differ, and yet there is a geometrical, *somatic* aesthetic that transcends such differences. In the steady flow of historical time,
specifically within the conditions of modernity, races are increasingly blending
into each other, and all will eventually fall under the same imperative of geo-
metric balance.[39] I want to draw particular attention to this transition: the willingness of minority individuals to surgically change their appearances to better
blend into the image of the dominant becomes superseded as the hybridization
brought about by modern migration makes the image of the dominant less and
less distinct. Herein the notion of symmetry comes to be a placeholder of value
against which the hybrid is to be evaluated.

Millard, too, ends up arguing the superiority of a hybridized image:

> While Oriental ladies are having their upper lids made more Occidental, ladies
> of other races, covetous of the charm, mystery and intrigue associated with the
> slit and slant of the Oriental eye, devote much time and expense to makeup to
> create the sloe-eye to imitate the Oriental effect. Often blending of racial char-
> acteristics produces an exotic beauty *beyond the pure forms* much as the mixing of

species can occasionally produce an exceptionally beautiful hybrid [emphasis added]. (102)

The valorization of the hybrid is only partially explicable by the fact that total transformation is impossible ("It is not just nonsense but impossible to make an Oriental totally into a Caucasian or vice versa. The same goes for transformation of a black into a Caucasian or vice versa or an Oriental into a black" [105]). Rather, we find in these writings on aesthetic plastic surgery a recognition not only of the limits of surgical technique, but also of the historical occasion of hybrid value, which rescues plastic surgery from having to confess its inability to enact absolute transformation. Instead, we witness the instantiation of an "ideal norm" of beauty which goes beyond racially distinct norms. This transition between the specificity of race to a focus on the normativity of the geometrical and the ascension of the hybrid has to be read within the history of U.S. modernity, and specifically that of Asian/American formation, as the concern becomes not the impossible task of sequestering race within nations, but of inventing the terms upon which to negotiate the hybridization of the modern nation feeling its very interior penetrated by the formerly foreign.

Recently, sociological attempts to explain the trajectories of interracial desire as determined by class mobility, fueled by feelings of inferiority instilled by racist imaging, have been countered by biological studies that explained that "beauty" is altogether nonraced. The cover story of the June 3, 1996, *Newsweek* offers us "The Biology of Beauty." The cover features two "beautiful" naked young people, white and blond, strong and slender: one male, one female. The article presents research that claims that "people everywhere—regardless of race, class, or age—share a sense of what's attractive" (62). Such arguments pick up the thread of Gonzalez-Ulloa's notion that, while a "universal canon of beauty" cannot be obtained, there is a shared sense of beauty emanating from an appreciation for symmetry, but these studies have the benefit of reaching this conclusion by way of extensive scientific analysis.

After first presenting the argument that we are attracted to strong, healthy individuals rather than weak, sickly ones (obviously because we instinctively want to reproduce), the article explains that the "latest" scientific studies have found that healthy bodies are signaled by symmetry; individuals are predisposed to have sex with people they sense to be reproductively viable. The empirical data support this: "For both men and women, greater symmetry predicted a larger number of past sex partners" (63). Symmetry may now be measured against a general set of possible combinations: "Scientists can now average faces digitally, and it's still one of the surest ways to make them more attractive" (64). The effect of such studies is to quell anxiety about race (or anything else) as presenting significant difference.[40] Besides reaffirming some very problematic masculinist, heterosexual assumptions about "beauty" and behavior, however, the study has the effect of suggesting that race matters so little that issues of material history are irrelevant. But if we "all" desire the same bodies, then why is it that there is not much *more* interracial marriage, or that certain patterns of intermarriage persist and others don't?

Resistance to structural critique shows up in most discussions of interracial marriage, even those most sensitive to certain imbalances and distasteful practices. The decision to intermarry is rationalized as distinctly individualistic: "As long as they're individuals, that's all that counts."[41] While I am not suggesting that such impressions of individual taste are mistaken, it is crucial to see what else, *along with race*, might constitute that "individual" as an object of desire. To denounce race as a determining factor is one thing, but to disengage completely from the way that race is imbricated and made visible in a number of social discourses is another. The move toward privatization is an effective way to bypass such considerations.

It is crucial to note that this newly defined imperative to reproduce the "species" is now seen as eminently "human" in a (potentially) *hybridized* fashion. That is, the imperative of racial reproduction has been dismissed, overridden by attention to the individual's urge to reproduce him- or herself regardless of any desire to reproduce any particular racial identity.[42] Hence the common anxiety voiced to counter desire for intermarriage—"What about the children?"—has been superseded by an always open and flexible hybrid image. But this notion of nonracial desire comes into collusion with a rather defeatist conservative stance toward the multiracializing of America. Have we accepted hybridization simply because it is inevitable? Is symmetry a rationalization, a substitute that will hide the lack of a clear image of "the face of America," in this age of increased and intensified migrancy and transmigrancy, which circulate in a global economy adumbrated and euphemized in Park's notion of a vast "unconscious cooperation of races and peoples"? What does the "new America" look like? We still need a face, but which face are we comfortable with? How does symmetry *look*, and *look back at us*?

That the connection among sexual attraction, reproduction, and race in the political economy of the state is linked to new global economics and migrancy is unmistakable. *Newsweek*'s 1996 cover story follows a special issue of *Time* magazine published in the fall of 1993: "The New Face of America: How Immigrants Are Shaping the World's First Multicultural Society." Their common attention to the face, specifically the female face, within the thematic of race, is telling. The *Time* issue dramatizes the "multiculturalizing" of America with the image of a computer-generated hybrid, a fantasy that seeks to put a face on the end product of interracial marriage. While intermarriage is initially used as a trope for the process of multiculturalization,[43] it provides a particular site for imagining the telos of immigration and assimilation in the late twentieth century: "The process of assimilation, while perhaps a bit more hesitant and stressful than at times in the past, still marches on. . . . There is no turning back: diversity breeds diversity. It is the fuel that runs today's America and, in a world being transformed daily by technologies that render distances meaningless, it puts America in the forefront of a new international order" (9). And it is precisely this technology that also assists in imaging the product of such time/space compression, such self-perpetuating "diversity."

Lauren Berlant remarks upon the way this image tracks the messiness of material history into a cybernetic private world: "The new face of America involves a melding of different faces with the sutures erased and the proportions made perfect; she is a national fantasy from the present representing a post-historical—that is, post-white—future" (418). This absenting of history may be approached from another angle as well. The movement from similitude to symmetry, the displacement of value from a mimicking and approximation of whiteness onto a "color-neutral" objectivity may be ironically correlated with a shift from modernity to postmodernity. Instead of an attempt to create and recreate a face of the nation which marks the persistence of a clear historical value (whiteness), the notion of symmetry instantiates a postmodern "flatness" wherein different points of historical origin are made irrelevant and erased. What matters most is the present, in which everything has equal value. Herein we find one of the many contradictions of postmodernity. At the same time that it allows an occasion for dismantling inherited hierarchies, it leaves uncertain the availability of any history to ground progressive work. Liberation is attended to by conflation and an emptying out of historical content. Yet this very contradiction drives the dialectic in which one may indeed be able to map another sort of totality.[44] Here I wish to center precisely on the unsettledness of this "shift": in the late twentieth century, we find a vacillation between a modernity in which race retains its negatively differential function, in which the nation continues to be (supposedly) consolidated in one historical racial image (although the discursive production of this image might change and vary), and a postmodernity in which a value-neutral "hybridity" instantiates an ahistoricized symmetry in the place of similitude. The former bespeaks the persistence of racial thinking, the latter aspires to move beyond it but can do so only by eliding material history. Finally, this shift may be correlated with the historical movement to late capitalism: the increased and uneven transmigrancy of peoples across national spaces is driven by the new mode of late capitalist production. The sovereignty of the nation-state is now compromised by increased transnational interests; the very constitution of its interiority attests to the demographic changes that accompany globalization.

Time's description of the process that resulted in this image merits quoting at length:

> The woman on the cover of this special issue of Time does not exist—except metaphysically. Her beguiling and mysterious visage is the product of a computer process called morphing. . . . When the editors were looking for a way to dramatize the impact of interethnic marriage, which has increased dramatically in the U.S. during the latest wave of immigration, they turned to morphing to create the kind of offspring that might result from seven men and seven women of various ethnic and racial backgrounds. . . .
>
> The highlight of this exercise in cybergenesis was the creation of the woman on our cover, selected as a symbol of the future multiethnic face of America. . . . Little did we know what we had wrought. As onlookers watched the image of our new Eve begin to appear on the computer screen, several staff members promptly fell in love. Said one: "It really breaks my heart that she doesn't exist." We sympathize with our lovelorn colleagues, but even technology has its limits. This is a love that must forever remain unrequited. (2)

The editors reassure us that this "woman" does not exist except "metaphysically": that status endows the image with a fantastic existence that is imaginable and representable in a technologically "valid" manner. The convergence of technology and imagination underwrites this particular face of America; it also declares the limits of technology, noting that technology cannot produce a sexually viable cyborg commensurate with the image. The *quasi*-whiteness of the image is a correlate to the vacillation between image and reality, the present and the future, between the absence and the presence of race as a sign. In other words, the image is particularly desirable because it is like and yet not-like, a perfect rebus of what used to be called miscegenation, now rewritten in a modern age that must become reconciled to the hybrid. The image is familiar enough to be not too unsettling, but not so familiar as to breed contempt. Rather, it fosters desire.

Figure 6. Cover of special issue of *Time*, 1993. Copyright 1993, Time, Inc. Reprinted by permission.

Time's image thus participates in the narrative of beauty and corporeal transformation we've traced from the 1930s, a narrative that at each step attempts to stabilize the effects of migrancy, desire, and identification, and to exploit this harmony as a sign of America's ability to deal positively with the new world of increased globalization. And it does so by means of art and artifice, surgery and cybernetics.

The celebratory subtitle, awarding America the number-one status once again ("During the past two decades, America has produced the greatest variety of hybrid households in the history of the world" [64]) is predicated on the notion that hybridity is not only inevitable, but valuable and especially economically so. This recalls the eugenicist notion of "hybrid vigor," which argues that the more distant the strains that are interbred, the stronger the resulting product. Yet here there is both the aroma of triumph and the scent of fear and defeat. The playfulness insisted upon in this imaging is replicated in a chart published on pages 66–67, in which inquisitive readers can pair up seven different ethnic and racial groups in both female-male and male-female directions to "see" what "their" offspring will look like.[45]

Intermarriage can now be a spectator sport. The actual physicality of the "event" is held at spatial and temporal distance, cleansed of its material messiness, the asymmetry of the political economy of race, gender, and class in America. This jettisoning of the materiality of the body, its effects, and its products into a cybernetic morphology performs the notion of pacification mentioned by Barthes.[46] Yet the very obviousness of this erasure of not only race, but the politics of race, belies an anxiety over the actualization of multiracialization and an ardent desire to leap beyond such concerns to a future time of reconciliation, wherein, somehow, those concerns have already been sorted out. While one can understand and sympathize with that utopianism, this positive view of multiracialization masks deeper anxieties over national identity and privilege that must be attended to in the present.

Two images present quite different views of the transformation of America under immigration and illustrate the persistence of race despite the celebration of symmetry. The first, from a 1993 cover of *Newsweek*, is a graphic illustration of anxiety over increased, "uncontrolled" immigration "flooding" the United States to such a degree that the icon representing the ideal of America as refuge for the world is drowned by a world unexpectedly mobile (and note here the submersion of the face). The second image presents a radically different depiction of the effects of immigration. It accompanies an article published in 1985 in *The New Republic*, "The Triumph of Asian-Americans: America's Greatest Success

Figure 7. Cover of *Newsweek*, August 9, 1993. Illustration by Scott McKowen. Copyright 1993, Newsweek, Inc. All rights reserved. Reprinted by permission.

Figure 8. Illustration from *The New Republic*, July 15/22, 1985. Reprinted by permission of *The New Republic*. Copyright 1985, The New Republic, Inc.

Story."[47] How are we to explain, in the age of symmetry and hybridity, the morphing of the face of the Statue of Liberty not into a composite image of immigrants and citizens, but into the Asian face, which proudly presents itself *without* the epicanthal fold?

The author of the article, David A. Bell, begins by describing a scene from Ridley Scott's *Bladerunner* (1982): "It is the year 2019. In the heart of downtown Los Angeles, massive electronic billboards feature a model in a kimono hawking products labelled in Japanese" (24). He then writes, "Why did the critics praise *Bladerunner* for its 'realism'? The answer is easy to see. The Asian-American population is exploding. . . . The numbers are astonishing. But even more astonishing is the extent to which Asian Americans have become prominent *out of all proportion* to their share of the population" [emphasis added] (24).[48] The symmetry of "America" is thus destabilized as Asians exceed their share, but, notwithstanding the sensationalistic evocation of the dystopian world of *Bladerunner*, this is not a regurgitated image of Yellow Perilism. Bell goes on to assure us, "Most remarkable of all, it is taking place with relatively little trouble" (24).[49] In other words, demographic asymmetry is to be tamed by a psychic commonality.

How do we explain this nonviolent revolution? What does it mean that Ronald Reagan called Asian Americans "our exemplars of hope and inspiration"? What is signaled by the brilliant explosions in the background, announcing the triumph of Asian Americans, as "they seem poised to burst out upon American society" (31)? Bell's article, while acknowledging anti-Asian racism and the persistence of cultural difference, ends by asserting:

> Their triumph has done nothing but enrich the United States. Asian-Americans improve every field they enter, for the simple reason that in a free society, a group succeeds by doing something better than it had been done before: Korean grocery shops provide fresher vegetables; Filipino doctors provide better rural health care; Asian science students raise the quality of science in the universities and go on to provide better medicine, engineering, computer technology, and so on. . . . This Fourth of July, there is cause for hope and celebration. (31)

But if the symmetrical hybrid that blends in and elides its points of racial origin is now replaced by a distinctly racialized face, what has happened to the idea of symmetry? The normalizing function served by symmetry is displaced onto a body that conspicuously *shows* race, but this raced image is then absorbed by another sort of norm.

We find the familiar image of the model minority. As usual, it defers in significance to how such success vindicates American ideology (this Fourth of July). There is thus a double movement — the calculated shock effect of the ori-entalized Statue of Liberty and the recontainment of the "explosion" of Asians in America to specific and discrete areas of activity: vegetable sales, rural medical practice, and the sciences. If the careful excision of race performed by symme-try is disrupted and the racialized face not only re-emerges but in so doing takes over the face of America, then this reappearance of race serves even more dra-matically to both articulate that fear and pacify that unearthed, awful image of otherness by recontaining and appropriating it and making it safe for America.

But perhaps the most telling element in this illustration is not the Asiatic American face alone. Along with the dominance of the Asian gene in the recon-stitution of the American body is the fact that the backdrop is land, not the har-bor waters of New York. The transformation of the face of America, specifically the welcoming image set to face the new immigrant, has been transformed into a landlocked figure, testifying not to the process of immigration and assimilation (via either the Atlantic or Pacific), but the revision of the *interiority* of the state, led by Asian Americans. If the dramatic increase in Asian immigration causes panic, this panic is defused by asserting that things haven't really changed all that much, or at least they have changed in a direction that does not essentially pull America off course. This may indeed be a more potent agent of pacification than the cybernetic and insistently "metaphysical" image of the "new America." Asian America, in its delimited supporting role, displays itself in order to give itself over to the higher imperative of American triumphalism. Yet, just as the ideo-logical traffic of the Asian eyelid is multivalent — submissive and yet potentially subversive — Asians are also placed in a condition of potentially productive *asymmetry* and identification. The breaking down of the "racial frontier" under the weight of postwar policies in the Pacific and a globalizing economy produces a specific refacement of the nation.

The imaging of the fusion of Asian and American, read within the general theme of hybridization in modern American life, can thus be understood as imagined within a particular aesthetic which uses the body as both touchstone and sign. "Culture" is located within the imaging of the beautiful and within the materiality of the body and its historical conditions. But this imagining can be read more theoretically, and more concretely, by tracking the penetration of the Asian body within the space of America — its lived environments, its socioeco-nomic and political discourses. The vacillation between "race-neutral" symme-try and the visibility of race produced by demographic "asymmetry" discloses the contradictory impulses of America. Promoting the notion of symmetry and race-blindness as both ideal and a concession to the diversity produced by contemporary histories of migrancy and globalization, America cannot remain comforted by that rationalization completely. Race re-emerges at particular moments of historical crisis. The Asian face of America manifests that crisis (the shock of misrecognition); the text that frames the image attempts to contain that crisis (the familiar assurance that Asians are "just like" Americans). This oscillation characterizes the still unsettled status of Asia/America.

The next chapter extends this discussion of the body to the realm of literary aesthetics and the narration of Asian/American subjectivity. The notion of following the illusory ideal form of otherness into an assimilated core of national identity, as transacted upon the facial contours and bodies of the Asian/American, finds similar articulation in the imaginative constructions of the Asian body in Asian American literary texts. The plasticity that now informs a notion of modern and postmodern assimilation (not only imaginable, but now surgically and cybernetically and biologically enactable as well) informs as well the narration of Asian America. Culture, here, is thus placed within a politics of socialization and distantiation, the body in its narrative formation imbricated within a discourse of a particularly racialized negotiation of social subjectivity.

4 / Transacting Culture:
Bodies at the Seam of the Social

> *The issue of historicity must be discussed on more than one*
> *level: not only on the level of what is represented (which would*
> *reduce this project to some genealogy of the signified) but also*
> *on the level of who and what is representing. The point is*
> *to view these levels (the rupture between them as well as their*
> *interdependence) together and attempt to interconnect the*
> *semiotic problematic of signification and the extra-textual*
> *dimension of representativity, as involving shifting relations*
> *of writing, reading, social reproduction and political power.*
> —ROBERT WEIMANN, "Text, Author-Function, and Society"

IF, AS WE SAW ABOVE, the racial Other can communicate with the "nonracial" (that is, the "American") only if and when "their" masks become faces and they are thereby redeemed from the realm of mere abstraction, then the sphere of cultural production is a specific site for examining that manifest expressive content. Yet, as Weimann suggests above, the critique of cultural production would include an analysis not only of the "signified" but also of the relationship between that discursive object and the "who" and "what" that produces it. We thus find ourselves engaged in a complex tracking of articulation, interpellation, and objectification, in which culture becomes both medium and value, and the politics of representation become clearer.

In this chapter I examine a number of literary texts that each narrate specific embodiments of Asian America. I use the term "embodiment" here to underscore both the materiality that informs the cultural adjustment deemed to be so central to American ideology and the procedural nature of "becoming" American. This is never a matter of smooth and unilinear movement, but of complex transactions that take bodies as embodiments of certain psychic dispositions that might be read as indicators of acculturation or alienation, and as physical entities engaged in the circuits of labor and consumption, desire and contact, life and death. The Asian/American predication involves both psychic projection and specific materialities: "acculturation" involves bodies as well as minds, each interpellated differently by a "universal" dimension implicit in American hegemonic forms and the particularities of race, ethnicity, and history.[1]

East Goes West: Transacting the Body

Younghill Kang's *East Goes West* (1937) is a remarkable narrative of great complexity, touching upon issues of race, ethnicity, class, nationalism, and gender and sexuality. My reading of the narrative, which stresses the interlinked economization of the body and "culture," is thus partial, but by no means incompatible with those that might foreground other issues.[2] Here I wish to draw attention to the ways in which this narrative of immigration makes explicit the negotiation of an Asian/American subjectivity within cultural and political economies of race. The text at once extenuates and attempts to rehabilitate temporal and spatial distance by establishing "culture" in various formations as a mediating term, yet the author is relentless in grounding the "experience" of culture in the marketplace, a site for the formation, buying, and selling of Asian America.

The novel begins by locating the authorial voice in a universal, transcendent temporality guaranteed by the notion of a common, worldwide literary culture: "The same time that occupied the Roman lovers is the same that Hamlet was insane in, and in the same I write and think of time" (3). Yet simultaneously, Kang weighs down and compromises that ideation: while his first-person protagonist, Han, has acquired an education in Korea that has allowed him to participate imaginatively in a temporality in which east and west are synchronized across historical time, a recognition of spatial difference (as emblematized by national geographies) introduces a gap, a point of rupture and difference, in that chronotope: "My own life in actual books still extant in my Korean village was traced far back in this way to ancestors with the bodies of men and heads of cows. This lifetime, threaded to theirs over the mellow-gold distances of time, can it be the same which now sees New York City?" (4) The narrator's "life" is thus distributed across various ideations—the chronotope of universal culture, that of the cultural history of Korea, and the concrete pavement of the modern western metropolis. While he might wrestle out of the grip of temporal difference by virtue of imaginative projection (the mythological beings of Korea might be imaginatively linked to ancient Roman myth), the somatic concreteness of his body refutes that attempt and draws attention instead to its unsettled presence on modern American soil.

His body bears the trace of a primordial identity attached to the east, an identity out of step with the rhythms of the modern west: "In more ways than one, I looked alien to the Machine Age and New York" (13). His further reflections on his situatedness disclose the limits of his imaginative occupation of transcendent temporality; time and space refuse to be so easily disjoined. The body is contained within material history: "I brought little money, and no prestige, as I entered a practical country with small respect for the dark side of the moon. I got in just in time before the law against Oriental immigration was passed" (5). Whatever poetic value might inhere in the myth of the east is brought back into the sphere of the political and the exigencies of the modern state. Throughout the narrative, the image of the east as cultural relic is placed into the circuits of western capital—the spirit, which the narrator envisions as communing with a universal aesthetic, is put in service of the needs of the body. Indeed, the cultural capital that accrues to the premodern east (as uncontaminated by the vulgarities of the "Machine Age" but also inoperative in modernity) is relentlessly qualified and made conditional by a firm recognition of the political nature of migrancy: "We floated insecurely, in the rootless groping fashion of men hung between two worlds. With Korean culture *at a dying gasp*, being throttled wherever possible by the Japanese, with conditions at home ever tragic and uncertain, life for us was tied by a slenderer thread to the homeland than for the Chinese. Still, it was tied. Koreans thought of themselves as exiles, not immigrants [emphasis added]" (74).

The narrator's description of his friend Kim is presented as a meditation on the possible modes of harmonizing the Asian body with the modern west—how to integrate such seemingly disparate entities? The body is once again set within a discursive logic that is deeply lodged in the encounter of particularly constructed notions of "east" and "west." As in Capra's invention of the hybridized figure of General Yen, Kang produces an Asian at one remove from the "typical" oriental and hence eligible for a particular kind of integration:

> His was not a typical Oriental face, impassive, static. He suggested to me that flowing, seething life reserved in Oriental painting for demoniac faces. . . . The so-called Oriental peace he lacked. His brooding eyes of a greenish black color, unusually wide and glinting beneath their rippling Oriental lids, might be those of a poet, prophet, or madman; but they were held in check by the gentlemanly

reserve of his mouth which was youthfully scrolled and bland. Altogether, a handsome Easterner with nameless elegance. His clothes, which by no means determine Asiatic gentlemanliness, were of an excellent texture and workmanship. This curt, harsh Western dress sat on him too with ease, and to it he seemed long accustomed. An Asian evidently who had been long abroad. About him I sensed the unknown thought and subtleties of knowledge I longed to make my own. (92–93)

The character Kim is endowed with an active nature that is specific to the aesthete and the aesthetic. This energy distances him from the "passive" Asian (a passivity that Kang suggests is linked to the ancient, the past, the premodern state of Korea). His habituation to the west is signaled by the naturalness with which he wears western clothes (and we remember Albert Palmer's attention to this sign of assimilation). In short, Kim's portrait is Han's projection of an ego ideal—a figure that represents precisely that subjectivity that resolves the contradictions he senses in himself and also those between his temporal frame of reference and his spatial location. And this spiritual equilibrium is perceivable in the comportment of the body that houses it. The body is thus the expressive vehicle of this synthesis and reconciliation of antinomies.

Yet the body is also part of a materialist discourse. It is a cultural text that does not simply stand alone as an idealized presence; it is a corporeality imbricated within an economy of representation and power, which is itself situated within the logic of race and class in the United States. For instance, early in the narrative, the narrator is hired as a manservant by a middle-class white woman who tells the narrator and his friend, "My former cook was a very tall Negro. He was able to do the work of two. But I hired you to be presentable" (63).[3] The "presentability" of the "oriental" is thus of higher value than the productivity of the "Negro"; the east domesticated and put into service is a sign of cultural capital that surpasses the actual use value of the "Negro." But however much the "oriental" body might be reduced to a "presentable" sign for this employer, Kang insists on not allowing the body to be simply a symbol. The reader is constantly reminded of the body's somatic needs, desires, and limits.

The trope of sustenance is central to the narrative. The narrator describes his work as a dishwasher in such a way that the linkages between workers and the hierarchies of production and consumption, sustenance and excess, waste and profit are explicit:

We worked by the service door to receive the plates before passing them on to the dishwashing machines. Sometimes the dishes came out from the banquet with whole half-chickens and big pieces of steak or legs of duck intact. By rights these must pass in steady stream into the garbage can. Oh, how that garbage can was buttered! Butter on practically everything, even on fat steak or creamy vegetables. How rich and juicy and luxurious the French cook had made all these to feed the garbage can! Not that the hotel wanted them for the garbage can—but they had been paid for, and the management was proud of its A-grade class and its fine system of sanitation. So the foreman would shout out for stealing the hotel's paid time if any snatched at the left-overs. You should have seen how those extras watched out of the corner of the eye! The rule was against stealing time, not food, and it was still possible to grab a piece of that chicken on the march to the garbage can if it could go down in the mouth all at once.

Back-door banquets impressed me deeply, and I could never cease wondering. All that food passing along through hungry hands to feed the garbage pail . . . it was so wasteful, so fantastic, so American! . . . Food that would never be the same again . . . and just at that moment looking so savory. The hungry applicants for the banquet, turned away . . . would find by that time the chicken legs had been all mixed up with broken dishes and salad refuse. . . . I always felt unusually depressed after a banquet. Not because I had to stay until three or four in the morning. I was glad of that, because I then received extra pay. But there seemed some hitch in American business methods. Why, you could feed more people with the waste food than those that had already been fed!

At the end of the banquet, all the helpers, except the regulars like myself, were again dismissed with pay. They were not even needed to wash up the dishes, for the hotel had the latest, most modern dishwashing machines and these could easily take care of even the enormous number of dishes used in a hotel banquet. It always paid the hotel to invest in the best mechanical devices for decreasing hands. Perhaps in another fifty years the New Hotel can give even choicer banquets—delicacies brought from the North Pole and South Sea Isles—and by that time there will be some machine, some endless caterpillar thing that will make the connection between tables and garbage pails complete without human intermediaries. There will be no more back-door banquets then. (196–97)

The logic of modern capital insists on the production of waste—the creation of luxury is parasitic on the creation of expendability. The garbage can becomes food itself (it is "buttered"), and it is turned into a consumer. The machines too are fed. But the narrative goes further than simply counterposing this inhumane consumption against the hunger of the poor and the working class. The owners do not begrudge the refuse to the workers as much as they are jealous of the loss of time / labor; the rhythm of immediately sustaining the body must be interrupted by the logic of wage labor. Production and consumption are thus particularly delinked; workers are alienated in terms of the most elemental corporeal need and integrity, yet this state of dehumanization is preferable to the inevitable replacement by machines. In anticipation of the time/space compression of late capitalism, we find here an understanding of how the drive for the "modern" necessitates the production of exotica (food imported from the far reaches of the globe finds its way quickly to the tables of the "New Hotel") and the acceleration of processing and service.

Kang presents a variety of workplace situations. From the dishwashing stations to the modern department store; from brutal exploitation to the lure of profit-sharing. There is always a keen perception of the logic of these work environments, but also an insistence on the needs to which such sensitivities must be subordinated:

> Of course, in this system [the modern department store] only the owners made any profits. Still, the pretense was kept up of profit-sharing in the earnings of the store. . . . Still, like tips, even fifty cents or one dollar a week was something to work for, and everybody tallied up eagerly at the end of the day to see how the day had gone for him. It was enough to make him side with the store in doing business, and have the true salesman spirit. (309)

Again, the production of this "spirit" is marked against the disciplining of the body: "It did not take me long to form an opinion that life in a department store was a horrible life for all people. What appalled me was the regimentation. You could never go out to eat when you felt like it, but must be assigned a regular lunch hour. . . . There were lunchrooms for employees in the store indeed, but these were very bad, and served only the leftovers from the regular customers' restaurant" (312). The narrator is led to conclude: "This *is* American life. . . . All day long the moving multitudes of humanity, with busy legs, constantly darting false smiles to cover their depressed facial expression, the worn-out machine bodies turning round in the aisles of unmoving glass and china sets, slowly figuring with shaking hands—haste and moving too many heavy things made them so—now over to the tally they go, recording 50 cents" (318).

This state of commodification and alienation sullies the narrator's attempts to parlay his cultural capital into any "authentic" human exchange. While Kang imagines a cosmopolitan cultural capital that is supposed to guarantee social commonality, it simply cannot be transposed to the *material* demands of modern urban social life. One of his first exchanges provides a concise illustration of this point. The narrator checks into a cheap hotel and is confronted with a porter's outstretched hand: "He waited. He didn't seem interested in my conversation.

I asked him if he liked Shakespeare. He giggled and said coldly, 'Who, suh? Me, suh? No, suh!' I know now he was waiting for a dime" (11). In the next months, the narrator's love of Shakespeare runs up against a different sort of aesthetic awareness—that of his own body: "In my unheated room during the cold night hours, I spent some monstrous intervals in studying Shakespeare. But it was hard to concentrate. Even in the midst of Hamlet's subtlest soliloquies, I could think of nothing but food" (32).

Related to this realization of the effects of the material upon the ideal, the narrator gradually comes to register the differentials of cultural imperialism, which severely compromise his faith in the universal. He is told by his college professor that "English literature was rightly great because it was a mirror for a great people, backed by a great moral sense, expanding over the world in a great empire. English laws, English democratic government had shocked all races into study and imitation" (107). Under the regime of a "western education," the protagonist is demoted from being a participant in universal culture to a supplicant, an object of charity, as his "uncultured" state is assumed: "For me there was always the special favor, special kindliness, special protection . . . the white-man's-burden attitude toward dark colonies. Ralph's kindness . . . Leslie's brutal cruelty . . . I weighed them in my mind, and it seemed to me better to miss the kindness and not to have the cruelty" (126).

Thus the narrator's stance toward culture is tempered by both a recognition of the material conditions under which culture becomes cultural capital (and debt) and a specific sense of culture as raced and as a site of violence. In such a revised sense of culture and the consequences this awareness has upon any definition of self predicated upon "culture," the body becomes both a sign of difference and a token of exchange within a particular economy. The narrator comes to realize this link between the two as he is tutored in the art of self-presentation by his friend Kim:

There is a great future for Oriental scholarship in the West. Have you ever thought of that? Nowadays in the West we see a definite trend. . . . You have to eat. To eat, you must enter into the economic life of Americans. Listen then. First you should get a good Western foundation in education. But . . . don't lose touch with your own classical traditions. By chance you came here from an old-fashioned community. You arrived with an unusual training and inclination for the ancient classics. You complain that you find it hard to learn the American efficiency and to find in that a means of livelihood. Don't set too much store on American efficiency. In making a living, Oriental scholarship may help you more than your American education. (277f)

This advice builds upon a recognition of the exigencies of daily existence, the tempo of modern life, and the manner in which the "oriental" can now profit from his differences—of race, of "ancient culture," and as one who possesses both the ancient ethos of Korea and the skills of American liberal education.

More specifically still, the subject position of the "oriental" coming under the tutelage of the west can be integrated into the all-American formula of working one's way through college. Recruited to sell self-improvement materials (significantly entitled *Universal Education*) by a Dickensian character named Mr. Lively, Han finds himself implicated within an ethnicized market strategy that is reliant upon a particular mode of narration:

> "Your background may be a good thing. Only you must reap advantage out of that. You must select some field where that will help. New England, now. An Oriental salesman for books. H'm!" Mr. Lively paused, and looked at me inquiringly. "A fine clean Christian young Oriental earning his way through college." (143)

The narrator goes on to describe the formalization of their business relationship:

> Mr. Lively drew up a contract for me. I was overwhelmed when I read that. It was not like business at all, but was testimony to my outstanding ability in studies and to my Christian character, adding in a special clause that I did not drink or smoke. And it summed up the whole situation too, how I was working my way through college." (179)

The narrator is correct in stating that the "contract" does not seem to read "like" a business agreement, but he does not realize yet that the contract is, indeed, business, in the sense of its codification of cultural value and its usefulness in the enterprise of salesmanship. The "heathen" Asiatic is made at once palatable and an object of sympathy; the goodwill attested to in mind and body (Christian and chaste) is but raw material for a further refinement—that of "education." And it is that process of refinement, of acculturation, that his prospective clients are called upon to validate and underwrite.

Yet this strategy meets with an unexpected reaction that manifests the superiority of the "oriental" as cultural icon over the hybridized figure-in-transformation. Han finds a couple so anxious to recruit him as an "expert" witness of the orient that they buy his *Universal Education* without any need of it (already ensconced within Brahmin high culture, they seek now to colonize the east): "She showed me her Japanese prints and her lacquerware, and asked me questions about them. She said she had started her collections in the Orient, and what did I think of them?" (187). Han's attempt to sell his wares to the woman is superseded by her interest in displaying to him her purchases from the orient and asking him to validate her as a consumer of oriental culture and vouchsafe the value of her acquisitions. He exclaims, "So now I saw that it was not my good salesmanship at all! My sales talk had in no way convinced Lawyer Norton. He had bought *Universal Education* in the handsomest binding, just out of charity" (188). One might modify his last observation—it is not out of "charity" that his books are purchased, but out of Norton's sense that something must be given back to Han in exchange for his willingness to serve as oriental legitimizer of their positions vis-a-vis the orient—Han as embodiment; the Nortons as beneficent patrons and bona fide connoisseurs. Crucially, the instantiation of this relationship is anchored by the direction of exchange and their relative positions of economic (versus cultural) power. The economic, then, has a way of overdetermining the outcome of such negotiations of culture and "common" interest in the orient. Whatever benefit accrues to Han by dint of his racial and cultural identity is subordinated to the contingencies of making a living. Thus even the most "liberal" and sympathetic buyers place the narrative of "education" and improvement behind that of the narrative of orientalist antiquarianism.

In this novel, stories are always caught up in the production and presentation of "self" geared to an ameliorative effect. Every interpersonal encounter takes place through such narrations. Han attempts to romance a young Anglo-American woman (Trip). He senses that the way to her heart is by portraying himself in the midst of creating an autobiography. Not just any autobiography, but one invented by Han to conform to the cliches and conventions of the west's understanding of Asia. Kang thus invents a critique through this embedded self-reflexive narrative. Trip asks:

> "What about you? What is your book, the best-selling one?"
> "An autobiography!" I said promptly. . . .
> So I began to outline a book about my early life in Korea, spurred on by my need to interest her, fix her attention. . . . I touched the more personal note, she looked so gentle and persuasively smiling. "When I was born, it was a famine year." I paused, dramatically. "I never had a mother. She died. And I missed her so much."

After pausing for dramatic effect, Han is surprised to hear his friend retort: "'*That* was probably a help. They don't seem to get on well with their mothers over here.' And I was a little offended" (336f). The "personal" event Han presents, following the stock formula that he calculates will bring the conventional response of sympathy and engagement, ironically is rebuffed by a retort informed by another stereotype of "oriental life."

"East" therefore meets "west" in eminently narrative encounters, and, most crucially, these narrative acts are depicted as set within a logic of desire and need that is firmly rooted in the body. No matter what "universal" or transcendent chronotopes are imagined by Han, he is brought back to the contingencies of negotiating Asian American modernity in all its racialized, ethnicized, classed, and gendered materiality. Nevertheless, it is crucial not to imagine that such an awareness of these differential categories is, once evidenced in Asian American literature, always present, or always articulated in similar ways. Rather, the exposition of race and ethnicity is constantly located within specific, historicized social formations. Kang writes as an Asian subject in exile — caught in the moment of modernity, which holds a particular promise of a "new life" in America. In the next text, we find a very different narration of self and universality.

Reading Past the Material: Mori's "Japanese Hamlet"

In many ways Toshio Mori's "Japanese Hamlet" (published in 1939, and collected in *The Chauvinist*) is an extremely elusive text. It seems to offer a very clear and simple message in its brief three pages, but a strong and persistent tension informs its key moments — a tension between a faith in the power of Art to transcend race, ethnicity, and history; and a subtextualized problematic that deconstructs such presumptions by showing how strongly those differential forces impinge upon any notion of transcendence and universality. The critic Elaine Kim is justified in calling Mori the "Nisei Universalist"; Mori continually stated his desire to write stories that would describe the "human condition" (E. Kim, *Asian American Literature*, 163).[4] This desire, however, is haunted by a persistent subtext throughout his works, which suggests the gap between desire and achievement that demarcates the particular dimensions of Mori's "universal." And that is why Kim's adjective is so appropriate. The plot of the short story is easy to summarize: we are told by a dramatized narrator that his friend, Tom Fukunaga, has devoted his life to being a Shakespearean actor. He is constantly coming to the narrator's house and rehearsing his lines from *Hamlet*. Eventually the narrator becomes so disturbed by this obsession that he asks Tom to stop coming. End of story. Yet my reading posits in this narrative a set of issues that are conspicuous by their silences.

The narrator introduces Tom Fukunaga as a thirty-one-year-old "schoolboy." Tom lives on five dollars a week, spending his days studying to become a Shakespearean actor. Although he is beginning modestly, Tom sees no outstanding impediment between this effort and his ultimate goal: he firmly believes that someday he will be placed within the cultural history of the Other. The narrator writes: "He played other parts in other plays but always he came back to Hamlet. This was his special role, the role which would establish him in Shakespearean history" (Mori, 40). In this act of taking on the culture of the Other, we find an echo of Fanon's anecdote about "many people in Martinique who at the age of twenty or thirty begin to steep themselves in Montesquieu or Claudel for the sole purpose of being able to quote them" (Fanon, *Black Skin, White Masks*, 193). As in the citations of Shakespeare found in *East Goes West*, such recitation thus serves as a marker of cultural capital, a sign of belonging to and identifying with universal culture.

One relative alone persists in trying to dissuade Tom from his mission, and it is important to note the specific terms in which he attempts to do so:

> He tried a number of times to persuade Tom to quit his stage hopes and school-boy attitude. "Your parents have already disowned you. Come to your senses," he said. "You should go out and earn a man's salary. You are alone now. Pretty soon your relatives will drop you." (39)

Tom is called upon to repress his indulgent fantasy of joining the world of the universal author. He is asked to set aside the infantile imaginings of a schoolboy (I would stress the particularity of that designation), and give himself up as labor in order to be a socialized being—a "man."

But Tom instead insists on entering the aesthetic of the universal from another direction, identified as a representation (indeed, an embodiment) of its universal culture. Ultimately, however, he cannot represent himself there in that way. The text never tells us why. Although neither his best friend the narrator nor the other characters can name racial difference as determining the unavoidable failure of Tom's project of entering the dominant's symbolic space, as represented by the Shakespearean stage, their confused attempts to dissuade Tom betray their recognition of it.

In a world of racial difference, to be Hamlet, Tom cannot be Japanese; to be Japanese, Tom cannot be Hamlet. Yet the myth of universal art denies that there is any contradiction since, in being an artist, Tom can do both. In a similar manner, while Tom is marked racially as Asian, the fact that he is Japanese American likewise would seem to offer him admittance into the dominant culture, since by being American his race is no longer thought to be a prohibiting factor. Yet the text presents us with the frustration of this attempt. Rather than the fulfillment of the universal's, and America's, premises, we see instead a quiet retreat from the quest. This turning back is not done through any overt act on the part of the dominant culture, but is found instead within Tom's reluctance to audition at the theater. Hence we can infer the workings of a particular unconscious that informs Tom of the futility of his efforts.

Tom has two listeners: the narrator and, indirectly, the reader. Thus there is a certain link between the reader and the first-person narrator. The narrator occupies a central role, mediating between Tom and what he calls "Shakespeare's book." The narrator hears Tom's recitations and verifies their accuracy:

> He used to come to the house and ask me to hear him recite. Each time he handed me a volume of *The Complete Works of William Shakespeare*. He never forgot to do that. He wanted me to sit in front of him, open the book, and follow him as he recited his lines. (39)

The fact that the narrator ultimately rejects this "role" is evidence of the fact that he has recognized the futility of Tom's project and wishes no complicity in that self-destructive act. Yet he remains blind to the fact that it is not Tom who is destroying himself, but rather the logic of the universal that refuses Tom that particular mode of representation even while soliciting his emulation of it.

In his role of stand-in for the dominant Other, the narrator can either deny or grant Tom the identity he desires by approving or criticizing Tom's recitations. Significantly, he does neither, but, like all of Tom's acquaintances and relatives, simply chooses not to address the question. The narrator silently tells himself what he would explain to Tom:

> We were miles away from the stage world. Tom Fukunaga had never seen a backstage. He is just as far from a stage door in his thirties as he was in his high school days. Sometimes as I sat holding Shakespeare's book and listening to Tom I must have looked worried and discouraged. (40)

It is telling that the narrator constantly calls Tom's copy of Shakespeare, "Shakespeare's book"; we can see this as a symbolic restoration of the book to its "proper" owner: William Shakespeare. It is a heavy irony that the one relative who is most persistent in trying to disabuse Tom of his fantasy is named "Uncle Bill." (And we remember how uncles figure in *Hamlet*.) Even when the narrator says, "One day I told him the truth: I was afraid we were not getting anywhere, perhaps we were attempting the impossible" (41), he never explicitly tells us why it is impossible. Hence, despite the number of clues that lead us to see how utterly disenfranchised Tom is in the realm of "Shakespeare," Mori's text will not or cannot name "race" as a determining and negating difference.

Finally, the narrator finds it necessary to detach himself from this relationship:

> The longer I came to know Tom the more I wished to see him well off in business or with a job. I got so I could not stand his coming to the house and asking me to sit while he recited. I began to dread his presence in the house as if his figure reminded me of my part in the mock play that his life was, and the prominence that my house and attention played. (41)

The narrator has clearly switched allegiance from Tom's dream to the roles that his relatives would have Tom take on. Tom's Hamlet comes to haunt the narrator's house, forcing him to acknowledge his complicity in what he recognizes as an act of self-destruction. It is because of his fear of being indirectly identified in this "mock play" that the narrator retreats into "common sense" and breaks out of Tom's imaginary sphere, perhaps out of self-protection—for a recognition of racism would implicate him as well. This is turn forces the reader to declare his allegiance: will he or she follow Tom in his dream, or the narrator, in his cynicism?

That Tom "appreciates" Shakespeare is an assumed response (the dominant culture finds reaffirmation—Shakespeare is "universal"); that he recites Shakespeare may even be assumed as a proper reaction; but that he would aspire to be identified through Shakespeare, and present himself as representing Shakespeare, thus moving over from passivity to action, is problematic indeed. And it is a particular kind of action, emphatically staged and exhibited, that calls into question the transposability of the Universal Author across explicit racial orders. The narrator's discomfort at Tom's particular choice of representation indirectly confirms this prohibition: "Sometimes I told him I liked best to hear him recite the sonnets. I thought he was better with the sonnets than in the parts of Macbeth or Hamlet" (40).

Now one could say that reciting the sonnets puts Tom in a much more directly contestive position vis-à-vis the Author—he is now taking on Shakespeare's lyric voice as his own. But we must remember that this would be a quite private enactment of Shakespeare: the lyric "I" is not to be inserted into an intersubjective drama, and would thus be able to entertain more freely its identifications across boundaries of race. It is specifically the public attempt to represent his Self as the dominant Other, emphatically marked simultaneously as the Other in costume and as not-the-Other by his physical features, that shows up most pointedly the contradiction at hand.[5]

Tom is at once not-different, since he is called upon to "appreciate" the universality of Shakespeare, yet he is also different, since he is not allowed to identify himself with it because of racial difference. Thus the contradiction is not between a skewed representation of Self (that is, the "hyphenated dilemma"), but rather the fact that the Other invites the minority subject to identify itself within the dominant on the basis of its ideological interests (that is, the investment in universals and the denial of difference), while at the same time withholding the full rights and privileges that accrue to its cultural citizens.

Tom's cultural heritage is not with his "race." He is not "Japanese" in the sense of being a Japanese national; he is an American, and as such, the dominant ideology would say, he should be privy to all that belongs to that title. But the hyphenated term that seeks to represent him elides the contradictions that now manifest themselves in his choice of vocation. And it is those contradictions that are repressed not only by the workings of the dominant Other as manifested in the unconscious-censoring mechanisms of the hegemonic, but also by the Japanese Americans themselves (the narrator, Tom's parents and relatives), who cannot bring themselves to voice that contradiction in even its tamest form: "You'll never be a great Shakespearean actor because you're a Japanese in America." Hence, the full significance of the title of the short story becomes clear. Tom is "the *Japanese* Hamlet."[6] In contrast to Kang's protagonist, who, forced to enter into the world of labor and exchange, recognizes and at times seeks to exploit the mark of racial difference, Mori's protagonist is an idealist who refuses to give up his belief in the Universal, and yet this refusal locks him into an isolated existence outside the circuits of the social and the economic. Yet, like Kang's novel, Mori's work cannot but be understood through the optics of material history.

William Saroyan begins his introduction to Mori's collection, *Yokohama, California*, by telling us:

> Of the thousands of unpublished writers in America there are probably no more than three who cannot write better English than Toshio Mori. His stories are full

of grammatical errors. His use of English, especially when he is most eager to say something good, is very bad. Any high-school teacher of English would flunk him in grammar and punctuation.

In spite of this, Toshio Mori is probably one of the most important new writers in the country at the moment.

He is a natural-born writer. . . . He can see *through* the material image to the real thing. . . . He is a young Japanese, born in California, and the first real Japanese-American writer. He writes about the Japanese of California. If someone else tried to tell you about them, you would never know them. Even if another young Japanese without Mori's Eye and Heart told about them, they wouldn't be what they are in Mori's little stories. They would be Japanese; in Mori's stories they are Japanese only after you know they are men and women alive. (8)

Saroyan starts by announcing Mori's difference via his status as an outsider to the English language, something that of course has been historically used to bar minority writers from the aesthetic. Yet Saroyan recuperates Mori precisely on the grounds of a universalist aesthetic. Mori is a "natural-born writer," and thus bypasses all difference marked by race and ethnicity. According to Saroyan, Mori realizes this identity precisely in creating narratives that represent human conditions that are *only later* identified as having Japanese protagonists. It is Mori's identification as artist, rather than as Japanese, that authenticates his representation, his attention to a universal aesthetic rather than to racial particulars, which makes possible such truth and value. And such truth and value can only be arrived at by seeing "*through* the material image." Although such a sentiment is clearly rooted in a liberal, antiracist ideology, such dematerializations have the effect of preempting a critique of those very historical discursive formations that delimit and discipline *all* bodies, as they are placed in sociopolitical circulation.

And yet, like Mori's short story, Saroyan's text cannot help but inadvertently let the particulars of material history and race in by the back door. Saroyan ends his introduction with this parenthetical note:

The foregoing lines were written in San Francisco six or seven years ago. Publication of Toshio Mori's first book was postponed, but here it is at last, fresh as ever. I promise the reader a real experience in reading. (October 1948). (10)

Saroyan elides the possible reasons for the postponement of publication, originally to take place in 1941. What was it that kept the book from being published? And why do we have it now? We do not know, but Saroyan tells us that, after all, what is important is that now we have these narratives, "fresh as ever," unmarked by both the war with Japan precipitated by the 1941 bombing of Pearl Harbor, and by the fact that by 1948 the Japanese were beginning to be rehabilitated in the eyes of the United States as Japan was being "democratized" by the Occupation. At the same time, the Chinese Communists were edging toward a decisive victory; the position of the Japanese and the Chinese on the axis of "good Asian / bad Asian" was shifting. Nevertheless, like "Japanese Hamlet," the title for Mori's collection, taken from another short story ("Yokohama, California") shows Mori's sensitivity to the hybrid nature of his world, the particularities of the universal, and the weight of history. If Kang's novel narrates the alienation of Korean exile and diaspora in 1930s America, Mori's work tests the ideology of assimilation and acculturation just before the outbreak of World War Two, and America's entry into a new age of global war in East Asia, a war that would forever change Asian America.

Body as Evidence: "The Shoyu Kid"

> *Mrs. C. T. said last night that when the small children play around the block, often they say, "Let's play killing the Japs." The older people look at each other sadly, but they don't say anything because they think the children are too young to explain to them. They don't realize "Jap" and "Japanese" mean the same thing.*
> —ANONYMOUS JOURNAL ENTRY, Poston, 1943
> (Gesensway and Roseman, 90)

As in Kang and (albeit implicitly) in Mori, the racialized body is seen to anchor the imaginative identifications of the Asian and is read as evidence of its particular relation to power in Lonnie Kaneko's "The Shoyu Kid," written after and commenting on the Second World War (1976).

The problem is not that the children are too young; the answer is not that "Jap" and "Japanese" mean the same thing—they do not. The semantic difference between the two signifiers signals a critical difference in speaking positions and enunciative power, between representations of Japanese Americans engendered by dominant American ideology and the possibility of articulating a self within an "ideologically neutral" nomenclature. The latter, however, is frustrated by a limitation inherent in the structuration and maintenance of the symbolic space of the dominant Other, wherein investments of representation echo in the gap between "Jap" and "Japanese." Most particularly, the symbolic containment of identification becomes literalized in the historical occasion of the Japanese American internment.

"The Shoyu Kid" is an intensely visual text that openly and explicitly problematizes the embodiment of Asian America under the specific conditions of being interned by the state as racially alien. If Mori's text can entertain the possibility of race's invisibility, this is no longer the case here, as the internment reveals the indelible mark of race and its stigmatizing power. The central action of the story involves a number of attempts to stalk an other that are ultimately revealed to be replicas of the manner in which the hunters are themselves embodied *as racial objects* constituted by the dominant Other's gaze.

The text begins with the instantiation of the main act of stalking—three young Japanese American internees hunt down a younger boy (the Shoyu Kid) in an attempt to get him to divulge his source of a precious commodity—chocolate. In the midst of this hunt there is another hunt—the camp community goes after a nondescript animal variously thought to be a rat or perhaps a rabbit. This hunt, embedded in the larger one, prefigures the inscription of both within the englobing logic of the internment, which stripped away "American" from "Asian."

The text's obsession with the specular is linked to charting out these various positionings of self and other, each one mobile and occupying variously the role of subject and object. One of the dominant modes of "viewing" comes through the narrator's representations of his fellows and himself. His language is saturated with symbols gleaned from the popular culture of the Other—nearly every trope and figure rhetorically links the boys to America. The act of naming is a crucial example of this mode of representation. To begin with, the story's title mimics the rhetoric of the Hollywood western—the "Kid" is known only through this appellation foisted on him by the older boys. The name is both playful and mocking, coupling terms from separate discourses into an unstable amalgam that in turn destabilizes its object. The "Kid" is interpellated according to the secretion emerging from his nose—the boys imagine it is the color of shoyu. Thus, both in outward form and in his body's unwitting expression of a deep racial identity, the Kid is labeled as "Japanese," an utterly abject term for obvious reasons. It is that designation that separates Japanese Americans from the national body and places them in the camps. Here, Japanese names are avoided as tokens of weakness; in renaming themselves, the boys either substitute the Japanese name with an American one ("Jackson" for Hiroshi), or distort the Japanese into an Americanism ("Itchy" for Ichiro). Indeed, this aggressive denial of their racial ancestry and their attempt to deracialize themselves suggests a link to Fanon's description, in *Black Skin, White Masks*, of reaction to racial persecution: "In order to react against anti-Semitism, the Jew turns himself into an anti-Semite" (182–83). This strategy of naming is precisely the imaginative redefinition of the body—its "de-orientalization."

The ways in which the narrator represents his group replicate this sort of imaginative transfiguration and distantiation, and evince the empowerment they seem to bestow: "Jackson smiled his John Wayne smile and took the Kid by the overall straps where the lapels should be and shoved the kid up against the side of the garage. 'You'd better shape up and talk, Kid'" (7). These representations, so heavily prescribed by the iconographic bodily gestures of "American" culture, involve a specific mode of seeing: "[Jackson] flattened himself against the wall, and like a soldier in a war movie, peered around the corner" (2); "Itchy was already peering around the corner like an Indian from behind a tree" (3). As the boys take on various roles in their imaginary world, each becomes endowed with a particular power of vision, of seeing without being seen. They become subjects that subject others to their gaze while seeming to remain unobservable. In short, they are voyeurs who witness and define other bodies while thinking themselves dis-embodied, deracialized, and powerful, and this empowerment is not coincidentally linked to their "de-orientalization."

In the course of the story the subjugation of the Kid takes on an increasingly aggressive and sadistic character, best represented in the following accretion of metaphors. As Jackson attacks the Kid, "He was the calvary colonel threatening a turncoat Indian scout; he was a police interrogator breaking a burglar; he was an army intelligence officer ripping into a prisoner of war. His face was impassive. Perfect" (7). This particular chain of representations is overdetermined by the confluence of the power of America, the institutional power of the "subjects." The specific logic of the story involves precisely betrayal, theft, and, of course, prisoners of war. Jackson's stoic, detached mask underscores the power he has over his victim, again demonstrating his power to affect without being affected, predicated upon his imaginatively embodying the form of the dominant Other. Fanon notes that the colonized will always identify with the colonizer according to a logic of representation that one is interpellated within, beginning in childhood. He describes the way that the black child is saturated with images of the victorious nature of all whites. He quotes from Legman: "With very rare exceptions, every American child who was six years old in 1938 had therefore assimilated at the very least 18,000 scenes of ferocious tortures and bloody violence."[7] As Legman notes, the victims of these American films are the indigenous Indians who are depicted as evil and worthy of destruction. Fanon notes that "the young Negro subjectively adopts a white man's attitude. He invests the hero, who is white, with all his own aggression—at that age closely linked to sacrificial dedication, a sacrificial dedication permeated with sadism" (147).

In "The Shoyu Kid," the boys' imaginative aggression against Indians (enabled by the boys' identification with "white") becomes another moment of sadism ironically applied to themselves: the imaginative transformation of their bodies into the image of the dominant Other evaporates; they find themselves victims of their racial bodies. The "torture" of the Kid is a displaced act of masochism, for the Kid takes on the identification of the group as Japanese Americans. This aggression against the Self via such a displacement parallels the boys' hatred of the Indians, who, like them, represent a group of peoples historically disenfranchised from their land and property. Despite the boys' imaginary identifications with authority and their acts of brutality carried out under such projections, the text is punctuated by moments that clearly assert the limits and contradictions of such "out of body" projections and set into relief the boys' status as mere mimics of that power.

Unlike the boys, whose play-acting must ultimately submit to the reality of their impotence, the dominant Other has the power to strike deep into the boys' consciousness even in play; the threat to manifest *its* imaginary in reality, to pose its empowered body against their abject forms, is always present: "that's the same red-headed soldier who used to stand there at the fence and point his gun at me like he was going to shoot me" (4). The overriding fact is that the Other's power to objectify the Japanese Americans subsumes and reveals as sham all their attempts to appropriate that symbolic, to re-embody themselves.

The second "hunt," the stalking of a wild animal, provides the boys with a strange perspective on their own act of stalking the Kid. In it, they occupy the same position that they do in their private "hunt"—subjects after their prey (the animal / the Kid), but they are also slightly *apart from* the other hunters, for they come upon the hunt already in progress. Therefore, the boys are briefly *observers* of another's hunt. This places them in a position wherein they can unconsciously recognize their own actions as seen from the point of view of the other; as such, they witness their own weakness. This subtle insertion of a double perception of themselves (as both subjects and objects) is a necessary prelude to the final scene.

The hunt is initiated by the narrator's cousin's grandfather:

[He] was scurrying between the hollyhocks, leaping awkwardly every now and then as if he were stepping on nails. He was a skinny old man whose feet seemed to be moving in two directions at once while his body was heading a third. His arms, weighted by a heavy, blunt spade, seemed to be confused about moving in a fourth direction. (5)

This comic figure presents itself doubly: it represents the elder generation of Japanese American males, formerly figures of authority and power, now fragmented and ultimately impotent. The narrator's representations of the old man's actions contrast sharply with the ways that the narrator depicts his own group's movements—sly, smooth, strong, all represented figuratively *through the Other*. But in another way the old man's actions stand in for the boys' own fragmentation and powerlessness. Their gestures ultimately seem futile and ineffectual; their machismo (counterposed to the feminized elder generation) consists merely of bullying the Kid, chasing the animal, and "giving the finger" to the old women behind their backs. Now, in observing the old man hunting his prey, the narrator unwittingly sees himself.

Not only is that last gesture emptied of content, it actually rebounds against the boys—their gesture of defiance points rather to the weakness and self-canceling nature of the impulse. The text is full of the boys' false bravado regarding their sexuality, their masculinity and power; they seek to negate both the general stereotype of Asians as effeminate and the particular intensification of that stereotype in the internment. Elaine Kim writes of the effects of internment on the Issei males: "They were painfully cognizant of the fact that they could not protect their families. . . . Until the internment, they had reigned unchallenged as the supreme authorities in family and community life. Now they were as much wards of the U.S. government as their wives and children were, who put food on the table and organized the children's lives" (135). In her analysis of "The Shoyu Kid," Sau-ling Wong notes: "The preadolescent narrator and his gang operate on an unstated syllogism distilled from the experience of political subjugation: being Asian means being weak; being female also means being weak; therefore being Asian is like being female" (*Reading Asian American*, 99). The boys' ultimate failure to claim strength is reflected in their failure to be recognized by others as they would want. They wince at the fact that despite their renaming themselves, the old women insist on calling them by their Japanese names, and the boys have no choice but *to answer* to those names, betraying the power of the others to interpellate them as subjects regardless of their own attempts at self-definition. This negation of their power to name themselves as Other is exacerbated by the fact that the ones who *are* called by American names are those younger and weaker than themselves, notably the Shoyu Kid (George) and the young girl they spy upon bathing (Janice).

The notion of being named by the female takes on another shape, when the boys are horrified that the Kid has turned into a "whore" by taking chocolate in exchange for engaging in homosexual acts with the soldier. To them, that the Kid does not recognize his actions as such is not as significant as the fact that he has tainted them with his acts. Not only has he assented to the feminization of the Japanese American male by the dominant culture, he has furthered both the American's disdain for them and confirmed the stereotype. He is rewarded with the symbol of America (Hershey's chocolate) in exchange for confirming its symbolic ordering of his/their body. The Shoyu Kid has been stigmatized; his action has substituted one stigma for another—chocolate (the mark of his betrayal of his "Japaneseness") for shoyu (the mark of his Japaneseness).[8] Significantly, although he is stigmatized by this chocolate, it is shoyu that is seen to inhabit the Kid's body. The passage of American chocolate into the Kid's body results in the secretion of only tears and shoyu; his very body is thus imagined as a catalytic space that inevitably expresses the indelible and immutable sign of race.

Their final gesture of resisting and transgressing the Other's authority is to steal some signs from the camp to designate their club house. This appropriation of signs is one of the high ironies of the text, an irony Kaneko leaves to the end. To stake out their territory, the boys have placed up the signs: "Off Limits," and "Minitoka Relocation Center." This act is a concise allegory for the entire story—in order to imaginatively project themselves into other bodies and identities, the boys subversively steal the signs of the Other. Yet these very signs resubjugate them: their domain is ironically represented in the Other's domination of them. This inadvertently truthful representation of their imprisonment puts the lie to their attempts to imaginatively become cowboys, wartime heroes, and so on, but it also shows the rationality that informs this attempt.

Their final act of humiliating the Kid likewise turns to inscribe them as victims. They decide to "pants" the Kid, to strip him of his dignity and privacy. They are stunned as they gaze upon his penis:

> There staring at us with its single eye squinting in Jackson's face was a little white prick like a broken pencil between equally white but shapeless thighs. Jackson was immobilized, his face slack in surprise and Itchy moved away. (8)

The object has now objectified the subject—the penis "fixes" the boys in its stare. And here the curious position of the narrator as both involved in and detached from the action is rearticulated—the penis "stares" at "us," while "squinting *at Jackson*." As a signifier it imposes itself upon the boys, the weakness they see in it theirs, too; indeed, the story ends by metaphorizing Jackson into the hunted: "He was sitting very still, and his eyes were soft and wide like a rabbit's" (9). Here, at the end of the story, we find an exact reversal of the theme of looking at others—the image of the Eye has been transformed from having ultimate power to objectify others while escaping objectification (we remember that, in stalking the Kid, Jackson "inched an eye like a periscope around the corner") to being imbued with all the weaknesses of the object—the boys are now looked *at*.

On one hand, here the penis is stripped of all the symbolic mystique with which the boys have imbued it through their talk of erections and sexual mastery. It is no longer a phallus, but is merely literal, the purely physical anatomical detail. But at the same time the momentum of the rhetoric carries the sign in the other direction—it is diminished *below* the literal (penis) to the negation of being and a mark of dysfunction (the broken pencil). The metaphors that Kaneko employs strike out the possibilities of occupying that position of authority and power (seeing, but not being seen) discussed above, *but also* form a comment upon the Japanese American's failure to represent itself authentically—the body is variously construed as a symbolic and somatic site of power and the location of the negation of those very things.

An attention to the young boy's body and its functions (consumption and excretion), and the literalization of the phallus as "symbol" therefore does not negate or offset the *logic* of the demands and limitations placed upon him as a biological subject. However much the boys may imagine their transgressive powers, the fact of their internment forces a reassignment of significance to acts of the imagination and a recognition of the way the body is crosshatched with the signs of power.

Kaneko's desire and ability to articulate the problematic issue of Asian American representation is particularly striking in contrast to Toshio Mori's story, where this problematic is present only in a repressed form and contained within the trope of universality. This can be accounted for in part by the relative positions of Mori and Kaneko in Asian/American history. Mori was writing at the time of the Second World War; the temptation to represent the Self as Other was both more immediate and overdetermined, its problematic nature repressed in favor of the belief that Japanese Americans could find wholeness and unity despite the projected representations of the Other. This belief is underwritten by a configuration of the "universal" that had banished race and ethnicity to a political unconscious.

In contrast, writing much later and in the middle of a specific cultural history that allowed for and even demanded the articulation of the problematic of race, Kaneko is faced with the need to recognize the contradictions it presented in material history. If we return our attention to Kang's early narrative, we find yet another formulation of self, negotiated within the particular contingencies of the early 1930s: neither "unnaming" nor universalizing, Kang's early novel narrates the demystification of the Universal in the context of the aftermath of the Depression, the mechanization and commodification of life, and the loss of Korea. Each text is shaped according to its particular understanding of how the aesthetic must be read historically (the attempts of Kang's and Mori's characters to materialize "culture" as a social fact; the specific attempts of Kaneko's boys at mimicking cultural iconographies). The body is thus not only a symbol but a materiality situated within the contingencies of history.[9]

The body is a multiply inflected sign and a somatic entity demanding sustenance and satisfaction for its particular needs. The fulfillment of those needs and desires is in turn implicated within the discursive formations that award recognition to that body across and within a racialized social logic. Self-imaging may be seen not only in imaginative works of fiction that construct a particular textual subjectivity, but also in the very embodiment of identity itself. The final narrative I treat here complicates the notion of self-formation by commenting directly on gender.

Fifth Chinese Daughter: The Working Body on Display

Jade Snow Wong's *Fifth Chinese Daughter* (1945) is credited by Maxine Hong Kingston for inspiring her to imagine the possibility of writing. It drew immediate critical attention upon its publication; critics commented on the author's eloquent depiction of a young Chinese-American woman's battle against a stultifying traditional Chinese father and her emergence into young American womanhood. Particular attention was placed on the self-effacing humor of the book, the quaint appreciations of modern American life told from the perspective of an outsider who nonetheless was slowly being drawn into that social life.

The narrative provided such a persuasive and seductive account of Asian Americanization that the author was sent on a publicity (that is, propaganda) mission by the State Department:

> In 1953, the State Department sent me on a four-month's grant to speak to a variety of audiences, from celebrated artists in Kyoto to restless Indians in Delhi,

from students in ceramic classes in Manila to hard-working Chinese immigrants in Rangoon. I was sent because those Asian audiences who had read translations of *Fifth Chinese Daughter* did not believe a female born to poor Chinese immigrants could gain a toehold among prejudiced Americans. (viii)

We note the particular trajectory of her itinerary: from a Japan recently under a program of "Americanization" and occupation, to recently decolonized India, Burma, and the Philippines. In contradistinction to these Asian countries in the throes of (re)nationalization, America, as realized in the particular narrative persona of Jade Snow Wong, stands forth as the universal endpoint of their respective political and social projects (if only they would adopt the hegemonic ideologies of Americanization).

Wong's process of Americanization on the personal level adeptly traces the formation of social subjectivity by emphasizing gender as a critical site of cultural difference and specifically tracing the emergence of American individualism in the economic realm. The transition from Asian to American is most lucidly defined by contrasting Asian repression of women to American egalitarianism. Nevertheless, whatever sharp contrast is afforded by such a reduction of difference is blurred and complicated by the narrator's observance of unequal job opportunities and wages between men and women in the United States.[10] The true "genius" of the narrative is to create a protagonist who transcends both these systems of inequality by finding economic self-sufficiency. That is the highest mark of success, and, the narrative implies, the vindication of a particular process. We need to begin by being much more specific about this process—its genesis at a particular moment of Chinese history.

Most critical appreciations have done little with the fact that the father, for all his "traditional" precepts, is actually himself an important transitional figure: Christianized, he believes that women should be freed from certain oppressive rules. The most important for Jade Snow is the right of women to an education. Yet it is clear that her father is quite selective about these "liberated" beliefs. He insists upon the primacy of his authority, and qualifies the reason that Chinese women should be educated: "since sons and their education are of primary importance, we must have intelligent mothers. If nobody educates his daughters, how can we have intelligent mothers for our sons? If we do not have good family training, how can China be a strong nation?" (5). Women's education thus is to serve not their own development but that of Chinese males and the nation.

But along with this diasporic project comes another rationale for "liberating" women, one intimately attached to reorganizing the domestic: "While most Chinese women in San Francisco still had to conform to the Old-World custom of staying at home, her father believed that according to New-World Christian ideals women had a right to work to improve the economic status of their family. Because they couldn't come to the factory, Mr. Wong took their work to them, installed and maintained their sewing machines, taught them how to sew, and collected the finished overalls" (5). We have here two contradictory rationales for educating Chinese women—the first promotes the idea only to retract its liberal thrust and reinvest in only slightly modified Chinese patriarchal values. The second reinvents domestic space as the space of labor: women are "free" to donate their wages to "their family" by adding outside work to domestic work. Jade Snow's ascension into Chinese-Americanness is predicated upon a negotiation outside both these modes: it is for her to invest her education otherwise; her genius is to find a mode of socioeconomic subjectivity that reconciles her father's contradictory impulses and the imperatives of modern America. It is for her to invent female Asian America. But during this process, the "spirit" of independence has to face the contingencies of the body.

Throughout the novel, Wong is attentive to details of material life. She notes the effect of the payments her father must make on the sewing machinery in his factory: "These expensive machines were as necessary to complete one pair of pants as a thousand pairs, and for many years Daddy was burdened with the payments on them; somehow these had to be squeezed out of his earnings before he could feed and clothe his family" (53). Wong narrates the daily burdens of labor upon her father and mother, struggling to make ends meet. Against this drudgery is posited the world of American culture and entertainment.

Wong visits the public library: "Temporarily she forgot who she was, or the constant requirements of Chinese life, while she delighted in the adventures of the Oz books, the Little Colonel, Yankee Girl, and Western cowboys, for in these books there was absolutely nothing resembling her own life" (69). Equating the harsh realities of material existence to Chinese life leads her to equate the realm of the imaginary to American life, and to posit a strict separation between the two. Again, she tells of her mother taking the children to the movies: "She took her children to 'foreign' movies. At the neighborhood theater a few blocks from their home, the attractions of Western life or jungle thrillers was supplemented by the serial, which was one of Mama's greatest passions. For a few hours, she and her children forgot who they were, how hard they worked, or how pressing were their personal problems, as they shared the excitement of six-shooters, posses, runaway stagecoaches, striking cobras, the unconquerable Tarzan, and organized apes" (71).

The separation between "Chinese" life and "American" life thus reified cannot be retained if the narrative is to produce a successful subjectivity by its end—

what is required is a mode of transgression and transition, something to bridge these two realms of the material and the imagination and create a fully recognized ideology of Asian/American selfhood. This bridge is the American education of Jade Snow. In particular, she is presented with both the demand that she become "an individual," that classic mythology of American life, and, crucially, that she find a means of *expressing* that individualization: "The highlight of her second year was an English course which used literature as a basis for stimulating individual expression through theme writing" (132). Such "stimulation" forces Wong into a particular program of self-formation portrayed as distinctly at odds with that self (or lack thereof) demanded by Chinese tradition. Again and again, she tells of the pressure to distinguish herself: "Instead of giving his students ready answers to their numerous questions, he would encourage them to work out problems for themselves. . . . This method made learning slow and painful, for it meant that students made mistakes, but in the end they learned better and more, and they developed individual integrity" (176).

This leads Wong to apply to Mills College, in Oakland, California. Her college education provides an especially crucial site for the negotiation of Chinese-American subjectivity. And again, this negotiation is founded on particular economic contingencies. As with Kang's "sentimental education," here the "cultural" is imbricated into the economy. The route from "Asia" to "America" requires a particular set of negotiations and exchanges. Wong is told that her financial situation need not preclude her attending college: "Dr. Reinhardt will help you if you are interested in going to Mills because she has had a lifelong interest in the Oriental people" (147). This "interest" is shared by her classmates: "Jade Snow Wong found that the girls were perpetually curious about her Chinese background and Chinese ideologies, and for the first time she began to formulate in her mind the constructive and delightful aspects of the Chinese culture to present to non-Chinese" (161). This situation provides a particular motivation for Jade Snow to in turn make the transition from seeing "China" as merely the grind of obedience and labor to a "delightful" culture with which and through which she is identified and given value. In other words, she is transformed, in this process of recoding the orient, in the *bildung* of her young assimilating subjectivity. And it is a particularly materialized value, as she is allowed to supplement her financial aid with work in the dormitory.

Wong's figure is thus positioned liminally—between the vestiges of Chinese as laborer, Chinese as cultural curiosity (as bearer of the "delights" of the orient), and as emergent Asian American, as seen in this description of her campus housing: "This building housed over a hundred girls, and its kitchen staff was entirely Chinese, some of them descendants of the first Chinese kitchen help who worked for the founders of the college" (157). She, too, becomes part of this lineage of labor, but only transitionally, from the privileged position of part-time helper clearly on the way beyond such work. The question remains, however, how to constitute a subjectivity that will be able to reconcile the various demands of Chinese American life. How could she "work" while still retaining the integrity of individualism? The title of chapter 20 is particularly revealing: "She Finds Her Hands."

The Asian body is drawn out of the realm of labor into the world of artisanship: "This wonder and marvel of pottery never ceased for Jade Snow. The instructor now gave them simple lectures on the nature of clay, what they should and should not do with it, on glazes and firings, and then left them alone with their hands and the materials. . . . The clay forms became a satisfying reflection of personal will and skill" (177). Pottery making stands as a potent metaphor for self-fashioning, as it creates that necessary mode of expression of self which is the unmediated representation of the individual mind and body. Her teacher says to her, "You work and work with your materials, and you will find that with experience your eyes and hands will help you make better pottery than any theoretical analysis of form" (177).

But, along with this celebration of the individual will, pottery making produces a commodity. And in this endeavor, Jade Snow finds a link with the patriarchal tradition. Her father tells her, "My father, your grandfather, was artistically inclined and very interested in handwork. He always said that a person who knew a craft trade would be a better person, for he would have the assurance of never starving. When I was only a young boy he made me apprentice in a slipper shop for three years to learn how to sew on slipper soles by hand, to be sure that I knew at least one handicraft well. I received no wages but paid fourteen dollars a year for instructions. Your grandfather thought that slippers would be an item always in public demand. He would have been happy to see your work" (180). We witness a specifically constructed Asian American female subject, one able to enjoy the privileges accorded the "modern Asian American woman": freed from the absolute strictures of "traditional China," trained into individuality by the west, and receiving the sanction of her parents to work as a craftsperson.

This particularity has the effect of separating her from her neighborhood community in San Francisco's Chinatown. She has made the trip to college across the Bay, and has partaken of a specific educational program. This has indeed altered her perceptions of herself, and of those with whom she formerly identified:

> The first year out of college found Jade Snow searching for her own niche in
> Chinatown again. She called on her former American-Chinese girl friends. For
> several reasons, they opened their doors but not their hearts to her. . . . Jade
> Snow made a few attempts to adjust herself to their pattern of activities, but af-
> ter two years away from them and from Chinatown, she now felt more like a
> spectator than a participant in her own community. (199)

To overcome this alienation, she embarks on a program of "Rediscovering
Chinatown" (the title of the twenty-fourth chapter). This double movement of
alienation and recovery is necessary if Wong is to narrate the transformative
story she desires—something must be lost, and its recovery marks the ascension of a new form: Asian/American. It is crucial to note that this "rediscovery"
is undertaken with a particular will; just as the clay is shaped by her hands, so
her "re-experience" of her home is molded by a particular need.

The distance between her and Chinatown shows up again in her decision to
change vocational goals. We remember that her father had hoped that her education could be put to use in building a modern China. Later, she decides to enter community service work. Now, however, she abandons that goal: "For some
time she had been thinking seriously of abandoning her plan for a social service
career, for she doubted if within the existing organizations she could really reach
the people whom she wanted to help in Chinatown" (234). Instead, she decides
to write: "Behind her purpose had been a deep desire to contribute in bringing
better understanding of the Chinese people, so that in the Western world they
would be recognized for their achievements" (235). At this point we ascertain
the convergence of two narrative strands: the imperative of highly individualized self-expression meets the need for a cultural representative. Yet this apparent ideal fusion is frustrated by her ignorance of whether or not this work could
offer her a livelihood: "She didn't have the remotest idea whether one could
make a living at writing. She didn't know whether an article was worth ten or a
hundred dollars" (235). Yet she remembers that she has, after all, learned a craft:
"She would make pottery and sell it! . . . Jade Snow was deliriously happy. What
a wonderful way to live! Write when she wanted to, and make pottery when she
wanted to. She could call her soul her own, strike her own tempo as she carved
her own niche" (236).

This independence is thus to be predicated upon a particular synthesis of
pure, nonintellectualized artistic will, the expression of her "hands," and the
learned and highly mediated effort to represent China to the west. These two
elements form the core of Wong's final self-presentations, which draw together

neatly the ethnic, racial, cultural, and economic in a particular transaction. Seeking space to make her pottery, she finds a sympathetic store owner in Chinatown; but the only space available is in his display window. Yet this seeming hardship turns out to be entirely fortuitous:

> Even while the brick flooring was being laid, curious passers-by stopped. Jade Snow discovered that one had only to get into a window to attract spectators. . . .
> Soon the curious spectators began to murmur aloud, conjecturing as to the nature of the equipment in the elevated display.
> "She must be planning to make bricks for the housing project in Chinatown."
> "No, look at those white pies; she must be setting up a model kitchen."
> "You are both wrong; this is a rice-threshing machine. See the stick across it? I have seen them in China!"
> "Oh, look, and it is a China girl, too. Look, she has no permanent wave. Her braids are the way they wear them in Shanghai. Here is a Shanghai girl!" (243f)

Jade Snow's pottery-making thus becomes a unique public spectacle—a spectacle all the more because of its unprecedented and uninterpretable nature. The public display of commodities is not unusual: what draws attention is the gender of the individual and the location of that display, and the spectacle of work:

> The morning paper carried the picture and a two-column story of the new enterprise. Jade Snow had become a wonder in the eyes of the Western world. They declared that she had invented a new mousetrap.
> Chinatown was agog. A woman in the window, her legs astride a potter's wheel, her hair in braids, her hands perpetually messy with sticky California clay, her finished products such things as coolies used in China, the daughter of a conservative family, running a business alone—such a combination was sure to fail! (244)

Nevertheless, the point of view represented here is clearly that of the imagined Chinatown community, a community, we remember, from which Jade Snow has already become distanced. Their beliefs are still rooted in an old-world mentality; what she has to display is the entrepreneurial spirit of modern America, something not lost on the white world: "Caucasians came from far and near to see her work, and Jade Snow sold all the pottery she could make. . . . But the Chinese did not come to buy one piece from her" (245).

This gendered, racialized body at work occupies this liminal space, between communities, transacting and enacting the eclipse of the Chinese and the invention of Chinese America, and because of this transactional function it draws the gaze of both worlds. But this alone would not suffice to solidify this subjectivity as anything more than a spectral image of a curiosity. What anchors this subject is its validation in the political economy: "Then those [Chinatown inhabitants] who had laughed hardest stopped. After two months, the mud-stirring maiden was still in business! After three months, she was driving the first postwar automobile in Chinatown" (245). The transition from being named by an antiquated and alien epithet to being marked as the avatar of modern Asian America again underscores the subject's distance from the old world of China. That old world can only marvel at her and her sense of self-fulfillment—and most important, at the material evidence of that success. She is recognized (that is, defined) as importing the first postwar automobile into Chinatown.

If the community is still unable to fully recognize the value and significance of Jade Snow's endeavor, her family and friends certainly do. And these are the sources of approval most important to Jade Snow:

> It was Mama who epitomized the family's change of heart. Where there was formerly only tolerance toward their peculiar fifth daughter whom no one could understand, the tolerance was now tingled by an attitude of respect. . . .
>
> Daddy, typically, touched her heart in another way. First, he was critical of her daring in assuming a position in the window above her spectators' heads. But when he saw that she was getting the prices and the market she wished, he ventured a suggestion. "Perhaps you should drape printed percale around your wheel, so that people will not see how crude a piece of equipment you use to make fine things." (245f)

Her father, still wishing to guide her success whatever its various forms, not only does not hold to Chinese codes of modesty for women, he suggests shrewd ways to maintain and increase the mystification of the enterprise. This embellishment underscores the fact that Jade Snow's success is indeed predicated on her being put on display.[11]

It is at this point that her father's two contradictory rationales for educating women are resolved: the project to educate women simply to be better educators of their sons gives way to the logic of independence, but independence secured by economic self-fashioning. He tells Jade Snow that once he wrote a cousin who urged him to return to China: "'You do not realize the shameful and degraded position into which the Chinese culture has pushed its women. Here in America, the Christian concept allows women their freedom and individuality. I wish my daughters to have this Christian opportunity. I am hoping that some day I may be able to claim that by my stand I have washed away the former disgraces suffered by the women of our family'" (246). Familial approval is centered on Jade Snow obtaining her father's blessing, and his blessing is one that not only bestows upon her the approval of her Chinese male ancestors, but does so within the logic of American entrepreneurship: "I told you once that your grandfather would have been glad to see that you had learned a handicraft. I can add now that he would have been happier to see that you have established your own business alone, even though you must begin modestly for lack of capital" (246). The figure of success we are left with at the end of the novel conjoins with the classic image of American individualism, but its distinguishing character is its gendered, racialized specificity, a specificity rooted in a historical moment that reconstitutes a particular location for the body:

> [Jade Snow] knew that she still had before her a hard upward climb, but for the first time in her life, she felt contentment. She could stop searching for that niche that would be hers alone. She had found her self and struck her speed. And when she came home now, it was to see Mama and Daddy look up from their work, and smile at her, and say, "It is good to have you home again!" (246)

As much as this is a novel of self-fashioning, we should pause over this last phrase—for the strong implication is that in Jade Snow's ascension into American individualism, the "home" has been refigured as well—each individual has settled into a particular niche in a newly drawn Asian America.

In this section we have addressed the politics of particular enactments of "Asian America." The particular linkage between the materiality of the body as labor, commodity, and reproductive or sexual force is to be made precisely upon the unsettled terrain of the Asian/American predication. Modern migrancy has forced a reassessment and rearticulation of race and ethnicity, in both directions of the increasingly unwieldy dominant/minority, self/other binaries. Their mutual interpenetration has resulted in a retrenchment of conservative discourses as well as an explosion of recombinatory movements. While here I have focused on the way Asians have been drawn to track their approximations to "America," and how that approximation has been variously facilitated, obstructed, and reshaped according to "spiritual" adjustments as well as to particular negotiations of material history, in the following section I will address what appears to be the obverse—the particular *modeling* function Asians have been called upon to fulfil for the *American* psyche. The various modes in which America has situated Asians "positively" as models are deeply attached to America's various articulations of nationhood against the backdrop of "Asia." We will find a dialectical movement characterizes an ongoing and unsettled production of Asian America.

Part III / Modeling the Nation

5 / Citizens and Subnations

THE RATIO OF ASIAN/AMERICAN OTHERNESS is distributed through and across the images of the body and psyche. The adjudication of this identification and disidentification engages a particular vision of the U.S. nation and the discourse of race. In this section I argue that the introjection of Asians into America has always taken place within a complex *multi*-racial dynamic—the Asian presence has historically prompted a reassessment of not only the general ideological specificity of white America, but also of the presence of other racial minorities within American ideology. Different Asian groups were compared to the contemporary abstraction of an American citizenry and to the particular images that had coalesced around other racial minorities as they were situated within that abstraction. This "local" analysis is complemented by a global one: Asian/American subjectivity also has been produced by referencing Asia and comparing Asia to America and other nations. Were this always a simple matter of constant degradation and marginalization, the nature of Asian America would be relatively straightforward. Yet it is the specific nature of Asians in America *and* in Asia to be held up as models at various points in history, not only for other racial minorities to emulate, but for whites as well. Here I give particular attention to how these phenomena were connected to America's sense of its ethnic and racial affairs at home and to a reassessment of U.S. national identity regarding Asia, and how this continues to be so.

In the previous chapters we saw how the pejorative aspect of hybridity became complicated by the appearance of a notion of marginality that rehabilitated bi-*culturalism* in the form of a new cosmopolitanism closely associated with modernity. Yet we found resistance to such a reformulation when it came to speak of mixed-*race* relations. The particular modification of that image in the economies of sexuality, labor, and culture discloses the friction between the mental and the material, between an imagining of particular Asian/American predications and their blockage and rerouting in material history. This chapter examines how this hybrid deeply informs the notion of a "model minority," a concept that combines "tradition" and "modernity"—for example, Asian "Confucianism" fused with modern American capitalist democracy. The signifier "Asian American" has been produced under particular historical pressures, rescripting "Asia" in relation to its American projection and introjection, and in relation to other racial groups. This process has involved both identifying and disidentifying "Americans" with a particularly constructed image of Asians. Here I comment on two periods, the 1930s and the early 1960s, and address the issue of how the image of the Asian in America performs certain ideological functions that serve to secure certain racial and national identities for both Asians and whites. In Chapter 6 I extend this analysis to the positioning of other minorities in the United States, and show how that interethnic schematization is correlated with an international one. In each case I will be particularly interested in the correlation of the raced body and the national psyche.

Comparison and Capital

Starting in the 1920s, we find modern science recruited to aid in the measurement, comparison, and evaluation of racial groups, specifically for their compatibility within the teleology of America in the modern age. Rather than produce new information, however, this endeavor tended to rehearse common notions of racial difference and value and modulate them according to the historically specific discourse of "America." One of the primary tools used was the intelligence test, specifically the Binet Scale for the Measurement of Intelligence. Such tests were created to address the issue of feeblemindedness mentioned in Chapter 1, as a way to guard against the weakening of the American mind. This notion of the "mental," however, is both extended to encompass the racialized body *and* particularized to address the subject's ability to function psychically in the modern world. Thus, "assimilation" takes on a specifically psychic inflection, as it requires a particular address to the capability of the individual to understand and perform new technological skills and negotiate modern cultural formations. For instance, those to be placed at the "top" as managers and ruling elites were those endowed with the particular intelligence required to negotiate and control the social and economic machine; those in the middle were relegated to manufacturing jobs; those at the bottom were either given gross manual labor or deemed beyond usefulness. The deployment of intelligence tests provides a particular insight into the way America attempted to understand not only the present relations of races within the imperatives of modernity, but also their future adaptability. The use of intelligence tests to predict future performance legitimized specific social practices that were aimed at reforming minorities according to their potential as socioeconomic beings. Here I mention briefly four different views on the relative position of Asians within such discourses.

In 1931, Thomas R. Garth calibrated the relative positions of minorities on America: "The racial I.Q.'s are, by way of résumé: whites, 100; Chinese, 99; Japanese, 99; Mexicans, 78; southern Negroes, 75; northern Negroes, 85; American Indians, full blood, 70. If one says that what is fair for one is fair for another, then regardless of environmental difficulties, the Chinese and Japanese score so nearly like the white that the difference is negligible. Certainly they possess a quality which places them in a class beyond the Negro, the Mexican in the United States, and the American Indian, whatever that is. Perhaps it is temperament which makes the latter groups unable to cope with the white man's test."[1] Second, anatomy professor Robert Bennett Bean ascertained the relative mental capacities of races based on an overtly aesthetic analysis of brains:

> In general, the brain of the White Race is large, the convolutions are rich, with deep fissures. The mental characteristics are activity, nervous and physical vivacity, strong ambitions and passions, and highly developed idealism. . . . The brain of the Yellow-Brown race is about medium human in size, with medium to good convolutions, which are sometimes varied and deep. The mental characteristics of the Yellow-Browns need further study, but they seem to be less vivacious, with emotions and passions less evident when strong than in the other two races. They possess moderate idealism. . . . They are less subject to cares and worries and are less varied and intense in religious feeling than is the White Race and have few psychoses and brain affections. They are industrious, endure fatigue, and are less likely to succumb to many of the infectious diseases than is either the White or the Black Race.[2]

In these two examples of the "scientific" differentiation of races, it is important to note the adumbration of two paradigms that will persist and develop. First, foreshadowing the full articulation of Asians as the "model minority," we have the assertion that, for all intents and purposes, Asians were mentally as capable as whites (or in some instances, even more capable).[3] Nevertheless, this is an ambivalent compliment, for it is clear that "intelligence" could be deployed variously, and that other characteristics could be summoned forth to justify

reinscribing a border between white and Asian, for example, as we will see below, the notion of "creativity." Still, the first passage is noteworthy for its early
pronouncement on the intellectual proximity of Asians to whites, especially as
it gestures toward a future wherein such tests of intelligence might even be
superfluous in terms of differentiating Asians from whites. On the other hand,
the second passage collapses "yellow" and "brown" into a single race and imbues
it with a number of characteristics and capabilities which align it (again) with the
technological demands of the late 1930s: a relative lack of emotions and passions, which signal an anaesthetic psychology. "Moderately" idealistic, this race
could be imagined to be docile and manageable (less likely to unionize, for example), and less susceptible to "psychoses and brain affections" that plague other
modern men. Add to these mental and spiritual characteristics so perfectly
matched to the demands of modern Fordist production—their industriousness
and near-immunity to "infectious diseases"—and one has an image of the minds
and bodies of the laboring class needed to rebuild the United States after the Depression. And yet the author of this passage admits that his analysis is unstable
and incomplete—he remarks that the "yellow-brown race" is still in need of
"further study." This incompleteness, the inconclusiveness of his analysis, discloses the as yet unfixed nature of this modern racial discourse and the flexibility of the categorical schematization of Asians.

And yet some refused this "yellow-brown" category, and disaggregated yellow and brown. The *Saturday Evening Post* (March 15, 1930) editorialized:

> [Mexican peons] fail to assimilate and they delay by that much the harmony which
> is necessary to continued national success. . . . Nor do all the Mexican peon la-
> borers return to their own country when the various crops have been harvested.
> They seem to be pushing farther north and crowding into the city slums. Because
> of the difference in economic conditions in Mexico and the United States and the
> lack of immigration restrictions, there is a tremendous suction of labor from the
> former country to the latter. . . . We may be obliged to absorb great numbers of
> Porto Ricans [sic], Hawaiians, and Filipinos; indeed, the Philippine problem has
> already reared its head in California. With the Mexicans already here, with the as
> yet unassimilated immigrants from certain European countries, and finally the
> vast and growing negro [sic] population, we already have an almost superhuman
> task to bring about requisite national unity.

These phenomena lead the editorialist to this conclusion: "We are under no obligation to continue to make this country an asylum for the Mexican peon, and
we should not do so."

In this passage, the positioning of racial and ethnic minorities evinces the specific national histories that compel such distinctions and analyses of race. Here we find a rationale for differentiating brown from yellow, and excluding the former. Immigration laws reflect particular calibrations for the composition of the nation-state. While the Asian presence here is one of inconvenient "obligation" (since Puerto Rico, Hawaii, and the Philippines are as yet still variously annexed to America and able to send their people to the United States); and newer East European immigrants have already penetrated American domestic space; and blacks are presented as an unfortunately permanent residue of American development; Mexicans could and should be excluded. The passage thus succeeds in producing a legitimate object of exclusion. Thus we may read the "yellow-brown" equation as a particular and anomalous one, prompted by specific needs for rationalizing the belaboring of yellow *and* brown bodies. And yet we find in the first passage the claim that, of all minorities, Asians are most capable of approximating whiteness. In these three citations from the 1930s, we find an outline of the various elements of the complex and mutable ideologies of Asian American racial categorization, each disclosing both residual racist sentiments and emerging discourses of modern accommodation.

In my final example, I turn to a contemporary study that is remarkable for its anachronistic nature—more than half a century after the "scientific" calibration of race in modern America emerges, is critiqued, and is significantly discredited, we find a statement that deploys exactly the same strategies and yet offers its data and conclusions as new knowledge. Were it merely ignored and uncommented upon, this study would have little significance outside its anachronism; yet it has been cited and used by contemporary scholars as evidence for the categorization of race and for guiding policy. Earlier on, in the writings of Herbert Spencer, the fear of the physical overwhelming of "the race" was neutralized by a faith in the ultimate power of "the superior mind": "dominant races overrun the inferior races mainly in virtue of the greater quantity of energy in which this greater mental mass shows itself."[4] In Chapter 1, we noted the fear of the "Asiatic masses." Here was a rejoinder to that fear—the minds of Europeans would prevail by matching physical mass with *mental* mass. In the mid-1990s, psychologist J. Phillipe Rushton put forward a theory that is based on a particular, comparative schematization of size—this time of brains and genitalia—and counterposed these schemata to the capacities of intelligence, industriousness, and sociability.[5] He measures those elements (as well as "activity," "anxiety," "aggressiveness," "rule-following," and "strength of sex drive") to map out the relative characters of "orientals," "whites," and "blacks."[6] Rushton then correlates these data with the "ranking" he asks orientals and whites to make (obviously no blacks can provide useful views on the subject). He asks them to assess themselves, their "opposite number," and blacks.

According to Rushton, each of these groups arrived at exactly the same conclusion: a direct correlation between intelligence, brain size, and, inversely, size of genitalia (with the exception of size of brain—each felt they had larger brains, but both agreed blacks had the smallest). The smaller the genitalia, the more intelligent the person; the larger the genitalia, the less intelligent. Most interestingly (perhaps), both whites and orientals ranked orientals first in intelligence and smallest in genitalia. Whites ranked in the middle, blacks were last in intelligence (but first in size of genitalia). Rushton sums up: "the racial gradient of Oriental-white-black occurs on multifariously complex dimensions. From brain size, intelligence, and personality to law abidingness, social organization, and reproductive morphology, Africans and Asians average at opposite ends of the continuum, with Caucasian populations falling intermediately" (262).

The passivity of the model minority is explained by the fact that people with larger brains turn out to be more polite. Rushton finds that "larger brains . . . led to delayed sexual maturation and the creation of a complex interdependent social grouping with high degrees of altruism" (209). Thus, looking back at human evolution, he concludes that "with increasing complexity of social organization would have come the social rules necessary to keep the individual's personal drives and emotions concerning jealousy, fear, sex, and aggression under control" (211). Nevertheless, before one becomes too alarmed by law-abiding, sexually restrained, mentally superior orientals taking over (and one has only to read all that negatively to find Rushton's characterization of blacks), we must remember that Rushton inserts a particularization: Asians have superior "visuospatial" abilities, but their *verbal* skills are weak. Therefore, "the relatively strong visuospatial and weak verbal abilities of Oriental Americans may result in a tendency to do well in professions like science, architecture, and engineering, which call for strong visuospatial abilities, and less well in law, which calls for strong verbal abilities" (144). Thus, Orientals are not interested in politics and even if they were they couldn't be active agents. The ascension (such as it is) of Asians *über alles* is now complete, using precisely the formula that places mind over matter. Nevertheless, the Yellow Peril is contained by the slow reproductive rates of Orientals (their small genitalia a sign of their disinterest in sex) and their political impotence. Rushton's formula seeks to account for Asian success, but deploys the same analytic tools to contain that success. This strategy is endemic in all articulations of the Asian American as the model minority.

Before we leave the "science" of comparative studies of race, we should note one other element found in the social discourse on Asians in the late 1930s which will continue on into the elaboration of modern Asian America: a liberal, antiracist view that asserted that Asians were eminently suited for Americanization *if* America could curb its racist tendencies. Romanzo Adams, in his introduction to William Carlson Smith's *Americans in Process* (1937), declares with regard to Asian Americans:

No matter what one's views may be relative to the wisdom or unwisdom of our former immigration policy, these young people of American birth and Oriental ancestry are part of us. Most of them will remain and also their children and their children's children. They are ambitious, alert, intelligent. They are securing an American education. If America means opportunity they are preparing to make full use of that opportunity. No mean success will satisfy them. Their faces are definitely set toward the winning of a superior economic status. Many of them are ambitious for recognition in the fields of art, science, and scholarship. They would enter fully into the spiritual heritage of America and enrich it from Oriental sources.[7]

As we saw in Chapter 1, upon completing the exclusion of all Asian immigration, in the 1930s the United States now had to decide how to regard Asians already in America. In this early articulation of a significantly positive view of Asian integration into American life, the only impediment to full Americanization is American racism: "the response of these young people is not rigidly controlled by some inborn racial traits, . . . their behavior and attitudes are largely influenced by local social environmental factors. They will become what America makes them."[8] In this last instance, we find a challenge to the nation: presented with a group of diligent, highly motivated individuals, it is up to America to live up to its ideals. Asian Americans offer the amalgam of east and west, but this fusion will not take if American racism intervenes in the process of Americanization. America, then, is represented as a special crucible, in which the old and the new mix, and the best of both emerge as their negative elements are canceled out.

This general image of the melting pot carries specific imagery with regard to each group that enters it; in the case of Asian Americans, it is an idealized and mystified notion of Confucianism, which is to be coupled with American individualism and laissez-faire capitalism. These modalities formulated in the 1930s have persisted to characterize the positioning of Asians in America to the present day. Although along with this historical movement one finds specifically

altered rearticulations and complications of these paradigms of racial positioning, this historical alteration has not yet produced an essential change in the contradictory set of possible locations of Asians within America. This positioning
is affected by, and affects as well, that of both other racial minorities and of
whites. The assimilation of Asians to America has played an important role in
reimagining America in the middle and late twentieth century. One Hollywood
film toiled especially hard to present a vision of Asian American assimilation in
the early 1960s, a time of particular significance in terms of immigration and
national identity. This film attempted to sketch out the emergence of a new
immigrant community, and in the process reaffirmed the identity of that "America" into which these Asians were to be assimilated.

Flower Drum Song: Modeling Minorities and the Majority in Postwar Modernity

In 1961, Ross Hunter produced the film *Flower Drum Song*, from the successful
stage play of Rogers and Hammerstein, which in turn was loosely based on the
1957 novel of C. Y. Lee. Later in this analysis I will examine the particular nature of the adaptation. Here, I focus on the way that the film constructs, in a very
comprehensive manner, a prescription for two dilemmas: first and foremost,
the assimilation of Asians into America, during a period that had begun to see
the effects of the termination of anti-Chinese exclusion in 1943. The increased
presence of Chinese, as families sought to reconstruct themselves in the United
States, is seized as an opportunity by the film's producers to comment on the socialization and modernization of Chinese-Americans. But along with addressing
these issues, the film suggests that this particular mode of assimilation might also
serve to guide America in its own process of postwar development.

In general, in the narrating of Asian/American introjection in the Cold War
years, Asian Americans serve both to prove the rightness of American democracy as a *worldwide* model and to remind Americans of the traditional values it
had cast aside in its rush to modernization. For instance, in Lin Yu-tang's *Chinatown Family* (1948), the acculturation of the Chinese immigrant provides the occasion for the American teacher to rediscover the English language. Tom Fong,
a young boy just arrived in the United States to join his father, develops a particular relationship with his English teacher:

> Tom worshipped her. In his mind, Tom established an equation—English was
> Miss Cartwright, and Miss Cartwright was English. . . .

> Miss Cartwright was enjoying the words as much as Tom himself. She had never found a student like this, and she had never quite realized the drama of English sounds herself. (62–63)

From this point, Tom invents a system for learning English phonetics that his teacher adopts. This theme is replicated in a number of Asian American narratives to illustrate how the assimilation process not only draws Asians into America—it also performs the critical task of reacquainting America with itself. Interestingly, in this instance Tom's "learning" also distinguishes the Asian immigrant from others—a French girl, who thinks she knows English well, is shown to be deficient when faced with an exam based on Tom's system. The ardent nature of Tom's love of English is contrasted to the presumptuous quality of other, European immigrants and to America's loss of wonder over its own language. Learning language becomes an indispensible part of learning to be American. Most significantly, it suggests that the effort put into this process signals an ethical and moral strength now lacking in the "west," which has become complacent and spoiled.

It is also crucial to note that Tom's interest in the English language is due in no small part to his attraction to Miss Cartwright as a sexual and racial being, the amalgam of which elevates her to the status of the transcendental:

> She was Tom's great discovery. He had never believed it possible that there were such Americans. Miss Cartwright spoke with a kind of angelic sweetness, and her lips tightened and dipped in the middle in a sweet smile when she spoke to Tom, and her eyes were a pale blue and widened when she was shocked, and her hair was a beautiful shining silver. . . . Her accent was feminine, clear, softly vibrant, and seemed to Tom divine. (61)

It is through their particular pedagogical relationship that Tom is able to bridge this gap, but, crucially, it is not only a one-way pedagogy. Cartwright not only inculcates in Tom the desire to be Americanized; he revives in her the same impulse. In fact, there is an aspect of envy in the excitement that is generated in Miss Cartwright over Tom's learning experience. If she appears as an object of desire, his acquisition of English contains the gift of wonder. The sexual attractiveness of Miss Cartwright is overshadowed by Tom's acquisition of the English language. Thus this episode reveals at once the interrelationship between sexuality, race, and culture, and the complex impetus for learning to be American and its therapeutic effect on America: the "model minority" serves both as a model for other minorities to follow in the process toward Americanization and as a secondary modeling system for whites.

Flower Drum Song serves as another example of such narrations of Asian America's "model minority" status. This notion was to coalesce in the later 1960s, after the Watts riots, as a way to explicitly suggest the particularity of Asians within the landscape of American race relations. I will argue that its appearance here is linked to earlier notions of Asians within the frame of what Frank Chin has called "racist love." This is seen specifically within such discourses as the findings of intelligence tests in the 1930s that declared a specific affinity between whites and Asians, and in future articulations within journalistic and academic discourses on the "model minority" in the 1960s and later. But the various manifestations of such sentiments must be recognized as contingent upon specific historical phenomena that called forth the image of Asians as "models" for particular kinds of ideological functions, and hence the "modeling" function of Asians is specifically delimited. In *Flower Drum Song* we find a specific set of ideological functions that define the particularity of Asians in America, both with regard to whites and to Latinos, as whites may be seen to represent the dominant race coming to grips with the postwar age of advanced technology, modern socialization, and the increased assimilation of ethnic groups, and Latinos, the threat of a local and persistent illegal immigration across a nearly unregulatable border.

The main plot is as follows: May-li (Miyoshi Umeki), a young girl from Hong Kong, and her father arrive in San Francisco as stowaways aboard a freighter. She has been brought to America by a Mrs. Fong to marry her son, Sammy (Jack Soo), the owner of a popular North Beach nightclub. Mr. Li and his daughter go directly to the nightclub and introduce themselves. Linda Lowe, (Nancy Kwan), an entertainer at the club and the girlfriend of Sammy Fong, overhears their conversation and storms off, having expected Fong to marry her. He rushes after her and explains that this arrangement was against his will and that he intends to get out of it. Fong knows that a Mr. Wang Chi-yang (Benson Fong) wishes to find a traditional Chinese girl to marry his elder son, Wang-Ta (James Shigeta); Sammy then introduces the Lis to Mr. Wang. The latter is delighted with May-li, who is all that a traditional Chinese girl should be. Sammy goes off, thinking that he has made everyone happy. But Wang-ta has met Linda Lowe, and she has decided to try to marry him, hearing of his father's wealth. Wang-ta has become enamored of Linda, beautiful and aggressively "American," whom he finds exciting and new, having been brought up under his father's strict rule. Mr. Wang is thus astounded when, at Wang-ta's college graduation party (and on the verge of the announcement of his son's marriage to May-li), Linda declares that she is to marry Wang-ta. When Mr. Wang cries out that he will leave

Wang-ta without a penny if he does this, Linda leaves Wang-ta. Wang-ta eventually discovers that he actually loves May-li. At the same time, after finding that Linda would make good on her promise to leave him if he did not marry her, Sammy decides reluctantly to give up bachelorhood and proposes marriage. However, Sammy's mother insists May-li is still obligated to marry her son.

The film provides the occasion for a meditation on modern life, particularly on the process of assimilation. The Asian immigrant figures in the film represent the foreign, but more importantly, in tracing the particular negotiations of the foreign into the domestic, we find as well a comprehensive commentary upon the renegotiation of Americanism in the modern age, as it draws upon the figure of a "neo-traditional" Asian woman to rescue the protagonist from both an archaic and repressive Asiatic tradition *and* the excesses of an overly accelerated, modernized America that has lost its moral anchor. To do this, the film works out the problematic of gender definition and heterosexual marriage to represent the ideal process for the socialization and reproduction of Americans: romance signals the resolution of contradictions of desire and reduces multiplicity to its proper dimension. *Flower Drum Song* also demarcates the issue of immigration in a highly differentiated fashion and signals a particular definition of the relative place of ethnic and racial minorities in the United States.

Before moving into my main argument, it is useful to mention one small episode in order to show how, even at a microlevel, the film persistently inscribes its meditation on the modern and assimilation. May-li tells Wang-ta a joke she has learned from his younger brother.

A spaceman has gone to Mars and discovered that it is populated by tiny people. Amazingly, he falls in love with one, and, being a respectful and traditional sort, asks her father's hand in marriage. May-li acts out the scene, holding out both her palms, taking the role of the astronaut and addressing each one as if it contained a small figure: "Dear sir, I know I am very different from you, but I love your daughter very much and promise to make her happy. What, you say you give your approval? Oh, thank you, I am so happy!" With the last sentence, she claps her hands together in joy. Of course, she thus inadvertently smashes both the Martians. Reading this in the context of the age discloses a number of anxieties that are erased in that last gesture of comic destruction. First, and most obviously, the story locates us precisely in the age of Sputnik. This references both the fear of technological destruction by nuclear war during the Cold War era and the fear that the United States might fall behind the Soviets in the "race for space." Second, this vast spatial realm opened up by technology also presented both a figurative and real symbol of the problems of managing a world made more complex by decolonization and concomitant new nationalisms abroad, the Chinese Communist revolution, and, much closer to home, the Cuban revolution. Finally, the joke is anchored in the fear of miscegenation taken into the realm of outer space. It is clear that the worst fear attached to the highly accelerated pace of modern life and a shrinking globe is, once again, its effect on sexual reproduction and social identity.

On one level the anecdote shows the liberal view toward miscegenation; yet in a wider frame it comments as well upon a general liberal view toward difference in an age more and more keenly aware of the imperative of the modern to accommodate and manage difference. The actualizing of liberal ideology has to self-destruct. Its misguided goodheartedness springs from a sentimentality that in its irrationality spontaneously destroys the dream of a world without difference. Most striking is the fact that the narrative that serves as a vehicle for this message is the voice and body of the Asian woman, who has taken on the role of the white male "hero." Her carefully pronounced English, spoken in a quiet and still unsure voice, and the graceful movements of her delicate hands present an eerie vehicle to convey the narrative and suggest that she has internalized this particular mode of narrating American modernity. Even more haunting, she conveys its mode of addressing the question of her own presence within it. That the telling of this story helps cement her relationship to Wang-ta (rather than to a member of any other race) attests to the short-circuiting of liberal ideology and the containment of desire within strict parameters that the narrative enacts. The joke's violent reinscription of "racial" boundaries provides the release of anxieties regarding precisely the same topic of "chaotic" untamed sexuality. The definition of these parameters becomes the rationale for the narrative of *Flower Drum Song*.

The joke's implicit criticism of interracial marriage also conjoins with a set of particularized representations of gender and nation. Linda Lowe represents the Asian American woman assimilated to a very specific notion of the feminine. Her solo, "I Enjoy Being a Girl," not only emphasizes the pleasures of self-presentation and of a "girl's" ability to manipulate men with her beauty and "charm," it also tracks this manipulation into a liaison with a male identified as both masculine and American. Lowe's song culminates with a statement regarding her desire to be held in the arms of a "brave and free male" who enjoys holding "a girl who enjoys being a girl." The discourse of Americanism is thus imbricated within a rhetoric of gender, power, and nation.

Yet the predication of desire is explicitly obstructed by what Sau-ling Wong has called the "ethnicization of gender."[9] In the cultural hybrid "Chinese-

American," the Asian male is made passive both because of his infantilization before the Confucian patriarch and his feminization within the racial stereotypes of America. Wang-ta complains that, while his father is Chinese and his younger brother American, he is an uncomfortable mix of both. It is crucial to note how the status of "hybrid" takes on a particular ideological charge at the moment of its predication within specific instances. In this case, to be hybrid means that the "American side" of him wants to kiss Linda Lowe, but the "Chinese side" of Wang-ta is afraid. At this precise moment of undecidability, Linda reaches over, cups Wang-ta's face in her hands, and says, "We'd better work on the American side." Thus sexual desire is always articulated and performed, or derailed and displaced, within the logic of a particular view of race, ethnicity, and nation.

The presence of the discourse of nation within that of gender extends to the body in general. In a ceremony in which Wang-ta celebrates his college graduation and his aunt her citizenship, we find the co-articulation of an assimilationist model in both the verbal and kinetic structures of Asian America, yet, as with other treatments of assimilation, the nature and context of such integration are carefully contained. Linda Lowe appears, and Wang-ta's younger, highly assimilated pubescent brother ogles her. No blushing violet he (his assimilation, his evidence of *his* American side, is contrasted to his older brother's passivity), he approaches Linda and asks if she knows a particular pop song. She enthusiastically says yes, and they move into a spontaneous performance of the song and dance. This is abruptly cut short by the father. One might see this as complementing, in short form, the entire scene, in which the aunt leads the cast in singing and performing "Chop Suey," yet the performances are qualitatively different. While Linda and Wang-san's performance signals a unidimensional assimilative movement (dispensing with "Asia" and rehearsing a completely contemporaneous, ahistorical enactment of "America"), "Chop Suey" sets forth a powerful representation of what assimilation might mean.

Mr. Wang declares that his sister-in-law, now a naturalized citizen, is like the "dish the foreigners have invented." She agrees to the analogy, and says, in fact, she likes it. In her song, she puts forth a pastiche of references (for instance, "nuclear war and Zsa Zsa Gabor") that for her symbolize the complex yet strangely harmonious heterogeneity of American modern life, that is, "chop suey." The cast then begins a dance number, in which they move through all the major Euro-American dance forms—square dance, waltz, rock, jazz (the last announced by the dance caller, "Everyone, have a ball!"). And yet this free-form segment is obviously performed as just that, a prescribed "free" form. While the song segment purports to represent through its sheer (seeming) randomness the positive freedom of multicultural America, the dance stresses the Asian Americans' virtuosity in adapting to and embodying the *American* body not only in the contemporary mode of Wang-san and Linda Lowe's rock dance, but in a comprehensive and eminently historical *unfolding* and *synthesis* of American culture. The film's point is to underscore and celebrate assimilation; the discordances and contradictions that might inhere in that assimilative move, the terms and conditions of assimilation, are elided for the sake of a highly polished performance of accommodation. Its very seamlessness presents an idealized image of mastery of American cultural forms, while at the same time the performance by Asian bodies brings with it a sense of defamiliarization that is not altogether comforting. In this utopian text, the sight of an all-Asian cast moving through the repertoire of American dance also presents an alienation of white America from these forms. The fact that the dance is performed solely by Asians, that there is no interracial performance, thus articulates a highly rarified moment of assimilation that elides the question of interracial relations. The suggestion is that Asia must first adapt itself to these forms before any liaison can take place.

This model of assimilation thus comments indirectly (and negatively) on the possible connections between Asians and both other ethnic groups and with white Americans. It argues for the assimilative potential of Asians according to very specific routes of entry and forestalls the actual intercourse between Asians and non-Asians that would be the litmus test for any assimilationist ideology. Instead, the film insists upon the manners in which Asians might "adjust" first to American "life" before meeting any "Americans." This differentiation between a pre-assimilation conditioning and actual interchange with non-Asians produces a safely sequestered vision of Asian America. By extension, it suggests that a similarly reified utopia might be just the right habitus for white America — watching the ideal couple, Wang-ta and May-li, negotiate the Scylla and Charybdis of outmoded Asian conservatism (represented by the older generation) and overly conspicuous American material consumption and acquisition (represented by Sammy and Linda) to reach the modern state serves as a guide to its own journey from the war years into the newly affluent Cold War era.

However, this neo-traditional utopia has to defend itself against certain elements in modern life. In mapping out the intrusion of such elements into the utopia of *Flower Drum Song*, the film constructs a fascinating response that suggests that technology can be both the facilitator of a dystopic rupturing of whatever uneasy peace may be forged between the ancient and the modern, *and* the very instrument that discloses the ideological contradictions that inhere in that nexus. The first representation of technology and modern life, a positive one, is seen as Linda and Sammy embark on a fantasy of married life. As the fantasy sequence progresses, it becomes clear that the vision is governed by Linda, and feared by Sammy. They find themselves in a hyperreal, modernist apartment in some San Francisco highrise with full-view windows that disclose blue skies, faint clouds, and the outlines of other highrises. They are dressed in matching bright ocher silk pajamas. As they begin their musical number, they wander over to the window, and a wet bar magically rises, on which are orange juice, coffee makers, and a toaster. As Linda presses the toaster button, a piece of toast flies into her hand. At that instant, she extols the wonder of a quiet Sunday with Sammy all to herself, and presses his nose with the same gesture of mechanical efficiency: the female control of technology and domestic space is complete. Next she is seen whisking Sammy's former lovers out the door, and in their place come her relations, who are portrayed as deadly bores. Thus the female utopian vision becomes the dystopic vision of the male trapped in monogamy. This develops as the private scene is invaded by incomprehensible and uncontrollable offspring (beat teenagers, the woman dressed in a flesh-colored body stocking straddling a man in a beret and cradling a book as he crawls across the floor in front of Sammy and Linda and their guests; and a "cute" eight-year-old Chinese American girl dressed in a cowboy outfit firing a six-shooter). Misogynistic fear is multiply articulated through the most obvious stagings: the little girl persists in obnoxiously kicking down the cane upon which the male in-law is leaning, and in firing her pistol, a white male gardener follows the people about snipping at the ladies' flowered hats with pruning shears. As Sammy tries to discipline the little girl Linda cuts him off and the girl kicks his shins.

The scene becomes increasingly chaotic when the girl goes over to a large-screen T.V., which seems to float in midair. On the screen, in high-contrast black-and-white, a cowboy and Indian do battle. As the girl starts to fire at them, they pause in their struggle, and join forces to begin firing back at her. The Indian hits his rifle butt against the screen, shattering it, and the cowboy and Indian invade the "real" scene, chasing the characters through a parallel set of multiple doors. The scene finally ends when the Indian ropes Sammy and spins him off. As Sammy staggers across the front of the stage, Linda appears from behind and breaks what appears to be a glass milk bottle over his head, at which point he collapses in a stupor.

The fantasy/nightmare is distributed differently: for Linda, it outlines the new freedom and power the "modern woman" has acquired; for Sammy, it can be generally read as the loss of male control to an aggressive and assertive feminine (I will develop this below in my discussion of the character of Helen Chao), which reproduces itself in ever more sinister forms in later generations, and as the invasion of the private by mass culture. Most significantly, it inventories precisely those elements that present the greatest threats to male hegemony—the insistence on feminine agency, the notion that the machine might supersede the human, and in general, the uncontrollability of mass cultural and countercultural forms. The television in this sequence is a life-sized (that is, oversized) contraption whose borders are easily breached: television culture aggressively invades the private world and plays a role in containing the male viewer for the final coup de grâce bestowed by the New Woman. Here, she is presented in a prefeminist mode, a seductress retooled with the intellectual ability to negotiate and manipulate sexuality in the modern age according to the imperatives of individualism in capitalism. Linda Lowe is specifically cast as one who is able to exploit the rift between "tradition" and the modern, as this schism is represented in the psyche of Wang-ta.

But if television is an unruly conduit for American life, then it also carries with it the potential for unleashing the contradictions between tradition and modernity that are glossed over in hegemonic representation. The key dilemma of the film is how the Flower Drum Girl—who is produced in the course of the film as the perfect woman—will link up with the protagonist. She is perfect precisely because she is eminently adaptable to all that American life throws her way, especially the foibles of her man. In one scene Sammy tries to show her how she would hate being married to him. He takes her barhopping, flaunting his lovers before her; they go gambling—he throws money away with abandon. They finally end the evening as the milkman makes his delivery, but May-li has stayed by Sammy all night, enjoying his enjoyments and serving his needs. She has also fulfilled all of Mr. Wang's expectations of a Flower Drum Girl—she performs traditional songs to ease his worries about the modern age. And yet she is able to adapt the songs to address the present day as well, and when she falls in love with Wang-ta, she urges him to teach her what a "real" kiss is. Her virtue and acquiescence stand in sharp contrast to the self-serving, sexually aggressive and materialistic Linda Lowe, the Americanized Chinese woman. Yet "honor" and obligation to the family association would dictate that May-li set aside her own interest in Wang-ta, again, this time fulfilling her duty to marry the man she was brought to marry.

Everyone is invited to witness May-li's marriage to Sammy Fong. Wang-ta and Linda Lowe watch silently as Sammy drinks a cup of the ceremonial wine. Then it is May-li's turn. She lifts her veil, but then turns suddenly to address Mrs. Fong. She announces that she cannot marry Sammy, that she came into the country illegally, and that "my back is wet." Wang-ta and Linda burst into smiles as Mrs. Fong recoils in horror: "I cannot have my son marry a wetback!" But Wang Chi-yang has no compunction against Wang-ta marrying an illegal immigrant: for him, the credentials that matter most are those of filial piety. Nevertheless, the objections raised by Mrs. Fong take precedence, and the marriage ceremony turns into a double ceremony: Sammy and Linda, and Wang-ta and May-li. This coupling neatly defines two Asian American types: although Sammy and Linda are recuperated into monogamous heterosexual domestic life, they lack a certain essential moral and social grace: both are comically vulgar and too obviously materially driven and aggressively acquisitive. Obsessed with the surface (they are both in the entertainment business), they represent the hyper-Americanized Asian, and consequently the model of a process of Americanization gone wrong. They also must be seen as representing the excesses that Americans are warned to avoid: Sammy and Linda represent in a displaced form a modern America cut off from its roots. On the other hand, Wang-ta and May-li present the ideal balance of "Chinese tradition" and American individualism, which will stand as a model for both Asian Americans and Americans in general. They are properly respectful of the past, yet aware of both the demands and freedoms presented by the modern world of the United States. They reject the puritanical, but retain modesty; they disdain avarice but subscribe to upward mobility.

This paradigm negatively defines the "improper" modes of modern American assimilation; it also comments upon the particular issue of immigration in the early 1960s. While presented in a comical light, the issue of "wetbacks" articulates a particular set of differentiations. How does May-li come to use the term? The night before her marriage, she wanders disconsolately into the living room and absentmindedly turns on the television (this automatic gesture implies her quick acclimatization to the modern American habitus). An image of a buxom and beautiful Mexican woman appears, dressed in a peasant frock, speaking to a white sheriff. She is distraught. "I cannot marry Rodriguez, I came across the Rio Grande illegally, I am a wetback!" To maintain the echo of this term so that it might infuse itself into May-li's psyche, the film script defies logic: "He is a wetback, too!" May-li retools the woman's speech in her own confession: "I came across the Pacific Ocean illegally." In transposing an inter-American crossing to a trans-Pacific one, May-li inadvertently marks what will be the two most dramatic sites of new immigration in the second half of the century.

The film lets the particular judicial history and function of the term remain at the margins of the narrative; what is important is that May-li understand that the term will forbid her marriage to Sammy. She adapts the term thus innocently, or so it would seem, and this frees her from any charge of racism. Indeed, it sympathetically links her with illegal immigrants. But the film will not allow for any close examination of the assumptions and consequences that surround this performance of American discourse. There is a peculiar distribution of race and law within the film.

The racial Other for whites is here presented historically, but, significantly, its representations are mediated and conveyed by mass media: the television. Indians and Mexicans are represented only on television and only in the context of the old west: the Indian is locked in mortal combat with the white cowboy; the Mexican woman and sheriff also hark back to the late nineteenth and early twentieth century. Television's black-and-white medium is starkly set against the vivid wide-screen Technicolor of Ross Hunter's cinematic production. This difference sets the "past" cleanly apart from the modern age—thus issues of racism are asserted to be contained by historical distance; it is suggested that in the present age racial violence and prejudice are somehow ameliorated by modern enlightenment. When the cowboy and Indian break the television screen and occupy the space of the main filmic narrative to which they were subordinated, this becomes a token of high trauma representing the impossibility of sequestering the historical moment from the ramifications of the past: the power of mass media to control the imaging of the past breaks down, and the past takes on a life of its own, acting in the present in unpredictable ways.

The traffic between the past and the present is thus mediated but not entirely controlled by technology: what is more saliently at issue is the particular political economy that is operative in that liaison between past and present. What is crucially significant is that May-li's identification with the term "wetback" is *doubly* efficacious, in true utopian fashion. Immediately, it does what she desires—it frees her from her marriage to Sammy Fong. But more importantly, it brings with it *no* negative effects. Rather than be denounced to the INS and put on the next boat to Hong Kong, she gets to marry the man she loves. Her illegal status is to be erased by her marriage to a U.S. citizen.

Again, this narrative act reconfirms the delineations of good and bad modes of assimilation. Sammy's mother is attached only to appearance: she is constantly portrayed in furs; she only slightly disapproves of Sammy's "swinging" lifestyle of gambling and loose women; more important to her is the veneer of respectability that May-li is supposed to provide the Fong family. When it turns out that May-li cannot perform that function, her traditional virtue becomes irrelevant. The social stigma it will bring the family in terms of an assimilated bourgeois American point of view takes primacy. In contrast, Old Master Wang, whose heart has been set on marrying May-li to Wang-ta, has no objection to her illegal status. Law here is easily transcended under the imperative of a particular ethos of tradition and its necessity to any act of assimilation.

This circumvention of law is a rehearsal of immigration law in the United States: the supposed "assimilability" of particular groups allowed them entrance and naturalization; others were denied such "Americanization" because of their inability to psychically adjust to (that is, socially accept) American life. Yet this litmus test was of course itself a projection of stereotyped beliefs fueled by the interests of the dominant class: as noted above, a particular discursive constellation drew on scientific data, domestic and global economic prognostication, and psychological, physiological, and cultural imaging to determine and reproduce the classification of different races around the core image of America. In this performance of differentiation, the particular set of moral and mental features that comprise May-li authorize her transgression of immigration law, so much so that the law in effect disappears. This seamless fulfillment of social desire cannot but offset the realities of the mechanisms that underwrite the political and social functions of the term "wetback." Most significant, it makes an unproblematized and absolute differentiation between illegal Chinese, whose illegality is excused because of their assimilability to modern American life (facilitated by "traditional" Confucian values), and Latinos, whose original racist designation, "wetback," remains an absolute obstacle. Significantly, this episode (indeed, the entire framing device for the film's narrative) does not exist in C. Y. Lee's novel.

The modifications made to the original novel disclose an interest in staging a national assimilation narrative absent its international history. If Hunter *adds* a framing device that will illustrate the ideology of assimilation and immigration, scripting American inclusion and exclusion and defining the formation of modern America, he *deletes* the novel's address to Chinese national politics and its skepticism regarding modern American life. The facility and desirability of "Americanization" is questioned and its costs measured, and the diasporic identity of new immigrants articulated as not simply quaint attachments to folk songs, but deep political questions of allegiance. Such is Hunter's interest in making this an *American* film in yellow-face, that he erases its *Asian* component except in its most banal form and produces a very selective vision of Asian America.

In the novel, Wang-ta's very American name, Lawrence, announces a historical moment linked to China. It is explained as sounding like the Chinese words, *lao ren se,* "the old man dies," that is, the identity of the new Asian American is coterminous with the death of the older generation. Indeed, the novel is about many deaths, literal and figurative. One man is shot to death in a fight over Linda Tung; Helen Chao kills herself; and the elder Mr. Wang has chronic symptoms of tuberculosis. The final scene is reminiscent of the resignation of Charlie Chan, noted in Chapter 2: the "old world" is irrecoverable, and those who linger in its memory are doomed. They are also, by dint of those memories, prevented from fully participating in the present: "This was the world of the younger generation, everything was changing, slowly but steadily. Even he, old-fashioned as he was, was now deserting his herb doctor, his best friend, and the only man in Chinatown with whom he could happily associate."[10]

The theme of finding the perfect woman (the trope of the Cinderella tale)—and the manner in which this theme indicates both the proper modes of assimilation to the aspiring Asian American and the ideal of femininity for the American audience—is extenuated in the novel and explicitly linked to the theme of reproduction, an act that will supposedly regenerate the Chinese family. The matching of Wang-ta to a Chinese woman takes on a particular urgency and pathos, as each attempt fails. Rather than having only two main contestants for marriage, as in the film, the novel presents a number of marriage possibilities, which are variously dismissed on a number of grounds.

Like the earlier novel by Louis Chu, *Eat a Bowl of Tea,* C. Y. Lee's novel focuses on the theme of reproduction; specifically under the historical conditions of post-1943, the date when the Chinese exclusion acts were voided and the possibility of reconstructing the Chinese family in America was first imaginable. Like Chu's novel, Lee's underscores the uneven and highly problematic nature of that attempt to regenerate China in America. Compared to the film's utopian staging of the coupling of a sincere, highly adaptive yet ethically conservative pair, the novel narrates the disintegration of the presumptions and values of both tradition and assimilation.

As in the narratives we examined in Chapter 4, Wang-ta's decision to leave his medical training (an eminent symbol of upward mobility) and join a school friend in starting a grocery reads "assimilation" according to specific material needs and possibilities. This decision also motivates a disquisition on class and labor that weighs communism and capitalism in the balance—this "local" decision in America is framed within an international context. This friend, who acts throughout the novel as Wang-ta's mentor, is a former Ph.D. student in political science who has decided that happiness lies neither in intellectual work nor material wealth:

"Look at my hands," he said. . . . "A few months' hard labor did it. The hands of the typical proletarian. The most outstanding change since I quit my intellectual life is the change of my hands." . . . "The hands of strength and toughness help to bring food to my own mouth and potatoes to those of my fellow man. Ever since I became a grocery clerk, I've achieved a strong sense of being wanted and useful. . . .

"You must realize that in this country perhaps you are only refused the opportunity to do what you want to do; but in China you will be forced to do what you don't want to do. . . . Even I . . . find the communist medicine a bit hard to swallow. This sounds like propaganda, but it's a fact we have to face; and you have to constantly bear in mind that communism and capitalism are like fire and water, they will never mix. As long as there is capitalism, communism will fight it. And you can assure yourself that capitalism isn't some back-yard weed that can be uprooted easily." (102–3)

Wang-ta's decision to follow Chang, to "be with the people," is thus extremely significant in its rejection of class aspirations, aspirations closely linked to notions of immigrant "mentality" and ethnic assimilation. Rather than aligning himself with those ideals, Wang-ta finally subscribes to an ideology that is neither communistic nor capitalistic (that is, in line with contemporary socioeconomic discourses), but is rather in accord with a nostalgic brand of social populism. It is, in other words, an explicit foregrounding of the Cold War context of the narrative that "resolves" such issues (capitalism versus communism, the "China" transported to Taiwan and in some way resident in Hong Kong versus "Red China") in a remarkably synthetic manner.

This differs crucially from the film's synthetic ideology, which is underwritten by Wang-ta's and May-li's marriage. In contrast, it is not clear at all that Wang-ta and May-li will marry in the novel—their relationship seems more one of a sympathetic bond between two individuals equally confused by the life choices offered them by Asian America. The novel thus marks the complexities of Asian and American identification: Chang's comments on communism and capitalism define the "two Chinas" of the era—Taiwan and the People's Republic of China (P.R.C.); Wang-ta must negotiate the imperatives of "China" in America; and May-li's story narrates the movement between Asia and America. The film's utopian assimilationist narrative is radically different from the skeptical, problematic portrait drawn in the novel.

The film version of *Flower Drum Song* is remarkable for its nearly comprehensive inventory of (and pacification of) modern American anxieties over sexuality, race, ethnicity, morality, immigration, and national spirit. Perhaps more remarkable is the fact that it uses Asian America as the stage upon which to dramatize these anxieties. This is no accident. The utopia of *Flower Drum Song* supersedes the shadow of "Red China"—its very centrality in the novel is just the element that must be made invisible in the Hollywood film.[11]

It is critical to historicize *Flower Drum Song*: the film is able to articulate this assimilationist utopia in a way that could *not* be done for much longer. The 1965 immigration act, which removed the nation of origin quotas imposed in 1924, unexpectedly and drastically swelled Asian immigration to the United States. Immigration became more possible for Asians and other groups, and integration became more problematic in the eyes of the American public. While the model minority myth adumbrated in the film flourished after the Watts riots, helping to castigate blacks and Latinos and rearticulate the particular modes in which racial and ethnic minorities were to properly find themselves entrance into the American "mainstream," the utopianism of the film, particularly in its massive, all-Asian form, could not be presented after 1965. Instead we find local and particularized articulations of Asian assimilation, which reveal the imaginative limits of assimilationist ideology and the insistence on a particular national identity.

Modeling the Nation: Cynical Culturalism

The impossibility of actualizing and stabilizing "Asian/American" is directly linked to the distinction made between "Asian" and "American," the premise of their mutual exclusion. This impossibilty in turn may be linked to the failure of interpellation that characterizes ideology, an inevitable failure because the "call" for the subject—what, exactly, the Other demands of its subjects—is impossible to discern. This impossibility is rooted in the inherent contradiction that informs the constitution of that Other—which must always finesse this inner contradiction by projecting its lack, its radical incompleteness, upon the subject.[12]

Here, the undecideable element is precisely the constitution of "America" under the pressure of race and ethnicity. Asians are deemed inadequate to America, marginalized, or excluded in order to (re)consolidate the nation's image of its ideal self, whose democratic and universal premises are nonetheless contradicted by its white supremacist ideology. Thus the constitution of "Asian-American" (as well as other hyphenated subjectivities) seems never able to be completed, for the very ontological status of "America" depends upon a tenuous, historicized, provisional, and contingent consolidation of nation against "itself." The nation can only be named as a particular within an ideology that simultaneously claims universality: America is the corporate entity supposedly comprised of all American citizens, yet it is a *particularly* textured, nuanced, and functioning image of the nation, which foregrounds certain of its elements and suppresses the rest.[13] As noted above, in this scenario, it is better to view the "Asian/American" split as a vacillating, multidirectional attempt at predication, rather than a teleologically predetermined and irreversible phenomenon: the contents of "Asian American" vary as the ratio of "Asianness" to "Americanness" is manifested in social practice. Despite such practices, which have relegated Asian Americans to particularly constrained roles in the American imaginary, this repertory includes, significantly, the role of a "people" who, albeit marginalized, serve as *models* for Americans. How to read the contradiction of margin and model and not reevaluate the presumptions of the "center"? The deployment of the model minority myth is an exemplary instance of such negotiations of social and political subjectivity; it may be located in the historical context of domestic civil rights activism and an emergent "Pacific Rim discourse." Both appearances of the myth are haunted by a sense of America's weakened position at home and globally.

It is crucial to understand that while the signified of the model minority myth certainly broadened to include, variously, East, Southeast, and South Asian groups, the specific group named by the term, the group whose particular characterization defines the nature of both the myth generated and its ideological functions, was Japanese Americans. Along with the focus on domestic educational and economic "success" (which can be linked to a proliferation of studies claiming that Japanese Americans were the United States' most "exogamous" Asian group, thereby signaling both their biological infiltration of and socioeconomic assimilation to the nation), the particular attention given Japanese Americans was filtered through the optics of an international remapping of the United States' relation to the "Pacific Rim," in which Japan emerged as a newly hegemonic economic power. The genesis of the model minority myth, the "line" between Asian and Asian American, was indistinct, yet at the same time the myth was inseparable from a general anxiety regarding the manner in which "America" could be preserved in the midst of both domestic economic and political upheaval and international renegotiations of power.

At "home," it is no wonder that the invention of the modeling function of Japanese Americans was deeply ambivalent. Addressed both to other racial minorities, who were told to emulate Japanese American assimilation, *and* to white Americans, who were seen to have lost touch with the guiding ethical principles of America, the domestic model minority myth was to serve a salutary purpose.

Yet this presented a problem: the very fact that a model had to be posited at all signaled a recognition of the weakening of the American state, a recognition that cast suspicion on its triumphalist ideology. Swerving to avoid the disclosure of any structural crisis, reactionary pundits made this "problem" part of a larger and more important solution. Conservatives needed a weapon to use against liberals who were pushing civil rights legislation—they found it in Japanese Americans, whose reputed success showed that urban poverty and violence were not the outcomes of institutional racism, but of constitutional weaknesses in minorities that were only exacerbated by the welfare state. In short, the model minority myth provided the opportunity for conservatives to situate the causes of these problems *outside* a consideration of institutional racism and economic violence: the success of the Japanese Americans was used to dispute a structural critique of the U.S. political economy. Yet the very racism away from which conservatives tried to draw attention reappears strongly in the logic of the model minority myth.

I wish to note the particular mechanisms whereby the "successful" predication of "Asian-to-Asian American" was diverted and destroyed. Ironically, the journey to recovery was to be led by a people who, once that mission was accomplished, would literally self-destruct by virtue of the fact that they would have become *too* successful. That is, they had become *Americans*, but as such they were contaminated with exactly the weaknesses and complacency from which their marginal status had protected them. Asian Americans could show America how to be "great" again, but after doing so they were either remarginalized as "Asian" or brought down to more a pedestrian sphere: that of "normal" Americans. It was left to white Americans to be inspired by, but ultimately to surpass, Japanese Americans, aided by the resuscitation of "America" as an inherently white nation. It many ways, it appears that the domestic version of the model minority thesis is a retroactive positing of identity: after surveying the contemporary racial and economic landscape, model minority proponents then invent a name that will produce retroactively the reality of the model minority. The set of racist assumptions that allowed for this construction is at least as significant as the fictional product.[14]

The international manifestation of the myth, which promoted Japanese business ethics and methodologies as the wave of the future, was equally ambivalent. While the domestic myth was deployed to contain and divert civil rights policymaking, to neutralize activism, and to promote a laissez-faire domestic urban policy, the international myth challenged the United States to modify its modes of economic operation. This variant of the model minority myth can be traced to early Pacific Rim discourse, which emerged likewise in the early 1960s, but it became most prevalent and anxious in the late 1970s, after the recognition of China and the fall of Saigon, and during deepening economic crisis. While the American business sector began to turn toward Japanese economic success as a model for a revision of American business practices, the interpolation of a "foreign" mode of business and production, no matter how benign the guise it might take ("synthesis," "adaptation," "selective borrowing"), threatened to eliminate not only the weaknesses of the American way of business but also precisely those elements that had contributed for more than a century to the ideology of triumphant American exceptionalism.[15] These different contexts produce different modalities of the myth, yet what is most germane for our purposes is the way both texts reinstate "America" and contain and neutralize the model of Asian Americans and Asia.

A certain ressentiment informed both manifestations of the model minority myth, and led its adherents to cautiously reinstate the line between Asians and Americans. Admiration for the Japanese Americans and Japan was inextricably linked to self-doubt. Yet conservative ideologues adeptly contained this negativity in two ways. First, they placed the blame for the nation's troubles upon minorities and liberal do-gooders and aligned themselves with the image of Japanese Americans they had constructed. This dynamic has had historically profound and far-reaching effects. It has facilitated the splintering off of Asian Americans from progressive political engagement, by working to convince many Asian Americans themselves of their privileged status and the conservative logic that underwrites it, and by aligning Asian Americans with the white middle class in the eyes of progressive activists of other races. Second, critics rationalized their resentment by pointing up the supposed limitations of Japanese Americans—their constitutional unfitness for Americanness.

Reaction to Japan as a potential model for corporate revitalization produced an equally important set of effects—most noticeably the surfacing of the inherent contradictions of a capitalist system ostensibly predicated upon laissez-faire policies. While some argued for the continuance of laissez-faire domestic policies, letting the "fittest" prove their worth and gain their rewards, speaking out against state intervention in the form of social reform and civil rights, these same individuals could be heard demanding that an activist U.S. government put in place tariffs and controls on Japanese goods.[16] The excuse for this inconsistency was that this had to be done only because Japan had a protectionist policy in place anyway. Yet this alibi did not provide a convincing distraction from the endemic problems of U.S. manufacturing and marketing in late capitalism.

Rather, a way had to be found to resuscitate America, but from a position of *strength*. Here I explore the restorative strategies deployed to salvage America and distinguish it from Asia. These strategies produced an "Asian America" that existed in a liminal state.

The first articulation of the model minority thesis was made in an article by social demographer William Petersen, entitled "Success Story, Japanese American Style," published in the *New York Times Magazine* on January 9, 1966, less than six months after the Watts riots in Los Angeles. Several other journalists and commentators quickly picked up this theme, which focused on high educational achievement levels, high median family incomes, low crime rates, and the absence of juvenile delinquency and mental health problems among Asian Americans, and juxtaposed this "success" against the failure of blacks in America. The message was clear—patient and quietly determined hard work brings success; welfare dependence and sheer "laziness" bring economic disaster. Scholars have since questioned the data from which this myth was created; nevertheless, the predominance of the image of the quietly hardworking Asian American has persisted in the popular imagination.[17] While obviously there is nothing wrong with hard work, the model minority myth reifies Asian American identity and deploys this reification programmatically against other groups, mapping out specific positionings of minorities within the U.S. political economy. There is a substantial amount of scholarship on the model minority myth, both supporting and debunking its findings. Few, however, have remarked upon the inherently fatalistic and contradictory nature of Petersen's praise of Japanese Americans, and the suggestion that they might act as models for other minorities. Here I focus on Petersen's cynical analysis of the production of socioeconomic subjects based on his particular reading of Japanese national culture, and his pessimistic prognosis for the future of minorities in America. These conclusions, fueled by his comparative analysis, serve both to underwrite a radically conservative anti–civil rights agenda and, ironically, to isolate Japanese American "success" as an unrepeatable feat.

Petersen found that his essay was "well received both by knowledgeable readers of the *New York Times*, who sent more letters of commendation than [he] had ever received concerning work of mine, and by professional colleagues, who several times asked permission to reprint the article in anthologies on race or social problems" (ix). Prompted by such response from both "knowledgeable readers" and his academic colleagues, as well as his sense that he "had raised some very important questions to which [he] had found no satisfactory answers" (ix), Petersen wrote a book elaborating and substantiating his argument, *Japa-*

nese Americans: Oppression and Success (1971). One should note the particular audience for which the book was written: a class of readers who skim the *Times* and academics (mostly sociologists) who were pleased to find that, even in its short form, Petersen's essay seemed to answer *their* questions regarding the nature of Asians in America and American race relations two years after the passage of the Civil Rights Act. The book was published as part of a series, "Ethnic Groups in Comparative Perspective." In his introduction for the book, the general editor for the series, Peter I. Rose, notes that Petersen, "by his own admission, knew almost nothing about Japanese Americans prior to 1965" (vii). According to Rose, the resulting study is to be valued for its "compassionate detachment" (viii): "Petersen's book is unique in many ways. Most striking, I suppose, because the author . . . is not a member of the subject of his concern" (vii). Yet, while asserting Petersen's objectivity, Rose fails to note the historical context that led to Petersen's interest in the Japanese in the first place.

One of the core elements of Petersen's study is his unabashed admiration for a people who, faced with immense oppression, of which the internment was only the most explicit and dramatic instance, managed to become one of the most "successful" minorities in the United States. Petersen explains: "I started not with a feeling of identification or even particularly of empathy, but with an interesting analytical problem: why in the case of *this* colored minority past oppression had led to phenomenal economic and social success, contradicting the generalizations derived from the experience of Negroes, American Indians, Mexican Americans, and others" (ix). Although he includes American Indians and Mexican Americans in this list, it is clear that his main point of comparison is American blacks, who are seen as the primary motivation for civil rights laws, and whose inability to succeed in American society is the "cause" of the Watts riots.

Gary Orfield's essay, "Race and the Liberal Agenda: The Loss of the Integrationist Dream, 1965–1974," makes the important argument that after an initial period of dramatic success, the civil rights movement lost momentum as liberal whites backed off from a structural critique of institutionalized racism in the U.S.[18] Instead of addressing the profound systemic problems of American socioeconomics, specifically in the urban ghetto, liberals attacked the more superficial, albeit still significant, aspects of racism:

> The liberal program for urban poverty in the 1960s was built around preschool and compensatory education, job training, access to higher education, increased social services, and community organization and empowerment through community action agencies. The basic assumption was that no fundamental economic

or racial change was essential. Opportunities existed; the need was simply to prepare blacks for them and forbid discrimination. Civil rights required only relatively weak fair employment and fair housing laws to deal with individual cases of discrimination. (329)

This made it possible for racists to blame blacks for their failures, rather than the deeper structural contradictions of a racist America:

> If one looks only at the resulting inequalities, one's natural conclusion is that something is wrong with the people who are on the wrong side of the color line. . . .
>
> When no effective explanation is presented, the political and social initiative is decisively with those who assert that the subordinate group's inferior position is caused by some kind of inherent personal or group inferiority. . . .
>
> Once [liberals] abandoned an analysis rooted in an understanding of the history of white prejudice and the need for fundamental change in the ghetto system, the ground shifted in the entire debate on compensatory programs. These programs were seen as beneficence by the white middle class rather than as a right. When blacks asked for more, they were accused of ingratitude. (315)

Petersen's "explanation" of Japanese American success must thus be read as a specific rebuttal of Lyndon Johnson's belief that "the black experience was fundamentally different from that of other immigrants" (325).

Three points form the essential base of Petersen's argument: first, he stakes out his professional objectivity—his *non*identification with his object of study. As we will see, this lack of identification is not altogether feigned, for ultimately the study, after its praise and admiration for Japanese Americans, maintains a border between them and both other minorities and whites. Specifically, although Petersen suggests that they might be "models" for other Americans, the subtext of his argument negates the possibility of any mimetic act. Second, an argument is put forward that oppression, rather than stifling a minority group's ascent, actually *has led to* success for the Japanese Americans. By that logic, the more oppression, the greater success. This underwrites Petersen's attack on civil rights, which lies at the bottom of his study. The third element is, precisely, the "comparative" one—how to "explain" the signal success of Japanese Americans, who have made it in the country of their oppressors, in light of the failure of other groups to do so? Petersen argues that this success must be accounted for by examining both the Japanese Americans' particular national and cultural history, which equips them with core values of proud independence, stoic fortitude, group and family loyalties, and community cohesion, and the effects of liberal social welfare programs and civil rights, upon which other minoritiess have become reliant, and which deprive them of a hunger for competition and productive struggle.

Petersen lays out these two topics at the beginning of his book; he is not stinting in his exceptionalism: "By almost any criterion of good citizenship that we might choose, not only are Japanese Americans better than any other segment of American society, including native whites of native parents, but they have realized this remarkable progress by their own almost unaided effort" (4). Leaving aside the oxymoron of "native whites," Petersen's statement seems calculated to have a specific shock effect on the dominant group. Japanese Americans are described as "neither the hapless beneficiaries of social welfare nor the cause of militant placard-bearers" who "out of the elements of American democracy—universal education, the free labor market, citizenship for all native-born residents, color-blind justice—to the sometimes slight degree that these were made available to them, the Japanese themselves fashioned their identity as the nation's prized subnation" (5). Petersen's prose has a distinct accusatory tone, aimed not only at racial minorities: if "they" can make it, why can't *all* the rest of us?

The ability of Japanese Americans to rebound, and even take advantage of oppression as a stimulus for success, is due to not to the values of family, nor religion (since, under the force of assimilation, the influence of these things is modified), but rather to loyalty to something Petersen calls a "subnation":

> Except for their smaller size, subnations have the main features that we associate with nationality: an actual or putative biological descent from common forebears, a common territory, an easier communication inside than outside the group, a sentimental identification with insiders and thus a relative hostility toward outsiders. (216)

Petersen gives example after example of the Japanese American "subnation" at work: "Their education has been conducted like a military campaign against a hostile world, with intelligent planning and tenacity. Their heavy dependence on the broader Japanese community was suggested in a number of ways" (115). The picture that emerges from this analysis is of a minority's success based on its maintenance of both a social and spatial separatism: segregation has its benefits *if* this social space enjoys a particular subnational profile. In other words, the very forces that kept Japanese Americans apart from the "mainstream" (as Petersen envisions things) allow them to maintain both the purity and strength of their subnation. To this he counterposes blacks: "Negroes shifted their reference group: once pleased to have risen above their fathers' status, now many blacks are aggressively dissatisfied that they have not yet achieved full equality with whites. One consequence of massive civil-rights programs has been to exacerbate racial conflict, to encourage the rise of black violence and white backlash" (218). He implies that by not accepting their status as separate (and unequal), blacks have signed their own death warrants. But that is not as disturbing to Petersen as the manners in which black discontent has breached the segregationist barrier between black subnation and white nation, manifesting itself in civil unrest, exposing America's legacy of racism and ideological contradiction. The symbolic space of the nation is now variegated and particularized, and this segmentation has implications for the real occupancy of a place in America.

While one reading of Petersen's book might be that Japanese Americans are successful because they "earned" their status as super-whites, there is a more profound and vastly more cynical element in his narrative. His reliance on the concept of a rather militant Japanese American subnation ("education conducted like a military campaign"), with its definitive elements of spatial, social, and psychic difference, isolates it and particularizes it so much that it can be an object of mimesis only by approximation or, more specifically, by *bricolage*. That is, other groups can only "model" themselves on the Japanese Americans by improvising with the elements indigenous to their own particular and predetermined "subnation." This attempt at mimicry can only lead to failure, it seems, for no other group has the specific genetic material of *Japan* as a basis for their subnation.

Yet even as he celebrates this subnation he senses a waning of effect—assimilation has eroded (but not yet eradicated) the borders and inner strength of the subnation: "in many respects the Japanese Americans are now more American than Japanese—in political loyalty, language, and way of life. Let us hope, however, that the subnation is not to be completely melted into the melting pot" (232). The misfit between Japan and America, the impossibility of predicating a Japanese American subject that might retain its potency, is thus emphasized in Petersen's "discovery" that the more Americanized the Japanese in America become, the less "Japanese" they are, and the less able they are to succeed by drawing on that special sense of subnation. Petersen speaks of increased "social pathologies" that plague the Americanized generation: "They [Sansei] have grown up, most of them, in relatively comfortable circumstances, with the American element of their composite subculture becoming more and more dominant. Part of their full acculturation to the general pattern is that they are beginning to show some of the faults of American society that were almost totally lacking in their parents' generation" (141).

Thus, after segregating and particularizing the success of the Japanese American "subnation" as something no other group can replicate because of its specific origins in the emergence of modern Japan, Petersen proceeds to argue that successful assimilation into American society paradoxically produces a *negative*, debilitating effect on the Japanese Americans. To maintain their "success," then, Japanese Americans must remain locked in a liminal, segregated, detemporalized zone *between* Asia and America.[19] Indeed, this zone is the product of the pressures of the contradiction that underlies Petersen's argument: he is caught between his ideological allegiance to American democracy and his admiration for a Japanese success story, which emerges only from a particular reading of a Japanese social system that, by his own account, thrives on authoritarianism and the absence of "even a word for civil rights."

To conclude this discussion of Petersen's thesis, we should examine what, exactly, he means by "Japan," for upon investigation one finds that his invention of Japan contains a specific remapping of both the Japanese nation and the United States. Petersen traces the success of Japanese Americans to the emergence of Japan in modernity. He is particularly struck by its adaptation and modification of western technology, economics, and military systems. Such adaptation characterizes an inherent ability of Japanese that will equip them for success under the specific conditions of modernity. Witness his discussion of an instance of Japanese modernization:

> The intelligent pragmatism that suggested these choices dictated to absolute commitments. The army was reorganized by the French, but within a few months of France's defeat in 1871 Japan shifted to the German military organization. The banking system, based at first on the American model, was soon changed to include elements of British central banking, long-term credit institutions copied from the French, and some innovations particularly suited to the local scene. (157)

This ability to fabricate a modern Japan from the raw materials of the west points to a specific agency—that of a Japanese social subject that is distinctly adaptive to the conditions of modernity: "The individuals caught up in this transformation were expected to both retain the old and acquire the new. The psychological type that resulted from such counterpressures, at least as seen from the outside, is an array of self-contradictions. In a sense that was even true of the traditional culture, in which ancient Chinese borrowings often lay side by side with half-antagonistic native traits, together forming a composite that struck every foreigner as inordinately complex" (161).

Petersen tracks the "best of old while retaining the new" to a primordial instance which makes the case of Japan exceptional and neutralizes the modeling function of Japanese Americans. Correlating his comments on the Japanese-American "subnation" with his conception of the Japanese nation, one discovers again that one cannot *be* like them; one can only emulate particular *fragments* of a complex and irrepeatable (sub)national culture: "Virtually by definition, each nation is distinctive in its culture: and the inculcation of its specific beliefs, attitudes, and patterns of behavior, one can reasonably hypothesize, differentiates the modal national of each country from the rest of the world's population" (160). He suggests that "perhaps we should draw no greater conclusion than that Japanese were trained by their multilayered culture to live effectively with complexities; in this sense, even the villagers had an 'urban' cast, a readiness for industrialism" (162).

From this celebration of the success of Japanese modernization, a process that accessed an essential Japanese subjectivity so universal that even rural villagers moved smoothly into industrialization and modern complexity, Petersen moves to his main point—a link between this revisionist history of Japan and contemporary American institutions:

> The faults of such a social system, as seen by a Western democrat, have often been pointed out, and in any case they are obvious enough. Structural lines as strong and clear as those in Japanese institutions easily merge with authoritarian control; political democracy is possible, as several periods of modern Japanese history have demonstrated, but not easily achieved or maintained. American commentaries have less often stressed the virtues of the system. The lack of privacy, the *absence of even a word for civil rights*, are symptoms of an organic strength that, on the one hand, motivated each Japanese to contribute his utmost and thus, on the other hand, enabled the nation to jump from an almost pathetic weakness to parity with the greatest powers in half a century [emphasis added]. (165)

Petersen limits criticism of the negative effects of the "Japanese system" to the obvious; his task is pointing out the positive. Yet even as he implies the disjuncture between American democratic ideals and Japanese authoritarianism, he maintains his admiration for what such authoritarianism has produced. This contradiction between emulation and the admission of ideological difference (for instance, admiration for a success bred of "Asian" conformity and allegiance to "tradition" and adherence to "American individualism") haunts the interstices of the concept of the model minority. It is intimately linked to the contradictions of democratic capitalism, which argues for egalitarianism as well as class distinction, and the contradictions of a racist ideology that must contain or neutralize any challenge to white supremacy, even while arguing for its assimilative powers. If Japanese Americans are to be assimilated, their economic and spiritual potency, derived from their subnation, must be left at the door. If they are not assimilated, they will remain at a hallowed, but hollow space on the exterior seam of the American state.

One of the ways that this contradiction is discursively elided is to draw attention away from it by focusing instead upon the *tripartite* ratio, Asian / White / Other, in which one of the three is used to leverage a particular relationship among the other two elements within the space deemed "America." In this light we can review the manner in which the furor over illegal Asian immigration in 1992 was quickly overshadowed by an attention to illegal Latino immigration. After a flurry of journalistic and photographic essays on illegal Chinese immigration in 1992, the public was instructed that the level of illegal Chinese immigration was far surpassed by that of Latino immigration. If anything, illegal Chinese immigration (like Cuban immigration) was quickly rearticulated in a critique of the "Stalinesque" conditions of the socialist countries, the illegals granted the status of martyrs to an American government that would not fully extend its sanctuary. Yet concomitantly there was a subtext of relief that, indeed, after striking this moralistic pose, the United States was not to be threatened by the influx of more immigrant groups. This became obvious in a number of special issues of *Newsweek* and *Time* magazines whose surveys conveyed the fact that Americans overall felt that there were too many immigrants, and that this was largely responsible for the weakness of the American economy and quality of life.[20] In the next chapter we shall see how, as with other similar moments of reassessing the ideology of America as sanctuary and melting pot, this provided the occasion for a reevaluation of the capacity of particular racial groups to assimilate and contribute to American life. This re-evaluation is then correlated with inter-national "traits" and dispositions, evincing a reassessment of American interiority and global position.

6 / Disintegrations and Reconsolidations

DURING THE LATE 1980S AND EARLY 1990S, the fear that immigrants, legal and illegal, were flooding the United States and weakening its economic and social fabric reached a peak. The U.S. Civil Rights Commission's report on anti-Asian violence provides a key set of documents regarding the ways in which anti-Asian sentiment proliferated during a period when one would expect that the model minority image would have erased all symptoms of anti-Asian racism. The 1992 Rodney King verdict disclosed as well the persistence of anti-black racism, particularly under Reagan-Bush, and the INS sweeps which used the violence after the verdict as an alibi to conduct massive round-ups and deportations of Latinos revealed perhaps the most significant strain of American anti-immigrant racism. The anti-Latino movement deeply informed popular elections, especially in California, where even "liberals" felt compelled by political expediency to articulate some sort of anti-immigrant stance. Democratic senatorial candidates Barbara Boxer and Diane Feinstein both ran on anti-immigrant platforms, the former suggesting that a trench be built the length of the U.S.-Mexican border and that National Guard troops be used to reinforce the Border Patrol. More funds were to be devoted to hi-tech infrared cameras and helicopter surveillance—nothing would be spared in this era that witnessed at once the evisceration of social programs and a stupendous increase in prison building and the flourishing of a prison industry. The increased fervor over welfare reform, which sought to force more poor into the labor vacuum left by the expulsion of Latino workers, may be read as but part of a general realignment of a racist and classist political economy. The representation of Asians during the Los Angeles rebellion of 1992 provides a particular illustration of one of the functions of the signifier "Asian" within contemporary America.

L.A., Asians, and Perverse Ventriloquisms

> *We can perhaps do better than to take stock directly of the*
> *ideological contents of our age; by trying to reconstitute in*
> *its specific structure the code of connotation of a mode of*
> *communications as important as the press photograph we may*
> *hope to find, in their very subtlety, the forms our society uses*
> *to ensure its peace of mind and grasp thereby the magnitude,*
> *the detours, and the underlying function of that activity.*
>
> —ROLAND BARTHES, "The Photographic Message"

How to derive peace of mind from an image of utter chaos and violence? One of the most conspicuous figures of the L.A. rebellion that circulated among popular radio talk shows, T.V. news reports, and daily and weekly print media was that of the "vigilante Korean." The image of Koreans, and, by extension, Asians in general, formed an integral part of a powerful homology of race, property, violence, and "justice" that significantly reenforced white hegemonic identifications.[1] At the same time, it allowed the effective absence of whites within the framework of representation, thereby affecting the pacification of social trauma remarked upon by Barthes.[2] This news photo emblematizes the *function* of Asian Americans both in the specific public discourses surrounding the L.A. rebellion and within the late twentieth-century American political economy.[3]

Let us examine closely a color photograph that appeared in the May 11, 1992, issue of *Newsweek*: A young Korean American male in the foreground looks askance toward the left of the frame, holding a semiautomatic handgun upright. He is wearing a Malcolm X t-shirt with the caption, "By any means necessary . . ." Depicted beneath that caption on the shirt is a print of a black and white photograph of a black man in a suit and tie holding an automatic rifle, looking down to the right of the frame, peering through a set of blinds out a window. In the background of the *Newsweek* photograph, two red fire engines spray jets of water on a smoldering building; a street sign tells us this is Olympic Boulevard. *Newsweek*'s caption, quoting a Korean American witness to the riots: "This is not America."

How to decipher this intensely overdetermined set of signifiers? The pose seems (too deliberately)[4] to cast the Asian figure into ironic dialogue with the figure of Malcolm X, with reverse angles of vision, of perspective, and of object. Malcolm X guards against the attack of the white police state, while the young Korean American stands in for a police force that withdrew its protection of his property to protect white property against (predominantly) black and Latino

Figure 9. Koreatown during the 1992 Los Angeles riots. Photo by Jean-Marc Giboux, courtesy Gamma Liaison.

looters and burners. The photo in turn engages the caption, for although the caption would attempt to explain, to rationalize the content of the photographic image, the photo gestures toward a discursive space *beyond* and outside it.

The semiotic density engendered in the conjunction of the Malcolm X t-shirt with that Asian body, set within a complex social, economic, and political history that commonly is reduced to the abstractions of "race relations" in the United States, opens up a number of questions that evince the inadequacy of our usual paradigms of interpretation. Indeed, any interpretive strategy not open to the mutual *disruptions* of narrative and image, representation and history, goes only so far in teasing out the crosscurrents of signification at work. We could ask, among other things, how an icon of Black Power has been uprooted from its historical specificity and appropriated, now seeming to sanction and even prescribe counterviolence against blacks and others who might threaten the dominant ideology. That is, how have the words of Malcolm X, aimed at freeing African Americans and protecting them against the intrusive violence of the state, come to legitimize protecting property from blacks and other groups consistently disenfranchised in the judicial and economic machineries of the state, as evinced most emphatically in those days of late April 1992 by the acquittal of the assailants of Rodney King? Furthermore, we could ask how, in this re-scripted context of racial violence and counterviolence, Asian American property has come to stand in for white property. And how can we account for the incommensurateness between the Korean American "vigilante" and the "legitimate" police force to which the vigilante is symbolically correlate?

Finally, what, exactly, are the absent referents *beyond* the frame of the photograph (the metonymies of the photo implicate other buildings, other victims, other agents of violence)? Most important, the text implicates a reader/viewer whose moral sense is assumed to be represented (both in terms of mimetically re-presenting and ideologically speaking on behalf of those absent)[5] in the simple declarative, summary recitation of a Korean American's enunciation, which now *speaks back* to the photo ("This is not America"), creating the illusion that it is articulating the mentality of the photographed subject.[6] But most compelling and confusing in this frame is the particular double inscription between the image and caption on that t-shirt and the body that displays it, the body and the shirt that augments the representation of that multiply significant body (Asian, American, male, merchant, vigilante, etc.)—and their particular materializations in this historical moment.

The questions posed above map out a set of trajectories into the density of this image, a density that I would stress is linked intimately to the liminal position of Asian Americans in the United States. This photograph "documents" a crucial, interstitial element that breaks apart the black/white dichotomy that was the simple image retained in the general account of the events of May 1992.[7] In this photograph, indexes of the violence are eclipsed by the figure in the foreground, a seemingly ancillary player—not a black, or a white, or a Latino, but an Asian.

Why select an Asian for this focal space? The obvious reason is the fact that, supposedly, the main targets of black and Latino rage were Korean American businesses. This was in part explained in the press by the longstanding animosity between Korean Americans and (particularly) blacks. Blacks were especially bitter over the slaying of a black teenage girl by a Korean American grocer over the alleged theft of a bottle of orange juice, and the extremely light sentence meted out to the grocer.[8]

The hierarchy of presence is significant here: an Asian body occupies the foreground in this narrative; blacks are present as second-level images (Malcolm X on the t-shirt). Whites, however, are invisible, somehow not part of "this" America. Thus what is missing in the narrative implicated by this photo/text is any inquiry into the structure of an economic system that historically has placed Asians against blacks and Latinos, and exploits that antagonism in order to construct a displaced rehearsal of a simplified white / black, purely "racial" antagonism. To begin to account for this elision of whites and the restaging of race relations without whites (but nonetheless containing the *function* of a white supremacist ideology channeled through the historically convenient body of Asian America), one must understand the continuity of the function of Asian Americans in the recent U.S. imaginary.

Many have pointed up the parallels between the Watts riots of 1965 and the recent riots in Los Angeles and elsewhere over the Rodney King verdict—one such parallel is that of the ideological function of images of Asian Americans. Between 1966 and 1992 the key elements persist: hardworking, persevering, and not dependent upon state or federal largesse, Asian Americans serve as emblems of the inherent logic of laissez-faire capitalism and the inconsequential nature of race and ethnicity before such a logic.[9]

In 1992, a little over a quarter of a century after Watts, in another "race riot" in the same city, Korean Americans were represented as the frontline forces of the white bourgeoisie. Not only were they successful even under the most oppressive circumstances, they were not afraid to arm themselves against blacks and Latinos to protect what is not only their territory, but also the buffer zone between the core of a multiethnic ghetto and white middle-class America. The locating, real and figurative, of Asians *in between* the dominant and minor is made less tenuous and even rationalized by a particular element that situates Asians within the dominant ideology and frees them of the burden of their ethnicity and race while retaining (for obvious ideological purposes) the signifier of racial difference: the notion of *self*-affirmative action informs the core of the model minority myth.

During the late twentieth century, minorities in the United States have been told to stop complaining about oppression and to start drawing upon inner strengths. This formula conveniently absolves the state of responsibility for social justice, transferring that responsibility to (only) those groups affected negatively by injustice. The particular brand of self-affirmative action that is the linchpin of the model minority myth uses an exaggerated representation of Asians as embodying those "traditional family values" whose lack brought about the L.A. riots, according to Dan Quayle and the Bush administration.[10] Here, the "Asian family structure" represents the perfect apparatus for the reproduction of the ethos of diligent hard work, self-denial, and political quietude. Instead of collective activism outside the family, Asians enjoy self-supporting family units

whose "traditional values" (traced back to Confucian pragmatic education) ultimately triumph over whatever difficulties might lie in their way. As such, Asian
families reaffirm the values of conformity, of deference to civil and familial authority. This representation, of course, writes out a substantial history of social
resistance and protest as well as the wide range of familial structures evident in
the multiple Asian cultures whose insertion into American society has been extremely uneven and varied. Instead, this photograph ends up specifically impli-
cating "traditional family values" within the moral imperative to protect the
sanctity of private *property* that is viewed as the reward for the practice of those
values within a market economy. Indeed, in the aftermath of Watts, during his
campaign for the California governorship, Ronald Reagan told the California
Real Estate Association that fair housing was wrong because the "right of an individual to ownership and disposition of property is inseparable from the right
of freedom itself." [11]

The notion of "traditional family values" is of course an impossibly vacuous notion, since it has no purchase outside of *specific* ideological activities. In this case,
Newsweek's representation of Korean Americans creates a frame that sketches
out the endpoints of a particular narrative linking the personal, familial, and communal to the material objects around which negotiations between and across
those three take place. As the photo in question places the viewer in the middle
of an ongoing activity, eliding any representation of causality and picking up
instead at the point *after which* causality can be taken as relevant (before the
higher and more immediate imperatives of the protection of life, now), the photograph that concludes *Newsweek*'s discussion of the riots, published in the subsequent issue (May 18, 1992, page 30), shows three Korean American women
in mourning, weeping at a funeral. [12] This photograph fills in the end point of
"this" America.

This juxtaposition of photographs of Korean Americans, seeming to form
the essential parameters of their involvement in the Los Angeles uprising, becomes a convenient speculum of the tragic narration of the "traditional family
values" of the dominant culture come up against those who are popularly represented as lacking such virtues. The drama is scripted within an unproblematized idealization of Asians (who thus configured stand in for dominant white
ideologies, to which they have a tenuous and contingent relation) and an equally
essentialized depiction of the black family as "pathological" (and therefore bereft of the property earned by Asians), always on the margins by dint of some
inherent resistance to the ethos so well exemplified by Asians. Both these formations are the products of a process of reification that exculpates the dominant

ideology from its role in setting the stage for the mutual antagonism of ethnic communities.

This use of Asian Americans as a defamiliarized, and hence all the more compelling, image of the "traditional American" is confirmed by Elaine Kim. Kim recounts how *Newsweek* magazine solicited from her an opinion piece on the subject of Korean Americans and the Los Angeles riots. The editor insisted that Kim work into her essay some reference to "Korean-American cowboys," wishing to dramatize the "resistance" of Korean Americans to black violence.[13] Although Kim explains that the carrying of firearms would be something relatively unfamiliar to Koreans (since guns are outlawed in Korea), the opportunity was simply too great for *Newsweek* to pass up. What it perceived was a "photo op" that would neatly draw upon and intensify the model minority myth (self-affirmation, individual initiative, and, now most important, an overriding will to protect the fruits of the free enterprise system). As in 1966, in the coverage of the Rodney King incident Asians are again used as a fulcrum inserted between ethnic groups to leverage hegemonic racist ideology. A particular homology is set in place—Asians against blacks and Latinos as white settlers stood against "pillaging" Indians. The Korean American "cowboy" thus serves as a defamiliarized image of white America's manifest destiny.[14]

The intensely materialistic nature behind this idealization of the Korean American "cowboy" and self-affirmative action is revealed in *Newsweek*'s picturesque prose, which blends a calculatedly limpid style with references combining inventive American know-how, the signs of Korean American success sacrificed to protect the stores, the adaptation of hi-tech personal communications devices to paramilitary purposes, and a relentlessly practical entrepreneurial spirit:

> With the police in disarray, some Koreans formed their own vigilante groups for self-defense. They strapped metal grocery carts together [*Newsweek*'s thinly veiled allusion to "circling the wagons"?] in a line across the parking lot at the Korean Supermarket on Olympic. Then they drew their Volvos, Mercedeses and other high-end cars into a Maginot line. Behind the cars crouched a dozen men with shotguns and pistols. Some had cellular phones strapped to their belts; others set up fields of fire from a supermarket roof. "No trouble," said one of the defenders with a wave. "Come back tomorrow."[15]

In some way, the image serves as a twisted corollary to the image of the beating of Rodney King. If white America[16] was repulsed by the image of the anti-black violence of the King beating, it could react positively, immediately, and with ethical purity when viewing Asian Americans defending themselves against black and Latino looters. And just as Rodney King's beating was supposedly the result of his "controlling the action," so too does black America bear responsibility for violence aimed against them by Korean Americans. Only here there seems no ambiguity in the justness of the accusation. In this photograph this is doubly inscribed—by indices of burning buildings, by a series of articles on the riots, but most immediately by the words of Malcolm X himself—"by any means necessary"—which now come to endorse *repression* of *African Americans* "by any means necessary." The movement of repression/rebellion comes full circle by means of this appropriation and inversion of "necessity."

While it is difficult to condemn acts of self-defense, one should note that what was at stake in the images of Korean American vigilantes guarding their shops was not just life, but as I have been arguing throughout, property, and *particular* property (against a particular threat)—hence the evocativeness of the image.[17] For the riots were as much about the material conditions of economic survival as they were about police brutality—the judgment set into relief the "justice" of Reaganomics as much as the racism of the judicial system.

To sum up: the property so stalwartly guarded thus operated as a *signifier*. It was the product of a particular regimen of capitalism seemingly unfettered by the obstacles of racism and allowed for by political quietism, self-denial, and discipline. All this was condensed in the image of the model minority. As such, non-ethnic viewers could sympathetically identify with particular property, and assume the role of one who had (likewise) acquired such property—for example, a middle-class readership could look at the much-mentioned "high-end" automobiles used by Korean Americans and look into their own garages, imagining that their own cars were trophies of *similar* arduous labor and self-sacrifice, and, by extension, sympathize with the urge to protect such hard-earned objects against those Latino and black rioters whose pathological laziness prevented them from earning such objects "honestly." Thus, even more than any abstract "spirit" of free enterprise, what draws the identificatory moves of the viewer to the image is the notion of the protection of private property. The protection of private property creates a strong identificatory bond between both those who have it in abundance and those who may not, but who have nonetheless accepted the validity of the mechanisms whereby one is to acquire it in U.S. society, and therefore view themselves as *deserving* it.[18]

In the use of private property as a sign of racial and moral superiority, the "representation" of Asian America(ns) overtly coincides with the vested interest of dominant American ideology—in Asian America(ns) it finds a speculum of the function of white dominance. The representation of Asian American protection of property achieves particular weight exactly because it appears to be another "case," *different* from white supremacist ideology. It involves a racially different group, and therefore vindicates the "neutrality" of American capitalism. The supremacy, the ultimate "soundness," of the capitalist economics that have disproportionately favored whites over racial and ethnic minorities now seems colorblind because "yellows" have found it to work in their favor, too. And thus the underlying mechanisms that continue to work against blacks, Latinos, *and* Asians, too, are made invisible by the inflationary symbolic of the "model minority."

In U.S. history the Asian has served as a powerful signifier — at first, as a local illustration of European orientalist mythologies, and more than a century later, as a "model minority" used to vindicate American ideology. Nevertheless, there is a hard residue of old-style orientalism — the notion that Asians have no concept of the sanctity of human life (as articulated endlessly during the Vietnam War) plays a crucial role in the representation of the Korean American "cowboy." For if the whites are too "refined," too attached to western Enlightenment notions of law and order, then Asians, genetically bereft of such encumbrances, can act out the primal imperatives of capitalism.[19] Asian Americans provide the prescribed body for the pristine violent strain that America would euphemize in itself but exploit in others. In April 1993, when the federal trial of the Los Angeles police officers was near its end, the media coverage of the event resurrected the "vigilante Korean." So invested was the media in this image that it was used by the *Oakland Tribune* for a story entitled, "Judge chastises media for reporting about possible hung jury." The photo and its caption ("David Chu, manager of the Western Gun Shop in the Koreantown section of Los Angeles, says sales have been brisk as a verdict approaches in the Rodney King beating trial"), has *nothing to do* with the story. Instead, they only add "excitement" to it. We are revisiting exactly the same terrain as mapped out above.

The obvious inversion of property and propriety that takes place across that homology are striking, and forces us to return to the caption and its implied question: what is "America"? What legitimates such relations of property and race? Or better yet, "what have 'we' come to be?" And this query is both prompted by and articulated within the caption chosen for the photograph, which sets off a quest for a narrative capable of representing "America." This narrative is generated precisely in a dual semiotic *twice* articulated in the photo/caption.

In his early essay on "The Photographic Message,"[20] Barthes explains how the press photo inverts the "traditional" relation between text and image:

The text constitutes a parasitic message designed to connote the image, to 'quicken' it with one or more second-order signifieds. In other words, and this is an important historical reversal, the image no longer *illustrates* the words; it is now the words which, structurally, are parasitic on the image. . . . Formerly, the image illustrated the text (made it clearer); today, the text loads the image, burdening it with a culture, a moral, an imagination. $(25-26)$ [21]

However, in this particular case, the "texts" and "images" are exactly *doubled*—there is a scene quoted within the image, comprised itself of photo/caption. Moreover, in both instances there is a significant rupture (instead of collusion) between image and text along the grain of history and ideology.

The double function of the *Newsweek* photo/caption, which exploits *both* what Barthes calls the "traditional" direction of commentary (the image does, in fact, give illustration to the impossible-to-visualize declaration, "This is not America"); *and* the "modern" relationship between text and image—the text "burdens" the photograph with meaning. In the embedded image as well we find a similar doubling—the text ("By any means necessary") functions as the designator of the scene, and the image of Malcolm X particularizes the universal instrumentality referred to in the caption. In the two text/images at hand, this reciprocal effect produces "clarity" through its transparent illustrative designation—the raised gun supersedes the now vacant generalization. Yet it also points to that which it cannot designate: the chaotic scene at Olympic Boulevard eclipses the verbal statement, "This is not America," betraying an inability to articulate that which *is* America—an object perhaps only recoverable through another mythic construction. And such a construct is found within the interstices of the quotation, significantly made more compelling from an immigrant perspective. It again accentuates the difference between the idealistic (and successful) Asian American and the cynical, destructive black or Latino, who denies the "America" envisioned by the other.

Nevertheless, despite this seeming racial saturation, what this photograph actually performs is an *evasion* of racial terms, rather than their instantiation and confirmation. And as such, this photo/caption serves as an exemplary text of pacification. Barthes goes on to note:

Certainly situations which are normally traumatic can be seized in a process of photographic signification but then they are indicated via a rhetorical code which distances, sublimates and pacifies them. (30)

Having set up this problematic of the pacification of photographic "trauma" via the specifics of text/image rhetoric, we can begin to unpack more precisely the narrative that informs the composition of both the inset photo/text and its frame.

I return to the photograph within the *Newsweek* photo, the photograph of Malcolm X reproduced on the t-shirt, which was originally published in *Ebony* magazine. Peter Goldman asserts that this photograph was part of a series of staged photographs that Malcolm X set up to deter assaults by both white racists and his black enemies.[22]

Malcolm X's most well-known pronouncement on blacks arming themselves regards such acts as necessary for self-defense against racist attacks in an era when the police refuse to grant blacks equal protection:

> I must say this concerning the great controversy over rifles and shotguns. The only thing I've ever said is that in areas where the government has proven itself either unwilling or unable to defend the lives and the property of Negroes, it's time for Negroes to defend themselves. Article number two of the constitutional amendments provides you and me the right to own a rifle or a shotgun. . . . If the white man doesn't want the black man buying rifles and shotguns, then let the government do its job. It is constitutionally legal to own a shotgun or a rifle. ("The Ballot or the Bullet")

Now the context for Malcolm X's endorsement of arms does not completely coincide with the caption chosen for the t-shirt, which uses his general statement regarding the liberation of blacks to endorse specifically violent means. Goldman recounts a conversation between Malcolm X and a black reporter that provides a specific context for that enunciation:

> I'm for the freedom of the 22 million Afro-Americans by any means necessary. By any means necessary. I'm for a society in which our people are recognized and respected as human beings, and I believe that we have the right to resort to any means necessary to bring that about. (222)

The marketing production of the t-shirt (and I suspect this must be a poster as well) uses the vagueness of the original quotation and the unmarked context of the photograph to create a highly provocative endorsement of armed defense.

Ironically, set in the context of *Newsweek*'s photo, Malcolm X's comments on why and when blacks should arm themselves now legitimizes the case for Korean Americans to arm themselves against blacks: the police were drawn back from Koreatown by Daryl Gates, leaving it to burn. Hence, Korean Americans faced the necessity of protecting their property themselves "by any means necessary."

But however complex, fragmented, and twisted the crosscurrents of violence and oppression may be, staged in this photograph as involving the opposition black/Asian, the condensation of this ideology in this overdetermined representation neatly elides the key agent of this antagonism and leaves it free both to stand apart as spectator, and enjoy a vindication of its political economy. This distantiation and identification is reproduced in the formal structure of the photograph—there are no whites, there is one Asian, and an image of a black torn out of its historical context and appropriated to speak for another, who in turn serves the function of the absented dominant. We find an eerie convergence in the double captions—the decontextualized voice of Malcolm X meets the voice of the Korean American ventriloquized through the Asian body in the photograph. But any investigation into the "origin" of this enunciation must take into account the apparatuses of production outlined by Barthes that, in this series of displacements, shift the trauma of racial violence onto Asian America.[23]

I am not suggesting that the actual protagonists in this siege were or are simply passive, manipulated subjects. Nor do I wish to suggest that this very real event was somehow only an illusionary construct. And, perhaps most important, I do not want to suggest that the shift of violence onto Asian Americans is only symbolic—far from that. I do want to widen the scope of our inquiry, however, to see how the narratives that are set into motion by these text/images implicate as well the mechanisms by which the dominant ideology comes to account for, pacify, and use to its own advantage a seemingly inexplicable event, while seeming to stand outside and beyond violence. The photograph before us both solicits and constructs a *narration* of cause and effect, agency and rationale, that allows the political, economic, and ideological apparatuses that set the stage for the Los Angeles uprising of the summer of 1992 to obscure their workings. In particular, what is at stake here is not only the recovery of the specific histories that are written out of the picture, but also the programmatic effects of such representations as this photograph that draw upon and in turn solidify (in their powerful silences) structures of feeling around the issues of race, ethnicity, class, capital, and social justice.

Differentiating the National

In late-twentieth-century America, both liberals and conservatives resorted to particular rhetorical arguments to underwrite their mutual desire to ride the tide of anti-Latino sentiment. The liberal argument ingeniously tapped into the argument of pro-black civil rights. For example, in the October 1992 issue of *The Atlantic*, Jack Miles's article, "Blacks vs. Browns: The Struggle for the Bottom Rung" comments on Latinos taking away low-skill jobs from blacks: "By an irony that I find particularly cruel, Latino immigration may be doing to American blacks at the end of the twentieth century what European immigration did to them at the end of the nineteenth" (66). Miles's alibi for shutting the door on Latinos is founded on one version of American history at the exclusion of another. Playing on liberal guilt over the history of slavery under which blacks have been oppressed in the United States, he conveniently fails to ask how it is that there is a "bottom rung" that must be, perforce, "battled over" by these particular contestants. Rather than critiquing the unequal and contradictory nature of democratic capitalism, Miles focuses solely upon the fact of scarcity and the primary obligation white America has to compensate blacks. This ingenious liberal elision of racial dynamics in the United States for the sake of opportunistically jumping on the anti-immigrant bandwagon seems pale compared to the raw exhibition of racism found in conservative accounts. Yet it is effective in its own way in assuaging the guilt of liberals who are backed into a defense of exclusion and deportation. Rather than turn their gaze on the sources of scarcity, they opt for a facile treatment of immigration issues.

The effectiveness of such a rationalization in the liberal camp can indeed be correlated with a conservative argument that, true to form, calls upon a brand of rationalization found in the early twentieth century. Nonetheless, the conservative argument was repetition with a difference, for it explicitly linked its analysis of U.S. racial issues to a *global* text. In the September 1992 issue of *The National Interest*, Lawrence Harrison harks back to essentialist notions of racial characteristics and points to a particular vision of the contemporary world for confirmation:

> Immigrants of some ethnic and national groups do better than others. The principal explanation lies in cultural values and attitudes. There is a close correlation, for example, between the impressive economic and social development of Taiwan and South Korea since World War II, and of Japan since 1868, on the one hand, and the performance of Chinese, Korean, and Japanese immigrants in the United States, on the other. The Confucian ethos has profoundly influenced all three nations. Similarly, the poor performance of Mexican immigrants has reflected Mexico's—and Latin America's—history of slow growth, social inequality, and limited political participation, the chief consequences of the traditional, anti-progressive Iberian value system. (40)

Given their particular cultural and racial roots, certain groups are equipped differently for late capitalism.[24] But the essential element is not only this culturally determined predisposition, but its *modification* as it is introjected into western democracy: "The success of the East Asians in America is testimony to the virtues of an open political and economic system in which fair play is increasingly a reality." He goes on to elaborate this point:

> Immigrants from China, Japan, and Korea have brought the positive values of work, education, merit and family orientation—similar to the Protestant ethic —to an environment that substantially unburdens them of the negative Confucian values of authoritarianism, hegemony of the bureaucrats, and disdain for economic activity. They have made a successful transition to the American cultural mainstream, notwithstanding a history of racism and persecution. Asian-Americans today inject a commitment to achievement and excellence into a society where, over recent decades those values have eroded. (46)

This citation presents two common motifs: first, the argument that the introjection of Asians into America is fortuitous precisely because of the correlation of Confucianism with Protestantism. For example, John Brademas, then-president of New York University, is quoted in an article explaining Asian American success by the president of the Asia Society, Robert B. Oxnam: "When I look at our Asian-American students, I am certain that much of their success is due to Confucianism. And the more I see of Confucianism in action, the more I think it is the mirror image of the Protestant ethic."[25] This happy coincidence raises the question, however, of where "Confucianism" ends and the "Protestant ethic" begins, or whether, indeed, it is possible to ascribe Asian success solely to one or the other.[26]

But a second, equally essential theme is that "traditional Asian values" are specifically set within the *recontextualization* and historicization of Asia *in* America. The notion is that this process divests old-world "tradition" of its negative aspects even as it retains and adapts its positive ones. This is a common element in the twentieth-century production of the model minority. For example, Winnick argues that coming to America allowed both Jews and Asians to rid themselves of those aspects of their traditional cultures that could not conjoin with modernity in America:

> Both East European Jews and Asians have flourished far better after emigrating than they did in their smothering countries of origin. The submerged capacities of a striving people rise soonest, and perhaps only, where there is a sufficient dose

of economic and political freedom, where governance by caste and command are least, where rewards are distributed by merit and performance instead of ascription and birth. Thus, the Chinese diaspora fared demonstrably better in (pre-1975) South Vietnam and Indonesia than on the Communist Chinese mainland, still better in the benign autocracies of Taiwan and Singapore, exuberantly in economically unbridled Hong Kong, and best of all within the free and stable polities of the United States and Canada.[27]

This triumphant declaration is clearly used more to argue for the benevolent effects of American democratic capitalism than it is to "explain" Asian success, but the claims made regarding the reward structure of the United States and the success of a remarkably undisaggregated Asian population abroad do not hold up to closer scrutiny. In short, they ignore the persistence and reproduction of the elites, of those who indeed benefit particularly from government intervention (Winnick conveniently fails to mention corporate welfare, for example, and the international aid meted out by the United States to "friendly" governments and businesses in Asia). Now certainly there are a number of success stories of the rags-to-riches type that always are set forth to illustrate the essential and universal benevolence of the American system, but they are exceptional in every sense of the word. Few pay attention to the vast number of Asian immigrants who were not born of the upper classes and whose experience in the United States has been quite different. Finally, the persistent ability of racism to "reforeignize" Asian Americans, as evinced in the 1996 presidential campaign finance scandal that had Asian Americans redefined as "Asians," is conveniently ignored.

Instead, the perfect marriage between Confucianism and Protestantism remains in the foreground, especially as this infusion is seen to have a salutary effect on an America that has become complacently decadent. This argument is proffered by post-Confucian proponents such as Tu Wei-ming. Writing on Asian Americans for the *Far Eastern Economic Review*, Susumu Awanohara reports:

Sociologist Tu Weiming had his own diagnoses and prescriptions for the U.S. While extolling the strengths of America's civil society, political process, due process of law and its freedoms, Tu added: "We also see there is sickness in the American soul and poverty of the American spirit." He listed "economism, egoism, legalism, anti-intellectualism, triumphantism and exclusivism" as ailments and shortcomings. Tu suggested that Asia's "less individualistic, less self-interested, less adversarial, less legalistic" approach to organising society might have some application in the U.S.[28]

It is no surprise that Awanohara mistakes Tu for a sociologist (he is a Chinese historian at Harvard), for his pronouncements clearly are meant to serve as sociological data. Yet this primordialism is rarely found in such unadulterated form in contemporary China. However, it is precisely this vision of "Confucianism" that buttresses the discourse of the model minority. We should recall the "openness" of the psychic identity of America invented to meet the demands of the modern world as discussed in the first chapter. In the late twentieth century, "Confucianism" provides the general term that implies the common ground of Asian/America.

And nearly everyone seems to be an expert on "Confucianism," a key signifier in this social and racial discourse. Throughout its evocations, "Confucianism" is simultaneously envisioned as a particular product of the ancient "Orient" and a social form eerily like "our own." This produces the notion of Asians "out-whiting the whites," since "Confucianism" seems a primordial genetic predisposition, passed on from generation to generation and only strengthened by its transplantation in the free soil of American capitalism. This perception is so widespread, it taps into so many anxieties and desires and serves so many discursive purposes, that it appears across a number of discursive fields. Not only do "sociologists" articulate the argument of the salvation of America by its Asian immigrants, psychologists do too. This appearance is of particular significance, as it evinces the interpenetration of the national, the ideological, and the psychological in the popular imagination. For example, we find this excerpt from a 1986 article in *Psychology Today*:

> Politicians love to make speeches about the values that made this country great. A firm belief in the value of education and hard work, they tell us, is distinctly American. But these beliefs are not much in evidence among those of us who proudly sing that we were "born in the U.S.A." We may believe in talent, in luck or in prayer, but these studies suggest that we don't much believe in education and hard work.
>
> These values are to be found, however, among our immigrant citizens. This creates an interesting dilemma for those who would close the door on the outside world, for to keep out immigrants is to keep out the very values that are supposed to be as American as apple pie. It would seem that if we want apple pie, we will have to import it.[29]

Yet even as "America" seems ceded to the new immigrant, this picture is not complete without noting that the influx of highly successful, motivated Asian immigrants is attributed to the hyperproductivity of an imported *American* educational system in Asia: "After World War II, American-style mass education was introduced into many Asian countries. . . . Countries such as Taiwan, Korea, India and the Philippines now produce more college graduates than their economies can absorb, and many professionals come to the United States in hopes of using their training more fully than at home."[30] (What this article fails to mention is that the establishment of American educational systems in East Asia after the Second World War was part of the U.S.'s Cold War policy, which coupled educational institutions with specific economic policies; we will address this issue and its effects in detail in the next chapter.) We recognize here the dual phenomena of projection and introjection, the transposition of American ideology and its apparatuses abroad and the introjection of Asian subjectivities in various forms into the United States. In recent discussions on "new immigrants," the focus has been on a particularly identified immigrant. Although most articles and essays on the subject take care to mention poverty-stricken refugees and poor immigrants as well, the growing fascination seems to be with the wealthy, as a counterexample to the "huddled masses" and as a new population that exercises more than a merely spiritual regenerative effect on the United States. (In Chapter 10 I will return to this discussion of "post-Confucianism" as a consolidating discourse in East Asian regional economies and its relevance to Asian America; here I will remain focused on its domestic articulation.)

Not only do the new immigrants from Asia bring skills and education, they bring capital badly needed to revitalize a weakened America. In this scenario, the "huddled masses" become indispensible investors. This transformation is not lost on journalists, who repeatedly deployed the rhetoric of inversion: "The Statue of Liberty invites 'your tired, your poor, your huddled masses yearning to breathe free.' Late this year, the United States will pursue a new category of immigrants: wealthy foreigners willing to invest $1 million in the country. . . . 'We are presently trying to identify ways to ensure that California will receive the lion's share of the investments that Asian immigrants are willing to make in the U.S.,' said Ron Gray, the lieutenant governor's press secretary."[31] In July 1992, *Business Week* declared: "It is still those 'huddled masses yearning to breathe free' who will keep the American dream burning bright for most of us."[32] Rather than view the model minority as simply the product of the transposition of Asia (and "Asian values") to America, it is better to regard it as being imbricated within the complex circulation of Asian and American ideologies, and being called forth within the particular material histories that those who rush to equate Confucianism with Protestantism refuse to acknowledge.

This produces an interesting set of negotiations: if Asians are following the Jewish pattern of higher education, family tradition, and even leisure time (one journalist insists that the Jews have now become complacent—they've taken up sports. Asians haven't, yet), *and* Asians are successful because they share values with the Protestant ethic, then Jews and Protestants are as similar as Asians are to any one of them, no? Or is it that Asians are successful because they have synthesized the best elements of Jewish and Protestant tradition? The answer to this question depends on whom one asks.

In contradistinction to Asian success abroad, and its projection into a reading of Asian Americans in America, again we have the Latino, whose "failure" is ascribed to his "roots" across the border and across the sea:

> A principal element of Hispanic culture is familialism—emphasis on the interests of the family to the exclusion of the interests of the community and country. . . . Several other aspects of traditional Iberian culture are the major obstacles of progress in Latin America and Mexico: an excessive individualism, particularly of the upper classes, that expresses itself in authoritarianism in the one hand, and social irresponsibility on the other (passivity in the lower classes is also a consequence); mistrust of, even hostility toward, those outside the family; a flexible ethical code, and negative attitudes toward work, saving, and entrepreneurship, in part the consequence of a present-oriented, zero-sum world view. Thomas Sowell observes that "the goals and values of Mexican-Americans have never been centered on education." (44)

The crucial element here is the comparative one: while Asians flourish in the United States because it provides a particularly liberating and enabling location for a post-Confucian entrepreneurship (which has specifically therapeutic effects on the American spirit and economy), Latinos find the United States barren soil because they lack the essential germ of modernity. It is therefore not even necessary to argue for Latino exclusion. Closing the border, in fact, can be rationalized as an act of humanity, for it spares the Latino the false hope that he could succeed in the United States. Sorry—it's all in the genes. Yet equally remarkable is how this rationalization extends the body of evidence from the domestic to the international—the *world* is now a text to be read as confirmation of American racial ideology. The author assumes the equal penetration of late capitalism across the globe; the ability to perform under its conditions attests to each race's potential for survival. The vilification of Latino looters in the L.A. rebellion of 1992 and the martyrdom of the Korean small businessman thus are rearticulations of a logic of racial differentiation that can be traced to the early part of this century, but they each take on the particular contours of American ideologies of the late twentieth century.

Cross-referencing the foreign and domestic can also be seen in a unique foreign policy proposal offered by Gore Vidal at a P.E.N. conference in 1985. He assesses the state of the American empire:

> We are now at the end of the twentieth century. England, France and Germany have all disappeared from the imperial stage. China is now reassembling itself, and Confucius, greatest of political thinkers, is again at the center of the Middle Kingdom. Japan has the world money power and wants a landmass; China now seems ready to go into business with its ancient enemy. . . .
>
> There is only one way out. The time has come for the United States to make common cause with the Soviet Union. The bringing together of the Soviet landmass (with all its natural resources) and our island empire (with all its technological resources) would be of great benefit to each society, not to mention the world. . . . The Soviet Union and our section of North America combined would be a match, industrially and technologically, for the Sino-Japanese axis that will dominate the future just as Japan dominates world trade today. . . . The alliance of the two great powers of the Northern Hemisphere will double the strength of each and give us, working together, an opportunity to survive, economically, in a highly centralized Asiatic world.[33]

In a later article he summarizes his conclusion:

> For America to survive economically in the coming Sino-Japanese world, an alliance with the Soviet Union is necessary. After all, the white race is a minority race with many well-deserved enemies, and if the two great powers of the Northern Hemisphere don't band together, we are going to end up as farmers — or, worse, mere entertainment — for the more than one billion grimly efficient Asiatics.[34]

So powerful is this imagined conglomeration of "Asiatic" forces, drawing on Yellow Peril images that we traced to the late 1920s in Chapter 1 — Chinese mass and Japanese technologies, both driven by Confucian fortitude and single-mindedness — that America must ally itself with its Cold War foe in a last, desperate measure. (Vidal's comments may have inspired popular novelist Tom Clancy's 1994 narrative, *Debt of Honor*, which imagines that a U.S.-Japan trade war turns into a world war pitting Japan, India, and China against the U.S. and a reconstituted Soviet Union).[35]

In response to an angry letter of protest from Evans Chen of *China News Daily*, Vidal replied: "In my context, 'one billion grimly efficient Asiatics' is an ironic twist." He tries to disguise his racist remarks based on the notion that he was simply saying that the west might be subjected by the East as we subjected it: "As we have made the Asiatics suffer during the past two centuries, so might they be inclined, *economically*, to make us suffer once the Sino-Japanese alliance takes place." He then tries to, once again, articulate his plan for survival: "I propose that the United States and the Soviet Union—two economic wrecks, thanks to the arms race—as the two great powers of the Western Hemisphere, unite in order to compete, *economically*, with the Asiatic world. That is hardly racism. It is common sense." [36] There are several problems with Vidal's defense: for instance, he attempts to sidestep the issue of racism even as he insists (despite previous protesting letters) on using the term "Asiatic." But most significantly he tries to weasel his argument by insisting that he is only referring to an "economic" attack, even though in his first essay, he describes modern "warfare" as precisely economic: "Wars of the sort that the Four Horsemen [Alfred Thayer Mahan, Brooks Adams, Teddy Roosevelt, and Henry Cabot Lodge] enjoyed are, if no longer possible, no longer practical. Today's conquests are shifts of currency by computer, and the manufacture of those things that people everywhere are willing to buy." [37]

The image of the Asian as particularly well-equipped, by dint of "Confucian" discipline and rigor coupled with his ascension into the economic and political spheres of western modernity, to become the primary exponent of capitalism, thus informs the rearrangement of domestic and foreign political economies. The particular shape of these rearticulations of Yellow Perilism and model minorities are shaped by the specific material histories of a United States having to grapple with the effects of its collapse in late capitalism. In this scenario, the figure of the Asian takes on the contours of the economic survivor of the wreckage of modernity.

But no matter how "ideal" a subject might be constructed around the figure of the Asian, as noted above there must be "flaws" posited in the Asian as a way to reparticularize "America" and block the Asian/American predication. By inventorying them we might discover the particular compensatory strategies used to salvage American ideology. In a move that parallels the criticism that Asians applying to elite universities were not "well-rounded," and that Asians climbing the corporate ladder lacked essential top managerial qualities, critics responding to the success of Japan in the world economy had to particularize both the Japanese and the Americans in order to construct two types of "success" and thereby downplay Asian success and rehabilitate America. One of the most explicit examples of such a strategy of redefining America via a comparative, exceptionalizing analysis of America to Asia is James Fallows's 1989 liberal polemic, *More Like Us: Making America Great Again*.

In a climate filled with talk about the demise of America as the world's great-est economic power and Japan's ascension to that position, a plethora of books appeared suggesting that U.S. businesses might emulate the Japanese business style. This prescription bled into one regarding the rescue of American society in general. "Confucianism" was perceived as a convenient signifier for an im-portable mode of authoritarianism that could substitute for all those moral codes that America had formerly relied upon for its cohesion and order: the business sector was simply one of the many spheres that would benefit from such disci-pline and loyalty. The private space of the family unit, especially of the lower classes and racial minorities, was also in need of a neo–Neo Confucianism which remained (and remains) altogether vaguely defined. One of the classic and pio-neering texts in this regard is Vogel's *Japan as Number One*. While, ultimately, Vogel's argument follows exactly the trajectory of Petersen's book (emulat-ing but finally problematizing Japan and thereby maintaining the specificity of America), Vogel goes to some length to argue the *commensurability* of Japan and America. Herein we find a particularly vivid articulation of Asian/America:

> While Japanese practices are in many ways significantly different from American ways, they are surprisingly consistent with America's basic values. America val-ues free enterprise, and even more of Japan's gross national product is located in the private sector than is America's. America is committed to freedom of speech and freedom of the press, and so is Japan. America strives for a more equal society, and although the Japanese have higher requirements for performance before granting underprivileged groups equality, they have exerted themselves in reducing differentials of opportunity and have achieved income differentials smaller than America's. Japan is group-oriented, but as George Lodge points out, communitarianism is an integral part of the American tradition, going back to the early New England village. America's many voluntary associations, its history of community organization, and the positive value it attaches to teamwork suggest that group-oriented activities, if not dominant, are at least not alien to the Amer-ican tradition. (254f)

In contradistinction, Fallows, drawing on both his own family's background and his experiences as a journalist in Japan, argues for American exceptional-ism. He characterizes the emulative discourse of contemporary pro-Japan ad-vocates thus:

> Since the publication, in 1979, of Ezra Vogel's *Japan as Number One*, the idea that America should be more like Japan has been a constant theme in American po-litical and intellectual life. American industrial planning should be more like MITI's. American schools should be more rigorous, like Japan's. American labor

relations should be more consensual. American companies should treat their employees more like family and take the long, strategic view. Since the American
work ethic and American management values have let us down, we should emulate those of the Japanese. (46f)

This, according to Fallows, is a simplistic and unthoughtful reaction to America's weakened condition: the way to "make America great again" is to be "more
like us"; that is, to reconnect with what has historically distinguished America
and realize that the way of the future should not be along the Japanese path
(which, Fallows insists, like both Petersen and Vogel, can actually only be taken
by the Japanese), but along a road uniquely American: "The purpose of this book
is to remind Americans of how unusual our national culture is, and of why it is
important that we not become a 'normal' society" (1).[38]

In the course of his narrative, it becomes clear that what Fallows means by
"normal" is exactly a predictable, convention-bound society: "America will be
in serious trouble if it becomes an ordinary country, with people stuck in customary, class-bound roles in life" (3). Of all the national cultures in the world,
America's, claims Fallows, is characterized by a productive chaos, an element
of unpredictability. In contrast to the "Japanese Talent for Order" (the title of
his second chapter), he poses the "American Talent for Disorder" (that of the
following chapter). Rather than emulate a nation of rigid bureaucracies and entrenched elites (as he describes in his seventh chapter, "Confucianism Comes to
America"), Fallows argues that the American spirit has always flourished under
a condition of radical freedom, free from government interference in social life,
archaic allegiances to extended families and traditional ethnic identifications,
free from the strictures of mandated religion. It is precisely such freedom that
underwrites American mobility and guarantees that all vestiges of Old World
caste and class systems are jettisoned in the exhilarating rush to modernity.

Like Petersen, Fallows not only greatly admires the Japanese, but also argues
that the very things that produce such seemingly successful social subjects are
particular to the Japanese historical, racial, and cultural situation. But, unlike
the conservative Petersen, Fallows the liberal is careful to explain how the very
things Americans admire in the Japanese run contrary to the true values of
America: their sense of family loyalty and obligation creates uncreative conformists; their national pride is born of deep-rooted racist chauvinism. While
Petersen downplays such negative aspects of what he has construed as Japanese
"culture," for Fallows they demarcate a radical and definitive difference, and this
allows him to break out of the contradictory mode of the model minority myth
that compromises Petersen's disquisition.

Fallows's greatest attention is not, however, to the American spirit, but to the national political economy, and, by extension, the global economy. He argues that America's economic well-being is dependent on what he (after Schumpeter) calls "the creative destruction" of its capitalist system: "'Capitalism' usually calls up images of big machines or powerful financiers or perhaps class war, but what capitalism really means is change" (52). Upon performing this romantic reduction of capitalism to mere "change," Fallows proposes perpetual revolution driven by each individual's challenge to the status quo according to his or her particular goals (which might, indeed, change frequently according to whatever wrinkles might appear). What distinguishes America is that it provides the most fertile ground for a creative capitalism that thrives on such ad hoc, inspirational intuitions. While the Japanese seem to have gained economic superiority over the United States, the American model has the advantage in the long run. Simply put, and despite the fact that he never mentions the term "late capitalism," the American spirit of spontaneous, creative, capitalistic mobility conjoins perfectly with the flexible character of late capitalism. While Japan will remain mired in nationalist priorities and overly orderly methodologies, American "individualism" (and this individualism is but one step away from a *post*national individualism that is consonant with late capitalism's transnational corporate view) will carry America into the twenty-first century. In short, we have an argument on which national culture, America's or Japan's, is best equipped for a late-capitalist globalized economy, the key terms vacillating between American "flexibility" (Fallows) and Japanese ability to synthesize and discipline (Petersen).[39] By comparing the two terms we derive a clearer sense of the historical specificity of their analyses, the nature of Asian modeling, and their application of these analyses to the redefinition of "America."

Two things are crucial to recognize in Fallows's narration. First, as we have noted, is his rationalization for the rehabilitation of America in the face of Japanese economic power. "We" can only rebuild our economic strength if we recognize what made America great in the past—this same element will make it great "again" well into late capitalism. Second, even as he differentiates Japan from America (order versus disorder, and so on), there is an implicit argument that echoes prior articulations of Asians as the model minority: while "Asia," tied down to a bureaucratized Confucian system, will be overtaken by a more vital and imaginative "west," Asian *Americans* might well contain the perfect measure of both cultures. Specifically, rather than relegate them to the margins of the state, as Petersen does writing for a conservative agenda in the 1960s, Fallows's late-twentieth-century liberalism embraces Asian Americans as another successfully assimilated immigrant group.

Indeed, to the consternation of both liberals and conservatives, Fallows uses social Darwinism to rebuff arguments against increased immigration.[40] Brushing aside the notion that immigrants will breed fear and resentment, especially among racial minorities, Fallows remarks, "America's long-term strategic secret is that it can get the most out of people by putting them in surprising situations. Competition from other Americans is the source of most of this ultimately healthful disruption, but a continual supply of new competition is invigorating too" (204). This simplistic and euphemistic passage would nonetheless seem to still place Asians at a disadvantage, since they would remain under the sway of their native country's Confucianist strictures and traditional prejudices. Yet this is not so. Fallows describes the case of "the Nguyen family," whom he met in 1982. The father worked hard at menial manufacturing jobs in Los Angeles after leaving the refugee camps. Then, he had a "stroke of blind luck":

> In the resettlement office he bumped into an American refugee official whom he'd known in the camp. She said they needed more office workers to handle new arrivals. Although Nguyen still did not speak English smoothly, she agreed to put him in language school while starting him at $660 a month.
>
> From this point on, the Nguyen family saga had all the classic elements of the Cuomo or Dukakis family's rise: sacrifice, study, ambition, frugality, achievement based on family pride. (102)

This instance is steeped in a mystified notion of "luck" that is heavily reliant on the classic American narrative ("he had a stroke of blind luck, like those in Horatio Alger novels"); yet Fallows is careful to point up that "luck" must be complemented by individual effort ("the Nguyen family saga had all the classic elements of the Cuomo or Dukakis family's rise"). This, then, is the particular amalgam that distinguishes America and folds the Asian American narrative into the general immigrant narrative of America.

On one hand, Fallows argues closely for the particularity of nation, history, and culture. America's exceptionalism is established in Fallow's portrayal of America as that space wherein all the specificities of an individual's *past* identifications are erased under the imperatives of "change":

> Certainly there is little evidence in Asia or Africa that people can rise above racial, ethnic, or tribal divisions. But, to return to the point on which this book began, America *is* abnormal. It faced the challenge of immigration in much more intense form a century ago; and instead of being weakened, it was enriched. . . . Many of those now considered part of "mainstream" white America are descended from people seen as totally alien when they poured in. (206)

This argument neatly slides by the question of race (opening with Asians and Africans but using successfully assimilated white immigrants as his evidence) in order to validate Fallows's assertion that the new world of America should be precisely a class- and color-free realm of free competition and "fair play," which is distinguished from Japan's exclusionist trade policies, calcified caste prejudice, and insiderism. Asian "success" is neutralized and historicized particularly in order that a promising future for America might be articulated through a selective and highly revisionist reading of its past and contemporary history.

Petersen deploys Japanese Americans as a group whose reputed success bears witness to the essential justness and logic of American ideology, yet once they have been exploited as evidence, they must be recontained and neutralized. Fallows addresses a different historical period and approaches the subject from a different ideological perspective. Nevertheless, he employs a similar strategy of containment. Whereas Petersen argues against a liberal revision of public policy in order to retain a racist social and political system, Fallows shrewdly differentiates between Asian Americans, who are deemed worthy of emulation because they have adapted their talents and spirit to the American way, and those Asians in Asia, whose skills and ethic of hard work will always be mired in Confucian conformity and thus always be subordinated, ultimately, to the independent, individualistic spirit of America. The Asian American is precisely the Asian American purged of Asia. Petersen's conservative vision has Asian American success brought back into the realm of the unexceptional, so as to allow whites to regain hope of yet matching and overstepping Asian American success; Fallows reasserts American exceptionalism over and against the rise of Japan as a major economic player. In both cases, we witness a careful manipulation of the ratio of Asian to Asian American, deeply informed by a desire to rehabilitate the American state in the midst of decline and doubt. Both these manipulations are predicated upon a drawing a particular line between "Asian" and "American" that insists upon their separateness.

In 1994, Fallows published a book devoted solely to detailing the economic system of East Asia: *Looking at the Sun: The Rise of the New East Asian Economic and Political System*. This time, after describing the rise of Japan and the "phototropic" gravitational pull exerted by Japan over other East Asian states,[41] he counsels the west in general to "be more like us": "Western societies should first concentrate on whether and how to remake themselves. . . . Today's Western societies should take the steps they deem sufficient to protect their interests. . . . This does not mean imitating techniques that have proven successful in Asia; in some cases it may actually mean doing the reverse." For example, instead of insisting on national "purity," as Japan does, Fallows claims we should "absorb the energies of people from other parts of the world."[42] As vampirish as this sounds, Fallows is trying to be liberal. He goes on to say, "The most important response to the Asian achievement will come in the United States, if it is to come at all. . . . The United States resembles a handful of nations . . . in believing that it can absorb immigrants into a multicultural society; most European and Asian countries are suspicious of this attempt."[43] In other words, liberal multiculturalism is an indispensable political and economic tool for the west. We find thus a *national* argument for America elaborated into a "cultural" one in which the west is posed against the east. America's project to strengthen itself should be a model for western civilizations in general. Yet liberal multiculturalism drew an immediate and negative response from conservatives who saw it as a threat to American civilization, rather than its elaboration.

In the middle and late 1990s, a number of books stepped into the "anxiety gap" closed briefly by the disintegration of the Soviet Union and the fall of the Berlin Wall, which were celebrated in Francis Fukuyama's "end of history" thesis.[44] If communism was neutralized as a threat, then something else was to take its place in defining an essential ideological threat to the United States. These books subscribe to the same general logic as those others we've examined in this chapter—defining and neutralizing Asia, drawing particular borders around America, and assuming the particular essential contents thereof. One such book was Joel Kotkin's *Tribes*, which posited diasporic "tribes" penetrating and restructuring national spaces. South Asians in the United States are described as the "new Calvinists," and the Chinese diaspora in terms of "spacemen" who "have landed." The new global economy will be organized around such networks and affiliations that transgress national boundaries and force a revision of any understanding of national ethos. We will return to a more detailed discussion of transnationalism and the revision of America in later chapters. Here I want simply to use Kotkin's book to offset a more paranoid and sharply uneconomical configuration of the globe.

By uneconomical, I mean that, unlike Kotkin's interest in the shaping influence of global economies as diasporic subjects revise national terrains, and Fallows's in the recuperation of American exceptionalism on the economic front, Samuel P. Huntington's controversial 1996 polemic, *The Clash of Civilizations and the Remaking of World Order* subordinates economic concerns to a purely cultural thesis that argues that the multiculturalism heralded by Fallows is the bane of America's existence. His long book spends three hundred pages organizing the world according to "civilizations" in order to launch an attack on domestic cultural politics. More than twenty years before, as a participant in the Trilateral Commission's report on how corporations were to protect their profits in the face of worldwide progressive activism, Huntington claimed: "The essence of the democratic surge of the 1960s was a general challenge to existing systems of authority, public and private. In one form or another, the challenge manifested itself in the family, the university, business, public and private institutions, politics, the government bureaucracy, and the military service. People no longer felt the same obligation to obey those whom they had previously considered superior to themselves in age, rank, status, expertise, character, or talents."[45] This unraveling of respect would be explained in the 1990s as a product of multiculturalism, which filled in the conspicuously missing terms in Huntington's earlier list: racial and gender issues are on the table. There are obviously a great number of provocative claims to be found in this book; here I want to simply draw attention to the way it effectively and antagonistically separates out Asia from America and removes any notion of Asia/America from the "core" of the U.S. nation. Asia is, in this influential book, particularly singled out as the antithesis of "the West."

The basic thesis of the book is that in the post–Cold War world, the great "clashes" of nations will come about not through ideological conflict (capitalism versus socialism), but through "civilizational conflict."[46] In this account the world is made up of Sinic, Japanese, Hindu, Islamic, Western, and Latin American civilizations. To this list Huntington adds "African," but immediately adds a parenthetical comment, "possibly" (45ff). The historical occasion for the book motivates the author's alarm. If clashes are to be civilizational, the west had better wake up. Huntington describes a world in which the west is losing ground universally, while other areas of the world are gaining various sorts of advantage: "The balance of power is shifting: the West is declining in relative influence; Asian civilizations are expanding their economic, military, and political strength; Islam is exploding demographically with destabilizing consequences for Muslim countries and their neighbors; and non-Western countries generally are reaffirming the value of their own cultures" (20). Later on, he specifies both the "quantitative" and "qualitative" advantages of all that which lies outside the west: "Quantitatively Westerners thus constitute a steadily decreasing minority of the world's population. Qualitatively the balance between the West and other populations is also changing. Non-Western peoples are becoming healthier, more urban, more literate, better educated" (85). Ironically, the "rest" have benefited from modernization (or "westernization") while the west has declined.

After extracting the benefits of western modernization, however, these other civilizations have realized the importance of indigenous traditions. Huntington is not bothered by this (aside from his dismay that these countries have not had the good grace to be thankful)—this return to "native traditions" is exactly what he will instruct the west to do. He describes the "second generation" of modern national leaders: "Most of the much larger second generation, in contrast, gets its education at home in universities created by the first generation, and the local rather than the colonial language is increasingly used for instruction. . . . The graduates of these universities resent the dominance of the earlier Western-trained generation and hence most often 'succumb to the appeals of nativist oppositional movements.' . . . We are witnessing the 'end of the progressive era' dominated by Western ideologies and are moving into an era in which multiple and diverse civilizations will interact, compete, coexist, and accommodate each other. This global process of re-indigenization is manifest broadly in the revivals of religion occurring in so many parts of the world and most notably in the cultural resurgence in Asian and Islamic countries generated in large part by their economic and demographic dynamism" (95). The implicit but broad hint here is that the west requires a similar "resurgence," a withdrawal from certain global positions and a retrenchment of conservative (that is, "fundamental") values.

He is particularly troubled by how "culture" follows "power." That is, culture is enabled and disseminated by power, and power is increasingly defined in terms of Asian economic strength: "The economic development of China and other Asian societies provides their governments with both the incentives and the resources to become more demanding in their dealing with other countries. . . . According to most estimates, the Chinese economy will become the world's largest early in the twenty-first century. With the second and third largest economies of the world in the 1990s, Asia is likely to have four of the five largest and seven of the ten largest economies by 2020. By that date Asian societies are likely to account for over 40 percent of the global economic product" (102f).

Economic strength allows for East Asia to consolidate itself and form a trading block unto itself.[47] Is the hidden fear that of a return to the closed ports of the nineteenth century on a globally Asian scale? "While the immediate economic interest of East Asian societies is to maintain access to Western markets, in the longer term economic regionalism is likely to prevail and hence East Asia must increasingly promote intra-Asian trade and investment. . . . It is necessary for Japan and other Asian countries to promote 'Pacific globalism,' to 'global-ize Asia,' and hence to 'decisively shape the character of the new world order'" (109).[48] Economic interests are shared precisely in relation to cultural com-monality: "Meaningful East Asian regional organizations will emerge only if there is sufficient East Asian cultural commonality to sustain them" (132). And this cultural commonality both consolidates Asia and excludes America. Hun-tington claims the existence of "fundamental cultural differences between Asian and American civilizations. . . . The sources of conflict are in fundamental dif-ferences in society and culture" (225).

Given this segmentation of the world into discrete and potentially antago-nistic civilizational spheres, Huntington finds that "the central issue for the West is whether, *quite apart from any external challenges*, it is capable of stopping and re-versing the *internal* processes of decay [emphasis added]" (303). Now, finally, af-ter some three hundred pages, we move to the central (salvational) argument of the book. We have been prepared for this by Huntington's covert emphasis on religion (via the more neutral idea of civilization). Civilization or religion, it all comes down to a fundamentalist belief in the absolutism of national culture and identity. While one might have been led to think that the west is most threatened by teeming masses of Islamics or economically dominant and cliquish Sinics, the real enemy is *within*—the enemy is made up of those individuals who would de-prive the west of precisely that particular fundamental cultural identity to which all civilizations must hold if they are to survive: "Western culture is challenged by groups within Western societies. One such challenge comes from immi-grants from other civilizations who reject assimilation and continue to adhere to and propogate the values, customs, and cultures of their home societies" (304).[49] He then proceeds to define what, exactly, the fundamental identity of the west is. The west is, simply, America:

> Historically American national identity has been defined culturally by the heri-tage of Western civilization and politically by the principles of the American Creed on which Americans overwhelmingly agree: liberty, democracy, individ-ualism, equality before the law, constitutionalism, private property. In the late twentieth century both components of American identity have come under con-centrated and sustained onslaught from a small but influential number of intel-lectuals and publicists. In the name of multiculturalism they have attacked the identification of the United States with Western civilization, denied the existence of a common American culture, and promoted racial, ethnic, and other sub-national cultural identities and groupings. . . . The multicultural trend was . . .

manifested in a variety of legislation that followed the civil rights acts of the 1960s, and in the 1990s the Clinton administration made the encouragement of diversity one of its major goals. (305)

He does not mince words: "Rejection of the Creed and of Western civilization means the end of the United States of America as we have known it. It also means effectively the end of Western civilization" (307).

If, as he argues, "in this new world, local politics is the politics of ethnicity; global politics is the politics of civilizations" (28), then the local politics of ethnicity have to be erased so that the U.S. nation (or, as Huntington deems, the west) can compete for survival globally.[50] The consequences of not so doing are catastrophic: "The leaders of other countries have, as we have seen, at times attempted to disavow their cultural heritage and shift the identity of their country from one civilization to another. In no case have they succeeded and they have instead created schizophrenic torn countries" (306). This leads us to revisit the earlier citations regarding the "second generation": these people have done what is only natural and proper—they have rejected the West and returned to their indigenous heritage: if they had not, they would have suffered the consequences of "schizophrenia."[51]

Huntington's study therefore wipes out any legitimacy for multiculturalism, and in so doing obviously vitiates Asian/American identity. Asians can be Americans only in so far as they conform to Western social codings. Their "Asian" identity, as seen above, is diametrically opposed to "American" values and beliefs. Huntington returns to this theme at the end of his book, specifically rearticulating American difference from Asia as his prime example: "The futures of the United States and of the West depend upon Americans reaffirming their commitment to Western civilization. Domestically this means rejecting the divisive siren calls of multiculturalism. Internationally it means rejecting the elusive and illusory calls to identify the United States with Asia. Whatever economic connections may exist between them, the fundamental cultural gap between Asian and American societies precludes their joining together in a common home" (307).[52] Huntington's agenda is clear from the very title of his book—his argument will exhume essentialist (even fundamentalist) notions of "civilization" in order to rally the west to reclaim its territory (diminished as it is). Externally, that means strengthening the west against foreign incursions and erosion of international policy (that is, "American interests"); internally, it means wiping out any element that would differ from and thereby challenge

Anglo-Saxon hegemony. In both cases, the Asian/American predication is closed off absolutely unless, of course, the Asian component is made invisible.

It may be that by tracking the various positions of Asians in America one can achieve a sense of precisely those contradictions that inform American racism. In order to celebrate the triumph of American democracy, it is necessary to have a racial Other whose success bears witness to the legitimacy of such basic notions as upward mobility. Yet even an assimilation into the elite classes cannot erase the mark of racial difference and the psychic and cultural differences that are assumed to accompany it. Such differences are held in reserve, able to be activated and deactivated selectively for different purposes. The figure of the Asian has been used to differentiate and particularize other racial minorities within that space of representation, and acts as well as a *secondary* modeling system. The gap between Asian and American is both elided when it is to the good of the hegemonic to have it disappear, and retained when the minor threatens not only to join the dominant but to overwhelm and force a revision of it.

As Thomas Nakayama points out, the distinction between Asians and Asian Americans is not fixed or firm; instead, Asian Americans are still often regarded as primarily, if not entirely, Asian: "The distinction between 'Asian' and 'Asian American' is quietly ignored. Not only are Asian Americans who have lived in this country for generations treated, discursively, as identical to Asians who have never left Asia, they are often distinguished from 'Americans'."[53] Peter I. Rose, whom we might remember as the series editor for Petersen's *Japanese Americans: Oppression and Success*, asserts nearly twenty years after writing his optimistic preface to that work:

> While more and more Asian Americans have come to represent the best of what those who promulgate "Americanization" would like to create . . . they are not and will not be fully assimilated, at least, not in the foreseeable future. . . . No matter how adaptive in values and aspirations, no matter how similar to whites in mannerisms and actions, Asian Americans cannot be members of the majority.[54]

And yet this is not entirely true for a number of reasons. First, the statement begs the question of what "fully assimilated" would mean. Second, it collapses all Asian Americans, regardless of country of origin, of time in the United States, of class or gender, and so on, into one category. It would be more useful to regard the terrain of Asian America as a shifting one, its hybridity always constituted by a complex set of both interlocking and contradictory elements that show the effects of race, class, gender, ethnicity, and sexuality. Ultimately what drives the ratio of idealization and negation is the particular relationship of power to be distributed across different racial groups in order to create a productive disequilibrium in U.S. society—productive in the sense that it is at once stable and threatened with particular modes of instability that have to be continuously guarded against. This is certainly not to say that historically there might not be a time of Asian Americanization. In this section we have seen "it" taking place variously and consistently, just as we have seen it qualified and reformulated. This dialectical movement will undoubtedly continue to characterize and to produce *various* Asian Americas.

These speculations and hypotheses regarding the precise manner of Asian American assimilation, the ratio of Asian to American, and the possible elements that might cross over, all share in their disregard for the precise material historical inscriptions of Asians in America. In the following section, I move from abstract ideations of Asian America to concrete instantiations, tracing the particular invention of new Asian American spaces in the built environments of modern America. This reconstruction of space witnesses the remapping of the nation according to radical redefinitions of the local and the global, with particular linkages to late capitalism. How have American localities been reshaped according to modern influxes of immigrants and capital? How does urban space reflect new social structures which in turn disclose patterns of ethnicity and race? How did America's wars in Asia produce specific reassignments of Asians and Asian Americans in American space, and what do these reterritorializations tell us about the symbolic, political, racial, ethnic, and economic logics of Asia / America? As we move into the contemporary period, we find a strident anxiety regarding the "Third Worldization" of American space, which brings to the fore crucial issues regarding the redefinition of social and economic life in an age of increased transnationalism, and the sovereign space of the nation.

Part IV / Placing Asian America

7 / War, the Homeland, and the Traces of Memory

> *The fundamental Marxist conception . . . is of individuals*
> *and social groups, including classes, perpetually struggling to*
> *control and enhance the historical and geographical conditions*
> *of their own existence.* —DAVID HARVEY, *The Urban Experience*

THE PREVIOUS SECTIONS OUTLINED the production of a particular
set of Asian/American subjectivities, each partaking in different ways in a redefinition of "America" in the context of specific material histories. How did
Asians in America become recognized through an optics of modern domestica-
tion in the 1930s? How were Asian/American identities transacted then at the
nexus of culture, sociality, and the body? How did the Civil Rights Act and the
social programs that were produced under its aegis affect the way Asian Americans came to represent a particular mode of assimilation to the modern American state, and how was this modeling function renegotiated in light of Japan's
ascension as an economic power and the later developments of an East Asian regional economy?

Attempting to locate Asians in America more concretely, this section reads
Asian America as eminently situated in the politics of space. This analysis continues to view Asian America through the discourses of the body, the psyche, and
space—how have Asians been located psychically and physically in what is
deemed "American" space? How have they variously taken possession of a place
in the nation and been dispossessed of it? How have such negotiations evinced the
historical formations and reformations of Asian America? How have race and
ethnicity, those markers of difference, entered into the negotiations over "common ground"? And, finally, how have imagined claims to space and place clashed
with juristic ones or coincided with them, and how is the imagination of space
linked to political and racial ideologies of the nation? This section examines two
major forces in Asian/American history and their impact upon the constitution

of Asian/American space. Chapter 7, focusing primarily on agricultural and rural areas, is aimed toward understanding the effects of America's twentieth-century wars—how did the wars in Asia mark a specific set of engagements and how did they affect the formation of Asian America? I read the relocation of Asian populations in/to the United States as particular acts of redefining and rehistoricizing the nation, and consider Asian Americans' role in such reformations.[1]

As we have seen, the very beginnings of modern Asian America may be given context within a respatialization of the nation—the United States' increased involvement in the Pacific, specifically its annexation of the Philippines and Hawai'i. America's interest in the Sino-Japanese War, its war in the Pacific (and its postwar relations in that area), its concern with China's and Taiwan's position in the Cold War, its wars in Korea and Indochina, have all affected Asian Americans profoundly, both in terms of Asians already in America and Asians who migrated to the United States. I read these effects as they are inscribed within lived environments: how do those newly marked spaces disclose the sedimented, palimpsestic signs of different identities and identifications, understood within the particular nexus of subject formation and history? Here, the role of memory becomes increasingly significant, as individuals and groups trace their relation to place, even as those traces may be covered over or erased, overlaid with different memories and claims to possession, as well as with memories and histories from different lands that have been brought over as part of the psychic makeup of dispossessed peoples and which constitute an irredactable perceptual grid thorough which the diasporic landscape is read.

How does American space thus lodge the traces of both Asian and "American" memory work—each one seeking to reestablish in and through space an image of different pasts to guide the present? I begin with a discussion of the juridical refiguration of American space and the dispossession of Japanese Americans during the Second World War, and analyze a film that seeks to narrate the reconciliation of Japanese Americans. The reading of the reconsolidation of Asian America within the social construction of space is then continued in an analysis of more recent history. My specific focus will be on the issue of refugee resettlement and "transformation," and how the respatialization of Asian America carries with it a temporalization—that of the unfolding of a constructed, assimilative subject that *takes place* particularly. What sorts of social teleologies are legitimated by the attempt to overlay the model minority thesis upon late-twentieth-century Asian refugee populations? How do their stories contrast with those of assimilated Asian Americans, and those of the new immigrant class? How might they reinvent and occupy space in different ways? And what kinds of historical memory enables certain claims and disables others?

In Chapter 8, I turn to the city in order to trace the effects of late capitalism upon the constitution of modern Asian/American urban space. In locating Asian America, there is an appreciable tension between a nostalgic, heavily idealized vision of America as an eminently "traditional" self-determining place of social and political life, in which a carefully temporalized process of assimilation brings all races and ethnicities into balance, and a sense of instability, ungovernability, and unpredictability brought about by the complexities of the increased imbrication of the local within the global. As Gupta and Ferguson note, "The irony of these terms is that as actual places and localities become ever more blurred and indeterminate, *ideas* of culturally and ethnically distinct places become perhaps even more salient."[2] As in Chapter 7, memory here plays a crucial role in the politics of place. I will ask how memory is read into and through specific chronotopes of the Asian/American nexus—memory as traced within sedimented spaces occupied by diverse, highly variegated groups: how does "America" seek to retain possession of and determination over these spaces, and how has modern history recontextualized and deterritorialized them?[3]

Economic globalization plays a crucial role in America's stance toward the entrance of Asians into America. Chapter 8 explains how the reconstruction of Asian America may be read within the logic of globalization, how local places are refigured as the invention of the Pacific Rim remapped "Asia" in and onto America (and America within the Asian Pacific), and political economies of local spaces become crosshatched by newer and less predictable forms of migration and finance. I begin by discussing the representative spaces of Asian America and their revision in the 1970s under the influence of economic restructuring, urban development, and immigrant labor and capital. I then look at the remapping of geographic and social space in the "Third Worldization" of American suburbs, paying particular attention to the tensions between migrancy, assimilation, class, and race. The activities of Asians and Asian Americans within such remapped areas have projected new identities that are assumed to have tremendous economic power, but in conclusion, I question the modes of actualizing that power, its uneven translation into political, social, and cultural power—how does "Asian" money circulate in "America" and how does this newly invented "community of money" trouble the notion of national sovereignty and community self-determination?

A reading of Asian America through the concept of spatiality is entirely apt, given the particular ways American space has been modified historically and Asians in America located differently in that persistently reterritorialized domain. For instance, the language of the 1942 Japanese Relocation Order sets forth a particular discursive strategy. President Roosevelt declares:

> Now, therefore, by virtue of the authority vested in me as President of the United States, and Commander-in-Chief of the Army and Navy, I hereby authorize and direct the Secretary of War, and the Military Commanders whom he may from time to time designate, whenever he or any such designated Commander deems such action necessary or desirable, to prescribe military areas in such places and of such extent as he or the appropriate Military Commander may determine, from which any or all persons may be excluded, and with respect to which the right of any person to enter, remain in, or leave shall be subject to whatever restrictions the Secretary of War or the appropriate Military Commander may impose in his discretion.[4]

There is a sleight of hand here. The fact of dislocation is veiled by a wholesale redefinition of location. America is now open to segmentation and appropriation at the sole discretion of "the appropriate Military Commander." Dislocation of American citizens is seen only as a consequence of something that has been rationalized in terms of America's right to determine its own space. It is not so much that Japanese Americans are dislocated, but rather that America has exercised its sovereign right to redefine itself. The issue of race is thrown into the background. With this redefinition, all notions of citizenship and property are suspended, but again, rationalized in a flawless logic that does not seem to deny the constitutional rights of American citizens. This strategy of euphemistically redefining exclusion as negative inclusion (leaving intact the myth of the melting pot) is not uncommon—it takes as a precedent the discourse of the Naturalization Act of 1790 (I. Stat. 103 [1790]), which was interpreted to say that only those *included* in the definition of "white" could be naturalized: "The provision is not that Negroes and Indians shall be *excluded*, but it is, in effect, that only free white persons will be *included* [emphasis in the original]." It is this phrase from the Act that is cited in the 1922 case of *Ozawa vs. United States* (260 U.S. 195) as providing authority to deny citizenship to Japanese Americans.

This kind of evasive (yet certainly not ineffectual) strategy of redefinition is coupled with confidence in America's ability to define and protect its space. For example, the opening phrases of the 1882 Chinese Exclusion Act read, "Whereas, in the opinion of the Government of the United States the coming of Chinese laborers to this country endangers the *good order* of *certain localities* within the territory of . . . [emphasis added]."[5] It is not only the territory of America that has to be protected, but the "order" that is supposed to dominate within that social and economic space that takes place on those unnamed "localities." This imperative for order seems to supersede the question of race, and as with the order to "evacuate" Japanese Americans, the decision to exclude Chinese from America is seen as simply a natural desire for order, not for what it actually was—the only time ever in American history a particular racial group was explicitly targeted for exclusion. The Asian race itself presented a threat to American "order."

The confidence of the state in its ability to mobilize "neutral" legal discourse at will to target and dislocate by race is nowhere more clearly evident than in the following statement by James Phelan, a San Francisco city councilman. While some politicians were eager to exploit the chaos that followed the 1906 earthquake, and suggested that the Chinese be "relocated" outside the City, others argued that this would deprive the city of a valuable source of revenue. Phelan boasted, "Let the Chinese locate wherever they please. If they prove obnoxious to whites they can gradually be driven to a certain sector of the city by strict enforcement of anti-gambling and other city laws."[6] Whether it be in anonymous, euphemistic discourse or unbridled racist language, America rationalized its overt dislocation of Asian Americans by evoking as primary the indisputable need for socioeconomic order; this rationalization simultaneously and successfully affirmed and confirmed the status of Asians in America. Logic and historical fact share in a kind of circularity: if America was to protect its order, then it had to control the location of those who never had an "authentic" place (that is, a location not susceptible to racially motivated disenfranchisement). America's notion of the "order" it required shifted according to its ideological needs even as such needs disclosed the inherent contradictions of America.[7]

The modern disenfranchisement of "aliens" from California land had begun early in the twentieth century, specifically as a way to stem the flow of Asians to America, to block the formation of Asian America. California Attorney General Ulysses S. Webb, author of the 1913 Alien Land Act, explained that the Act "seeks to limit [aliens'] presence by curtailing their privileges which they might enjoy here; for they will not come in large numbers and long abide with us if they may not acquire land."[8] In a letter arguing for the prohibition of land ownership by Japanese Americans, California Governor William D. Stephens wrote in 1920:

> We stand today at this point of western contact with the Orient, just as the
> Greeks who settled in Asia Minor three thousand years ago stood at its eastern

point. And while Mesopotamia and the country to the East thereof were the highways of the intercourse between the Orient of that era and the Occident of that era, and while historically, there was much of contact and conflict between the types representing the two standards of civilization, history does not show any material fusion of either blood or idea between the two peoples.[9]

The logic of exclusion, aimed at preserving a particular national space that accommodates a transhistorical, absolute racial separateness between Asia and America, is deployed throughout Asian American history, but most overtly and dramatically in the internment of Japanese Americans during the Second World War.[10] Here, the history of the nation is turned back in order to erase the presence of Japanese Americans and restore a pristine image of the nation. This nation nonetheless held Japanese Americans behind barbed wire as a reminder of the state's power to perform such revisionist acts. Of course, in doing so it had to elide the contradictions that act presented: the unearthed racist strain of America.

As noted above, after the bombing of Pearl Harbor in December 1941, the U.S. government mandated the redefinition of American territory according to the logic of national defense, thereby aggressively "evacuating" Japanese Americans from their land and stripping them of property and rights. Within its very first three briefings, the Department of Justice announced the creation of eighty-six "prohibited zones" from which the Japanese Americans were to be removed.[11] The identification of these crucial areas coincided with their having sizeable Japanese American populations—for the government, this presented more than a coincidence: "Whether by design or accident, virtually always their communities were adjacent to very vital shore installations, war plants, etc. While it was believed that some were loyal, it was known that many were not." To complicate the situation, "no ready means existed for determining the loyal and the disloyal with any degree of safety. It was necessary to face the realities— a positive determination could not have been made."[12]

The logic of this passage is remarkable, as it discloses the particular relationship between space and psychic identification. After first seeming to concede that Japanese American presence in these areas may be simply an "accident," DeWitt goes on to indicate that the only way to tell whether this "accident" was significant would be to test the loyalty of those Japanese Americans. Unfortunately, there is no way to do that, so the (impossible) burden of proof must fall on the Japanese Americans. More interesting still, even though DeWitt claims that it is "known" that "many" are not loyal, his speech undercuts the very possibility of founding that knowledge, since "a positive determination could not have been made." TenBroek notes that in actuality "many if not all of these and other installations, especially military installations and war-production facilities, were built long after the settlement of the Japanese."[13] In their anxiety to uncover a well-planned and intricately carried out conspiracy, the government had to ignore history; it had to simultaneously rehistoricize and respatialize these areas in order to remove the Japanese Americans from them.

At the heart of all this is the sense that Japanese Americans are not really Americans; the difficulty of determining loyalty is sidestepped in this passage from the "Final Recommendation of the Commanding General, Western Defense Command and Fourth Army, Submitted to The Secretary of War."[14] The document begins by designating the subject: "Evacuation of Japanese and other Subversive Persons from the Pacific Coast" (immediately, the Japanese are assumed to be subversives). The report goes on to say, "The Japanese race is an enemy race and while many second and third generation Japanese born on United States soil, possessed of United States citizenship, have become 'Americanized,' the racial strains are undiluted. To conclude otherwise is to expect that children born of white parents on Japanese soil sever all racial affinity and become loyal Japanese subjects, ready to fight, and, if necessary, to die for Japan in a war against the nation of their parents."[15] DeWitt dismisses any notion of Japanese becoming "Americanized," but he does so in a very interesting fashion—by comparing Japanese in America to Americans (more explicitly, American whites) in Japan.

While this may seem a universalizing (humanizing) gesture, it also cannot help inadvertently dismantling the very exceptionalism upon which America was founded, namely, that America, with its ideology of freedom and liberty, was *not* like any other nation. Unlike every other country, America was claimed to be able to work a particular transformation upon its immigrants, and this ideology of course was accessed frequently and loudly throughout and after the war in order to put forward the American cause in the postwar refiguration of the world.[16] DeWitt gives all that up in order to cut off any possibility that Japanese Americans could ever be anything other than Japanese. American space has to be secured, but in the course of this pronouncement, America has ceased to be the same historically idealized and rationalized space. Like his humanizing gesture above, DeWitt's memo to Laurence I. Hewes, regional director of the Farm Security Administration, orders Hewes to, in a "fair and equitable" manner, "institute and administer a program which will insure continuation of the proper use of agricultural lands voluntarily vacated by enemy aliens."[17] But while he argues for "fair and equitable" arrangements, it becomes clear that one of De-Witt's primary concerns is the continued productivity of this land so "voluntarily vacated."

While some have argued that economic considerations played only a minor role in the evacuation, an article in the *Oakland Tribune* (November 17, 1943) notes: "The vegetable growers, more keenly appreciative of what they face in Japanese competition than other groups, appear to be unanimous in wanting the Nipponese kept out. A number of growers frankly admitted they preferred white competition." But in order to argue for evacuation, it was necessary to deny the fact that the Japanese American farmer was an important contributor to the economy — that is, racists had to at once argue that the Japanese were and were not competitive and significant producers. The politics of evacuation thus reveal the intimate and often contradictory relations between racism and economics. To make clear the evacuation's actual economic cost to the country was to reduce the chances that the government would take the step of removing the Japanese Americans from their fields.

Indeed, U.S. Department of Agriculture data showed that in 1941, the Japanese grew between 30 and 35 percent of all commercial truck crops in California.[18] The final report of the Tolan Committee (the committee in charge of the House of Representatives' hearings on "National Defense Migration" in 1942) stated, "representatives of producers' associations, who it might be presumed are adversely affected by Japanese competition, minimized the importance of Japanese production."[19] To assure the evacuation, the fields themselves were even argued to contain "signaling devices."[20] We have then the refiguring of Japanese American land into a strategic area from which Japanese, never to be Americans, are to be excluded and removed. Yet the contradiction the evacuation posed with regard to economic considerations (were the Japanese a significant component of the agricultural economy?) still had to be addressed.

Okihiro and Drummond point out that "the immediate concern was the very real possibility of Japanese tenants defaulting on the loans issued and, further, the loss of what promised to be a very bountiful agricultural season."[21] In March 1942, over six thousand Japanese farms had to be transferred over to non-Japanese operators without significant loss of money. These non-Japanese operators were "anxious to avoid any risk in operating these farms." Therefore, a *parent* corporation financed by the government was the solution sought and obtained.[22] Okihiro and Drummond explain that "the fruit companies obtained generous, risk-free government loans to subsidize their operations (loans were secured on the assets of Japanese farms)."[23] In other words, the government itself provided the means by which the contradictory status of Japanese American agricultural work was finessed, thereby allowing for the internment while guaranteeing the uninterrupted productivity of the fields.

In general, Asian American history has been grounded in such spatial politics. An understanding of this has guided Asian American activism since its beginnings. As the U.S. government ingeniously remapped the nation's interior during the Second World War in order to erase the legal rights and presence of Japanese Americans, so Japanese Americans and others have sought redress via a rememorialization of land and space, to restore the evacuated histories they silently contain. Most significantly, the efforts to gain compensation for the internees through the Civil Liberties Act of 1988, to radically revise the script of history and the reading of the politics of space, occupation, and identity, was undertaken to do more than legitimate the historical record and symbolically draw a response from the state. A counterdiscourse was also enacted, one that exposes the contradictions of the internment, answers the surviving directly, and attempts to forestall the reenactment of such an act.[24]

The covering up of the contradiction between racist and economic interests and the overriding interest in maintaining American democratic ideology shows up in a number of cultural texts of the postwar era; one example is King Vidor's 1952 film, *Japanese War Bride*.[25] Like Capra's film, Vidor's *Japanese War Bride* is able to bracket ideological contradiction by focusing on the resolution of romance; the very last image of the film, in reconciling America with Japan within the shared expanse of the Pacific, takes our eyes away from the materiality of the land and the abiding struggle over agricultural markets.[26] I use this representation of the reintegration of Japanese Americans to America after the war to narrate the movement from pre— to post—World War Two Asian America, specifically, the movement from the "hot" war of World War Two, through the Korean War, and onto a mapping of Asian American assimilation. If Millard wonders how the East Asian "war bride" will appear on Main Street, U.S.A., and thereby implicitly raises the question of how Asians will take places in the nation, Vidor gives us one answer.

Vidor's film tells of an American soldier (Jim Sterling) and his romance with a Japanese Red Cross nurse (Tae) in Japan, their marriage and return to his family farm in Salinas, California. There they meet his friends and relatives, some of whom are sympathetic, others openly antagonistic. By weaving together the various responses to the marriage and creating a particular resolution to these tensions, Vidor seems to suggest the proper way for America to deal with not only the trauma of the Second World War, but also of actually bringing the effects of the war home to the Central Valley. The presence of Tae in Salinas, and especially her status as Jim's wife, opens up old wounds and reengenders bitterness. The narrative economy of the film requires that certain characters are restrained, diverted, disciplined, or simply relegated off-stage—their combined prejudices are neatly collapsed under one general category. Roughly speaking, Vidor sets up a dichotomy between those who cannot and will not forget the trauma of the war, and those who are able and willing to divert their attention to the present and future. Yet, as will become clear, the film's closure is dependent on the disciplining of a single character whose involvement in the story line is removed from the issue of the war. While this allows the film's resolution, it also draws attention away from a series of issues involving historical memory and the persistence of racism. Like Capra's *Bitter Tea of General Yen*, *Japanese War Bride* invests its narrative in romance. However, Vidor's film more clearly sets up a series of historical terms that form a strong, although ultimately muted, subtext.

The opening credits are displayed against the backdrop of a series of sweeping aerial shots circling the Pacific coast—details of pounding waves set against huge panoramic vistas, with the title of the film set out in "oriental brushstroke" calligraphy, suggesting at once the inscription of the "war bride" upon that terrain. But the diegesis begins in a dark and misty field of death in Korea. The camera pans across a number of American bodies—there seem to be no survivors. But a moment later a flashlight sweeps slowly across the ground to reveal a moving figure whose eyes slowly angle up to view the holder of the light—a member of a small group of American infantrymen. Next we find ourselves in a clean, bright hospital ward in Japan. The survivor is lying in bed, watched over by a female Japanese nurse. We find out her name is "Tae," and she has been writing letters home dictated by Jim, whose arm is injured. He explains that he was originally stationed in Japan as part of the occupying forces; then he was transferred to fight in Korea. The film thus sets Tae up as participating in the rehabilitation of America and implies an Asian (that is, Japanese) endorsement of postwar American policy in East Asia, a fusion of interests in the newly mapped region of the Pacific. He tells Tae that this time back in Japan he's much happier, having now made a friend in her. The theme of movement, between Japan and Korea, and back again to Japan, moves us between various historical frames, revealing America's various engagements in East Asia. This sets up the final "link": the move back to the United States.

Jim flirts directly with Tae, who is embarrassed and insists that he stick to the task at hand, writing letters home, and she to her proper role as his scribe. Yet her very ability to write *his* letters home establishes her at the seam between Asia and America. Jim indirectly addresses her by dictating to her a fictitious letter to an unnamed friend. He tells of being cared for by a beautiful Japanese nurse who, "in a Red Cross outfit looks like any other girl—I wonder what she'd look like in America." Jim's attraction to Tae is racialized ("Japanese nurse"), but then the issue of race is immediately subsumed to her identity with a frame that universalizes her ("any other girl"). Finally, and most tellingly, the rhetorical question Jim dangles before Tae can be read as a literal enigma that will drive the narrative—what, exactly, *does* Tae "look like" in "America"?

Before coming to America, however, Jim and Tae must first secure the blessing of her grandfather, who has taken care of Tae and her mother ever since the death of Tae's father. The grandfather surprises Jim by speaking fluent English— he explains he studied in America, and that he was the one who taught Tae English. Despite this "westernization," he is adamantly traditional, and does not believe that the interracial marriage is a good thing: the cultures are simply too different.[27] To prove this, he pretends that it is Japanese custom to perform blood sacrifice to honor special guests. He proceeds to pretend to slaughter two monkeys. Jim runs off horrified, only to be brought back by Tae, who tells Jim that it was all a show to frighten Jim off ("my grandfather's ways are not your ways"). The grandfather apologizes: his deception was intended merely to dramatize the essential gulf between Japan and America. Finally, although saddened by their plans and entirely skeptical about the marriage, the grandfather gives his blessing. Vidor uses this scene to delineate Japanese prejudice, but more important, he defines Jim and Tae as young, idealistic adults unwilling to remain in the grip of past history—specifically, that of the war between Japan and the United States. Conversely, the grandfather establishes one of a series of characterizations of the inability to move beyond the past, especially as it is manifested in a belief in the incommensurability of Asia and America. The development of the narrative becomes a movement away from this way of thinking, exemplifying faith in the transformative nature of the future. When asked if she knows what it will mean to go to America, Tae answers, "It means I'll be an American."

The point of entry to America is San Francisco, but this is done offstage. The film's depiction of Tae's first step onto American soil is at the train station in the agricultural center of Salinas, California. Jim's male relatives are there to greet him—his father; his older brother, Art; and his younger brother, Ted (Jim's mother and Art's new wife, Fran, are preparing the welcome home). His father's first words to Tae (dressed in kimono by Vidor to accentuate her foreignness) seem to bode well, "Welcome home, Tae." Art and Ted are equally welcoming and gracious. But before arriving home, Vidor tracks the family car as it drives past field after field, thereby establishing the central theme of the family's economic life—agriculture. Jim remarks at one point, "Looks like a good crop, who's farming it now, McNally?" His father answers, "No, the Hasegawas have it back—they're good farmers." Vidor thus interrupts Tae's encounter with Jim's family to set up another key problematic of the film—the reenfranchisement of Japanese Americans. Yet this issue is bracketed quickly by the next scene—Jim and Tae's homecoming.

While the men of Jim's family seem to welcome Tae, Jim's mother and his new sister-in-law do not; they are polite but cold, and Tae notices this. She becomes so nervous that she drops a plate and breaks it while trying to help out in the kitchen. Jim's mother strains herself trying to pick up the pieces, and goes off to bed. Tae is distraught and offers to use Japanese massage to ease her mother-in-law's pain. Jim's mother declines, but later Jim prevails upon her to let Tae try. This "laying on of hands" (which domestically replicates Tae's nursing of Jim in a foreign Asian war) works—Tae and Jim's mother are isolated in a scene in the mother's bedroom, and enter into conversation, finally. It comes out that Tae's family owns a number of farms, and the women bond: not only has Tae paid proper deference to Jim's mother and indicated that she will "take care of" her, but they also share a love of farming.

But Fran, Art's new wife, is an anomaly. No one in town expected her to settle down, least of all with Art. Fran reads *Vogue* magazine, dresses up in city clothes, and is portrayed as a vulgar, bigoted egotist who has always had, in Jim's mother's words, a "schoolgirl crush" on Jim. Counterposed to this possible competitor for Jim's romantic feelings is another hometown girl whom many in the town, including Jim's parents, felt would be Jim's choice for marriage—Emily Schafer. In contrast to the bleached-blonde Fran, Emily is a natural blonde, and seems altogether angelic, accepting of Tae and warmly greeting Jim. She is the "typical" girl back home who is above resentment, either against Jim for marrying another, or against the Japanese ("we can't carry hatred for the rest of our lives"). In these three women we find a complex set of desiring positions vis-à-vis the white American male. Each represents both racial and national gender ideologies. The hometown girl is cast in two molds: one with wily and immoral urban aspirations, the other reinstating the heartland. Tae represents the best of both. She is cosmopolitan and worldly, yet domesticated nonetheless and happy for it. While Fran dresses like an urbanite and sets her sights on seducing her brother-in-law, Emily spends her time caring for her bereaved mother, who is still mourning the loss of her only son at Bataan. If these figures each represent a different sort of mate for Jim, his marriage to Tae represents a step *outside* these counterposed "American" alternatives, and a move toward a liberal utopian vision. Crucially, their union is predicated upon a selective forgetfulness, one that allows that crucial transit between a newly invented Asian American domestic space and the economic sphere.

As Jim and Tae form a pair of young people unwilling to sacrifice their lives to the past, so too we are introduced to Shiro and Emma Hasegawa, Mr. Hasegawa's children. The encounter between the two sets of young people takes place at a particular venue. Tae is taken to town to do some shopping, but we never see that initiation to American consumerism. Instead, she is first taken by Jim's father to the vegetable packing plant. Mr. Sterling is especially interested in showing Tae the new farm machines ("See how much time these save?"). Thus, instead of shots of Salinas's department stores, we have detailed shots of the modern agricultural plant, as Tae is offered a tour by Shiro and Emma. Vidor establishes the centrality of the biracial marriage, yet he also insists on maintaining a focus on the subtext of land and agricultural business.

The symbolism of this heartland of agricultural life within the trope of Asian America is obvious, and underscored by the constant reference to the internment—when Emma first meets Tae she welcomes her in particular language, "Welcome to *our* country." Their claim to America is underscored by the fact that Shiro, lured to Japan by a friend before Pearl Harbor, is imprisoned there during the war for not supporting the Japanese (as his friend does). Emma and her parents are sent to the Tulare relocation camp, but Emma maintains her American patriotism. But even such acts of loyalty and the young Hasegawas' willingness to forget and forgive cannot dispel the persistence of economic and racial conflict. The relationship between the Sterlings and the Hasegawas is strained. Even Jim, who is portrayed as the most nonracist figure, when asked by Tae if the Hasegawas are friends, hesitates before he deliberately forms his answer, "Well, not exactly—they're neighbors." He may marry a Japanese, but he doesn't imagine that he can be intimates with these particular economic competitors; he can only recognize their presence adjacent to his land.

It becomes clear to Jim that to really have a life of their own, he and Tae need to leave the family home (where they have been staying in Jim's old childhood room), and build a house of their own. The space of the Sterling house embodies a particular set of traditional rural American values.[28] The front yard in particular—its borderland between the private and public—becomes the site of various negotiations between the family members and their neighbors and friends. Mrs. Schafer indeed refuses to set foot in the Sterlings' home as long as

Tae is there, and Jim's mother regretfully concedes the loss of "a dear friend." Another person who refuses to enter the Sterling home (not because of Tae, but because of the Sterlings) is the elder Mr. Hasegawa. We are told that he holds a grudge against the growers association, which tried to take over his farm while he was in the internment camp; Jim's father even makes the likeness of Mrs. Shafer to Mr. Hasegawa explicit. This set of positions against forgetting is counterposed to the younger generation. Vidor represents this space as the place where the best instincts of American inclusion strain against racism and prejudice. Ultimately, however, Jim and Tae must live elsewhere and let the rural family sort out its conscience; the Asian American couple's destiny is to invent a new locale.

It happens that there is one spot on the Sterlings' property that, to Tae, looks exactly like a place on one of her grandfather's farms. Furthermore, it just so happens that Jim's father had promised this piece of land to him. Tae tells Jim he'd better start to work soon—she is expecting a baby. Vidor thus sets up the theme of establishing the first biracial Asian American family at precisely the *new* symbolic nexus of Asia and America on the edge of the Pacific.

Perhaps because of the birth of her new grandson, Mrs. Sterling, Sr., becomes closer to Tae. Fran, having lost Jim to Tae, cannot stand this added insult. One day, the men come home from a growers association meeting in great consternation.[29] Someone has placed an anonymous letter in Mr. Sterling's association mailbox, insinuating that Jim is not the father of Tae's baby—Shiro is. This attribution of fatherhood symbolically works to set back the optimistic notion of an Asian American biracial child manifesting the new, positive postwar Asian America and reinstalls the impossibility of such a liaison. The letter suggests that unless Jim's father throws Jim and Tae out of his house (and thereby restores the proper constituents of the domestic), he will be banned from the association; his socioeconomic world cannot stand such contamination. Tae's supposed infidelity to Jim is cast as symbolizing her high loyalty to her race; it suggests that Jim's marriage to her, as Tae's grandfather argues, is an impossible attempt to transcend such racial loyalities. In short, it rehearses the same argument used to intern Japanese Americans—that no matter how "American" they seemed (to want to be), their essential loyalties were with Japan. It is the film's ideological task to negate such a rehearsal.

While his wife and Art worry about the economic ramifications of being barred from the association, Mr. Sterling insists on standing his ground. Jim is simply amazed at their assumption of the letter's veracity, and tells Tae to pack. When she says nothing upon learning about this affront, he demands that she speak ("Why can't you people be more like us?"). This first, explicit articulation of his own racism shows the entrenchment of racism in even the "best" of Americans. When Tae refuses to either confirm or deny the affair, Jim drives off in a fury. When he returns, he discovers that Tae has left with the baby. Fran accosts him, saying that this is how it should be, that Tae understood that their marriage was wrong, and that she has decided to go back to Japan. In fact, Fran tells Jim this is all his fault ("There wouldn't have been trouble if you hadn't brought Tae here"). Jim begins to suspect that it was Fran who wrote the letter; finally she admits to it. She tells Art: "I wanted to let him know how people felt." At this Art slaps Fran to the ground.

It is clear by this point that the film has isolated Fran and condensed its distribution of hatred and bigotry in her and her alone. Her disciplining is couched in terms of the reinstatement of proper domestic order—Art tells her, as he drags her back into the house, "You've been throwing too many curves, we're going to straighten them out." Fran's sexuality (her "curves") will be redisciplined—she is taken out of circulation and reinstalled in her proper place, her independence tamed.[30] Once Fran is removed, Mr. Sterling tells Jim to seek out Tae, and presents a collective apology to Jim that rebuts Fran's claim that she speaks for "how people feel." Jim's father tells him that "we've all made our mistakes," and that they will make it up to Jim. Jim rushes off and finds Tae with the reluctant help of Shiro and Emma, who have been asked by Tae to keep her whereabouts a secret (Shiro convinces Emma that "it is wrong to keep a husband from a wife"). The film's dramatic finale is a parallel shot to the scenic backdrop of the opening credits—aerial views that sweep along the coastline, where Tae has fled in despair. She seems perched upon a cliff, ready to jump, when Jim takes her in his arms. She embraces him; there is one close-up of her relieved and passionate face against his chest, then the camera pans back for a wide shot of the couple against the coast, which captures them in a freeze frame.

As noted above, the film raises the essential question of how Tae will "look" in America. This question is of course linked to that of transposing Asia into America after the Second World War. But even though Vidor reduces this issue to the romantic by locating the key element of resistance in Fran, and then seemingly neutralizing the harshest feature of racism by placing Fran, now chastised and defeated, back into "the house," certain issues remain.[31] Vidor devotes a significant amount of narrative time and space to the issue of land and its economy. The fact that the action takes place in Salinas is highly motivated; the attention given to the new technologies is crucial, but more crucial still is the fact that these technologies are now in the hands of Japanese Americans as well. The meeting that the Sterling men have attended regards the new threat posed by the fact that "the Japanese are farming again." While the romantic tension and the family's relation to the interracial marriage have been dealt with, the film never resolves the economic and racial issue it takes so much care to raise. Instead, the film reconciles the difference between Japan and America by its persistent equation of Asia with America via their shared symbolic space—the Pacific. In Vidor's film, there is a coordinated reoccupation of the land: Jim returns from the Korean War, preceded by the Hasegawas' return from the camps. And, crucially, a third party is involved—Tae, the postwar Asian immigrant, the Asian American to be and the mother of one who will by natural right be American.[32]

All this takes place on the border of the Pacific, and it is in that common space that the new utopia of Jim and Tae, America and Asia, will be created. The opening shots could be California, but they could as well be the Japanese coastline—no houses or people intrude onto the scene to specify the exact location. But rather than being so open-endedly optimistic, the film's attempt at settling issues of race, sexuality, but also of the internment, agricultural strife, and so on, is incomplete. What will happen at the next growers association meeting? How is it possible to extend the enlightened views of the Sterling family into that space? What sorts of contradictions abide? Will Sterling leave the association or has the revelation of Fran's villainy defused that situation entirely? The land, in Vidor's film, is relegated to the purely *symbolic* arena; this allows its weak ideological resolution because it has removed the actual economic realm from sight.

Finally, I would draw attention to another strange detour. Why is the film titled "*Japanese* War Bride"? The war with Japan has been over for a number of years before Jim's encounter with Tae. The film serves to focus our attention upon the effects of the Second World War, but it is only able to make it a contemporary issue by using the Korean War as a pretext. In so doing, it brings up but immediately subdues the *current* engagement of the United States on Asian soil, in order to attempt to enact the romantic reconciliation of Asian America. "Asia" here can *only* be Japan, which has been occupied by the United States and reconstructed as a "democractic" capitalist state, *not* Korea, split between capitalistic and socialistic regimes, which remains represented only in the opening shot of a dark field of death from which Jim is rescued and placed into the bright convalescent space of Tae's Japan. Vidor's film thus evokes contemporary history only as a pretext to "resolve" the effects of past history. Contemporary history is flattened out, but so is the past, as the romantic resolution of the narrative leeches out the abiding problematics of race and economics.

As we've seen, during the Second World War, the United States government had to invent a way to reconcile precisely such economic and ideological interests. One essential strategy was to redesignate the land upon which the Japanese Americans lived—Asian American bodies were dispossessed of the space that they occupied through a government edict declaring that land to be different and the conditions of their occupation particular. In so doing, reclaiming the land after the war necessitates a particular act of archeology, of tracing back the marks of prior occupation and ownership in a historically and politically palimpsestic landscape that bears the imprints of competing visions and (re)appropriations. It also calls for a reimagining of new possibilities of occupation and place-taking.

Shiro Fujioka's *Traces of a Journey* (1957) contains just such an imaginative revision of the California landscape:

> If we follow the example of China's history of three kingdoms and divide the Imperial Valley in three parts, leaving out the cotton growers on the border, there was Mr. Kikutaro Nishimoto in the southern area, Mr. Shonan Kimura in the central part around Holtville and El Centro, and in the northern area around Brawley was Mr. Rita Takahashi. They were, so to speak, Wu Ti, Shu Han and Wei of the three kingdoms.

Citing this passage, Karen Leonard aptly asks, "But why did Fujioka locate his kingdoms in China rather than Japan? Probably he did so because Japanese history features several periods of *two*, but not three, kingdoms feuding and also because the Japanese immigrants were a relatively well-educated group, conversant with Chinese history as well as their own" (123). I suggest that another reason the Chinese image may have been chosen is because the Chinese were not dispossessed of their land, the Japanese were. The claim to a more primordial history (Japanese tracing their cultural heritage to China) retemporalizes as well as respatializes the land. Again, Leonard claims "they were *seeing* similarities to an Asian landscape and imagining themselves free to farm and fight on it . . . they were using that broader identification to contest subordination, to assert a different vision of the political landscape" (124). I would argue that it also imagines positive, nonalienated space of potential commerce in a common American economy—that is, what Tae and Jim imagine as a common *place*.[33]

World War Two produced in its wake a dramatically new formation of Asian America. If the 1930s anticipated the development of an America deeply linked to a Pacific trajectory, the Second World War and the Korean War drove home that reality. Asian America begins to show the markings of new global strategies, alignments, and notions of "development" at the same time as the presence of Asia within America is informed by particular identifications with both Asia and America. The dominant historical frame installed in the 1920s nonetheless holds sway until the mid-1960s, wherein we find the revision of immigration laws in 1965 and the wars in Indochina. The reception of influxes of Asians during this period is deeply shaped by a domestic crisis regarding racial minorities and poverty, and foreign interests. To manage the "flood" of refugees from Southeast Asia required a convergence and correlation of the narrative of the model minority (which would assure America that this new population would follow along the path of previous Asian groups) and the narrative of reconciliation and forgetting (or a particular remembering, let us say) of the war in Vietnam, which would assure it that the material histories that had delivered the refugees to America's shores would not complicate their subjectivation in any significant manner. Indeed, their subjectivation would in some way help vindicate America's bloody engagement in Indochina.

Refugees, Reinventions, and the Politics of Memory

The arrival of refugees from Indochina into the United States in the 1970s and 1980s evinced the particular interest of the state in accelerating assimilation because of specific historical contingencies. To this end, the dispersal of communities was seen to be essential to that process. Yet I want to address as well the reformation of community and reinvention of "ethnic" life implicit in this redefinition of space. The flood of refugees from Indochina to the United States presents an altogether different sort of diaspora from that of willed immigration, one that links up international and domestic agendas in specific ways. In a statement before the Subcommittee on Immigration and Refugee Policy of the Senate Judiciary Committee on September 7, 1985, Secretary of State George Schultz gave a relentlessly reductive analysis of how this refugee population was produced: "The root cause of the refugee problem in Indochina . . . is . . . the imposition of communist oppression on the people of those countries."[34] In response, Tollefson rightly notes: "Such simplistic statements ignore the economic and social consequences of a generation of warfare, bombing, and chemical defoliation, as well as the successful U.S. economic embargo designed to strangle the Vietnamese economy. The official version of history—that communists create refugees while Americans save them—disguises the U.S. role in creating and sustaining the ongoing refugee crisis."[35]

The invention and implementation of refugee policies—from refugee centers in international and foreign spaces to asylum and social welfare programs in the United States—likewise evince the convergence of multiple agendas. These agendas disclose a complex set of strategies for the formation of a new Asian/American subject out of the fragments of postcolonial struggle; these processes should be read as indices of a particular imagining of Asian America in historical time that attempts to write out the specificities of forced migration and the legacy of the wars in Indochina. Crucial to our understanding of this phenomenon are both the distinction between immigration and refugee policies *and* the blurring of this distinction under the willed forgetfulness of the American imaginary. This blurring of categories points up the overriding imperative to place all Asian migration, forced or not, under the same processes of assimilation and social subjectivity, despite tremendous historical differences. There is, in other words, a willed amnesia of the state, countered by the persistence of refugee memory.

In the late 1980s, press coverage of Indochinese refugees acknowledged their material differences from other Asian groups now identified as the model minority, yet it also declared their essential point of commonality: an abhorrence of welfare. In February of 1987, *U.S. News and World Report* ran a story detailing "trouble" within "the model minority": "Indochinese refugees are touted as an American success story—in fact, a staggering number are poor, out of work, and on relief."[36] Indeed, the article focuses precisely on the issue of welfare, beginning the essay with the story of a young Vietnamese girl who won a national essay contest that celebrated the Statue of Liberty, but who was compelled to return the prize (a new automobile) because it would have meant giving up public assistance monies. Its one subhead is titled, "On Welfare"; it ends the piece with two quotes—one from an academic who praises the refugees as making "exemplary use of the welfare system," and another from a young mother who says, "I'm unhappy to receive welfare." Throughout these essays, comparisons are made to blacks and other minorities and their use of federal assistance. In short, the refugees' relation to the welfare state presents a litmus test of assimilation. Of most concern throughout is the identification of refugees as welfare recipients: the world of welfare is a world radically segmented off from viable sociality. It is emphasized over and over that these welfare recipients are to be distinguished from welfare's *pathological* populations. Thus, the "American" subjectivization of Asian refugees comments not only upon their adaptability but also, by contrast, upon the failure of other populations.

Fortune's 1986 essay on Asian Americans upped the rhetoric, with this description of America's "super minority": "Asian Americans have wasted no time laying claim to the American dream. They are smarter and better educated and make more money than everyone else. Now they are vaulting the last obstacles that stand between them and this country's corner offices."[37] The lead photograph shows Robert Nakasone, "top officer of Toys R Us," with his wife, four children, and white rabbit, in Ridgewood, New Jersey. The hyperidentification of Nakasone as "super" is presented in the suburban coding; the family is set off against their impressive Tudor-style home, they appear an altogether attractive bunch, beaming out at the camera. Another sign of his having made it in America is his white wife. Nakasone is made even further American by the fact that he is a top executive for that universal toy mart, Toys R Us. The perfect combination of leisure, recreation, and childhood as a corporate product, and all this is measured against a particular history. The article begins: "In the trunk of Robert Nakasone's car is a brown government-issue blanket. It was the blanket handed to his mother when she, like thousands of other Japanese Americans, was 'relocated' into camps during the anti-Japanese hysteria of World War II. The blanket, which Nakasone's family now uses for picnics, reminds him of how far he has come." Yet, after touting psychological and economic data to support his claim of Asians' superior brainpower and initiative, the author (or his editor) includes a sidebar: "The Super Minority's Poor Cousin." It cites statistics regarding the plight of Indochinese refugees of the second wave, and cites a researcher who claims that "part of the problem is that it doesn't pay for refugees with families to work."[38]

The juxtaposition between the Nakasones and their "poor cousins" sets off the generation that has left the legacy of anti-Asian racism (which appeared in the last "big" war in Asia) in the dustbin of history, and those who are striving to take the first step beyond the war in Indochina. But, most important, the author's citations of the biodeterministic argument suggest that as long as the genes are there, the newest group of Asians in America, if disabused of welfare, will make it *in time*. The process of Asian American subject production is inherently replicable.

The problem is the welfare system, not the circumstances that force people onto it. As we saw earlier, "dependency" on welfare has long been the litmus test by which American sociability is gauged. An analysis of Asian American subjectivation during this period reveals the intimate link between the forgetting of history (that particular complex set of material forces that produced the refugee) and the elision of ethnic differences among Asian groups. Such differences are set aside as incidental to the imperative to locate refugees on American soil and to shape them into social subjects no different from other Asian Americans. In the late 1970s and the 1980s, the need to "locate" refugees was pressed by an economic slump and civil unrest.

Refugees do not fit into one group. There were two major waves of refugees: those arriving in 1975, as part of American-sponsored evacuation and coming directly to refugee camps on the U.S. mainland, and "boat people" and overland refugees, who spent considerable time in refugee camps in Thailand, Malaysia, Singapore, Hong Kong, and other parts of Indochina. These refugees were not part of the U.S. evacuation, but left their country out of opposition to the new government's economic and rural resettlement programs. Also, between 1975 and 1980, Cambodians, Laotian minorities, and ethnic Chinese fleeing Vietnam came to the United States as a result of civil war, famine, war with Vietnam. The economic and social status of these two groups differs significantly: while the first wave of Indochinese refugees tended to be relatively well-educated, proficient in English, and experienced in urban living, this second wave was poorer, less educated, typically did not possess the skills needed for employment in a technologically complex society, and was in greater need of federal assistance. Comprising the "largest nonwhite, non-Western, non-English-speaking group of people to enter the country at one time," they became trapped in low-wage service sector jobs.[39]

These differences bear importantly on the manner in which the refugees were integrated into American society. These different waves had different angles of entry into two tiers of work opened up by a global economy: professional, managerial, and service workers; and low-skill, low-wage labor. Moreover, a large portion of the second wave were relegated to the welfare state. As we have seen, despite these differences, both were embedded within a generalized narrative of immigration and ethnic assimilation that served specific ideological purposes of erasing the signifiance of history for expediency's sake. Nevertheless, and crucial for our understanding of this particular imagining of Asian America, refugee populations have resisted that narrative in important ways and "adapted" to America particularly. It is therefore critical to examine the complex dialectic between the imposition of certain narrations of assimilation, the contradictions within and between such narrations, resistance to such narratives that result in eminently hybrid cultures and subjectivities, and the complex status of such cultures.

Refugee policy may be traced back to the first international apparatuses established to deal with refugee issues. In 1951, the United Nations established its High Commission for Refugees (UNHCR), the major agency in the field. The original mission of UNHCR was to protect refugees from the crisis and aftermath of World War II. However, the large flows of refugees from Indochina in the 1970s "led to the development of doubts about the capacity of the international community to respond to the problems of forced migrations."[40] Given the size and nature of the Indochinese refugee crisis, and the UNHCR's inability to manage that crisis adequately, the management of the refugee crisis fell to the mercy of an ad hoc set of procedures that largely depended on the willingness of First World nations to absorb and aid the refugees. The relative willingness (or lack thereof) of various nations to absorb and house Indochinese refugees was dependent on their individual domestic agendas as well as their international ones.[41]

In the United States, refugee policy has always been intimately connected with international policy and national domestic interests, developing since the end of the Second World War and the beginning of the Cold War. The 1952 McCarran-Walter Act granted the attorney general discretionary authority to "parole" into the United States any alien for "emergent reasons or for reasons deemed strictly in the public interest."[42] This authority was originally intended to be applied on an individual basis, but it was actually employed for the mass parole of those fleeing Communist oppression (Hungarians in 1956, Chinese after 1949, more than 145,000 Cubans after Castro's 1959 coup). This authority was also used to handle refugees from Indochina, but their admission should be seen in the context of the U.S.'s larger anticommunist program:

> The attorney general [permitted] over 400,000 refugees from Indochina to enter between 1975 and 1980. By 1980, 99.7 percent of the more than one million refugees admitted under the parole system were from countries under Communist rule. The preference afforded refugees from Communist countries is also reflected in the 1965 reforms, when Congress created the first permanent statutory basis for the admission of refugees. Incorporating prior refugee language into a seventh preference category, conditional entry was provided for refugees fleeing Communist-dominated areas of the Middle East. . . . Until its repeal in 1980 the seventh preference was used by tens of thousands of refugees fleeing China, the Soviet Union, and other Communist societies.[43]

In other words, the influx of Indochinese refugees to the United States was part and parcel of a larger ideological effort to lean the balance of the Cold War toward the Free World; the insertion of these Indochinese refugees into America took place within a narrative of Americanization and global politicking. A 1990 study by the Lawyers Committee for Human Rights found that, even with the Refugee Act of 1980, significant ideological bias persisted; the implementation of the Act was still weighed toward offering entrance to refugees coming from communist countries.[44]

Yet even the desire to promote a certain image of America as the Free World came under pressure, because of the sheer number of Asian refugees seeking entrance.[45] Anxiety over the number of Indochinese refugees coming to the United States prompted a new set of policies that placed particular emphasis on the proper way to locate these Asians in America without destabilizing its social core.[46] Initial proposals for locating refugees included putting them on an uninhabited island or removing them from countries of first asylum and placing them in "holding centers" for indefinite periods of time (China's Hainan Island, Japan's Okinawa, America's Guam, north Australia). Such "solutions" disclose exactly the desire of the First World to dispatch history to the margins of visibility, to erase the effects of colonization and neocolonial policies in Asia. They also give the lie to the current celebration of postmodern migrancy, and remind us of the essential political functions of nation-states in securing rights and privileges. Grant's observation of these facts is eloquently phrased and worth quoting at length. He asserts that such measures (of isolation and containment)

> do not touch the central issue, which is that refugees should not be left stateless by the refusal of other nations to accept them. . . . A person who is forced to live outside the authority of the nation-state becomes, in the modern world, a person without the rights and duties of a citizen. The idea of an "international citizenship" is attractive in principle, as is the idea of living in isolation in a utopian community. But each is a way of opting out of the issues posed by the boat people who, like the Indo-Chinese refugees generally, are too intensely connected to the forces of history and politics that have erupted to displace them, for them to become citizens in limbo, sanitized against time and space.[47]

In particular, we might note the way such solutions take these subjects outside the narrative of assimilation into any "modern" state and bypass the specific character of forced migration. For instance, they gloss over the fact that refugees most often did not come directly to America, but were forced to live in refugee camps before arriving here. Such camps were worlds of their own, extraterritorial spaces of liminality and statelessness.[48]

Counterposed to such policies of segregation and containment are policies that attempt to deal with the presence of refugees on national soil. The goals of U.S. refugee policy became assimilation and self-sufficiency. Such policies simply overlaid the "classic" narrative of immigration upon the refugee crisis: "The historical pattern of resettlement in the United States has been established by the experiences of European immigrants who arrived at the turn of the century. First, the immigrant population adapts economically but not socially. With time, a slow process of acculturation and adaptation is accomplished through education. But this pattern of assimilation has not as accurately characterized Asian ethnic groups or involuntary migrants. These migrants have special problems in accepting and adapting to a society they do not prefer."[49]

The fact that such a particularly constructed "American culture" may not be the preferred cultural formation of refugee populations results in the nonconvergence of policy goals, material circumstances, and refugee interests. Instead, we find the production of hybrid social formations. There is some flexibility in such formations, both in terms of their character and practice and in terms of the state's accommodation of them. That accommodation is predicated upon a particular notion of that social subject's psychic disposition—read against the parameters of acceptable sociality, the psyche becomes used to track social assimilation and becomes available for observation precisely by way of the subject's ability (and desire) to perform economically.[50] "Self-sufficiency" as a goal reflects the state's desire to see economically independent (and therefore nondemanding) subjects produced at the end of the assimilation process, subjects able to perform in the circuits of production and consumption. Conjoined here is the Asian as model minority and as *homo economicus*—he or she is reduced to a simple, independent, biopolitical subject.[51] This reduction is an ideal subject who reflects the positive nature of Americanization, even in the most trying of times. While there is certainly nothing wrong with helping individuals become economically self-sufficient, in refugee "transformation" policies we find that the priority seems to be instead on *selectively* disobligating the state of its responsibility for the refugees it had a strong hand in creating. Their successful reformation as American exculpates the United States for any involvement in producing that huge flow of refugee populations in the first place.[52] In the extreme, it suggests that refugees should be grateful to the United States for rescuing them from a backward culture in Indochina and providing them with the opportunity for a truly modern life. Such a reduction conspicuously ignores other resettlement issues, especially the heterogeneity of refugee subjectivities and cultures.[53]

The locating of refugees on American soil followed a policy of dispersal and forced integration. Once again, the politics of space intervene to make the narration of refugee life particular and distinct from the universalized and romanticized story of the immigrant. An essential part of refugee policy was that of spreading out refugee populations throughout the United States. The U.S. government feared both a drain on resources and violent reaction against refugees by various local inhabitants, and sought to mitigate those effects by forestalling or breaking up ethnic communities and simultaneously forcing a more rapid assimilation to American life.[54] This policy of course had its contradictions—was it better to disperse the refugee population in order to decentralize it and diffuse the impact of the arrival of tens of thousands of Indochinese, or would it be an easier management situation to cluster them together?[55] Yet the decision for dispersal was countered by refugees' overriding desire to reconstitute their communities: "While initial resettlement in the United States reflected a pattern Vietnamese had little power over, by June 1976 these first-wave refugees relocated, abandoning their sponsors and often their isolation. Their movement was from rural to urban areas, from northeastern states to southern and western states. By 1978 one-third of all refugees were concentrated in California; another 10 percent were in Texas. As of 1983, 90 percent of all refugees were in 10 states."[56] Although the government offered various financial incentives to refugees, trying to move them from the city back into rural areas, such incentives were rarely taken.[57] The state's desire was obviously not only to defuse potential concentrations of refugees in the tinderbox of depressed urban areas, but also to render them less visible.

Resistance to the will of the state to manage the refugees' insertion into American social space is read negatively by administrators, who cast this resistance in terms of a rejection of the proper mode of socialization.[58] Once again, a psychic profile of the refugee is produced by administrative agencies in order to explain such resistance. Tollefson notes: "These stereotypes influence policy by justifying America's continuing power over Indochinese. Resettled refugees have little involvement in deciding what new arrivals must learn in special pre-entry training programs. Government officials criticize refugees for moving from state to state, claiming without evidence that they are relocating to increase their welfare benefits, when in fact they do so to reunite divided families and reconstitute communities. The State Department complains that refugees are ungrateful and uncooperative, blames unemployment on their eagerness to be dependent on welfare, and concludes that the resettlement program has done everything it can for them."[59] In short, we have the invention of a subject exactly counterposed to that of the model minority. Instead of the pride of Japanese Americans unwilling to stoop to welfare, we have the instance of Asians willing to participate in the welfare state. This "willingness" is read not according to the specific histories and cultures of refugee populations and the history of U.S. imperialism in Asia, but according to the generalized domestic narrative of welfare and minorities. The Indochinese refugee presents the American imaginary with both the presence of the past and a puzzling contradiction to the myth of the Asian American model minority.

The administration of welfare is carried out within a complex set of apparatuses essentially geared toward "reducing dependency."[60] In the process, the goal is to effect a "transformation" of the refugee—from social dependent to a subject able to negotiate American life.[61] This process is intimately linked to the production of a particularly assimilated subject.[62] "Refugee transformation" is transacted via "[the] critical phases of adaptation, capability building, and disengagement" which change a "displaced person" into "An Individual Well-Equipped for Life in His Country of Final Destination."[63] As Ong puts it, "The transforming myth of the Overseas Refugee Training Program (ORTP) was to instruct refugees to 'speak good English, be employable, be unwilling to accept welfare, and be happy' in America."[64] This leads us to understand that "assimilation" has to be disaggregated and specified according to particular historical instances and agendas.

Tollefson gives a detailed account of the nature of these programs and their methods for effecting the transformation of refugees into good workers who will not place a drain on welfare rolls. One publication from the International Catholic Migration Commission instructs the refugee to "get along with everybody" and warns, "If you are a bad worker, the company can fire you. Then it might be hard for you to get another job."[65] Crucially, English language instruction does not give refugees a vocabulary for complaint or criticism, or indeed, civic life. Instead, the classroom is set up to represent an idealized American workplace, with clear hierarchies and duties, focusing on employers' needs. Pamphlets are circulated describing how refugees are regarded by employers as a means to suggest proper behavior, reward, and punishment.[66] One State Department publication explicitly notes: "Instruction must be directed toward meeting refugees' employment needs. Such needs are best determined by an employer needs assessment."[67]

The reverse of being a good worker is of course to be a welfare recipient—a game is played wherein participants are divided into two groups—one group is given employment and receives a paycheck, another receives welfare coupons:

Both teams must pay for housing, food, transportation, education, and other necessities with the money they receive. . . . The students are told that the purpose of the game is to practice handling U.S. currency, while the real aim stated in the curriculum is to discourage use of welfare.

This takes place through systematic differences in the treatment the two teams receive throughout the game. Blue Team members (those who receive a paycheck) are addressed by name, while Pink Team members are addressed by a number, which they must wear around their necks. Blue Team members sit on chairs, while Pink Team members must sit on the floor. Teachers who hand out paychecks and welfare checks treat Pink players rudely, while they treat Blue players courteously and respectfully. Only Blue players are permitted to sponsor relatives still in Southeast Asia; Pink players are forbidden to apply for relatives' resettlement.[68]

This game is called the "Free Money Game." The issue here involves more than the stigmatization of welfare (and the color scheme effects a degraded feminization of all welfare recipients)—it assumes that refugees' dependency on welfare is the result of their failure to learn the proper lessons, and not the result of institutional racism, classism, or labor practices. "Success" is carefully delineated within a complacent, depoliticized subjectivity.

Yet that passivity is not absolute: refugees are trained, above all, to become consumers, to circulate their earnings back into the national economy. One English language drill contains this streamlined version of buying an automobile:

> A: How can I get a loan?
> B: Why do you want the money?
> A: To buy a car.
> B: How much money do you need?
> A: $2,000.
> B: Please fill out this application.
> A: When do I get the money?
> B: Next week.[69]

The simplicity of this catechism instills a sense that any obstacle to its realization in real life is the result of the refugee's incomplete or faulty learning, not the actual mechanisms of the banking system.

Finally, the very positioning of refugees in the camp itself reflects the segmentation and segregation of space, "the very layout of the Center reflects the status of individuals and agencies."[70] The closer one is to the central area, the greater one's importance, authority, rights and privileges. And these rights and privileges include the right to transsect certain areas. Even the means of loco-motion are segregated—only teachers are allowed to ride on buses within the camp; refugees must walk, even though they are located furthest out on the pe-ripheries. Ironically, this regimen reflects more the realities of American life than the ideology the refugees are taught: "The refugee is told that in America all people are believed to be created equal, while he can see plainly from his lowly status among Americans in the [Processing Center] that this is not the case."[71] Yet a crucial element here is the notion that the refugee, once "pro-cessed" successfully, will graduate from that subaltern position. Thus, all these disciplinary practices, universally inscribed in the temporal and spatial organi-zation of the camp, are geared toward escaping it.

If, as Mortland argues, the effect of these programs was to intensify the lim-inal experiences of refugees, as they were trained to recognize and respond to a particularly scripted "Americanization," then we have another case where the "Americanization" of Asians takes place according to a slow catechism installed within a specific ideological terrain. Just as wealthy Asian entrepreneurs in Mon-terey Park were accused of leapfrogging the slow ardous temporality of subject-production (by dint of their imported capital), so the refugee is, in radically dif-ferent circumstances, asked to undergo a particular process of transformation and reidentification.[72] The impatience of administrators and social workers re-garding the speed and nature of refugee adaptation to "American life" may be in-terpreted as emanating in large part from a desire to bypass the radical histori-cal differences between immigrant and refugee.

In contrast to overtly stigmatizing processes that marked the unassimilated refugee as backward, primitive, and obdurate, the distinctly opaque character of the refugee also prompted some liberal anthropologists to enlist ethnographic analyses to enlighten public policymaking.[73] This disciplinary approach made recourse to a structural analysis of features shared by the Other and the Same. A common mode of understanding the mental state of refugees was via the pathology of post-traumatic stress, which in 1994 was defined by the World Health Organization as "a delayed or protracted response to a stressful event or situation (of either brief or long duration) of an exceptionally threatening or catastrophic nature. . . . Typical features include episodes of repeated reliving of the trauma in intrusive memories (flashbacks), dreams, or nightmares, oc-curring against the persistent background of a sense of numbness and emotional blunting, detachment from other people, unresponsiveness to surroundings."[74] Such readings allowed a convergence of two casualities of the wars in Indo-china—Vietnam veterans, and the Vietnamese themselves.[75]

America's "access" to the mind of the refugee took place at one remove: the American public could not be placed in a position equivalent to the actual combatant in Indochina. Hence there was no guarantee that such homologies would bring the refugee closer to the American horizon of understanding. Would an identification with the American war veteran allow such a fusion of perspectives, or would it instead sequester the veteran *and* the refugee in a particular imaginary space and time *out there and back then*, leaving "America" as a singular vantage point still retained as the norm? This displacement, like all such displacements, was not complete — if America attempted to relegate its memories of the war to the dramatically dysfunctional and damaged psyches of the "refugee" and the "Vietnam vet," their combination of numbness and hyperalertness, then the American imaginary discloses nonetheless a persistent if repressed and ambivalent memory of the war.[76] Such identificatory indecidability reflects the ways in which drawing the refugee into Asian/American subjectivity is always caught up in the various and sometimes contradictory agendas of domestic and foreign policies.

These forced migrants were made visible in American space against the backdrop of America's failure in Vietnam and a general political economy of race in America. No matter what their background, "Vietnamese were not exactly welcomed into this country. Many Americans opposed granting them asylum; they saw the Vietnamese as reminders of a war that America should never have fought. . . . Compounding the war-related hostility toward Vietnamese was the timing of the Vietnamese arrival. The year 1977 marked the beginning of the American economic recession; unemployment among Americans peaked. . . . American blacks charged local governments with discriminating in favor of Vietnamese in job placement services and allocating public housing. Similar incidents were repeated in Albuquerque, where Mexican American resentment against Vietnamese ran high."[77] One letter revealed exactly the desire to redefine America's underclass in an effort to remove the Indochinese from view: "I am sick, sick of Vietnam, the boat people, and Southeast Asia. How many Americans who are poor, elderly or disabled and living in our ghettos can buy their way out with gold? Instead of bringing in 14,000 Indochinese and spending half a billion dollars on them a year, we should spend the money on our own refugees."[78] This letter writer's strategy is to directly invert the situation: if what qualifies the Indochinese for "special consideration" is the term "refugee," then why not apply it to "our own" people living in poverty? This inversion is made possible only by erasing the historical link between the refugee and U.S. national policy (who has "brought" them in?), and claiming the poor as "ours" and the refugees as somebody else's. If guilt is the driving force, what about our moral responsibility for our own? The distinction between "our" history and "their" history separates the two at a time when their interlinkage could not be more clear.

In the mid-1970s, even liberals questioned federal refugee policy. As if in anticipation of the liberal argument against immigration from Mexico and Asia cited previously, which took as its moral high ground the need to deal first with the legacy of slavery, it was argued that such efforts meant, in then California governor Jerry Brown's words, "neglecting people who are living here." Senator George McGovern claimed, "Ninety percent of the Vietnamese would be better off going back"; and Congressman Burt Talcott of California argued, "We have too many Orientals already . . . the tax and welfare rolls will get overburdened and we already have our share of illegal aliens."[79]

The particular imagining of the assimilation of Indochinese refugees into America took place across and within a number of narratives, each with its own design. The refusal to house refugees in First World countries disavowed the role of those countries in creating that population; the role of the United States was to act as a responsible party, but to feel more responsible to the sanctity of its domestic state. Refugees were dispersed and "processed" through a regime that sought to produce a particular ethnic subject, stripped of history and perched on the brink of assimilation into the bourgeoisie. Yet this integration via a conventional story of ethnic assimilation was frustrated both by the contradictory feelings of Americans with regard to the war and by resentment from other minorities who were angered by the state's use of these refugees to salve collective guilt and at the same time use the obligation to help these products of American involvement in Asia to supersede the responsibility to help groups disadvantaged by institutional racism. Working-class whites who felt their jobs and livelihoods were threatened by these newcomers were also resistant.[80]

"Integration" and "transformation" were also subverted by the desire of these refugees to maintain communities and forge differing modes of adaptation, resisting the promise of the mainstream. Oral histories collected from refugees present a set of narratives that may begin to restore the complex material histories of forced migration, the effects of administered "transformative" policies, and the economies of race and power that refugees had to negotiate. Refugees were not simply passive subjects; they could and did (and continue to) interpret and deploy variously the discourse of non-dependence, even though their poverty rates remain startlingly high. We thus witness not submission but struggle in the transformation of refugees into Americans. The common interest of both the state and the refugees in integrating and empowering refugees is clear; but equally clear are different notions of what this integration is to look like and how it is to occur.

There is ample evidence of a counterdiscourse of resistance, invention, and modification which draws heavily upon the refugees' memories of the war and the deep recognition of their current historical circumstances.[81] While one cannot ignore the mediated quality of such narratives, they do offer some indication of how Indochinese refugees' narrations of American life locate different points of emphasis and value than those attached to the stereotypical "immigrant narrative" through which the refugees were commonly perceived.[82] The following excerpt eloquently describes the dislocation of time and space: "When I stepped on the plane, the time was 4:35. The weather was changing. Dark clouds rose up in the sky and the winds violently blew sand on the ground and formed some twisters. 'The first rain of the rainy season may happen!' I thought. I gritted my teeth and went up to the plane. I felt lonely with a broken heart. For the first time in my life I knew the sadness of one who must leave his country."[83] Gazing at the landscape of his home one final time, the speaker reads it according to a temporality and cultural life that will be alienated from him in a moment, as he enters a radically different chronotope. Thus, the simple observance of the external world—weather signs, climates—becomes a vehicle for the narrator's sense of his disengagement from familiar patterns and their absence in his new space of exile. This disjuncture forces upon the speaker the exact nature of his act of migrancy.

In contrast to one of the key features of the "immigrant narrative" (the primacy awarded money-making), we find in this next excerpt an entirely different set of needs and expectations: "My sons and I are not wealthy people. We are just workers who want to survive. We are not ambitious. We do not wish to go into business and get rich. We live like poor people but we are happy and do not envy others. We like living quietly and simply."[84] Nevertheless, this resignation to and acceptance of circumstance is not universal—individuals caught up in different situations participate in the "American Dream" in various ways. One such life is documented in the film *AKA Don Bonus*. Part of a project that had Indochinese high school students in San Francisco film their own lives, the life of "Don Bonus" takes place in the shifting terrain of the underclass and the welfare state. His fatherless family is relieved to be transferred to better public housing, further away from crime and violence. Bonus works hard at school, taking remedial classes in which he is nonetheless insulted and berated by a teacher for his "attitude." Yet he graduates from high school. Mother and siblings cannot attend the ceremony, however—they feel their presence is needed more that day at the sentencing of one of Don's younger brothers for attempted murder. Don does not begrudge them their absence from his graduation. His life has taught him the different and contingent priorities of American life. The film illustrates the way the "American Dream" is tracked differently, open to compromise, modification, reinvention, and that all these strategies disclose the impact of material history upon the Indochinese refugee.

Even the simple act of controlling one's movement across space is a struggle:

> I regret that we moved. I wanted to stay there [at their first home in the U.S.]. My children insisted that we move. Now I would like to go back, but my children are here, so I cannot. I prefer to live in the countryside, as we first did when we came to America, and not in a city as we do now. It is like Vietnam. I didn't want to leave Vietnam, but all my children were gone; I'm old, and they have to take care of me. So I had to follow them. That's what I did again in America.
>
> The main problem that I have in America is that I don't know how to speak English. Second, if I wanted to go somewhere, I cannot. I would have to use a car, but I cannot drive. If I use the bus, I am afraid that I will become lost.[85]

This passage directly addresses the issue of movement across various spaces—from Vietnam to the United States, from one city to another, from the rural to the urban; in each case the elderly woman is carried along by the course of history, by the transfer of authority and power away from her and her generation. Her inability to determine the placement of her own body is paralleled by her lack of English—the physical and the psychic become alienated. In such cases, what does it then mean to be "free" in America? Another speaker remarks: "Even though I am told that the United States is a land of freedom, I feel no freedom at all. Freedom, to me, is being able to farm our own land, raise our own cattle, and own our own homes without obligation to anyone."[86]

If such an ideal situation is forced to remain simply utopian, Indochinese refugees have nonetheless fashioned hybrid cultures in very different communities—there are Laotian refugees in middle Tennessee, Mien in Alabama, trailer-court communities in Kansas; the Marian Days Catholic festival in Missouri draws forty thousand Vietnamese immigrants annually.[87] This hybridity is produced at the nexus of specific and particular situations of labor, leisure, community life, and general life circumstances, and discloses uneven and complex alliances, affiliations, and segregations. Of particular interest for this section's topic is the issue of land, space, and sovereignty. As noted in these refugee narratives, these issues press hard upon the self-conception of refugees. The Vietnamese enclave of Versailles in New Orleans is particularly notable for its real and symbolic arrangement of land and land usage.

About forty percent of the twelve thousand Vietnamese who live in New Orleans reside in the Versailles subdivision.[88] Although many of the younger generation have moved to the metropolitan area, many older Vietnamese, who are largely poor and from agrarian backgrounds (that is, part of the second wave of refugees from Vietnam) have chosen to remain in Versailles. They have invented a "cultural milieu remarkably similar in many respects to that which they were forced to leave."[89] That culture includes a particular spatial arrangement. A commercial strip evinces the same kinds of shophouses found in Vietnam, arranged in similar patterns, and offering a full complement of services. But more interesting, perhaps, is the presence of an intricate system of vegetable and herb gardens set off across from the commercial strip by a canal. About thirty different Vietnamese crops are cultivated in residents' yards, in the backyards of duplexes and single-family residences, as well as on unused land between an artificial levee and the drainage canal. Crops are grown for consumption, and also sold to the local markets and restaurants. These spaces and this usage is not mentioned here merely to note their quaintness, but rather to remark upon the way they restore some sense of recognizable cultural and economic identity to these older refugees, instead of the identity foisted upon them as refugees by their adopted country.[90] The sense of dislocation, compounded by that of immobility and inaction found in the narratives above, is ameliorated in this re-creation of culture.[91]

This may be contrasted to the displacement, alienation, desperation, and violence evident in the highly publicized actions of Vietnamese gangs. The April 1991 shootout in Sacramento gives us a view into the nature of such violence. On April 4, more than a decade after the end of the Vietnam War, four Vietnamese men took over a Good Guys electronics store in Sacramento and held forty-one people hostage. The particular demands of the hostage-takers were described in the local newspaper as "bizarre": a helicopter to fly to Thailand so they could fight the Viet Cong, four million dollars, four bulletproof vests, and forty pieces of one-thousand-year-old ginseng roots. The background of these young men was especially odd in relation to this deed—all four were altar boys; three had dropped out or been expelled from school; none had been able to find a steady job.[92] Andrew Lam's report on the case notes the convergence of a number of issues—in particular, the staging of this deadly takeover (in which three of the four Vietnamese young men were killed, along with three hostages) in an electronics store filled with video goods, where these men, accustomed to watch Rambo-like films (in Lam's words, these men were "daily worshippers in this secular temple of high-tech consumerism"), could watch themselves on a panoply of television screens; their desire to return to Vietnam to continue a dead war; and their demand for ginseng roots that, according to Vietnamese mythology, were supposed to make them invulnerable. The event compels us to examine more closely the notion of the "Americanization" of refugees, in particular the idea that, once in America, the slow work of "transformation" (facilitated by consumer culture) slowly but inevitably carries the refugee forward out of memory.

Frank Smith's study of Cambodian television viewing likewise points out that the interpretive activities surrounding cultural consumption disclose radically different ways of relating media culture to refugees' lives—indeed, the line that separates the fictional and the real is severely blurred and indistinct. Watching *The Killing Fields*, which represents in intense visual and aural media climactic events now far away and in the past, engages the Cambodian refugees in a very specific process of participation and verification.[93] The Vietnamese youths' desire to finish a war long over is not entirely uncommon, as one refugee narrative demonstrates: "They [acquaintances of the narrator] dream of fighting the Communists, throwing them out, and returning to live out their days peacefully in their homeland. But this is only a dream."[94] In short, the temporal and spatial distance between the United States and Indochina is at once extenuated and shortened, participation in "American life" is mediated by the specific material histories of refugees and bound together by a particular sense of memory.

Many feel that only in death will the fragments of their lives, dispersed across different temporal and spatial frames, be made whole: "Day after day, I long to return to my country. My heart is not here in America. I fear that when it comes time for me to leave this world, my children will not give me a proper funeral."[95] For Hmong peoples such as the speaker just quoted, burial customs are especially significant. Tapp notes, "Given the importance of the geomantic system for burying the dead in formulating Hmong ethnicity, it is not surprising that the most serious threat to Hmong cultural traditions is felt to be that posed by the very different burial and mortuary practices . . . which they must now often adopt in dealing with death (*kev plog kev tuag*). . . . Many elderly Hmong, both in France and the U.S., were gloomy about future prospects for the Hmong in the countries, since burial sites could not be properly aligned."[96] In California's Central Valley town of Tollhouse, the burying of Hmong dead has become involved in a negotiations over space. Over a hundred years ago, a pioneering family donated land for a cemetery. One local resident remarks, "This cemetery was donated by the Yancey family for the mountain people. The Hmong come in and have taken it over. I don't begrudge them for a needing a place. But why our place?"[97] The answer is that the Hmong chose that site because of its similarity to their own mountain villages.[98] The three-acre site has been segmented into three areas, "Local folks with their plain flat markers over here. 'Hmong Hill' is over there, with its incense sticks, American flags, and giant headstones."

The presence of the American flag is not at all gratuitous—many gravestones proclaim the line of work of the deceased, "He served for the CIA."[99] The Hmong tribespeople were embroiled in complex political and cultural battles between U.S., Vietnamese, and Cambodian factions, and were recruited by the Central Intelligence Agency to fight against the Viet Minh. Now, because of animosity from townspeople (despite the fact that there are ten unused acres of land in the cemetery), the Hmong are no longer willing to visit existing graves. What is significant for our discussion here is the way negotiations, usage, and representations of symbolically charged space evince the will to forget America's engagements in Asia, to forget how and why exactly refugees come to be in America, how, indeed, American history is written on those tombstones as well, and the urge to preserve one sort of memory and memorialization over another.[100]

Like the struggle over the space and construction of memorialization in Tollhouse, the controversy over the design of the Vietnam Memorial in 1982 manifests the politics and problematics of representing and symbolizing the history of America's engagement in Indochina.[101] The debate raised complex issues regarding the adequacy of representational forms; specifically, the debate itself also was a battle over the Vietnam War: the memory of the war would retroactively reanimate and redefine the historical record. The plain black wall proposed by architect Maya Lin was described by critics as "unheroic," "a black hole," a "nihilistic statement." Charles Krauthammer wrote that the design did not mention "Vietnam, war, duty, country, sacrifice, courage, or even tragedy."[102] In other words, the memorial did not literalize the war in the expected lexicon of monuments and history. After fierce debate, a compromise of sorts was struck—a "realistic" depiction of three Vietnam veterans armed with weapons and battle gear would be placed in proximity to Lin's memorial. She complained that that sculpture would intrude upon the "artistic integrity" of the memorial. Besides, she said, the original design gave "each individual the freedom to reflect upon the heroism and sacrifice of those who served."[103] An article in the *National Review* confirmed that interpretation, calling it an "open book memorial" which was "beautiful, imposing, and fitting."[104]

The battle between "realistic" and abstract memorials involves a number of issues.[105] Here I only note that, in providing a relatively open space for interpretation and the giving of meaning, the abstract memorial rejects the literalizing and therefore stabilizing and codifying function of the realistic memorial. Such a stabilization of memory attempts to fix it in time, to sequester it away from the mutability of human consciousness. As Pierre Nora notes, "The less memory is experienced from the inside, the more it exists through its exterior scaffolding and outward signs."[106] The problem here, of course, is the constitution of that particular interiority. Whose memorial was it? How can "Asian" and "American" history be separated in this instance, in the commemoration of their common engagement? The presumption of that interiority is one question. The other question raised by realistic memorials is the "message" that the viewer is supposed to process, and this question is of course intimately linked to that of the ideologically saturated lexicon of memory. Lin's abstract design left the message open; the memorial was in that sense a pre-text, a catalytic occasion sanctioned by the state by the very presence of the sculpture within the memorial grounds of the nation. The issues of space, location, ownership, identity, and memory which we have traced throughout this chapter link up ultimately to the question of history and the politics of memory.

Amerasians: Coming Home for the First Time

If Jim and Tae's biracial child is the harbinger of postwar Asian America, an optimistic figure to inhabit that seamless continuity of Asia Pacific America in the mid-twentieth century, the history of biracial children of the Vietnam War symbolizes the compromise of such utopian thinking and evinces instead the violence of the wars in Indochina and America's will to forget. The case of the Vietnamese Amerasians exemplifies the battle over America's sense of responsibility, and, more deeply, as in the Vietnam memorial, the battle over how and what to remember. In 1989, as many as thirty thousand children of American servicemen were thought to still remain in Vietnam. The term "Amerasian" was coined by Pearl Buck in *East Wind, West Wind*, and referred to children of Asian mothers and American fathers left fatherless in Asia; its redeployment signals the historical continuity of America's engagements in Asia and the effects of those engagements.[107] The various policies set up to facilitate their "homecoming" (as it was called) reveal the contradictions and ambivalences surrounding the Vietnam war.[108]

Called *bui doi*, or "dust of life," these individuals, some very clearly marked as products of liaisons with the west, are damned in a country where not only cultural belief but legal and economic practices revolve around patriarchal prerogatives.[109] To not have a father is to not be a viable social subject. Added to this stigma is the particular sign of miscegenation, the sin of the mother. Although they are theoretically Vietnamese citizens, they are excluded from Vietnamese life and face systematic discrimination: they are ineligible for ration cards and often "beg on the streets, peddle black market wares, or prostitute themselves. . . . The mothers of Amerasian children are not eligible for government jobs or employment in government enterprises and many are estranged from their families and are destitute."[110] Upon arrival in the United States, the Amerasians are hardly welcomed "home": they do not speak English, are not comfortable with American culture (their "American" identity was a black mark against them in Vietnam; their Vietnamese identity may now make them a target of racism in the United States), and only a tiny percent are ever reunited with their fathers. Such "hybridity" reveals the scarring produced at the nexus of American imperialism and libido. Furthermore, the fact that the American soldiers were disproportionately drawn from poor minorities makes these individuals objects of liberal compassion but marked more precisely by skin color.

The drama surrounding the Amerasian issue reads much like an amplified version of the narrative of the abandonment of illegitimate children by their fathers. But the amplification is striking for the way it embroiled the "father" in a particular discourse of national forgetting. Although as early as 1980 a special "Presidential Determination" (No. 80–17, 45 Fed. Reg. 29,785) declared Amerasians "of special humanitarian concern to the United States," it was not until the 1982 amendment to the Immigration and Nationality Act that the United States expressed any responsibility for the children and granted them citizenship status, although it did *not* do so for the children's mothers (it would seem that the Asian/American split was located precisely at this boundary).[111] Previously, under the Immigration and Nationality Act, Amerasian children were not exempted from numerical restrictions placed on immigration since they were not "legitimate" children of American citizens. The use of such moralistic and sexist restrictions casts the onus back upon the Vietnamese woman and the child of the American father.

It took until the 1987 "Amerasia Homecoming Act" for the United States to attempt a coherent, expeditious, specific program that broadened eligibility to other family members and attempted to help Amerasians navigate their way through the bureaucractic nightmare between refugee and immigrant status (in

1985 there was already a backlog of twenty-two thousand cases).[112] The Act declared that while Amerasians and their close family members were to be admitted to the United States as immigrants, rather than refugees, once here they would be treated as refugees and thereby given full refugee benefits and access to training programs.[113] Such manipulations not only critically disclosed the ambiguous status of these individuals in the American political psyche, in an important way they also commented implicitly upon the unsettled status of the American memory of Vietnam. The state's recognition of these children as its own, the idea of a "Homecoming" act, is a generous rhetorical move that suggests a particular reidentification, yet the material histories of these individuals in Asia and in America disclose the complexities that are hidden underneath such a broad verbal performance of reconciliation.

In the next chapter, I will continue this analysis of the reshaping and reclaiming of American space. If the wars in Asia reterritorialized Asian America and forced a redefinition of what it was to be in the twentieth century, the postwar emergence of transnational economies reshaped the local in particular ways and threatened to revise national space in a more subtle yet more effective way.

8 / Demarcations and Fissures: Reconstructing Space

> *The same human motives, which have led men to spread a*
> *network of trade-communication over the whole earth, in order*
> *to bring about an exchange of commodities, are now bringing*
> *a new distribution of populations. When these populations*
> *become as mobile as the commodities of commerce there will*
> *be practically no limits — except those artificial barriers, like*
> *the customs and immigration restrictions, maintained by*
> *individual states — to a world wide economic and personal*
> *competition. Furthermore, when the natural barriers are*
> *broken down, artificial barriers will be maintained with*
> *increasing difficulty.* —ROBERT PARK, *Race and Culture*

ROBERT PARK'S VIEW OF MODERN LIFE is inseparable from his writings on urban geography. Park himself was of course deeply engaged in urban policy — as an unofficial adviser to the Chicago Commission on Race Relations and as the first president of the Chicago Urban League.[1] According to Park, the dual characters of the modern age were a new global economy and dramatically increased (and increasingly disorderly) migrancy. These forces were reshaping urban life — the cities themselves would "become the centers of vast numbers of uprooted individuals, casual and seasonal laborers, tenement and apartment house dwellers, sophisticated and emancipated urbanites, who are bound together neither by local attachment nor by ties of family, clan, religion or nationality." What makes Park's definitions so significant for this study is the fact that these passages are taken from his introduction to J. F. Steiner's *The Japanese Invasion* (1917). If there were any doubt as to how the Chicago School's notions of modern America took as a central facet the Pacific "racial frontier," its possible transgressions, and the consequences of such transgressions for the United States, the link between political economy, urban geography, migration, nation, and race is unmistakable here:

> Already the extension of commerce and the increase of immigration have brought about an international and interracial situation that has strained the inherited political order of the United States. . . . Whatever may have been the immediate causes of the [first] world war, the more remote sources of the conflict must undoubtedly be sought in the great cosmic forces which have broken down the barriers which formerly separated the races and nationalities of the world, and forced them into new intimacies and new forms of competition, rivalry, and conflict.[2]

The focus on competition as the greatest shaping force in modern life is well established in Park's writings.[3] Without putting too fine a point on it, one might conjecture that the mystified "cosmic force" referred to here takes one form in modern capitalism on a global scale. Among its numerous effects, as evident in all these citations, is the alienation of human beings. This alienation is reflected in the very shape of the modern American city. Park's studies of the modern city focused on the spatial distribution of groups and their interrelationships in maintaining the city's economic equilibrium—in the modern age people related to each other not via a common culture, but via the logic of the market.[4] Against such alienation Park hopefully posed the idea of a new American "culture" that would provide the means to make new bonds and commitments and allow people to move outside the fearfully isolated space of the private home, besieged as it was by the new demands and conditions of modern life.

It was within this context that, for Park, ethnic communities might be "redemptive," as they carried within them the residual traits of traditions lost in the move to modern America and its industrialized cities. This led Park to argue against the notion of absolute assimilation and instead for the persistence of ethnic communities that, by their very exclusion from the mainstream, were allowed to retain certain traditions.[5] Nevertheless, he also saw that persistent disenfranchisement from the core of social and economic power would inevitably lead to the deterioration of the ethnic group. This made the modern city a unique space of both modern alienation and segregation, but also of new combinations and interfaces that challenged any simple notion of assimilation.[6] Park's notion of mobility was thus complicated by two strains of thought. On one hand, he posited the socioeconomic need for racial minorities to assimilate. Such assimilation would come only when "social distances are overcome through participation in a common cultural life."[7] Yet Park also worried about the cost posed by assimilation to the separate groups' "culture." Surveying the cityscape, he wondered if separate ethnic and racial communities did not reflect the fact that more binding and logical ties drew such groups together—that is, unlike other "moderns" who were linked solely by economic logic, ethnic and racial minorities were held together by a common culture.

The result of this, for an understanding of the place of race in the modern city, is the following: first, that the spatialization of the cityscape reflects the segregation of groups according to an economic logic—the members of these different groups might, as they "modernize," loosen their ties to the community and join the mainstream as they recognize there a different "common culture," that of the market. Second, this gain is also a loss—the specifically racial identity can never be completely erased (as we saw previously), rather, racism would always differentiate the raced subject. Third, only through racial conflict would groups be able to enfranchise themselves, and the occasion and opportunity for conflict was presented in the modern city, a still new space of potential reterritorialization. The tableau of the modern city was a virtual grid of representation upon which the rate and nature of ethnic and racial assimilation could be read.

Moving more closely to view this reconstructed urban space, one finds that in the effort to escape these alienating and conflictual effects of modernity, the home becomes a particularly contrived sanctuary: "Man invariably builds himself somewhere and at some time a home, a retreat, a refuge, where, surrounded by his family and his friends, he can relax, and, so far as it is possible for so gregarious a creature, be wholly at home and at ease, and in more or less complete possession of his own soul."[8] Private domestic space will house the fragile "soul" of modern man and woman. "Home" is constructed within the context of a particular remapping of domestic space which nonetheless must acknowledge its new neighbors. Witness, for example, these two citations from Stonequist:

> The expansion of Western civilization over the globe has brought about marginal areas of conflict and produced persons living within both cultures. Such culture conflict is particularly evident in the urban centers. These are the points of maximum cultural interpenetration. From such centers the new influences radiate out along the paths of communication and transportation.[9]

> New countries like the United States are only the conspicuous examples of a world-wide condition. Consequently we need not search far in order to find

acute instances of the marginal man. He may be our next-door neighbour: the economically successful but socially unadjusted immigrant who as a young man left his peasant environment in some distant country to make his fortune in newer and richer lands. . . . Farther away perhaps lives the man of Negro, Mongolian, or mixed blood who carries in his face the tell-tale evidence of an alien background, but whose inner personality may be indistinguishable from that of our closest neighbor.[10]

Stonequist's general observation is articulated in a particularly localized, personal narrative that evinces precisely those complex forces that weigh against any simple, psychologistic analysis of the production of social space: this "worldwide condition" is not to be found (only) in an abstractly imagined urban space —one's own domicile is likely to be contiguous to that of the "successful but socially unadjusted immigrant." But that is only the most benign form of foreignness (benign, since this immigrant's foreignness, attested to by his or her as yet unadjusted social subjectivity, is counterbalanced at least in part by material success, evidence of suitability to American economic, if not social, life).

As we follow the rhetorical sweep of this redefinition of urban space "radiating out" of the city in the first citation, so do we, in the second, follow a trajectory out from the center (located, obviously enough, in one's domicile) to find those whose racial markings have cast them further out into the peripheries— the ethnic immigrant and the racial minority are to be found on a particularly drawn continuum of modern city space. What is seemingly left intact is the center, sequestered in its protective interiority, fortified by assumptions of its wholeness and adjustedness. And yet even the center is not immune from the effects of this new "worldwide condition." For the very neighborhoods we inhabit are now variegated, unevenly mapped spaces of immigration and racial difference which refuse to be read simply. We find that, "beneath" racial difference, the same universal psychic revision is to be found (even) in "our closest neighbor." If "culture" is to be that redemptive force that binds people together in the absence of "tradition" in the modern age, then what we find is a particular crisis in the cultural life of modern America which can be read in the very shape and nature of its urban spaces, which are marked differentially by race, ethnicity, and migration.

In the late twentieth century, the anxiety apparent in Park's 1917 introduction to *The Japanese Invasion*, which anticipates the beginnings of modern Asian America set within the modern global economy, becomes fully realized under the condition of transnational capital. One of the many books declaring a "Pacific Century" wonders what happens when people note that "our monthly rents and mortgage rates are controlled by new financial markets that depend as much or more on the Bank of Japan as they do on the Federal Reserve Bank. How did we arrive at this juncture in our history? Where will it take us?"[11] The modern formation of Asian America, the refiguration of American space now informed by modern Asia, is a persistent theme from Park's time onward. This chapter will focus on the particularly alienating effect of Asian transnational capital on "American" space—in the contemporary manifestation of Asian America.

As noted in Chapter 7, the production of Asian American social subjectivity must be seen as *taking place*—that is, as emerging within a specific set of variously produced symbolic and actual spaces. Contemporary understandings of the built environment see the symbolic and literal precisely as interpenetrating. The publication of Henri Lefebvre's influential book, *The Production of Space*, marks the consolidation of a theory of space that departs significantly from earlier readings. The traditional mode of doing urban geography characterized by Park's Chicago School read the modern city as a particular organism with its own logic of survival and equilibrium: "We may, if we choose, think of the city, that is to say, the place and the people, with all the machinery and administrative devices that go with them, as organically related, a kind of psycho-physical mechanism in and through which private and political interests find not merely a collective but a corporate expression."[12] For Park, the complexity of modern life engendered new modes of organizing the built environment; the best way to understand these new formations was by way of the rhetoric of the organic, which assumed that a "natural" logic informed these new social spaces. In short, these new formations did not require a new analytic language; rather, they could be understood as following certain natural (transcendent) laws. At the root of this model was the assumption of an equilibrium-seeking organism that sorted out its priorities and efficiencies in an inevitable way, even if it was not always harmonious.

Later theorists of urban geography have contested these assumptions and have provided a way to open up our analysis to transnational capital. The hermetic integrity of Park's organic city is breached by an analysis that insists on the linkages between localities and larger structures of social, economic, and political life. Gottdiener summarizes his position vis-à-vis Park thus:

> Both the cities and the suburbs are sustained and nurtured by national, even global processes of advanced industrialization. Business, finance, and government all converge on urban space to alter or transform it, because in most cases class frac-

tions of capital require it, the property sector produces it, and the government has made it profitable to do so. Although local areas still grow "by themselves," the really broad aspects and problems of contemporary urban expansion, conceptualized as massive systems of regional growth, require [a theory of the social construct of space].[13]

Edward Soja's work similarly defines space as socially constructed according to a more heterogeneous model than Park's. Not only does Soja include the effect of complex material forces on the local as mentioned in Gottdiener, but, following Lefebvre, he also ties together the objective realm and the psychic realm in the perception and analysis of space:

> The assertion of (social) spatiality . . . forces a major reinterpretation of the materiality of space, time, and being, the constructive nexus of social theory. In the first place, not only are the spaces of nature and cognition incorporated into the social production of spatiality, they are significantly transformed in the process. This social incorporation-transformation sets important limits to the independent theorizations of physical and mental space, especially with regard to their potential applicability to concrete social analysis and interpretation. In their appropriate interpretive contexts, both the material space of physical nature and the ideational space of human nature have to be seen as being socially produced and reproduced. Each needs to be theorized and understood, therefore, as ontologically and epistemologically part of the spatiality of social life. . . .
>
> The production of spatiality in conjunction with the making of history can thus be described as both the medium and the outcome, the presupposition and embodiment, of social action and relationship, of society itself. Social and spatial structures are dialectically intertwined in social life, not just mapped one onto the other as categorical projections.[14]

Of particular importance is the production of space by various agents, the production of space as an act of conflict and consensus.

Lefebvre differentiates between "representations of space" and "representational spaces," between "space" and "place":

> Representations of space are certainly abstract, but they also play a part in social and political practice: established relations between objects and people in represented space are subordinate to a logic which will sooner or later break them up because of their lack of consistency. Representational spaces, on the other hand, need obey no rules of consistency or cohesiveness. Redolent with imaginary and symbolic elements, they have their source in history—in the history of a people as well as in the history of each individual belonging to that people. (42)

Represented space is the terrain of ideology, representational space that of "absolute space," or "place," which, although given certain latitude, is weakened by its remove from power. Lefebvre makes the issue of power explicit:

> In *spatial practice*, the reproduction of social relations is dominant. The *representation of space*, in thrall to both knowledge and power, leaves only the narrowest leeway to *representational spaces*, which are limited to works, images and memories whose content, whether sensory, sensual or sexual, is so far displaced that it barely achieves symbolic force. (50)

Here, I will retain an attention to both space as understood as the overarching ideological effects of late capitalism, and place as a particular site of work, labor, and everyday life, which manifests the force of capital and yet also resistance to or deflection of it, and attempts particular reinventions. Taking up these perspectives, and broadening them to include an address to the fundamental issues we've traced throughout this study—migrancy, race, ethnicity, and the global economy—help us to better read both the situatedness of Asians in America and their inscriptions within and upon both the cityscapes of the United States and the American imaginary. Sassen likewise observes the connection between the symbolic notion of otherness and concrete material practices: "Immigration and ethnicity are constituted as otherness. Understanding them as a set of processes whereby global elements are *localized*, international markets are constituted, and cultures from all over the world are de- and reterritorialized, puts them right there at the center along with the internationalization of capital as a fundamental aspect of globalization [emphasis in the original]." [15] How Asians in America "appear" is thus linked intimately to the chronotopes that frame that appearance. And, as we have traced from the 1930s, that framing has everything to do with the linkage of "Asian" to "American" in the modern state. It is this struggle for symbolic *and* actual power that characterizes the ideological, political, and cultural practices of Asian America.

The chronotopes in which the figures of the modern and postmodern Asian/American are drawn are vastly complex and offer a number of contradictions to various ideologies of assimilation and the production of the individual American subject. For instance, reading race into the "society" that constructs space provides a way to understand the ways that a reading of place as the product of capital reaches a point of negation, or at least containment and contradiction when race and ethnicity are factored in. While, as Dirlik notes, "capitalism . . . accepts the destruction of places as a condition of its success," [16] we will find that capital, even in rolling over distinctions of place, may have a specifically

raced value: even as foreign direct investment is sought to prop up a weakened domestic economy, the racial appearance of those investing that capital in those actual locations (as inhabitants, instead of invisible account holders) forces a rethinking of the priorities of such communities (what price are they willing to pay
for economic viability?). The logic of capital also runs up against the primordial
values of self-determined community that would contain and domesticate the
foreign. This tension can be excavated from Park's own writings on urban geography: we may read his self-enclosed and self-regulating organic model as
motivated in large part by the ideology of self-determination so much at the
heart of American belief. The "sanctuary" built in the midst of radical change in
the neighborhood, now peppered with the newly mobile foreign, may be read
as the last bastion against the effects of that "vast unconscious cooperation of
races and peoples." But that refuge is hedged on all sides by unevenly assimilated
"marginal" people, brought to the interior of the nation by the logic of modern
economies. This movement has historically produced the attempt to contain
such groups spatially. It also has led to a readjustment of the notion of community: not only its composition demographically, but its modes of symbolic identification and sustenance.

Here the different claims on place will be read as a struggle to anchor social
identity in place even as the constituent elements of place are rewritten, "out-
sourced," reterritorialized, and cross-hatched by various claims made by various agents. Dirlik's essay usefully points out the complex political issues involved in any reading of place, citing the "rich interplay of politics, psychology
and esthetics" (9). Rather than accept an entirely passive model, Dirlik argues
the necessity to "question and transcend such notions which make places into
playthings of a globalizing capital, and to reaffirm places in terms of the values
implied by the concept of place; not out of a utopian or nostalgic urge to restore
to places some irreducible (or even unimaginable) pristine purity but in order
to differentiate clearly places as projects" (36). Turning specifically to the case
of Asian Americans, we should note, along with Ong, Bonacich, and Cheng,
that, like Asian immigrants, they "are not merely filling the positions that are being created as a result of restructuring. They are actively helping reshape the
economic landscape." [17]

The (Re)Formation of Community

Saskia Sassen has pointed out that in today's world, any notion of national borders becoming more porous has to specify the contents circulating across such

weakened borders with ever-increasing speed. She notes the coexistence of different regimes for the movements of capital and people: "Current immigration policy in the highly developed countries is increasingly at odds with other major policy frameworks in the international system. There is a combination of drives to create border-free economic spaces yet intensify border control to keep immigrants and refugees out. . . . There are, in effect, two epistemological communities: one dealing with the flow of capital and information; the other with immigration."[18] Simply put, the circulation of bodies, rather than the more neutrally characterized commodity or cash, calls attention to another index of desirability. The question of what we import runs up against the question of who we live next to.

In this chapter I tackle the problems that recent Asian immigration has presented to the mapping of American space. Throughout, I follow Sassen's debunking of the common myth of immigration: that immigration is either simply a matter of individual choice or the relative desirability of the land emigrated to as compared to the country of origin. Instead, she instructs us to examine "the impact of the internationalization of economies on, first, the mechanisms connecting emigration and immigration countries and, second, the organization of labor markets in both types of countries."[19] Thus, the logic of global capital binds the relevant countries in such a way that individual national economies cannot be read purely locally.[20] For instance, the need for cheap labor, semi-skilled labor, technicians, and particularly skilled workers is not simply produced by the country of immigration, but that need itself is the product of the globalization of national economies.[21]

In 1917, the same year that saw the publication of *The Japanese Invasion*, the United States envisioned a particular mapping of the "Asian" world. Driven by the fear of a flood of unassimilable immigrants and an attendant mentality of containment, on February 5 Congress passed an act creating an "Asiatic Barred Zone" which extended the Chinese exclusion laws to all other Asians: "The zone covered South Asia from Arabia to Indochina, as well as the adjacent islands. It included India, Burma, Thailand, the Malay States, the East Indian Islands, Asiatic Russia, the Polynesian Islands, and parts of Arabia and Afghanistan. . . . Together these provisions [Chinese exclusion laws and the Gentlemen's Agreement] declared inadmissible all Asians except teachers, merchants, and students. Only Filipinos and Guamanians, under U.S. jurisdiction at the time, were not included."[22] Only in 1965 did that "zone" collapse under the directive of the Immigration Act, and the juridical segregation of Asia from America gave way to a new historical formation.[23]

The nature of Asian immigration to the United States after the Second World War has been qualitatively different from that which preceded it; this immigration has been particularly influenced by U.S. policies established during the occupation of Japan, the Cold War struggle with regard to China (1945−49), and wars in Korea (1950−53) and Vietnam (1962−75), and by the globalization of a new world economy. During the 1950s and the 1960s, the United States poured vast sums of money into East Asia with the intent of establishing its hegemony over that area; for instance, Japan was occupied so as to be "Americanized," its economy and politics made to conform to a particular image of an American-dominated Asia. Between 1945 and 1990, without factoring the staggering amount spent on the Vietnam War, the United States contributed "some $71 billion in development aid, loans, technical assistance, and other means of economic support to the Asian nations on the western side of the Pacific Rim. The sums were far greater than earlier outlays for the Marshall Plan in Europe. In fact, the American effort in the Asia-Pacific region consituted a second and continuing Marshall Plan in all but name." [24] The stabilization of economies in East Asia was affected by U.S. support of particular authoritarian regimes; the United States pressed these countries toward export-based economies suited to U.S. needs. As Liu and Cheng put it: "Taiwan and South Korea used tight control over labor to build manufacturing industries, turning trade deficits to surpluses. U.S. capital was available for foreign ventures because rising domestic labor costs pushed business interests to search for more profitable outlets abroad. To attract these investors, Taiwan and Korea offered favorable terms of return and facilitated the local recruitment of professionals to work in the transnational corporations. The hiring of locally recruited personnel integrated these professionals into an economic network that required a mobile labor force not bound by national boundaries." [25]

Thus, while some Asian immigration (primarily refugees from Indochina, but other immigrants as well) still provides cheap labor in the United States, joining Latino immigrants as low-wage workers, since the 1960s this "traditional" component of Asian immigration to America has been complemented and nearly overshadowed by a highly educated stratum of technicians and professionals who are playing an increasingly major role in restructuring the economy, providing skills, entrepreneurial energy, and capital. [26] The education of this group, as well as the particular need for their training, is itself another outcome of U.S. domestic and foreign policy: while the U.S. made drastic cuts in social spending (for example, in education) to cope with a postwar economy, Asia had a surplus of highly educated individuals whose skills have not yet found niches in their home economies (this situation is of course in flux). As many Asian homelands are still "developing," professional employment in the private sector, particularly suited to advanced economies, is hard to find. These countries in general are producing more highly trained people than they can absorb, while the U.S. produces fewer than it needs. Individuals trained by an educational system modeled on the U.S. system and heavily weighted toward a capitalist ideology of individualism are drawn to the higher salaries to be found abroad.[27]

In the cases of immigrants coming over as low-wage workers as well as those filling niches in the managerial and entrepreneurial classes,[28] one witnesses the convergence of factors pressing these immigrants to leave Asia and the creation of specific slots in the U.S. economy within the service sector and a flourishing informal economy. In the 1980s and 1990s, while Asian professionals offer technical and other sorts of highly educated support to the upper stratum of this service economy, "the swollen professional and managerial stratum of the global city has a need for hotels, restaurants, entertainment, and other personal services, such as house-cleaning and child care."[29] To this one may add the physical labor required to support the projects of re-gentrification and construction in the revision of major American cities, which call again for low-wage, semi-skilled and unskilled workers.

Asian immigration since the Second World War thus derives both from the effects of postwar foreign policy and from the general process of globalization of which those policies are a part. While changes in the 1965 immigration law and the prior existence of immigrant communities are important factors, they are not alone sufficient to explain the continuation of this flow at even higher levels.[30] Immigrants and their communities are used to lower costs of production; they raise the organizational flexibility of formal sector industries (the garment industry, for instance) while neighborhoods engage in the informalization of work that is created by, among other things, competitive pressures in certain industries to compete with low-wage Third World countries; the rapid increase in volume of renovations, alterations, small-scale new construction; and inadequate provision of services and goods by the formal sector.[31] Therefore, Sassen suggests that "a good share of the informal economy is not the result of immigrant survival strategies, but rather an outcome of structural patterns or transformations in the larger economy."[32]

The pervasive attitude toward the increased visibility and centrality of immigrant labor (witness the difficulty of the Clinton administration in filling high-level appointments with individuals who had not engaged in one way or another in supporting illegal immigrant labor) engenders the notion that America is being turned into a "Third World country."[33] This notion takes as its evidence the more pronounced presence of ethnic populations in assumed "American" spaces —their storefronts, products, commodities, and bodies are all taken as signs of America's inability to maintain its borders and to self-sustain. But rather than being the result of the haphazard convergence of the wills of a mass of individual immigrants from abroad, seeking to take advantage of American "weakness," we have seen that the "Third Worldization" of America is a result of complex geopolitical and economic phenomena. This remapping of American cities was and is accompanied by both racial and class anxiety. Anxiety surrounds the basic notions of community sovereignty in an age of increased transnationalism and the correct path of ethnic assimiliation in an age of increased and uneven transmigrancy. Basic questions of the nation-state—who belongs here and who controls "here"—become all the more pressing and more difficult to resolve.

One of the primary modes through which the land itself is given over to the control of the market is, of course, speculation, which plays a central role in the radical and violent restructuration of American communities. Harvey theorizes real estate as a "second circuit" of capital, and outlines the mutual engagement of three activities that we will find in each of our cases of restructuration: "The activities of the property circuit have actually created and exaggerated demand by three main methods: by 'land speculation,' by channeling capital flows, and by state support for both."[34] Reconstructing Asian/American space has involved precisely these three methods—the effects of foreign and domestic speculation, the divergence of capital, and the involvement of the state in the "public-private" venture of urban redevelopment. Each of these phenomena has a profound effect on the production of Asian/American subjectivity, and on the sense shared by many that their control over their communities has been given over to others.

Restructuring the Asian/American City

An "informal" case of such restructuring of ethnic communities and the particular nexus of local ethnic capital and labor and foreign speculation is the resurgence, growth, and overdevelopment of New York City's Chinatown.[35] This re-invigorated Chinatown was expected to develop along the lines of a typical ethnic enclave, to become, in Peter Kwong's words, a "Little Hong Kong."[36] The fact that it did not reveals much about the new economic world of the late twentieth century. In the late 1960s, New York's economy was in deep decline, as the withdrawal of corporate headquarters and manufacturing industries resulted in a steady loss of jobs. This created a crucial depression in property values that in turn allowed for local Chinese investment in self-employing, small-business activities. One of the primary industries was garment making, which fed into New York's need for a cheap, flexible workforce. In the mid-1960s, New York's garment industry had declined because of competition from southern states and the Third World; between 1969 and 1982 there was a 40 percent loss of jobs in that sector. During this same period, the number of Chinese women working in New York Chinatown garment factories grew from eight thousand to twenty thousand.[37]

By this time the 1965 Immigration Act had opened the way for dramatically increased Asian immigration. As the pattern of immigration switched to families rather than individuals, a particular ethnic economy flourished around the garment industry: Asian women participated as flexible, second-income providers who could absorb long periods of unemployment. They did not speak English and were dependent on Chinese subcontractors, who took advantage of their flexibility and status. Besides taking advantage of this new workforce, sweatshops have flourished because they require little capital to start up. In 1960 there were only 8 factories, in 1965 there were 34, in 1974 there were 209, and by 1984 that number had climbed to 500.[38]

Suddenly, more and more Chinatown families became two-income households, with both greater wages to spend and particular needs. The participation of women in the garment industry created a multiplier effect: restaurants sprang up to provide food for families with working women, and other service-related businesses followed suit.[39] This created a boom in Chinatown business. During this period Kwong finds that "the desire of Chinese retailers to locate in the heart of Chinatown is so strong that they are paying unbelievable prices. According to a study done by the Real Estate Board of New York, the annual rent per square foot for retail space on Canal Street is $275. That is higher than rents on Madison Avenue above Forty-second Street ($255) . . . and it is far higher than on Wall Street, where the rents are around $175 per square foot."[40]

At the same time, Asian foreign capital, fed by the prosperity of Chinese in Hong Kong, Taiwan, Macao, Malaysia, Indonesia, Thailand, Burma, and the Philippines, was particularly anxious to find investment opportunities, particularly after the recognition of China, the fall of Saigon, and the uncertainty over the fate of Hong Kong made foreign investment more and more attractive.[41] Many banks were set up in Chinatown to facilitate the transfer of transnational capital: from 1981 to 1986, fourteen Chinese-owned banks opened, making a total of twenty-seven banks in the Chinatown community, two-thirds of which were Chinese-owned. Their combined assets at that time were estimated to be over $2 billion in reserve.[42] Kwong reminds us that it is crucial to note that this money came only when it was deemed profitable, and it was made profitable by the garment industry and the restaurant industry that supported it. The implosion of the Chinatown community may be read within a critique of capital: "Communities have to be disrupted by speculative activity, growth must occur, and whole residential neighborhoods must be transformed to meet the needs of capital accumulation. Herein lie both the contradictions and the potentials for social transformation in the urbanization sphere at this stage in our history."[43] In the course of this radical revaluation and restructuring, community members were displaced. Against arguments for restricted growth, investors put forth the imperative to develop a "first-class Chinatown" and "to build to what the property here is worth." This amounted to the redefinition of Chinatown solely as a space of economic production.[44]

Ultimately, true to the contradictions of capital, this strategy of over-accumulation backfired. Higher rents cut into profits of restaurants and other small businesses and industries; wages fell; workers were laid off. "Loans for restaurants and garment factories are harder to get, since they are considered high-risk ventures. In fact, those who made money in garment and restaurant businesses are now moving into real estate. This exodus of capital has created a situation where only the large enterprises can survive. Thus there is a concentration of capital in the community economy; fewer and fewer individuals own more and more businesses."[45] Thus, from being a small business community whose owners, workers, and customers were largely part of that community, Chinatown became a space of speculation and foreign investment, with more and more of its economy given over to a small economic elite with few ties to the community.[46] The narrative of the ethnic minority achieving the "American Dream" was subverted as the benefits of that dream were diverted into the hands of big real estate interests and foreign capital.

But the penetration of foreign capital is, as we have seen, only one part of the story. To fully understand what happened in New York's Chinatown, one must read its remapping within the logic of late capitalist flexible accumulation, which created specific openings in the devalued landscape of the city, a niche within garment manufacturing, a pool of Asian labor, a need and opportunity for an informal economy, and, finally, the context for foreign investment.[47] Thus the increased visibility of a "Third World" (both in terms of ethnic labor and foreign investment) within and upon American space, cannot be read as simply infiltration from without, but instead must be understood as evincing the mutual participation of the domestic and the global economy in the restructuring of social and economic life. Notions of the individual's sovereignty over his or her private space become exploded, as the logic of what Harvey calls the "community of money" hijacks any notion of a self-determined community.[48]

The connection between these phenomena and the concept of "culture" is doubly clear: as the context for cultural production is dramatically shifted out of a simply articulated local space and placed instead within the nexus of forces that exceed the immediate influences of the local, "culture" takes place on a shifting terrain that is increasingly contextualized within a dialectical reformation of local and global. The usual expectations of life, the trajectories of subject formation, become increasingly displaced and regeared. This displacement and regearing has everything to do with the production of space for economic growth, the diverting of public funds from social programs, and the consequent redefinition of social, political, and cultural citizenship—who and what *belong* here? Under such conditions, the remapping of the city coincides with the redefinition of ethnicity and race within the modern, postwar American political economy. The very nature of "assimilation" and the backdrop against which it is to take place are defined within specifically revised historical conditions.

Redevelopment and the Reassignment of Space

The switch from investing in social programs to investing in urban "redevelopment" in the Nixon years followed the need to refuel an economy in the throes of recession.[49] One manner of doing so, and of attracting foreign investment as well, was state-sponsored destruction of ethnic communities undertaken to "redevelop" and modernize the cityscape. In this case, the pejorative imagery of the Third World was deployed to describe domestic poverty, backwardness, crime, filth, and decay. In short, "urban blight" was a deeply racialized and ethnicized term. Urban redevelopment was to be an enlightened and progressive reformation of such spaces, designed to rescue America from the Third World. This project was actually a thinly disguised pretext to lay claim to valuable land.

After the Second World War, the U.S. government embarked upon an intensive drive to restructure its major cities. Urban development programs needed a proactive government to assure that cities developed profitably and efficiently: "The capitalist state must provide the infrastructure and subsidies which will ensure the profits of monopoly capital; it must subsidize and protect the accumulation process, while continuing to permit the private appropriation of profits. . . . Government agencies provide the authority to make and enforce decisions affecting the spatial efficiency of the urban economy, in the form of zoning plans, the development of industrial parks, urban renewal projects and, increasingly, metropolitan planning activities."[50] We thus have a systematic reinvention of "public works" that is characterized by an inherently private enterprise benefiting from public dollars. Redevelopment had a particular impact upon ethnic neighborhoods, as these spaces were embroiled in a sweeping program to reformulate American urban space for the late-twentieth-century economy.

Postwar urban renewal is characterized by a land-clearing strategy that removes "undesirable" populations from potentially valuable land, and the use of public funds for private goals instead of direct funding of social programs. The impetus for renewal was twofold: the need to make the city economically vital and competitive, and the need to eradicate "urban blight." In redevelopment propaganda, both the lethargy of cities and their decay was identified not with basic structures of inequality, but with particular pathological populations. This historic reformation presented not only the occasion for a specific strategy of economic "revitalization" (that is, restructuring), but also for a renewal that was predicated upon the stigmatization, relocation, and containment of minority and low-income groups.[51] It was argued that "a better city is a more middle-class city even when the majority of citizens are poor and working-class people."[52] Removal of such populations was necessary to make them and their effects invisible, and to acquire the land that once housed them; this in turn would "bring back the middle class" into the reinvigorated city. Urban development would "maintain and reestablish racial and class territorial segregation through locational decisions involving clearance, zoning, public facilities (especially schools), transportation routes, and publicly subsidized housing [and] encapsulate the lower classes in peripheral locations."[53] To facilitate the acquisition of land, cities such as New York declared "special districts" that altered zoning laws in unpublicized hearings. The wholesale delegitimation of poor and minority communities was facilitated by using the pretense of attacking the universally abhorred condition of poverty. This was a thinly disguised strategy for class and race warfare.

Herbert J. Gans's 1961 essay, "The Balanced Community: Homogeneity or Heterogeneity in Residential Areas," blatantly discloses the social, economic, racial, and "cultural" segregation that lay behind "urban renewal," supporting an agenda for redevelopment that would spatially maintain strict class divisions:

> Architectural and site plans can encourage or discourage social contact between neighbors, but . . . homogeneity of background or of interests or values [is] necessary for this contact to develop into anything more than a polite exchange of greetings. . . . Positive, although not necessarily close, relations among neighbors and maximal opportunity for the free choice of friends both near and far from home [are] desirable values, and . . . a moderate degree of homogeneity among neighbors [is] therefore required. (141)

Further into this essay, Gans tries to argue that class, not race, is of central importance. Without common "values" and tastes, neighborhoods will be sites of "cool" politesse, not communities. He suggests that the state pay greater attention to improving the economic status of the poor, rather than forcing open housing and depriving the American citizens of their inalienable right of choice.[54] While this rationalization is incomplete without ameliorating the condition of the poor, whose class values are alien to the idealized middle-class neighborhood that Gans sketches for us, the argument for segregation and displacement *without* compensation is the historical reality of urban redevelopment.[55] The "removal" of the poor underclass was supposed to benefit all parties concerned.[56] Two policies aimed at improving the cities seemed to go hand in hand: federal funding for redevelopment, and funding for low-income housing. The notion was that as urban decay was uprooted and slums torn down, new federal housing would be constructed. Yet municipalities were not required to replace housing units demolished under renewal programs.[57] Space-clearing was performed by evoking the power of eminent domain, which allowed city governments to seize land and then sell it to private developers, who in turn would be subsidized by federal monies.[58]

After the early 1970s, urban redevelopment takes on an entirely new dimension, although its basic premises remain the same. Harvey notes Jencks's particular dating of the postmodern: "Christopher Jencks . . . dates the symbolic end of modernist architecture and the passage to the post-modern as 3.32 P.M. on July 15th, 1972, when the Pruitt-Igoe Housing development . . . was dynamited as an unlivable environment for the low-income people it housed. Shortly thereafter, President Nixon officially declared the urban crisis over." Harvey continues: "1972 is not a bad date for symbolizing all kinds of other transitions in the political economy of advanced capitalism. It is roughly since then that the capitalist world, shaken out of the suffocating torpor of the stagflation that brought the long postwar boom to a whimpering end, has begun to evolve a seemingly new and quite different regime of capital accumulation. . . . The new regime is marked by a startling flexibility with respect to labor processes, labor markets, products, and patterns of consumption."[59] Urban development policy shifted from direct federal aid to block grants in 1975, and gave over administrative power to "virtually autonomous redevelopment authorities."[60] Federal oversight was decreased and the private nature of this public enterprise became more clearly evident. This may be read as part of the new strategies of late capitalism, which impact significantly on the determination of land usage and the composition of American social life.[61] As more and more public funds were devoted to subsidies and incentives for private business, they were diverted specifically from social programs aimed at helping the poor. The compensatory logic behind this, of course, was that a healthier business climate would produce better jobs for all. Yet, as Squires argues, "The principal beneficiaries are often large corporations, developers, and institutions because the tax burden and other costs are shifted to consumers. And perhaps the most important public benefits—jobs—are either temporary and lowpaying or, in the case of good jobs, go to suburbanites or other out-of-towners recruited by local businesses."[62] The selling point for urban development, while including an appeal to civic duty, largely redistributed public monies to select private enterprises that did not pass on their profits. Instead of improving the public lot, urban redevelopment usually created greater inequities. For example, more jobs were created in New York City in 1983 than in any year since 1950; however, the city's poverty rate increased 20 percent between 1979 and 1985— the jobs created paid less than those manufacturing jobs (usually unionized) they replaced.[63]

The case of San Francisco's redevelopment exhibits many of these features. Furthermore, the city has its own particular history with regard to Asian America. San Francisco's early transformation toward a service economy and its position vis-à-vis the emerging "Pacific Rim" worked to its advantage during the postwar years.[64] In the period after the war, there was a tremendous boom in high-rise construction in the central business district.[65] The city's business elites looked forward to reaping huge profits from San Francisco's strategic location in the state, nation, and Pacific. In 1970, Rudolph Peterson, president of the Bank of America, makes the neoimperialist subtext of Pacific Rim discourse perfectly clear in his redefinition of local and global spatial identities. If 1917 is

characterized by the invention of an Asiatic Barred Zone, 1970 finds a vertiginous expansion of America into the Pacific and beyond:

> When I speak of the Pacific Rim, I am putting the broadest possible construction
> on the term—the western coasts of South America, Central America, our own
> continent, and extending beyond Australia and the Far East to India. There is no
> more vast or rich area for resource development or trade in the world today than
> this immense region, and it is virtually *our own front yard*. . . . Were we Califor-
> nia businessmen to play a more dynamic role in helping trade development in the
> Pacific Rim, we would have giant, hungry new markets for our products and vast
> new profit potentials for our firms [emphasis added].[66]

This redefinition of the local discloses the transfer of power to multinational and
transnational interests. With a mixture of fear, fascination, and hungry anticipation, Viviano and Chinn write in 1982:

> The simple truth is that San Francisco's economy is no longer unfolding in the
> boardrooms of New York, the committee rooms of Washington, or the back
> rooms of Sacramento. . . . The Bay Area is slowly being drawn into a second great
> frontier of new possibilities: a transpacific urban community that will be the
> globe's most formidable economic powerhouse by the end of the decade. . . . In
> short, the cities of the Far East [Singapore, Seoul, Kuala Lumpur, Hong Kong,
> Taipei (*sic*), Tokyo, Bangkok, Jakarta] are emerging as the nodal points of the
> twenty-first century—and no other western city is in a better position to join
> them than San Francisco.[67]

The move to acquire land for the expanding business sector was thus prompted
by an intent to reconfigure the city as a "nodal point" in a larger circuit of trans-
Pacific capital that now read this expansive, rich, global space *locally* as "our
front yard" in the new cartography of the Bank of America.

This restructuring had a profound effect upon ethnic and racial minorities
and the poor, who were to have no place in this reinvention of the city. To clear
land, San Francisco redevelopers targeted the Western Addition (occupied by
an older Japanese American population); Hunters Point (largely African American); the heavily Latino Mission District; and Chinatown.[68] Indeed, the term
used by developers to describe this landgrab was "Negro removal."[69] Redevelopment in a city which has increasingly defined itself economically as the gate-
way to Pacific Rim economies also "removed" Asian/Pacific Islanders precisely
to make way for Pacific Rim investment. The transformation of American city

spaces into parts of the "global village" are made possible by the influx of Asian capital and the "availability" of Mexican and Latin American labor.[70] In San Francisco, two cases directly affected Asian American communities — the International Hotel (I Hotel) in Manilatown at the edge of North Beach and Chinatown, and the Nihonmachi development in the Western Addition. In both cases, the interconnection of local, national, and trans-Pacific interests took place against a particular historical backdrop.[71]

In the late 1960s, the International Hotel was home to about two hundred elderly Filipino men. They had been recruited to labor in the United States, and later fell victim to Asian exclusion: unable to bring over Filipinas and subject to anti-miscengenation laws, these men formed a unique community within the larger enclave of Manilatown. This hotel, located in the area that was to become the expanded and renovated Financial District of this new Pacific Rim city, was targeted by developers.[72] In 1968, Walter Shorenstein of the Milton Meyer Company initiated demolition proceedings in order to turn the site into a multilevel parking garage. Filipino tenants marched in protest, represented by the United Filipino Association. Because of strong community resistance, Shorenstein backed off from that plan, and was compelled to sign a new lease agreement.

Between 1969 and 1970, thousands of individuals and various groups from around the Bay Area came together to completely renovate the hotel. Nonetheless, in 1974 the hotel was sold to the Four Seas Investment Corporation of Hong Kong, and in September of that year the corporation ordered the demolition of the hotel. This announcement was protested by a large coalition of tenants' rights groups from Japantown, Hunters Point, the Western Addition, and the South of Market area; racially diverse tenants' rights advocates were perfectly aware of the larger structural consequences of local redevelopment. The State Supreme Court ordered a stay of eviction in July of 1976, and Mayor George Moscone proposed that the city exercise its right of eminent domain to buy the hotel from the Four Seas group and sell it back to the tenants as a nonprofit venture. The Board of Supervisors ultimately agreed to this plan under tremendous pressure from the mayor's office and the community, but the Four Seas group refused to accept an offer that would have provided them with a 50 percent profit. They insisted on going forward with the demolition of the hotel.

On January 16, 1977, six thousand people formed a barricade around the entire block. Superior Court Judge Charles Peery rejected the city's attempt to exercise eminent domain, and in July the State Supreme Court lifted its ban on the eviction. On August 4, 1977, the San Francisco police and sheriff's departments deployed over three hundred armed officers in full riot gear to remove three thousand people who had maintained a vigil against the eviction for several days. The police cordoned off a two-square-mile perimeter to prevent tens of thousands of other protesters from joining the vigil, and, using firetrucks and axes, battered down the doors at both ground level and higher levels, smashed down apartment doors, and removed protesters and tenants. The "fall of the I Hotel" marked the destruction of the last piece of Manilatown, which had slowly been eroded and consumed by urban expansion. Yet the story does not end there.

For the next twenty years, if one visited the site of the I Hotel one would not have found a highrise, or even a parking garage. Instead, a huge gaping crater has marked the site for two decades. The Four Seas corporation discovered that, ironically, the protest had forestalled development until the site was not as profitable as they had envisioned. The corporation was therefore content to simply let the land stay vacant. In 1994, the U.S. Department of Housing and Urban Development awarded the city $7.6 million for low-income housing. The San Francisco mayor's office promised to add $5.5 million to that for constructing a new International Hotel, which will house as well a community school serving seniors and a museum for Manilatown. Estella Habal points out that a central component of community activism was the connection between younger Asian American activists and the elderly Filipino tenants. While the media attempted to portray the tenants as innocent dupes of activists who were seeking an issue, Habal stresses the fact that the tenants themselves had initiated the protest, and were in many cases themselves well versed in labor activism. The history of the I Hotel manifests at once the interrelationship between economic restructuring, private-public enterprise, and community resistance, cast within the redefinition of local space as nodal point of the Pacific Rim. The "Asian" identity of San Francisco was thus battled over by two groups with entirely different visions of Asian America.

During this same period, developers had their eyes on another older Asian American community across town. Fainstein et al. explain: "The centerpiece of the Western Addition project was the Japanese Cultural and Trade Center, which houses commercial and office space of firms specializing in Japanese-American trade, a Japanese-style luxury hotel, and the Japanese consulate. It symbolizes the new economic ties between the Bay Area and Japan. The replacement of a neighborhood of low-income Japanese [sic] residential occupation by a high-rise center of corporate commercial ventures reflects both the changed nature of U.S. relations with Japan and the prominence of San Francisco in ministering to them."[73] The Japanese American community, deemed in need of "redevelopment," was dispersed and never reconstituted in the low-income housing promised them. Ironically, many of these people were interned during the Second World War — this second relocation reaffirmed their dispossession from American space.[74] Tatsuno notes that the condition of that area had indeed deteriorated, yet the policies of redevelopment here, as elsewhere, "focused primarily on the technical and economic aspects of rehabilitation and clearance of physical deterioration in central cities and . . . ignored the social and political effects of displacement."[75] Resistance to development was overwhelmed by a coordinated press campaign that equated redevelopment with civic responsibility, clearly defining "the City" against those in the ethnic community who fought the plan. The August 1, 1967, issue of the San Francisco *Examiner* carried a story that described the area as "a disease of the heart and lungs," and interpellated the "silent majority" of Japantown residents who supported the plan as the voice of the city: "[The quiet majority of residents who are cooperating with the renewal program] should speak out, lest the dissident minority voice be mistaken for a majority. When they speak out, they will be speaking not only for themselves, but for the city."[76] This invitation to join the hegemonic worked — a weakened community could not resist the combination of private-public interests. This "reinvention" of Japantown has strong parallels to the development of Little Tokyo in Los Angeles; in this case the confluence of local and transnational interests, the redefinition and occupation of the community by the transnational, is abundantly clear.[77]

Like San Francisco's Western Addition, in the late 1960s this area in Los Angeles was in need of rebuilding, and sought federal funds. Activists had a particular notion of what redevelopment should entail: "Redevelopment should mean rebuilding and improving a community for the people who live in that community." Yet those funds were aimed not at the betterment of the community, but to rebuild the city's tax base via incentives to big businesses. The 1965 "Master Plan" included as its main focus the development of an "International Zone" which would include Little Tokyo, Chinatown, and Olvera Street. In 1972 the L.A. Central City plan proposed the development of "unique, one-of-a-kind, cultural, recreational, and tourist facilities." Little Tokyo, once its residents were displaced with the promise of low-income housing to come, was to become totally dependent on tourist trade. City documents announced: "The relationship between the Central Business District and Little Tokyo is symbiotic. Little Tokyo relies on the district for tourist trade and the district relies on Little Tokyo for the *added amenity value* it provides to a rich and varied downtown." Community space is thus reduced to being merely a supplement, a scenic backdrop, dependent upon the central business district for its existence but with the bulk of the profits and capital siphoned out. The "ethnic" thus became simply an appetizer, a novelty. And this transformation could not have occurred without first downgrading the ethnic inhabitants who lived on that land and substituting for their culture a corporatized view of the ethnic-as-amenity.

This change was entirely an outcome of the logic of development; redevelopment was to "pay for itself" via increased tax revenues—the political economy of Little Tokyo was thus geared toward revenues that would not *necessarily* be channeled back into the community rebuilding projects the community had proposed as the ends at which redevelopment was to be aimed. Rather, those funds were dispersed to finance other redevelopment projects. One such project particularly discloses the transnationalization of the local. The New Otani Hotel was to be built by the Kajima Corporation under the name of the "East-West Development Corporation." Kajima, a multinational Japan-based corporation made up of thirty of Japan's largest financial institutions, had established itself as the fourth-largest construction company in the world (by the late 1990s, it had become the second-largest). The relation between Kajima and the redevelopment agency (the Community Redevelopment Agency, CRA) included what became the norm for such private-public ventures. For instance, Kajima sold a parcel of land to the CRA for $407,000, and then bought it back for $179,000, pocketing the difference of $226,000. Although charged with gathering revenue to finance community redevelopment, the CRA thus acted as a mechanism for Kajima profiteering. Despite community outcry, the hotel was built in 1977; low-income housing for those displaced in this landgrab was put on hold, while profits from the hotel are placed into offshore accounts.

Today, the rule of this multinational over this Asian American community and its environs continues. Community activism over recent labor disputes at the hotel discloses a history that gives further depth to our understanding of the density of global capitalism and racism, particularly at the nexus between transnational capital and an enlarged low-wage working class drawn from across various borders.[78] Today, suites at the New Otani go for between $475 and $1,800 per night, while its workforce (70 percent Latino, 25 percent Asian) earn bottom wages. In 1996, staff at the New Otani Hotel went on strike, protesting unfair working conditions that included the demotion of Mexican and Salvadoran waiters and their replacement by Anglos, nonfraternization policies between ethnic groups, banning Spanish, and the firing of union activists. During this struggle, it came to light that during the Second World War, Kajima operated a slave-labor camp at the Hanaoka copper mine in Akita Prefecture. About one thousand Chinese peasants and P.O.W.s were forced to divert a river near the mines. Such were the inhuman conditions and acts of violence against the workers that on June 30, 1945, there was an open revolt. The workers were captured and tortured, and *after* the surrender of Japan, a dozen of these former prisoners were put on trial by the Japanese government and sentenced to life imprisonment.[79] They have filed suit in a Tokyo court, asking for a corporate apology and monetary compensation. This transnational historical dimension produced a transnational multiethnic response when the strikers of 1996 called for an all-out boycott of the Otani, and a multiethnic coalition of workers and sympathizers from the Anglo, Latino, and Asian communities (some forty-six Asian Pacific Islander groups) wrote an open letter to Emperor Akihito calling for more social accountability for Japanese firms doing business in the United States. Progressive Asian American response to transnational capital has been anything but quiet.

A similar case is the strike against the Japanese mega-grocery chain, Yaohan.[80] In 1988, Yaohan led other Japanese supermarket chains in international earnings capacity. Its strategy has always been to avoid saturated markets (such as Tokyo and Osaka), and to invest instead in untapped markets abroad. In the late eighties, Yaohan had a hundred markets in places such as Japan, Singapore, Hong Kong, Brunei, Malaysia, Taiwan, Costa Rica, Brazil, and the United States. With regard to the latter, Yaohan realized the tough competition posed by U.S. chains such as Safeway, and began targeting Asian neighborhoods, as well as black and Latino ones. It particularly located in economically depressed areas, where it was welcomed as a source of jobs; Yaohan advertised itself as "catering to the needs of the community." After eliminating local stores, however, Yaohan marked its prices above what the community was used to paying and charged food stamp users a 10 percent surcharge. As far as its attitude toward its workers was concerned, Yaohan imposed a Japanese-based "Yaohan culture" (which included a mandatory daily salute to the Japanese flag), sexually harrassed its black and Hispanic female employees, discriminated on the basis of race, engaged in illegal anti-union activities, and abused government incentives.

Most relevant for a discussion of the restructuring of Asian American space is the fact that Yaohan excused these practices on the basis of "cultural difference": for all its claim that the market was there to serve the community, it became clear that that space was more an extraterritorial zone. We usually associate such "export processing zones" with the *maquiladoras*. When safely sequestered at the horizon of U.S. borders, such zones remain at the outer limit of American concern.[81] What the Kajima and Yaohan cases bring forth, however, are the ways in which transnational capital claims a space in America that far exceeds the simple signposting of deterritorialization—Asian capital has played an instrumental role in the restructuring of communities and the re-scripting of national histories. Organizers of the Yaohan boycott were careful to steer clear of reducing the conflict to one of race and nation: the "mispercep-tions" of Yaohan executives as to the American way of labor and business were to be regarded as a class conflict, not a national or racial one.[82] Similar strate-gies were adopted in the workers' strike against the Koreana Wilshire/Hyatt in Los Angeles.[83] Nevertheless, while the definition of such struggles solely in terms of class is strategically necessary, this elides the messy issues of how *eth-nicity* and class interact. For example, the Korean ownership in the latter case was delinked from its Korean American employees on the basis of both class and ethnicity; certain classes achieve a particular position of privilege in transna-tional actions, and, as subordinated workers and yet "compatriots" as well in a "foreign" land, ethnic groups stand in particular relation to members of their nation of origin.

In historically tracking the development and transformation of Asian Amer-ican space, again and again we find the progressive detachment of space from community, fed by the logic of capital and the struggle to represent and reclaim that space differently. And this is precisely what links ethnic space to *ethnicized* space in the formation of new, "postindustrial" America. As in San Francisco's, Los Angeles's, and New York's ethnic neighborhoods, we find in the ethnicized community of Monterey Park, California, that "the adversary of community groups . . . mostly ceased to be the government and [became] instead the im-personal forces of the marketplace."[84] As in the case of New York City's China-town, the community is taken over by the "community of money." Anxiety re-garding the ability to determine the particular nature of communities in the face of Asian immigration is fed by a specific material history intimately linked to the same forces of economic restructuring that were manifested in the policies of urban redevelopment.

Monterey Park

If the case of New York Chinatown shows the effects of the global economy on the ethnic enclave—specifically, on the labor of Asian women and the commu-nity it helped to create and make thrive—the destruction of the I-Hotel and Ni-honmachi and the Little Tokyo projects evince the further disenfranchisement of ethnic peoples from their community and land under the imperatives of "development," then we find a more complicated situation in Monterey Park,

California, during the 1970s and 1980s. In the first case, we witnessed the making-visible of an image of the Third World within specific locations; in the other cases, we saw efforts to eradicate, rearticulate, and recommodify that image, as the specific markings of economic violence are glossed over and the built environment is made to reflect an entirely different order of things. However, in Monterey Park we find a particularly white suburb "taken over" by "Asia" and transformed entirely into a specific image of "Third World America," one that is all the more threatening for its unbridled and explicit link to the contradictions of global capital read in a national frame.[85] As a suburb, Monterey Park was conceived under a well-established vision:

> The spatially fragmented form of residential life we identify most with suburbanization has been constructed around a definite *mode* of reproduction carved out by the early bourgeoisie and carried forward since by the upper middle class (new petty bourgeoisie or managerial-professional class) since the later nineteenth century. This mode has as its basic building blocks the so-called "nuclear family," the single-family home, homeownership, the neighborhood school, and a certain limited type of "community" conjoined with a localized political jurisdiction.[86]

It is in this reformulation of space in late capitalism that, as Dirlik notes, the local as "traditional" becomes less and less tenable, but at the same time more and more important a notion to secure:

> Global capital represents an unprecedented penetration of local society globally by the economy and culture of capital; so that the local understood in a "traditional" sense may be less relevant than ever.[87]

Monterey Park occupies some 7.7 square miles, 8 miles east of Los Angeles; it is one of 84 cities incorporated within Los Angeles County. It has the particular distinction of being the only city in the continental United States with a majority Asian population: some 56 percent of its 60,000 inhabitants are of Asian origin.[88] Between World War II and the 1960s, the city grew in the aftereffects of the wartime economy, with new housing developments and GI loans. By the 1960s, it had become a modest middle-class suburb, attracting Latinos from East L.A. and Japanese Americans from West L.A., as well as Chinese American professionals moving out of Los Angeles's Chinatown.[89] In short, Monterey Park symbolized not only a small town successfully transformed into a characteristic suburb in the postwar period, endowed with all the idealized features of non-urban existence (crime- and pollution-free, detached from the obsolete manufacturing industries of the past and instead at the forefront of the service sector, at a safe distance from urban decay and yet accessible to urban attractions by automobile), but also a community whose new members represented ethnic mobility, the culmination of a particular social telos.[90]

This social identity is intimately linked to an assimilationist narrative that conjoins with that of American individualism: "We can . . . interpret the preference for suburban living as a created myth, arising out of possessive individualism, nurtured by the ad-man and forced by the logic of capitalist accumulation. . . . The American suburb, formed as an economic and social response to problems internal to capitalist accumulation, now forms an entrenched barrier to social and economic change."[91] Thus, the move to the suburb by assimilated ethnics underscores the perpetuation of a particular narrative of ethnic mobility deeply linked to a closing off of space to any who have not passed through a specific process of becoming American.

This produced a critical problem in Monterey Park, for by the late 1970s, the city was suffering from a seriously weakened economy, its inactive commercial district decimated by the flight of capital to areas receptive to large-scale developments such as malls.[92] The preservation of the suburban community was at a crisis point when there appeared what seemed to be a godsend. On one hand, more and more Angelenos were attracted to Monterey Park: "The two gasoline crises of 1973–74 and 1979 helped cause a rapid increase in the city's population as Los Angeles–based workers sought to avoid the hassle and expense of a long commute. Monterey Park was a safe, clean, and convenient option" (Waldman, *California Journal*, 207). But, far more significantly, large numbers of affluent, well-educated Chinese from abroad began coming to Monterey Park and investing their money. One developer in particular, Frederic Hsieh, energetically promoted Monterey Park both in the United States and in Asia. He drummed up support from the city council; one individual ironically had a prescient view of what was to happen: "Everyone in the room thought the guy was blowing smoke . . . then when I got home I thought, what gall. What ineffable gall. He was going to come into my living room and change around my furniture?"[93] We have then the convergence of assimilated, upwardly mobile migrants from the Los Angeles urban areas, and Asian immigration from overseas. It was the latter whose arrival was the most conspicuous.

Local residents had a particular memory of this influx: "First it was the real estate people, and then trading companies, heavy investors, people that come with hundreds of thousands of dollars in cash."[94] This specific image of the "new" Asian immigrant departs significantly from the image of the poor, hard-working immigrant; these newcomers followed the logic of investment rather than labor. Instead of locating in traditional niches such as restaurants, groceries, and garment work, these new immigrants were involved in banking, real estate, health services, computer technology, and international trade in Los Angeles and, crucially, connected to Pacific Rim economies as well.[95] Monterey Park entered the circuit of transnational economy under the sponsorship and management of Chinese, who owned between two-thirds and three-fourths of all businesses. This capital produced a "brief but furious period of land speculation in the late 1970s and early 1980s [which] led to uncontrolled construction and an unprecedented escalation of property values."[96]

Not only did the locals see their economy taken over by these investments, but, more visibly and startlingly, the built environment became a sign of this transformation, as former shoe stores, tire stores, veterinary hospitals, even doughnut shops became converted into banks, banks that had conspicuously posted Chinese business signs and advertising.[97] Because of the inflated cost of property, owners had to charge high rents that most individual proprietors could not afford. The owners' only option was to carve up the property into smaller storefronts and charge high enough rent for each lease to realize a return on the investment. Thus, the "appearance" of the Third World in Monterey Park (cramped, high-density, foreign-language "cubicle" storefronts) is directly tied to the logic of capitalist innovation and its "creative destruction" of prior forms for the sake of greater accumulation. Here, that accumulation is attached to the particularities of transnational capital's penetration of national space. Besides the business district, residential areas evinced the steady remapping of private lives: neighborhoods of single-family homes were peppered with more commercially valuable high-density apartment buildings, condominiums, and additions to existing houses, which created what came to be known as "monster houses" (homes built to the limit of the property line, sacrificing landscaping for square footage, and thus producing an intensification of the high-density image).[98]

The people who ran and patronized these businesses and owned, managed, and lived in these structures shared with them a particular identification with money. "Residents spoke with disdain of the sudden increase in luxury cars in town, of $100 bills flashed in restaurants, of business people wearing tailor-made suits and sporting expensive jewelry."[99] Yet these appearances were not the only disturbing "lifestyle" imported into Monterey Park. Timothy Fong notes, "In fact, huge profits were not the primary concern; the overriding objective was to gain long-term stability over short-term profits. Some investors were even willing to take a loss for several years in order to secure a place in the United States. . . . Opening a business here allowed the individual and his or her immediate family to obtain visas to reside in the United States. After a while, the business owner could apply for permanent residence. And the automatic American citizenship of a child born here gave the family a firm foothold in the United States." [100] Thus what we witness in Monterey Park is a particular disruption of various temporalities deeply attached to America's self-conception. For example, the above instance shows the stalling or deferral of capital accumulation for the sake of citizenship status, whereas the image of wealthy, acquisitive Chinese immigrants shows the leap-frogging of the slow, arduous, and eminently didactic experience of assimilation.

One local resident narrates this difference: "Before, immigrants were poor. They lived in their own neighborhoods and moved into ours after they learned English, got a good job, and became accustomed to our ways. Today, the Chinese come right in with their money and their ways. We are the aliens." [101] Instead of following the path of the earlier Japanese Americans and Chinese Americans, and Latinos who moved into Monterey Park in the 1960s, these new immigrants were seen to have sidestepped the rigors of that particular, *time-consuming* act of *Americanization*, and, crucially, this perversion of the normal chain of events has resulted in the *alienation* of "natives." Specifically, these new immigrant subjectivities disrupted the idealized notion of the local as traditional and introjected a global economic subjectivity that displaced the local, pointing up the fact that even its quaintness was no longer able to exact any ideological purchase in the new age of late capitalism. Seagrave's rhetoric reflects the general paranoia of loss and alienation: "Whites who worried in the past about immigrants lowering standards in their neighborhoods are now alarmed because incoming Chinese are raising the standards, causing property values to soar. The newcomers are better-dressed than the locals, serious professionals with a keen business sense and a shrewd knowledge of how capitalism really works. This arouses more than a little envy." [102] But what of the reverse? Were these diasporic subjects Americans? Or did they not inhabit a particular transnational space and time? In which case, we have to ask, where and what is America? That is, from what, exactly, were the old Monterey Park residents alienated? And what did the landscape now represent but the space of a radically revised America? [103]

This alienation penetrated as well into the established Asian American community; many of whose members had internalized a particular sense of identification with the assimilationist narrative and distanced themselves from the new immigrants both in terms of the lifestyle they seemed to represent and because of the effect they supposedly had upon the community. Fong notes that the "ethnic enclave" became a "predatory" one, feeding off the already established ethnic community, and at the same time undercutting its stability with rabid speculation and construction.[104]

Although "time is money," money may obliterate time. The particular problematic here, of course, is the way that money has also overturned racial hierarchies—Asians have bypassed the steps necessary to make them equal to whites economically. To some degree, as Harvey has explained, *money is democratic*. Harvey writes, "There is . . . something very democratic about money. It is a 'great leveler and cynic,' says Marx, because it eliminates all other marks of distinction save those contained in its possession."[105] Race and ethnicity appear to be removed as significant elements once a certain threshhold of wealth is crossed.

One particularly telling anecdote that circulated widely in Monterey Park captures a number of these issues. People talked of "an elderly Chinese gentleman riding his bicycle down the street with a satchel slung on one of the handlebars, and if he saw anybody in the front yard, he would approach them and ask, "Would you like to sell your house? I've got the money."[106] Like all myths, the story is less important than the terms used to tell it. The suggestion of harmlessness (the elderly old gentleman), the particular mode of locomotion (an innocent vestige of Main Street, U.S.A.), takes on a tone at once comical and sinister—the bicycle seems capable of moving across any space, the satchel on its handlebars does not contain the Sunday paper, but cash, and lots of it. And the rider's polite inquiry jars against the absolute power of acquisition he wields, indiscriminately, almost on a whim. No matter what your price for your domestic space might be, he has the money, whose source remains mystified. Under such conditions, the power of the individual is dwarfed by the logic of capital:

> Individuals come to sense their own helplessness in the face of forces that do not appear amenable, under given institutions, even to collective political mechanisms of control. As we cross this boundary, we move from a situation in which individuals can express their individuality and relate in human terms to each other to one in which individuals have no choice but to conform and in which social relations between people become replaced by market relations between things.[107]

In Monterey Park, the dispossession of space, the re-gearing of social time, and the mystification of money brought about a reaction that complicates the notion that money is democratic. It becomes clear that certain money, and its effects, is *out of place*. Instead, an attempt is made to resurrect, from the debris of the past, some notion of life before transnational capital. Harvey notes, "the search for 'authentic community' and a 'sense of place' became all the more fierce as the community of money became more powerfully felt."[108] Monterey Park was torn apart by the conflicting demands for development and capital accumulation, and a no-growth movement that sought to tame the gravitational pull of capital. The intense acceleration of capitalist accumulation and investment literally took control of the city. One consultant brought in to handle the crisis commented, "by the time we got through satisfying the opposition, speculators would come in and raise the property value another $20 a square foot so that the economics of the plan would be obsolete by the time it got adopted."[109] Such speculation offered "no short- or long-term community benefit, created inflated property values, rising rents, and a shortage of productive businesses."[110] In such a crisis, local residents responded by taking recourse to the familiar but intensely threatened narrative of American subjectivity. Monterey Park became the birthplace of the English-Only movement.

It is crucial to note that English-Only was the perfect means by which to separate out the two Asian American groups: the assimilated, English-speaking Asian American who had paid his or her dues and had passed through the specific waiting period of assimilation, and the new Asian immigrant, whose wealth had bypassed that catechism, and whose *trans*migrancy signaled a distinct ambivalence. If anything, to speak English was to be a minimal yet highly symbolic sign of acquiescence to the notion of how things should be. It provided a means to discipline the new immigrants and check the credentials of even assimilated Asian Americans, since by that time the two had become collapsed as one in the racist fears of the non-Asian community.[111]

Various observers wished to reduce this complex case by erasing the racial aspect. For example, Nicholas Lemann wrote in *The Atlantic*:

> The issue in Monterey Park that looks like the short-term future of Southern California, though, is not racial tension, which I went there to find, but development. Of course, anti-development politicians will pick up on racial sentiment, but this doesn't mean that talking about development is some sort of ruse. The anti-development passion is heartfelt. . . . The post–Second World War migrants to Los Angeles from the American heartland are getting old. Their tolerance for change isn't what it once was, they have plenty of time to express their dissatisfactions, and the city *has* changed. It feels like a city now, and that is exactly what the postwar migrants weren't looking for when they came to Los Angeles.[112]

The details that Lemann omits would provide a more careful inventorying of the precise nature of "the city," which is particularly foreign-seeming. As Friedland notes, "Even without the mediation of urban political structures, it is probably at the local level that nonclass forms of political identification such as territory and ethnicity are most acutely felt."[113] It is not simply a matter of money being raced or race-neutral; rather, it is its particular function within the discourse of the nation in the throes of a global political economy that is of significance. To defend against the erosion of national identity, in Monterey Park we find that a rebuttal of the logic of capitalism is necessary to preserve "America": "the populist and anti-capital thrust of slow growth is continually attenuated and transformed by nativism into the politics of ethnicity."[114] Against this effort to claim back local space is posed not only the increased imbrication of the local in the global, but the decentering of even suburban life, a process Kling, Olin, and Poster have dubbed "postsuburbia."

In these negotiations between the local and the global, the ethnic immigrant and the Americanized ethnic, and claims to an essential core of "America," the valence of the term "Chinese" is unstable and contingent. Asian Americans are desired for capital, but not their race. Aihwa Ong notes: "their symbolic capital as a 'race' in America places them on the horns of a dilemma: they are perceived both as America's front troops in the economic competition with Japan in the Pacific Rim *and* as the embodiment of Japan as America's post–Cold War enemy. . . . Asian American cultural belonging is defined within U.S. corporate and legal strategies to appropriate Asian labor, capital, and knowledge in the Pacific Rim region. . . . This view of Asians as capitalist resources accounts for the [fact that the] 1990 Immigration [act] has a special 'investor' category to compete with Canada and Australia for the world's flight capital. A green card can be obtained for a $1 million investment that creates at least ten jobs. Seminars directed at Chinese Americans offer suggestions on how to get 'U.S. citizenship through real estate investment and acquisition' [*Wall Street Journal*, February 21, 1992, B1]."[115] Nevertheless, as seen in our examination of Monterey Park, the capital brought to America from Asia may not be "laundered" as it moves across the border (or through the Internet): it may retain the mark of origin and transfer, even as its path forks and rejoins other sources and flows. When given the political cause of reestablishing a sense of sovereignty, these sources can be traced back to reracialize cash and capital and "(re)foreignize" Asians in America once again. This is exactly what we find in the late 1990s "scandal" over "Chinese money" finding its way into U.S. political coffers.

The "Chinese Money Scandal"

If Dooner's and Rohmer's visions of Asiatic invasions now seem to be quaint and simplistic (see Chapter 2), the current furor over Chinese money "buying" an American presidential election is not essentially any more sophisticated. Nonetheless, despite sharing several features with generic Yellow Perilism, the Chinese Money Scandal has its own particular texture and historical context. The issue of Chinese contributions to the Democratic National Committee has the elements of both old-fashioned influence peddling in a Yellow Peril mode and the modalities of transnational capitalism. One figure who emblematizes the former is Charles Yah Lin Trie, who, along with John Huang, is said to have raised over $1.8 million for Clinton. We are told that Trie first met Clinton in Little Rock, where Trie, now the owner of an international trading company, was then merely a struggling businessman whose small Chinese restaurant Clinton frequented. The narrative of hometown intimates in Arkansas chatting over an inexpensive Chinese meal becoming partners in mapping out U.S.-China relations is a particularly American narrative.[116] Trie was later supposed to have handed over a bag of money to influence the Democratic National Committee: "the bag contained only $167,000 in checks and money orders, plus a stack of inflatable Asian novelty items that Trie was planning to market in the United States."[117] Like the figure of the Chinese bicyclist in Monterey Park, this story would have merely the status of a surprising and comic coincidence without the scaffolding of the scandal of transnational money on a massive scale.

The fear that the American government might be merely a front for a complex set of transnational corporate interests (and this fear obviously applies to all national governments) was fed by the prominent involvement of the infamous Lippo Group, a transnational corporation based in Indonesia. John Huang served in the employ of this entity before his stint in the Commerce Department, and then as fundraiser for the Democratic National Committee. (Particularly worrisome concerning the Lippo Group is that it is headed by the Riady family, a cornerstone of what has been termed "Greater China," a complex network of economic relations between southern China, Hong Kong, and Taiwan. We will consider this phenomenon in detail in Chapter 10.) But most significant, of course, has been the way that this nightmare has been replaced by an even worse one. Now, it seems, the bogeyman of transnational capital may have simply been the servant of the Evil Chinese Empire. A scandal of illegal campaign contributions was transformed into a breach of national security. The redeployment of Cold War rhetoric carried the inflections of Elliot Ness; a Boston *Globe* editorial on the subject makes reference to "the Communist cosa nostra," "Beijing's . . . efforts to mold U.S. policy to Chinese designs," the "liquidation" of U.S. jobs.[118] Richard Bernstein's and Ross H. Munro's prediction of China's "Coming Conflict with America" explicitly reanimates the Cold War: "The primary American objective in Asia must be to prevent China's size, power, and ambition from making it a regional hegemon. Achieving that goal requries maintaining the American military presence in Asia and keeping it vastly more powerful and effective than China's armed forces. Furthermore, preventing China from expanding its nuclear weapons arsenal should clearly be an American goal. In the worst-case scenario, Sino-American relations would witness the reappearance of a nuclear standoff reminiscent of the Cold War."[119]

Prominent in this charge is the 1993 sale of Lippo's Hong Kong Chinese Bank to the China Resources Holding Company, a Chinese government–affiliated trading company: The Washington *Times* declared, "A U.S. intelligence source said China Resources was essentially owned and operated by the Chinese Army and that Chinese military intelligence officers were free to penetrate its operations for economic espionage." There have been myriad conjectures about what is actually going on: is this a plot by Taiwan to divert attention from its own significant influence over Washington? What is behind Clinton's attempt to portray himself as an innocent dupe of the Red Chinese (rather than the unwitting beneficiary of "overzealous" campaign staffers)? If before we saw the *New Republic*'s orientalization of the face of the Statue of Liberty as an homage to the model minority, the *National Review*'s infamous cover that "orientalized" the Clintons and Al Gore renarrates the Yellow Peril's ability to change the face of American politics.

This insinuation set off a series of articles, including a February article in the *Washington Post* by Bob Woodward suggesting that intelligence sources revealed a Chinese plot to buy influence. This prepared the stage for the Congressional hearings in July, which Chair Fred Thompson opened with these "basic findings": "The committee believes that high-level Chinese government officials crafted a plan to increase China's influence over the U.S. political process. . . . Our investigations suggest it affected the 1996 presidential race and state elections as well." This infiltration was supposed to have both immediate and long-term effects, as the Chinese scheme would launch a virtual virus into the American body politic: "Another aspect of the plan is remarkable because it shows that the PRC is interested in developing long-term relationships with persons it has identified as up-and-coming government—up-and-coming officials at state and local levels."[120] These allegations launched a full-scale incursion into Asia; one report noted: "The search for evidence of a new Asian plot against the U.S." has caused investigators to embark on a journey where they are described as having "traveled thousands of miles, ridden ferries in Macao, dodged anti-U.S. protests in Jakarta, and even trekked to a Buddhist order's mountaintop headquarters in Taiwan."[121] Nevertheless, despite this dramatic infiltration of Asia in pursuit of an answer to American political schemes, their target seemed to fade into the dense Asian underbrush like so many Viet Cong. It was ruefully noted that "'the committee's authority stops at the Pacific Ocean line,' the Governmental Affairs Committee's chief agent from the FBI had to remind the senators this week as the tantalizing money trail of Yah Lin 'Charlie' Trie faded from sight somewhere over the horizon in Asia."[122]

Within a few days, however, Thompson's conspiracy theory began to unravel. News stories noted the "failure to establish a conclusive link between the well-documented plan and any of the suspect contributions that went to the Democratic National Committee."[123] The Justice Department quickly distanced itself from Thompson: "'There was a campaign by the Chinese to infiltrate Congress and a campaign by the Democrats to gain contributions from wealthy Asian-Americans. . . . Were the two linked? Where's the proof? [quoting an FBI official]."[124] By the end of the week, it was disclosed that the issue of Chinese espionage was merely planted without belief by Republicans.[125] Nonetheless, the insinuation of a Chinese plot had a crucial effect outside the issue of campaign finance reform. It fed a remilitarization of U.S.-China national security discourse. A news story printed on July 13, 1997, revealed that "House Republicans are trying to get the country's national security apparatus to focus more attention on Beijing's intelligence and military operations. . . . The House had already approved, in the fiscal 1998 defense authorization bill, creation of a $5 million center for the study of Chinese military affairs at the National Defense University. . . . According to intelligence sources, only the Soviet Union, at the height of the Cold War, was singled out for such a special report to Congress and then only because KGB officers with diplomatic cover had been discovered meeting with Capitol Hill staff and Moscow was placing disinformation about the United States in newspapers around the world." In an amazing exercise in diplomatic doublespeak, "the legislation said the center to study Chinese military affairs should be created not because the United States views the Beijing government as an enemy, but because 'stated geopolitical ambitions of China will pose challenges that will require careful management in order to preserve peace and protect U.S. national security.'"[126]

This diversion, this displacement of causality into a rehash of Cold War rhetoric is symptomatic of a deeper fear that business has changed (much for the worse) under the logic of late capitalism.[127] This reduction ignores the fact that the Taiwan government has always played a powerful role in American politics.[128] Nor should one forget the fact that China has for some twenty years had a significant number of U.S. lobbyists (including former secretaries of state Alexander Haig and Lawrence Eagleburger, with Kissinger and Associates being the most influential) promoting its interests in Washington and elsewhere, and how those interests coincide with those of American corporations.[129] Finally, one should be aware that the U.S. government has a long history of intervening in other countries' affairs, one such instrument is the National Endowment for Democracy, created fifteen years ago. It spends about $30 million a year influencing political parties, labor unions, dissident movements, and news media in dozens of countries, including China. For example, for the Nicaraguan election of 1990, it provided $3 million in "technical assistance," and $1.6 million in 1996 in China for "institution building."[130]

But here I want to focus on how the redeployment of a simple Cold War formula willingly forgets the more complex imbrications of the national economy within the global one. Similar to the "politics of ethnicity" that emerged in Monterey Park and that were galvanized by the issue of "Asianized" American space, so here the sanctity of the body politic is to be guarded against *Chinese* infiltration with little address to how the vulnerability to such "infiltration" was created by the American political system, or to the fact that such "Chinese interests" as there may be are often the same as American corporate interests. The arbitrary quality of national corporate identities was made clear by Boeing's CEO, who proclaimed that he wanted Boeing workers in China to believe that Boeing was a *Chinese* company, and workers in Brazil to believe it was a Brazilian one, and so on. Rather, the focus of the Chinese Money Scandal is on the uncomfortable proximity of China to the United States.[131] The eerie respatialization of the United States is reflected in one journalist's comment: "Asiagate, in short, is what happens when Dogpatch meets international intrigue. Maybe Little Rock and Canton Province aren't so far apart after all."[132]

Rothkopf notes that a "deep shift" is evident in recent U.S. pronouncements on China: "The real issue is the deep shift in American perceptions about the world, our place in it and threats to our nation. . . . The second half of the twentieth century can be seen to mark a shift in U.S. foreign policy toward a fundamental, ongoing confrontation between the world's dominant power, the U.S., and the rising powers of Asia."[133] Yet that is only part of the story. He leaves in place the binarism of U.S. /China in order to foreground the new (and very real) discourse of confrontation urged upon Washington by many, both liberals and conservatives. Kissinger's logic will most likely prevail: such confrontation is likely to be unproductive in an era of powerful transnational corporate interests. Indeed, as Rouse points out, the seeming conflict between the nation and transnationals may often be a political distraction: "The state and corporations, as institutions dominated though not totally controlled by the capitalist class, have tended overall to experience the crisis [in the influence and authority of the nation-state in transnationalism] in similar ways and to work in tandem to resolve it."[134] That is, the state and transnationals are not necessarily opposed, but may be united in class warfare against the proletariat. Rouse summarizes this point: "The relationship between the state as emblem of the nation, the population that resides within its borders, and the corporations that do business there is more disjunctive than at any time in the country's history" (368).[135]

The specter of transnationalism and the global economy it inhabits and forces us to inhabit haunts the Chinese Money Scandal. With the reinstantiation of the east/west binary this specter evaporates, and in its place is the more familiar and therefore more comfortable anxiety over the Free World and the Unfree World, the nation and its sovereignty are reinstated, community is recollectivized around a common, manageable enemy whose borders are equally distinct. But the logic of late capitalism has already fused itself into the landscape and the social subjects whose lives are lived within the particular coordinates of a much different time and space.

The link between identity and place becomes tenuous indeed in the postmodern age. The particular "cosmic forces" noted by Park and identified here as global capital increasingly force apart certain linkages and identifications previously thought to be secured by and in space. Our sense of "cultural" Asian America (that is, its forms of life and representation) have been examined here according to its specific historical condition in the middle and late twentieth century of migration (forced and otherwise), internment, dispersal, and reformation. In the term "Asian America" I again insist upon embedding the complex interpenetration of race, ethnicity, and nationhood, even as such concepts evince the pressures and effects of transnationalism. In the concluding section of this study, having now discussed the reshaping of Asian American space, I address more closely the historical modifications of Asian/American identity, which seek to name a psychic identity *across* such spaces. I will trace the modification of a particular set of psychic identifications that embed within themselves specific notions of race, ethnicity, and nation. From the 1970s to the present day, I read a movement from the psychoanalytic modality of "schizophrenia" to that of the "transnational," and to various consolidating discourses such as the "postindustrial" and "cyberspace," which promise a new "borderless world" but often enough reinscribe the differentials of Asian America.

Part V / Mind Readings

9 / Double Trouble: The Pathology of Ethnicity Meets White Schizophrenia

THROUGHOUT THIS STUDY, I have been concerned with the predication of "Asian" to "American" as read in and through the discourses of body, psyche, and space. Rather than discovering a clear end point to that teleology, we have found instead a series of partial predications and uneven integrations into political and cultural spheres. This uneven, incomplete relation has everything to do with the ways in which American identity itself has been reformed and redefined in the twentieth century.

The rescripting of America in the twentieth century has been done in relation to migrancy and movement, redefinition and replacement of borders, and the presence of newly defined populations. These new definitions of America have engaged particular notions of both "bedrock" assumptions of national identity *and* new kinds of flexibility in the construction of the modern state, here specifically in its relation to Asians in America and to Asian states. In the first section we reviewed the rearticulation of Yellow Perilism in the 1930s and the way America sought to redefine its identity as a "nation of immigrants." The introduction of a new notion of hybridity paralleled a reconsideration of life under new global arrangements and economies. The historical development and modification of the Asian as "alien" in America was then traced according to the representation of the body at the nexus of cultural and national identification, economic life, and reproduction—we addressed the aesthetics of Asian/American ethnicity within a material frame.

In the third section, the ascension of the Asian as model for America in the contexts of the Civil Rights era, Japan's growing influence in the international marketplace, the development of East Asian regional economies, and the cultural "crisis" in the West was complemented by the containment and qualification of these models and the resuscitation of American particularism. This dialectic between the emulation and reparticularization of Asians speaks to the shifting visions America had of itself and of the persistence of racial differentation despite all the incentives to imagine Asian American success as intimately linked to American subjectivity.

Last, in the fourth section, we witnessed how Asians "took place" in America, with specific attention to the way new historical circumstances disrupted the grounds upon which America has laid claim to sovereignty. The location and dislocation of Asians in America were seen in conjunction with the way American space itself was reconstructed in late capitalism, and in the context of America's various engagements with East and Southeast Asia in the middle and late twentieth century. In such a remapping of national space, the nostalgia for a simple, sovereign, self-determining community was put into a state of doubt, as other forms of memory were rehabilitated and imported. In short, Asian America was crosshatched by heterogeneous narratives and occupied by subjectivities produced at the intersections of race, ethnicity, gender, and class on a national, international, and transnational scale. In each case, it is crucial to see the formation of Asian/American identity as a co-product of both Asians and non-Asians—that is, to refuse the notion of Asians as hapless and contentless "subject postions." Rather, Asians in America have participated in the shaping of modern America, both as active agents and as presences that called for a rethinking of America's ideological claims. Throughout we have witnessed the modification, but ultimately the persistence, of the racial divide.

It is precisely these vacillations of identification that were to be gathered up and rechanneled singularly in the process of "assimilation." As we have seen, since at least the time of the Dillingham Commission, the American state had been anxious to understand the precise nature (and limits) of integrating new immigrants into its social, economic, political, and cultural life. Looking more precisely at the period with which this study begins, in the mid-1930s we find "an authoritative definition" of "acculturation" presented by the Subcommittee on Acculturation of the Social Science Research Council. According to this report, acculturation "comprehends those phenomena which result when groups of individuals having different cultures come into continuous first-hand contact, with subsequent changes in the original cultural patterns of either or both groups."[1] This definition has the uncommon merit of noting the mutual (rather than one-way) influence exerted by one group upon the other; however, it conspicuously sidesteps the issues that most concerned Americans: How were these influences to be enacted? What would be the precise ratio of "influencing" versus being influenced? On what terrain would influence be transacted? A decade earlier, Robert Park and Ernest Burgess had come up with a more precise definition: "Assimilation is a process of interpenetration and fusion in which persons and groups acquire the memories, sentiments, and attitudes of other persons or groups, and, by sharing their experience and history, are incorporated with them in a common cultural life."[2] There is a particular economy here: of acquisition, shareholding, and finally incorporation, but the commodities we are talking about have a specific *psychic* content—memories, sentiments, attitudes.

As we have seen throughout this study, this psychic phenomenon is deeply linked to the actual physical occupation of space—the psychic and political economies of Asian America are intimately linked. The question is *how* this sharing is to "take place." For that, we find the authors' recourse to a thinly veiled organic biologism: "interpenetration and fusion." This rhetoric becomes elaborated later on: "The nature of social contacts is decisive in the process. Assimilation *naturally* takes place most rapidly where contacts are primary, that is, where they are the most intimate and intense, as in the area of touch relationship, in the family circle and in intimate congenial groups [my emphasis]."[3] The final component to add to this definition of assimilation, which explicitly ties together the psychic and the physical, is the notion of race and nation: "assimilation" is "the name given the process or processes by which peoples of diverse racial origins and different cultural heritages, occupying a common territory, achieve a cultural solidarity sufficient at least to sustain a national existence."[4] The convergence of territory and contiguity, culture and national "existence," endows assimilation with a particular identity and social function—it is to vouchsafe the smooth operation of the national in reproducing itself coextensively in mind, body, and space.

This reproduction is to be manifested in a particular morphology, wherein the psychological element is crucial. The national is to be secured by a specific process of memory transfer: the migrant's past is to be rescripted and given a content of secondhand histories and values, integrated with his or her own into a functioning psychic reality, and this will allow the state to continue its course through modernity.[5] We find again the particular coalition of territory, memory, history, and nationhood. Although the precise nature of the "sharing" of experience and memories of them does not come forward in these sociological definitions, the very presence of such a concept discloses the centrality of a particular *mentality* to any notion of assimilation to "America."

In this final section, I examine how the key tropes used to identify the Asian/American subject are related to the redefinition of national identities, and how this redefinition has taken place in political, social, and cultural discourses. Specifically, I am interested in the tropology of the *psychic*, which posits in the Asian / American subject a particular set of mental and spiritual capabilities and weaknesses, dispositions, encumbrances, and values. For example, if social identity and community membership are so attached to common memories (let alone experiences), is memory dependent on direct experience, or does a collective memory not rest instead upon a tradition of narration and performance? What is the nature of the various "collectivities" that might vie for primacy in our *re*collective processes? How does recourse to such collectivities inevitably bracket out other modes of identification? How does the use of psychologistic discourse both pathologize and propose remedies for the not-yet-assimilated subject? And, finally, what is the nature of memory in a transnational or cross-cultural situation? I begin by examining the trope of "schizophrenia," which has been used to describe the "dual personalities" of hyphenated Americans, who are thus depicted as unable to engage unproblematically in that invented hegemonic memory. In Chapter 10 I turn to the production of a series of psychic identifications that grapple with the transnational age—diaspora, "Greater China," and the elaboration of the "Pacific Rim" into that mass psychic hallucination William Gibson has dubbed "cyberspace."

Deployed as a diagnosis of cultural and racial duality, racial and cultural "schizophrenia" is predicated upon an absolutist, nation-based notion of identity, which is put into crisis by migrancy and racial difference. In the United States, this points up the fundamental dilemma of inclusionist and assimilationist doctrine. This mental pathology may be linked to the historical schisms of the 1970s, the period in which this trope is most often articulated. There are certain, fundamental questions: How was this pathology an outgrowth of earlier notions of the "marginal man"? How was the recourse taken to "cultural nationalism" the logical response to this stigma, and yet how does this alternative remove from view other modes of identification? Crucially, how can we turn the schizophrenic pathology reserved for racialized peoples back on the pristine notion of "whiteness," which seeks to project schizophrenia solely onto the minds of racialized peoples and therefore allow itself to stand above such concerns?

The tropology of alienation, fragmentation, and conflict so common to modernity has, as we have seen, been adapted particularly to designate and diagnose the racial Other. Yet with every instantiation of this tropology there is a movement of recombination, if only to make some graspable, perceivable entity available for ideological circulation. The standard reading of the modern migrant subject has been the image of the "marginal man," which we have traced from the influential writings of Robert E. Park. The "margin" can be mapped at the fringes of American society; however, that was not the site of Park's original formulation. As we have noted, Park extends "marginality" to a wide range of individuals who are caught between the old world and the new. The "margin" is read in that *liminal* space: the mental processes that inform the negotiation of that space then form a key component of the modern psyche. Those people who are marginal are those who have lost contact with the values, customs, and mores proper to the old world—they are inscribed instead in the logic of modern economies without, as yet, cultural coherence. Yet this general notion of a seemingly universal decline of modern men and women becomes particularly attached to those whose racial markings set them off most dramatically and tellingly from the first waves of American immigration.[6] These people are *particularly* marginal; they are marked by their more distant and distinct racial and ethnic identities. Marginality thus is transformed from an overall condition to one that applies specifically to racial others. The marginal in its racial formulation is thus located not in a temporal and geographic gap (between old and new worlds, premodernity and modernity), but at the outer fringes of American subjectivity. The process of assimilation narrates the gradual movement from the margin haunted by race to the supposedly colorblind center of American idealism.

This racialization of marginality is linked to DuBois's early notion of "double consciousness," expounded through his seminal study *The Souls of Black Folk* (1903; last revised 1953). The key difference between the concept of the marginal man and double consciousness is of course that, rather than naming Marginal Man's cultural conflict between old and new worlds, DuBois's concept explicitly connects double consciousness and political power: while the American black was part of a nation without power, they were also nationals without citizenship. In the first chapter, DuBois writes:

> It is a peculiar sensation, this double-consciousness, this sense of always looking at one's self through the eyes of others, of measuring one's soul by the tape of a world that looks on in amused contempt and pity. One ever feels his twoness,— an American, a Negro; two souls, two thoughts, two unreconciled strivings; two warring ideals in one dark body, whose dogged strength alone keeps it from being torn asunder. The history of the American Negro is the history of this strife— this longing to attain self-conscious manhood, to merge his double self into a better, a truer self. . . . He simply wishes to make it possible for a man to be both a Negro and an American."[7]

This merging would not entail the loss of either, but rather a depathologized new whole.[8] DuBois used double consciousness as a metaphor to describe the effects of racialization upon the African American psyche. To do so he removed the onus from individual psychic dysfunctionality and placed it on institutional racism. Yet in later periods the superficial and ideologically expedient reading of "double-consciousness" as "dual personality" tended to repathologize the individual racial and ethnic subject and make the psychic instability of the subject a product of his or her own inability to make cultural choices.[9] In other words, the mapping of marginality was *internalized*, taken from the topography of margin-to-center movement across the American grain and situated in the deeply troubled psychic recesses of racial subjects.

One essential point needs to be made here, and recalled throughout our discussions of racial psychologies: deeply embedded in the notion of double consciousness and dual personality, making particularly logical its affinity with the pathology of the schizophrenic, is the sense of being watched. Yet the ontological grounding for racial duality is produced by the fact that the racial subject is at once marginal *and* central, like *and* not like. The very fact he or she can imagine being looked at *just so* means that his or her alienation is predicated upon a sense of difference installed *prior* to the act of self-consciousness—he or she has already internalized the dominant's point of view ("they view us as such").[10] Thus, even though DuBois notes that the Negro is allowed to see himself only "through the revelation of the other world," it is clear that the racial subject must have *already* had intimations of that alterity.[11] In short, the work of "assimilation" does double duty, producing a subject who has those "memories" implanted in his or her psyche, and yet those memories, dispositions, intuitions serve only to remind him or her of the gap that lies between them and those memories—in other words, of their borrowed, not shared, nature.

For example, one early sociological study of Japanese Americans uses the trope of being watched to describe the essential difference between Japanese Americans and whites—Japanese Americans are discovered to differ from whites because the former are more sensitive to social conventions; whites are relatively free from such inhibition. The researchers hit upon this analogy:

> A simile is useful in pointing up the similarities and differences between Japanese American and white middle class achievement orientations: the ultimate destinations or goals of individuals in the two groups tend to be very similar; but the Japanese Americans go toward these destinations along straight narrow streets lined with crowds of people who observe every step, while middle class persons

go toward the same destinations along wider streets having more room for maneuvering, and lined only with small groups of people who, while watching them, do not observe their every moment.[12]

One could not ask for a better example of how body, psyche and space converge in mapping out the coordinates of Asian/American social ontology—why does it surprise these sociologists that racially marked people might have a particular intuition of being watched?

In the 1970s, two Asian American psychologists, Stanley and Derald D. Sue, published an article that took up this way of describing the "dual personalities" of racial minorities in the United States. They complicated the formula slightly, inventing three "personality types" under which U.S.-born Chinese Americans could be classified. Seeing the "traditional Chinese family," "western influences," and racism as major forces shaping Chinese American self-consciousness, the Sues asserted that if the pressure from the convergence of these forces became too great, the Chinese American mind would have to make an identificatory commitment in order to keep from being pulled apart: "When these sources of stress become too great, mental health problems are frequently the result."[13] Either one became a "traditionalist" and adopted Chinese values; embraced western values, thereby becoming a "marginal man"; or one "rebelled" against such a choice and committed oneself to developing Asian American values, thus becoming an "Asian-American."[14] While the Sues seem to lean toward approving the last choice, they caution that the rebellious nature of the Asian American, if taken too far, can result in a "hypersensitivity" to racism. This schematization immediately drew fire, most particulary from Ben R. Tong, then a Ph.D. student at the California School of Professional Psychology and psychology instructor at San Francisco State.

Tong was particularly incensed at the Sues for writing out or distorting history. In his rebuttal, he accused the Sues of having an "ahistorical frame of mind."[15] In a later article, he elaborates: "The critical issue is that they [Sues] and their colleagues *explain* their findings with the . . . racist assumption that there has always existed an unbroken continuity between Chinese America and certain 'cultural values' of ancient Cathay; values which have somehow remained unaltered for centuries above the exigencies of history."[16] Tong argues instead that the bulk of Chinese immigrants were in fact distanced from those orthodox values—coming predominantly from Canton, they had an entirely different cultural and historical identity, deeply ensconced in resistance and rebellion.[17] Tong seems to avoid the accusation that he too is holding fast to an ahistorical, essentialized notion of Chinese American identity, now simply redefined as Cantonese American.

But his reason for such a reductionist move is to define a sharp contrast between this essential character of rebellion and resistance and the present-day Chinese American: "The question then arises as to how Chinese-Americans became what they are today if their forebears were *not* groveling chinks."[18] His answer is that this "groveling" is actually a strategy of subterfuge: "Locked out of legitimate economic enterprise by white law, the Chinamen invented *fake Chinese culture* to survive. . . . To Chinese-Americans, *kawk jieh* is the act of cheating, deceiving, outwitting or exploiting another. . . . It expresses—all at the same time—the anger, the ingenuity, and the audacity of the old Chinamen."[19] Thus, taking advantage of "racist love" (191), the Chinese in America faked submission and exploited white America's appetite for such a "culture." Nevertheless, Tong acknowledges a danger to such a strategy: "A distinction can be drawn between schizoid behavior that is *creative* and schizziness that is *pathological*. What starts out as a creative response to an insane social reality can itself become a form of madness. This occurs either by virtue of the person (displaying such behavior) *being labelled sick*, as in the case of R. D. Laing's clientele and whites in this culture, or by the fact of *remaining withdrawn*, like Chinese-Americans [emphasis in original]."[20] Thus, in crossing the line dividing creativity and pathology, Chinese Americans have been both "the agent[s] and victim[s] of their alienation from their humanity."[21]

I want to draw forth three key issues from this debate: first, the tension between a psychologistic reading and a pragmatic and ethical one; second, the importance attached by all parties to some sense of "national" or racial character; and finally, to the fact that this "character" is adaptive to specific historical contingencies. In sum, there is an essential "politics" of identity. But in order to go beyond the obviousness of such a statement, one has to maintain an attention to the elements sketched out above—the morally fraught condition of multiple choices; the recourse inevitably made to a overwhelmingly broad cultural "character," and the way the psyche is deployed pragmatically in the socioeconomic realm.[22] Tong's "creative schizziness" seeks a way out from underneath the forced binarism of either/or that Surh insists is the key characteristic of racial psychologies: "The Asian American, like all racial minorities in the United States, is like a man on a tightwire drawn between the two halves of himself."[23] Instead, Tong argues that "the so-called identity crisis, belabored to death by hack writing and glib rhetoric, simply refers to that growing number among acculturated (but never assimilated) native-born Chinese-Americans who cannot accept the alternatives of this 'either-or' syndrome."[24] But that strategy falters even as it is articulated—Tong cannot yet map out the politics that would be called for to secure the creative schizo from falling into pathology: "The sickness of Chinese America . . . is *not* to be treated by psychotherapy. Something else is required. Something of a radical political nature that has yet to be seriously considered."[25] Missing here is a sustained analysis of the political economy of race in America. All Tong can do is insist upon that tenuous, heroic "creativity" that always threatens to be internalized and taken as "real." It also is of no help politically beyond its self-involvement.

If the culture of resistance is all that survives in an idealized and limited fashion, it is still that to which activists in the 1970s held as the potential grounding of a resurgent movement. This culture had to avoid the radically unstable creativity of the schizo and posit instead a foundational identity. That identity would be found in combination of cultural nationalism and a politics of place.[26] What emerges in the 1970s is a constant three-way tension among the abhorrence of the pathological schizoid personality, a suspicion of its "creative" manifestation, and the promise of the Asian American cultural nation that took the "community" to be the site of a positively construed difference. It is this locus of political activism that most sharply evinces the practical agendas of Asian America (here we refer back to the struggles over local space and community self-determination seen in Part 4).[27] Drawing on the positive energy of cultural nationalism, activism was successful, ironically enough, to the degree it could bypass a thoroughgoing critique of whether the tenets of cultural nationalism, drawn from African national liberation ideology, could be commensurate with the political situation of Asian America. What was unquestionably germane, however, was their common critique of power. The struggles of that era are thus better understood not as taking the founding of a cultural nation as an end point, but as a co-effect of the effort to reform (if not revolutionize) the nation and its assumptions with regard to race, class, ethnicity, and gender, and its distribution of power. And this reformation necessarily included a revision of psychic pathologies.[28]

Asian Americans having recourse to cultural nationalism sought to ground identity outside of the debilitating dualism of schizophrenic pathology. Chin et al. remark on the way the dual personality concept installed a permanent disenfranchisement: "Fourth-, fifth-, and sixth-generation Asian-Americans are still looked upon as foreigners because of this dual heritage, or the concept of dual personality, which suggests that the Asian-American can be broken down into his American part and his Asian part. This view explains Asian assimilation, adaptability, and lack of presence in American culture. This sustaining inner resource keeps the Asian-American a stranger in the country in which he was born."[29] In contrast to the pathology of dualism, which "deprives the Chinese-American and Japanese-American of the means to develop their own terms,"[30] the invention of Asian American cultural identity was to make possible the articulation of difference from both elements of the dual personality concept: "The assertion of distinctions between Chinese and Chinese-Americans is neither a rejection of Chinese culture nor an expression of contempt for things Chinese, as the whites and the Chinatown Establishment would make them out to be. It is calling things by their right names."[31] The distancing of China as a point of reference was a necessary move: it allowed the rupturing of the genetically ensured passing down of "tradition" into the psychological makeup of Asian Americans and established instead the possibility of a discontinuity which would allow for a new formation. This rupture takes place even as blacks, with whom many Asian American activists identified, sought to regain a sense of roots in Africa: it was precisely because Asia had historically been established as an abject realm within an orientalist discourse that Asian Americans were dubious about finding "strength" in searching back.

The two decades between the 1970s and the 1990s form a critical transition in Asian/American identifications.[32] In the early 1990s, the AIIEEEEE group reinstated Asia as a point of reference. This move was facilitated by the resurgence of East Asia as an economic power (the reformation of "Asia" historically in the years between the two AIIEEEEE anthologies of 1974 and 1991), as well as two crucial developments of the 1970s: the installation of Asian American literature both in the academy and in popular culture, beginning with Maxine Hong Kingston's The Woman Warrior (1975), and in 1978 the appearance of Edward Said's enormously influential book, Orientalism, which opened the way for a thoroughgoing critique of the discursive production of "other" spaces. Chin's long contribution to the Big AIIEEEEE! directly addresses the popularity of Asian American literature. Deeply suspicious of the sources of this popularity, Chin attacks the ideology of the autobiographic form adapted by Chinese American authors, which, he asserts, perpetuates a situation wherein the Chinese American author is constantly deferential, subordinate, and confessional. For Chin, these narratives willfully ignore the presence of a tradition of resistance and affirmation:

> Then, as now, the Christian autobiographers [i.e., those Chinese American authors adopting the autobiographical form] are blind to the presence of the heroic

tradition in every shop in every Chinatown, in the tongs, in the Cantonese opera they bring to local theaters and feature at their New Year's banquets, and in the huge gold dragons and phoenixes clawing the walls of Chinatown restaurants everywhere. If Louis Chu were alive today, he would be surprised to see that we have to fight to have his *Eat A Bowl of Tea* understood as *Three Kingdoms* and *Water Margin*, Sun Tzu and Confucius fermented into a language of pure Chinese psychology, and writing in English as if it were a dialect of Cantonese.[33]

Chin's referencing of China has the effect of at once reinstating the dichotomy of dualism ("the differences between Western and Asian civilization are real, sharply defined, profound, and easily stated: Western civilization is founded on religion. Asian civilization—Confuciandom—is founded on history")[34] and suggesting the invention of a hybrid form ("writing in English as if it were a dialect of Cantonese"). In so doing, he is actually recalling Tong's argument for a revision of Chinese American history according to a newly discovered lineage passed down as Cantonese militancy. Where Tong confines his claim to a "subversive element" that could easily slip into neurosis, Chin proposes a heroic tradition that launches a direct assault on the residual elements of Asian passivity found in Tong's hypothesis. Nevertheless, while Chin's mode of rehabilitation, like Tong's, at once provides the positive grounds for a rebuttal of the image of the Chinese and Chinese American as constitutionally weak, it reestablishes the essential gap between Asia and America. Importantly, however, Chin opens up one particular space for appropriation and hybridization—the cultural sphere.

Even in recent discussions of Filipino identity, the psychologistic remains the most powerful analytical device. With the particular dynamics of postcoloniality in mind, Strobel argues for a "decolonizing of the mind" to be brought about by "the process of undoing the effects of colonization on the Filipino psyche by recognizing the master narratives that constructed colonial identity and replacing them with indigenous narratives."[35] She cites the American Association of Filipino Psychology, as well as V. Enriquez's *From Colonial to Liberation Psychology: The Philippine Experience* as particular sites for the discursive production of a postcolonial psyche.[36] The "recognition" and "replacement" motif here vies with the psychological exposition of assimilation, which insists on transposing and "sharing" memories, experiences, sentiments. But still missing is a sense of how, exactly, these operations are to occur and what material conditions obtain to facilitate, block, or reshape psychic content. In her recent reformulation of Asian American "panethnicity," Yen Le Espiritu also touches upon the psychological as a key arena of identification: "The construction of Asian American identities is not only a response to conditions in the mainland United States but is also deeply bound to collective memory, historical struggles, and the real or imagined 'homeland.'"[37] Here, again, we find the recourse to memories and imaginations, struggles and "real" homelands. There is no doubt that these key tropes are critical elements to our presentation of Asian American ethnicity, but the problem of discerning the particular content, weight, and valence of certain terms remains: what is the correlation between real and imagined nations, how are memories shared (or not) intersubjectively?

With this focus upon the psychological, it is no surprise that Asian Americans would have recourse to cultural nationalism, that discourse which itself is so historically linked to psychologizing power and its effects. Cultural nationalism specifically provides a way to map ethnic identity even while acknowledging the uneven and inconsistent ways that the "ethnic" traverses various terrains. Barth's concept of ethnicity has important ramifications for the adaptation of cultural nationalism. He writes:

> It is clear that boundaries persist despite a flow of personnel across them. In other words, categorical ethnic distinctions do not depend on an absence of mobility, contact and information, but do entail social processes of exclusion and incorporation whereby discrete categories are maintained *despite* changing participation and membership in the course of individual life histories. . . . [An ethnic group] shares fundamental cultural values, realized in overt unity of cultural forms.[38]

This description implies that "ethnicity" can be maintained among noncontiguous individuals under specific conditions. Its nonconvergence with territory is crucial, for this notion of ethnicity allows for a common cultural identity independent of space, and links up the notion of ethnicity with that of diaspora.[39]

In the colonized context, where cultural nationalism is first articulated, this has the effect of grounding national identity under a condition of disenfranchisement from the land. Where the physical and historical are crosshatched by dispossession, the possibility of resurgency is founded upon a common cultural identity that bears both the mark of colonization and that of a future beyond it. Cabral notes: "The value of culture as an element of resistance to foreign domination lies in the fact that culture is the vigorous manifestation on the ideological or idealist plane of the physical and historical reality of the society that is dominated or to be dominated."[40] In this struggle, the psychological forms a key role in national liberation: "A reconversion of minds—of mental set—is thus indispensible to the true integration of people into the liberation movement."[41]

Yet Fanon will argue that the revolutionary mind will not be committed to restoring a precolonial *memory*, but to being conscious of the political contingencies of the *present*: "It is not enough to try to get back to the people in that past out of which they have already emerged; rather we must join them in that fluctuating movement which they are just giving shape to, and which, as soon as it has started, will be the signal for everything to be called into question."[42]

One of the main problems, of course, is the fact that the context for cultural nationalism is quite different when one turns to the situation of Asian America, and the transformed terrain of Asian America between the 1970s and the 1990s.[43] This is true even while acknowledging the usefulness of the "internal colonialism" model. While we can engage Fanon's important focus on the production of emergent formations, we must remember that for Fanon, culture is absolutely linked to nation: "The nation is not only the condition of culture, its fruitfulness, its continuous renewal, and its deepening. It is also a necessity."[44] This forces a discussion of the constitution of that "nation" to which Asian American culture is to be aligned. Cultural nationalism in this case would have to imagine a particular political encasement for "the nation." For Asian American activists in the 1970s, this encasement, the site for a war of position, was the community, and, indeed, the local enactment of a cultural nation provided the indispensable grounds for progressive political work, the most lasting effect of which might well be the reshaping of American consciousness of ethnicity and race. Nevertheless, the relation of "culture" to "nation" has *always* been haunted not only by the open question of their precise interface politically, but by the identification of "nation" in communities deeply influenced by both national and international politics, and now, increasingly transnational operations.

An anecdote from Frank Chin reveals the nonconvergence between Asian nationalism and Asian American cultural nationalism. Chin talks about teaching a college class in the San Francisco Bay Area in the 1970s. The class has been singing anti-Asian racist songs as a parody of white racism—but the parodic element is lost on certain people:

> The gang council decides we're too controversial. They call me to a meeting. The leader of the Chinatown Red Guards taps me on the shoulder and says, "I want to talk to you." I turn around and just like in the movies, his fist is coming toward me. He knocks me down, my glasses go flying, he punches me in the stomach. . . .
>
> He says, "Identify with China!" I say, "Wait a minute. We're in America. This is where we are, where we live and where we're going to die. There's not going to be any revolution. That's crazy." He can't hit me anymore. He's already done

that and it's not working. . . . He curls his lip and says, "You cultural nationalist!"
I go, "*What?* What's a cultural nationalist?"[45]

The Red Guard's exhortation to "identify with China" is complemented by his insult—"cultural nationalist!" Either one identifies with the "country of origin" or one has fallen into faulty identification with a phantom Asian American nation secured only by "culture" suspiciously close to "American" in its identity. Yet both Chin and his antagonist are caught up in a pernicious circle that avoids the interactive, dialectical history that produces Asian America.

The precise nature of "dual" personality cannot be grasped without a specific sense of the forces that create that schism, the assumptions that underlie the imputed *separateness* of the two realms of experience, and the nature of the "wholeness" sought. Rather than assuming simply a free-floating land of neurosis and schizophrenia, we should see that the separation of "Asia," "America," and "Asian America" is *itself* a psychic rationalization that, in seeking to simplify complex forms of identification and disidentification, blinds us both to the precise politics of separation, and, concomitantly, to their grounds for interpenetration. The question behind cultural nationalism is therefore not the availability of a "nation" to secure "culture," but rather the historical materiality of a culture produced in a psychic space wherein a particular and contingent formation of the nation appears *in relation* to multiple identifications which are themselves driven by specific contingencies.

For instance, taking the most *literal* phenomena of binationality, Asian America is marked by a longstanding history of continued involvement with Asia: both Hawai'i and the U.S. mainland have been the homes of governments in exile—Lyu's history on Korean nationalist activities in the U.S. is a valuable document in this regard, as is Lee's study of the Overseas Chinese Affairs Commission. The work of Him Mark Lai has traced the double focus of the Chinese Marxist Left on both China and the United States, and the importance of the Chinese language press in establishing a North American diasporic community; Bernard Wong reports the impact of events in China on Chinese American communities. Likewise Edward Chang and others have studied the effects of the 1980 Kwangju uprising on Koreans in America; and Bello and Reyes have reported on the effects of the overthrow of Marcos on Filipino communities. Recent political activism with regard to events in Asia has included a Los Angeles protest against the Thai government's suppression of pro-democracy demonstrations that left thousands killed (Arenson), and against the Japanese government's eviction of Korean laborers taken to Japan in World War Two.

Karl Lo's study of the Chinese vernacular press in North America between 1900 and 1950 points out that these presses' attention to nationalist struggle and political formations had the effect of not only raising large sums of money from Chinese American communities, but also of instantiating a particular "social memory" which waxed and waned according to historical events: "When the contributions became a part of the social memory of the Chinese Americans, they reinforced the volition, which prompted more copies and more titles of newspapers. This in turn led to more contributions, and so forth. The cycle reached its height in the 1943–44 period. After the defeat of the Japanese, the volition was weakened and the cycle lost momentum."[46]

Asian national politics continue to be a critical part of Asian American life: there is a persistent history of anti-communist Vietnamese "death squads" and other sources of pressure on Vietnamese American communities (Grossman; Harrison); the 1985 murder of Henry Liu in Daly City, California, by Taiwanese agents brought particular focus on the workings of the KMT in the United States (see Dowie and Millman; also Cohen). Recently, Kotkin and Diau sensationally claimed that "China's next revolution may start here." They report on a group of pro-democracy activists in Silicon Valley:

> Largely unsung, such small, highly motivated bands of California Chinese are increasingly the ones taking the lead in doing the dirty work of the anti-Communist insurgency—smuggling dissidents out of China and smuggling pro-democracy cassette tapes, facsimiles, letters and newspapers. In the not too distant future [they assert], they also may literally supply the weapons that can spark the revolution. Earlier this year, the Chinese Democracy Movement held seminars featuring former officers in the People's Liberation Army on the possibilities of a military coup against the current Beijing government.[47]

Whatever the alarmist tone of this piece, it is superseded by the sense that America (specifically the Silicon Valley) is now the site to launch the last war against communism: American space is now identified with "anti-Communist insurgency"; the ideological warfare carried on in California attests to the continued identification of America as the Free World. Even as America's defense industry has seemingly been put on warning by Congressional budget-cutters, the high-tech capabilities of the Silicon Valley are regeared to do battle elsewhere. Kotkin and Diau point out enthusiastically that the 1911 revolution was also launched by Chinese revolutionaries in the United States.

Asian American novels persistently foreground diasporic politics—Kim's *Clay Walls* narrates the nationalist activities of Korean immigrants in California's agricultural spaces; in Wendy Law Yone's *Coffin Tree*, the psychic damage created by CIA-sponsored coups in Burma is carried over to America by Burmese exiles; Karen Tei Yamashita traces the reappearance of a Japanese fascist mentality even in the new utopian spaces of Brazil in *Brazil Maru*. Ty Pak's short story "A Second Chance," which narrates the journey of a Korean correspondent to Manchuria during the Korean War, succinctly pulls together the several historical strains of Korean history and endows our understanding of Korean American "identity" with a particular density:

> He [the correspondent] could have died for them, stayed there for the rest of his life working with them. Every cell in him tingled and reverberated with the story of the race—the vagabondage that originated from Central Eurasian steppes, trekking and meandering across the mountains and deserts of two continents, the persecutions, discriminations, genocides that hounded them everywhere they went and kept them on the move, the narrow escapes, constant packings-up and movings-on, panting runs, exhausted droppings on the road, children smothered in their cries, the uneasy settlement of the peninsula coveted by the hostile nations, Chinese, Russian, Mongolian, Manchu, the thousand years of invasions, national emergencies, midnight alarms, vigils, widows' keenings. The ten millennia of Korean history paraded past him like a grim tableau. The whole time he was there, he lived in a trance-like state of exaltation.[48]

Rather than see these phenomena as defining the persistence of Asian identification with Asia (and not America), we should understand that the historical reality of Asian America has been produced by a number of factors, including but not limited to the ongoing influence of Asian national identity, America's continued identification of Asians as not Americans, and transnational capital's persistent merging and delinking of the interests of "Asia" and "America" at precise moments. In other words, the symptoms of "schizophrenia" read into Asian Americans are the outcomes of specific material histories and not the *inherent* mental pathologies of bicultural peoples. Likewise, the referent for "cultural nationalism" is now increasingly linked to a particular transnational identity, whose contents vary with historical contingency. Asian/American identity politics is therefore not a matter of simple choice between Asia or America, but rather produced within a complex set of material histories. Elaine Kim, writing after the Los Angeles uprising, puts it this way:

> I have been critical lately of cultural nationalism as detrimental to Korean Americans, especially Korean American women, because it operates on exclusions and fosters intolerance and uniformity of thought while stifling self-criticism and en-

couraging sacrifice, even to the point of suicide. But *sa-i-ku* makes me think again: what remains for those who are left to stand alone? If Korean Americans refuse to be victims or political pawns in the U.S. while rejecting the exhortation that we go back to Korea where we belong, what will be our weapons of choice? . . . It is far easier for Anglo Americans to call for an end to cultural nationalisms than for Korean Americans to give up national consciousness, which makes it possible to survive the vicious racism that would deny our existence as either Korean Americans or Americans. . . . What is clear is that we cannot 'become American' without dying of *han* ["the sorrow and anger that grow from the accumulated experiences of oppression"] unless we think about community in new ways.[49]

Indeed, it could be argued that Korean American "identity" has been particularly characterized as "dispersed" both in terms of the exile and diaspora from Korea, and because Koreans have been forced across and out of the country because of colonial wars and civil schisms within.[50]

The consolidation of identity around a common core masks both the homogenizing process of consolidation and of difference-making that secures one set of identities while necessarily subordinating others and obviating certain critical possibilities. Kim's comment focuses on the equally bad choices of "Americanization" and "Asianization" if these choices are made according to the presumptions of absolutism. As Brackette Williams argues:

This equation of homogeneity as nation is thus part of a broader assumption that has served to undermine deconstructive analyses of political consciousness, group identity formation, and sociocultural integration. . . . [Assimilation and acculturation] link the homogenizing process to a form of hegemonic dominance that, following Gramsci, we refer to as a transformist hegemony. This ignores the fact that both the creation of heterogeneity and the production and legitimation of classificatory systems to order it are ongoing parts of all human society, no matter what the stability of putative homogeneity or the stability of a particular hegemonic moment.[51]

If this attention to heterogeneity promises a better description of social realities and of the degree to which the hegemonic must tame such realities, then we find a specific containment in the notion of ethnic dualism, which will insist on pathologizing the schizophrenic. Politically, this means that the ethnic subject has to either be identifiable within that abject paradigm, risk dismissal as overtly "Asian," or declare allegiance to the nation, even while suspecting that the nation has no specific allegiance to it. This is the question that haunts the narratives of 1970s Asian America.

In and Out of Disguise

Daniel I. Okimoto's *American in Disguise* was published in 1971, with an introduction praising it by James Michener. It met with some critical success: one critic claimed that in Okimoto's novel "provocative ideas are expressed with such scholarly restraint that they may go unread in the current racial uproar," and another praised it for talking of "the Negro problem sympathetically and yet not without the racial pride of one from a subculture which always worked hard and had a devotion to education as a spur to achievement."[52] Clearly, this was a novel that was appropriated by the mainstream press to confirm the model minority myth. Yet a less directed reading of the novel reveals a subtly nuanced and deeply ambivalent narrative. Moving between growing up in the United States and the author's postgraduate study in Japan, it is sharply critical of both American racism (and the passive response to it of many Japanese) and Japanese nationalism, among other things. However, the narrative ultimately resolves this personality conflict by squarely identifying with "America."

The title itself is taken from an instance wherein the author insists that he is just as "American" as any other American—his Americanness is simply not immediately visible: he is in the "disguise" of Japanese.[53] But his defining moment comes when the author tells of his dilemma over whether or not to register for the draft during the Vietnam War: "How would I resolve the dilemma between my strong opposition to the Vietnam War, based upon the dictates of my conscience, as against the legal responsibility of each citizen to accept the obligations of citizenship no matter how inconvenient or distasteful?" (165).[54] The narrator proceeds to provide ample evidence of just how much he disapproves of the war, especially as he cites instance after instance of American racism against Asians and other racial minorities. Yet he finally decides to register: "For all its faults, for the immensity of the gap between myth and reality, the United States still had many redeeming virtues; it was a nation to which I felt an instinctual allegiance" (168).

It is exactly this unexamined "instinct" that discloses the author's absorption of American nationalist ideology, an instance eminently *cynical* in Žižek's terms: "The cynical subject is quite aware of the distance between the ideological mask and the social reality, but he none the less still insists upon the mask."[55] Rather than debate issues of false consciousness, it may be more useful to focus upon the way Okimoto at once legitimates himself as a politically aware "ethnic author" and brackets all his criticism, which is superseded by an ultimate deferral to the "myth" of America. Crucially, it is a myth much more pernicious than the one he seems to straightforwardly dismiss at the beginning of his rationalization. Its perniciousness lies in the fact that it is more than the externally identified "myth" so easily debunked by social reality, it is rather the more deep-seated myth of America's ultimate justness *despite every social fact*. As such, what Žižek calls the "mask" coincides ironically with the "disguise" Okimoto identifies as his Japanese face—it is a mask that persists and finally conquers the subject, as witnessed in the all important manners in which the subject *performs* ideology. The nation keeps reappearing as the nodal point of identification, both here and generally in 1970s literature, whether it be in a primordial retrieval of Cantonese identity or American patriotism. The "schizophrenic" once again is better seen as produced by the contradictions of state ideology and practice rather than in the "confused" state of the Asian/American psyche—a confusion that in *American in Disguise* is only resolvable by pledging allegiance to one nation.

A provocative point of comparison to Okimoto's narrative, which like Okimoto's travels between Japan and the United States (although from the opposite direction), is Yoshimi Ishikawa's *Strawberry Road*, originally written in 1991 and published in Japan as *Sutoroberī rōdo*. This autobiographical novel tells of Ishikawa's journey from Japan to California in 1965 and his reunion with his older brother, Daiku. The novel is set within a context of historical transition, wherein the residual effects of the American occupation of Japan, the rise in the Japanese economy, the Vietnam War, the burgeoning of the countercultural movements of the sixties, and North American agricultural economies and immigration policies are all conjoined. Regarding this text as a countermovement to Okimoto's narrative, we find a common concern with identity, but the stakes and conditions of negotiating Asian/American identity are vastly different.

Ishikawa begins his narration with clear attention to the differentials of class and the shifting, unstable histories of emigration. The transit points of emigration calibrate a trajectory that follows specific class distinctions, yet the fixity of those distinctions is counterposed to the unpredictable revision of global economic relations. He writes:

> Our ship, the *Africa-maru*, was making its last journey. It carried more than one hundred and sixty immigrants, a few businessmen, and five exchange students. Although the ship was destined for the immigrant regions of Paraguay, Brazil, and Argentina, it would stop off in America for the businessmen and the students. . . . All had their own reasons for coming, but all had the same goal—success. We were poor people.

That year a huge economic boom started in Japan. No one on that ship would ever have guessed it; the people back home would have found it even harder to believe. (2)

Ishikawa's decision to emigrate is prompted by both his brother's prior act of emigration and by his early familiarity with American culture. This familiarity is produced through specific material exchanges—the economics of the Occupation which couple young Japanese women with the American occupation forces, the circulation of tinned goods and candy bars from U.S. military stores into the island economy, the flow of "culture" into the public sphere, all serve to establish a particular representation: "American culture permeated my small island, so I felt familiar with America before I ever set foot there" (7). The very materiality of "America" is perceived by contrasting American objects with their Japanese counterparts. "America" is represented by its commodities, which have an economic value entirely correlated with the aesthetic: "Japanese magazines were cheap and rough to the touch, whereas American magazines were so incredibly shiny I had to squint while looking at them" (10).

Nevertheless, Ishikawa's narrative picks up the historical complications of such idolatry. As we move forward in time, the Japanese become "more and more familiar with foreign countries, and anti-American views appeared in Japanese media and public opinion because of the escalation of America's intervention in Vietnam" (16).

Just as international relations between America and Asia complicate the figuration of America in the narrator's mind, so does the development of the U.S. agricultural economy and its new dependency on migrant labor open up a particular angle of entry for Japanese: "In the early fifties, the state [California] began hiring 350,000 workers a year from Mexico under the *bracero* program. As migrant workers, the Mexicans became the backbone of American agriculture. When Japanese farmers heard about this, they sent Hiroshi Nasu, the chairman of the Japan International Farming Friendship Association, to America to ask that Japan be allowed to join the bracero program. After some initial setbacks, they sent their first contract laborer to America in 1956" (13). *Strawberry Road* thus prepares the stage for some sort of critique of capitalism, U.S. imperialism, and neocolonialism. Yet the narrative veers off in another direction. Landing in America, Ishikawa is both disillusioned at the hard labor in the fields, and caught up in the American Dream.

While he can "identify with" the Mexicans who labor side by side in the strawberry fields with him, as the two Japanese brothers come to own a bit of land they become altogether ambivalent about the Mexicans. They appreciate the critical part Mexicans play in the economy, but lack enough sympathy to transcend their interests as owners. After the Mexicans go on strike, several Japanese workers intervene; racial identifications take precedence:

> The Japanese farmers who took part in the strike breaking felt that it was time to show Americans how hard they could work. During the summer of 1966, the Japanese had also risen in a fervor, like the blacks, [and] the Mexicans. . . .
>
> "The whites are havin' to take another look at us. But you know, even though I understand what the Mexicans are feeling, they went too far, and the whites got mad. Call it civil rights, call it whatever you want, but whites get angry when Mexicans say those kind of things." (212)

Yet no matter how much the Japanese try to align themselves with "America," there is a persistent sense of alienation in this new land. Ishikawa's brother notes the temporal disjuncture of diaspora: "You lose all sense of the seasons in America," my brother explained. "Sometimes it feels like time has stopped. There's no New Year's celebration here or Festival for the Dead, and you never go picnic under the cherry blossoms—everything's a muddle" (39).

Ishikawa's alienation from America is only intensified by his different class status—his friends still in Japan are students embroiled in intellectual and political activities; he is a small farmer in the United States. He makes friends with a local Japanese: "Starved for news of Japan, I read the enclosed newspapers and pamphlets in his letters and pored over books by important Japanese critics, which the same friends had recommended to me. I felt the gap between my life on the farm and my friends' lives back home widening" (163). A few pages later, he puts it succinctly: "I now had a farmer's body" (170). That diasporic body seems intractably mired in labor. The only way to reempower that body is through sexual conquest. Nevertheless, this body's libidinal energies are constantly frustrated by the fact that the fantasies engendered in the narrator's imagination—fantasies of sex with full-breasted American blondes, with a female Mexican fieldhand, with "flower children" in the Haight-Ashbury—are never realized.

The resolution of the novel is brought about precisely by the narrator's retreat into Japanese identity via a sexual liaison. He takes up with a Japanese businesswoman, who has been betrayed by her white lover. Both she and Ishikawa have become vulnerable by disillusionment with the United States. She deigns to sleep with this poor Japanese farm boy because of the latent nationalist identifications he awakens in her. In their affair, naming is everything—it cements the tenuous "relationship" that could never have taken place under any other circumstances. Their class differences are superseded by their mutual alienation in America. At first her names for him maintain the gap that lies between them in terms of class and age; he is identified solely by the commodity he proffers ("Mr. Strawberry") or infantilized as "Strawberry Boy." Their sexual act is underwritten by her final submission to the fantasy of nationality: "I want you, a Japanese man" (232). His "boyhood" as an American fieldhand is triumphed over by his interpellation as a "Japanese man."

This moment caps Ishikawa's narrative; the bonding of the two figures evaporates, and the novel ends with the reinstantiation of doubt. The author climbs aboard a Greyhound bus heading for New York: "which America was the true one—the America of the photos, the America before my eyes, or the America of the farm? I sat riveted, a kaleidoscope of images flashing before my eyes. For an instant I was struck by an odd fancy that America exists only in the mind" (263). This catalog of mutually exclusive possibilities for "America," this "kaleidoscope" of images, fits well with the narrator's status as perennial spectator of American life. With the sole (and crucial) exception of his work on the farm, all other realms of experience are accessed only through a mist of alienation—he is never a participant in any real sense. Rather, his self-consciousness is formed against the backdrop of a number of imagined possible relationships in and to America.

This narrative of dual alienation (from America and from Japan) differs from Okimoto's in two significant ways. Most obviously, it is written from the point of view of a migrant, whose preconceptions of the land he is entering are formed in the context of the American occupation of Japan. The very nature of the promise of America is thus to be read within the program of democratizing Japan—Ishikawa's "Americanization" begins there. His entrance into American life separates him from the telos of Japanese subject formation—his friends continue on the path into the middle-class intellectual sphere, while he is relegated to the laboring class of an interethnic American workforce, and then lifted slightly into the lower echelons of the small farming class. Whatever "split consciousness" Okimoto suffers is not applicable to Ishikawa, for Ishikawa's "Americanness" is alienated in materialist terms. "Race" is thus read with class, and "native" against "diasporic" to produce two radically different articulations of Japanese Americanness, and two incommensurate representations of duality. While Okimoto is able to, as a last resort, reaccess "America" and declare his allegiance to this admittedly flawed ideal, Ishikawa is unable to do so because for him America is not available to such understanding. Reading these texts historically and with attention to the particular ethnic/diasporic status of the speaking subject allows us to grasp the various functions of "nation" in the representation of Asian/American "hyphenation."

If the 1960s and 1970s drew largely on cultural nationalism to found community activism, Chang Rae Lee's novel *Native Speaker*, written in a quite different historical frame, outlines a utopian vision of overcoming and subverting dualistic (that is, hyphenated) thinking, but ultimately declares that that moment is not yet ripe. Again, the focus is on a split between ethnic and diasporic subjectivities. The title itself gestures toward an open question at the same moment that it makes a declaration: Henry Park, the protagonist, is a "native speaker" of English, yet the precise nature of his being "native" is a question that Lee poses in terms of agency in the political economy.

This question would seem to solicit a negative reponse—far from being an active participant in the political and social world, Park is employed as a "spy": his liminal status between Asia and America is especially useful in tracking down the targets his company sets for him: "Each of us engaged our own kind, more or less. Foreign workers, immigrants, first-generationals, neo-Americans. I worked with Koreans, Pete with Japanese. We split up the rest, the Chinese, Laotians, Singaporans, Filipinos, the whole transplanted Pacific Rim" (16). The "schizophrenic" here is set forth in Henry's doubling of consciousness—he is both spy and spied upon, as he must invent a persona that will draw out the confidence of his target. Yet he increasingly finds it difficult to separate his life from its fictional mask: "I wasn't overtly concerned in the beginning . . . that I was employing my own life as material for my alter identity. Though to a much lesser extent, a certain borrowing is always required in our line of work. But this assignment made it, in fact, quite necessary to allow for more than the usual trade. When the line between identities is fine (and the situation is not dangerous), it's preferable not to build up a whole other, nearly parallel legend" (168).

His very ability to spy on his target, a rising politician named John Kwang, is predicated on their similarity:

> I had ready connections to him, of course. He knew I was Korean, or Korean-American, though perhaps not exactly the same way he was. We were of different stripes, like any two people, though taken together you might say that one was an outlying version of the other. I think we both understood this from the very beginning, and insofar as it was evident I suppose you could call ours a kind of romance, though I didn't know exactly what he saw in me. Maybe a someone we Koreans were becoming, the latest brand of an American, that I was from the future. . . . Before I knew of him, I had never even conceived of someone like

him. A Korean man, of his age, as part of the vernacular. Not just a respectable grocer or dry cleaner or doctor, but a larger public figure who was willing to speak and act outside the tight sphere of his family. (129)

Their bond is thus constituted both by their inherited roles as Korean Americans and by a shared vision of a future subjectivity fully participant in the public sphere. It is this public identity as a post-ethnic subject that distinguishes Kwang.

Two things characterize Kwang's politics. First is his refusal to be an "ethnic" politician: "He wasn't going to be just another ethnic pol from the outer boroughs, content and provincial; he was going to be somebody who counted, who would stand up like a first citizen of these lands in every quarter of the city. . . . He was how I imagined a Korean would be, at least one living in any renown. He would stride the daises and the stages with his voice strong and clear, unafraid to speak the language like a Puritan or like a Chinaman and like every boat person in between" (283). In other words, while not being a "native speaker," Kwang is tied neither to the absolute value of nativity nor of ethnicity. He will insist on laying hold of and revising the term "American": "He began to think of America as part of him, maybe even his, and this for me was the crucial leap of his character, deep flaw or not, the leap of his identity no one in our work would find valuable but me" (196).

It is precisely this "leap" out of the ordinary bounds and conventions of Asian American (specifically, Korean American) identification that will be unrecognizable to Park's company and clientele (and indeed everyone else), who can only think in the simplest oppositional terms.[56] Their paranoia concerning subversion drives them to Henry Park's company, yet it limits their attention only to specifically conventional modes of insurgency. They are unable to understand a new world of transmigrants, post-ethnics, diasporics, transnationalism "from below." Park describes their clients and targets: "Our clients were multinational corporations, bureaus of foreign governments, individuals of resource and connection. . . . Typically the subject was a well-to-do immigrant supporting some potential insurgency on his old land, or else funding a fledgling trade union or radical student organization" (16). Instead of "old-style" politics, which fall within these parameters, Kwang's constituency presents his second point of distinction: "They were of all kinds, these streaming and working and dealing, these various platoons of Koreans, Indians, Vietnamese, Haitians, Colombians, Nigerians, these brown and yellow whatevers, whoevers, countless unheard nobodies, each offering to the marketplace their gross of kimchee, lichee, plantain, black bean, soy milk, coconut milk, ginger, grouper, ahi, yellow curry, cuchi-frito, jalapeno, their everything, selling anything to each other and to them-selves, every day of the year, and every minute. John Kwang's people" (77).

To pull such seemingly disparate groups together, Kwang knocks down bar-riers by drawing out historical similarities of oppression and exclusion. He tells a group of Koreans who are complaining about blacks:

> Know that the blacks who spend money in your store and help put food on your table and send your children to college cannot open their own stores. Why? Why can't they? Why don't they even try? Because banks will not lend to them because they are black. Because these neighborhoods are *troubled, high risk*. Because if they did open stores, no one would insure them. And if they do not have the same strong community you enjoy, the one you brought with you from Korea, which can pool money and efforts for its members—it is because this community has been broken and dissolved through history.
>
> We Koreans know something of this tragedy. Recall the days over fifty years ago, when Koreans were made servants and slaves in their own country by the Imperial Japanese Army. How our mothers and sisters were made the concubines of the very soldiers who enslaved us. I am speaking of histories that all of us should know. (142)

In recognition of the economic violence perpetrated against both blacks and im-migrants, Kwang sets up an underground economy, adapting a piece of ethnic history to a multi-ethnic condition: "He models our program on the *ggeh*. A Ko-rean money club. . . . In this sense we are all related. The larger *ggeh* depend solely on this notion, that the lessons of the culture will be stronger than a mo-mentary lack, can subdue any individual weakness or want. . . . My father would have thought him crazy to run a *ggeh* with people other than just our own. Span-ish people? Indians? Vietnamese?" (261).

Yet in the end, Kwang is brought down by the enormity of his vision, but also by his political opposition. They have placed their own spy in Kwang's organi-zation. Kwang's reaction is to have the person killed. This fall back into the worst violence of common politics drives Park to betray Kwang. Henry finally turns even more cynical than we found him at the beginning:

> But can you really make a family of thousands? One that will last? I know he never sought to be an ethnic politician. He didn't want them to vote for him solely be-cause he was colored or Asian. He knew he'd never win anything that way. There aren't enough of our own. So you make them into a part of you. You remember every one of their names. You are the model by which they will work and live.

You are their hope. And all this because you are such a natural American, first thing and last, if something other in between. (303)

The answer to the final question—who exactly are Park's clients (even he doesn't know)—comes out when the media describe the *ggeh* that they have uncovered: "The club is like a private bank that pays revolving interest and principal to its members, many of whom are Korean, lending activities that aren't registered with any banking commission and haven't reported to tax authorities. The information, oddly, originates from the regional director of the Immigration and Naturalization Service" (305).

The schizophrenic diagnosis, which insists on separating Asian from American, and other groups from each other, seems to have won out. Henry's biracial child, Mitt, dies accidentally at an early age. It is this death that drives a wedge between Henry and his wife, Lelia, and adds to Henry's alienation and withdrawal. Lelia wonders, "Maybe it's that Mitt wasn't all white or yellow. I go crazy thinking about it, don't you? Maybe the world wasn't ready for him. God. Maybe it's that he was so damn happy" (120). Mitt's happiness, innocent of a racial and ethnic history that demands a diagnosis of schizophrenia, cannot last. One thing particularly identifies Mitt for Henry: "Mitt always spoke beautifully" (222). This nonpathologized, fluent and happy mixedness is thus not for the world at present. Lee narrates the specific historical and political incompatability of Kwang's dream. Nevertheless, it is a deeply ambiguous ending: are we to read the failure of this utopian vision as emanating out of the intractable corruption of American politics, the unrelenting pressure to ethnicize and marginalize, or out of a more amorphous sense that the time is "not yet" ripe for the dream of postethnicity? Is *Native Speaker* thus to be read as a postethnic utopian narrative or a cynical, reactionary closing off of social utopias and a retreat to a safer, privatized space? What loyalties can bind, what betrayals are justified, and to what ends are actions to be taken in such a world?

In this context, it is no wonder that paranoia runs deep. If the 1970s named Asian Americans as dual personalities, the 1980s and 1990s have produced a particular vision of the schizophrenic, one intimately linked to transnationalism. This is a crucial element in *Native Speaker*: the agency's clients and objects of surveillance are all participants in the complex processes of transnationalism, transmigrancy, and uneven and discontinuous "assimilation" that marks the age and puts into crisis the notion of nationhood and citizenship. Recalling the previous section's address to the variegation of space and the restructuring of place in late capitalism, we might incorporate the notion of "racial" cultural duality / schizophrenia into a more general and fundamental splitting apart of social and political subjectivity in postmodernity.

As we saw above, as whites worried about the "Third Worldization" of local space, the very semantic charge, the very integrity of certain key words (white, American, traditional, and so on) came under pressure and doubt. What we find is a close rehearsal of Robert Park's early disquisition on "marginal man," which began as a general descriptor for "modern man," and was then reified to name and pathologize specifically *racial* marginals. What I am suggesting here is a reversal of that trajectory of pathologization and a reinscription of subjects heretofore "unmarked" by race within a more global sense of fragmentation and unanchoring. Within this examination of ethnic duality and schizophrenia, I will argue that such duality and schizophrenia should be extended as well to whites.

If Park's original notion of marginality was intended to account for the gap between the loss of old-world tradition and the not-yet-proven protocols of modern America, then we should restore that "universal" concept of a crisis in modern social being in our own investigations of late modernity. Here the fear of the racial other is complemented by a concomitant doubt of the purity and integrity of whiteness, and, reading this in terms of nationalisms, of "Americanness." As noted above, Park's original notion of marginality was intended to account for the gap between the loss of tradition and modern America. Modern man was psychically riven, placed in the margins of, on one side, loss of traditional ethical and political beliefs, and, on the other, the not-yet-clear vision of what would replace them in the modern world. Although this psychic split was not entirely smoothed over for the Euroamerican subject, it was qualitatively different for the raced subject. It became characterized by a racial and cultural double default. The neither-nor formula of marginality was not as pernicious for the Euroamerican subject, since it was still placed at the center of a modern teleology. Whichever way modernity was moving, that subjectivity was carried along in its flow. For the American racial subject, however, that forward motion was not in the least guaranteed. Indeed, the psychic split for the racial subject threatened constantly to sidetrack and stall that particularly designated forward progress of racialized subjects: assimilation.

The discourse of postmodernity has, however, presented the occasion to rethink that historical bifurcation which tracked differently the white and the nonwhite in American discourse. Much has been said about the new "condition" of postmodernity that collapses prior distinctions and sets all subjects under an equal condition of "hybridity," "fragmentation," and so on. This has both positive and negative effects on issues of race and ethnicity (among other things).

Setting aside for the moment the liberating and counterhegemonic potential of this conceptualization of the postmodern, we might stop to examine how the postmodern harbors within it a particular anxiety with regard to race and culture. The dark side of postmodernity is haunted by a loss far greater than its modern variety, since the loss is not mourned—indeed, it may be hardly noticeable. We have ceased to sense the loss of the modern. But a particular sense of disorientation still pertains.

The positively inflected notion of equality under postmodern hybridity is complemented in its negative formation by a paranoid and indeed schizophrenic sense that what was formerly Other is now the Same (as the schizophrenic sees no limits on the proliferation of personalities). Precisely the mark of distinction which privileged some over Others is now erased—everything and everybody is mixed, pastisched, multiple. Here the fear of the racial Other as no longer "other" is complemented by a concomitant doubt of the purity and integrity of whiteness, and, reading this in terms of nationalisms, of "Americanness."[57] One particularly brilliant and ambivalent reading of postmodernity in which we discern this anxiety is found in Jameson's *Postmodern Condition*.

Jameson's discussion of schizophrenia considers it to be a characteristic feature of the postmodern. Specifically, following Lacan, Jameson diagnoses schizophrenia as produced in a breakdown of the signifying chain:

> When that relationship breaks down, when the links of the signifying chain snap, then we have schizophrenia in the form of a rubble of distinct and unrelated signifiers. The connection between this kind of linguistic malfunction and the psyche of the schizophrenic may then be grasped by way of a twofold proposition: first, that personal identity is itself the effect of a certain temporal unification of past and future with one's present; and, second, that such active temporal unification is itself a function of language, or better still of the sentence, as it moves along its hermeneutic circle through time. If we are unable to unify the past, present and future of the sentence, then we are similarly unable to unify the past, present, and future of our own biographical experience or psychic life. (26f)

The "flatness" which for Jameson characterizes the postmodern age is produced by the evaporation of historical density, of temporality itself. There is simply nothing to anchor identity, since no "story" obtains: no narrative can link up random events into a meaningful statement; no personal identity can be formed when one cannot locate oneself in history: "The breakdown of temporality suddenly releases this present of time from all the activities and intentionalities that might focus it and make it a space of praxis" (27). Not only is history depleted of any weight, it becomes simply one "optional" narrative among many.

Deeply linked to this notion of radically interchangeable narratives (or non-narratives) is the idea of Difference. How can the idea of "difference" exist in this indifferentiable atemporality called, provisionally, "now"? If time is flattened, space too evinces a particular horizontality, and on this "level playing field" emerges, in new proximity, visibility, and likeness, with what was formerly called the racial Other. In a remarkable move, Jameson connects the disappearance of history to the *appearance* of Others as precisely, now, *not* different:

> The apparent celebration of Difference, whether here at home or on the global scale, in reality conceals and presupposes a new and more fundamental reality. Whatever the new liberal tolerance is, it has little to do with the exotic range of the emblematic Family of Man exhibit, in which the Western bourgeoisies were asked to show their deeper human affinity with Bushmen and Hottentots, bare-breasted island women and aboriginal craftsmen, and other of the anthropological type who are unlikely to visit you as tourists. These new others, however, are at least as likely to visit us as are immigrants or *Gastarbeiter*; to that degree they are more "like" us, or at least "the same" in all kinds of new ways, which new internal social habits—the forced social and political recognition of "minorities"—help us to acquire in our foreign policy. (357)

The "fundamental" condition of postmodernity induces a deeply unsettling effect in Jameson's analysis, precisely as it sets up an uncomfortable sameness among heretofore discrete others *and* the Eurocentric Self: all former modes for understanding the relative positionalities of raced and "non-raced" are taken from us. This presents at once an ontological and an ethical dilemma. Jameson suggests: "We need to explore the possibility that there exists, in what quaintly used to be called the moral realm, something roughly equivalent to the dizziness of crowds for the individual body itself: the premonition that the more other people we recognize, even within the mind, the more peculiarly precarious becomes the status of our hitherto unique and "incomparable" consciousness or 'self'" (358). Note the figure Jameson deploys: to approximate the new, postmodern sense of vertigo in social space, one can hark back to the famous Baudelairean image of the crowd, stifling and disorienting (even as it exhilarates) the bourgeois individual. Does this not indeed remind us of those schizophrenic moments of modernity wherein the racial schizophrenic, the dual personality, is at a loss to cohere its fragmentary allegiances, and senses itself spied upon by multifarious others, which might well include itself (is "it" "them")? The crowd that engulfs the Self is made up of Others, but their frighteningly "new" proximity may be attributed to the fact that in postmodernity, they are precisely like "us." Both "they" and "we" are subjected to and by a "fundamental": the mode of production called late capitalism, wherein all former narratives are shredded.

What is left for us is something Jameson calls "schizophrenic nominalism," which includes "the rubble and the ruins of much of that—place, personal names, etc.,—without the personal identity or the temporal and historical progression, the coherence of the situation and its logic (however desperate), that gave bourgeois realism its tension and substance" (360). Again, this loss of identity, of distinction, is inseparable from a loss of historical consciousness. The "present" has superseded and obviated both past and future time. Jameson's analogy for this "overcoming" is profoundly provocative and germane for our discussion of racial schizophrenia, for he equates the new "present" with a "demographic" change that alienates the Eurocentric Self from history. It is worth quoting at length:

> The dispersive impact of demography is another very different and perhaps more characteristically postmodern effect, felt first and foremost in our relationship to the human past. It would seem, according to some reports, that the quantity of human beings now alive today on earth (some five billion) is rapidly approaching the total number of humanoids who have already lived and died on the planet since the beginning of the species. The present is thus like some new thriving and developing nation-state, whose numbers and prosperity make it an unexpected rival for old traditional ones. *As with bilingual speakers in the United States*, one can at least predictively calculate the moment when it will overtake the past: that demographic moment is already at hand, as a rapidly approaching point in the not so distant future, and thereby to that degree already part of the present and the realities with which it must reckon. But if this is so, then the relationship of the postmodern to historical consciousness now takes on a very different appearance, and there is some justification, and a plausible argument to be made, for consigning the past to oblivion as we seem to be doing; now that we, the living, have the preponderance, the authority of the dead—hitherto based on sheer numbers—diminishes at a dizzying rate (along with all the other forms of authority and legitimacy). It used to be like an old family, old houses in an old village with only a few young people around, who had to sit in the darkened rooms at night and listen to the elders. . . .
>
> What the past has to tell us is therefore little more than a matter of idle curiosity, and indeed our interest in it . . . comes to look like an in-group hobby or adoptive tourism. . . . The salute to non-great-power languages or extinct provincial traditions is, of course, politically correct and a cultural spinoff of the micropolitical rhetoric discussed earlier [emphasis added]. (361)

Let me try to untangle this depressing and yet potentially counterhegemonic scenario. The present, represented in the live body count of the world's extant population, virtually overnumbers the past. The "old family" (of modernity) is consigned to a mythic "darkened room." But, most significantly, the numerical superiority which has produced that relegation is *not* simply a matter of *more* people, but of *newly visible* populations, those "Bushmen and Hottentots, bare-breasted island women and aboriginal craftsmen" that are now to be not only *counted*, but counted as *the Same*. Jameson's choice of analogy (bilingual speakers in the United States) is not accidental, and we may link it to his later remarks about non—major power languages and "extinct" provincial traditions. In the flattened-out temporality of the present, everything can claim equal status. The "old family" is dead; nothing can cohere the disparate and dense population of the present since History (secured by the traditional tale passed down from elder to child in that cold dark space of tradition and history) is simply one tale among many. (That is, unless one follows Jameson in naming late capitalism as that nonstory, that non-narrative, that links "us" all under its spell.) Jameson is distinctly ambivalent about this state of things ("there is some justification, and a plausible argument to be made, for consigning the past to oblivion"). He cannot foreclose the possibility of "mapping a totality," of imagining the possibility of again thinking historically. One central question is what can count as history now, given this newly populated terrain.

Now the schizophrenic can be read racially. If before it was simply a matter of a lack of history in late capitalism, now it is (also) a lack of history because "new voices" have joined in the cacophony of the postmodern. Postmodern schizophrenic meaninglessness is directly correlated with the fact that racial others are now too much like us in this flat(line) space of postmodernity—there are no hills or valleys to secure our geographies, no way to "map" a position. "We" are just as randomly postmodern subjects as "they." In other words, "white" is no longer distinct. This particular brand of colorblindness is part and parcel of Jameson's end of History. It is no accident that William Gibson's work, singled out by Jameson because its "representational innovations . . . mark his work as an exceptional literary realization [of global paranoia]" (38), equally reflects what I will call "postmodern white schizophrenia." This new schizophrenia may be seen as a contemporary elaboration of the notion of "marginality" introduced in Park's sociology. While that troubled notion of modern life was later exclusively foisted upon racialized peoples as "dual personality," here I read those symptoms back into whiteness (although admittedly that formulation may be too symmetrical). In the next chapter I will substantiate my case for Gibson as conveyor of Jameson's postmodern racial anxiety, as I develop a context for cyberspace as an extenuation of Pacific space; here I consider this notion by way of an examination of three earlier science fiction texts: Ridley Scott's *Blade Runner* (1982), the novel from which it was adapted, Philip K. Dick's brilliant *Do Androids Dream of Electric Sheep?* (1968), and another novel by Dick.

Postmodern White Schizophrenia

An entire literature has evolved around Ridley Scott's film *Blade Runner*. I will not attempt a lengthy analysis of the film, but focus on it as a text of white schizophrenia. One of its first scenes, of the grey, sepulchral, dystopian landscape of post-apocalyptic Los Angeles, is often noted for its teeming masses of "ethnics" hawking their wares in densely packed street shops.[58] The streets are pressed on all sides into narrow channels by precipitously tall buildings with massive video screens. Above all this float police helicopters and advertising ships. Conspicuously present are Asians—both on the streets and, in the form of the image of a female Asian face displayed on a video screen, as advertisement. Billboards and storefronts carry signs in Chinese characters, but also in a hybrid language, a mixture of German, Japanese, Spanish, and English.

Despite the masses of Asian faces, and the particular iconography of an ad featuring a Japanese woman's face, which is broadcast across a video screen that takes up the entire facade of a building,[59] it is obvious that whatever "peril" might be posed by their numbers is vitiated by the fact that *actual* Asians are relegated to the ground level: power resides above, in super high-rise structures and in the various flying vehicles of the security forces that skim the surface, make arrests, and then lift back up again. Deckard, a former "blade runner" (the state police that hunt down renegade cyborgs called "replicants"), is blackmailed back into service with the threat that, without the status of a blade runner, he will be simply another powerless inhabitant of the ground level. Thus it is quite telling that the image of Asians in *Blade Runner* has been so appropriated and cited as an image of the Yellow Peril, when it is in fact so contained.

The real concern of the film in fact seems to be with the distinction between two groups of whites—white humans and white replicants; the struggle is to identify, hunt down, and terminate the replicants. Since replicants are virtually identical to humans, an overriding tone of paranoia sets in—anyone could be "the other." Concomitantly, one's sense of self is unanchored from its intersubjective mooring—we no longer know who we are, except via a notion of human being that is constantly being approximated by "genetic designers." To determine who is what, blade runners make use of the Voigt-Kampf empathy test, monitored by observing retinal patterns at the time of interrogation: these eye movements are taken to be infallible manifestations of psychic makeup. This test, probing the human content of the one interrogated, forms one aspect of the film which calls for a reading of schizophrenia. The "dual personality" read into the bicultural individual pathologizes him or her as one unable to cope with multiple demands and the finitude of their psychic resources; they remain forever split between the two cultures, and unable to map out a third possibility. I suggest that *Blade Runner* narrates precisely a racial schizophrenia, located not within a white / racial other split, but within an internal schism to be found at the core of whiteness, which always suspected the integrity of its "purity," its unmixedness.[60]

The 1990s have witnessed a burgeoning of interest in critically scrutinizing whiteness.[61] Such critiques attempt to denaturalize "white" as a given and unified category. Ross Chambers links the ideal of unity to that of visibility: "It is not enough, it seems, for whiteness to pluralize its other [that is, to pose its "unity" against a fragmented set of other specificities]. It must also protect itself from scrutiny. . . . That is, it needs to be not only indivisible but also invisible."[62] In *Blade Runner*, that attempt at invisibility is put into crisis by the appearance of ones whose visible exterior shows no marked difference from white humans, but whose interiorities pose an essential difference. Although this crisis is presented as one between the human and the inhuman, the very representation of race in the film specifies "human" as white. Thus the questions of "human" being are at once questions regarding whiteness; the fissures and irregularities of what constitutes "human" are to be correlated with those of whiteness.

This reading is indeed strongly implied in the film. While the replicants are all depicted as white (made in the image of their creator), they are referred to as "skin jobs," which Deckard tells us is the equivalent to the word "nigger." The novel is more explicit: a television advertisement for replicants claims that these robots duplicate "the halcyon days of the pre–Civil War Southern states! Either as body servants or tireless field hands, the custom-tailored humanoid robot." (14). This abject designation serves to maintain the essential, inhuman character of the replicant against that of the human. Nevertheless, reading the human/nonhuman schism as a racialized phenomenon, we find that the lack of clear distinction between the form and behaviors of replicants and humans injects a schizophrenic element into "whiteness" itself: it is always suspicious of its assumed nonraciality, that is, its essential difference from that "thing" named by race. One standard definition of schizophrenia in fact notes that "the disturbance involves the most basic functions that give the normal person a feeling of individuality, uniqueness, and self-direction."[63] Indeed, Ernest Becker, whose work we will examine below, asserts that schizophrenics may not be able to sustain meaning at all.[64] Rather than see this condition as only applicable culturally to "minority groups," as Snyder and Forsyth suggest, I will argue that this invidious state is found in all racial crises, including that of whiteness.[65] Just as early debates over the notions of monogenesis and polygenesis placed before whites the possibility that their "species" was not absolutely distinct from racial others, so too does *Blade Runner* present the question of essential white difference in the guise of the human/inhuman question, which, after all, was the distinction that rationalized the western colonial enterprise by characterizing the racial other as not human.

Now surely this is a secondary interpretation of the film, but I pose it as a possible subtext because, as noted above, *Blade Runner* is so often remembered and described precisely as portraying in its opening scenes the contemporary representation of the Yellow Peril *par excellence*. Scott obviously "plays the race card"; the question is, why introduce race into the film so conspicuously only to elide it? Why suggest a treatment of race only to divert the narrative into a human/replicant dilemma? I would suggest two things: first, that the issue of race is not erased, but rather compacted within a four-term homology that correlates Deckard's meditation on human (in its pure and unimpeachable form) versus replicant "skin job," with white purity versus white as raced and impure. The play of surface similitude masks the unfathomable mystery of both human and racial essence; this mystery, or mystique, is seemingly resolved in phenotypical markings declaring difference. Yet within whiteness itself there resides a schizophrenic disequilibrium, an essential uncertainty of its boundaries and contents, and, especially, its ability to *reproduce* itself as such.

In this sense, whites are now subject to that paranoid schizophrenia that anchors accounts of ethnic subjectivity. One has only to recall the imagery of DuBois's double consciousness or of DeVos's Japanese Americans walking those "straight narrow streets lined with crowds who observe every step" to discover the connection between the tropes used to describe racial self-consciousness and paranoid schizophrenia. In *Blade Runner* we find *whites* are now forced to walk those narrow streets, to feel the eyes of both replicants and humans upon them: questioning gazes probe their behavior to discern their humanness, but also their own racial wholeness—the ontological chasm opened up by technological (re)production draws into its terrain of self-doubt the purity of "the race" as well—of the "skin job / 'nigger'" within. Schizophrenia's environment is haunted by a multiplicity that is absolutely linked to social dysfunction. Finally, the critique of capitalism draws these threads together—isn't Deckard, in submitting to the disciplinary regimes of the state, simply a higher level "nigger"? This overarching commonality of subordination is the "fundamental" bond of similarity that Jameson evokes in the "postmodern condition."

The standard definition of schizophrenia is found in the *Diagnostic and Statistical Manual of Mental Disorders* (IV): "Schizophrenia is a disturbance that lasts for at least six months and includes at least one month of active-phase symptoms . . . including: delusions, hallucinations, disorganized speech. . . . These signs and symptoms are associated with marked social or occupational dysfunction. . . . The characteristic symptoms of schizophrenia involve a range of cognitive and emotional dysfunctions that include perception, inferential thinking, language and communication, behavorial monitoring, affect, fluency and productivity of thought and speech, hedonic capacity, volition, drive, and attention" (273f). Schizophrenics are dysfunctional precisely in their inability to perceive reality and process it in socially sanctionned ways. This may be manifested in the splitting off of different cognitive and identificatory functions.

The crisis in *Blade Runner* that sets off its schizophrenic diegesis may be read as emanating from a reproductive project run amok. Replicants, after all, are bred as colonizers—white beings sent off to colonize heterotopias "off-world." The constantly regenerative project of conquest may be seen as correlated with the production of humanoid forms, a project intimately tied to an ego-driven agenda of immortalization. Imperialism therein joins up with the propagation of the race in ersatz form: if the weaknesses and contingencies of white human reproduction and colonization are too great, what better use of technology than to guarantee the illusion of white purity not through eugenics but cybernetics; and what better use of that product than to carry on the work of imperialism as surrogate colonizers?

Yet a number of contradictions haunt this formulation: the replicants are "white" colonizers, but they are also slaves to white humans. The doubleness of master/slave, the slippage between human and inhuman (subject and object), is found again in the contradictions of colonialism: just as colonization sought to finesse the inherent contradictions of violent enlightenment by focusing solely on what Conrad calls "the Idea"—that of sheer productivity—and ended up producing instead the "unmethodical" Kurtz, so too does pure capitalist-driven technology, in seeking even further refinements in its production of replicants, endow replicants with human memories, which make them in some instances more human than humans (Batty's grieving over Pris, his last act of saving Deckard).[66] In both cases, replicants are produced with the aim of extending the human past its natural boundaries.

If the late nineteenth and early twentieth centuries manifested the fear of "race suicide" (see Chapter 1), then the middle and late twentieth century ponders the eclipse of the human. My analysis here suggests the linkage between these two anxieties. The cybernetically produced "New Face of America" appears with *Time*'s disquisition on immigration and racial mixing. This is the "positive" articulation. *Blade Runner* presents the negative. In this discussion of white schizophrenia, we may see the dual anxieties over the perpetuation of the human and the perpetuation of the race as stimulating schizophrenia. Ernest Becker's book *The Denial of Death* provides a reading of schizophrenic symptomology that is perfectly in keeping with our reading of *Blade Runner*. The Frankensteinian, hypercapitalistic figure of Tyrell, who fabricates life out of death, surplus value that has its necessary date of termination (planned obsolescence), produces replicants in order to carry on the work of colonization. At once he extends the human/white domain and reduces the risk of its demise by having the replicants carry on the work. Their rebellion is nothing less than an attempt to claim the full rights of humanity. Provided with emotions and past memories, replicants turn against their master precisely because they wish to know their expiration dates. In so doing, as Deckard realizes, they are exactly like humans; they, too, are seeking a way to deny death, or to at least know its moment in advance.

Becker's reading of schizophrenia places its dysfunctionality at the limits of life: "normal" human beings have evolved social protocols to keep mortality at the fringes of thought; schizophrenics, incompletely socialized people, cannot deny death:

> The schizophrenic feels these [dread of death and the overwhelmingness of life] more than anyone else because he has not been able to build the confident defenses that a person normally does to deny them. The schizophrenic's misfortune is that he has been burdened with extra anxieties, extra guilt, extra helplessness, an even more unpredictable and unsupportive environment. He is not surely seated in his body, has no secure base from which to negotiate a defiance of and a denial of the real nature of the world. . . . It is a failure of humanization, which means a failure to *confidently deny* man's real situation on this planet. (63)

In order to cope with this unsociable knowledge, the schizophrenic denies the correlation of mind and matter—the coterminality of the symbolic and the physical body. For him, multiple symbolic bodies can split off from the physical body contaminated by mortality. In this, Becker sees "science fiction": "It took a long time for us to understand this state because we are dealing with a phenomenon so strange it seems truly like science fiction. I mean the fact that human experience is split into two modes—the symbolic self and the physical body—and that these two modes of experience can be quite distinct. In some people they are so distinct as to be unintegrated, and these are the people we call schizophrenic. The hypersensitive individual reacts to his body as something strange to himself, something utterly untrustworthy, something not under his secure control" (218).

The human/replicant split reproduces this alienating effect—as soon as the subjectivity of "replicant" is instantiated, it ruptures the heretofore unbroken surface of the "human" and installs a radical doubt of the nature of human society: who or what exactly constitutes one's intersubjective universe? This uncertainty, even while allowing for a temporary freedom from the thought of death, is ultimately the social death warrant for the schizophrenic: "In this sense, what we call schizophrenia is an attempt by the symbolic self to deny the limitations of the finite body; in doing so, the entire person is pulled off balance and destroyed" (76). Finally, it is important to note how the limitations of the physical body, its confinement within the sphere of mortality, has a particular connection to the imagination: "Depressive psychosis is the extreme on the continuum of *too much necessity*, that is, too much finitude, too much limitation by the body and the behaviors of the person in the real world, and not enough freedom of the inner self, of inner symbolic possibility" (78). The schizophrenia of whiteness in postmodernity is produced by, among other things, a vertiginous proximity to Other bodies with which it can and yet cannot identify. The urge to transcend "finitude" has no viable locus, and as this is the case, *anything* and *any body* can serve as a site for schizophrenic projection and identification. The "mind" has no body either to secure its somatic drives or externalizing and internalizing psychic anxieties. If there are no borders, what can contain and protect the "inside"? Is not "whiteness," in its very desire to transcend its vulnerability, now ironically threatened with its loss? Jameson's mode-of-production analysis may thus be read as a racial crisis as well.

The above reading of schizophrenia in *Blade Runner* is based on problematizing the human/inhuman binary, seeing the production of replicants as a schizophrenic production meant to master finitude and death by claiming for humankind the ability to create life and projecting not only humanity, but also its concomitant mortality, upon those creations. But I specifically want to draw attention to the subtextual element of race in *Blade Runner*, the white-on-white

paranoia that inquires ceaselessly into its own constitution and frailty. If replicants are "skin jobs/'niggers,'" whites in disguise, then their presence instantiates the need to constantly survey whites, and, as the narrative suggests the possibility that Deckard himself might be a replicant, the need to constantly question one's own raciality. The contradiction found within the reading of
human-as-schizophrenic is that one creates replicants to endow oneself with the
illusion of immortality, of godhood; yet the "perfect" act of replication makes
that product so human as to radically problematize the ability to distinguish between the human and nonhuman. Racial schizophrenia, the paranoia found
within whiteness, finds itself in a similar contradiction. To make the
white/other distinction work, the boundaries between the two must be secured. Yet the very existence of the racial Other suggests a viability that questions the premises of whiteness. In *Blade Runner*, whites can no longer tell who
is human and who is not, who is a "skin job" and who is not, who will aid and
abet colonization and who will identify with the colonized (we should underscore the fact that those in power are, indeed, white—the figure played by
James Olmos is merely the comprador class personified). But rather than distinguishing between self and an easily identified racial other, one finds here the
attempt to delineate the fissures of whiteness, the internal indecidabilities cus-
tomarily reserved for nonwhites. Here, whites (in the person of Deckard) attempt to wrestle with the essential violence that supports their claim to enlightenment, and to reproduce whiteness, if only mechanically.

Scott seems much more interested in explicitly defining the struggle in solely
human (that is, "universal") terms, and so uses race as a kind of local color—the
penetration of the human world by the inhuman is made more mystified and sinister by contrasting it to the more visible and yet more controllable "invasion"
of the white world by the Third World. It is precisely in Scott's choice of symbols that a racial *and* national crisis may be extrapolated. The double play between the colonizing enterprise and the fear of one's own colonization, the contrast between the horizontal and vertical dimensions (power and lack thereof),
the constant probing of the contents held within white skin, all may be correlated with a crisis of the national.

Let us revisit the famous resolution of the version of *Blade Runner* released to
theaters—Deckard and Rachael fly over to a new world of nature unspoiled by
technology, but also absent other beings: the issue of difference is suppressed,
muted, in regaining Deckard's humanity and compassion. What, exactly, are
they running away from? Of course, it is the fear of other blade runners out to
discipline the renegade Deckard and fulfill the "contract" against Rachael. It is

also the entire "combine" of technoculture. But *Blade Runner* may be read as well as a case of *multicultural* anxiety: a forestalling of contact with the ground-level inhabitants of multiculture and a displacement of that anxiety upon the reproduction, biological or cybernetic, of whiteness. This is a reading of Scott's film, not of Dick's novel, which is quite different in its historical context and its aims. But Scott's film inserts this glimmer of attention to race. It does so for sensationalism and to tap into our age's fear of race, but not to openly critique it. If one wanted a more explicit articulation of nation, race, and ethnicity in Philip K. Dick's work, one finds a more explicit address in another, earlier text.

Dick's 1962 novel, *The Man in the High Castle*, is founded on a nationalist paranoid fantasy that prominently features Asians—what would happen if the Allies had lost the Second World War? Dick's novel imagines the United States after the war: the Japanese and Germans have emerged victorious; America is now split into two geopolitical regions on an east/west axis; the western United States is annexed to the "Pacific States of America," governed by "the Home Islands," that is, Japan. There is a critical differentiation of "Reich Trade" versus "Pacific Trade"; the two superpowers of Germany and Japan have an uneasy alliance, and what used to be the western United States is incorporated into a Pacific "Co-Prosperity Alliance" (10), Dick's fictional fulfillment of what the Japanese had proposed in the Second World War, a "Greater East Asia Co-Prosperity Sphere." If in the film *Blade Runner* we have a paranoid vision of radical ontological doubt, *The Man in the High Castle* presents a paranoid narrative about national failure and historical unanchoring. It is in this novel that we find a true representation of Asians taking over a post-apocalyptic United States.

In this world, America has been reduced to a set of nostalgic commodities for Japanese consumption. America has become *ethnicized*: one protagonist runs the "American Artistic Handicrafts" company, which specializes in selling "authentic" historical objects (everything from Civil War arms to Mickey Mouse watches) to the Japanese, feeding off a "Japanese craze for Americana" (3, 28). One character presents one such object: "This is most authentic of dying old U.S. culture, a rare artifact carrying flavor of bygone halcyon day" (44). However, in true Dick fashion, there is always the problematic of authenticity and of illicit reproduction: "Using an elaborate variety of tools, materials, and machines, W-M Corporation turned out a constant flow of forgeries of pre-war American artifacts" that are virtually "indistinguishable from the real" (48, 56). What forms the basis for reality is, ostensibly, "history," the anchoring of the object in space and time, yet history too is problematic: "What is historicity?" "When a thing has history in it." (63). Yet the salesman Childan remarks, "'This whole damn historicity business is nonsense. . . . Look at these. Look the same, don't they? Well, listen. One has historicity in it. . . . Don't you feel it?' he kidded her, 'The historicity?'" (63). Ultimately, "history" is "all in the mind," a willed belief in value (64).

As with *Androids*, Dick's concern here is with the thin (if not invisible) line between reality and illusion, history and fantasy, the objective world and its subjective encasements. One key motif in the novel is, in fact, the effort to find the elusive author of a novel entitled *The Grasshopper Lies Heavy*. He is Hawthorne Abendsen, who lives in his refuge, the High Castle. Abendsen has narrated another ending to the war, one in which the United States has won. This narrative has captured not only American readers, but both German and Japanese readers as well—everyone seems to intuit the illusory quality of American defeat. In the end, we are told that Abendsen's fiction of American victory is indeed "true," but by this point one is not even sure what counts as "truth" in this fictional world.

Schizophrenia here is read precisely along economic and racial lines—interracial relationships are inscribed within a logic of exchange which alienates even as it intimates humanness. Childan is invited to a Japanese customer's home:

> Very shortly, as he ascended the stairs to the Kasouras' apartment, he thought, Here I am, not invited in a business context, but a dinner guest. He had of course taken special pains with his attire; at least he could be confident of his appearance. My appearance, he thought. Yes, that is it. How do I appear? There is no deceiving anyone; I do not belong here. On this land that white men cleared and built one of their finest cities. I am an outsider in my own country. (104)

Even as he nurses the hope that he and the Japanese have struck common ground, he realizes that this is not true:

> Face facts. I'm trying to pretend that these Japanese and I are alike. But observe: even when I burst out as to my gratification that they won the war, that my nation lost—there's still no common ground. What words mean to me is sharp contrast vis-à-vis them. Their brains are different. Souls likewise. Witness them drinking from English bone china cups, eating with U.S. silver, listening to Negro style of music. It's all on the surface. Advantage of wealth and power makes this available to them, but it's ersatz as the day is long. (112)

The power of the Japanese to create a surface similitude via the acquisition of American history and the mimicking of American tastes (food, jazz, and so on) falls apart precisely because it is a *pastiche*——a copy of something that has no real existence. What is this "America" referenced and reproduced on the basis of objects that are themselves forgeries?

If this is the dystopic landscape of a particular Asian America, what is the "truth" contained in Abendsen's novel? This excerpt from *Grasshopper* shows the particular wish-dream of postwar America; it is a vision of nothing less than an *American*-invented and -centered Pacific Rim economy:

> And these markets, the countless millions of China, set the factories in Detroit and Chicago humming; that vast mouth could never be filled, these people could not in a hundred years be given enough trucks or bricks or steel ingots or clothing or typewriters or canned peas or clocks or radios or nosedrops. The American workman, by 1960, had the highest standard of living in the world, and all due to what they genteelly called "the most favored nation" clause in every commercial transaction with the East.[67] The U.S. no longer occupied Japan, and she had never occupied China; and yet the fact could not be disputed: Canton and Tokyo and Shanghai did not buy from the British; they bought American. (159)

Is the reality that Japan and Germany lost the war? If so, then why and how was the hallucination that they won produced if not in a hyperparanoid American nationalist nightmare? In this novel, we find anti-Semitism on the now "Reich-held" east coast, where all are suspect and Jews are tracked and sent back to Germany for execution, and a Japanese annexation of the west coast into a particular vision of the "Pacific Rim," where American whites grovel. It is a world made up of Japanese business whimsy and inscrutability, and German genocidal policies in Africa and its fascistic plan to take over the planets. All this seems to evaporate at the end. Juliana Frink decodes *Grasshopper*'s narrative and confronts Abendsen with the accusation that his novel was actually produced through the oracular text *The Book of Changes* (the *I Ching*). The final irony is of a "reality" of a rectified vision of a triumphant America produced only by way of an ancient "oriental" text.

The Man in the High Castle is written in the midst of Cold War politics, as the aftereffects of the Second World War are being most strongly felt. The suggestion of an "alternate" outcome for the Second World War has less to do with the obvious caricatures of fascism than with the reaction of "America" to its dispossession, especially read within a prescient view of a global economy in which America is no longer hegemon of the Pacific. While *Blade Runner* narrates white paranoia over technologies and artificial intelligence, the dehumanizing of the human realm, I have suggested that within that frame there is a strong subtext of racial paranoia. In Dick's earlier novel, paranoia persists at the interstices of national longing (for the restorative narrative of American victory) and xenophobic fear of national loss. If in Scott's filmic adaptation of *Blade Runner* the figure of Asian America is relegated to the deepest sections of the vertical sphere, only to reappear indirectly through the meditation on white humanity, then in *The Man in the High Castle* America (at least the west coast) is made Asian in a constantly destabilized double illusion that splits "America" off into a pastiche of commodified "history."

The discourse of schizophrenia deployed to pathologize Asian Americans while leaving the "norm" unexamined may serve as an index to precisely the assumptions that undergird our notions of the social and the national, and the place of race therein. If ethnic "schizophrenia" is a modification of a global malaise of modernity, then in the postmodern age we find contemporary modes of rehabilitating such "schizophrenic" identities in increasingly complex transnational and "postindustrial" spaces. Specifically, in the final chapter of this study we will address the vacillation between "borderlessness" and the reinstallment of national and cultural borders as this vacillation reflects and manifests the reshapings of Asian America.

10 / Asia Pacific: A Transnational Imaginary

IN THE 1980S AND 1990S, the reading of Asian America according to
a pathology of schizophrenia (or, less dramatically, according to an unhealthy
and persistent duality) is complicated by different discourses that seek to rationalize and accommodate new perspectives on this entity. Asian America is now
seen as taking form within increasingly complex spatio-temporalities. In tracing
the various formations of modern Asian America, I have characterized it within
both the general framework of modern migrancy and the particular encounters
of America with East Asia. Within this broadly sketched context, modern America is defined in terms of its neocolonial westward gaze, its discovery of "national interest" in the Pacific, as well as in terms of its steady revision of identity
according to the introjection of Asians into its national space, a movement that
is a result of these new national activities and engagements, of specific historical contingencies in East Asia, and of the development of world economies.

Asian America is formed within specific and complex chronotopes—the
transformation of Asian to American, the evidence of these historical projections and introjections, involves particular movements across time and space
toward a destined identification. In this final chapter I want to draw these issues
together in order to address the ways that, in the late twentieth century and on
the horizon of the early twenty-first, we witness a perverse warping of this telos: Asia presents to America a specific temporal disjunction in postmodernity.
The rise of East Asian economies has had, to say the least, an unsettling effect on
American self-identity. Has Asia arrived at the twenty-first century *before* America? How has Asia leapfrogged ahead of the United States, which has traditionally claimed the leading role of the modern world?[1]

The image of the Pacific has been radically revised under late capitalism—the former open space for Euro-American imaginings of natural wealth and exotic sensuality, the new frontier that was to manifest a trans-Pacific *American* destiny, is suddenly discovered to be already occupied by an alternative postmodernity marked as Asian, one that cancels out Weber's assumptions of Asia's unfitness for modernity and suggests that Asia has only benefited by not being mired in a futile project to gain modern status. It has bypassed that stage entirely and has arrived before the United States at the postindustrial, late-capitalist global economic summit. In trying to explain this phenomenon, critics have accessed an image of "Asia" that has profound implications for Asian Americans, as it forces a reevaluation of that persistently evasive notion we have tracked throughout this study: America, and, specifically, its Asian facet. It may be, ultimately, that Asian Americans are (once again) what America at once secretly admires and fears.

This temporal warping takes place within a newly mapped space. The growing phenomenon of transnationalism (economic, cultural, political) has vastly complicated modern notions of immigration and assimilation. In the previous chapter, we investigated the dispersal of Asian American psychic identity between the cracks of clear national identities during the era centered in the 1970s; now we find new modes of reconsolidation. This chapter examines a number of formations of Asian identity in Asia Pacific as they bear upon an understanding of Asian American subjectivity. I begin with an account of an American view of the Pacific, and then link the historical revision of that image to the emergence of what has been termed "Pacific Rim Discourse."[2] I examine the projection of diasporic identity within this newly mapped space and the appearance of a certain chronotope for Asian diaspora in the 1970s, and then trace the rise of a set of newer terms—"Greater China," "Cultural China," "Asia Pacific." Each of these terms has added a particular inflection to the representations of the region and its inhabitants and transmigrant populations; in my analysis I attempt to articulate the particular productive forces behind such conceptualizations and their relevance to Asian America.

From those discussions we find the emergence of a subjectivity that is seen as particularly well equipped for the current age (and beyond), operating within a specifically constructed social, political, and economic sphere in the Asia-Pacific region. How does that subjectivity fuse Asia with America (or, more important, how can America join itself to the presumed core of this region)? I end by addressing a new formation of Asian America in cyberspace, as the appeal to a "borderless world" masks a very particular finanscape that takes off from the seeds of Pacific Rim and Asia Pacific discourse. Within this chronotope, a post-national subjectivity implicit in these inventions becomes the idealized figure of postmodernity and late capitalism. Nevertheless, I argue that literary representations of this borderlessness, with the cyberspaces of William Gibson taken as examples, recover and reinstate national borders, east and west binarisms, and recuperate a specific western individual at the core of reality.[3]

The Pacific as the Repository of the American Imaginary

A recent book on the "Pacific Century" suggests a particular remapping that re-visualizes Asia as a Pacific, *oceanic* entity rather than a huge, inert land mass:

> The nature of the change can be best visualized by holding up a globe and posi-tioning its center at Beijing, then repositioning the globe to focus on an early maritime center such as Manila. The two worlds of Pacific Asia become readily apparent. . . . Until the nineteenth century, China dominated the region with its continental-centered world view. The Great Wall symbolized this overriding concern with threats, new influences, and opportunities emanating from within the Asian mainland where, from a very early time, the inhabitants of fertile river valleys competed with one another and with intruding nomadic tribes from the steppe. When at last this vision began to shift toward a recognition that the fu-ture lay at the ocean's edge, it symbolized a major turning point in Pacific-Asian history.[4]

From the other side of the Pacific, we find in United States history that par-ticular moment in the nineteenth century when America turned its gaze west-ward along that same body of water as the space necessary to transsect if the United States was to meet its Manifest Destiny. In the late nineteenth century Hubert Bancroft's voice is both adventurous and a bit desperate as he articulates an ambition that has been welling up for decades: "We are no longer a virgin continent to develop. Pioneer work in the United States is done, and now must take the plunge into the sea." As Arrell Morgan Gibson remarks, "There in the contiguous oceanic hemisphere—the Pacific Basin—was a frontier province in which the pageant of American expansion continued."[5] This westward gaze is informed not only by the logic of expansion, but also by the ideology of west-ern civilization being carried forward spatially and temporally by the United States. At the turn of the century, Governor John Hay declares: "The Mediterranean is the ocean of the past, the Atlantic the ocean of the present, and the Pacific is the ocean of the future."[6]

Nevertheless, as we have noted in our examinations of Asian American discourse of the 1920s, there is at once an ever more acute understanding of the United States' western destiny and a recoiling before the otherness of this new civilizational frontier.[7] East Asia is seen as particularly *occupied*. The state of California is depicted as "an outpost on the western edge of Occidental civilization": "the mind's eye takes its gaze and sees on the other shores of that great ocean the teeming millions of the Orient, with its institutions running their deep roots into the most venerable antiquity, its own inherited philosophy and standards of life, its own particular races and colors."[8] Yet what this governor of California ironically forgets is that it was precisely members of this "Orient" that had made it possible, through their labor on the Transcontinental Railroad, for the United States to join its Atlantic and Pacific seaboards—in other words, for the states to be united in westward, trans-Pacific intention. The "deep roots" that anchored "particular races and colors" to East Asia had already been pried loose by the history of the west's engagement in China. The numbers of immigrants were, however, not as significant as the ideological revision of the United States, the Pacific, and movements of people and goods across it. Whatever "cultural difference" might exist between America and Asia, it certainly didn't interfere with imperialist activity; indeed, the imputation of difference sanctioned imperialism. From the mid-nineteenth century to the age of the Great Depression, America's capitalist rise in the world economy was coordinated with the purchase of Alaska in 1867, the staging of a *coup d'etat* in Hawai'i in 1893, with seizing control of Philippines, and the final annexation of Hawai'i. Between 1913 and 1929, U.S.-Pacific trade increased nearly four hundred percent.

The Second World War and the Korean War showed both the weakening of European hegemony and the intensification of America's Pacific identity. In 1967, in the midst of the Vietnam War, President Richard Nixon declared in an influential article: "The U.S. is a Pacific power. . . . Europe has been withdrawing the remnants of empire, but the U.S., with its coast reaching in an arc from Mexico to the Bering Straits, is one anchor of a vast Pacific community. Both our interests and our ideals propel us westward across the Pacific, not as conquerors but as partners."[9] In the twentieth century, for the United States, this "Pacific" is formed in the historical frame of wars in Asia from 1941 to 1975. If America is but "one" anchor for the region, there is no doubt that Nixon intends it to be the weightiest one, which will not only root us in American interests even as we are "propelled" westward, but root the region in them as well. The "partnership" is not of trading equals, but of a new cartel to be chaired by the United States. America's perception of the rise of East Asian economies was haunted by the notion that Japan's imperialist plan of economic hegemony during World War Two, the "Greater East Asia Co-Prosperity Sphere," was manifesting itself even after Japan's defeat.[10] As we noted in Chapter 9, this fear is made explicit in Philip K. Dick's *The Man in the High Castle*, a narrative of a postwar Pacific Rim. It was the invention of a "Euro-American Pacific" that was to contain and neutralize such a fear.

Arif Dirlik explains that historically the "Asia-Pacific Idea" is informed by a number of contradictions and conflicts from its very inception: "From the beginning there was a strong Asian component present in the Pacific economy that complicated this logic and introduced into it a contradiction that disrupted the region's status as a periphery to a European core. This was the Chinese economy, a world economy in its own right. . . . The Pacific economy as it took shape through the interaction of alternative centers with their contradictory demands."[11] In the present moment, he notes that the dominant direction of influence has been reversed: "The Pacific region took shape originally through Euro-American activity that was oriented to an Asian world economy (China); it is now shaped increasingly by an orientation to a North American market through the activity of Asian peoples."[12] While insisting on the importance of the category of geography, Dirlik maintains that the "Asia-Pacific Idea" collects within itself a variable set of noncontiguous elements that each serve a particular function in constructing that ideation: "What do we miss when today we place California on the Pacific rim, yet ignore an Asian-American population in North Carolina that has economic ties to the Pacific?"[13] I would suggest that their noncontiguity has critical implications for Asian Americans, which we see here as indeed a part of this specific "Asia-Pacific discourse."

This discourse was enabled by the fact that, in contradistinction to previous notions of a "radically Other" Orient, we find in the 1970s a recognition of common capitalist identity. Connery argues that "Pacific Rim discourse" was a "tentative move into the anxious mythology of a putative new era, an era during which that fundamental characterization of the hegemon's view of its other—Orientalism—loses some of its utility."[14] Instead of positing an Asiatic "other," Pacific Rim discourse sought to consolidate a particular economic identity, a transnational capital sphere in which "Japan and the NICs represent capital's transformative promise—their recent history is capital's teleology," and in which "China is the certain future."[15] In the exuberant rhetoric of futurologists John Naisbitt and Patricia Aburdene, this consortium is both Asian and

American, possessing American youthfulness augmented by the recent growth of East Asian economies, and flexing its muscle in unprecedented ways, linking American frontierism with a transnational imaginary: "The Pacific Rim is emerging like a dynamic young America but on a much grander scale."[16] The resulting "world" will be, precisely, utopia: "we possess the tools and the capacity to build utopia here and now."[17] Gao Fang, an outspoken critic of the futurologist Alvin Toffler's notion of a "Third Wave," names this utopia more precisely when he speaks of an "international capitalist utopianism."[18]

Scholars have noted that the Pacific Rim serves as a trope for a process of what Harvey calls "spatial fixes," that is, receiving points for the endemic over-accumulations of contemporary capital: "capital transfers by transnational corporations and international lenders (e.g., the World Bank) to productive sites throughout the 'Asia-Pacific' represent precisely such spatial displacements."[19] Capital investment in the Pacific included the proliferation of off-shore operations, export-processing zones that, under the North American Free Trade Agreement, produced a particular link between East Asian and Mexican EPZs, and the creation in China of "special economic zones" to facilitate the integration of China into the Asia Pacific economy.[20] The new "open ports" of China, the export processing zones of East Asia and Mexico, are all extra-territorial zones of exploitation that create a particular porousness and heighten the rate of influx and reflux of global capital.

The entire region was remapped according to the logic of flexible accumulation set within the particular political and social economies of the Pacific.[21] The island of Saipan provides a particular instance of such reinvention of Pacific space coupled with the use of controlled migrant labor. Thousands of Chinese, Filipinos, and other Asian nationals are flown to Saipan routinely, working at half the U.S. minimum wage and producing garments (some $280 million worth annually) that will be shipped out bearing the "Made in the U.S.A." label. This is possible because Saipan, five thousand miles from the continental United States, is part of the U.S.'s Northern Mariana Commonweath in the western Pacific. Nevertheless, in a 1976 agreement, the islands were exempted from minimum wage restrictions. The production of low-wage laborers in the depressed regions of the Pacific finds an open but term-limited home in Saipan, as workers are flown in and out of this putative American space to make "American" garments at wages that are illegally low in the United States, and then are shipped back to their home countries. The porousness of the Pacific for capital accumulation and spatial fixing thus is invented by transnational capital in ways that use the national as a convenient fiction.

But these smaller enterprises pale before the envisioning of America's participation in immense trading blocs such as a "Greater China Common Market," or a "Greater Chinese Economic Bloc."[22] Woodside details the particular construction of a new economic psychology: "The language of the Asia-Pacific myth, with its invocation of 'Third Wave' civilizations and its focus upon the 'basic commonalities' of economic prosperity, rhetorically reconciles the tensely coexisting multiple rival capitalisms and usefully blurs potential battle lines among them. Its votaries on both sides of the Pacific Rim become imaginative shareholders in a common utopianized marketplace."[23] The most significant proposal for the purposes of this study founds a new vision of Asian America: Zbigniew Brzezinski's neologism, "Amerinippon."[24]

In 1989, Australia's prime minister, Bob Hawke, formally proposed an intergovernment organization, the Asia-Pacific Economic Cooperation (APEC): Australia, Brunei, Canada, Chile, China, Hong Kong, Indonesia, Japan, Malaysia, Mexico, New Zealand, Papua New Guinea, the Philippines, Singapore, South Korea, Taiwan, Thailand, and the United States. Originally it was assumed that the Russian Republic, which inherits virtually all of the old Soviet Union's Pacific real estate, would also enter. Within this newly invented space of the Asia Pacific, Asian Americans were posited as the Pacific Rim subject par excellence, emissaries of commerce and cultural translators. L. Ling-chi Wang points out the historical depth of this phenomenon, as the overseas Chinese (*huaqiao*) "were first and foremost an economic asset as sources of remittances and promoters of international trade."[25] From former "sojourners" to "parachute kids" and "astronauts," the Asian American subject has come to symbolize the shifting identities of Asian transnational diasporas and suggest a particularly productive, postindustrial subjectivity.[26]

Transnationals and Diasporics

The notion of diaspora has been deployed both literally and figuratively to designate a particular opportunity for reinvention and liberation from various naturalized categories, set within historical contingencies that weigh into the production of such subjectivities. In this vein, Ong and Nonini's recent collection of essays, *Ungrounded Empires*, contains several provocative readings of Chinese diasporas and marks a signal development of research in this area. While cognizant of the fact that no state can absolutely dictate or predetermine the "identity" of diasporic subjects, one should not downplay the complex process of identity formation that, in one way or another, involves state apparatuses.[27] Simply put, there is no diaspora without borders and no borders without states. The imperatives of states (even under transnational conditions) contest and constrain the psychic identifications that make up diasporic identity and the identity of diasporas.

In his contribution to Tu Wei-ming's landmark collection, *The Living Tree: The Changing Meaning of Being Chinese Today*, L. Ling-chi Wang proposes a materialist critique that discloses the profound contingencies of such "meaning." He disaggregates and specifies the terrains upon which "identification" takes place: "Each identity is dynamic in character, constantly undergoing transformation. Motivating this transformation are factors such as race relations in the host country, public policy toward the Chinese, the state of the host country's diplomatic relations with China, and China's policies toward overseas Chinese" (211). Wang's shrewd disaggregation of various strands of identification and his analysis of the ways such identities are produced historically and materially is a welcomed intervention in discussions that tend too often to be couched in only the most mystified terms.[28] One way of approaching an analysis of this complex dialectic is to consider how diaspora involves a revision of time and space.

The production of diasporic identity takes place in a confrontation between two distinct time/space constructions, a chronotope characterized by atemporality and seclusion, and one of dominant historical time and sociopolitical space. These are interpenetrating terms in a dialectic within which the *diasporic* subject is produced unevenly and in relation to a newly fashioned *ethnic* subjectivity. The concept of diaspora begins of course with dispersion of the Jewish people. In the Jewish diaspora, the subject attempts to perpetually reinstate the State, but in the *fictional* form of the cultural Nation. It is fictional in the sense that it has no status as a political entity beyond the imaginations of its constituents. From the observance of collective ceremonies to the disciplining and regulation of the body, what Foucault calls the technologies of the self, we find a ritualistic reaffirmation that the absent State lives on in a displaced form, in the form of an imagined Nation, but more specifically, in the subject's particularly imagined relationship with it. In the Jewish case, this displacement of the state into the cultural nation is evinced in the increased attention to the hermeneutic reconstruction of the Law, which is critical precisely because it is a consolidating discourse that nonetheless must be secured and manifested without benefit of being institutionally underwritten and practised by a State. Rather, it is realized only within communal and domestic space. Thus, in the collective imagination, the compensation becomes the thing itself—the cultural nation is the state. The time/space coordinates of the cultural nation are substituted for those of the State; the cultural nation exists in a particular temporality distanced from that of the historical present.

But in the case of the Jewish diaspora, we find history intervening in this ceremony of locating the State in the displaced form of the cultural nation and identifying oneself within that space. In 1948, the state of Israel was proclaimed and the idea that the State resided within, psychically and ethically, that one's subjectivity was indeed constituted as a vessel for that manifestation, was challenged by the reality of an actual state, no longer displaced into the imaginary, no longer utopian, but real, with its own temporal contingencies and pragmatic demands. In terms of social subjectivity, then, a question arose. Who was the "real" Jew—the person who "returned" to the state now *realized* geographically, historically, and politically, or the person who abided by the timeless ritual that said the State was wherever Jews of good faith lived? Did leaving the diaspora mean that one was belying the fictionality of the compensation, that bargain with history, that had kept the Jewish people intact for centuries? But more vexingly, what did it mean to *remain* in diaspora when the state was now there, available and viable, and one's political identity realizable in an actual political state? We tend to focus on the psychic constitution of diaspora, the "feeling" of displacement and the psychic drive for attachment. Here I link the psychic to the political, the imaginary to the real, as it is precisely that *dialectic* relationship that gives each diasporic instance its particular identity in relation to ethnicity.

The psychic, manifested in the memory of the homeland and the consciousness of the diasporic new land, locates itself in a liminal space that may be correlated with a temporal frame. This temporality is the stalled rhythm of social integration; of attaining citizenship, both cultural and political; in other words, of becoming *ethnicized* and integrated particularly into the state. This concept of diaspora and ethnicity, which has its affinities with that of "dual personality" schizophrenia in a more explicitly spatial schematization, becomes complicated as transnational capital and its effects have loosened the hold of the nation-state on the psychic imaginations of diasporic subjects. I want to mark a tension between a "cross-cultural" version of diaspora that might be read in the ethnicization of subjects, and a "transnational" one that describes more transmigrant, multiply situated identities. To make the case of the importance of such a distinction for the construction of "Asian America," I will need to work through the issue of how this tension is elided by the discourse of "traditional Asian values," which is used to explain the ascension of Asians in postmodernity and gloss over the disruptive effects of transnational capital. In this process, the "Asian" is conjoined to the "Asian/American." Only after doing so can I discuss the postmodern appearance of Asia in the cybernetic, intensely accelerated vision of authors such as William Gibson, and link it to precisely this theme of temporal and spatial disjunction and recombination.

Diaspora always takes place after a border crossing. In the Asian American narratives we will examine, I understand this movement to produce *at once* diaspora *and* ethnicity: the reconstitution of the subject as a subject in diaspora takes place at the same moment that the subject is labelled "foreign" in its new location. As the point of origin slips into the distance, the regimes of the new location impose their own political identities. Border-crossing thus requires passports and green cards that disaggregate and specify the particular status of diasporic subjects. Even if one is "naturalized," that process of becoming is indelibly part of one's identity and abides in one's identity as an *ethnic* person. But at the same time, part of the nature of the diasporic mentality may be to see in its remove from Home a compensation and even a salvation—the distance from the home state is seen as a positive, enabling phenomenon. It is enabling precisely as it is imagined as *delinked* from state apparatuses.[29] Thus we find an appreciable tension between transnational identifications that inscribe a diasporic subjectivity, and a "cross-cultural" dialectic that exerts its own pressures locally, as a new ethnic subjectivity is produced in its new geographic topos.

This sanctuary is often depicted as having a particular temporality. Consider this passage from Carlo Levi's antifascist novel, *Christ Stopped at Eboli*. LeGoff argues that, in exile, the narrator discovers "he shares a common hatred of Rome with the peasants abandoned by the government, and slips into a state of ahistoricity, of immobile memory":

> Shut up in a room, and in a closed world, it pleases me to return in memory to that other world, closed in on pain and customs, outside the reach of History and the State, eternally patient, in this land of mine, with neither consolation nor sweetness. . . .[30]

But this sanctuary in the country, away from the center of the fascist state, is a fragile one, for it can only exist within that particular space seemingly sequestered from the flow of historical time which is also the characteristic of social life.[31]

If we extend this reading of exile to the topos of diaspora, we find a tension between the freedom open to the diasporic imagination at a distance from home and residing in an idiosyncratic temporality, and the juridical and ethical requirements placed upon the subject by the new state with its particular historical time. A number of Asian American literary narratives focus on precisely this spatiotemporal problematic manifested in the tension between diasporic and ethnic identity. In Nièh Hùalíng's 1976 novel, *Sangqing yú Taohóng* (translated as *Mulberry and Peach*), we find this tension driving the formation of a new diasporic subjectivity, as the protagonist, Mulberry, develops a second personality, Peach, in the course of her flight from China.

Some of the most striking images of this text are of interior spaces. The protagonists endeavor to create particular places from which history is bracketed out, and a new atemporality takes over: the refugees' boat and the camper trailer, the house in Beijing, an abandoned water tower in the Midwest, a basement retreat in New York. It is no coincidence that this ahistorical space is imaginable only when the state is relegated to the exterior. When that space is violated, time resumes; this temporality is particularly identifiable as one dictated by the state.

Mulberry's retreat as a fugitive from the law to an attic in Taibei allegorizes what kind of time and space is invented within that removal from the law of the state. This sanctuary is governed by a strictly idiosyncratic temporality—the clock perpetually reads 12:13. Although this sanctuary is permeated by the social and historical—voices are heard coming from the street, old newspapers remind the fugitives of the past and the present—the occupants are barred from actively participating in that social space. The question becomes one of how to invent a viable identity within such a time/space construction. As the fugitives' time away from historical time lengthens, we find the gradual production of neurosis and psychosis particular to social isolation. In her diary, Mulberry's daughter Sang-wa writes, "Mama says that people in attics don't need identity cards." She discovers, however, "Even cats and dogs have identity card chains. I don't have one and I'm afraid" (175). One cannot imagine an existence outside of the social; it is there that identities are produced. Despite the diasporic subject's identification with the home it left behind, and despite any attempt to freeze time and fix space, the diasporic subject must give itself up to the temporal and historical as it is resituated in a new sociopolitical sphere.

It is no accident at all that the mediating term that propels the narrative forward in the United States is precisely the figure of the immigration agent who tracks Peach. It is his interrogation that marks the intervention of the state in the construction of ethnic identity and attests to its need to recuperate that fugitive subject into its political field. The first line of the novel is an address to the immigration agent: "I'm not Mulberry. Mulberry is dead!" To which he replies,

"Well, what is your name, then?" One might even say that without this inter-rogative force and its symbolization of the state, Peach could never have been invented, that her invention takes place within the discourse of the state, which calls for an *account* of diasporic identity so that it might contain it, domesticate it, absorb it. But, ironically, this intervention may also be seen as an enabling one, for it forces just that remove from atemporality necessary for a new dias-poric subject to be produced. This narration forces a reassessment of the home-land—Peach must account for herself, and that account is inseparable from an account of China. Leo Ou-fan Lee points out, "it is precisely Peach Red's tor-mented and anxiety-ridden outcry about her exiled existence on the edge of American society that compels her alter ego, Mulberry Green, to encompass the entire historical span of her personal past. In other words, it is her newly ac-quired American side—and the need to explain why she is in America—that forces her Chinese side to be engaged in a search for meaning through her per-sonal journey in Chinese history."[32]

Kingston's *The Woman Warrior*, published in the same year as *Mulberry and Peach*, provides an example from Chinese American literature of this problematic of ethnic and diasporic identification within and outside social space and historical time. In this case, diaspora is not read within the problematic of exile but within a problematic of uneven assimilation. Yet the essential issues remain—both au-thors grapple with the question of identity posed against a shifting, "ghostly" figuration of China. One of the most anticlimactic moments comes in the chapter entitled, "At the Western Palace," when Moon Orchid confronts her husband in America. Having left China thirty years ago, he has never suggested that she join him. He is now living in the United States with a new wife. Moon Orchid's sister, Maxine's mother, Brave Orchid, is a strong-willed woman who insists that her sister come to the United States and claim her marriage rights:

> "You have to ask him why he didn't come home. Why he turned into a barbarian. Make him feel bad about leaving his mother and father. Scare him. Move right into his house with your suitcases and boxes. Move right into the bedroom. Throw her stuff out of the drawers and put yours in. Say, 'I am the first wife, and she is our servant.'" (126)

When asked why he never sent for Moon Orchid, the husband replies, "It's as if I had turned into a different person. The new life around me was so com-plete; it pulled me away. You became people in a book I had read a long time ago" (154).

We should pause to examine the language of these two passages. Brave Orchid's solution to her sister's dilemma is for Moon Orchid to invade the space of her husband's American home, to *re*domesticate it and install herself. This involves precisely a *retemporalization* of that space—she will say, "I *am* the *first* wife," conjoining the historical past of China to present-day America. But her husband's pronouncement, his alibi for forgetting her, argues exactly the opposite: pulled into the temporal flow of the new country, he *becomes* something else, and, conversely, his Chinese family is objectified, frozen in his memory as a *past* narration. The husband is freed of the constraints of China; this also means that his wife is unable to call on him to account for himself. While he has been re-identified in diaspora, her diasporic transfer to the United States is not commensurate with his—she is burdened by her gender, and by her age. In short, she is denied both temporal development and the rights that are particular to the past existence that she and her husband originally shared.

The differing temporalities of ethnicity and diaspora are captured in this exchange between Maxine and her mother. Brave Orchid remarks:

> "Time was different in China. One year lasted as long as my total time here; one evening so long, you could visit your women friends, drink tea, and play cards at each house, and it would still be twilight. It even got boring, nothing to do but fan ourselves. Here midnight comes and the floor's not swept, the ironing's not ready, the money's not made. I would still be young if we lived in China."
>
> "Time is the same from place to place," I said unfeelingly. "There is only the eternal present, and biology. The reason you feel time pushing you is that you had six children after you were forty-five and you worried about raising us."[33]

Unable to comprehend the impact of economic hardship upon the immigrant body, Maxine refutes ("unfeelingly") her mother's experience of time by recourse to the "universality" of biology. She recognizes gender but not economics, local familial identifications but not diasporic ones. In short, she cannot understand the difference history makes.[34]

While the novel ends with the notion that Maxine has been able to find a mode of translating the "foreign" into the domestic, of negotiating a discourse of Asian Americanness, Moon Orchid falls victim to precisely the untranslatability, the *non*transference, of Chinese ethics onto American soil. Moon Orchid is sacrificed as an illustration of the damage done by seeking to correlate disjunctive time—she goes mad, and her madness has exactly the character of the dysfunctional chronotope we saw in *Mulberry and Peach*. The ascension of the Chinese American generation, integrated (albeit painfully) into the chronotope of

"America," occurs simultaneously with the demise of the immigrant generation. Maxine's coming into being is predicated upon her coming to speak; this occurs simultaneously with her mother's transformation into a listener, not a talker.[35]

The formation of diasporic identity is thus inscribed within a dialectic tension between two time frames; the crucial issue is the ways in which the social and political imperatives of the new state enable the formation of ethnic identity in diaspora. Under such conditions, the role of diasporic culture comes to occupy a central role, for it is in this realm of representation that the psychic displacements and spatiotemporal disjunctures we've remarked upon may be reconciled—the diasporic *imaginary*, in consolidating disparate elements of cultural life under one rubric, is looked to for a unitary moment in an otherwise fraught existence.

Bienvenido Santos's *What the Hell for You Left Your Heart in San Francisco* (1987), narrates one such attempt to gather up and give a content to diaspora via the representation of "culture." In this narrative, the protagonist, David Tolosa, is stranded in San Francisco. He finds work as the editor of a magazine on Filipino American culture which a group of wealthy Filipino doctors are starting. They have no idea what the magazine should be; the protagonist has his own ideas:

> If I could have my way we would have to establish a policy steering away from politics, the so-called New Society in the Philippines that the martial law government was supposed to create. The question was at best divisive and would hurt circulation one way or another. Concentrate on human-interest stories, toned-down success stories, no superlatives and embarrassing assumptions that sound like bragging. All features would have to be relevant to the life of the Filipino in America, particularly the new breed of Filipino immigrants like the members of the Board, with an occasional special about old-timers, their little successes and big problems, the more factual, the more effective (no sob stuff). Helpful hints covering the more prevalent needs and problems of the Filipino in the States. Profiles on those who have distinguished themselves in whatever field, no matter how humble. Movements, worthy causes that need to be sponsored. Seemingly perennial problems of the new, and sometimes ignorant, arrivals. Solutions or attempts at solutions. Get experts to contribute articles with corresponding payments or honorariums. Interviews. Fiction? Maybe. Poetry, rarely. Fillers.[36]

Tolosa is faced with producing a magazine that will represent precisely the formation of this "new breed" of Filipino diasporic culture, but he recognizes at once the limits and protocols. It will have to avoid certain formulae, and yet in so doing it replicates others—it will be novel yet innocuous, useful but only in a limited manner. Most tellingly, it will minimize literature. "Culture" in this formation is entirely pragmatic and depoliticized—perhaps the world of the "old-timers" is precisely the world of the political and historical.

The novel tracks the disintegration of the magazine (which it turns out is really only being used as a tax write-off)—the entire narrative is filled with discontinuities and alienations, which each in their own way comment on the impossibility of constituting diasporic "culture." Instead we find David moving between and within discrete, isolated spaces: a fleabag hotel in the Tenderloin, the home of his mentor (a professor at San Francisco State who houses welfare recipients on the side), the basement apartment given him by the chief sponsor of the magazine, a wealthy surgeon who specializes in vasectomies. The thematic of discontinuity and sterility, the inability (and even lack of desire) to continue a tradition in diaspora as well as the inability to "take root" in this new space, is carried throughout the novel, which ends on a note of existential angst:

> There are no stars blinking at our feet, no encrusted jewels, such as you might imagine, winking over our heads. We are flesh and blood, tired before the day is over, seeking to find after the rains, a welcome door, a smiling face, both the familiar and the strange. Surrounded by strangers, we look for friends on a continuing search against despair. . . . We have left our native land but our hearts are still there, not here.[37]

Santos significantly does not narrate the story of a Filipino creating a novel in isolation (the figure of the artist as creator in his or her own world only lightly touched by material history), but rather tells of an attempt at a textual production of culture inscribed within a particular set of economic and political conditions. This attempt to fabricate "diasporic culture" within a new diasporic collectivity thus runs up against a precise set of historical and ideological contingencies.

Nevertheless, Santos does provide a glimpse of collective "culture" outside such constraints, and it is here that we find its only viable, affective articulation: his students put on a performance of Filipino and Filipino American skits, songs, and dances, ending with the audience joining them in singing *Kayan Ko* (My Country):

> I sang from memory, from the heart and soul, damn it! I had sung the same lyrics with other homesick Filipinos many times when we met together to celebrate a holiday—in the mid-West, in New York, in San Francisco. The year was 1975, three years after martial law had been declared in my country. Always I sang the

song with my heart in my throat, thinking, how long, God, how long martial law would keep me here wandering in exile.[38]

It is because he has been able to draw out from his young students an understanding of the historical and cultural forms of the Philippines that he in turn is able to realize the liminality of exile. While he recognizes the illusory nature of his magazine project, removed as it is from the political, he comes to understand another possibility for the transmittal of culture, which is available because it allows the political and historical to intrude into its space of isolation. And, crucially, that performance of culture is specifically removed from the circuits of commodification. That rupturing of alienation (however transitory) allows for a moment of intersubjective connection.[39]

If the diasporic here constituted tenuously in Santos's novel in a muted political context, Carlos Bulosan's novel, *America Is in the Heart* ardently foregrounds the political in global terms. As a point of contrast to Santos's short novel, Bulosan's text anticipates a critique of global capital in its particular analysis of immigration from the Philippines to the United States. Bulosan's narrative begins, as Ishikawa's *Strawberry Road* will several years later, by establishing a particular historical context: as Ishikawa maps the emigration of Japanese out from Japan to America and Latin America in the postwar period of American occupation, so Bulosan begins his narrative by setting the context of his protagonist's departure from the Philippines in the late 1920s: the "enlightened" neocolonial U.S. administration has joined forces with the entrenched Filipino elites that serve its purposes; the peasants are doubly dispossessed of their land. And yet, American ideology, in the form of an imported school system and political administration, has convinced many of the potential benefits of "democracy." Carlos's view of "America" is thus prescribed for him long before he ever sees it. And yet when he comes to America, he finds not the enlightened land of democracy, but a land that shares many of the same oppressive features as his homeland. *America Is in the Heart* synchronizes the two different spaces in the shared (albeit uneven) rhythms of capitalism.

Sau-ling Wong has noted the tremendous amount of sheer *movement* in the novel, from the Philippines to the U.S., and then all around the western region of the U.S., circling back and forth.[40] Correlated to that circling is a persistent repetition of narrative elements, which creates a sense of fatality, broken at irregular intervals by moments of difference and hope. This particular spatiotemporal scheme discloses the viselike grip of capital upon the bodies of the field workers; the logic of migrant labor drives the workers from field to field. Thus,

rather than an incoherent set of ramblings, Bulosan narrates the precise and contradictory logics of agribusiness and nationalist politics. The "diasporic" here is
located within this chronotope; the decisive moment of difference comes when
Carlos is placed in a sanatorium for treatment of tuberculosis. It is in this space,
isolated from the material demands of labor and resistance, that he is afforded
the opportunity to become a cultural worker—he reads voraciously and comes
to sense his vocation as a writer. Bulosan's early narrative anticipates recent
work on diaspora under transnational capital. Although it appears restricted (or
even conservative) in its treatments of gender and race (and even class), it breaks
out of the debilitating mold of immigrant literature that, in its fixation on the
movement from one country to the next, refuses attention to global forces that
pertain in both.

Some recent narratives also explicitly address the imbrication of the "ethnic"
in global capitalism. One text that is intimately congizant of the deployment of
Chinese ethnicity within the narrative of American capitalism and its transnational aspirations is Steven C. Lo's 1989 novel, *The Incorporation of Eric Chung*.
The narrative begins by disclosing the end point of this "incorporation," which
places the protagonist at the edge of a final "downsizing": he is sequestered in a
tiny office with his secretary; they are the last survivors of a company set up to
do business with China. The narrator's appraisal of his situation reveals that he
has been thoroughly conditioned to capitalist logic: "In the final analysis, everything that happened happened because it made perfectly good sense. Nothing
came out of the blue. Nothing was evil, corrupt, or diabolic enough to make the
blood boil. No heroes, either. No one tried to be one, not that there was any
need" (1). The narrator's refusal of sentimentality is a refusal to grant capitalism
an otherworldly, abstract existence. For him, it is entirely logical that the venture to "incorporate" a young foreign student from China should run aground
on the shoals of an American entrepreneurialism completely ignorant of China.

Eric comes to Texas Technical Graduate School in 1972, and, after a series of
low-paying part-time jobs, he is recruited to be the "Chinese expert" for an enterprise invented by a young American, Roger Holton. Accidentally placed in
contact with a wealthy insurance man, Holton blurts out an off-the-cuff plan to
sell electronics to China. He knows nothing about either, but is playing into the
standing myth of the "China market." (This is of course meant to be ironic. Written in 1989, the novel looks back upon the tenor of Nixon's trip to China.) Soon
he is embroiled in endless schemes to get an audience with Chinese officials—
the only ones he finally meets are low-level types who are only interested in selling, not buying. This intensely black comedy parodies the "immigrant" myth as

well as American corporate hunger to seize the opportunity to market in China and attain instant wealth.

In the exposition of the narrative, we find time and again the alternation of stalled time (the seemingly endless waiting for a reply from the Chinese "contacts"), played against rushes of enthusiasm, venture capital, a telegram from China, which all disrupt any smooth linear development or unfolding. Similarly, Lo pays great attention to the details of place and space: from large corporate boardrooms to the tiny cubicle Eric ends up in, from the dirt roads of Seminole, Texas, to the superhighways leading to the metropolitan mecca of Dallas, Eric's final destination:

> Everything went beautifully as planned until I got lost on the highway coming into Dallas. Too many road signs and intersections suddenly came up—driving in Lubbock had never been so complicated. I missed an exit on I-20 and ended up driving up and down on Loop 12 where I didn't belong. I drove aimlessly and finally headed toward a group of tall buildings which I could see from miles away, hoping to find the Taltex building somehow. And also I wanted to see Dallas better. The tall buildings with tiny dots of lights made quite a scenic skyline in the night. I turned into the downtown area at about ten and spent a good thirty minutes circling the streets. I was impressed by all the buildings. It was hard to decide whether Taltex was anywhere close. I couldn't ask people either, there was virtually no one on the streets. At this time in my home city, I thought to myself, people would be standing on each other in downtown. And we didn't have tall buildings. (198)

Searching for a single point of orientation, the Taltex building, Chung winds around the highways and loops, finding a landscape filled with buildings but not the one he wants. In a single, seemingly random thought, he bridges the time and space between his home city in China and Dallas, if only to note their disjuncture. But what he cannot recognize is his role as a mediating subjectivity that occupies one chronotope while imaginatively projecting upon it another. This disregard is entirely in keeping with the disjuncture traced throughout the novel between the corporate world of America and the not yet ready for the free market economy China of the 1970s. Holton's greedy scheme gears the narrative precisely, yet futilely, toward that nexus of capitalist interests in future time. Concomitantly, the slow-paced *assimilation* narrative (Chung's assimilation into America via the "foreign student" route) is superseded by Holton's efforts to immediately *incorporate* Chung in *transnational* capitalist speculation, speculation evident in the built environment of the Texas skyline. Each of the texts above addresses the problem of ethnic and diasporic identity, understood not simply as the result of individual psychologies but as the product of complex historical chronotopes. The differences among these several narratives should alert us to the uneven and irregular historical manifestations of what is recognized as "diaspora."

Recently, much work has been done on the concept of diaspora. What has become clear in these studies is that there is a wide set of possible interpretations and definitions. What has interested me more than seeking some theoretically uniform concept of diaspora is rather the ideological purchase different articulations of the term allow. It becomes clear that one can't name diaspora until *after* the fact. I prefer, then, to regard the concept of diaspora as an enabling fiction, as a pretext for the exposition of profound notions of the national, of race, ethnicity, and history. From this perspective, "diaspora" does not consist in the *fact* of leaving Home, but in having that factuality available to representation *as such*—we come to "know" diaspora only as it is psychically identified in a narrative form that discloses the various ideological investments. And these investments give each particular articulation of the concept its specific charge. It is that narrative form that locates the representation of diaspora in its particular chronotope.[41] This spatiotemporal construct approximates a psychic experience particularly linked to material history. It is only after the diasporic comes into contact with the material history of its new location that a particular discourse is enabled that seeks to mark a distance, a relation, both within and outside that constellation of contingency.[42]

"Diasporic identity" is historically deployed to secure particular claims on cultural authenticity, and these claims are predicated on adjusting and manipulating notions of spatiality and temporality. What does space matter if we are psychically all "together"? What does time matter if we are all synchronized in a particular albeit sputtering telos (into the postmodern, the postindustrial, the postnational, the post-ethnic, and so on)? Recently, of course, such claims of uniformity have been countered by ones arguing for the impossibility of such notions under the conditions of postmodern hybridity. My intent here is not to rehearse this debate, but rather to shift it to another terrain. The question here is what, exactly, "diaspora" claims and why and how those claims are of any importance. In other words, what do such identifications imply and what kinds of social, political, economic relations are facilitated or denied as we entertain a more liberal framework for postnational cultural identity? Turning to a specific case that is intimately linked to Asian America, that of recent Chinese diasporic discourse, the question is not so much what the "center" was, is, or could be, but rather what allows any particular discourse to convince us that a periphery exists *as such*.

Obviously, there is an incommensurability between the totality of people who have left China, those who still abide there, and the multiplicity of ways their existences are made available to representation. We need to examine the modes in which any *discrete* notion of diasporic experience comes to stand in for an *essential* experience—what has been finessed, bracketed out, in that articulation. In short, the term "diaspora" may be understood as retroactively naming the discursive effects of the production of knowledge about *diaspora*. This is similar to Hobsbawm's suggestion of how one might study the nation: "it is more profitable to begin with the concept of 'the nation' than with the reality it represents."[43] This critical, particularizing, and historically aware mode may be a more productive and instructive way of "defining" diaspora than trying to do so by defining the reality it represents. It reveals more strikingly the ideological and ethical necessity of such fictionalization in terms of the production of social subjects and insists that we locate ourselves within that problematic and within material history. The discourse of "being Chinese" is one produced at a particular historical juncture, which reads "Chinese" within a condition of late capitalism and constructs a specific transnational subjectivity in dialectic relation to an ethnic subjectivity produced as the diasporic subject "takes root" in the particular regimes of its new geographical location. This process has deep implications for Asia/America.

Being Chinese

Reviewing the situation of contemporary East Asia, Wang Gungwu notes:

> The ability of many Chinese abroad to turn multinational trading systems to their advantage has been remarkable. The massive growth of international trade has enabled these Chinese, especially in the Asian-Pacific region where they are so numerous, to combine cosmopolitan culture with an increased capacity to associate and trade with other Chinese—both in China and around the world—in ways never seen before.
>
> Their faith in education and their position in the world economy invariably enhances the ability of the Chinese to live and prosper with equally committed non-Chinese. What this does to the quality of their Chineseness is open to question. One may even wonder how long being Chinese will continue to be relevant under such circumstances.[44]

What Wang Gungwu suggests is, for many, astounding: he envisions the disappearance (into irrelevance) of a question that has captured the imaginations of modern China scholars for decades—what does it mean to be Chinese? At the horizon of global economic integration, that question may be worse than unanswerable. It may be demystified entirely. In precise terms, Wang suggests a scenario that implies the erasure of ethnicity—Asian America, under such conditions, is both impossible and eminently real. Ethnicity is invisible: Asians may not be distinct from Americans in this manifest utopia of transnational economic development. Of course, this is an extreme position, but a very useful one, in that we may use it to anchor one end of our discussion, which we will return to when we come to a "world without borders."

In a wider perspective, the question of "Chineseness" has involved a series of complex identificatory movements, wherein "culture" and political economy interact with the particular semiotics of race and ethnicity. "Chineseness" is read across various landscapes to yield particular and often contradictory understandings of both its tenacity transhistorically and its historical malleability. Asian American identity in late capitalism has occupied a central role in the imagining of how Asia and America may or may not be partners in a late capitalist, postindustrial world. The consolidation of Chinese identity has brought forward a particular discourse of "Asianness" in its wake, and that discourse evinces a specific blend of ethics and economics, morals and monetary habits, customs and consumption. I want to use the discussion of Chinese identity for our examination of Asian/American identity in late capitalism precisely because it has occupied a central role in the imagining of how Asia and America may or may not be partners in a late capitalist, postindustrial world.

There has been one discourse that has maintained Asian identity in the face of such variability, one that has transcended national distinctions within Asia and been adjusted to conjoin with the definition of a new late capitalist subject. In the late 1980s and 1990s, "Confucianism" (or, as this incarnation is known, "post-Confucianism") has been rearticulated in particular ways that not only bind together Greater China but by implication reach into domestic American space as well. The particular attention to the notion of "Greater China" is evidence of a most powerful consolidation of Asian subjectivity that has a particular mode of interfacing with Asian America. It is economic to be sure, but underpinning that identity are a set of imputed "values" and dispositions that bear importantly upon our sense of Asian America. I will move from a discussion of Greater China to address the reconsolidation of identity under the twin rubrics of Confucianism and capitalism, and the various modes of inventing a new Asian/American subject in the context of Asia Pacific.

Over the past decade, the notion of "Greater China" has been produced to name the particular phenomenon of overseas Chinese investment flows among China (specifically the southern provinces of Guangdong and Fujian), Taiwan, and Hong Kong, and sometimes extended to incorporate various ASEAN states.[45] As self-contained as what has been called the "Bamboo Network" may appear, Ash and Yueh point out the intimate and crucial links this "network" has to other financial flows. While detailing the economy of Greater China, they suggest that "the economic symbiosis inherent in integration counsels caution in interpreting these figures. Shipments of commodities between the Chinese mainland, and Hong Kong and Taiwan do not all derive from self-contained, indigenous activities. Rather, they have increasingly reflected the integrative impact of FDI [foreign direct investment] and outward-processing operations" (723). Indeed, one of the critical tools used by China in moving into a market economy was the designation of "special economic zones," special import and export sites that traded more freely with foreign capital. Furthermore, the deployment of capital in the Southeast Asian region has produced tremendous fissures even as it has integrated states into this regional economy. For example, because the Chinese make up a disproportionate share of the commercial class in most of these countries, many have locked the Chinese out of certain sectors of the economy as part of an effort to promote indigenous business.[46]

Despite this more complex understanding, however, the predominant image of Greater China has been colored by western fears of Asian insiderism and anti-westernism (to be sure, this image is aided and abetted by the promulgation of Asian self-portraits in this mode, as we will see shortly). Weidenbaum and Hughes assert:

> The massive cross-investments among these nations are evidence of a new but poorly understood economic power in the region. This force is both a potential ally and a formidable competitor of Western business. It possesses tremendous financial wealth, and has repeatedly demonstrated the ability to capture large profits from emerging markets, in spite of political fragmentation and economic uncertainty. This power that we refer to is the bamboo network of ethnic Chinese entrepreneurs who have relocated to the Southeast Asia diaspora.[47]

Wang Gungwu usefully disaggregates the concept of "Greater China" into three different arenas: political, economic, and cultural.[48] The predominant object of scrutiny has been the economic one, yet it is crucial to see how the cultural realm has been, despite the desire of many of its various proponents, linked intimately to the former. The most influential and controversial formulation of contemporary Chinese culture and diasporic identity to date is found in Wei-ming Tu's collection, *The Living Tree: The Meaning of Being Chinese* (originally published as a special issue of *Daedalus* in 1991). This collection opens up many provocative avenues; here I concentrate on the formation of "Chinese identity" as it may pertain to a study of Asian America and transnationalism. Crucially, I want to map out the linkages between a materialist reading of transnationality and, continuing our focus on the formation of identity around mental dispositions, a psychologistic reading. I contrast this psychological trope with that of schizophrenia, which we examined in the previous chapter. In all these movements there is a critical linkage between the psychic content which is deemed to secure identity and the larger ideological structures that form the implicit bedrock for that psychology.

In his Preface, Tu in fact expresses this connection—while "being Chinese" may be racially cohered, birth alone is no guarantee; one has to "learn" to be Chinese, and "learning to be truly Chinese may prove to be too heavy a psychological burden for minorities, foreign-born, non-Mandarin speakers, or nonconformists; for such people, remaining outside or on the periphery may seem preferable" (Tu, "Preface," viii). Again: "Still, learning to be Chinese, especially for minorities and the foreign-born, is an attainment rather than a given" (ix). Crucially, the status of Chinese Americans is thus always problematic, as they may or may not have access to a hidden "structure": "Perhaps a deep structure underlies the psychocultural life of the Chinese, a structure so ingrained in the 'habits of the heart' that, tumultuous modern transmutation notwithstanding, it has not lost its enduring strength" (ix).

It is the flow of history that has swept Chinese out of the bosom of the homeland; it is precisely a deep psychological structure that may form the bridge back, not to China as it exists, but to an idea of "Chineseness." For Tu, this bridge is indeed the instrument that reconciles the gap between "Chineseness" and China as it exists today, between the unmistakably Confucian ideals that undergird Tu's Chineseness and the transnational pragmatics of the contemporary world. The relationship between the two seems entirely dialectical: "To Chinese intellectuals in industrial East Asia, the awareness that active participation in the economic, political, social, and cultural life of a thoroughly modernized community does not necessarily conflict with being authentically Chinese implies the possibility that modernization may enhance rather than weaken Chineseness. Still, the meaning of being Chinese is itself undergoing a major transformation"

("Cultural China," 9). Again, the persistent attention to the mental (awareness, recognition, and so on) produces a very particular nexus that psychically reconciles culture with economics and politics. "Cultural China" is a "psychological as well as an economic and a political nexus" (16).[49]

In resisting the impulse to racially determine Chineseness, Tu resorts to the figure of "culture," which accommodates particular psychologistic identifications (and that "psychological structure" here is synonymous with a moral and ethnical system). At the core of this "Cultural China" are those living in China, Taiwan, Hong Kong, and Singapore; they form the "first symbolic universe."[50] The third has an extremely interesting set of participants—all those who are active in the discursive production of China (albeit "discourse" in the particular sites of academia, politics, policymaking, and advocacy). It is the second symbolic universe that is most pertinent to our study, for it is comprised of the diasporic Chinese. While he concedes, "The impression that the overall cultural orientation of Chinese settlers has been shaped predominantly by the magnetic power of the homeland is simplistic" (19), Tu still asserts, "the diaspora Chinese cherish the hope of returning to and being recognized by the homeland" (19). It is this focus on "cherishing" and "recognition" that reinforces the sense that Tu's "Chineseness" is predicated on a psychological profile which links this latest and most compelling notion of "Chineseness" to a discussion of Asian/American identity as psychological. This psychology is underwritten by an ethical and emotive discourse that has supported the production of a particular Asian/American subjectivity: it is the discourse of Confucianism. Tu passionately and emphatically declares: "Without being able to continue the Confucian rhetoric, with all its manifestations, the meaning of being Chinese is so fundamentally challenged that there is no way for the Chinese to connect themselves up with the traditional concept of being Chinese. In other words, there is a fundamental disintegration of the Chinese identity itself."[51]

Post-Confucianism has been the subject of much scrutiny both in America and in Asia. Rather than rehearse that voluminous body of work, I focus here on its implications for the study of Asian America. Post-Confucianism rewrites in extremely significant ways the liaison between "Asian" and "American" that took place in the 1970s. We recall that one of the central tenets of Petersen's thesis was that the Japanese American "subnation" succeeded in America largely because of its very separateness. In particular, to account for Japanese *American* success, Petersen posited the notion that "traditional Asian" social beliefs did not contain a term for "civil rights." The idea of capitalist success *without* democracy was an alluring notion, and fed into the conservative pipe dreams of that era. In the 1980s and 1990s, such ideas were carried forward and read specifically in a transnational tableau as the "bubble economy" of Japan burst and a new Asian regional economy took its place as the most formidable economic force presented to the west.

If the Pacific Rim was to be the site of the major economic battles of the late twentieth and twenty-first centuries, then this space was occupied by an image that was at once retrograde and futuristic, combining the romanticism of a bygone age with the cutting-edge expansionism of late capitalism, which manifests itself not only in foreign direct investment but also in a nesting instinct which, as we saw in Chapter 8, has in turn transformed the cityscapes of the First World. Chinese entrepreneurs are depicted in one account as "an adventurous crew of modern-day Phoenicians fanning out across the Pacific, seeding their new homes—mostly Canada, Australia, and the United States—with wealth and entrepreneurial savvy." [52] At a 1990 conference at the University of Tsukuba, Chung-hsun Yu presented a paper entitled "Ethnic Chinese as the Shadow Leading Actor in the Age of Asia-Pacific" (29). The mystification of transnationalism in Greater China is couched in terms that assert a profound continuity throughout the region:

> Capital moves throughout the network in circuitous ways, providing safety against unforeseen political and economic events. Bankers speak of transactions that involve six or seven countries, with the funds flowing back to their original source at the end of it all. Even when Taiwan had strict exchange controls, it was possible for an individual in the network to deposit a large sum with a gold shop in Taipei and for a relative to withdraw the equivalent on the next day from an affiliated gold dealer in Hong Kong. [53]

Despite the obvious fact that, as Ong and Nonini point out, "not all Chinese engaged in transnational moves are capitalists," [54] the overriding image is one of an arcane cabal of Asians pitted against the west, of traditional cultural formations rallied forth to facilitate a particularly culture-based transnational enterprise. Communism is no longer the greatest threat—capitalist competition is; instead of the "Bamboo Curtain" of the Cold War, we find the "Bamboo Network" of the 1990s: "The *guanxi* of the overseas Chinese family business provides a perfect complement to high-tech western firms that lack the necessary economic and political connections to navigate a treacherous foreign business environment." [55] The problem is how to penetrate this Bamboo Network—the co-participation of non-Asians is not a given, and in fact may run aground on the shoals of essential cultural difference. As Singapore's strongman, Lee Kuan Yew, asserts, "The day Chinese lose their Confucianness . . . that day we become just another Third World society."[56] Confucianism is the signifier that consolidates all those essential attributes that position Asians particularly in the global economy. Without "it," the Chinese and other Asian groups that are identified with Confucianism lose both their cultural and economic identities and fall backwards into the retrograde detritus of the Third World, or, by implication, meld into a subordinate position in western capitalism.

Instead of acknowledging the centrality of such historical elements as the state's repression of the consumption rates of subaltern social groups and classes and the closely knit relations of labor and global outsourcing in late capitalism, especially in the garment, automobile, and personal computer industries, in the particular rise of Pacific Rim economies,[57] the most highly publicized and popularized explanations of Asian economic success dwell on "traditional Asian values," often most emphatically promoted by Asians themselves. This New Orientalist discourse is a self-orientalizing one that deploys a retrospectively invented "tradition" to support its claims of exceptionality in modernity: "In their outward appearance these East Asian *nouveaux riches* are Westernized. Yet behind this facade the people of these countries pursue a way of life that remains essentially Oriental. . . . This combination of Western capitalism with Oriental culture has exerted a significant and pervasive impact on the economy of these countries."[58] What is the particular content of this "Oriental"? More important, how does this content explain the "success" of East Asia economically?[59] The answer commonly given, both in Asia and in America, is "self-reliance and the Confucian virtues of thrift, discipline, industriousness, family cohesion, and reverence for education."[60] (As noted above, there is in most accounts a slippage that equates "Asian" with "Chinese" according to a monolithic, "commonly shared" belief in "Sinic" Confucianism.)

Such explanations always take this "fact" as a refutation of Weber's thesis that Confucianism in China is an obstacle to its modernization.[61] The key element here is the *timing* of this phenomenon. What was before a hindrance has reappeared in the historical context of late capitalism as a boon.[62] Thus, where in the 1920s the Pacific Ocean was a graphic border between mutually alien ethical, philosophical, and cultural systems, in the late twentieth century we find an intense interest in mapping the common economic ground, and this project is dependent upon ascertaining a *psychological* commonality. Crucially, if such a commonality is not discovered, one has to submit to the grim absolutism that places the west behind Asia: "Societies based upon the Confucian ethic may in many ways be superior to the West in the pursuit of industrialization, affluence, and modernization."[63] Tu Wei-ming puts the question this way: "Seemingly outmoded Confucian institutional imperatives and preferences have reemerged as more sophisticated ways of dealing with an increasingly complex pluralistic world than the single-minded attention to instrumental rationality."[64]

This revision of Confucianism as the ethical and cultural system *par excellence* for the contemporary world is predicated on a dramatic revision of modernity. Under the various contingencies and imperatives of this rescripting of the modern, we find a concomitant revision of its key terms. In particular, as east/west binaries are put under pressure by a shared (if unevenly so) participation in the global economy, the cross-trafficking of ideologemes is dizzying. As the west is counseled to emulate the newly relevant belief systems of Asia, we will find a particularly selective appropriation of Confucianism, what I call "Confucianism as a pretext." Similarly, the acceptance of western ideas of democracy has its particular pragmatic inflections in Asia: "Together, the ideas of capitalism and democracy have accelerated the modernization process in Pacific Asia even if, in their assimilation, 'capitalism' and 'democracy' were transformed in ways that now set them apart from their Western origins."[65]

All this rescripting would be useless were it not underwritten by the invention of a particular psychological profile—a subjectivity that could perform according to this multiple, hybrid belief system and thereby manifest and legitimate its precepts. Confucianism is predicated upon (and within) a particular, modern sense of self at the nexus of the economic, social, political, and cultural. Tu conceives of it as a "new type of psycho-cultural dynamics" that, while tapping into traditional values, is undergoing modification in modernity. It is in this psychic space that east and west together encounter modernity. Tu insists he wants to "highlight the American presence in the East Asian consciousness both as an historical fact and as a symbol for modernity."[66]

While Tu sees the cultural as linked to the economic (sometimes quite intimately), his notion of "Cultural China" clearly subordinates everything to a specific understanding of the superior explanatory force of "culture." Still, it is crucial to stress the engagement of the cultural with the economic in the performance of Confucianism. Where the focus on culture allows Tu to champion the notion of a non-race-based cultural identity, "Confucianism" has been deployed as racially specific in order to explain and legitimate a political economy of the Pacific Rim. It is in this form that Confucianism as both an exclusive racial and cultural signifier presents a challenge to the West. Lee Kuan Yew has stated the belief that "people feel a natural empathy with those who share their physical attributes. This sense of closeness is reinforced when they also share basic culture and language. It makes for easy rapport and the trust that is the foundation of all business relations."[67]

Given this racial gap, it is natural that the west has sought to find that common ground mentioned above. Especially since "the overseas Chinese network is often 'maddeningly impenetrable' to outsiders,"[68] it is crucial to make use of business consultants such as John Kao, who claims non-Chinese entrepreneurs can "both tap and create the opportunities" for a "symbiotic" relationship with China.[69] Again, this "symbiotic relationship" is predicated not only upon particular business strategies, but also upon the production of political/cultural subjectivity that transcends this Asian barrier to America.

This new subjectivity is eminently sociopolitical, and exists in a realm that, in suggesting this particularly "symbiotic" economic ecology, has profound implications for Asian America. As we saw in the 1970s, the model minority myth was predicated upon the creation of a mythic social space in which civil rights were irrelevant at best, obstructive at worst. The rearticulation of Confucianism carries within it a specific address to issues of authoritarianism and collectivity. As Aihwa Ong notes, "there is . . . a move beyond the simple reiteration of Chinese (Confucian) values to the articulation of a pan-Asian humanitarian model that is based on ahistorical and homogenizing descriptions of Asian cultures to legitimize overall state policies of capital accumulation, labor control, and social control."[70] Even the laudatory discourse that encases Confucianism takes care to mention, however much in passing, the way it may underwrite authoritarianism: "In government, Confucianism supports enlightened authoritarian rule by a centralized bureaucracy, not popular democracy."[71] The flatness of this enunciation masks the manifest disjuncture of Confucianism and Americanism. Tu himself suggests that while Confucianism might be "an alternative way of capital formation,"[72] there is also a contradiction between its authoritarian strain and democracy.[73]

While the focus here is the opposition of Confucian authoritarianism and democracy, the elided (and key) term is capitalism. Under the logic of Confucianism as an "alternative modernity," democracy may be a nostalgic relic at best, an ideal that has to be sacrificed to the imperatives of global economic competition. Lee Kuan Yew asserts: "Contrary to what American commentators say, I do not believe that democracy necessarily leads to development. I believe that what a country needs to develop is discipline more than democracy. The exuberance of democracy leads to undisciplined and disorderly conditions which are inimical to development."[74] Thus, the reaction of the American public to the Michael Fay caning case in Singapore is instructive: public discourse ranged from liberal cultural pluralists, who argued that the miscreant should be held liable in the home country's terms, to staunch patriots who saw his punishment as an affront to an American citizen in a primitive Third World country. Yet there was also a sense of admiration for the authoritarian regime, a sense that, if only America could act with such impunity, the country would be better off. Indeed, Singapore became a surrogate disciplinarian, curbing the excesses of American youth. Most important, perhaps, some felt that America might in fact be able to successfully compete with Asian nations if it were freer from democratic encumbrances.[75]

To ameliorate the harshness of authoritarianism and thereby make possible a connection between Confucianism and American capitalism, another facet of Confucianism is championed—collectivity. If a perceived absence of individuality in Asia was formerly seen to be an obstacle to creativity, innovation, and entrepreneurship, today the west's woes are attributed to rabid individualism and loss of collective responsibility. The modern United States has a tradition of admiring Asian "communitarian values" specifically as a vestige of traditional values lost by the west in the transition to modernity. For example, earlier, in Vogel's *Japan as Number One*, we find this passage:

> America's problem of recreating a sense of community now that group ties have been attenuated is infinitely more difficult than Japan's problem of maintaining group ties that were never dissolved. But there is no reason why, with greater central direction and sensitivity to the needs of various groups, to the mechanisms of maintaining solidarity, to the practice of broad consultation, America could not adopt policies more suited to the postindustrial age and recreate a sense of community on a form adapted to postindustrial society. (255)[76]

As attractive as this call to civic responsibility in a capitalist frame may be, this liberal humanism comes to be deployed to argue against "western individualism" and for greater central control.

This heavily idealized notion doesn't specifically name the "collectivities" that are to be formed and loyally supported. Ong and Nonini make it perfectly clear: "The essentialization of Chineseness as Confucian has become a convenient meta-inscription of, and prescription for, pan-Asianness among the elites of the so-called new dragon nation-states of the Asia Pacific."[77] This idealized "collectivity" is to be a tool of managerial capitalism.[78] And if the West is to emulate this new imperative of collectivization, one can imagine the nature of those collectivities. In his response to a paper suggesting the "de-ideologization" of Confucianism for pragmatic economic development, Peter Duus aptly points out:

"I guess the question that tickled the back of my mind was whether this paper in fact suggests ways to "re-ideologize" Confucianism. . . . There might be in Confucianism a kind of ideological tool for either managerial control at the state level through the creation of some sort of public ideology propagated through the educational system . . . , or a similar kind of management ideology in the hands of corporate managers that would try to privilege harmony and loyalty as values to be pursued not simply to maintain labor peace but also to justify what some might call an inequitable distribution of the profits and output of the production process."[79] But rather than acknowledging the primacy of cartels and other transnational entities as the real identity of these sentimentally evoked "collectives," the notion remains amorphously anchored as solely an oppositional term to "western individualism." Behind that lies the real target—the civil rights and liberties of the non-elites.

The strategy of using the rise of East Asian economies to leverage the manifestation of raw capitalism, an antidemocratic repudiation of individualism, has profound implications for Asian America in late capitalism. "Asian" authoritarianism may be adopted by the west so as to compete with Asia—democracy in its fullest sense may be a disadvantage, a relic of "modernity." Asian Americans are therefore the test case of how much of either can co-exist in the new *homo economicus*. I extend this critique in order to revisit the invention of the model minority myth. We recall Petersen's unmasked admiration for a country that "doesn't have a word for 'civil rights'." The production of the new transnational Asian capitalist subject, eminently equipped for the postmodern political economy, allows for the reactivation of an antidemocratic authoritarianism in America as well as Asia, and, once again, Asian Americans are taken as living proof of its validity. Berger's question "Could it be that East Asia has successfully generated a nonindividualistic version of capitalist modernity?" is precisely that wish for a capitalist modernity that is more "humane" for its neutralization of rapid individualistic acquisition, yet without a real consideration of the power and composition of the new collectives, the presence or absence of social conscience therein, or of the loss of democratic principles that comes with that pipe dream.[80]

The rhetoric of Confucianism as cultural and ethnic discourse has been appropriated as a political tool by capitalists, western and Asian, and, most germane for this study, this discourse has been tied to a particular civil discourse in the United States that reveals a particular set of affinities between this "global" discourse of post-Confucianism and late capitalism and various disciplinary regimes in the United States. More than the florescence of a particular individual subjectivity, there is the instantiation of a specific *social* entity. If the Asian American contains within him- or herself the essential ingredients for the new world economic order, the "collective" sensibilities that keep Asia strong are also guiding principles that Americans need to adapt, according to certain champions of corporatedly reinvented Confucianism. Indeed, William Ouchi's "Theory Z" evangelically takes the managerial style of collectivism/corporatism as the last bastion of social life: "Family members regularly interact with other organization members and their families and feel an identification with the organization. . . . If it is true that American society in general is moving toward a low affiliation state, if it is true that neither the church, the family, the neighborhood, the club, nor the childhood friendship is likely to make a comeback, then it falls to the work organization to provide the glue which will hold this society together."[81]

Amid the proliferation of "Asian values," it is essential to note Dirlik's observation that "culturalist explanations unfailingly avoid distinguishing a cultural legacy from what is *constructed* as a cultural legacy in the projection upon the past of present perceptions. . . . Confucianism has been reconstructed, beyond recognition to any hypothetical Confucianism of the past, in accordance with the demands of a contemporary East Asian capitalism. . . . Rather than 'traditionalize' modernity, . . . they have modernized tradition."[82] To this I would add America's own domestic use of "Confucianism as a pretext": this revision has attracted the fantasies of western capitalists who see in it a view of both the "good old days" of raw capitalism and the avatar of late transnational capitalism that reenlists Asian Americans as a particular set of subjects able to negotiate and facilitate both the literal transactions of capital between Asia and the United States and the various cultural liaisons of Asia and America that break apart the Asian cartels and map out a common place in the Asia Pacific. The collectivism that produces a benign (and, most important, profitable) political economic system is more accurately depicted in Reagan's contemporary (and equally paternalistic and authoritarian) notion of a "trickle-down economy," which specifies the exact hierarchies that underlie these notions of "collectivity." The charge that Asian Americans are "clannish" and conformists is thus mobilized to underwrite a specifically corporate and professional identity, and to eclipse individualism. At once, Asian Americans are cast into particular roles as exemplars of "collective" mentalities and divorced from the primary values attached to individualism—free-thinking, creativity, imagination. What, then, is the new terrain of this new, trans-Pacific economic and social subject?

Cyberspace as Equal Space: Pacific Rim and Beyond

Even as the discourse of the Asian Pacific economic boom moved along at a steady pace in the 1990s, the rumblings of regional economic destabilization after the return of Hong Kong to China in the summer of 1997 and the first signs of a weakening Thai economy in August and September prepared the way for the dramatic stock market crash of Hong Kong and South Korean markets in October 1997, a crash many Asian analysts blamed on the unbridled application of free market economic polices in East Asia. Besides injecting a heavy dose of sobriety into the celebration of Asian economic success, the immediate ripple effect from Asia to the west wiped out any lingering innocence concerning the interlinkage of world markets, most particularly, the intimate link between Asia and America. Such a relation had already been suggested by Kenichi Ohmae in his book *The Borderless World*. Ohmae's vision is of importance to our study precisely in its remapping of the Asian Pacific onto the globe, its attendant recasting of politics in a moral vein, and the particular nature of the crosscurrency of Asia and the west necessary for any mapping of such a "borderless world."

The centerpiece of this vision is the foreign exchange market, what he calls the "FX Empire": "The FX market has become an empire of its own, no longer vulnerable even to the actions of determined governments. . . . At the root of these developments is the recent explosion of superliquidity in the Triad's [New York, Toyko, London] financial markets. In Japan, for example, private savings and the corporate sector generate more than $1 billion in surplus capital *every day* that has to be invested somewhere. Real consumption—more plants, more equipment—can only absorb so much" (158f). Within this scheme, the Pacific is reterritorialized in a global, borderless, postnational world made possible by the convergence of capital and cybernetics.[83] The globe itself presents seemingly infinite sites for spatial fixes; we find a universalized "oceanic feeling" that, as Connery points out, correlates oceanic with capitalist discourse: flows, streams, liquidity, are now extended into every cybernetic "port." Crucial to note in this global capitalistic reterritorialization is its supposed evasion of national government control. Ohmae writes: "The global, interlinked, tradable FX empire allows money literally to travel around the globe in seconds. Even if, for instance, the Bank of Japan decides to tighten up the money supply at home, desired funds are instantaneously available from abroad" (162). Herein, the usual instruments nations use to control their economies become of lesser import; for instance, "the opportunities to make profits through FX-based speculation have diminished the importance of interest rates" (162).[84]

For Ohmae, such loosening of national determinations results in the realization of utopia in the form of a radical economic democratization of the globe. Not only is "everyone" now a potential partner in the global speculative market ("current data available to any PC user through Reuters, Quotron, Telerate, and the like can turn novice investors into wealthy individuals [and vice versa] in short order . . . the FX . . . , is widely available to anyone who wants to play" [161]), they are also now truly and equally global consumers of a global marketplace. The Internet has made possible not only universal accumulation but also universal consumption. It is in this latter sphere that the discourse of "democratization" is foregrounded, for obvious reasons—the reality of a globally available and "playable" speculative market is less easy to defend amid radical inequities of purchasing power and insiderism than is the vision of a marketplace where we can all shop at our own levels of disposable income and computer access time.

It is in the world of consumption that Ohmae locates "value," read here as both economic and, eerily, ethical: "This flow of information is nothing new. It is not segmenting consumer taste or choice. Instead, it is making it possible, at last, for the many variations in taste around the world to find concrete expression. . . . There is no universal style, nor even a style that holds firmly at the national level. . . . What has changed in the past few years is the ability of the interlinked economy to accommodate that variation and that multiplicity of styles" (185). In this universal, postmodern, late capitalist, cybernetic aesthetic, we can each be all we can be, given this brave new world, which presents for our consumption all that is there to consume in this strangely conceived and highly particular virtual public sphere.

The ethical dimension is extended to a discussion of the proper role of government. To have a truly pluralistic world of consumption (and in keeping with this bizarre and rather alienated correlation with a public sphere), we cannot accommodate the vestiges of old-fashioned national government controls: "[People] want to find expression for their diverse mix of tastes and preferences. . . . The role of government is not to make these choices but to ensure that people can and do. No system can provide a good life for its people that is not sensitive to, that does not develop out of, the irreducible fact of pluralism. And that is the fact upon which the interlinked economy rests" (192).[85] Here, the true disappearance of borders takes place within the ideological merging of laissez-faire capitalism west and east, which overturns the neat binary proposed by, among others, James Fallows: "In Anglo-American theory the state gets *in the way* of the economy's growth and the people's happiness" while "in the Asian model it is an indispensible tool toward those ends."[86] Ohmae's appeal to the West is precisely located in his disingenuous appropriation of western democratic discourse to underwrite the new cybernetic world economic order. In the borderless world, the state authoritarianism identified with Asia disappears and in its place is universal laissez-faire policy.

Finally, and perhaps most significantly, this new world order of absolute freedom brings with it a particular psychic effect that finalizes the disengagement of the subject/consumer/investor from the grip of the national: "We are finally living in a world where money, securities, services, options, futures, information and patents, software and hardware, companies and know-how, assets and memberships, paintings and brands are all traded without national sentiments across traditional boundaries" (171). In this heavily teleological description of a "borderless world," we have the ironic deployment of "democracy" as opposed to outmoded, authoritarian national interventionism. Yet, just like the "collectivism" of the post-Confucian age, this triumphalist discourse that evaporates the borderlines between east and west in the radical extension of the Pacific Rim to the entire world masks the realities of uneven access, uneven starting points of accumulation, the limits of consumerism, the shaping and warping forces of market economies, not to mention the raw physicality of labor and material.[87] The absolute and instantaneous fluidity of capital in cyberspace, which imaginatively lifts capital off the ground into the ether, cannot long mask for the even minimally skeptical reader the rough traction of the contradictions that anchor capital in material history.

Jean Chesneaux looks upon such a "borderless" state with barely hidden contempt; yet his often trenchant critique of this viewpoint has the unsettling tendency to cast Asia as *specifically* alienated by the modern. Asia is marked as a place where the impact of modernity is particularly disjunctive. Where Ohmae evaporates east/west distinctions, Chesneaux reinstates a rigid east/west binary, the transgression of which marks the melting of essential borders that would preserve Asia, for better or worse, always outside the modern. Modern time itself is non-Asian: "Time squeezed into the immediate instant, time rigidly programmed and priced, quantitative time—isn't that the time of the modern West, as much as of modernity itself? That sort of time is utterly foreign to non-Western cultures" (18).

Most germane for the topic of this section, such alienation (re)produces in Asia that schizophrenic pathology attached to modern Asian America: "Perhaps even more violently than Westerners, the Japanese have been struck on the head by the modernity world. Their experience is almost clinical, bordering on collective schizophrenia" (42). If in the 1970s Asian Americans were susceptible to a schizophrenia produced by biculturality, here we have that pathology projected onto a global frame. Somehow, Asians and modernity don't mix. This perspective obviously is the mirror image of that which takes Asians as the modern subjects *par excellence*. Yet the contradiction we find inherent in all pronouncements that seek to place Asians in some relation to modernity shows up in Chesneaux as well. For as much as he accesses the notion of Asia as outside modernity, he sees Asians as *within* it, too. In this passage we discover exactly that discursive realm that allows the fusion of contraries, Asia and the west—global capitalism:

> Hong Kong itself is nothing but an enormous "off ground" system, overpopulated, over-motorized, over-built, over-programmed, which keeps its balance only in the perpetual agitation of financial speculation, commercial novelty, traffic congestion, hurrying pedestrians, in an endless rush.

> Hong Kong functions in a situation of planetary ubiquity. Impeccably dressed in their three-piece suits, portable telephones in hand even in the street, Chinese raiders place orders to buy or sell on the stock exchanges of New York, Sydney or London. International shipping schedules and currency exchange rates are posted everywhere. (11)

This representation of Hong Kong becomes the representation of the new global economy itself; the Chinese "raiders" the living embodiment of modern capital inhabiting that "special place of modernity": "As a tightly interdependent network, the world's great stock exchanges comprise *one of modernity's special places*, a globe-encompassing place whose spatio-temporal structures are no longer consistent with classical geometry. . . . Carried along the successive time zones by computer interconnections, the world financial market functions 24 hours a day with instant ubiquity . . . [emphasis in the original]" (49).

The fusion of Asia with modernity has come at a cost to the west, for such a transgressive act, even as it increases the sphere of capitalism, denies the west any essential priority therein: "The *reproducible* character of this globalized economic system has been confirmed by the emergence of the four industrial centres of the Far East: Hong Kong, Singapore, Taiwan and South Korea. Modernity-world has appeared there with surprising malleability, setting itself up on a non-Western socio-cultural terrain which has turned out to be particularly favorable. . . . It is these countries that have denied to the West exclusive historical rights over the cultural and social conditions considered as the unique prerequisites of modernity" (59). Thus, for Chesneaux, "the Pacific, long the ultimate locus, somewhere at the far ends of the earth, for what was deemed by Westerners to be strange or exotic, has been integrated into the world geopolitical field."

Nevertheless, he denies that the new center of economic gravity has now shifted to the Pacific: "Fashionable current theories according to which the Pacific is the 'new centre of the world,' if taken literally, are incompatible with the fundamental ubiquity, the non-centrality, of the modern world. They can only be understood as Nippo-California propaganda, useful as it happens to the French political leadership in justifying and rationalizing its fantasies of a 'Franconesia.'" (67f).[88] This assertion outlines the trajectory from the west to Asia Pacific to a "borderless," cybernetically enabled world of virtual finance moving instantaneously throughout the globe. This movement has, at each step along the way, paused to contemplate the subjectivity that would inhabit that space, and each of those subjectivities—immigrant, diasporic, "culturally" bonded or not, has had its particular Asian/American inscription.

Throughout this study we have contemplated the predications of Asian to American; the postindustrial, postmodern, late-capitalist worldviews that have been recently promulgated each in their own way anticipate a fusion of Asia and America. Triumphalist discourses of post-Confucianism and globalism offer, respectively, a particular ethical commonplace in which culture underwrites economics, and a global market, made possible by cybernetics, which allows a re-spiritualization of the world. Yet in the literary imagination of such cybernetic encounters, we find a particular reinstantiation of orientalist mappings and a very specific simulacra of Asian America that respecifies the particular national identities that triumphalist cyberspace discourse tries to ignore.

Connery notes the particular inversion of national and global teleologies that occurred in the 1980s. Where before "the Western present was the East Asian future," it became the case that "if Japan was anywhere in time, it was in the future."[89] Yet the literary imaginations of writers such as William Gibson were able to construct a simultaneous (if unevenly so) arrival in futurity, and the chronotope of that futurity was precisely cyberspace. Common to much of the pathbreaking works in science fiction is an elaboration of cyberspace that shares Ohmae's imaginative, economistic trajectory from Pacific Rim to cyberspace, as well as Chesneaux's sense of alienation. Crucially, in these various visions, the homogeneous, "democratic" world envisioned by Ohmae is unmasked as a site of contention, specifically between the rise and fall of the east and the west. Out of this turbulent encounter in the nonwaters of cyberspace, there emerges a particular surviving (and therefore prescriptive) subjectivity, whose formation comments back upon the defining struggle between borderlessness and borders in which it is triumphant.

Here I examine two of William Gibson's works in order to explore how these visions of a liaison between Asia and America (as representatives of the ascension of a Pacific-centered world view and the decline of a Euroamerican one) underwrites the cyberspatial imaginary. The connection between cybernetics and psychology, the pathology of modern schizophrenia read somatically within the "wired" and frayed nerves of cyberspatial inhabitants, is connected by Csicsery-Ronay to cyberpunk's interest in global economies, and provides us with a way to attach these issues to the extension of the Pacific Rim into cyberspace:

> By the time we get to cyberpunk, reality has become a case of nerves—that is, the interfusion of nervous system and computer-matrix, sensation and information, so all battles are fought on feeling and mood, with dread exteriorized in the world itself. This distance required for reflection is squeezed out as the world implodes; when hallucinations and reality collapse into each other, there is no place from which to reflect. . . .
>
> The advantage these metaphors [linking the organic to the electronic] have over the more deliberate and reflective symbols that usually go into the cybernetic fiction discussed in David Porush's *The Soft Machine* (1985) is that they are embedded in the constantly shifting context of a global culture drawn into ever newer, even stranger webs of communication command and control. (190)

Gibson's *Neuromancer* is most often regarded as containing the first articulation of "cyberspace": "A consensual hallucination experienced daily by billions of legitimate operators, in every nation, by children being taught mathematical concepts. . . . A graphic representation of data abstracted from the banks of every computer in the human system. Lines of light ranged in the nonspace of the mind, clusters and constellations of data" (51). Yet while cyberspace seems entirely digitally induced, we should note the correlation of cyberspace with the "nonspace of the mind," for it is in resurrecting and rehabilitating the "mind" that Gibson is most interested.

In *Neuromancer*, the world is remapped into specific sectors, most notably, Chiba (Japan), and the "Sprawl" (the U.S.). Chiba is particularly the site of neurosurgery, the repair of nervous systems torn apart by encounters in cyberspace, and, in the case of the novel's protagonist, burnt out in revenge for his betrayal of a client. The name of the protagonist, "Case," is of course calculated—the central human figure is exactly a "case" of hypersensitive, logged-on mentality, whose adrenalin and amphetamine rushes are prompted by the fact that tiny sacs of poison have been surgically attached to his nervous system, timed to dissolve slowly. The only way he can save his life is to steal a code for what turns out to be an AI (artificial intelligence) and thus gain the password that will stop the process. As both a data thief and a decoder, Case exemplifies the human compulsion to gain information; his very nervous system is geared toward that end. In the world of cyberpunk, information, as much or more than knowledge, is power. But in whose hands? In *Neuromancer*, it is possessed singularly:

> Power, in Case's world, meant corporate power. The zaibatsus, the multinationals that shaped the course of human history, had transcended the old barriers. Viewed as organisms, they had attained a kind of immortality. You couldn't kill a zaibatsu by assassinating a dozen key executives; there were others waiting to step up the ladder, assume the vacated position, access the vast banks of corporate memory. But Tessier-Ashpool wasn't like that, and he sensed the difference in the death of its founder. T-A was an atavism, a clan." (203)

In this crucial dichotomy, multinational corporate power is specifically exemplified by Asia, incarnated as Asia, in the form of *zaibatsus*. In contrast to this immortal "organism" stands the vestige of Euroamerica—the Tessier-Ashpool conglomerate, clan-based in the "old-fashioned way."

Perhaps in recognition of the ascension of the new world of the zaibatsu, the matriarch of the T-A conglomerate invents what turns out to be a fatal scheme. According to the last of the line, 3 Jane, she "commissioned a construction of our artifical intelligences. She was quite a visionary. She imagined us in a symbiotic relationship with the AI's, our corporate decisions made for us. Our conscious decisions, I should say. Tessier-Ashpool would be immortal, a hive, each of us units of a larger entity" (229). While the immortality of the zaibatsus is guaranteed by the perpetual regeneration of corporate material, the T-A clan would give itself over to the logic of artificial intelligence. Nevertheless, in constructing a world sequestered away from all other time and space, 3 Jane notes that the result of this acquiescence to AI was that "all direction was lost, and we began to burrow into ourselves" (229). In the counterposing of the Euroamerican, AI-dependent, T-A to Japanese zaibatsus, the atavistic remainder of western civilization to the new Asian multinationals, the result is an ever-inward turning, self-consuming "artifact," eclipsed by an ever-expanding globalizing corporatism. The demise of T-A is brought about precisely by the fusing of its two opposite (yet complementary) AIs: "Wintermute" and "Neuromancer": "Wintermute was hive mind, decision maker, effecting change in the world outside. Neuromancer was personality. Neuromancer was immortality. Marie-France must have built something into Wintermute, the compulsion that had driven the thing to free itself, to unite with Neuromancer" (269). In the end we find the ascension of AI, the demise of T-A, and the survival of the zaibatsus.

The particular function of Asia in this narrative joins a "political" critique of the new transnational elites to a particular interpersonal crisis. The trope of Asia America is deployed specifically in Case's sexual activities and emotional bonds, and the resolution of loyalties and mentalities comes at the end of the novel in a truly schizophrenic set of images. Case's main emotional bond is with an Asian American woman, Linda Lee, whose murder is a part of the larger scheme to manipulate Case. In the course of the novel, he is paired up with Molly, a Japanese "samurai," whose physical skills at murder and mayhem parallel Case's neurological and cybernetic ones. They become lovers, briefly. The end of the narrative calls on Case to either give in to the hallucinatory and join Linda Lee there, or renounce that lure and claim his "mind." The novel ingeniously has it both ways: Case emerges from cybernetic hallucination *and* resides in it; this formula finesses the impossible liaison between Asia and America by (schizophrenically) creating two "Cases" out of one.[90] In the "first case," which provides the major rehabilitative closure, Case survives precisely because he is able to see through the hallucination that is cyberspace. He is able to step outside the "consensual hallucination" and in so doing rehabilitate the western individualistic (male) subject. His conquering of cyberspace is predicated on nothing less than recovering his mind, that human thing that supersedes cyberspace. After all, "the cyberspace matrix was actually a *drastic simplification* of the human sensorium [emphasis added]" (55).

Now, the pernicious formula that claims that Asia is the future and Euroamerica the past is negated. America is restored in the figure of the antihero Case—"the Sprawl" is contained and redefined, identifiable in less pejorative language via the ascension of the male hero who is its denizen. Harking back to our earlier discussion of schizophrenia and nationalism, we should note the seemingly minor mention of experiments undertaken to "reverse schizophrenia through the application of cybernetic models" (84). Reading through the logic of this formula, we can posit that the disjunctive dualism of cyberspace and reality, correlated with the twin telos of Asian ascension and Western decline, is negated by the "application" of cybernetic models that are, after all, themselves modeled upon the human mind. What emerges as dominant and surviving all is the Western Mind, encased in the white male body cleansed of its poisons and healed of its neurological and spiritual wounds. As the hallucination of a borderless cyberspace breaks apart, race and nation re-emerge.

Figure **10.** Illustration by Lou Beach from *California Magazine*, September 1990, p. 24.

The identification of this overriding, supreme entity with Case allows a re-habilitation of the western male individual subject (which is indeed correlated with nothing less than the Human) as somehow standing above and beyond the hallucinatory, schizophrenic world dominated by Asiatic zaibatsu corporatism and haunted by the ghost of old Euroamerica. Case disentangles himself from the net of both corporatisms the moment he walks away from hallucination, and in so doing raises an essential question to the matrix as he asks Neuromancer, "So what now? . . . Where do we go from here?" It replies, "I don't know, Case. Tonight the very matrix asks itself that question. Because you won. You have already won, don't you see? You won when you walked away from her on the beach [a hologram of Case's dead lover]. She was my last line of defense. I die soon, in one sense. As does Wintermute" (259).

Nevertheless, the novel compromises that solution—for in its very last scene, we find that a "second case" exists in cyberspace, still hooked into the hallucination in which he and Linda Lee are together:

> And one October night, punching himself past the scarlet tiers of the Eastern Seaboard Fission Authority, he saw three figures, tiny, impossible, who stood at the very edge of one of the vast steps of data. Small as they were, he could make out the boy's grin, his pink gums, the glitter of the long gray eyes that had been Rivera's. Linda still wore his jacket; she waved, as he passed. But the third figure, close behind her, arm across her shoulders, was himself.
>
> Somewhere, very close, the laugh wasn't laughter.
>
> He never saw Molly again. (271)

These two Cases each find a particular existence with regard to Asia—in one, Asia exists as part of cyberspace, his liaison with the dead figure of Linda Lee is possible there, alongside Wintermute. In the second case, he is saved in body and spirit by his rejection of that hallucination; however, in this condition of survival and enlightenment, Molly cannot exist. The recovery of the mind, specifically, the western white male psyche, is made possible through a particular narrative strategy that allows impossible desire, intimately identified with Asia, to live on in cyberspace, alone, at the same time that it can live in reality, but without Asia. One has one's cake and eats it too. If this restorative and compensatory fiction nevertheless seems predicated on a doubling maneuver and therefore is all too close to "two Cases" of schizophrenia, the radical separation of the two realms—the fantastic one in which the Asian American liaison with Linda Lee takes place in that hallucinatory realm of cyberspace and the "real" world that exists precisely *without* the Asian American liaison—allows for sanity to be reinstalled.

We find another narrative of the liaison of technology and the human, Asia and America, in a novel that Gibson wrote after actually visiting Japan.[91] Gibson plays with a theme set up in Philip Dick's brilliant and immensely influential *Do Androids Dream of Electric Sheep?*, and in particular the ending invented in Ridley Scott's film version, *Blade Runner*, which, as we discussed in Chapter 9, leaves off with the human "blade runner" Deckard escaping from the corporate, colonizing world with Rachael, a replicant. The human and the inhuman find a point of commonality in their mutual rejection of capitalism (in the form of the Tyrell technoempire, which produces the replicants as colonizing instruments).

In Gibson's *Idoru* we find a human/inhuman match between Rez and Rei Toei. Rez is a racially hybrid rock star, one-half of the band Lo/Rez. Lo is a

Chinese guitarist (the "next Jimi Hendrix") and Rez is half Irish and half Chinese. This hybridity deeply informs his psychology: at one point he propounds the notion of a "Sino-Celtic mysticism" (170). This enthusiasm for the hybrid attains new levels when Rez proposes "marrying" Rei Toei, a virtual "idoru" (Gibson's version of the Japanese term, "aidoru," or "idol").[92] Rei is described as a "personality-construct, a congeries of software agents, the creation of information-designers" (121). In other words, it (she) is information endowed with sex, beauty, corporeality. Reaction to this suggestion is typified in these words from his manager: "Rez . . . he says he's going to marry this Japanese twist who doesn't fucking *exist*! And he *knows* she doesn't, and says we've *no fucking imagination!*" (98). The imagined liaison of Asia and America (which we've traced from Capra's film of the 1930s) is thus rewritten in the late twentieth century as the interface of data (Japanese) and hybrid imagination ("Irish-Chinese-American"). Rez's viewpoint is represented by a disparaging friend thus: "Evolution and technology and passion; man's need to find beauty in the emerging order; his own burning need to get his end in with some software dolly wank toy. Balls. Utter" (187).

This hybridity is enabled precisely by the nature of culture in cyberspace. The "now" of youth culture is "digital, effortlessly elastic, instant recall supported by global systems she'd never have to bother comprehending" (17). Whereas the hero of *Neuromancer* is a data thief, the protagonist and orienting point of view in *Idoru* is Laney, a "cybernetic water-witch" who has the uncanny ability to intuit and navigate the hidden patterns of this elastic digital medium: "He had a peculiar knack with data-collection architectures, and a medically documented concentration deficit that he could toggle, under certain conditions, into a state of pathological hyperfocus. . . . The relevant data . . . was that he was an intuitive fisher of patterns of information: of the sort of signature a particular individual inadvertently created in the net as he or she went about the mundane yet endlessly multiplex business of life in a digital society" (30f). That is, he pinpoints the truth of each individual, the residue left after the vapor of cyberspatial hallucination fades away, and he can also predict certain media trends for the benefit of corporate culture. Laney is prized for his ability to "locate key data in apparently random wastes of incidental information" (49). Nevertheless, Rez presents to Laney a particular frustration: "I can't pull a personal fix out of something textured like corporate data. He's just not *there*" (217). Rez's marriage to Rei Toei is in fact the marriage of two corporately produced hallucinations—one made of flesh and the other emanating from a metal canister resembling a thermos bottle (a genie from the bottle?).

Even the physical landscape of Japan is revealed to be a construct—created after a cataclysmic earthquake: "Look at a map. A map from before? A lot of it's *not even where it used to be*. . . . They pushed all the quake-junk into the water, like landfill, and now they're building that up, too. New islands" (61). But if Japan is now a reconstruct attempting to resurrect itself from the rubble of its past, then the Western World mapped by Japan is merely a deeper and more tenuous construct, an outlawed nightclub carved out of the belly of a "nanotech building" decorated with frozen urine:

> The Western World occupied the top floors of an office building that hadn't quite survived the quake. Yamazaki might have said that it represented a response to trauma and subsequent reconstruction. In the days (some said hours) immediately following the disaster, an impromptu bar and disco had come into being in the former offices of a firm that had brokered shares in golf-club memberships. The building, declared structurally unsound, had been sealed by emergency workers at the ground floor, but it was still possible to enter through the ruined sublevels. . . . As the reconstruction began around it, it had already become a benchmark in Tokyo's psychic history, an open secret, an urban legend. (212f)

The contact between east and west is detailed as disjuncture. If the construction of the west within Japan is subterranean and high-rise, hidden and legendary at once, then the appearance of *street-level* Japan to western eyes is disjunctive and alienating. When Chia, a teenaged girl from Seattle, is sent by her local chapter of the Lo/Rez fan club to find out what's happened to Rez, she encounters a particular culture shock in Tokyo:

> She felt like everything, every little detail of Tokyo, was just different enough to create a kind of pressure, something that built up against her eyes, as though they'd grown tired of having to notice all the differences: a little sidewalk tree that was dressed up in a sort of woven basketwork jacket, the neo-avocado color of a payphone, a serious-looking girl with round glasses and a gray sweatshirt that said "Free Vagina." (181)

Gibson blends cyberspace with real space—here the pretense of futuristic Tokyo jibes with elements of an actual Tokyo landscape—the unlikely notion of culture shock existing in such an intimately and immediately linked globally cultured future world is made possible by instating, anachronistically, a view of *real, contemporary* Tokyo (of trees protected by straw shields, avocado-colored public phones, and the common sight of the famously and bizarrely pastiched English slogans).

This anachronism suggests an essential and abiding foreignness to Japan and creates a stereoscopic effect temporally, superimposing one temporality over another even as they share in the same psychic quality of alienation. Despite Gibson's immense imaginative vocabulary, the "shock" of future Tokyo is the same as the shock of present-day Tokyo. We remember that although Gibson's work had always used Japan as a particular topos, it wasn't until *Idoru* that he actually traveled there. We might ask, did what he actually discovered there surpass the alienation produced in his own imagining of it? I will suggest that whatever Gibson may have discovered in Japan was prejudiced by a deep set of assumptions regarding discrete national spaces, assumptions that postmodern Japan, real or imagined, confused for Gibson. This confusion was apparent long before he went to Japan; it was present in his mind as he wrote *Neuromancer*.

Gibson's visions of cyberspace contain the lurid figures of yakuza, an amphorous atmosphere of transnational corporate capitalism, the hallucinatory domain of cyberspace. Yet, essentially, despite the premium placed on exoticizing the future in a postmodern and ultimately orientalist frame, the recuperative logic of these two narratives reinstates "reality" and rescues the human from illusion. Most significantly, for all intents and purposes it reinstates national boundaries and in particular the east/west, Asian American binaries, with the latter terms now in (re)ascension. This segregation comes as no surprise, given the rationales Gibson gives for staging his novels in Japan.

In an interview with Larry McCaffrey, Gibson is asked how he came to use Japanese settings. His answer reveals a set of issues that are deeply linked to the study of Asian America:

"Terry and the Pirates" probably had more to do with it than personal experience. I've never been to Japan, but my wife has been an ESL teacher for a long time, and since the Japanese can most afford to send their teenagers over here to study English, there was an extended period when this stream of Japanese students turned up in Vancouver—I'd meet them a week off the plane, see them when they were leaving, that sort of thing. Also, Vancouver is a very popular destination for Japanese tourists—for example, there are special bars here that cater exclusively to the Japanese, and almost no one else goes into them because the whole scene is too strange. I'm sure I got a lot of this in when I wrote *Neuromancer*.[93]

This particular set of circumstances, of Gibson's "encounter" with Japan, is remarkable: first, he cites the midcentury comic strip, "Terry and the Pirates," that championed American heroism against the Red Chinese. But aside from this common orientalist source of information, Gibson notes the specific opportunity to meet Japanese students coming and going (and nothing, it seems, in between). His wife's vocation puts him in contact with these economically advantaged Asians who are here to learn *his* language. But third, he mentions a situation that is perhaps most revealing of all, and to which he attaches the specific composition of *Neuromancer*. He mentions the "special" Vancouver bars that "cater exclusively" to Japanese. "No one else" goes into them because "the whole scene is too strange." Crucially, Gibson never tells whether *he* ever went in. Did the scenes in his novel thus come from his imagining of the goings-on in those heterotopias? Or did he venture in and actually witness such "strangeness"? The permeation of Canadian space by these transient Japanese brings the exotic home to Gibson, and, fueled by popular cultural images of the Far East, he creates with impunity the necessarily separate spaces of Asian America. The fusion of the two in cyberspace must be ultimately separated out, reaggregated into their distinct spaces, if "reality" is to survive. Recalling our discussion of Jameson's reading of postmodernity as schizophrenic, Gibson's narrative *re-compartmentalizes* the "flattened" spaces in which former heterotopes became part of a great, sweeping *homotopia* which Gibson calls cyberspace—the consensual hallucination is now broken and disaggregated, things and people are returned to their "proper," discrete, places.

Takayuki Tatsumi, writing on the translation and reception of *Neuromancer* in Japan, suggests that both Japan and America read each other through the other's optics—Japanese see themselves in Gibson's novel, but, Tatsumi argues, America likewise sees itself in Japan. The meeting ground is cyberspatial culture, and, as such, it contains the hallucinatory quality proper to that space: "Cyberpunks perceive 'semiotic ghosts' of the present-day Far East; meanwhile they are perceived as the 'ghost-writers' of our future."[94] But what is left out of this neat symmetry is the ideological consequence of the modes of closing off these narratives, of reconciling and re-settling "sense."

Suvin correctly notes the ideological ambiguity of Gibson's narratives: "his plot oscillation between defeatism and kitschy happy endings . . . is an indicator of a real dilemma this very intelligent writer finds himself in as to the direction of history and even as to the possibility of meaningful action within it." Noting that Gibson's "balancing act accepts the status quo a bit too readily," Suvin asserts that this ambiguity is "simultaneously an acknowledgment of the overriding role of History and a flight from it."[95] I would specify that Gibson's ambivalence regarding the very nature of cyberspace is intimately linked to the possibilities of imagining it as a relation to Asia.

Following the imaginative trajectory of western capitalist development to the edge of the Pacific in the early 1920s, we have traced the wholesale leap into Asia during and after the Second World War, and the dual intensification of transnational capital and the cybernetic world that allows for a particular re-imagining of capital as not only liquid, but "virtual." In such a trajectory, Asia stands as both, by dint of its "success" in postindustrialism and its identification with technology, an avatar of postmodern late capitalism, and as (still) a frontier that, once crossed, disrupts the identity of "America." Cyberspace fiction is the arena of the imaginary which allows such formations and tensions to be repre-sented. Gibson's fiction is both traditionally racist and "progressively" anticapi-talist, but the primordial values of "reality" to which he would return are co-ordinated with a recompartmentalization of Asia and America as well.

If Asian America is posited as the postindustrial space par excellence, and its subjectivity the one best suited to navigate the Pacific "net," and if this subject anticipates the ultimate state of borderlessness, then in the most imaginative, far-out narratives of cyberspace we discover once again the reparticularization of race and nation. And yet here this respatialization, while resecuring "Amer-ica" as reality, *limits* the nation as well. It takes it out of the corrupt circuits of the Matrix, but also out of the utopian mappings of cyberspace. It restores American capitalism (however grudgingly) as vastly preferable to transnational capitalism, but this evasion is itself simply a matter of remythologizing the past (of monopoly capitalism and monoracialism). Where does this leave Asian America, then? Is the triumphant florescence of Asian America in cyberspace it-self just another hallucination? The Asian American narratives we have exam-ined in this chapter suggest a more concrete set of liaisons, and in that con-creteness enable us to step outside the Euroamerican imaginings of Gibson and view the specifically material manifestations of Asian America in late modernity.

Conclusion

IF THERE WERE ANY LINGERING DOUBT as to the significance attached to Asia and Asian America in discussions of the United States' domestic and foreign interests and, indeed, its very constitution in the late twentieth century, that doubt would be dispelled by a series of essays commemorating the seventy-fifth anniversary of *Foreign Affairs* in 1997—four explicitly foreground Asia and, indirectly, Asian America.[1] Most significantly, each of the central concerns of the present study is reflected in one or more of these essays: the modern redefinition of America, the impact of Asian immigration and ethnicity on the United States, the development of "Asia Pacific," the invention of a "borderless" world, and, finally, the effects of all of these issues on America's sense of its national sovereignty and identity in an age of transnational flows and diasporas. This is certainly not to say that *Foreign Affairs* should be taken as the arbiter or predictor of Asian America; rather, we should recognize that these essays indicate how the importance of these issues moves far beyond the narrow, self-enclosed boundaries imputed to "ethnic studies." It shows the nation's own deep involvement in issues of race and ethnicity both locally and globally, and the fusion of the particularity of ethnicity in the general construction of national identity.

For example, beginning with the most general contribution, Brzezinski's essay conceives "Eurasia" as the most significant part of the globe. The United States will face the formidable landmass that begins in the west of Europe and is "anchored" by China to the east. Eurasia is emphatically "home to most of the world's politically assertive and dynamic states. . . . Collectively, Eurasia's potential power overshadows even America's" (50). Turning to China as "the Eastern Anchor" of Eurasia, the former assistant to the president for National

Security Affairs (1977–81) declares emphatically, "There will be no stable equilibrium of power in Eurasia without a deepening strategic understanding between America and China and a clearer definition of Japan's emerging role" (58). The meaningful geopolitical world therefore is located in that mass of land; it is America's responsibility to maintain a particular balance in that Eurasian space, whose one anchor calls for a particular set of negotiations between the United States, China, and Japan.

Mahbubani's essay focuses on the Asian Pacific facet of that triangulated Eurasian American confederation, a facet that he views as nothing less than "the hinge of history" upon which the twenty-first century will turn (149). Herein he discovers a "new order" which transcends prior binaries and creates a particular common ground inhabited by specific subjects:

> Those who live and travel in the region realize that a new order is emerging. While governments and newspapers highlight differences, the quality of people-to-people relationships are bridging the cultural gaps, even between the United States and China. Tens of thousands of Chinese students have returned to China after studying in America, and it is these thousands who are moving up the political ladder, assuming key posts as mayors and vice ministers.
>
> When this generation of Asia-Pacific residents gathers, whether they are American and Chinese, Australian and Indonesian, Japanese and Thai, there is little discomfort or distance. They do business with each other with ease. It is not uncommon for a Hong Kong developer to build a shopping center in Jakarta, with the architectural design done in Vancouver. Or for a Singapore shipping line to shift its accounts department to Manila while acquiring a second shipping line in California. (156)

As noted in Chapter 10, this is of course a particular "collectivity." The "conversation" that cements the east to the west takes place solely within a group of transnational capitalists and political operatives whose main interests are keeping "good government" in place so as to secure their investments and prerogatives. Here, Asian America appears as the geopolitical, economic space of interpenetration and accumulation, populated by these specific subjectivities. Thus, in these two essays, we find a specific attention to geopolitical balance in the newly designated "most significant" world of Eurasia-America and the presentation of Asia Pacific as a specific piece of "evidence" that proves the viability of post-dualistic economic cultures. If the former ponders the daunting task of keeping things in political balance between Europe, America, and Asia, the latter attests to the smooth-running exercise in global economies and cultures evident in the transnational regional economy of Asia Pacific, even suggesting that it serve as a model for transnational "communitarianism."

Schlesinger's and Huntington's essays turn to the domestic and find a particular crisis therein. In both cases, this crisis is identified with ethnic and transnational influences on America. If Brzezinski wonders about geopolitical balance, Arthur Schlesinger, Jr., wonders if the nation can maintain in any way its democratic ideals. He names a number of forces that are exerting powerful historical pressures on democracy. The first is that of racial protest: "The democratic adventure must confront tremendous pent-up energies that threaten to blow it off course and even drive it onto the rocks. . . . Minorities seek full membership in the larger American society. Doors slammed in their faces drive them to protest" (5). This "door" is particularly defined as economic exclusion. Schlesinger worries about "unbridled capitalism," particularly when its operations are accelerated by technology: "The computerized world poses problems for democracy. . . . Those who skip or flunk the computer will fall into the *Blade Runner* proletariat, a snarling, embittered, violent underclass" (6). In such a world, there is no way for a national or even international ethos to take hold. The smooth liquidity of the borderless world is for Schlesinger a slippery slope: "Cyberspace is beyond national control. No authorities exist to provide international control. Where is democracy now?" (8). The trajectory of Schlesinger's essay moves particularly to Asia. If the greatest threat to democracy at home is "unbridled" capitalism and racial and ethnic protest, the greatest threat to world democracy is Asia: "The new salience of Asia on the world scene, the absence of historical predilections for democracy, and the self-interest of rulers who see democracy as a threat to their power suggest a period of Asian resistance to the spread of the democratic idea" (10).

Herein we find a particular assignment of meaning to Asians and Asian Americans—both form some sort of threat to democracy. If Asian Americans might be identified as part of a racial minority demanding full democratic and economic participation at home, Asians abroad turn deaf ears to the moral and ethical claims of democracy. Now I am less concerned with the "reality" presented by this imputed threat than with the racist sentiment that comfortably allows such blatant reifications of Asians and Asian Americans (and the two are often confused in these articles), and why these reifications work to comment on the separateness of the Asian American in American democractic ideology.

Finally, and remarkably, to resolve these tensions domestically, Schlesinger has recourse to the idea of interracial sex: "Sex—and love—between people of different creeds and colors can probably be counted on to arrest the disuniting of America" (11). This is a rather noteworthy prescription to find in *Foreign Affairs* (one can't help but note the unintended pun on the journal's title). It discloses a particular notion of the interfaces, positive and negative, between the "foreign" and the domestic. It also reveals both a deeply human notion and a rather desperate one as well. It reiterates Robert E. Park's prescription in the 1920s and discloses the problem that has plagued America since its modern incarnation—the accommodation of migrancy, race, and ethnicity. Schlesinger's downhearted liberal mode of reconciling America with its disunified self stands in stark contrast to Samuel Huntington's diatribe, which represents a continuance of another tradition of thought.

Concerned as always with the "erosion" of national interests (and deflecting attention from the murkiness of such a supposed consensus), Huntington claims that one of the factors contributing to this erosion is the absence of a clearly defined enemy against which to consolidate the nation. Following the path laid out in his *Clash of Civilizations* book, he claims a contemporary need to find an "opposing other" in the absence of the Cold War, which readily provided one in the Soviet Union. Why must we find an "other"? Because the "other" at home is eroding the nation from within: "Given the domestic forces pushing toward heterogeneity, diversity, multiculturalism, and ethnic and racial division, however, the United States . . . may need an opposing other to maintain its unity" (32). Huntington believes the most likely candidate is China, but he notes, with some disappointment, that "China is too problematic and its potential dangers too distant in the future." He is only half right—China certainly continues to serve as a powerful other against which America may define itself. It is just that China is no longer such a neatly defined other as before, thanks to its move toward a market economy and the imbrication of both the United States and China in new transnationalisms. And this of course has had specific consequences for the formation of Asian/American ethnic identity.

Indeed, the very "other" needed to consolidate the United States in the face of widening chasms created by ethnic and other minorities turns out to be those ethnic minorities *themselves*, who are now more visible and vocal than ever before because of "changes in the scope and sources of immigration and the rise of the cult of multiculturalism" (32). *They* are the others against whom "we" may set our identity politics, for they have hijacked the entire set of apparatuses essential to the running of the state: "The institutions and capabilities—political, military, economic, intelligence—created to serve a grand national purpose in the Cold War are now being suborned and redirected to serve narrow subnational, transnational, and even nonnational purposes. Increasingly people are arguing that these are precisely the foreign interests they should serve" (37).

There is thus a double "erosion" of the national character, carried out on one hand by multiculturalists (ethnic minorities) who skew America off course and weaken its resolve, and on the other hand by newly internalized "others," diasporics who retain allegiance to their homelands and work from within the United States to focus its interests in their favor. Indeed, we see that the two groups might indeed be the same — ethnic Americans are now recast as diasporics, un- or non-Americans, in a rehearsal of the logic of the Japanese American internment. This recasting is made explicit here:

> The growing role of ethnic groups in shaping American foreign policy is reinforced by the waves of recent immigration *and by* the arguments for diversity and multiculturalism. In addition, the greater economic wealth of ethnic communities and the dramatic improvements in communications and transportation now make it much easier for ethnic groups to remain in touch with their home countries. As a result, these groups are being transformed from cultural communities within the boundaries of the state into diasporas that transcend these boundaries [emphasis added]. (38)

In sum, "diasporas in the United States support their home governments." Huntington uses Asian Americans as one specific example: "Chinese-Americans . . . overwhelmingly pressure the United States to adopt favorable policies toward China" (39). This is a blatant and stupid untruth, which collapses Chinese from China, Hong Kong, Taiwan, Southeast Asia, and elsewhere together and ignores the sizeable anti-communist, pro-democracy element (even Schlesinger acknowledges various Asian democratic movements, although he still wonders if they are not anomalies). But facts simply seem to get in the way of Huntington's need to mark off "America" by demonizing everything that looks different from him. Each of these essays identifies the parameters of American interests and anxieties; each uses a specific modality of Asian/American discourse and maps out a particular ground of both potential consensus and disjuncture.

A different definition of this space and this subjectivity would reject the three main points of identification we have traced, beginning in the 1930s, and which are manifest in all these essays from *Foreign Affairs*: first, their reduction of "Asian American" subjectivity to that of "transnational capitalist," that is, the fixing of Asia/America into solely a rarified space of economic common interest among transnational capitalists; second, the demonization of Asian/Americans as perpetual ethnic/diasporic foreigners (most evident in the racist remarks of Huntington); and, finally, the vestiges of schizophrenic duality, that drive a pathological schism at the point of the hyphen. Each of these prevalent forms of identification have been (and must continue to be) challenged and deconstructed variously if we are to secure a deeper understanding of the production of Asia/America. In this conclusion, I take up the above points in reverse order: schizophrenia, diaspora, transnationalism.

Coming out of 1968's radical impetus to reject the standard demarcations of political, social, and sexual life, Deleuze and Guattari's critique and radical revision of schizophrenia retains even today much of its suggestive power. In particular, they contend that under capitalism, with its constant cycle of production and excess, under- and over-consumption, and destabilized wages, values, and employment, there is no fixed authority to anchor and legitimize a schizophrenic diagnosis. Therefore, the libidinal energies pent up and oppressed in the clinical definition and pathology of schizophrenia are to be freed up in Deleuze and Guatarri's *schizoanalysis*, a mapping of newly understood multiplicities of subjectivities.

Yet within this opened space, I have insisted on acknowledging the particular, uneven surface presented to ethnic and racial subjects, especially as they transect national spaces. For both diasporic subjects and ethnic subjects, I would argue, "culture" presents a particular site for (re)negotiating subjectivity, a site cross-hatched by multiple interests and agents. Allen Chun argues for viewing discourses of identity "as interpretive mechanisms through which specific people, institutions or cultures localize (or indigenize) diverse global flows in order to negotiate a meaningful life space or position themselves within a situation of power" (69). As Chun notes: "Underlying the call for multivocality of the kind constitutive of current notions of multiculturalism is the notion that place can be imbued with multiple meanings" (70). Yet I would also argue that such projections require what I call an "echo effect." This term describes the confirmation of "voices," the resolution of discrete acts, the interplay between individuals, groups, and the state that marks the intersubjective political world, which is necessary for idiomatic "meaning" to become politically effective. It is within this dialectic of articulation and power that Asia/America is produced. A new collection of essays edited by Evelyn Hu-DeHart, *TransPacific Articulations*, considers precisely the complexities of this dialectic.

One thing crucial to add to this discussion is a notion that has guided this study throughout—that "the State" or "the Nation" should not be read as a monolithic (that is, not contradiction-free) entity against which the "ethnic" is simply posed. It has its own multiple and often contradictory interests. If Deleuze and Guattari point out the destabilized nature of the capitalist state and propose the liberating effects of a "schizoanalysis" that would recover and unleash pathologized multiplicities formerly contained and disciplined within a discourse of unity and singularity, Wallerstein observes within capitalist "culture" a duality and a contradiction that links up with our prior discussions of schizophrenia and race.

I have argued that modern Asian America should be read within a context of multiple subjectivities whose multiplicity can be depathologized through a close and critical reading of Asian, American, and Asian/American history, *and* that the unity presumed to be enjoyed by "America" is in fact better read as a set of adjustments and reformations that disclose the fact that America is always in process itself. And a large part of this process in the twentieth century has *particularly* involved Asian America. We have noted that this interrelationship has been glossed over by the attribution of essential difference to Asian Americans. Nevertheless, we have also noted the attribution of various possibilities of predication, even of the suitability of Asians to serve as models for America. It is this contradiction that discloses the contradictions between race, national interests, and identity. That is, Asians and Asian Americans have been incorporated variously into America as their image has coincided with particular historical American interests; yet they have been reparticularized by race as well. We have, in other words, the tension between ethnic particulars, whose particularity is read in their "split" nature, and the presumption of the nation's "universal."

Wallerstein argues that within that supposed universal itself resides a split; he focuses on the interplay between capitalist culture's assertions of transhistorical universalisms that seek to unify and consolidate power (what he calls "culture I"), and assertions of difference that rationalize inequities and particularities within that universal (this is "culture II"). Wallerstein uses as his examples of culture II discourses of racism and sexism, which capitalist culture uses to "explain" the uneven participation of differently marked groups according to race and/or sex. That is, if capitalist culture insists on its universality, it still has to rationalize the empirical evidence of its unevenness. The interworkings of these two notions of "culture" thus finesse the inherent contradictions of capital; Wallerstein's essay is geared toward explaining "how the ideologies of universalism and of racism-sexism help contain [six contradictions of the capitalist world system], and why therefore the two ideologies are a symbiotic pair" (42):

> The "culture" . . . of this capitalist world-economy is the outcome of our collective historical attempts to come to terms with the contradictions, the ambiguities, the complexities of socio-political realities of this particular system. We have done it in part by creating the concept of "culture" (usage I) as the assertion

of unchanging realities amidst a world that is in fact ceaselessly changing. And we have done it in part by creating the concept of "culture" (usage II) as the justification of the inequities of the system, as the attempt to keep them unchanging in a world which is ceaselessly threatened by change. . . . Therefore, the very construction of culture becomes a battleground, the key ideological battleground in fact of the opposing interests within this historical system. The heart of the debate, it seems to me, revolves around the way in which the presumed antinomies of unity and diversity, universalism and particularism, humanity and race, world and nation, person and man/woman have been manipulated. (38f)

If we recognize this split within the capitalist culture (and focus particularly on America and the case of Asian America), we see the state's own struggle with itself projected onto and through racism. America must work both to secure its identity and *invent* one to suit the new historical contingencies of the late twentieth century, contingencies that conspicuously include its relation to Asia Pacific.

Along with recognizing the destabilized nature of America, which will allow for a deeper and more complex understanding of Asian America, it is crucial to recognize the agency of Asian Americans in fashioning their own existences and how that refashioning has impact on Asian America. In the case of the diasporic subject, Purnima Mankekar, drawing on the work of Karen Leonard and Roger Rouse, points out the need to see diasporic subjects as forging coalitions based on a politics of location and accountable engagement with struggles in both the homeland and diaspora. That is to say, diasporic subjects act as political and social agents within coalitions geared toward the specific material contingencies of the place of location, those with an eye toward the homeland, *and* those *outside* both those configurations. "Ethnic choice," in Karen Leonard's phrase, foregrounds both the contingent nature of action and the pragmatics of agency, and argues for a particular kind of agency to be read into discussions of diasporic identities.

In the case of ethnic subjects, we might use a rather unlikely text to argue for the positive agency of Asian Americans, Easurk Charr's *The Golden Mountain*. This autobiography tells of Charr's childhood in Korea and emigration to the United States. There are a number of remarkable aspects to this narrative—the author's discussions of his ardent Americanism and Christian belief are read within the context of anti-Japanese and pro-Korean nationalist politics. The novel, when it appeared in 1961, was criticized by some for its overwhelmingly positive depiction of the United States, and in particular its elision of racism.

But missing in that critique is the struggle Charr undertakes to obtain citizenship for himself and his wife. Having served in the American armed forces in the First World War, he expects that he will fall into that category of persons eligible for citizenship for having served in the military. He discovers that that ruling is unevenly applied, and when it comes to his case, he is denied citizenship.

He goes through the usual bureaucratic channels, but what is notable is that after many efforts, he not only mobilizes the church, his former college, and the American Legion, but he also publicizes the case in the media.[2] He is finally successful. Charr's actions call on America to fulfill its promises; when it does, Charr is unstinting in his praise and affection for his new country. How are we to read this? On the one hand, we could skeptically note the singularity of his case, which benefited from Charr's particular set of backers and supporters, and we could note that no change in the law occurred because of it. We could criticize his patriotism for being based solely on his own good fortune. But on the other hand, we could, bearing all this in mind, see his act as an affirmative, noncompliant gesture which brings to the fore the inherent contradictions in America in such as way as to produce a positive result. Charr's story suggests that even in the most unlikely narratives one might find a rebuttal to the stereotype of the complacent and apolitical Asian.

The participation of Asian Americans in antiracist, anticlassist, profeminist and pro–gay rights struggles, and their ardent work for community interests, give the lie to the depiction of Asian Americans as the unvocal and uncritical minority. The work of Yen Le Espiritu and Lisa Lowe have in different ways grappled with the issue of accommodating both "pan-Asian ethnicity" and Asian America's "heterogeneity," and the possibilities of exploiting both in political work. In terms of ethnicity and race, we must recognize and analyze the ways race itself is indeed much more complex—the issue of interracial subjectivities, which has indeed been one key trope in modern national discourse, forces us to confront assumptions of race and its interfaces with ethnicity and nation.[3]

Turning to the topic of transnational cultures, the work of Aihwa Ong, Sau-ling Wong, and others has usefully pointed up the way that transnational movements displace and variously reinstall hierarchies of gender, class, and ethnicity, and Colleen Lye has shown how the transposition of Asian American texts across borders produces readings that prompt us to recognize the contingencies and interestedness of ideological work. Numerous studies have alerted us to the fact that the neat boundaries of the nation are now less tidy, as the local and the global continue to affect one another. In the particular case of Asian

America, even as we witness the effects of transnationalism and ethnicity upon it, we find American culture as well penetrating and affecting Asian cultural space. Yet here too we find "culture" reinterpreted and deployed variously.[4]

Finally, I would like to return to a subject found in the introduction to this study—South Asia. In the introduction, I explained why I have not treated South Asia in this book. Yet here, in closing, I want to suggest that the two trajectories of Pacific Asian America and *South* Asian America might produce a very meaningful set of discussions. It may be that a focus on transnationality and postcoloniality, read within the differentials of ethnicity, class, gender, and race, would result in a better understanding of each, and of the historical composition of America. The particular meeting ground promoted by American economic interests, that of the Pacific Rim, reifies "Asia" at a specific point, and, as I hope to have proved, this reification has everything to do with the modern appearance of Asian America. Having noted the formation and functions of "Asia Pacific" in mapping modern Asian America, I would suggest the importance of deconstructing this identifying *topos* if we are to move beyond its reifications.

The recent partial collapse of Asian economies has driven an element of doubt into the discourse of Asian triumphalist discourse. Capital has flown out of Asia Pacific for the moment, showing that its economic surges may be accompanied by equally dramatic falls. This meltdown has had the consequence of putting deflated Asian economies at the door of the International Monetary Fund; the strings attached to the astronomical loans they seek from the I.M.F. serve to (once again) coerce Asian economies to conform to western interests: "The financial crisis is thus a golden opportunity for Washington. Indeed, the rollback of protectionism and activist state intervention is already incorporated into the 'stabilization' programs the I.M.F. is negotiating."[5] Herein we find a reinflection of "Confucianism": no longer the guiding discourse of late capital, it is read as oriental despotism and *guanxi* as corrupt Asian insiderism: "Many of the same institutions and people who recently celebrated the Asian 'tigers' as the engine of world growth into the twenty-first century now speak of them as a source of financial contagion, even as the trigger for global deflation."[6]

Thus we may sense a slow decline in a particular narrative arc, yet another modification of American identity as linked to Asia Pacific. These fluctuations mark a particular set of historical inscriptions of Asian America. This historical moment presents the occasion to critically reevaluate the America—Asia Pacific paradigm and its attendant Racial Frontierism, which we have traced from the early twentieth century and asserted as the dominant paradigm for modern Asian America. It may be that now we can engage South Asia in a new American "modernity" (or postmodernity), especially as new global economies have brought a sizeable growth in the numbers of South Asians in the United States. Indeed, by incorporating a study of South Asia into the "modernity" assumed to be contained in Asia Pacific, we might arrive at a productive convergence of issues heretofore obstructed from view by the dominance of America's Asian Pacific "destiny."

Asian America is always in process; the twenty-first century will undoubtedly present yet another set of manifestations that press the particularity of race against the universalities of the modern state. The subjectivities produced within such a context will, no doubt, continue to try borders and revise interiors, and is so doing leave a particular impress upon history.

One way that the dynamic vision of Asian/American has been stabilized, ironically, is by embracing that version of postmodern thought that attempts to make race simply a random and optional element in our "multiple" identities. I say "ironically" because this utopian vision is altogether commendable—I truly hope that race might indeed cease to be a negative and destructive element of identification. But despite the fact that certain readings of the postmodern proffer us the notion that now we are all one (for better or worse), I remain skeptical of the sustainability and pragmatic purchase of such notions. Among other things that stubbornly point up the incompleteness of such notions of postmodernity, I sense we are still awaiting that disappearance that early twentieth-century American sociologists deemed necessary for "real" assimilation—the disappearance of race. The degree to which race remains a powerful and negative signifier is the degree to which the *modern* project is left incomplete.

Appendix / Model Minority Discourse and the Course of Healing

IT IS TAKEN AS AN UNSPOKEN TRUTH that to realize its counterhegemonic potential, minority discourse must access hegemonic apparatuses. Nevertheless, the hegemonic also holds certain identificatory lures for the minor subject that subtly solicit and enjoin its participation in particular modalities.[1] Thus, given the increasing appearance of various discourses apprehended as "minority" in various positions and guises within locations traditionally regarded as privileged spaces of cultural production and reproduction (for instance, popular media, corporate boardrooms, academic institutions, public school textbooks, and so on), we are led to ask: are such presences signs of deep social change or indices of the appropriation and containment of minority discourses? The burgeoning interest in contemporary Asian American literature, evinced by its high profile on both university syllabi and popular book shelves, in the increased number of newly published authors, and the canonization of established writers such as Maxine Hong Kingston (who is, according to some accounts, the most widely taught living American author on college campuses), provides a particularly strong case of the ascension of a "minority discourse." How can one account for the tremendous popularity of novels such as *The Woman Warrior*, *The Joy Luck Club*, *Typical American*, and *China Boy*, among others? Here I wish to look more closely at this specific "minority discourse," and suggest one answer.

A critical reading of these texts, and of the way they are represented in press releases, author interviews, book jacket blurbs, newspaper reviews, and academic essays, discloses a common thematic. The most popular texts tend to be perceived as resolutions to a generalized "problem" of racial, ethnic, and gendered identities.[2] Such perceptions deeply inform the contracting, marketing, and distribution of Asian American literature, which in turn influences the (re)production of representations of the successful formation of a particularly constructed Asian American subjectivity, as well as the institutionalization of these texts within academic and popular culture. This cycle of representational and ideological function places Asian American literature in a particularly strategic position vis-à-vis both dominant ideologies and other minority discourses — it marks out a transitional space in which the "minor" emerges into the dominant by way of a specific set of negotiations of subjectivity. There is, therefore, a doubleness in Asian American literary texts, which serve as representatives of an eccentric "ethnic" literature as well as models of successful assimilation to the core. This double function oscillates between the persistence of a fetishized "ethnic dilemma" and a specifically achieved "healing."

Like the representation of Asian Americans as the "model minority," the recent explosion in the production and marketing of Asian American literature betrays a particular ideological strategy — the "myth" of Asian American success took hold only because it suppressed specific differences in the material histories and contemporary realities of many different Asian groups in America and foregrounded the rise of certain Asians (primarily among second and third generation Chinese and Japanese Americans) while ignoring the continuing struggles of others. The current popularity of certain *Chinese* American texts (which far exceeds that of the literatures of any other Asian American subgroup) may in large part be attributed to a discourse that likewise suppresses material differences of sociopolitical being and fixes upon an ideology of depoliticized self-healing primarily concerned with the psychological adjustments of ethnic subjects and enabled by a presumption of a particularly constructed ethnic malaise.[3]

Before proceeding any further, I would stress that, like the model minority myth, what I refer to as "model minority discourse" is an ideological construct not coextensive with the texts themselves, but rather designating a mode of apprehending, decoding, recoding, and producing Asian American narratives. I am not accusing the authors of the novelistic texts I treat of consciously setting out to construct texts that prop up dominant ideologies. Rather, I want to point out that a particular formula of subject construction has evolved and has been naturalized as a central component of popular Asian American literature. It has come to serve both as a model for Asian American literary production (a convention of fiction *writing*), and as a literary object (the product of a particular convention of *reading*) in which the historical and political are displaced and/or repressed while a particular subjectivity emerges as the consequence of this narration of coming-into-health.

Russell Berman's discussion of literary institutions is descriptive of the function I am assigning "model minority discourse": "The term 'institution' . . . suggests the norms which define a hegemonic model of literature within a given cultural setting, i.e., a model that is by definition never identical with real practices but which constantly describes the borders of normalcy, thereby allowing for the possibilities of acceptance and transgression."[4] Instead of attempting to locate the "real practice" of Asian American writers, an endeavor that ultimately cannot account for the more complex and significant political unconscious nor for the larger issues of author function and social ideologies, I want to extrapolate the "normalizing" function of a discourse that bears a particular relationship to a larger set of social practices.

The prescribed route out of the ethnic subject's psychic impasse of "dual personality" evinces the production/retrieval of a specific interiority that absorbs ideological contradiction into one's Self, signaling its identification with, and in, the hegemonic. Model minority narratives constitute a specific model of assimilation, held to be the natural working out of the "ethnic dilemma," that reroutes social critique into introspective meditation. In much the same way that the model minority myth worked to place the responsibility for the minority subject's success or failure squarely within his or her personal "capabilities," so the logic of model minority discourse argues that an inward adjustment is necessary for the suture of the ethnic subject into an optimal position within the dominant culture.[5] In both cases the sociopolitical apparatuses that perpetuate material differences remain unchallenged and sometimes even fortified.

The role of Asian American narratives as vehicles for such notions of self-recovery is highly overdetermined, for in its discursive space the Asian American novel combines the introspective "ethnic gaze" (that sees in its self the root of both pain and cure), and the privatizing function of modern western novelistic discourse (which tracks the emergence of ego out of chaotic indistinction). Moreover, as a specifically "American" discourse, Asian American literature finds this novelistic phenomenon compounded by the "romantic" strain of American letters, which foregrounds the fulfillment of the individual's "destiny."[6]

Rob Wilson notes in American biographies a similar project which takes "American culture as a consensual adventure toward achieving states of freedom." As such, cultural production reproduces a particular socioeconomic ideology: "Any immigrant soon learns that 'America' comprises . . . a set of cash-value ideas that the self is enjoined to interiorize and, believing in, enact into a circular, self-fulfilling prophecy of liberal modernity in which the success-failure of the individual is metaphorically equated with the success-failure of 'America' itself."[7] Linking these points up with Asian American narrative, we might see the *ethnic* and *racial* problematic, which compromises and forces into contradiction the assimilation myth of America, neutralized in the resolution of Asian American novels, in any manner of forms. This success, as Wilson notes, redounds upon the nation. Thus, even in celebrating the acquisition of the Self, we find that this private self, whose constitution is the informing substance of the narrative's progress, is an eminently *conventional* recipient of identification—one learns what it is to be an individual through the negotiations of *this* prototype.

I am not positing any causal link between the new evocations of self-affirmative action and "model minority discourse," but rather discerning an overarching sociopolitical space of which these discourses are symptomatic—a space that accommodates each of these elements as complementary to its logic of contemporary American subjectivity. Most important, I want to argue that in model minority discourse we find the instantiation of a collective psychic identification that constructs a very specific concept of the negotiations between social trauma and private health, assigning the ways that minority subjects are to "mature" through achieving a specifically prescribed understanding of their place in the national community. Model minority discourse provides a particularly potent site of subject construction and ideological containment because it achieves its force from the fact that it *appears*, by dint of mobilizing "ethnic dilemmas," to be contestatory. Yet the sublation of ideological contradiction within the recuperative operations of individual "healing" vindicates the dominant ideology while rewarding the subject with a particular form of individual well-being freed from both the constraints of collectivity (that is, "I am no longer 'labeled as Asian American,' I am an *individual*") and its obligations ("I am my*self* first, and my 'Asian Americaness' only partially coincides with that Self, and I can access it at will"). In these discourses one sees examples of what Gramsci calls "common sense": "Common sense is not rigid and immobile but is continually transforming itself, enriching itself with scientific ideas and philosophical opinions which have entered ordinary life."[8] The temporality at which practical applications of common sense are aimed is precisely a future *happiness* promised to those who subscribe to certain attitudes regarding the way the world works—that is, hegemonic ideologies.[9] In model minority discourse and self-affirmative action, the route to happiness (that is, health) follows the path of a specific *bildung* that reinforces dominant notions of subjectivity.

The efficacy of the discourses I examine here in constructing and reproducing particular notions of subjectivity, their similar *pedagogical* functions (which will be discussed in more detail near the end of the essay), cannot be underestimated. The technologies of self underwritten here repeat the requisite initiations into the hegemonic, which operates effectively only when subordinated groups see their interests (protocols of self-formation) as aligned with it. In tracing the connections between the work ethic of self-affirmative action and model minority discourse's representation of healing, we can see the coincidence of these technologies of self with the hegemonic—the juncture of the interests of dominant ideologies in perpetuating a specific political economy and the interests of minority groups in attaching themselves successfully to the promise of upward mobility on the strength of inner conviction and self-help. Psychic, social, and economic well-being become one.[10]

Nevertheless, despite the overall skepticism that informs such conclusions, I would maintain that model minority discourse might not close off the potential for *subsequent* social action. That potential hinges upon a particular negotiation between the notion of the personal and the political. Here the work of bell hooks (especially in her *Sisters of the Yam*)[11] is suggestive. Hooks's contribution is notable for its attention to both personal recovery and institutional violence to the collective subject, and its sensitivity to their interrelatedness. The interstices between the personal and the political form a central problematic for minority discourse in the United States; the justification of progressive redefinitions of ethnicity, class, race, and gender lies largely in the practical application of energies derived from such redefinitions that can be deemed "political," that is, affecting social change. The problem lies in determining the particular relation of what is called the "personal" and political. For instance—does every assertion of a "reconstructed" minority subjectivity count as a political act, and, if so, how do we distinguish among the multiplicity of "political" acts? Is the "personal" indeed even available as an object of critique?[12]

If Asian Americans represent the model of assimilation to which other groups ought aspire, if their assimilation (as represented by and in the dominant culture) is the proper end point of ethnic mobility, and, finally, if the popularity of certain kinds of Asian American literature can be taken as indices to particular modes of narrating minority subjectivity and subject construction consistent with the model of minority assimilation, then such readings can serve as important sites of cultural critique. I will first outline the conjunction between the model minority concept and self-affirmative action. Then I analyze a number of Asian American literary texts for their relation to model minority discourse. Finally, I address the historical functions of reading Asian American texts in this particular mode, and conclude with a discussion of healing and minority discourse.

The self-affirmative action that informs the center of the model minority myth uses an exaggerated representation of Asians as embodying those "traditional family values" whose lack brought about the Los Angeles rebellion, according to Dan Quayle and the Bush administration.[13] This "independence" is a sign of recovery from racism, a generous (and highly pragmatic) gesture of leaving such issues aside. This valorization of self-affirming individualism and the use of Asian Americans as exemplary cases may be correlated with the more general de-politicized climate of the 1980s and 1990s. The rise of the cult of the Self during the Reagan/Bush era could only reinforce notions of self-affirmation assumed to take place on an unproblematic economic stage; and the various "movements" to do away with affirmative action and welfare in the 1990s simply confirm this trajectory. But it is crucial to see what had to be erased in order for that Self to be freed from all that limited its "potential." In short, this involved a serious re-thinking of social relations and ethics.

Both self-affirmative action and model minority discourse are predicated upon subsuming or erasing the political under the force of an idealized individ-uality that transcends the specificities of material history and underwrites an ideology that is seen to be timelessly true, valid, and ethical—individual hap-piness is only limited by one's own inner resources. What draws these two dis-courses together is the fact that both their cures either preempt or postpone confrontation with material (rather than "strictly personal") history. Everything moves inward, and in both cases that movement takes place in a particular act of *narration*.[14] This memory work involves a particular technology of the self. In each case, the liberating move is at once the sublation of the sociopolitical and the ascension of a subject made whole by its liberation from the historical and collective memory.[15] This pathologizing of racial individuals is endemic in American race relations; the jettisoning of ideological contradiction into the realm of a privatized individual psychology is consistent with American think-ing on race since the late 1930s. Adolph Reed, Jr., describes the influence of Myrdal's *An American Dilemma*, commissioned by the Carnegie Foundation in the late 1930s: "The key feature of the new regime of race relations were a rejec-tion of fundamental racial differences, a pro forma commitment to racial equal-ity as an ideal and an insistence on defining racism in individual, psychological terms rather than in relation to state action."[16]

The ethnic subject can only blame itself and a tradition of beliefs for what-ever alienation or lack of success he or she might find in America. It is crucial to note that from its early modern history, Asian American literature has been exploited to affirm dominant ideologies in this respect. Elaine Kim notes this model of self-incrimination and self-assertion with regard to the use of Asian American narratives during the post–World War Two period:

In 1950, *Fifth Chinese Daughter* helped popularize the notion that American racial minorities have only themselves to blame for lack of success in American life. Wong herself writes that members of racial minorities who try to blame social conditions for their difficulties are merely lazy. . . . Wong sings the praises of American opportunities and life, and attributes to her own individual effort her success here. Such a view, especially as expressed by a member of a racial minority group, was important in the post-war era, when charges of racial discrimination in the United States were circulating in developing countries, which, having recently been freed from colonial rule, were questioning the validity of American world leadership. The U.S. State Department, having already negotiated for the rights to publish *Fifth Chinese Daughter* into a number of Asian languages, arranged for Jade Snow Wong to be sent on a speaking tour in 1952 to forty-five Asian locales from Tokyo to Karachi, where she was to speak about the benefits of American democracy from the perspective of a Chinese American.[17]

Twenty years later, in the aftermath of the Watts riots, books such as Daniel Okimoto's *American in Disguise* (1971) and Jeanne Wakatsuki Houston and James D. Houston's *Farewell to Manzanar* (1973) were praised for similar evaluations of racial discrimination and social unrest. One critic noted that in Okimoto's novel "provocative ideas are expressed with such scholarly restraint that they may go unread in the current racial uproar," and another praised it for talking of "the Negro problem sympathetically and yet not without the racial pride of one from a subculture which always worked hard and had a devotion to education as a spur to achievement." Likewise, *Farewell to Manzanar* was praised for being "remarkably lacking in either self-pity or solemnity."[18] What is remarkable about the genesis of the novel in model minority discourse is the continued lack of sustained engagement with the agency that has prescripted this arena of disease and cure.

Now, this is not to say that issues of racism, sexism, and class distinction do not appear. In fact, to satisfy the conditions of minority literature, such issues are *required* to appear as pretexts for the elaboration of the "ethnic split," the "crisis of identity," and other elements of ethnic malaise, and to satisfy a liberal audience that these are not simply works by closet whites, that is, "inauthentic" ethnics. But model minority discourse resolves a personal crisis by finessing the political after providing the requisite amount of criticism of the nation. A classic instance of this is found in Okimoto's *American in Disguise*, when the author tells of his dilemma over whether or not to register for the draft during the Vietnam War: "How would I resolve the dilemma between my strong opposition to the Vietnam War, based upon the dictates of my conscience, as against the legal responsibility for each citizen to accept the obligations of citizenship no matter how inconvenient or distasteful?" (165).[19] The narrator proceeds to provide ample evidence of just how much he disapproves of the war, especially as he cites instance after instance of American racism against Asians and other racial minorities. Yet he finally decides to register: " . . . For all its faults, for the immensity of the gap between myth and reality, the United States still had many redeeming virtues; it was a nation to which I felt an instinctual allegiance" (168).

It is exactly this unexamined "instinct" that discloses the author's absorption of ideology, an instance eminently *cynical* in Žižek's terms: "The cynical subject is quite aware of the distance between the ideological mask and the social reality, but he none the less still insists upon the mask."[20] In other words, rather than debate issues of false consciousness, it may be more useful to focus upon the way Okimoto at once legitimates himself as a politically aware "ethnic author" and brackets all his criticism, which is superseded by an ultimate deferral to the "myth" of America—crucially, it is a myth much more pernicious than the one he seems to straightforwardly dismiss at the beginning of his rationalization.

Its perniciousness lies in the fact that it is more than the externally identified "myth" so easily debunked by social reality. It is rather the more deep-seated myth of America's ultimate justness *despite every social fact*. As such, the "mask" coincides ironically with the "disguise" Okimoto identifies as his Japanese face— it is a mask that persists and finally conquers the subject, as witnessed in the ways in which the subject *performs* ideology. This dramatic encounter is unusual; more commonly the dialogue between the dominant and the ethnic minority is, in model minority discourse, displaced upon such generic topoi as the "generation gap," the "coming to terms with a split identity." Rather than placing demands upon the dominant culture to account for itself, model minority discourse most often takes its own illness as a given, implacable part of its inherent nature, and retreats inward to diagnose itself.

Tracking the *historical* modifications of what I have been calling "model minority discourse" discloses the specificity of this discourse as it comments on the particulars of American cultural politics. The difference in the movement toward ethnic "enlightenment" in Maxine Hong Kingston's *The Woman Warrior* (1975) and in her later work, *Tripmaster Monkey* (1987), illustrates the operations of such narratives and the way model minority discourse, as a practice of reading and writing, must be historicized. *The Woman Warrior* begins with the famous injunction not to tell: "'You must not tell anyone,' my mother said, 'what I am about to tell you'" (3). From that moment on, however, the narrator proceeds to test that injunction and circumvent it; the resulting narration resembles in form the "memory work" of the recovery movement's renegotiating and retelling of the past:

> Whenever she had to warn us about life, my mother told stories that ran like this one, a story to grow on. She tested out strength to establish realities. Those in the emigrant generations who could not reassert brute survival died young and far away from home. Those of us in the first American generations have had to *figure out* how the invisible world the emigrants built around our childhoods fits in solid America [emphasis added]. (5)

In this "figuring out," a phrase that works well as a description of the tropic activities that take place as Maxine tries to adapt what is useful in her mother's stories to her American life, we find a brutal split between the China reconstructed as a kind of mythic "other world" and the mundane "solidity" of America. For example, while Kingston begins the novel with what promises to be a sustained attack on misogyny, when we arrive in America that attack is diluted and displaced. As Maxine herself notes, "My American life has been such a disappointment" (41). While here she is referring to the gap between her mother's expectations of her and her own achievements (saving a village versus getting all A's), the novel locates the possibilities for heroism in the mythic past and deflates political action in the present. Maxine refuses her employer's order to type up invitations to a banquet given in a restaurant that is being struck; she "marches to change the world at Berkeley" (47); but these isolated gestures pale before the heroism she feels is expected of her by her mother.

The most striking illustration of the sublimation of the political into the personal is the symbolic parallel drawn between the act of narrative vengeance of the Woman Warrior and that of the narrator, Maxine. The Woman Warrior becomes the embodiment of a communal moral imperative—upon her back are written the grievances of the people; her moment of revealing herself as a woman is coextensive with her articulation of those wrongs: "'Wherever you go, whatever happens to you, people will know *our* sacrifice,' my mother said. 'And you'll never forget either.' She meant that even if I got killed, the people could use my body for a weapon" (34). When she confronts the baron who has robbed and plundered her village, she rips off her shirt to show him her back, but his eyes are fixed upon a sign of her sex: "When I saw his startled eyes at my breasts, I slashed him across the face and on the second stroke cut off his head"

(44). At the end of the "White Tigers" chapter, Maxine likens herself to the Woman Warrior:

> The swordswoman and I are not so dissimilar. May my people understand the resemblance soon so that I can return to them. What we have in common are the words at our backs. . . . The reporting is the vengeance—not the beheading, not the gutting, but the words. And I have so many words—"chink" words and "gook" words too—that they do not fit on my skin. (53)

Here the narrator draws out the connection between the mythic grievances of the peasant class and the female sex in old China, and American racism. Yet the parallel act to this "reporting" in Maxine's American scenario evinces *not* a political and collective act of vengeance, but an interpersonal reckoning.

The Woman Warrior ends with the narrator negotiating the translation of Chinese myth to Chinese American solidity, reconciling herself to the absolute distance between the mythified past of China and the concreteness of American life by way of an adjustment of expectations and values, identities and potential. This moment takes place precisely as Maxine dares, however weakly, to talk back:

> Maybe because I was the one with the tongue cut loose, I had grown inside me a list of over two hundred things I had to tell my mother so that she would know the true things about me and to stop the pain in my throat. When I first started counting, I had had only thirty-six items: how I had prayed for a white horse of my own. . . . How I had picked on a girl and made her cry. How I had stolen from the cash register and bought candy for everybody I knew. How it was me who pulled up the onions in the garden out of anger. . . . (197)

We note here that the narrator is performing the act opposite to accusation—she is confessing her own sins. But this confessional has an important aspect of defiance in it—she challenges her mother to react, to exert her will. Most important, it is an attempt to find a place for herself: "If only I could let my mother know the list, she—and the world—would become more like me, and I would never be alone again" (198). The result of this reporting is precisely that coming-to-terms with not only her mother, but indeed, "the world," in *Maxine's* individual terms: through this confrontation, Maxine will work both a transformation of her mother, and, politically, the world itself: both will be remade in her image. This in turn will guarantee a new sociality to Maxine, who will never "be alone" in this new world. Most important, as I discussed above in Chapter 10 of this study, the novel consists of two different trajectories: the ascension of

Maxine as the new Asian American female subject is pegged to the decline of her mother's immigrant generation. As the former gains a voice, the latter's becomes demythified and muted. Kingston is not without sympathy for this, as we saw above, yet the direction that dominates this narrative is clear—to be American is to take on a specific individualist character.

This privatizing trajectory is found elsewhere: there is the suggestion that the reporting of crimes and collective grievances can only be done blindly and with incomplete knowledge—after all, how can Maxine *read* what is written on her back? In contrast to the mere display of a text she cannot read, Maxine's final act of articulation transforms her from reporter to author, from a collective agent to the private individual. The close of the novel is a moment of enlightenment in which all illusion and fear drop away. Through talking, she exorcises her demons:

> The very next day after I talked out the retarded man, the huncher, he disappeared. I never saw him again or heard what became of him. Perhaps I made him up, and what I once had was not Chinese-sight at all but child-sight that would have disappeared eventually without such a struggle. The throat pain always returns, though, unless I tell what I really think, whether or not I lose my job, or spit out gaucheries all over a party. I've stopped checking "bilingual" on job applications. (205)

Whereas the Woman Warrior's speech is a communal grievance at oppressive exploitation, this counter-discourse manifests Maxine's "coming to terms" in a way that is ultimately the result of her own self-healing.

Finally, issues of race and ethnicity are cast in doubt by a supposition that this "ghost" was simply the product of the *universal* experience of childhood, and as such, could have been resolved in the simple passing of time. The "ghosts" of her childhood then, conceived in the mythic shadows of her mother's China, are exorcized, but so too are the politically identified issues of feudal oppression and sexist violence. Like the phantom "huncher" in the world of American individualism, they are normalized by being *translated* into personal terms. The seamless subjectivity achieved here is manifested in the act of rejecting the "bilingual" split, or the need to admit one's (imperfect) bipolarity, and in the declaration of monolingualism (that is, subjectivity as evinced in language, words that are not heteroglossic but now recuperated into an idiom of wholeness). In the "translation" of the "Song for a Barbarian Reed Pipe," the language of origin is that of the conflicted, ghostly remnants of tales of China; the "target" language appropriates those forms but casts them in the light of a young Chinese American woman's self-fashioning.

The "reports" that bracket the novel clearly show a transition from the explicitly and militantly collective politics of class and gender to the overriding logic of personal healing that sets those issues into the amber of a higher imperative. The ascension of the personal overshadows those concerns and makes them components of the personal that can be readjusted and defused by the agile manuevering of psychic, rather than materially constituent, forces. This is made possible only by the narrator's act of "talking" out the grievances repressed by her intimidation before her mother's supposed wholeness. Maxine has verbally negotiated her own terms of selfhood.

The monologue in which this "memory work" takes place is strikingly different from the one that informs Kingston's second novel, *China Men*, which was begun simultaneously with *Woman Warrior*. In that text, Kingston inscribes memory work deeply in Chinese American history, from the nineteenth century to the days of the Vietnam War, and sees the production of individuals within collective and national histories. The same attention to public history ends her third novel, *Tripmaster Monkey*. At the end of *Tripmaster*, we find a monologue articulated by Wittman Ah Sing, the protagonist of the novel, an emblem of 1960s community activism. His long speech (some thirty-three pages) is a critique of American racism and imperialism, and a meditation on notions of multicultural communities and activism. In short, Wittman comes to politicized terms that resemble more the articulation of grievances of the Woman Warrior, rather than the "reporting" of Maxine that furnishes *The Woman Warrior* with its closure. And this, along with the dense interjection of history and cultural politics *into* the personal accounts for both the latter novel's power and, I would argue, may in part account for its relative lack of success among a readership that expects a quite different formula. It is most telling that Whitman delivers his speech to a *community audience* and stages himself as part of that community, while Maxine's audience consists solely of her mother. Both Maxine and Wittman are ultimately left alone after their respective enunciations, but the trajectories marked out for them differ significantly. Maxine is posed on the threshold of an individual subjectivity that knows no preexisting labels—it is declared as a unique and irrepeatable Self; Wittman, on the other hand, is to become a pacifist and antiwar activist, that is, he will conjoin his subjectivity to a social collective formation. It is intensely ironic, and a comment on the logic of cultural production within history, that Kingston's retrospective of the 1960s (*Tripmaster Monkey*) invests its healing operations in collective politics, while her first "novel" (*The Woman Warrior*), written in a time more proximate to the period, holds politics at arm's length, skeptical as Kingston was of the political rhetoric of the time.

If *Tripmaster Monkey* sets itself up as a politicized revision of history, Amy Tan's *Joy Luck Club* represents a return, with some modification, to the discourse of inward healing found in Kingston's narrative. Tan's novel differs from *The Woman Warrior* on a number of points. Most important, its narrative strategy distributes the memory work among a set of mother/daughter pairs, creating an impression of a complex and comprehensive inventory of inter-generational Chinese-American relations. Yet at base it merely updates the narrative motivations and resolutions of Kingston's earlier novel. Issues of class, I would argue, appear as developments of a contemporary narrative of Asian America that ultimately serve to complement and underscore (in however complicated a fashion), rather than displace or challenge, the mother/daughter differential. Mother/daughter understanding in fact is even less ideologically embedded in Tan's novel—where Kingston strives to address issues of cultural identity and categories, Tan's novel, perhaps because it disperses its problematic across these multiple pairs, is less focused on the general and more upon a resolutely bourgeois individual ideology that derives its power from sameness disguised and made more attractive as multiplicity.[21]

The resolution of *The Joy Luck Club* takes place only as the various personae recognize their individual traumas as the products of particular intergenerational and intercultural gaps, gaps that supersede other considerations or causalities. We remember that the Joy Luck Club's genesis is, after all, written against the backdrop of the Sino-Japanese War. Refusing to give in to despair, the response to war and famine is to convert one's inner world:

> We decided to hold parties and pretend each week had become the new year. Each week we would forget past wrongs done to us. We weren't allowed to think a bad thought. We feasted, we laughed, we played games, lost and won. . . . And each week we would hope to be lucky. That hope was our only joy. And that's how we came to call our little parties Joy Luck. (12)

While fighting madness with madness is a commonplace trope, what is troubling in *The Joy Luck Club* is that this mentality becomes transposed uncritically to a radically different political and cultural context. The cynicism and hopelessness in the face of war brings forth a psychic adjustment that cannot be correlated with the daughters' situation in the United States without opening several problematic issues. Interestingly, the mothers of the novel are endowed, despite such a traumatic past (or perhaps because of it), with a will and energy that surpasses the capacities of their daughters, debilitated as they are by the unfinished business of personal coming-into-being.

As counter-examples to this kind of narrative closure, I will briefly mention two lesser-known Asian American texts. Milton Murayama's *All I Asking For Is My Body* (1959) casts an entirely different light on the ideas of hope, luck, and individual recuperation. This novel's ending appears to echo the formula of ethnic self-help — the protagonist's family has inherited a huge debt, and as workers on a Hawaiian sugar plantation, there seems little chance that they will ever pay it off. The protagonist enlists in the Army at the beginning of the Second World War, and hits upon a formula for playing craps. He wins the six thousand dollars needed to pay off the debt and frees his family from this overwhelming burden. What better example of self-motivation? Yet the context of the novel problematizes such a reading.

It locates the "debt" squarely within the convergence between an anachronistic and corrupt Japanese system of obligation and an exploitative American capitalist labor system that disallows any accumulation of savings and deploys uneven wage scales to set different ethnic groups against one another. The intergenerational conflict here is inscribed within a cultural and political economy that negotiates parent/child relations in terms of bodies and their capacity for labor, which is seen to produce wages that are in turn seen not as sustenance, but as money that will go to pay off the debt. Nevertheless, this money is never accumulated simply because the labor / living wage ratio is too unbalanced — the family can only proceed to get themselves deeper and deeper into debt. The only way out of this explicitly historicized contradiction is therefore left to chance, for a faith in the moral and economic logic of hard work is absolutely deconstructed. But even attempting to read the ending as an endorsement of self-motivation fails, since the protagonist is caught padding the dice and must trust everything to "chance." Thus what appears to be cosmic justice can equally be read as a cynical reflection on the devastating double contradiction between the political and labor economy of American capitalism and an ethical Japanese tradition made absolutely exploitative in its displaced context in America: the only way out is through "divine intervention."

Another example of an Asian American literary text that refuses to attempt to elide historical materialism for the thematics of individual transcendence is Janice Mirikitani's poem, "Breaking Silence," in which the act of speaking is an eminently collective act.[22] Mirikitani sets up two discursive registers in this poem — one, "lyrical" and poetic, presents the poet's voice, embedding the second — her mother's testimony before the Commission on Wartime Relocation and Internment of Japanese American civilians. These two strains, lyrical and prosaic, philosophic and emotive, become entwined in the course of the poem, which ends with a recognition that the poet's voice and her mother's are fused in a common identity particularized by history:

> We are lightning and justice.
> Our souls become transparent like glass
> revealing tears for war-dead sons
> red ashes of Hiroshima
> jagged wounds from barbed wire.
> We must recognize ourselves at last
> We are a rainforest of color
> and noise.
> We hear everything.
> We are unafraid.
> Our language is beautiful.

The "language" shared is exactly that language which joins the personal and the political, refusing to attempt to detach one from the other. The "transparency" of their souls is achieved by the splitting apart of the subjective "shell" that prevents the minority subject from articulating a *collective* grievance against the state.[23]

While it may seem simply a matter of the prerogative of creative writers to write as they wish, the importance of model minority discourse to the containment of minority discourse cannot be overemphasized. Not only does such literature serve as a "model" for minorities, it also both represents Asian Americans in a particularly paradigmatic fashion and presents a subject whose suture into the larger symbolic of dominant ideologies solicits a particularly strong identification from a *general* audience predisposed to seeing in this recovery a displaced image of its own ideological presumptions. Thus, model minority discourse reproduces specific minority subject positions within the hegemonic, reinforces the dominant culture's notions of model minorities (and by extension, negative impressions of those recalcitrant "other" minorities), and underwrites a larger ideology of individuation. Ultimately, the *pedagogical* function of model minority discourse is its most significant aspect.[24]

Habits of Reading

In her history of Asian American literature, Elaine Kim provides a brief but tremendously provocative anecdote. A friend of Kim's was presented with a copy of *The Woman Warrior*. The bestower exclaimed that, having read the novel, she finally understood her friend.[25] Somehow Kingston's novel had the power to explain human beings in a way that direct personal contact could not. In its particular discourse the novel provided a mode of understanding that surpasses and can even stand in for human relations. What about that text allowed it to achieve such a potent reality effect? Here we have an exemplary case of the predisposition to read popular Asian American texts according to particular psychosocial needs. Somehow, the woman was inaccessible to her friend in some essential way; somehow that novel made "her" accessible and present to her friend. In short, the text *made sense*. My point here is that the sense was immanent in the reading. It has animated exactly the expected themes of subject-split, cultural alienation and confusion, and coming-to-terms that fits the stereotypical image of the model minority. Most important, the way that the narrative negotiates its healing is consistent with the model minority subject's construction.

The perpetuation of the marketing of Asian American literature as the literature of an assimilated group now at peace after a "phase" of adjustment is dangerous in its powerful closing-off of a multiplicity of real, lived, social contradictions and complexities that stand outside (or at least significantly complicate) the formula of the highly individuated "identity crisis." Not only do representations of the model minority obfuscate these complexities, the identification of Asian Americans via the representation of a narrow group of Asians in America finds confirmation in the readings of redemption found in works that are now set forth as the representative texts of Asian American literature.[26] For example, *Time* magazine offers us an essay tellingly entitled, "Fresh Voices Above the Noisy Din" (June 3, 1991, pages 66–67). It lauds the new works by Gish Jen, David Wong Louie, Gus Lee, and Amy Tan (all *Chinese* American authors). These "voices" are not only heard, but given substantial advances on their novels because, according to Jen's publisher, Seymour Lawrence, "They're second generation, and they're better educated and ready to tell about their experiences." From that pronouncement, we can extrapolate what the "noisy din" is — those uneducated, unassimilated, agrammatical writers ignored and marginalized by the culture industry. In other words, those voices that do not reproduce the conventions of healing. On the other hand, literary texts by the "fresh voices" are received as "New works . . . [that] splendidly illustrate the frustrations, humor and eternal wonder of the immigrant's life." Now obviously this rhetoric is meant to sell books—the question is, how does this discourse work? On what presumptions does it rely?

Here we mark the collusion between the rhetoric of healing and the discourse of advertising that is applied to the marketing of Asian American literature that at once exploits its "exotic" potential and conflates that exoticism into a universalized narrative of "immigration" (put at a distance by focusing on the "educated" second-generation writer's representations of immigration) in order to elide problematic historical specificities. The co-presence of a defamiliarized, exotic narrative and an identifying regimen of interpretation is also the key element linking model minority discourse to the imagination of self-affirmation psychology. Interestingly, the recent hysteria over "illegal Chinese immigrants" has forced a radical reassessment and repoliticization of the representation of the "Asian immigrant." Some argue this hysteria foretells a return of anti-Asian sentiment in a time of economic crisis. This issue promises to intensify the tension between the bourgeoisified, "assimilated" class of Asian Americans and recent immigrants and to demand a rethinking of the inscription of the ethos of the model minority. Asians as the model minority now come into contradiction with Asians who, within the context of a post-Fordist late capitalism, have helped place the "native" U.S. economy in crisis by either economic "aggression" (Japan or the East Asian "tigers") or illegal infiltration (thereby glutting the labor pool and draining the welfare state).

An audience situated within a deeply depoliticized, inward-turning United States wherein thousands seek to recover their "inner child" while others are told that *only* their lack of character (brought about by an *inherited* dependency on welfare and affirmative action) prevents them from realizing their full human potential, can find in model minority discourse a displaced, defamiliarized, and mythically amplified re-enactment of their own struggle.[27] For example, instead of a mother with a particular, localized past, they have a mythologized mother with the weight of Chinese tradition behind them. Sexual oppression takes the form of an entire race of *necessarily* misogynistic Asian men, spawned as they were by the arch-patriarch Confucius. But at the end of the novel the trauma recedes into the fictional. Here we can see that cathartic (and politically disengaging) emptying-out-of-self-through-identification of which Brecht speaks. Most significant, however, is the fact that in this case, the identification is *complemented* by a certain estrangement. One can identify with the Asian American protagonist largely because of its honorific status as model minority.

Yet that Asian American is made attractive by its particular mode of narrative—it is exoticized, mythified, essentially weak yet resolutely determined to liberate itself.

One short but extremely telling example can serve to illustrate how model minority discourse coincides with a set of social discourses. In a 1991 talk at Stanford, Gus Lee explained that his Chinese-American editor asked him to remove a chapter from *China Boy* and put in its place a chapter in which the protagonist, a young boy, is invited to a gathering of the Chinatown clan elders. Lee said he had never heard of such a thing, and asked his editor if he himself had. No, replied his editor, but it would make a better read. Lee thus wrote in a chapter in which the boy not only is invited by the elders, but placed at the center of their ceremony, and toasted as the new generation:

> My uncle coughed discreetly, and cleared his throat. "Tonight, we meet the new hope of China," he said, using his dramatic poet's voice. "A boy with a Kiangsu father who works for Amethyst Jade Cheng. With an American stepmother who went to Smith College. . . . But this toast is to all of us. We are wood, my brothers. We are sinewy, old wood, old trunks, with fading limbs and few leaves! Right? Is it not so? . . . We were all born in the nineteenth century. We are men of the past age. This little boy . . . is our memory. . . . We drink to the boy . . . because we have our youth back for a night. Ha! When would we have ever *stood* for a child back in the Middle Kingdom? *Never!* But here, we have only the memory of what a child represents to us. We ask him to remember us, and thank him for being our collective Only Son. *Gambei*, Before Borns!"[28]

This is a highly idealized, and, as even the uncle himself puts it, far-fetched scene, yet its imaginative logic fits perfectly with the model minority narrative. The elders have *recognized* the ascension of the child; the child has found a place to be both child and adult, China has been founded in America, but only as a memory. The past is confronted and recognized for its pastness; the new age is heralded (we may note how this replicates the double trajectory found in *Woman Warrior*). The new individual receives the ultimate recognition of his coming-into-being—his ascension over his cultural past. The past is *collective* and moribund (signaled in the calculatedly misleading translation of *xiansheng* ("prior-born"; that is, "elder," but a common honorific, "sir") as "before born," that is, born in a time before the valorized present. Here we find the conversion of respect into pity (the past is pathetic, the present the term of value). The present (America), *unique* and vital, now has the ultimate power of life or death over the past (China)—the elders ask his indulgence for their survival *in memory*.

It is easy to see the psychological function of this revision of ceremony for the old men; what is less obvious is the way this revision elevates the "boy" in precisely the terms we have been discussing. In an almost suicidal articulation, the older generation graciously invites and views the spectacle of its own death, and the emergence of a new age youth from these ruins. Lee has willfully killed off the past (despite all his own experience of it) in order to script a satisfying recitation of its weakness.[29] The result of this process of subjectivization is an eminently healthy individual, cured of the residual effects of history and politics, ready to meet the modern world. As such, he becomes a compelling object of identification. If the tendency of Asian American novels is to close by asserting that the healing of the protagonist's wounds is made possible only through these kinds of acts of psychic adjustment, acts that leave the ideological questions and contradictions of the social space bracketed out, then what we have is the recapitalization of the dominant ideology's stock of belief. Obviously, this dynamic is not confined to ethnic narrative—western narrative in general signals the emergence of individuality from the group; what I am most concerned about are the consequences of such a formula superimposed upon the *racial* and *ethnic*, especially as they pertain to the historical and political.

Now one could argue that I am reading model minority discourse *into* these narratives, and doing them a great disservice. While this criticism is more appropriate to some texts than others, I am more interested in the ways that the most popular Asian American novels lend themselves to such readings and the way such readings have become highly conventionalized and disseminated. The crucial point is that a mode of creating, marketing, and interpreting Asian American literature has emerged that lends itself to these prescribed formations and installs both a particular pedagogy for Asian Americans and a way of "reading" race in America. Another criticism has been that I have devalued the "personal." I have nothing against personal growth and well-being, nor against the fulfillment of "potential." I am suspicious, however, of two things: first, the almost automatic acceptance of the "fact" that all Asian Americans are victims of this particularly reified identity crisis. I want to ask why and how we accept this condition *so constructed* as a necessary fact. It is not clear to me that the formula as it has evolved (the hyphenated state, intergenerational misunderstandings, cultural alienation), *particularly* constructed and evenly distributed among all Asian Americans, is (or should be) a *predominant* concern for all Asian Americans, given quite different historical contingencies. I wonder how this prescribed illness serves particular discursive purposes; I also wonder about the unproblematized flattening out of the notion of "potential" across a range of different socioeconomic, political, ethnic, and racial situations.

The Personal, The Political, the Line In-Between

I have tried not to use prescribed definitions of "personal" or "political," but rather let my analysis illustrate the parameters of both as they apply to this specific case. Roughly speaking, I have reserved the "personal" to describe that psychic space that fixes upon a notion of selfhood foregrounding individuality and considering its construction in social history to be something to be transcended. This transcendence is *qualitatively different* from a liberation from oppressive hegemonic identifications. The "personal," as I use the term, seeks out a space for its "freedom" *within* the logic of the hegemonic—in fact, it identifies with it precisely because it views the dominant ideology as fostering, rather than suppressing, individual initiative.

For "political" I have in mind a collective social practice that engages individual action with an aim of appropriating, reconfiguring, or deconstructing the hegemonic. In this respect, it is contestive on a larger scale than individual complaint or grievance. This distinction is similar to Deleuze and Guattari's "second characteristic" of a minor literature:

> The second characteristic of minor literatures is that everything in them is political. In major literatures, in contrast, the individual concern (familial, marital, and so on) joins with other no less individual concerns, the social milieu serving as a mere environment or a background. . . . Minor literature is completely different; its cramped space forces each individual intrigue to connect immediately to politics. The individual concern thus becomes all the more necessary, indispensible, magnified, because a whole other story is vibrating within it. In this way, the family triangle connects to other triangles—commercial, economic, bureaucratic, juridical—that determine its values.[30]

While one might argue over this rather rough distinction, my concern here is with the ways that model minority discourse may be deemed "minor" for its appeal to issues of race and ethnicity, *even as* its narrative logic results in a denial of both as ultimately determinative of subjectivity, relegating such concerns to a lesser position of importance, even to the extent that they are seen as obstacles to the individual's well-being. That is, the "minor" *slides back* into the dominant.

In the case of *The Woman Warrior*, we can see both these facets. Published in the mid-1970s, the novel was a landmark in both ethnic and women's literature. Although its author denied that she had written the book with a "feminist" or "ethnic" message in mind (rather, she said, such perceptions on the part of readers were the result of the fact that such topics were in the air at the time), the novel became a rallying call to "break silence." Feminists saw in the novel a sustained critique of misogyny; ethnic critics saw a critique of racism; but most important, perhaps, was the formulation of the notion that "pain is political." From this necessary and enabling moment, however, there was little critique of the parameters of either pain or politics.[31] Instead, in the eighties and nineties that followed (and during which the novel has not ceased to be popularized, even more so than any subsequent work by Kingston), what one finds is chaotic attempts to calibrate pain and politics.

A similar blurring of distinctions and degree occurs when ethnic literature is seen as constitutively contestive and its effects guaranteed, and, more important, when its relation to the dominant hegemony is glossed over or dismissed too readily. Instead, we find a valorization of ethnic individuals now empowered by the very "fact" of being "minor." This can lead to a situation in which minority individuals become the repositories of a reified "difference." Chandra Talpade Mohanty writes forcefully of the collusion of this movement toward individuation and neoconservative politics:

> There has been an erosion of the politics of collectivity through the reformulation of race and difference in individualistic terms. . . . The 1960s and 1970s slogan "The personal is political" has been recrafted in the 1980s as "The political is personal." In other words, all politics is collapsed into the personal, and questions of individual behaviors, attitudes, and lifestyles stand in for political analysis of the social . . . this process of the individualization of race and its effects dovetails rather neatly with the neoconservative politics and agenda of the contemporary United States government.[32]

My argument has been that model minority discourse has provided a blueprint for the deliverance of minority subjects from collective history to a reified individualism. The problematic addressed in this essay might be located in the predication of minority subjectivity into a counterhegemonic politics. This negotiation is, unfortunately, obscured by the proliferation of supposedly contestatory acts. Furthermore, even if we accept the notion of such identifications, we have yet to ascertain the necessarily contestive nature of acts predicated upon such subjectivities—that is, because I'm oppressed do my actions necessarily un-oppress me, or anyone else, or is that simple act already loaded with "contesta-tory" implications?[33] Ultimately, we have yet to arrive at a satisfactory theory of culture's effect on politics.

In model minority discourse, the personal/political (collective) opposition is fractured (but not broken), precisely because of the ideological doubleness mentioned above—the model minority text is both "political" in the sense that it appeals to its subject's status as "minority," and yet it is "personal" to the de-gree that it reinscribes that minor status as emergent only insofar as the individ-ual ethnic subject transcends its subalternity. The critical question remains as to the site of relocation and the resulting positionality of the subject. There is no clear answer to these questions of the personal and the political. If we can take the case of model minority discourse, it is precisely because of this that minor-ity discourse's containment and its utopian potential are both present at once.

Reference Material

Notes

Introduction

1. The "availability" of Chinese labor should be understood within the context of the Opium Wars of the mid-nineteenth century, that modern crisis of western imperialism and geopolitical interests in East Asia.

Chapter 1: Pacific America

1. See Connery's contextualizations of this quote in his two essays. In January and February of 1938, Christy published two essays in this journal arguing for the study of "intercultural relations" between American and Asia.

2. Arrell Gibson, *Yankees in Paradise*, chap. 17.

3. Quoted in Zinn, 306.

4. R. E. Park, *Race and Culture*, 246.

5. See essays by Paul and Matthews for studies of the social science discourses on nineteenth-century immigration from Asia.

6. Densch, 219.

7. See J. Chang, "Local Knowledges," for a discussion of this topic.

8. R. E. Park, *Race and Culture*, 228.

9. Hunt, 227. See his chapter in the effects of Chinese exclusion in U.S. China policy, pp. 227–57.

10. Haller, 153. See Handlin, chap. 5, for a critique of the Commission's work.

11. Haller, 153f.

12. This phenomenon bears a striking resemblance to the representation of the working class in the first half of the nineteenth century in Paris. Balibar notes:

> There forms the phantasmatic equation of "labouring classes" with "dangerous classes," the fusion of a socioeconomic category with an anthropological and moral category, which will

serve to underpin all the variants of sociobiological (and also psychiatric) determinism, by taking pseudo-scientific credentials from the Darwinian theory of evolution, comparative anatomy and crowd psychology, but particularly by becoming invested in a tightly knit network of institutions of social surveillance and control. (Balibar, "Class Racism," 209)

13. Konvitz, 14. All further references to Konvitz in this section are placed in text within parentheses.

14. Cited in Corwin, 19.

15. McDougall, quoted in Haller, 162. Some might say that the caste system was informally already in effect.

16. See Martin, *Flexible Bodies*, 28ff. Claude Lefort notes the deployment of such imagery by totalitarian regimes:

At the foundation of totalitarianism lies the representation of the People-as-One . . . the constitution of the People-as-One requires the incessant production of enemies. . . . The enemy of the people is regarded as a parasite or a waste product to be eliminated. . . . What is at stake is always the integrity of the body. It is as if the body had to assure itself of its own identity by expelling its waste matter, or as if it had to close in upon itself by withdrawing from the outside, by averting the threat of an intrusion by alien elements. . . . The campaign against the enemy is feverish; fever is good, it is a signal, within society, that there is some evil to combat. (Lefort, 297f)

Quoted in Martin, "Toward an Anthropology of Immunology," 421. I am indebted to Herman Beavers for recommending these works to me.

For a study of the legal history of this topic, see Colker.

17. Quoted in Haller, 146.

18. See Madison Grant.

19. Haller, 68.

20. Frederick S. Crum, "The Decadence of the Native American Stock," quoted in Haller, 79.

21. Quoted in Haller, 148.

22. In Carlson and Colburn, 342f.

23. Bellah, 181. Photograph in Marzio, 373. I thank David Goldberg for referring me to this photograph.

24. Gelderman, 56f.

25. Cros, 141.

26. Kevles, 111f.

27. An entire sanitorium and community was founded by Kellogg (famous now mostly for his corn flakes), who invented electroshock machines to prevent masturbation and who counseled against sexual gratification. See Boyle.

28. Kevles notes: "In 1936, the University of Heidelberg voted an honorary degree of medicine to Harry Laughlin . . . Laughlin, who accepted the degree . . . wrote to the Heidelberg authorities that he took the award not only as a personal honor but also as 'evidence of a common understanding of German and American scientists of the nature of eugenics'" (118). (In 1933 Hitler's cabinet had promulgated a Eugenic Sterilization Law.)

29. In Kevles, 110f.

30. Osumi, 15.

31. Sucheng Chan, *Asian Americans*, 47.

32. R. E. Park, "Our Racial Frontier on the Pacific." In *Race and Culture*, 252. Essay originally appeared in *Survey Graphic* 9 (May 1926): 192–96.

33. Kawakami, 39.

34. See E. F. Wong, 80, 117. This of course was the beginning of Japan's notion of an "East Asia Co-Prosperity Sphere," which we will address specifically in Chap. 10.

35. Obviously Park is not endorsing Japanese imperialism, but rather pointing to the complexity and strength of this "process" that links race to geopolitics.

36. R. E. Park, 151.

37. See S. Chan, *Asian Americans*, Okihiro, *Margins*, Takaki, *Iron Cages*, for histories of these acts.

38. Hing, 19. See also 47–71, for the effects of these laws during the 1930s and 1940s upon the Asian populations in the U.S.

39. E. F. Wong, 103; see Moy, 87f.

40. Isaacs, 103.

41. Melendy, 61.

42. Osumi, 19. Osumi presents a comprehensive view of anti-miscegenation laws and Asians in California.

43. Isaacs, 42, 44.

44. Ibid., 100.

45. See Gossett, chapter 7.

46. And it is this fear that haunts the model minority myth.

47. Richard Austin Thompson, 185.

48. These citations come from Isaacs, 101f.

49. Balibar, "Class Racism," in Balibar and Wallerstein, 211.

50. Quoted in Martin, 28f.

51. Takaki, *Iron Cages*, 236.

52. Ibid., 248.

53. Melendy, 195.

54. Isaacs, 357.

55. For an excellent study of this case, see Lyman, "Marginalizing the Self." Lyman shrewdly probes the discursive strategies of creating "color." See also Ian Haney Lopez. I thank Professor Lopez for our conversations on this topic during our stay at the Stanford Humanities Center.

56. In *Re: Sadar Bhawab Singh*, 246 Fed. 496 (1917). Quoted in Jensen, 255.

57. Jensen, 258.

58. Buaken, 169.

59. Posadas, cited in Okihiro, *Margins*, 54.

60. See DeWitt.

61. DeWitt, 49–69.

62. Catapusan, 174.

63. See Puette.

64. In W. C. Smith, *Americans in Process*, xi.

Chapter 2: Bodies and Souls

1. See Tu Wei-ming, "A Confucian Perspective," 29.

2. Rohmer, 15.

3. The issue of Bragg's funding should not be missed, as today Congressional hearings probe the issue of "foreign" contributions from Asian Americans to the 1996 Presidential campaign.

4. Wu, *Yellow Peril*, 35.

5. Rohmer, 299.

6. Richard Austin Thompson, 423.

7. In *Daughter of Fu Manchu* (1931) and *Fu Manchu's Bride* (1933), Rohmer fixes on the subject of racial hybridity.

8. One appreciates Cruso's anticipation of 1970s Japan bashing.

9. For a historical disquisition on racial hybridization and the state, see Vasconcelos.

10. In Goldstein, Israel, et al., 132–47.

11. Hawley, 141f.

12. See Hom, "Chinatown Literature," for a study of Asian American literature of this period.

13. For the relation of leftist political activism and the Chinese working class, see R. Yu.

14. For overseas Chinese nationalistic activities, see L. Ling-chi Wang, "Roots," 192f.

15. Capra, 140.

16. McBride, 281.

17. Lyman Van Slyke, in a personal communication, suggests that Yen may be derived from Yan Xishan, a warlord who ruled Shansi province. See Gillin, 1967.

18. See Spence, *The Search for Modern China*, 393.

19. Capra conspicuously signals the relationship between Yen's demise and the West: the tea is prepared in a western-style pot and cermamic cup.

20. Marchetti, *Romance and the "Yellow Peril,"* 50.

21. Capra, 485.

22. Mulvey, 59. See also Mulvey's later elaboration of this essay, also in Penley, "Afterthoughts on 'Visual Pleasure and Narrative Cinema'."

23. See Gaines, and also Browne.

24. Staiger, 20.

25. For these figures and other historical data used, see Spence, *The Search for Modern China*, 382.

26. See Griswold for a discussion of how the invasion and colonization of the Philippines at the turn of the century signaled a new Far Eastern policy. Hunt (182) notes the particular relationship between the annexation and Far East policy: "Control of territory adjacent to China improved the American claim to a voice in China's ultimate disposition, while a Philippine naval base put Washington in a better position to back that claim." The specifically neocolonial aspect of this leverage is also clear: "The next logical step in an independent policy might have been to take a slice out of Chinese terri-

tory. But McKinley publicly proclaimed in December 1898 that that was a step the United States would not take. Though coastal China might fall under foreign control, he confidently predicted that somehow the 'vast commerce' and 'large interests' of the United States would be preserved without departing from traditional policy and without the United States becoming 'an actor in the scene'." Nevertheless, the possibility of U.S. annexing territory was always present.

27. Griswold, 3f.

28. Ibid., 380f. I do not mean to suggest that the specific program of U.S. imperialism in Asia is set in the late nineteenth century; rather, that a posture that commits the U.S. to a neocolonialist project is taken.

29. Spence, 353.

30. Griswold, 386ff.

31. Spence, 352.

32. Ibid., 353f.

33. For example, the events of April 1927 were seen by Stalin to confirm his reading of the internal politics of the KMT under Chiang Kai-shek. See Spence, 354.

34. Cited in Israel, "Carl Crow, Edgar Snow, and Shifting American Journalistic Perceptions of China," 151. For a contextualization of Crow's writings, see MacKerras, chap. 5.

The allure of China as a mass market and the ideological effectiveness of commodity culture seems a permanent fixture in American ideology. In October 1996 retired Army General Colin Powell noted, "If you give 1.3 billion Chinamen access to home-shopping on television, communism is over, because there is no way communism can compete with a salad shooter for $9.95" (Associated Press Newswire, Oct. 7, 1996).

35. Crow, *Foreign Devils*, 326.

36. Spence, 385.

37. Hunt, 258.

38. MacKerras, 77.

39. Willis, 94.

40. Turner, 105.

41. See, for example, his *L'Analyse du film*.

42. Fiske, quoted in Gina Marchetti, "Ethnicity and Cultural Studies," 283.

43. See Jespersen for an interesting study of how events in China were "produced" for American consumption, and Winks's and Rush's collection for essays on fictional representations. Both studies emphasize the various mediations and politics of presenting Asia to the American public during this period.

44. Isaacs, 51f; see also 167f.

45. See Marchetti, *Romance and the Yellow Peril*, 54. Josselyn Marsh also pointed out, in a personal communication, the echoes of Griffith's *Broken Blossoms*.

46. Marchetti, ibid. 54.

47. Capra, 141.

48. The process of transforming the white into the Asian can be taken as an allegory of a nearly masochistic endeavor to master the negotiation between Asia and America. In later years, Hollywood became fixated with just how much it could achieve the

"desired Oriental shape." Eugene Franklin Wong cites a detailed description of the "advanced" techniques used to transform Shirley Maclaine into a geisha in a film (*My Geisha*) that explicitly thematizes the ability of a white to pass as Asian:

> The technicians mixed a batch of dental plaster—a highly refined and smooth type of plaster of Paris—and poured it into the wax impression [of Maclaine's eyes]. When that hardened, we removed the wax and had a perfect reproduction of the top half of the familiar Maclaine face. It was on this model that we then proceed to work with modeling clay, curving the eye to the desired Oriental shape. Through another series of wax impressions and dental-plaster castings, we were finally able to bake rubber eyepieces fashioned from the clay additions we had sculpted into the plaster reproduction of her upper face.
>
> These complicated procedures took four days, at the end of which time [Wally] summoned Shirley back to the lab. [He] glued on the eye-pieces with spirit gum, and to give the eyes a further slant [he] glued an invisible flesh-colored plastic tab to the skin near each of her temples. Rubber bands, attached to the tabs and hooked together at the top of her head, under a concealed wig, pulled up the corners of her eyes. With brown contact lenses obscuring her bright blue eyes, Shirley looked as Oriental as the Japanese Empress. (42–43)

49. *Variety* 17 (Jan. 1933).

50. Priscilla Wald (personal communication) points out that Asther's "yellow face" can be contrasted to Megan's partial transformation into May-li in the film's diegesis. Crucially, in both cases this "transformation" is partial, and discloses in stereoscopic fashion both the image aspired to and the traces of the former identity. Wald points out that Capra says Asther doesn't appear Caucasian, which is different from saying that he appears Asian.

51. Spence, 387f. See also Isaacs, 155f. For Pearl Buck, see Peter Conn, *Pearl S. Buck: A Cultural Biography* (Cambridge: Cambridge University Press, 1996).

52. See Isaacs, 79, for interviews with Americans who stated they preferred to see Asians in books and films, rather than encounter them in reality.

53. In James, 123.

54. Ibid., 127.

55. Althusser, 28f.

56. Jameson, *Political Unconscious*, 56.

Chapter 3: Written on the Face

1. Bryan Turner, 190. See also the essays collected in Featherstone et al. for a useful set of meditations on the sociology of the body. Among other things, this anthology connects recent scholarship with the all-important work of Foucault, as well as with the work of Deleuze and Guattari. See in particular the essay by Scott Lash. Also see Donald Lowe for a Marxist analysis of the body in late capitalism.

2. See Szwed for a study of the racial body as expression of racial culture.

3. "Human Migration and the Marginal Man," originally published in *The American Journal of Sociology* 33, no. 6 (May 1928): 881–93. Reprinted in R. E. Park, *Race and Culture*, 353.

4. R. E. Park, ibid., 346. See R. Young, *Colonial Desire*, for further discussion of the history of hybridity in colonialist discourse.

5. R. E. Park, introduction to Stonequist, xviii.

6. Ibid.

7. Stonequist, 2.

8. Ibid., 221.

9. R. E. Park, *Race and Culture*, 379, note 3.

10. Ibid., 379.

11. *Abstracts of Reports of the Immigration Commission*, vol. 2, 505. For a discussion of these findings with regard to contemporary issues of "refugee transformation" (addressed in Chap. 7), see Tollefson, *Alien Winds*, 45ff.

12. *Immigration Report*, 2:505.

13. Ibid.

14. Ibid., 506, 527.

15. R. E. Park, "Racial Assimilation in Secondary Groups," *Publications of the American Sociological Association* 8 (1914): 71. Quoted in R. E. Park, *Race and Culture*, 353.

16. In R. E. Park, *Race and Culture*, 244–55. First published in *Survey Graphic* 56 (May 1926): 135–39.

17. R. E. Park, 247.

18. Ibid., 249–50. Goffman's work reads social behavior precisely as a "performance" played according to intuited rules and protocols in order to gain certain benefits. Yet the reception of this performance is always fraught with the possibility of failure, of "losing face." We might read the increasing anxiety over performance and identity in the corporatized world of the 1950s and 1960s as taking place at the same time as racial tensions manifest another threat to white male identity. We will touch on this subject again in Chap. 9.

19. R. E. Park, 247.

20. Ibid., 244

21. Ibid., 250. Here he is mistranslating—the term is to "lose face," not to "lose one's face." The latter is far too individually focused, and detached from the intensely collective phenomenon of "face."

22. Ibid., 250.

23. Ibid., 251.

24. Ibid., 248.

25. Stonequist, 105.

26. Palmer, 163f.

27. Chieng Fu Lung, "A Chinese Student and Western Culture," 24–38.

28. McCurdy provides the estimate of "in excess of 250,000 double eyelid operations performed annually in the Orient" (4).

29. The fact that Matsunaga is Asian American is not lost on Irene Chang, who writes on the subject for the *New York Times*. See "For Asians in the U.S., a New Focus on Eye Surgery."

Eugenia Kaw's excellent article discusses the evolution and perpetuation of normative discourses of occidental beauty and the stigmatization of the Asian face, and is attentive to the economic logic of this esthetic industry. Indeed, all the accounts I read of the new popularity of this surgery abroad (in both daily newspapers and professional journals) contain some hierarchy of First World/Third World cosmetic industries. The most expensive (i.e, the best) surgery is performed in the United States, of course; those wanting to save money suffer from botched jobs: sutures in Korea come loose, etc. For a first-person account of motivations for the surgery and reflections on the operation, see Iwata.

30. The specifically *schizophrenic* aspect of this notion of imagining another observing one and assuming certain identificatory dynamics therein is discussed in detail in Chap. 9.

31. For a discussion of using racial features to ascertain and predict behavior, see Szwed.

32. Cited in Kaw, 85.

33. DuCille, 13.

34. See Kaw.

35. Millard, "Pereginations," 325.

36. We might thus locate Palmer in between R. E. Park's and Millard's positions— Palmer believes that the physical and the psychic are mutually forming.

37. And here it would not be inappropriate to draw a link between such "progressive" attachments to science and the claims of eugenicists in the early part of the century. For example, see Haller, and Kevles.

38. Deleuze and Guattari, *A Thousand Plateaus*, 178.

39. Millard, *Principalization*, 98.

40. *Newsweek*, June 3, 1996, page 60.

41. Nachman, "The Lure of Interracial Romance," 21.

42. Currently, "mixedness" is enjoying a highly publicized, positive articulation, due largely to the rising fame of the young multiracial golfer Tiger Woods. In early May of 1997, both *Time* and *Newsweek* ran stories on interracial marriage and changing attitudes toward mixed race in the United States. See Jack E. White, and Leland and Beals.

43. *Time* tells us: "The face of America has been dramatically altered in the final years of the twentieth century. America's face is not just about physiognomy, or even color. . . . It is about the very complexion of the country, the endless and fascinating profusion of peoples, cultures, languages and attitudes that make up the great national pool" (3).

44. Berlant's essay gives a provocative reading of this *Time* cover, and compares it to *Time*'s 1985 special issue on immigration. In Chap. 9 I further develop these ideas on the shift from modernity to postmodernity and its relation to issues of race and ethnicity.

45. *Time* describes the process:

Time chose a software package called Morph 2.0, produced by Gryphon, to run on a MacIntosh Quadra 900. The Morph 2.0 is an offspring of Hollywood's sophisticated special-effects equipment. . . .

Morph 2.0 enabled *Time* to pinpoint key facial features on the photos of the 14 people of various racial and ethnic backgrounds chosen for the chart. Electronic dots defined head size, skin color, hair color and texture, eyebrows, the contours of the lips, nose and eyes, even laugh lines around the mouth. The eyes in particular required many key points to make them as detailed as possible; otherwise the results would be very erratic. Similarly, miscalculating the dimensions of an upper lip only slightly, for example, could badly skew the resulting face. . . .

Sometimes pure volume counts. The more information extracted from a given feature, the more likely that feature is to dominate the cybernetic offspring. Even when the program is weighted 50–50, if an African man has more hair than a Vietnamese woman, his hair will dominate; the same thing applies to larger lips or a jutting jaw. One of our tentative unions produced a distinctly feminine face—sitting atop a muscular neck and hairy chest. Back to the mouse on that one. (66)

46. For pacification and race, see Chap. 6.

47. Bell, 24–31.

48. Similar arguments of Asian Americans appearing in certain valued venues "out of proportion" to their demographic representation are of course found in the college admissions controversies of the 1980s. See Dana Takagi for an excellent study.

49. In Chaps. 9 and 10 we will specifically address the narrative of Scott's film, as well as the issue of cyberspace.

Chapter 4: Transacting Culture

1. A "classic" text in this regard is Milton Murayama's *All I Asking For Is My Body*, which I discuss in the appendix to this study.

2. I thank Sau-ling Wong for first bringing this novel to my attention with regard to this topic.

3. Throughout this chapter's discussion of the "presentation" of the Asian/American subject, one can profit from Goffman's *The Presentation of Self in Everyday Life*, in which Goffman, on observing "everyday life," discovers an open theater of specific social "performance." He considers "the way in which the individual in ordinary work situations presents himself and his activity to others, the ways in which he guides and controls the impression they form of him, and the kinds of things he may and may not do while sustaining his performance before them" (xi). Here this analysis is complicated by the racial and ethnic aspect of such performances, how the racial other may not be able to assert such control, and how his or her racial identity may be deployed by others.

4. See my "Toshio Mori and the Attachments of Spirit" for another mode of reading Mori.

5. Frank Chin notes that Chinese American boys were enlisted in minstrel shows as blackface performers (see Chin, "Come All Ye Asian American Writers," 18–19). The dynamics of staging race are being studied by, among others, James Moy and Vincente Rafael. The issue of the presentation of one race by actors of different races of course informs the core of the *Miss Saigon* debates.

6. And to make the entry into the "universal" more fraught, even when the minority subject acquires the cultural capital of the Other it may not be enough. In the cultural politics that leverages a racist national subjectivity even as it presumes upon universal value, entrance can be constantly deferred, as is evident in the epigraph that

begins this chapter. Hence "entry" can be constantly withheld, and the universal cautiously protected against fulfilling its promise of inclusivity against its will. Etienne Balibar notes precisely the same strategy: "If it must be admitted that French nationality includes innumerable successive generations of migrants, their spiritual incorporation will be justified by their capacity to assimilate, understood as a predisposition to Frenchness, but the question can always be raised (as in the past about the *conversos* under the Inquisition) whether this assimilation is not superficial, mere appearance" (Balibar, "Class Racism," 285).

7. "Psychopathologie des Comics," in *Les temps modernes*, May 1949, 919ff. Cited in Fanon, *Black Skin, White Masks*, 147.

8. Shoyu itself is an ambiguous symbol. At once it marks ethnicity, but, in the context of the internment, it marks a weird kind of misrepresentation—internees were given shoyu has an all-purpose condiment for everything from rice to pancakes. The boys, upon hearing that the Kid's constant nose-drippings are caused by eating too much shoyu, stop using it themselves. Their disgust stems from a striking, conflated image of themselves as Japanese *as imagined by the Other*—they are irrevocably "Japs."

9. Nevertheless, despite the negativity found in each of these narratives, the sense I have underscored of predetermination and, indeed, the overdetermination of identification, it is crucial to note as well the complex and uneven deployments of identifactory markers. For example, Hayashi and Abramson's study of "self identity" of Japanese American internees reveals at once the need to disaggregate any analysis of this phenomenon by gender and generation, as well as other differential categories. Such analyses show how Asian/American subjects renegotiate even the given terms of Asian Americanness, to different effect. Besides Hayashi and Abramson, see Gordon Nakagawa's essay on the subject.

10. She is told by a prospective employer: "I'm just tipping you off. If you want to make a decent salary or to be recognized for your own work, and not as somebody's secretary, get a job where you will not be discriminated against because you are a woman, a field in which your sex will not be considered before your ability" (234).

11. I thank Priscilla Wald for her careful reading of this analysis, and her suggestions.

Chapter 5: Citizens and Subnations

1. Garth, 71, 75f, 83f. Quoted in Carlson and Colburn, 35f.

2. Bean, 94ff; in Carlson and Colburn, 105f. See Gossett, chapter four, for an extensive account of craniology and racial categorization.

3. This schematization has not always been true historically. In the nineteenth century, studies claimed that "black and Asian immigrants . . . were culturally deemed to be somewhere between 'half civilized' Mexican and 'uncivilized' Indian populations" (Almaguer, 8). In other instances during this period, Asians were likened to the "lowest" group—California Indians—on the basis of the theory that the North American and Asian land masses were once contiguous. The shift in perspective is thus quite significant.

I thank Michael Omi for contributing information on this topic, and for his many good suggestions.

4. Quoted in Gossett, 150.

5. Rushton is heavily cited in that contemporary classic of scientific racism, *The Bell Curve*.

6. This schematization is found in Rushton, 162, fig. 7.4, which reproduces a graph from a 1992 study.

7. Smith, xiv.

8. Ibid., xiv.

9. See Sau-ling Wong's essay "Ethnicizing Gender" for a fine discussion of ethnicization and gender.

10. C. Y. Lee, *The Flower Drum Song*, 244.

11. See Hamamoto for a wider examination of televisual representations of Asians in America and the relation to national and international politics to such productions.

12. See Žižek, *Sublime Object*, 120f.

13. See Balibar, "Paradoxes of Universality." See also the special issue of *differences* (vol. 7, Spring 1995) on the politics of the universal.

14. See Žižek, "Identity and Its Vicissitudes."

15. I would insist that, as similar as each evocation of the model minority myth may be to another, it is crucial to note the specific historical context of each evocation and the functions it serves.

16. Cf. Cumings (40), who notes "the inability of elites to do more than oscillate between free trade and protectionism, between admiration for Japan's success and alarm at its new prowess."

17. For a critique of this thesis and specific data that disaggregates and specifies "success," see Cacas; S. Chan, *Asian Americans*, 167–83; Grove and Wu; Hazlett; Hurh and Kim; Bok-Lim Kim; Osajima; Sue and Okazaki; and essays in Yun. For a comparable case in Britain, see Errol Lawrence.

18. See Orfield, "Race."

19. John W. Connor's findings seem to confirm Petersen's notion that the more assimilated Japanese Americans become, the lower their academic achievement. See Connor, "Changing Trends in Japanese American Academic Achievement." Also see McLeod, "The Oriental Express."

20. For example, *Time*, July 8, 1985 ("Immigrants: The Changing Face of America"); *Newsweek*, August 9, 1993 ("America—Still the Melting Pot?").

Chapter 6: Disintegrations and Consolidations

1. I want to underscore that I will be discussing the *image* of Korean Americans. As Elaine Kim notes, Koreans were not heard from within the mass media's coverage of the rebellion, *except for* highly selective and fragmented representations. I want to make clear that I am arguing for a particular understanding of the functionality, and *not* assuming

that Koreans themselves endorse any specific representation or are complicit with that functionality.

Kim conducted a number of interviews with Korean Americans shortly after the rebellion, and incorporated these interviews into her film *Sa-I-Gu*.

2. The police officers, the actual perpetrators of the beating, I would argue, were curiously *disembodied*—their status as "human" obviated by the constant reiteration by both their attorneys and by sympathetic media of their mental disorientation at the "scene," their fear for *their* lives. They were, for all intents and purposes, transformed into phantasmal forces, (merely) reacting to a situation, "incited" by King, who, we were told, was "controlling the action."

3. See Abelmann and Lie for a study of Korean Americans and the Los Angeles uprising.

4. Barthes points out that the press photograph "benefits from the prestige of denotation: the photograph allows the photographer to *conceal elusively* the preparation to which he subjects the scene to be recorded" ("The Photographic Message," 21).

5. This double semiotic of "representing" is the formulation of Gayatri Spivak in "Can the Subaltern Speak?"

6. The caption as commentary thus functions both as an objectivized mentality within the frame and a subjective response to the larger context—both ostensibly representative of "the" Korean American perspective when in fact both are subsumed beneath the editorial *coupage* of photo and essay editors "representing" that "community."

7. The minimal attention given to the predominance of Latino involvement in the rebellion, and, more important, the essential part the Latino community plays in race relations in the U.S., particularly in Southern California, is noteworthy. I would argue that just as the representation of Asian Americans in this event served as a "positive" surrogate for dominant white ideology, so did the media's representation of Latinos serve to underwrite the basic premises of dominant ideologies—the presence of Immigration and Naturalization Service agents engaged in sweeps of Latino neighborhoods after the rebellion rivaled the presence of the LAPD, without comment from the mainstream news media. The INS used the riots as a pretext to round up *any* "suspicious" Latinos and detain them without warrant or charge. Thus we have the Asian American as white surrogate in the battlefront of capitalism versus chaos, and Latinos as deportable surrogates for a black population that cannot be "legally" disenfranchised because of their birthright. This essay is a preliminary attempt to account for the various symbolic displacements of racial "functions" distributed among different groups.

8. Here I am referring to the killing of 15-year-old Latasha Harlins, who was accused of stealing a bottle of orange juice by a Korean American grocer. Upon being accused, Harlins shouted back at the grocer, who then tried to detain her. Harlins broke free and struck the woman. When she turned to leave the store, the grocer reached under the counter, pulled out a handgun, and shot Harlins. The entire event was caught on the videotape of the store's security camera.

9. The other side to this image—a rising number of "gang-related crimes," as well as the not-so-appreciative response to Asian success, Asian-bashing—is left out of the picture.

10. This element is transposed to other minority groups as well, as was clearly seen in the confirmation hearings of Clarence Thomas, and the tremendous success of Shelby Steele's and Steven Carter's books. For a fine rebuttal to such neoconservative arguments, see Robin D. J. Kelley, *Yo' Mama's Disfunktional!*.

11. George H. Smith, 96.

12. The caption: "While mourning their dead, Koreans were living proof that the old vocabulary of race no longer applies."

13. Kim's talk was given at a conference on Minority Discourse held at the University of California–Irvine's Humanities Research Institute in June 1992. Her *Newsweek* piece appears in the May 17, 1992, issue.

14. In the appendix to this study I again treat the doubleness of defamiliar/familiar found in the interpolation of Asian America into the U.S. imaginary.

The image of the "cowboy," and particularly the *lone* cowboy, as depicted in this photograph, of course resonates with the imaginary of Reagan/Bush (television and film cowboy / Texas urban cowboy).

15. *Newsweek*, May 11, 1992, page 38.

16. Here and throughout the essay, I want to admit the generalization "white," but retain it provisionally to denote the dominant's constitution of a majority consensus which, as is clear from this essay, can be bought into by any number of individuals of varying racial and ethnic identities.

17. It was standard journalistic practice to couple the body count of the riots with statistics regarding the damage to property in millions of dollars.

18. Patricia Williams points out the economic basis for our notions of private and public: "I have been thinking about the unowning of blacks and their consignment to some collective public state of mind, known alternately as 'menace' or 'burden'— about the degree to which it might be that public and private are economic notions, i.e., that the right to privacy might be a function of wealth" (21–22).

19. Films such as *Straw Dogs* play out this notion of the American male's impotence and reluctance to engage in violence until his "property" is threatened.

20. Barthes, 15–31. Barthes attempts to account for the semiotic structure of press photographs:

> The press photograph is a message. Considered overall, this message is formed by a source of emission, a channel of transmission, and a point of reception. The source of emission is the staff of the newspaper, the group of technicians certain of whom take the photo, some of whom choose, compose, and treat it, while others, finally, give it a title, a caption, and a commentary. The point of reception is the public which reads the paper. As for the channel of transmission, this is the newspaper itself, or, more precisely, a complex of concurrent messages with the photograph as center and surrounds constituted by the text, the title, the caption, the lay-out and, in a more abstract but no less "informative" way, by the very name of the paper. (15)

21. This notion of the "naturalization of the cultural" is developed more fully by Barthes in *Mythologies*.

22. Goldman, *The Death and Life of Malcolm X*, 155–56. Goldman's text reproduces the photo, following page 170.

Clayborne Carson documents the numerous threats to his life Malcolm X reported to the police, and their response.

23. There is something here that reminds one of Foucault's famous analysis of Velasquez's *Les Meninas* in *The Order of Things*, in which he notes how the orienting point of view, the "human subject," is everywhere implicated but radically absented from the painting. I would argue that here we have an allegory of the way that dominant ideology is inscribed everywhere in this photograph, but made invisible by the way Asian America has been used as its stand-in.

In Chap. 9, I will return to this phenomenon of racial "excision."

24. One of the most interesting aspects of Peter Gourevitch's analysis of the "current debates" regarding the Pacific Rim in 1989 is his comparison of two Pacific Rim regions—Asia and Latin America. He tries to account for their very different situations in late capitalism. See Gourevitch, especially pages 11–13.

25. Quoted in Oxnam.

26. In Chap. 10 I examine the deployment of Confucianism in global capitalism.

27. Winnick, 24f.

28. Awanohara, "Backlash," 31.

29. Chance, 52.

30. McLeod, 50.

31. See Leung.

32. "The Immigrants: How They're Helping to Revitalize the U.S. Economy."

33. Vidal, "Requiem for the American Empire," 18, 19.

34. Vidal, "Empire Lovers," 350.

35. See M. T. Berger, *Yellow Mythologies*, 100.

36. Vidal, "Exchange," 602.

37. Vidal, "Requiem for the American Empire," 18.

38. The question of imitating Asia persists: an article in the April 13, 1996, issue of *The Economist* asks, again, "Should Asia Be Copied?"

39. Among the many analyses of Japan's ready-made postmodern, global culture, see Robertson, *Globalization*. Robertson argues that Japan's ability to think globally is predicated upon its historically "syncretic" religion. For a rebuttal to such culturalist explanations, see Tomoji Ishi, "Less a product of some mysterious Japan culture, Japanese corporate culture derives from historically concrete economic and political structures and conflicts" (122).

40. See Skerry's review of Fallows's book, "Individualist America and Today's Immigrants." For an example of the conservative argument for more immigration, see Wattenberg and Zinsmeister, "The Case for More Immigration." One should note that this argument specifies that these new immigrants should be admitted *only if* they possess the specific skills and capital needed by the United States.

41. Fallows, *Looking at the Sun*, 249.

42. Ibid., 441.

43. Ibid., 442.

44. See Fukuyama.

45. Huntington, "The United States." See Omatsu, 35.

46. Huntington's "clash" theory was complemented by Robert D. Kaplan's "The Coming Anarchy" article in *The Atlantic*, whose cover reads: "Nations break up under the tidal flow of refugees from environmental and social disaster. As borders crumble, another type of boundary is erected—a wall of disease. Wars are fought over scarce resources, especially water, and war itself becomes continuous with crime, as armed bands of stateless marauders clash with the private security forces of the elites. A preview of the first decades of the twenty-first century."

47. In 1996, a series of articles appeared, stating with some relief that Asian power had lapsed. See, for example, Desmond: "The Failed Miracle: Rarely has a country fallen so far so fast as Japan has in the past five years"; and "Asia's flagging alliance," *The Economist*, April 13, 1996, pages 13–14.

48. Quotes are taken from Yoichi Funabashi, "Globalize Asia," *New Perspectives Quarterly* 9 (Winter 1992), page 23f; Kishore M. Mahbubani, "The West and the Rest," *National Interest* 28 (Summer 1992), page 7; Ogura Kazuo, "New Concept of Asia," *Japan Echo* 20 (Autumn 1993), page 41.

49. In my conclusion I address the latest manifestation of Huntington's thesis—his attack on "diasporics" in the United States, by which he essentially means any immigrant, new or old.

50. For an earlier analysis of the Civil Rights and antiwar movements, read in the context of an overarching thesis on American politics and idealism, see Huntington, *American Politics*, 167–220.

51. In Chap. 9 I will focus on the issue of schizophrenia and national identity.

52. It is hard to leave Huntington without mentioning the scenario for the next world war he invents, with its particular slap at Asians, Latinos, Africans and African Americans, and an "American public" (read liberal no-nothings) whose weakness led to the defeat of America in the first place: "The United States, Europe, Russia, and India have thus become engaged in a truly global struggle against China, Japan, and most of Islam. . . . Large segments of the American public blame the severe weakening of the United States on the narrow Western orientation of WASP elites, and Hispanic leaders come to power buttressed by the promise of extensive Marshall Plan–type aid from the booming Latin American countries which sat out the war. Africa, on the other hand, has little to offer to the rebuilding of Europe and instead disgorges hordes of socially mobilized people to prey on the remains" (313–16).

The lure of imagining a war between the United States and China seems irresistible (and perhaps morally imperative to some). See Bernstein and Munro, *The Coming Conflict with China*, 186–202, which begins, "We do not think that a war between China and the United States is likely. *But* there *could* be a conflict in the South China Sea if . . . [my emphasis]". Before long the authors have detailed the precise timetable, armaments, and players in this "war game." The seductiveness of such an imaginative "game" is telling.

53. Nakayama, 68.

54. Rose, "Asian Americans," 212.

Chapter 7: War, the Homeland, and the Traces of Memory

1. Studies which address the specific issue of Asian-American urban space and the ideological and political impact of the city as a social and cultural form are too numerous to mention. For representative pieces from different perspectives, see articles by Arreola, Posadas ("Crossed Boundaries"), and Erica Y. Z. Pan.

2. Gupta and Ferguson, "Beyond 'Culture'," 39.

3. The topic of memory has in the last decade or so been increasingly researched. The most influential thinkers from earlier periods are Maurice Halbwachs and, later, Pierre Nora. Recent work has particularly focused on the politics of memory, especially as related to postcolonial and minority discourse studies (one rather problematic reading of this is David Lowenthal's notion of postcolonials' adaptation of "western identity").

Huyssen links this interest in memory to the project of modernity: "The current obsession with memory is not simply a function of the fin de siecle syndrome, another symptom of postmodern pastiche. Instead, it is a sign of the crisis of that structure of temporality that marked the age of modernity with its celebration of the new as utopian, as radically and irreducibly other" (6). Nevertheless, this notion of modernity and its celebrations ignores precisely the differentiation and reification of "memory" as the possession of some and not of others.

4. United States Department of War, *Final Report: Japanese Evacuation from the West Coast* (hereafter, *Final Report*), 26f.

5. Commager, 560.

6. Cited in Lyman, *Chinese Americans*, 84.

7. The claim to "authentically" laying claim to U.S. land brings up the ironic fact that the person placed in charge of the War Relocation Authority, Dillon S. Myer, proved so "adept" at dislocating racial minorities from their land that he was later appointed by Harry Truman to direct the Bureau of Indian Affairs. Wrote Truman, "Myer has established a precedent for equitable treatment of dislocated minorities" (quoted in Drinnon, 163). This assignment wasn't exactly a plum one—Truman hoped that the Bureau would "get out of the Indian business" and privately told associates that he had "a shitty ass job I want [Myer] to do" (cited in Drinnon, 166).

8. Quoted in Okihiro and Drummond, 168.

9. California Board of Control, *California and the Oriental* (Sacramento: State Printing Office, 1922), 10. Cited in Dirlik, "Asia-Pacific in Asian-American Perspective," 318.

10. While our focus will be on the removal of Japanese from California, it should be noted that the dislocating of Japanese occurred globally. Japanese were removed from their homes in Alaska, Canada, Mexico, Central America, parts of South America, Haiti, and the Dominican Republic. See Weglyn, 56f. Also see essays by Ogawa and Fox, Hirabayashi, and Gardiner, on Japanese internment outside mainland United States.

It should be noted that scholarly interpretation of the role economics played in the argument for evacuation is split—tenBroek et al. argue against Grodzins's assertion that economics and racism played significant roles in the decision. From the evidence it becomes clear that certain argumentative hurdles had to be cleared in order for the evacuation to make economic sense. Okihiro and Drummond's essay explains how that came about.

11. "Eighty-six prohibited zones were delineated in the first three Department of Justice announcements . . . seventeen areas along the coast, typically several miles in length and running inland from the shore to the nearest highway. There were thirteen areas around San Francisco Bay, including the dock areas of the bay cities, airports, terminals, industrial sections, and military and naval installations" (tenBroek et al., 106).

McCloy (of the War Department) instructed DeWitt (the military commander designated by Roosevelt to carry out the executive order): "From these zones you will provide for the exclusion of all persons" who are "Japanese aliens, American citizens of Japanese lineage, and any person suspected of being a spy, saboteur, or fifth-columnist" (tenBroek et al., 112).

12. *Final Report*, 9.

13. He continues: "In Southern California, for instance, Japanese had farmed at Signal Hill near Long Beach for years before oil was discovered there. The Los Angeles municipal airport, the Northrup and the North American air-craft plants were built in the midst of the extensive Japanese truck farming area near Hawthorne and Inglewood. In some cases where oil and electric installations preceded the Japanese the companies concerned especially encouraged Japanese American farmers to work land on the rights of way and between the oil derricks" (tenBroek et al., 268).

14. Written by DeWitt and published as part of the *Final Report*, 33.

15. *Final Report*, 33.

16. See Chap. 2 for a discussion of the transformative powers of America.

17. *Final Report*, 56.

18. The contradictions of pro-evacuation forces becomes clear. Grodzins notes that, even as it published a pamphlet entitled *No Japs Needed*, "The Grower-Shipper Vegetable Association . . . could admit that resident Japanese controlled 'the astoundingly large figure of 60 percent' of California's tomato crop" (168). Agricultural data is provided in Grodzins, 168.

19. Quoted in Grodzins, 169.

20. Ibid., 176.

21. Okihiro and Drummond, 171.

22. *Japanese Evacuation and Resettlement Study*, Bancroft Library, University of California, Berkeley, "Operation of Evacuated Japanese Farms," A 18.06, 1–2. Quoted in Okihiro and Drummond, 172.

23. Okihiro and Drummond, 172.

24. Specific efforts were launched in the late 1960s to repeal the Emergency Detention Act. Okamura, Takasugi, Kanno, and Uno explain:

> During the McCarthy era, a great fear of subversion by domestic Communists led to the passage of the Internal Security Act of 1950, with its Title II provisions for detention camps. This law, known as the "Emergency Detention Act," permitted the attorney general to apprehend and to place in detention camps any person or persons he suspected of "probably" engaging in acts of espionage or sabotage. The constitutional rights of due process and trial

by jury would have been ignored. Furthermore, the government would not have been required to prove that the suspect was "probably" dangerous.

In keeping with the provisions of Title II, six detention camps were prepared and maintained from 1952 to 1957. Eventually the McCarthy era passed, and in 1957 Congress ceased to appropriate maintenance funds for the detention camps. Most of the camps were gathering dust and most people forgot about it.

[But in early 1967] rumors spread rapidly through the Black communities that concentration camps were being prepared for Black people in order to end their "riots." Black leaders such as Stokely Carmichael, H. Rap Brown, Malcolm X, and eventually Martin Luther King, Jr. claimed that if Japanese Americans could be placed in concentration camps, so could Black people. Rumors also spread through the anti-war movement that mass incarcerations were being planned to thwart its protest of the Vietnam war.

It was in this setting that a four-year campaign to repeal the Emergency Detention Act was launched.

Okamura et al, 71f. (Title II was successfully repealed on September 21, 1971).

For a study of the passage of the 1988 Act, see Hatamiya.

25. See Bok-Lim Kim, "Asian Wives," for a brief study of "war brides," as well as Evelyn Nakano Glenn's work.

26. There is a wealth of studies on the internment; more and more seek to restore the voice of the internee within a historical context. Two diaries are of particular importance: see studies by Modell and Gordon Chang.

Peggy Choy's essay, "Racial Order and Contestation," gives an interesting comparative analysis of the treatment and actions of Japanese American internees and Japanese American soldiers stationed in the same compound.

27. We may contrast the conservative attitude of this embodiment of cosmopolitan East/West culture to that of Capra's General Yen, whose *prewar* libidinal and spiritual interests lead him to imagine the possibilities of such a liaison.

28. See Marchetti, *Romance and the "Yellow Peril,"* 167.

29. And here is where I depart from Marchetti's otherwise excellent analysis of the film. She asserts that the Sterling home "is free from all the economic and psychic stress of advanced capitalism" (168). Vidor certainly establishes it as that initially, but, as we noted, the viewer's very introduction to the home is preceded by first passing by and noting the Hasegawas' farm, and Jim's explicit query to his father as to who owns that land sets up a question about land ownership, economic competition, and race. Furthermore, as we've again noted, Tae's first "shopping trip" into town (her initiation into consumerism) is diverted into a tour of the packing plant. These shots set up the final breaching of that inviolate space of the private home—the letter blackmailing the Sterlings into banishing Tae if they want to retain their membership in the growers' association.

30. A great deal can be said of Fran's sexuality and assertiveness, and of the way the film establishes nearly every other female character as her antithesis in one way or another, which serves to further isolate and stigmatize Fran.

31. Marchetti remarks upon Fran's role in her analysis of Vidor's film, 158–75. Indeed, the identification of female sexuality and independence with "danger" to American domestic space is well established.

32. The issue of the product of this liaison of East and West, the birth of the biracial child, brings to mind the particularly sexist policy of the United States government with regard to interning biracial children. The judgment was based on the gender of the non-Japanese parent: those born of a Japanese American mother could leave the camps and return to their "Caucasian" homes; those of Japanese American fathers were allowed to leave the camp but not to return to the west coast. See Spickard, "What Must I Be?", 49.

33. One postwar narrative from a different national history, which is founded on a particular remapping of the land, a redefinition of common place, and a restoration of history is Joy Kogawa's *Obasan*, a novel of the Japanese Canadian internment. The entire novel is a series of displacements and erasures that make knowledge of the ethnic subject impossible without a revisionary return to the land. One of the most striking episodes in *Obasan* regards the landscape. Years after the end of the evacuation, the protagonist Naomi and her family return to their former homes and attempt to find traces of that existence:

> We looked for evidence of our having been in Bayfarm, in Lemon Creek, in Popoff. . . . Where on the map or on the raod was there any sign? Not a mark was left. All our huts had been removed long before and the forest had returned to take over the clearings . . . the Slocan that we knew in the forties was no longer there, *except for the small white community which had existed before we arrived* and which watched us come with a mixture of curiosity and fear. Now, down on the shore of the Slocan lake, on the most beautiful part of the sandy beach, where we used to swim, there was a large new sawmill owned by someone who lived in New York" [emphasis added]. (117–18)

Only a few bones remain: "The part of the cemetery that holds [the] bones [of the Japanese Canadians] is off by itself in the north-west corner of Forest Lawn. Perhaps some genealogist of the future will come across this patch of bones and wonder why so many fishermen died on the prairies" (225). It is precisely these "bones" that have the potential to "speak," yet we must remind ourselves that this potential is contingent upon the "*possibility* for it to be true"—some archeologist of a vaguely distant future must find the graves, recognize the contradiction between the patrimony of the dead and their place of burial, and, furthermore, find *significance* in this alienation.

See my essay "The Politics of Memory" for a fuller discussion of Kogawa's novel, which explains the notion behind the "possibility" for truth.

34. *Department of State Bulletin*, Nov. 1985, 21.

35. Tollefson, "Indochinese Refugees," 263.

36. Whitman, 18.

37. Ramirez, 148.

38. Ibid., 156.

39. Citation from "Trouble for America's Model Minority," *U.S. News and World Report*, Feb. 23, 1987, pages 18–19, see also Hing, 135f.

40. Strand and Jones, 4.

41. See Bruce Grant, 193, 195ff.

42. Hing, 124.

43. Ibid., 124f.

44. See its report, "The Implementation of the Refugee Act of 1980: A Decade of Experience." See also Silverman.

45. Hing, 125. Hing notes that between April and December 1975, 134,000 Indochinese refugees were admitted, 125,000 of whom were Vietnamese: "By 1978 thousands more were admitted under a series of Indochinese Parole Programs, authorized by the attorney general. The number of Indochinese refugees swelled to 14,000 a month by the summer of 1979. Following the tightening of Vietnam's grip on Cambodia, several hundred thousand 'boat people' and many Cambodian and Laotian refugees entered between 1978 and 1980. In fact, annual arrivals of Indochinese refugees had increased almost exponentially: 20,400 in 1978, 80,700 in 1979, and 166,700 in 1980" (Hing, 126).

46. "A major catalyst for the new refugee law [of 1980] was a disturbing anxiety felt by some members of Congress that thousands of Indochineses would destabilize many communities" (Hing, 127). See Kaplan's apocalyptic vision of the effects of refugees on local spaces, a key element for this chapter: "I would add [to Huntington's "clash of civilizations" theory] that as refugee flows increase and as peasants continue migrating to cities around the world—turning them into sprawling villages—national borders will mean less, even as more power will fall into the hands of less educated, less sophisticated groups" (Kaplan, 60).

47. Grant, *The Boat People*, 205f.

48. For descriptions of refugee camps, see works by Hein, Rose ("From Southeast Asia" and "Links in a Chain"), and Tollefson (*Alien Winds*), and oral histories by refugees (Chan, *Hmong Means Free*; Freeman; and Lando and Sandness).

49. Strand and Jones, 10. They go on to observe: "The goal of any policy of resettlement is the successful assimilation of refugees into the country of final asylum. This implies the integration of refugees into the cultural fabric of the host country. It also implies the resocialization of refugees into the political and social norms of the society. However, it does not in any sense imply the accommodation of refugees as suggested by Zangwill's 'melting pot.' Indeed, the characteristics of the melting pot society have seldom been the American immigration experience. In a pluralistic society such as this, assimilation is not characterized by a uniform culture. Therefore it is not likely that the cultural patterns of refugees will disappear" (128).

50. "If assimilation is a process characterized by decreasing differentiation between subcultures and the dominant culture, then it may be impossible to distinguish between a socially well-adjusted refugee and a well-assimilated refugee" (ibid., 128).

51. See Ong's "On the Edges of Empire" for a detailed treatment of this issue.

52. Pointing to success stories (as Reagan did in a State of the Union address) "not only sets an unrealistic standard that contributes to frustration among both refugees and resettlement officials, but they also serve to absolve Americans of their responsibility to provide funding for programs to aid in resettlement" (Tollefson, "Indochinese Refugees," 271).

53. Strand and Jones, 237. In particular, the emphasis on the formation of an individualized American subjectivity ignores the myriad reasons for refugees' sense of collective identity.

54. "While resettlement was the province of voluntary agencies, the U.S. government put considerable pressure on them to disperse refugees throughout the country and prevent the development of large ethnic communities that might create tensions between local, state, and federal governments or put undue strain on local community resources" (Kelley, "Coping," 143).

Refugees were sent to California, Texas, Pennsylvania, Florida, Washington, D.C., Illinois, Louisiana, Minnesota, New York, Oklahoma, Virginia. "Eighteen [other] states became the destination of fewer than 1,000 refuges each" (ibid.).

55. On April 18, 1975, President Ford created a temporary Interagency Task Force (ITF) to coordinate activities. It was the policy to disperse refugees as widely as possible: "For those who wished to maintain control over the Vietnamese, assigning them to a few central locations seemingly promised to keep them where they could be more easily monitored and manipulated. At the same time, however, it increased opportunities for refugees to communicate with and reinforce each other, perhaps enabling them to form alliances and mobilize. Dispersal had its own appeal. It might help avoid acute economic stress in host communities, force a more rapid assimilation, and diffuse the potential for solidarity and organization. . . . By compelling them to disperse and rely on outsiders, IATF hoped to domesticate the refugees, easing their transition into and their burden on mainstream culture" (Hing, 128f).

56. Kelley, "Coping," 145. Howell (123) points out how this reveals the persistence of ethnic identities. Some communities were "not flexible enough to accommodate them. Yet the preference and need for ethnic community support and familiarity contribute to the secondary migration of many refugees even before they are capable of supporting themselves, sometimes severing them from sponsors and removing them from the agencies which have received funds to provide services to them."

57. Hing, 131.

58. As Aihwa Ong notes, "The biomedical gaze is not such a diffused hegemonic power but is itself generated by the complex contestation of refugee subjects pursuing their own goals" ("Making the Biopolitical Subject," 1243).

59. Tollefson, "Indochinese Refugees," 273.

60. Haines, 46. For the reinvention of refugees as "problems," see William Liu, 9.

61. Ong argues, "Welfare states, public health, educational and housing agencies administering the needs of citizens can be said to participate in the creation of biopolitical subjects of a particular kind" (Ong, "Making the Biopolitical Subject," 1243).

62. See Hein, chap. 1, for a discussion of the ideology of assimilation. The state's role in mediating and producing certain "minority" subjectivities is well researched. See Roxanna Ng for a fascinating account of the Canadian state's transformation of minority women into "immigrant women" and the relation of that strategy to labor practices.

63. Mortland, 385.

64. Ong, "Making the Biopolitical Subject," 1245.

65. Cited in Tollefson, *Alien Winds*, 58.

66. Such data is invaluable for this pedagogy, as well as for social workers and job placement officers in the United States. See Latkiewicz and Anderson for one example.

67. Cited in Tollefson, *Alien Winds*, 67.

68. Ibid., 72.

69. Cited in Tollefson, *Alien Winds*, 58. In 1983, one trade magazine bemoaned the fact that, as of that date, Asian refugees were still "an invisible market": "They seem to have dissolved into the manmade thickets of this international city [Seattle] as effectively as they once disappeared among the tropical jungles of their native lands" (Bruce Williams, M-58).

70. Mortland, 393.

71. Ibid., 401.

72. Not following that pedagogy resulted in being interpellated within a pathologized "immigrant psychology," conceived of within the regimes of the psychoanalytic treatment institution: "'Talking medicine' [interviews with refugees seeking a particular regime of health and disease] in fact buttresses a disease narrative whereby stereotypical Asian patients' beliefs are integrated and transformed within the medical paradigm. In practice then, 'cultural sensitivity' becomes a strategy that uses cultural difference not so much to understand particular experiences of illness as to read symptoms that confirm universalized states of biomedicine" (Ong, "Making the Biopolitical Subject," 1249).

In the following chapter I will address the case of Monterey Park.

73. The connection between academic knowledge production and public policy is made clear in a special issue of *Anthropological Quarterly* is dedicated to applying anthropological data to refugee policy. For these authors, the case of refugees calls for ethnographic readings. Its editor writes:

> For the anthropologist, many issues involved in refugee resettlement in the United States reflect concerns which traditionally have been part of the profession's domain, and, therefore, should invite professional interest. First, there are the refugees themselves, who as foreign nationals, are often culturally different from most residents of the United States. Thus, their resettlement in this country involves processes of change and adjustment, on both individual and group levels. Second, due to these cultural differences and to the circumstances of their departure from their countries of origin, most refugees have significant needs for assistance in reconstructing their lives and for establishing means of supporting themselves—financially, socially, and emotionally—in this country. In order that these needs be met succssfully, the development of program activities to assist refugees and the analysis of the relevance and effect of policies require an understanding of their varied cultural backgrounds. (Howell, 120)

Howell argues for "applied anthropology"—showing how "policy" is related to "politics" and arguing that the study of refugee culture should contribute to policy-making.

74. World Health Organization, 82.

75. Tollefson, "Indochinese Refugees," 267. He continues: "Though research on the psychological adjustment of refugees in the United States is inadequately funded, what little has been done shows that many refugees suffer post-traumatic-stress disorder. Hyperalertness, extreme startle reactions, fear of the sounds of airplanes and other noises, flashbacks, and recurrent dreams are well documented" (269).

There have been several studies of the modes of "remembering" of Vietnam, for example, Rowe and Berg. For a review of veterans' narratives, see Uhl.

76. There have been numerous studies of the cultural production around Vietnam. See Allen and Ngô for particularly useful sets of essays.

77. Kelley, "Coping," 148. Bruce Grant quotes a General Be: "When there is a new housing project going up, or services being handed out, the white community will often support the Vietnamese as a way of getting rid of blacks" (Grant, 164). For public opinion polling, see Haines, and Starr and Roberts. Stern includes data from Great Britain, Canada, and Australia.

78. Cited in Kessner and Caroli, 67.

79. Quoted in Starr and Roberts from, respectively, *U.S. News and World Report*, May 5, 1975, page 22; *Time*, May 12, 1975, page 26; and *Time*, May 12, 1975, page 24.

80. For the argument that refugees would massively take over American jobs, see William T. Liu, 67. For an analysis of how many refugees were *not* able to fulfill the destiny of the "model minority," see Gold and Kibria.

81. See, for example, Ong, "Making the Biopolitical Subject."

82. A 1993 special issue of *Amerasia Journal* contains three interesting critiques of refugee narrative gathering. See Thomas A. DuBois, Truong, and Franklin Ng, "Towards a Second Generation."

Rasbridge, writing as an anthropologist, goes so far as to say, "Beyond merely providing catharsis for the refugee, then, the refugee life history endeavor provides us with the opportunity to gain a level of empathy which is usually not obtainable through a participant observation approach typically employed by most of our anthropologist colleagues" (62). The tone and perspective of this passage is remarkable indeed—the effect of the narration upon "the refugee" is reduced to a "mere" product; empathy becomes a prize awarded to this special group of anthropologists who venture into territory unexplored by "most" of their other colleagues.

83. Hieu Tran, "The Day I Left for the USA." In Lando and Sandness, 71f.

84. Chan, *Hmong Means Free*, 75.

85. In Freeman, 371.

86. Chan, *Hmong Means Free*, 116. As R. Radhakrishnan notes, speaking of the Indian immigrant: "Her naturalization into American citizenship minoritizes her identity. She is now reborn as an ethnic minority American citizen. Is this empowerment or marginalization?" (205).

87. See, respectively, Blanchard, Sanders, Benson, Beyette. To these one may add studies of Chinese diasporic communities in Arkansas (Tsai), South Florida (Cindy Wong), Mississippi (Loewen and Quan). See also Hein, *From Vietnam, Laos, and Cambodia*, 5–68.

88. Data for this discussion comes from Airriess and Clawson.

89. Ibid., 5.

90. Here I am elaborating on a point made by Airriess and Clawson, 8.

91. See Leonard, *Making Ethnic Choices*, for a very interesting study of Japanese and Punjabi reivention of land and cultural formations in California.

92. This data taken from Lam. For a discussion of media coverage of the event, see Song and Dombrink.

93. Among other things, Smith's study tracks the particular effects of specific cinematic and televisual formulae, such as John Woo's films and American films on Vietnam and Cambodia.

For an interesting discussion of how religious and philosophical beliefs play a specific role in Cambodian attitudes toward life in America, see Welaratna.

94. In Freeman, 379.

95. Cited in Chan, *Hmong Means Free*, 117.

96. Tapp, 34f.

97. Data taken from Arax, "Final Turf War."

98. And one can contrast this common topos with that of the Pacific coast, where Jim and Tae will settle the new Asian-American family in King Vidor's film.

99. For an excellent summary of the complex history of the Hmong, see Chan, Introduction to *Hmong Means Free*.

100. See Leonard, "Finding One's Own Place," 127, for an interesting discussion of Japanese and Punjabi burial practices in California's Imperial Valley.

101. Franklin Ng's essay on the subject draws together valuable background information.

102. Krauthammer, 7f, quoted in Ng. Ng presents a number of statements that show too the racist attitude presented to Lin, whose Asian American ancestry was held to be suspicious and a probable motive for her "attempt" to besmirch the memory of American soldiers fighting in Asia.

103. Quoted in Scruggs and Swerdlow, *To Heal*, 132.

104. Hannah, 1476.

105. I refer the reader to James E. Young's excellent and provocative work on holocaust memorials.

106. Quoted in J. E. Young, 5.

107. See Root, 30. For a useful article that probes the intersection of patriarchy, nation, gender and refugee policy, see J. Bhabha.

108. Data derived from articles by DeMonaco and Robear. See also Bass and DeBonis. This historical event was staged as a revision of the Madame Butterfly theme in the Broadway musical *Miss Saigon*.

109. Nationality, race, and personal identity essentially derive from the father (DeMonaco, 648).

110. Indochinese Refugee Resettlement and Protection Act of 1987, Pub. L. No. 100−202, 101 Stat. 1329-183, 1329-184. Cited in Robear, 127.

111. DeMonaco, 643, 661.

112. The broadening of eligibility not only meant that Amerasians could bring over family members; it also meant that these *bui doi* were preyed upon by the same population that ostracized them previously—more and more "relatives" appeared, or bribed Amerasians to name them as relatives.

113. DeMonaco, 680.

Chapter 8: Demarcations and Fissures

1. Lal, 4.

2. R. E. Park, *Race and Culture*, 225.

3. See Schwendinger and Schwendinger, chap. 48. They describe Park and Burgess's notions of competition as universal: "Migratory, demographic, interracial, economic, and ecological relationships [are] also provided as concrete illustrations of competitive relationships . . . the authors [make] the point that 'a competitive order' has existed everywhere and always among living things" (388).

4. "Human ecology, as Park conceived it, was of interest because social relations were often reflected in spatial patterns and 'social distances' were frequently expressed as physical distances" (Lal, 29).

5. See Lal for a discussion of the various sorts of criticism that these suggestions drew, and compare this to William Petersen's idea of the ethnic "subnation" mentioned in Chap. 5. Also, see Piven and Cloward for another angle onto this notion of segregation.

6. See Lal, 152.

7. Lal, 44.

8. R. E. Park, 361.

9. Stonequist, 213

10. Ibid., 3.

11. Borthwick, 3.

12. R. E. Park, 1936, page 2; cited in Gottdiener, 28.

13. Gottdiener, 68. See also Castells.

14. Soja, 120, 127. To this he adds the specific link to capitalism: "Time and space, like the commodity form, the competitive market, and the structure of social classes, are represented as a natural relation between things, explainable objectively in terms of the substantive physical properties and attributes of these things in themselves" (124).

15. Sassen, "Analytic Borderlands," 190.

16. Arif Dirlik, "Place-Based Imagination: Globalism and the Politics of Place," 11. I thank Professor Dirlik for sharing this excellent essay with me.

17. Ong, Bonacich, and Cheng, 29.

18. Sassen, *Losing Control*, 86f.

19. Ibid., 76.

20. See Sassen, "Whose City Is It?" 218.

21. The restructuring of city space partakes of a number of regimes. Mike Davis observes: "There is no single, master logic of restructuring, rather the complex intersection of two separate macro-processes: one based on the overaccumulation of bank and real estate capital (most recently, from the recycling of East Asian trade surplus to California); the other arising from the reflux of low-wage manufacturing and labour-intensive services in the wake of unprecedented mass immigration from Mexico and Central America" (*"Chinatown,"* 67f).

22. Hing, 32.

23. As many have pointed out, the architects of that piece of legislation had no idea that the lifting of quotas set in the 1924 National Origins Act would have any particular effect on immigration from Asia. Rather, they saw it as encouraging and facilitating emigration from Europe: "Attorney General Robert Kennedy estimated that perhaps only five thousand immigrants from the Asia-Pacific region might immigrate in the first year. . . . Johnson, who was critical of the Asia-Pacific triangle in his 1964 State of the Union address, usually emphasized the corrective nature of the law for southern and eastern European immigrants without reference to Asian immigration" (Hing, 39).

Instead, the Act radically changed the composition of Asian America, and this fact brought about a compensatory move to reduce the flow of Asians into the United States: "That Asians constitute almost half of the legal immigrants to the United States today and that European immigration has declined greatly are perceived as conclusive evidence that the design of the 1965 law gave too much to Asians while disadvantaging Europeans. The truth is that the 1965 amendments were intended not to encourage Asian immigration but to advance European immigration. Yet a section of the 1986 Immigration Reform and Control Act was deliberately designed to advantage non-Asians by adjusting quotas for two years" (Hing, 7). See Hing, pages 81, 88, 95, 101, and 107, for statistics for individual groups.

Besides adjusting quotas, other laws have been deployed to harrass and exclude Asians: "In August of 1978 immigration inspectors in Honolulu began a systematic interrogation of returning elderly Asian Americans who were lawful permanent resident aliens of the United States. The airport interrogation went far beyond the customary questioning as to purpose and length of stay abroad. It focussed on whether they were then, or had ever been, recipients of Supplemental Social Security Income (SSI). . . . If SSI had ever been received by the returning alien, immigration inspectors took possession of the person's alien card and passport and instructed the person to report for further inspection and interrogation. . . . At the inspection they were informed that they were excludable from the United States as 'public charges' and were generally given three options: return to their native country, request an exclusion hearing, or terminate SSI benefits and post a public-charge bond of $5,000" (Hing, 113f).

24. Gibney, 517.

25. Liu and Cheng, 77.

26. Ong, Bonacich, and Cheng, 13, 19, 24, 27.

27. "Export-oriented economies and the infusion of Asian educational systems with United States/Western modes of thought, patterns of action, and ideals predisposed the Asian middle class and professionals to emigrate. Both factors depended on the a priori existence of a more general economic linkage. For the United States, its connection to the Philippines, the three Chinese-speaking regions, India, Vietnam, and South Korea emanated from its emergence as a hegemonic power after World War II." Ong, Bonacich, and Cheng, 89. See also 26f.

Reimers points out that, along with the introduction of U.S. military and educational apparatuses, U.S. culture became increasingly widespread in East Asia after the war, and American cultural values disseminated widely. See Reimers, 97.

28. Ong, Bonacich, and Cheng, 27.

29. Ibid., 30.

30. Sassen, *Global City*, 316.

31. Ibid., 290ff. Sassen points out that the common view is that immigrants provide low-wage labor to a declining, backward sectors of capital. She argues that this view is correct in part, but incomplete. There are two additional roles for immigration that are particularly relevant for our discussion:

1. Providing labor for the low wage service and manufacturing jobs that service both the expanding, highly specialized service sector and the high-income lifestyles of those employed in the specialized, expanding service sector. They service the most dynamic sector of the city's economy.

2. Occupation of areas that would otherwise have had a high proportion of abandoned housing and closed stores.

Sassen writes: "Basic traits of advanced capitalism may promote conditions for informalization. The presence of large immigrant communities then can be seen as mediating in the process of informalization rather than directly generating it: The demand side of the process of informalization is therewith brought to the fore."

32. Sassen, *Global City*, 294.

33. A running joke publicizing a recent release from Disney (*Jungle To Jungle*) shows a young boy brought to New York from the Amazon by his newly discovered yuppie father. He is shown how to hail a cab, and remarks, as the cab screeches to a halt: "A miracle!" His father replies, "No, a miracle would be if he understands English." Thus the modern American and the innocent primitive both occupy a more pristine space than the migrant integrating into the political economy. For a study of Philadelphia as imbricated in the "Third World," the notion that American urban sites are indeed endowed with many of the markers of the "Third World" as a consequence of public policy, see Koptiuch. For a sustained narrative of America's dissolution into the Third World, see Edward Luttwak, *The Endangered Dream of America*.

34. Walker, 402. With regard to the first element, Walker finds that "land speculation has been a hallmark of American urbanization, equalled nowhere else in the advanced capitalist countries until the recent past. The role of speculation has been recognized by urban geographers, but without systematic analysis. What is loosely known as land speculation—where it is not merely a pejorative for land investment—consists of two active forces: the manipulation of land and land uses to create rents (the main source of profits in property investment) and self-sustaining property bubbles" (402). See also Fegan's discussion of speculation.

35. In this discussion I am indebted to the excellent work of Peter Kwong.

36. See Kwong, "New York is Not Hong Kong."

37. Kwong, *New Chinatown*, 32.

38. Ibid., 32.

39. See Dong Ok Lee for a discussion of the development of ethnic economies, and Tseng for a description of Taiwanese immigrant business practices.

40. Kwong, *New Chinatown*, 51.

41. Ibid., 44.

42. Ibid., 46.

43. Harvey, *Urban Experience*, 123.

44. Loo, *Chinatown*, 75.
John Wang points out that residents predicted the disintegration of their community: "Many community residents . . . expressed the fear that the continuous influx of foreign capital would put more and more pressure on the already scarce space, pushing rents for small businesses and working people to outrageous heights. Well-financed businesses will force out many of the smaller businesses. And when that happens, they predict, Chinatown will cease to exist as a viable community for those who live there" (78).

45. Kwong, *New Chinatown*, 53f.

46. For instance, in 1976, New York Telephone sold 18 lots to Thomas Sung, Tommy Lee, Helmsey-Spear (at that time the largest private real estate corporation in New York), and Raymond Wu, who all wanted to condominiumize the land. See Kenneth R. Ong, "New York Chinatown: A Community Fights Gentrification." Ong also describes the victories gained in court by tenants rights groups.

47. See Kwong, *New Chinatown*, 25–56.

48. See Harvey, *Urban Experience*, 164–99.

49. "The use of increasingly scarce resources to capture development meant that the social consumption of the poor was neglected in order to provide benefits to keep the rich and powerful in town" (Harvey, *Urban Experience*, 272).

50. Friedland et al., 198, 201. The authors make the further point that the government in such instances is anything but neutral or democratic: "The formal structure of the state is not socially or politically neutral . . . urban governments attempt to absorb and limit the scope and impact of political participation by channeling it to agencies of limited power and high politicalization" (Friedland et al., 212). Cf. Squires: "Redevelopment initiatives throughout the nation have historically shared an ideological commitment to private-sector growth and to the notion of the public sector as a junior partner in efforts to stimulate that growth. . . . The increasing integration of the United States in the world economy, coupled with the restructuring of the national economy in the past two decades, has placed constraints on public resources while at the same time reinforcing traditional relationships between the public and private sectors" (Squires, 2).

51. "On the whole, older American cities became vehicles for the encapsulation of minority groups and low-income whites in obsolete sectors of the economy and deteriorating physical environments" (S. Fainstein and N. Fainstein, "Economic Change," 4).

52. N. Fainstein and S. Fainstein, "Regime Strategies," 252.

53. Ibid., 253.

54. Piven and Clowards's argument against desegregation makes a more rationally framed structural critique.

55. In his introduction to *The Japanese Invasion*, Park touches precisely the same notion of class, space, and identity: "Immigration brings with it a new and disturbing form of competition, the competition, namely, of peoples of a lower and of a higher standard of living." Reprinted in R. E. Park, *Race and Culture*, 226.

56. The 1969 report of the National Commission on Urban Problems, entitled "Building the American City," contains a chapter rationalizing the substitution of the term "urban renewal" for "slum clearance":

The Commission believes that the record clearly and unmistakably supports the view that the three primary purposes of the urban renewal title of the act of 1949 were: (a) to speed up the clearance of slums and badly blighted residential areas; (b) to facilitate the provision of decent, low-income housing by helping to finance the acquisition and preparation of appropriate sites, including insite preparation of public facilities that would contribute to "a suitable living environment," and (c) to give private enterprise 'maximum opportunity' to take part in redeveloping these areas. (152)

Despite such rhetoric, see essays by Marcuse and by the Citizens Commission on Civil Rights for a critique of such sentiments.

57. N. Fainstein and S. Fainstein, "Regime Strategies," 248.

58. "During the period 1954–74 the federal urban renewal program, established under Title I of the 1949 Housing Act, became the principal weapon used by government to combat urban 'blight.' Under this program, local authorities used the power of eminent domain to acquire privately held land, then, once a site appropriate for redevelopment had been aggregated and prepared, they turned the land over to a public agency or private developer at a lower price. . . . Although the act declared that the redevelopment area should be predominantly residential in character and that all displaced families be relocated in suitable accommodations, it included no mechanism to induce private developers to build housing for low-income households. Implementation of urban renewal resulted in displacement of poor, predominantly minority residents and use of vacated land mainly for commercial, high-rent and institutional purposes" (S. Fainstein and N. Fainstein, "Economic Change," 17).

59. Harvey, *The Urban Experience*, 256. For more on Pruitt-Igoe, see Rainwater.

60. Levine, 20. He notes, "The partnerships that emerged after 1970 differed from the earlier versions mainly in the expanded scope and complexity of their activity, and in the increased public resources and power that were made available to support private development and create a good business climate" (Levine, 22).

"Both Model Cities and urban renewal terminated with the 1974 passage of the HCDA, which introduced the Community Development Block Grant (CDBG)" (S. Fainstein and N. Fainstein, "Economic Change," 18). It was part of President Nixon's "'new federalism' of special revenue sharing and increased authority for local governments. . . . The years after 1974 saw an increasing emphasis on using private investment to redevelop cities" (ibid., 18).

61. Under these new management conditions, "Municipal democracy is compromised . . . as business control over public resource allocation is increased, and as economic development policy is removed from the normal channels of municipal governance and lodged in public-private institutions. . . . Because public-private partnerships reflect the agenda of urban business elites, they tend to have little impact on the central economic problems of urban areas: inner-city poverty, neighborhood decay, and the shrinking number of quality employment opportunities available to city residents" (Levine, 13).

62. Squires, 3. He states, "A central objective of the emerging strategy has been to secure larger subsidies and financial incentives from the public sector and to reduce corporate taxes and other contributions to . . . social welfare programs" (5).

63. Levine, 25. See Michael E. Stone's classic essay on housing, financing, wages, and capitalism for a discussion of how these elements come into contradiction in U.S. mortgage markets.

64. "San Francisco established a service economy—one based on financial dominance of trans-Pacific capital flows, as well as corporate headquarters functions, conventions, and tourism. . . . Combined with changes in core land use and population, sharp employment growth in these sectors indicated that San Francisco was the quintessential restructuring city" (S. Fainstein and N. Fainstein, "Economic Change," 12).

65. "Between the end of World War II and 1979, 52 high-rise office buildings were constructed in the central business district. . . . The period 1966–75 witnessed a spurt of office construction that added 15 million gross feet, with an estimated 11 million more to be completed by 1980" (S. Fainstein, N. Fainstein, and P. J. Armistead, "San Francisco," 211).

66. Quoted in Paul Rupert, "Corporate Feast in the Pacific." *Pacific Research and World Empire Telegram* 1, no. 4 (Jan.–Mar. 1970): 3. Cited in Hartman, *The Transformation of San Francisco*, 3.

Of course, in 1917, the element to be barred was immigration; in 1970, that which is to be incorporated are commodities and capital.

67. Viviano and Chinn, "The Hong Kong Connection," cited in Hartman, *Transformation*, 4f.

68. For full accounts of this "transformation" and the response of activists, see Chester Hartman's two studies, *Yerba Buena* and *Transformation*.

69. "The Western Addition A-1 stands as a glaring example of early renewal projects, in which housing for low-income minority groups was removed, usually without relocation payments to the occupants, and replaced by office, commercial, and institutional structures and middle- and high-income housing." Hartman observes, "It was from Western Addition A-1 and projects like it around the country that redevelopment and urban renewal became known as "Negro removal"'" (S. Fainstein, N. Fainstein, P. J. Armistead, "San Francisco," 218; citing Hartman, *Yerba Buena*, 100).

Davis notes that, ironically, the Watts Rebellion facilitated precisely such a "removal": "By raising the spectre of Downtown and USC engulfed by a militant Black population, the traditional corporate patrons of the CRA (Community Redevelopment Agency) were able to galvanize broader ruling-class support for the renovation of Downtown" (Davis, "*Chinatown*," 69f).

70. For an excellent discussion of the impact of Pacific Rim capital in California, specifically California, and with regard to the restructuring of other ethnic communities, see Davis, ibid. See also Peterson, "The Southland Emerges as a Global Village."

71. See Hartman, "San Francisco's International Hotel," for an excellent contemporary report on the events and issues. I thank Chester Hartman for providing me with this article, and Michael Stone for discussions on this issue.

72. I follow the historical data provided generously by Estella Habal, of the Manilatown Heritage Foundation. I am grateful to Ms. Habal for speaking with me on this subject. Estella Habal has authored a dissertation on the I-Hotel struggle and the history of Manilatown for the Department of History at the University of California, Davis.

For a vivid depiction of the struggle and events surrounding the I Hotel, see Curtis Choy's documentary film, *The Fall of the I Hotel*.

73. S. Fainstein, N. Fainstein, and P. J. Armistead, "San Francisco," 217.

74. See Schoch, 98.

75. Tatsuno, 36.

76. Quoted in Tatsuno, 42.

77. Data for this discussion comes from the report of the Little Tokyo Anti-Eviction Task Force. For redevelopment in Los Angeles, see also Davis, "*Chinatown*," *City of Quartz*, "Monop-L.A." The similarities between the development of Los Angeles' Little Tokyo and the development of San Francisco's Nihonmachi are striking.

78. Data for this discussion comes from Davis, "Kajima's Throne of Blood." For an analysis of Japanese corporate responsibility and local activism, see Ishi.

79. See Ian Buruma, *Wages of Guilt*.

80. Information for this discussion derived from Iwai and Simi, which includes a valuable report on the Fresno Organizing Project which organized the anti-Yaohan movement.

81. For a good discussion of contemporary Asian womens' labor in the context of Asian American culture and history, see Lisa Lowe.

82. Indeed, Asian business practices in America are not necessarily essentially any different from American practices of union-busting. See Lazarovici's discussion of the strike against the Taiwan-based Tuntext company. See also Tseng for a discussion of the specific transnational nature of Taiwanese businesses in Los Angeles.

83. See Namju Cho.

84. S. Fainstein, N. Fainstein, P. J. Armistead, "San Francisco," 241.

85. For a discussion of racial segregation in suburbs, see Keating. Chen (*Chinatown No More*) and others have pointed out that the character of recent immigration from Taiwan has not been toward Chinatowns in large urban settings, but rather toward suburban space, at least for middle-class immigrants.

Fujioka and Gong note that in 1990, the total number of Asians in the Californian suburban counties of Alameda and Contra Costa Counties exceeded the total Asian population in the city of San Francisco. The Asian population of Santa Clara county alone is expected to exceed that of San Francisco. In contrast, "without international migration, San Francisco would have suffered a net loss in its Asian population" (Fujioka and Gong, 83). The authors point out, however, that geographical redistribution does not necessarily mean social integration.

See Kotkin and Grabowicz, 243f, for important data on California's solicitation of foreign direct investment in the late 1970s and early 1980s.

86. Walker, 392.

87. Dirlik, "Global in the Local," 28.

88. Timothy Fong, *The First Suburban Chinatown*, 3. Of the rest, thirty-one percent are Hispanic and twelve percent are white. I am indebted to Fong's excellent study of Monterey Park.

89. Ibid., 20.

90. Orfield comments on the excitement raised when 1980 census data indicated that there was a significant increase in the number of African American families moving

into the suburbs. Orfield points out that a closer examination of those spaces reveals that they were suburbs in decay, hardly "suburbs" at all, nor the proper signs of "success." See Orfield, "Minorities and Suburbanization." I point this out merely to indicate the highly symbolic nature of space and the subject's ability to move between specific sites. I do not necessarily agree that moving to the suburbs in itself can be taken at face value.

91. Harvey, *Urban Experience*, 122.

92. Fong, 46.

93. See Arax, "Nation's First Suburban Chinatown."

94. Anonymous businessman quoted in Fong, 48.

95. Horton, *The Politics of Diversity*, 31.

96. Fong, 174.

97. Ibid., 49.

98. Ibid., 43.

99. Fong, 48. Mitchell tells how, in Canada, the discomfort felt by many Canadians over the influx of such conspicuous Asian investors prompted the state to put in place certain programs to teach these individuals to blend in better, thereby not only settling civil unrest, but also facilitating investment: "In reaction to burgeoning social and cultural antagonism, the Canadian and Hong Kong capitalist elites, backed by the Canadian state, established the acculturation program Meet with Success in Hong Kong. This program was primarily targeted at middle-class emigrants to Vancouver, who were educated about Canada and about the necessity to adopt a more flexible, cosmopolitan subjectivity" (Mitchell, 252). This program thus promoted Vancouver's integration into the global economy and at the same time produced a particular transnational Asian subject able to negotiate that integration as "Canadian."

For a particularly racist and paranoid view of the "threat" which was supposed to be diffused, consider this excerpt from Sterling Seagrave's *Lords of the Rim*:

> While Anglo vitality remains dormant, the Chinese develop and operate a parallel economy, gradually gaining economic leverage and the political swat that comes with it—as they have done so thoroughly in Thailand, for example. Big money is hard to resist, and the Chinese are pouring money into BC [British Columbia], with benefits already apparent to all. Once addicted, nobody will want to turn off the dollar flow. (270)

100. Fong, 48. He describes the production of a particular transmigrant community: "In the late 1970s it was not uncommon to see wives and children living in Monterey Park while the husbands commuted across the Pacific. Sometimes both parents stayed in Asia and the children were sent over as students; they were set up with a home and sometimes a car. . . . Once the children were established as permanent residents, they could help the parents immigrate" (Fong, 49).

101. Quoted in Horton, *Politics of Diversity*, 21.

102. Seagrave, 273.

103. For other cases, see Christopher J. Smith's study of Flushing, New York. He points out that the earliest appearances of Asians in this community are traced back to two international events: the fact that the United Nations was briefly headquartered in Flushing in 1946, and that the World's Fair was held there in 1964–65. The spread of

Asians into suburban space thus correlates with the postwar development of suburbia as well as the effects of America's geopolitical and international cultural activities, in which East Asia plays an increasingly important role.

Also, see Harris's article on the debate in the Los Angeles suburb of Artesia over the proposed road sign for "Little India." "Locals" fought the placement of that sign, despite assurances that it will bring business (ethnic Indians own about 80 percent of the 900 businesses in the 1.6 square mile city). The mayor declared: "This is Artesia, not India. If you don't like our decision [not to have the sign] please pack up and leave this city and move to some other place or go back to India."

104. "For the many minimal-profit family entrepreneurs in Monterey Park, high property values and rent-gouging by ethnic property owners are not conducive to a symbiotic relationship. In this city we may very well be seeing an enclave economy that is more predatory than supportive, because of land speculation, too much competition within the enclave, and the inability of the enclave to reach out to a broader market" (Fong, 166).

Richard H. Thompson's study of Toronto's Chinatown also points out that the "traditional elite" of that Chinatown, arguing against development, came into collusion with the new "entrepreneurial elite" of Asian capital when it became clear that it had to do so in order to maintain its hegemony as spokespersons for "the community." See Thompson, 307–19.

105. Harvey, *Urban Experience*, 168. The effect on commodities is similar: "'To the extent that money, with its colorlessness and its indifferent quality can become a denominator of all values,' Simmel wrote, 'it becomes the frightful leveler — it hollows out the core of things, their specific values and their uniqueness and incomparability in a way which is beyond repair. They all float with the same specific gravity in the constantly moving stream of money'" (166). Harvey goes on to remark: "The grand diversity of actual labor processes given over to the production of all manner of goods of specific qualities . . . gets averaged out and represented in the single abstract magnitude of money (exchange value)" (167). For further discussion, see Harvey, *Justice*, 234–41.

106. Cited in Kwong, 38.

107. Harvey, *Urban Experience*, 123.

108. Ibid., 183.

109. Cited in Fong, 54.

110. Fong, 54. Nevertheless, as Harvey points out, even recognizing the destructive rapaciousness of "development" cannot erase the contradictory lure of its supposed benefits. Here we can substitute "race" for class without losing the essential point, as non-Asians and many Asian Americans argued against growth: "Urban regions wracked by class struggle or ruled by class alliances that take paths antagonistic to accumulation (toward no-growth economies or municipal socialism) at some point have to face the realities of competition for jobs, trade, money, investments, services, and so forth" (Harvey, *Urban Experience*, 158). Cf. Harvey, ibid., 122: "The exclusion of further growth creates a . . . problem, for if a 'no-growth' movement gathers momentum, then how can effective demand and capital accumulation be sustained? A phenomenon created to sustain the capitalist order can in the long run work to exacerbate its internal tensions."

111. "Though only a minority of Chinese immigrants are developers and speculators who command large financial resources, once growth is associated with them, all Chinese become a suspect homogeneous group to non-Chinese" (Fong, 169). Thus we find that "assimilated" Asian Americans may very well identify with the non-Asian community and be targeted as still "alien." They may, indeed, internalize that suspicion of themselves.

112. Lemann, 62.

113. Friedland et al., 213.

114. Horton, "Politics of Ethnic Change," 591. See Calderon for a discussion of interethnic politics in Monterey Park.

115. See Ong, "On the Edge of Empire."

116. The event that drew particular attention to Trie was his bringing a Chinese arms merchant, Wang Jun, to the White House. Trie was said to have "dreamt of opening a Chinese restaurant-cum-Asian business center near the White House" (Clines).

117. See Rosenbaum.

118. March 2, 1997, D6.

119. Bernstein and Munro, 31. They elaborate this argument in their book *The Coming Conflict with China*.

120. Senator Fred Thompson's opening statement, Associated Press, July 8, 1997. Sen. Sam Brownback added: "Did foreign governments or foreign conglomerates infiltrate our political process with a scheme to influence our election for their own ends?" (Associated Press, July 8, 1997). I thank L. Ling-chi Wang for providing much of the data on the "Chinese Money Scandal."

121. Sun, A14.

122. See Clines.

123. See Woodward, "FBI Cleared China Funds Revelation."

124. "Justice Distances Itself from Thompson Charge Regarding China." Capitol Newswire, Washington, D.C., News Bureau, July 14, 1997.

125. "No Republican looking into the campaign-finance scandal actually believes John Huang is a spy. . . . But Clarke's comments come a little late for the GOP, which for five days has been trying to paint Huang as a cross between a Cold War era spy and a practitioner of a more modern type of industrial espionage. Sen. Sam Brownback, R-Kan., had argued that Huang had helped endanger American lives, and several senators had posed scenarios that had Huang leaking everything from nuclear power plant secrets to military base information to the Chinese" (Sheila Kaplan, "GOP Backpedals on Huang Accusations," MS-NBC broadcast, July 20, 1997).

126. See Pincus.

127. As early as April of 1990, there had been the resurgence of China as the Evil Empire. FBI director William S. Sessions warned the House Judiciary subcommittee on civil and constitutional rights of the "widespread use" of Chinese nationals in the United States as communist spies.

In the same testimony Sessions reported on the FBI's investigation of a twelve-year-old American schoolchild for his letter to the Yugoslavian embassy for information for a book report. The Director "credited arms control agreements, business opportunities

both here and in the Soviet Union, U.S. emigration policies, and cultural and educational exchanges giving Soviet intelligence services 'greater opportunity than ever before to exploit the United States and its citizens.'" See Ostrow.

One former U.S. ambassador to Beijing (and veteran of twenty-seven years at the
CIA), James Lilley, went so far as to say that "They [the Chinese] have been kicked out
of more countries in Africa than we have, they've been at it all the time, influencing
people with guns, politics, and money." See Zuckerman.

For a later report by the FBI on Chinese influence, see Woodward.

128. See articles by Brauchli and by Zuckerman.

129. See Silverstein. Also, see Bernstein and Munro, *Coming Conflict with China*,
105–29. See Kissinger's defense of a pro-Beijing policy and his insistence on his objectivity: "The Folly of Bullying Beijing" (*Los Angeles Times*, July 6, 1997).

130. See Broder. See also Layoun for a discussion of the operations of the Endowment
in Greece, the Middle East, and Japan. Norman Solomon's article, "Money Scandals:
'Mr. Smith' Goes to Washington," details a longstanding history of U.S. clandestine operations in foreign politics. The article was sent out on the Internet via the Creator's
Syndicate in March 1997, and reprinted in many newspapers, including the Minneapolis
Star Tribune (Mar. 16, 1997); and the Sept./Oct. issue of *EXTRA!*, the magazine of Fair-
ness and Accuracy in Reporting (FAIR).

131. See "America's Dose of Sinophobia" for a discussion of the dual appearance of
Francis Fukuyama and Samuel P. Huntington at a Washington dinner: Huntington's
"clash" theory was all the rage, and was used to fuel fear over China that overshadowed
the actual issue of illegal campaign funds.

132. Rich Lowry, "Selling Out? China Syndrome." *The National Review* (Mar. 24,
1997).

133. See Rothkopf.

134. Rouse, 360.

135. Cf. Ong and Nonini, "Toward a Cultural Politics": "The imbrication of the
nation-state with capitalism challenges the popular view that transnational capitalism
is eroding state power everywhere and in the same way" (324).

Chapter 9: Double Trouble

1. Redfield et al., quoted in Gordon, 61.

2. R. E. Park and E. W. Burgess, 735. For a fuller discussion of Park's theories of
assimilation and a critique in terms of Asian-American issues, see Paul Takagi, for a critique of Park's race relations cycle theory, see Lyman, "The Race Relations Cycle of
Robert E. Park."

3. Park and Burgess, 736f.

4. R. E. Park, "Assimilation, Social," 281.

5. Below I will speak in greater detail about Ridley Scott's film *Blade Runner*; here I
simply mention the similarity of the Tyrell Corporation's endowing the replicants with
memories (e.g., Leon and Rachel's photographs), and this act of memory invention.

6. One might also note that, accompanying the transfer of "marginality" from modern individuals in general to the racialized subject, was a new pathologization of modern life that spoke of the alienation brought about by the corporate world. This pathologizing was especially prevalent in the 1940s through the 1960s. The new corporate subject was torn asunder by the falsity of the boardroom. The notion of hypocrisy, of false fronts, of performance of social roles, appears in Whyte's notion of the "organizational man," Fromm's "market-oriented personality," and Riesman's "other-directed personality." See Brian Turner, page 110. Here he cites W. F. Whyte, *The Organizational Man* (New York, 1956), Erich Fromm, *Escape from Freedom* (New York: Reinhart, 1941) and David Riesman, *The Lonely Crowd: A Study of the Changing American Character* (New Haven: Yale University Press, 1950).

7. W. E. B. DuBois, 102.

8. In forming this concept, DuBois drew on a long psychological tradition that began with the 1817 case of Mary Reynolds, as described in the journal *Medical Repository*. The case involved a woman who at age nineteen fell into a deep sleep. When she awoke she had no memory of her prior self, and took on an entirely new personality. Over the next four years she alternated between these personalities. Francis Wayland's *Elements of Intellectual Philosophy* again referred to the case and category; finally William James, DuBois's teacher at Harvard, treats the subject in his *Principles of Psychology*. In France, Binet (known in the U.S. for his I.Q. tests) took up the subject. See Bruce.

9. One of the most ardent writers in this "school" was Vita S. Sommers, who asserted that "problems of identity constitute the most serious and distinctive psychological disorder of our time. . . . Greenson, one of the major contributors to the understanding of this problem, has gone so far as to call it 'the American disease'." After opening her study at this level of generality, however, Sommers focuses exclusively on "the cultural hybrid, or multiethnic patient." See Sommers, 332.

Cf. Grewal and Kaplan's observation that even the current, valorized notion of "hybridity" is racially asymmetrical: "what seems to get *theorized* in the West as 'hybridity' remains enmeshed in the gaze of the West" (7).

10. This notion is present, of course, in Fanon. See also Butler for a discussion of subjection.

11. DuBois, "Strivings of the Negro People," 194f.

12. Caudill and DeVos, 1117.

13. Sue and Sue, 40.

14. Sue and Sue, 38.

15. Tong, "Ghetto," 8. As noted before, this ahistorical and vague notion of "Asian values" played a crucial role in constructing the model minority myth. We return to it later in this chapter.

16. Tong, "Living Death" (hereafter LD), 183.

17. Tong, LD, 184.

18. Tong, LD, 186.

19. Tong, LD, 190. While disagreeing with Tong on several issues, Surh shares his disdain for the Sues' "ahistorical" thesis, and suggests that the marginal man adapts as a survival strategy not because he has made a moral choice: "the Marginal Man does not

turn his back on his own kind out of malice or evil intent, but as a mode of survival" (Surh, 163). For an interesting case history of dualism as strategy, see Ichioka.

20. Tong, LD, 193.

21. Tong, LD, 178.

22. Indeed, one of Tong's critics targets mainly his ethnography, and reaches back to the ninth century to do so. See Abbott, 69f.

23. Surh, 162.

24. Tong, "Ghetto," 19.

25. Tong, "Ghetto," 24.

26. See Dirlik, "Place-Based Imagination."

27. See Omatsu, and other essays in Aguilar-San Juan.

28. See Omatsu, 21.

29. Chin et al., xxiv.

30. Chin et al., xlviii. In another essay, Chin and Jeffrey Paul Chan argue the case more specifically: "The concept of dual personality successfully deprives the Chinese-American of all authority over language and thus a means of codifying, communicating, and legitimizing experience" ("Racist Love," 65f).

31. Chin et al., xxv.

32. For an analysis of this transition in other terms, see Dirlik, "Asians on the Rim."

33. Chin, "Come All Ye Asian American Writers," 50.

34. Ibid., 34.

35. Strobel, 38.

36. Published in Manila by De La Salle University Press in 1994.

37. Espiritu, "Crossroads and Possibilities," viii.

38. Barth, 9, 11.

39. This idea will be developed in the next chapter.

40. Cabral, 54.

41. Ibid., 57.

42. Fanon, *Wretched of the Earth*, 227.

43. For an analysis of this topic, see Dirlik, "Asians on the Rim."

44. Fanon, *Wretched of the Earth*, 244.

45. Quoted in Terkel, 311.

46. Karl Lo, 176. For more information on nationalist activities in the United States, see Okihiro, *Margins and Mainstreams*, 165, and Melendy, 148–60 and 209–16.

47. Kotkin and Diau, 24.

48. Ty Pak, *Guilt Payment* (Honolulu: Bamboo Ridge Press, 1983), 114–15. Cited in Abelman and Lie, 50.

49. Kim, "Home Is Where the *Han* Is," 229f.

50. See Abelman and Lie, especially pp. 49–84.

51. Williams, 147f. A summary of her argument may be found in this passage: "To-day, studies of nationalism and of the politics of cultural struggle which shape and sustain it must be part of a broad cultural history focussed on the way that the precepts of linking territory and culture, which produced the initial generic Western European ideologies of nationalism, resulted in emphases on fixity, stability, homogeneity, and

presumed linkages among these as against the reality of heterogeneity. At the same time such a study becomes a synchronic examination of how new national ideologies, based on the precepts of older ones, often actively retained or passively took for granted the physiognomic premises they contained as they became free to reform the ideological orientations that preexisted European colonial expansion" (166f). See also Lisa Lowe's influential article on heterogeneity and hybridity in Asian America, reprinted in *Immigrant Acts*.

52. *Saturday Review World*, Nov. 6, 1973, page 34; *Library Journal*, Nov. 1, 1973, page 3257. Cited in Kim, *Asian American Literature*, 81f.

53. And here we can think back to Park's scrutiny of the young Japanese American woman—seeking traces to confirm her Japanese identity.

54. Okimoto.

55. Žižek, *The Sublime Object of Ideology*, 29.

56. Park delineates Kwang from the stereotype: "I am here for the hope of his identity, which may also be mine, who he has been on a public scale when the rest of us wanted only security in the tiny dollar-shops and churches of our lives" (304).

57. Hayden White has made the point that the anxiety over the exact content of whiteness/civilization has long been an issue. He correlates the progressive annexation of Other spaces with a psychic interiorization of wildness: "As one after another of these wildernesses was brought under control, the idea of the Wild Man was progressively despatialized. This despatialization was attended by a compensatory process of psychic interiorization. And the result has been that modern cultural anthropology has conceptualized the idea of wildness as the repressed content of *both* civilized *and* primitive humanity. So that, instead of the relatively comforting thought that the Wild Man may exist *out there* and can be contained by some kind of physical action, it is now thought . . . that the Wild Man is lurking within every man" (White, 153f). I thank Arif Dirlik for suggesting this essay to me.

58. See, for instance, Bell's use of a particular description of this scene to characterize the presence of Asian Americans.

59. The notion that Scott may be borrowing from Dick's novel, *The Man in the High Castle*, to create the image of an Asian "invasion" is supported by the image from that novel of "enormous neon signs with their permanent ads obliterating the front of virtually every large building" (22).

60. Csicsery-Ronay claims that such fear of the internal characterizes the link between the genre of horror and cyberpunk, and suggests as well a link between these genres and the trope of schizophrenia: "The horror genre has always played with the violation of the body, since it adopts as its particular 'object' fear—the violent disruption of the sense of security, which, precisely because it is a sense, works from within the house/body, the house of the senses. Hence, in horror, the house/body's integrity is generally threatened from within, using analogues of disease and unconscious psychosomatic pathology" (188).

61. One of the first such attempts was Ruth Frankenberg's *Social Construction of Whiteness*. See Shelly Fisher Fishkin, "Interrogating 'Whiteness,'" for a comprehensive listing of "white studies."

62. Chambers, "The Unexamined," 191.

63. World Health Organization, *Lexicon of Psychiatric and Mental Health Terms*. Geneva, 1994, p. 82.

64. And this is the thematic linking this notion of schizophrenia to that of Jameson.

65. See Snyder and Forsyth, 29.

66. Here we might look back upon our discussion of assimilation as involving precisely a sharing of memory, and a memory transfer.

67. We should note here that it is the United States that is endowed with this status, not China; it is a weird echo of the Open Port treaties of the nineteenth century which endows the United States with the power to dictate the terms of trade.

Chapter 10: Asia Pacific

1. The recent "crash" of many of these Asian economies has forced a rethinking of this, as we will discuss in the conclusion to this study.

2. See Connery's and Cuming's respective articles which each bear this term, as well as Dirlik, "Asia-Pacific Idea."

3. Throughout, my usage of "postmodernity" is influenced by Jameson and Harvey, rather than stemming from the formation of the term as a purely ethico-aesthetic effect.

4. Borthwick, 9.

5. Hubert Bancroft, quoted in Kotkin and Grabowciz, 224. This spirit is neatly condensed in the first chapter of Arrell Morgan Gibson's book, entitled "America's Last Frontier: The Pacific Basin." For a history of American images of the Pacific, see M. Consuelo León W., and, for its particular imperialistic textuality, see Rob Wilson, *American Sublime*.

6. Quoted in Gibson.

7. I am referring here to Park's notion of a "racial frontier" in the Pacific, for example.

8. California State Board of Control, *California and the Oriental* (Sacramento: State Printing Office, 1920), page 10. Quoted in Leonard, 119.

9. Nixon, "Asia After Vietnam." Quoted in Cumings, 33.

10. For a discussion of this Japanese concept of neocolonial expansion, see Peter Duus, "Imperialism Without Colonies." See also Tomiyama Ichirō: "'Cooperativism' is nothing more than the 'Greater East Asia Co-Prosperity Sphere' ideology, which attempts to justify Japanese invasion in contrast to 'white' colonial rule" (387).

11. Dirlik, "Asia Pacific Idea," 67. He maintains that "there is no Pacific region that is an 'objective' given, but only a competing set of ideational constructs that project upon a certain location on the globe the imperatives of interest, power or vision of these historically produced relationships" (56).

12. Ibid., 73.

13. Ibid., 63.

14. Connery, "Pacific Rim Discourse," 33f.

15. Ibid., 36.

16. See the discussion in Naisbitt and Aburdene, "The Rise of the Pacific Rim," 184–227. This passage cited in Wilson and Dirlik, 5.

17. Naisbitt and Aburdene, 336f.

18. Gao Fang, *Ping disanci langchao*. Quoted in Woodside, 16.

19. Nonini, "Ethnographic Grounding," 165. Nonini raises the important historical precedent, which I have remarked upon in Chap. 8: "It was the existence of *prior* spatial displacements of surplus U.S. and European capital during the late 1940s, the 1950s, and the 1960s that allowed Japanese, Korean, and Taiwanese capitalist enterprises, under strong state direction and encouragement, to develop their economies to become competitors with U.S. capital to begin with" (165). In my previous discussion, I noted that this influx of U.S. money into these areas was part of a general "Marshall Plan"; state direction was mandated by U.S. overseers, and the notion was (obviously) *not* to develop these countries' potential as competitors, but as suppliers and markets for the United States.

20. See Van Kemenade, 161. These zones were set up by future Chinese president Jiang Zemin. On East Asian EPZs and Mexican *maquiladoras* under NAFTA, see Castillo and Acosta. For "special economic zones" in China, see Xiangming Chen.

21. For instance, "while American wholesalers found new sources of supply in Asian manufacturers, American corporations, in their single-minded search for increased profits, took advantage of cheap labor (and strong central governments) in the Asian NICs to set up their own 'off-shore' plants. These then proceeded to ship goods back to the United States, for sale under familiar American brand names" (Gibney, 246).

22. See Xiangming Chen, 98.

23. Woodside, 24.

24. In Brzezinski, "America's New Geostrategy," 680.

25. Ling-chi Wang, "Roots," 186.

26. Ong and Nonini go so far as to identify this subjectivity in these terms: "Chinese transnationalists are thus *prototypical people of modernity* who, like diaspora Indians, emerged as modern trading subjects under European imperialism and are now extending their entrepreneurial and professional interests to former metropolitan countries [emphasis added]" ("Towards a Cultural Politics," 327).

"Sojourner" was a term commonly used in the nineteenth century to refer to Chinese workers who had come to the United States. Nowadays, the latter two terms describe the more complicated situation—"parachute kids" refers to children from Asia sent alone or with one parent to live in the United States, "astronauts" refers to transnational Asian business people. In both these cases dual residencies are kept.

27. As Ong and Nonini flatly state, "There is nothing intrinsically liberating about diasporic cultures" (ibid., 325).

For discussions of the appropriation and manipulation of diasporic identities, see Vincente L. Rafael, "'Your Grief Is Our Gossip'" for an account of the "nationalist attempts [in the Philippines] at containing the dislocating effects of global capital through the collective mourning of its victims" (267), and Katharyne Mitchell's analysis of the production of Chinese capitalist subjectivities in accordance with Canadian economic desires. The "flexibility" of Southeast Asian transnational identities noted by Ong and

Nonini raises the question of "authenticity" mobilized to secure, for various interests, certain national and ethnic subjectivities at particular times and others at different moments.

28. See Waldinger and Tseng for a close study of two different manifestations of Chinese diaspora in the United States.

29. Leo Ou-fan Lee writes on this question from the point of view of the intellectual activities on the "periphery" ("On the Margins"); Sau-ling Wong's recent work on immigrant literature has also approached this subject from the perspective of gender and politics.

30. Quoted in LeGoff, 136f.

31. See Thomas Luckmann's discussion of time and sociality.

32. Lee, "On the Margins," 230.

33. Kingston, *Woman Warrior*, 105f.

34. Chesneaux makes a similar point: "Immigrant workers . . . have left behind their ethnic cultures solidly based in another space-time, and are suddenly confronted with the spatio-temporal contradictions of modernity" (29f).

For a fine poetic elaboration of Chinese American diasporic and local identities that spans a broad stretch of historical time, see Leong.

35. Now why is this episode anticlimactic? It is because everyone, including the reader, occupies a time/space different from Moon Orchid and can see what is to occur. We are synchronized with historical time; she is not. In the sisters we are presented with two portrayals of this disjuncture—we must remember that Brave Orchid also believes, or wants to believe, that her sister can claim her rights. Indeed, Moon Orchid's reluctance to do so indicates that she may be wiser than Brave Orchid in her sense of the historical difference that separates her from any social institution that would interpellate her husband in the way they expect—he simply will not answer the "call" to perform.

36. Santos, 24f.

37. Ibid., 191.

38. Ibid., 176.

39. For a thoroughgoing contextualization and critique of Santos and Filipino literature in general, see E. San Juan, Jr.

40. See Wong, *Reading Asian American Literature*, 135f.

41. Similarly, LeGoff suggests: "Just as the past is not history but the object of history, so memory is not history, but both one of its objects and an elementary level of its development" (129). See also Balibar and Wallerstein, 86, for the idea of the nation form as retrospectively produced.

42. It should be pointed out that different "waves" of diasporic and immigrant populations often hold very different views toward one another. There are various divergences between diasporic Asians and American-born Asian Americans, as exposed in David Henry Hwang's play *F.O.B.* and evident in Asian American narratives. See Marlon K. Hom, "A Case of Mutual Exclusion," which gives numerous examples of how each group stereotypes the other.

43. Hobsbawm, 9.

44. Wang Gungwu, "Among Non-Chinese," 146.

45. For an overview of the genesis of the term, see Uhalley. For detailed economic description, see Ash and Yueh. Representative studies among a vast and growing number are the 1993 special issue of *The China Quarterly*, Van Kemenade, and Weidenbaum and Hughes.

46. For instance, in Malaysia, "the race riots [of May 1969] hastened the recognition that unless something was done to redress the economic balance between the haves (who happened to be mostly Chinese) and the have-nots (whom happened to be mostly Malays), the racial divide would widen. The answer the politicians came up with was the New Economic Policy (NEP)" (Lynn Pan, 226). See Szanton Blanc for an excellent discussion of the local production of "Asian capitalism" in the Philippines and Thailand.

47. Weidenbaum and Hughes, 8.

48. Wang Gungwu, "Greater China and the Chinese Overseas," 926.

49. Wang Gungwu asserts the difficulty of answering the question of what "Cultural China" might be: "As for the cultural debates that have followed, they have led to both pride and incomprehension" (ibid., 929).

50. Tu, "Cultural China," 13.

51. Tu, *The Confucian World Observed*, 113.

52. Clark, 38. The author notes that this image is confirmed in its cultural production: "The topic is hot enough to have spawned a new four-color glossy magazine, *Emigrant*" (39).

53. Weidenbaum and Hughes, 30. These authors, seeking a western equivalent, take recourse to the Jew-Asian analogy, saying that this phenomenon resembles nothing so much as the Rothschild empire (10).

54. Ong and Nonini, "Towards a Cultural Politics," 325.

55. Weidenbaum and Hughes, 57.

56. Lee Kuan Yew, quoted in Gibney, 254.

57. See Woodside, "Mobilization Myth," and Gereffi, "Global Sourcing," and essays included in Bonacich, Cheng, Chincilla, Hamilton, and Ong's collection.

58. Tai, 2.

59. Borthwick puts it, "Why do these East Asian economies have such high savings rates? Why have their societies been able to adapt so readily to industrialization, seemingly with a minimum of social disruption? What accounts for the apparently harmonious relations between government and industry or between management and labor? Why is income relatively equitably distributed in these countries, and why, when it is not, does the inequality attract so much attention?" (309).

60. *Forbes*, July 18, 1994, pages 140–43; quoted in Ong, 188. See also Weidenbaum and Hughes, 28.

61. Weber's thesis is found in *The Religion of China*. Cf. Peter Berger's flat reassessment: "Weber wrote extensively on Asia, notably China and India, concluding that Asian cultures and religious traditions were deeply uncongenial to modernization. I think one may say today, simply, that Weber was wrong" (6f).

62. As Arif Dirlik puts it: "What had hitherto been viewed as an obstacle to Chinese modernity was transformed into a dynamic force of modernity for others to emulate." See Dirlik's excellent study, "Confucius in the Borderlands," 236.

63. Kahn, 121.

64. Tu, "A Confucian Perspective," 34. For Confucianism as facilitating capitalism, see Nakajima. See also Eisuke, Morishima, and Tai for East Asian proclamations of how Confucianism presents an "oriental alternative" to a weak western economic and cultural model. For a fuller discussion, see Mark Berger. For "Chinese values," see Farquhar and Hevia.

65. Borthwick, 542.

66. Tu, "A Confucian Perspective," 32f.

67. Quoted in the *International Herald Tribune*, Nov. 23, 1993, page 4. As Aihwa Ong notes, "It is precisely this continual invocation of Chinese cultural affinity and racial exclusivity that has disturbed some Western observers, who are struck by the increasing number of regional business meetings restricted only to entrepreneurs of Chinese ancestry" (Ong, "Chinese Modernities," 182).

For an analysis of current deployments of race in the discourse of East and Southeast Asia, see Sautman.

68. According to *International Investor* magazine, as cited in Weidenbaum and Hughes, 29.

69. See Ong, "Chinese Modernities," 182; quoting Kao, *South China Morning Post*, Nov. 25, 1993, page 31.

70. Ong, "Chinese Modernities," 191. In another article, co-written with Donald Nonini, she points out: "Much of the new capitalism of the Asia Pacific is state-driven and state-sponsored, and Chinese transnational capitalists, like those in other parts of the world, represent forces that nation-states can deploy and discipline to strengthen themselves." Indeed, "transnational Chinese capitalists within the region have been the linchpin securing economic dynamism to authoritarian state systems. . . . The imbrication of the nation-state with capitalism challenges the popular view that transnational capitalism is eroding state power everywhere and in the same way" (Ong and Nonini, "Toward a Cultural Politics," 324).

71. Borthwick, 309.

72. Tu, *Confucian Ethics Today*, 164; quoted in Dirlik, 259.

73. Tu notes: "The success of Japan and the Four Dragons . . . may have a great deal to do with the authority of the central government to forge bonds of trust with the business community, the intelligentsia, the working class, and the populace as a whole. However, this concerted effort to achieve vertical integration makes it difficult to develop Western-style democratic institutions and ideas such as civil society, loyal opposition, an independent legal system, a sense of privacy, and individualism" ("A Confucian Perspective," 35). In 1988, Tu Wei-ming gave a speech entitled, "Confucian Humanism and Democracy," which "offered a devastating critique of hierarchy and the absence of democracy in the Confucian tradition" (Dirlik, "Confucius in the Borderlands," 257).

74. *Far Eastern Economic Review*, Dec. 10, 1992; quoted in Ong, "Chinese Modernities," 184.

75. Internally, Heng and Devan have also pointed out how the instantiation of "Confucian patriarchy," attached as it is to the overriding imperatives of order and social harmony, has been deployed to produce a particular female subjectivity for the Singaporan state.

76. Gibney, in ending his book on "the Pacific Century," makes a similar point: "It is in fact the Chinese idea of the family and the community—as reinterpreted by Japan, Korea, and others—which should give us a new perspective. Economy, in the root meaning of the Greek *oikonomos*, means a stewardship—that is, to manage and distribute the work and goods of a household or community. It is more, far more than the pursuit of private gain" (Gibney, 563). Cf. Lee Kuan Yew, in Van Kamenade, 378.

Tai Hung-chao quotes and endorses a newly valorized collectivism as the "Oriental alternative," which treads between the Scylla and Charybdis of unbridled capitalism and totalitarian socialism: "East Asian countries, by relying on their cultural strength rather than following a Socialist strategy, have been able to accomplish precisely what many Socialist developing countries have avowed but failed to achieve" (27). Finally, note Nakajima: "Marxism, socialism, or theories of a planned economy are no longer valid models for modernization. The American model for modernization based on rationalism, or pragmatism, aimed at a highly consumptive mass society has also reached a stalemate these days" (115).

77. Ong and Nonini, 328. Further, note Mitchell's observation that "Hong Kong capitalists can manipulate images of both the transnational cosmopolitan and the 'ethnic Chinese,' enabling them to position themselves at the lucrative center of Pacific Rim business" (236); i.e., these identities are flexible and adaptive.

78. Dirlik, "Asia Pacific Idea," 74. The most famous exponent of this management technique is William Ouchi. See his *Theory Z: How American Business Can Meet the Japanese Challenge*. He is following the lead of Ezra Vogel.

79. Duus, "Discussion," 6of.

80. Peter Berger, 6.

81. Quoted in Kotkin and Grabowicz, 238.

82. Dirlik, "Confucius in the Borderlands," 266f. Dirlik goes on to specify the historic moment: "It may not be coincidental that East Asia emerged as a 'model' almost simultaneously with the appearance of a Global Capitalism. And it has been a model, if not for a new kind of social paradise, at least for new models of social control and management of the exploitation of labor. And it has been successful, judging by the popularity in the United States, at least, of 'Oriental' texts that promote at one and the same time a New Age philosophy of social humility and management" (Dirlik, 268).

83. See Wilson, "*Goodbye Paradise*," for a provocative discussion of this respatialization of the Pacific and cyberpunk fiction, and Wilson's "Imagining Asia-Pacific" for a more general, but just as useful, discussion of the ideological formation "Asia-Pacific."

84. Nevertheless, Ohmae concedes that governments may affect (but not "manage") the "FX empire" by adjusting exchange rates.

85. In this regard, Ohame has particularly harsh words for America: "There is, unfortunately, much in the American soil that undermines the kind of steadiness global cultivation requires. The legal system in the United States, for example, is a wonderful mechanism for spoiling the soil for business" (208). This "borderless world" is obviously a response to American tariff wars with Japan.

86. See Mark Berger, 96f, regarding the increasingly prevalent notion that Asian economic success is predicated on the activist state. Fallows quoted here.

87. See Bonacich, Cheng, et al., "The Garment Industry in the Restructuring Global

Economy" (8–13), for a good discussion of the uneven effects of globalization in Asia Pacific. See also Paul Virilio's work on cybermonde, speed, and politics.

88. See Chesneaux, *Transpacifiques: observations et considerations diverses sur les terres et archipels du Grand Ocean*, Paris: La Decouverte, 1987.

89. Connery, "Pacific Rim Discourse," 34.

90. See Bukatman's chapter, "Terminal Flesh," which notes that this double resolution is typical of the genre.

91. After writing *Neuromancer*, Gibson wrote several other novels before writing *Idoru*. One major novel written during this intermediate period was *Mona Lisa Overdrive*, which like *Neuromancer* deploys Japan as a key topos.

92. For a discussion of *aidoru*, see Ching, "Imaginings."

93. McCaffrey, interview with Gibson, 284f.

94. Tatsumi, 373.

95. Suvin, 357f.

Conclusion

1. *Foreign Affairs* 76, no. 5 (1997). In order of appearance, they are: Arthur Schlesinger, Jr., "Has Democracy a Future?"; Samuel P. Huntington, "The Erosion of American National Interests"; Zbigniew Brzezinski, "A Geostrategy for Eurasia"; Kishore Mahbubani, "An Asia-Pacific Consensus." Walter B. Wriston's "Bits, Bytes, and Diplomacy" also touches upon the issues raised in the last chapter regarding cyberspace and the Pacific.

2. The editor notes Charr's petition filed in Missouri: "*Petition of Easurk Emsen Charr*, 273 Fed, 207 (1921). A similar case in California was *in re En Sk Song*, 271 Fed. 23 (1921). Both grew out of the legislation enabling certain war veterans to become naturalized citizens and affirmed the ineligibility of Koreans for naturalization. Forty-four Koreans in Hawaii were naturalized under the same legislation, but their naturalization was subsequently voided" (307).

3. For Asian American studies, see the special issue of *Amerasia Journal* (vol. 23, no. 1, 1997) dedicated to this topic.

4. See, for example, works by Wee, Gregory Lee, and others. For an interesting discussion of the way "modernity" has restructured Asian urban geographies, see Tadiar. Recently, Academica Sinica in Taiwan has begun a series of conferences on Asian American studies; these reveal a particular set of concerns and interpretations of Asian America from Asia.

5. Walden Bello, 19. It is crucial to note that "western" interests do not necessarily depart from the interests of some Asians. While the middle class and workers may be further disadvantaged, Bello notes that "Washington's free-market agenda is not without partisans among the political elite in Asia. In their view, the U.S. corporate sector's embrace of downsizing and other ruthless measures in the early nineties accounts for America's marked edge over Japan and Europe. According to this school, state-assisted capitalism may have worked in achieving high growth in the early phases of industrialization but is dysfunctional in an era of globalized markets" (19). Thus we have another

swing in the relative value of American and Asian capitalisms and a concomitant modification in the valuation of Asian/American.

6. Bello, 16.

Appendix: Model Minority Discourse

This essay was written for the conference on Minority Discourse at the Humanities Research Institute, University of California—Irvine, in June 1992. Although I have modified my views somewhat since this essay's inception, because it has been widely cited and since plans to publish a conference volume have been set aside, I have decided to append it to this larger study. Certain sections have been omitted because they are to be found in earlier chapters. I thank Homi Bhabha, Abdul JanMohamed, Henry Giroux, King-kok Cheung, Lisa Lowe, and David Lloyd for their comments at the conference.

1. See my "Universalisms and Minority Culture" for a study of this issue.

2. This pathologizing is discussed above in Chap. 9.

3. This may also be read globally—there has emerged a genre of post-Mao, post–Tianmen Square China/United States narratives that demands similar critical attention.

4. Berman, 155.

5. By "optimal" I mean that subject position seemingly most free to predicate itself within the dominant.

6. For two different accounts of the romantic element in American literature, see Jay and Porte. The practical application of individualism in the psycho-economic field is well established in modern American mythologies by figures such as Norman Vincent Peale (*The Power of Positive Thinking*, 1952) and Napoleon Hill (*Think and Grow Rich*, 1960).

7. Wilson, "Producing American Selves," 106, 109. This essay presents a number of provocative ideas that link up well to the present study.

8. Gramsci, 362, n5. Stuart Hall explains that for Gramsci, "Ideology consists of two distinct 'floors.' The coherence of an ideology often depends on its specialized philosophical elaboration. But this formal coherence cannot guarantee its organic historical effectivity. That can only be found when and where philosophical currents enter into, modify and transform the practical, everyday consciousness or popular thought of the masses. The latter is what he calls 'common sense'." See Hall, 20.

9. In this, Foucault notes that "happiness is not only a simple effect. Happiness of individuals is a requirement for the survival and development of the state." Foucault, *Technologies*, 158.

10. See Hall, especially 14–15.

11. See hooks.

12. The contradictory and highly charged character of our notions of the "personal," and this notion's ability to critique the social, was made clear at various presentations of this essay, when many audience members became (in one of their words) "anxious" at my inclusion of popular psychology into a discussion of minority discourse. Somehow the connection between popular psychology and a set of literary texts that have already become canonized as "ethnic" literature was seen to trivialize them. I understand by this criticism that the "personal" as it appears in mass culture was taken to be ontologically

distinct from the "personal" that could appear in academic, institutional culture. One is discredited as the victim of a false consciousness, the other is privy to more elevated traumas and remedies. But "mass" cultural phenomena need to be treated with great seriousness and not trivialized themselves as simple curiosities or somehow beneath academic scrutiny. They are crucial signifiers of sociopolitical and cultural ideologies that might well have a more profound effect on our social lives than texts of elite academic status to which minority literatures would aspire. Therefore, I want to take the conjunction of the discourses of self-affirmative action, recovery, and model minority discourse as critical indices of the contemporary cultural and sociopolitical space we inhabit; I want to take their intercourse as not only possible but always immanent.

13. This element is transposed to other minority groups as well, as was clearly seen in the confirmation hearings of Clarence Thomas, and the tremendous success of Shelby Steele's and Steven Carter's books.

14. This connection is not merely accidental. Amy Tan tells the story of her coming to write—in therapy she became disconcerted that her therapist would fall asleep during the sessions. Tan then turned to writing as therapy.

15. See, for example, Halbwachs's influential work on collective memory. One may also refer to my essay "The Politics of Memory: Remembering History in Alice Walker and Joy Kogawa."

16. Reed, 506.

17. Kim, *Asian American Literature*, 60. For a provocative discussion of the relationship between confessional, autobiography, and Chinese American literature, see Chin, "This Is Not an Autobiography." A longer exposition of this thesis is found in Chin's "Come All Ye Asian American Writers: The Real and the Fake," in *The Big AIIEEEE!*.

18. Cited in Kim, *Asian American Literature*, 81f.

19. For a fuller discussion of Okimoto, see Chap. 9 of this study.

20. Žižek, *The Sublime Object of Ideology*, 29.

21. Lisa Lowe's "Ethnicity, Hybridity, and Heterogeneity" (in *Immigrant Acts*) argues an opposite case for the novel. For an extensive critique of this novel's complex contradictory qualities, see Sau-ling Cynthia Wong's "Sugar Sisterhood."

22. Collected in Bruchac, 189–91.

23. While certainly open to critique, the works of Frank Chin, Wendy Law-Yone, David Wong Louie, and Marianne Villaneuva also display sustained attempts to acknowledge history in a way that postpones the ascension of the individual long enough to seriously consider the political and collective construction of individuality. For a novel that significantly rewrites the subject position of "recovery," see Fae Mynne Ng, *Bone*.

24. Here I use "pedagogical" in a manner similar to the sense outlined in Homi Bhabha's "DissemiNation: Time Narrative, and the Margins of the Modern Nation," where the pedagogical refers to the particular forms of objectification to which the "people" are subjected in order that the nation have some founding mythology. Thus, the *modeling* function of the model minority myth involves a chain of production that takes particular subject positions as (objectified) pedagogical models for future subjectivities.

25. Kim, *Asian American Literature*, xix.

26. The fact that the novels I have discussed in terms of model minority literature are written by women (with the exception of my references to Daniel Okimoto and Gus

Lee) is determined not by any interest in discrediting Asian American women's writing, but rather by the fact that it is precisely Kingston and Tan who are clearly the most popular and widely read Asian American authors, and this fact presents their writings for particular scrutiny.

It is also true that the two examples I give of "contestive" texts are by Japanese American writers, while those of "model minority literature" with the exception of Daniel Okimoto are Chinese American. Here is not the place to unpack the different historical contexts of the literatures of Chinese and Japanese Americans and their effect on the literature. For such discussions, see the introductory essays in Chin, Inada, Fusao, and Wong, *AIIIEEEEE!*

The fact that the novels of these writers are so widely read has important consequences for the reproduction of subjectivities. As Hazel Carby, John Guillory, and others have pointed out, the "inclusion" of minority and women writers in college syllabi, for example, gives the illusion that such "representation" is the same as political representation. The problem lies in the fact that simply being read does not guarantee that the potentially contestive aspects of the novels are recognized or debated. On the contrary, texts can be read in ways that reconfigure potentially contestive elements as homogeneous correlates to dominant paradigms of subjectivity. By extension, such textual arrangements have significant impact on the (re)production of stereotypical representations of minority subjects, as seen in Kim's anecdote. In my critical introduction to *The Ethnic Canon* I discuss further the hegemonic uses of ethnic literature and suggest a critical multiculturalism.

The work of Paulo Freire, Henry Giroux, and Jonathan Kozol on radical pedagogy is of particular interest in terms of the reproduction of subjectivities through pedagogical protocols. For an excellent discussion of these issues and their connection with the rise of literary studies in Britain, see Hunter.

27. Clinton's "welfare reforms" are the most current manifestation of this line of thinking.

28. Gus Lee, *China Boy*, 311–12.

29. In this respect it is interesting to compare this treatment of the figurative "death" of Chinese male elders with that in the work of Frank Chin, whose texts (e.g., *Year of the Dragon*) are filled with death. In each case the elders blindly and tenaciously refuse to admit their illnesses. It is that hard edge of resistance to being displaced by modern America that is blunted to effect a specific purpose in Lee—here elders willingly admit their pastness, and thus the ascension of the young is stripped of any moral or historical complications or contradictions. In this, Lee's emendation strikes a resonant tone with recovery discourse, which legitimates the morally imperative prioritization of the present over the past, no matter who should be attached to either.

30. Deleuze and Guattari, *Kafka*, 17.

31. In this respect Joan W. Scott's influential essay, "The Evidence of Experience," is critically important.

32. Mohanty, 204–5.

33. In British cultural studies, Georgia Born has similarly questioned the necessarily contestive act of consuming mass culture.

Works Cited

Abbot, Kenneth. "Chinese-American Society." *Amerasia Journal* 1, no. 4 (Feb. 1971): 68–73.

Abelmann, Nancy, and John Lie. *Blue Dreams: Korean Americans and the Los Angeles Riots.* Cambridge, Mass.: Harvard University Press, 1996.

Abstracts of Reports of the Immigration Commission. 2 vols. Washington, D.C.: Government Printing Office, 1911.

Aguilar-San Juan, Karin, ed. *The State of Asian America: Activism and Resistance in the 1990s.* Boston: South End Press, 1994.

Airriess, Christopher A., and David L. Clawson. "Versailles: A Vietnamese Enclave in New Orleans, Louisiana." *Journal of Cultural Geography* 12, no. 1 (1991): 1–14.

A.k.a. Don Bonus. By Sokly Ny and Spencer Nakasako. San Francisco, Calif. Distributed by NAATA / Cross Current Media, 1995.

Allen, Douglas, and Ngô Vinh Long, eds. *Coming to Terms: Indochina, the United States, and the War.* Boulder, Colo.: Westview Press, 1991.

Almaguer, Tomás. *Racial Fault Lines: The Historical Origins of White Supremacy in California.* Berkeley: University of California Press, 1994.

Althusser, Louis. *Reading Capital.* Trans. Ben Brewster. London: New Left Books, 1970.

"America's Dose of Sinophobia." *The Economist* (Mar. 29, 1997): 35.

American Psychiatric Association. *Diagnostic and Statistical Manual of Mental Disorders* (DSM-IV). Washington, D.C.: American Psychiatric Association, 1994.

Appadurai, Arjun. *Modernity at Large: Cultural Dimensions of Globalization.* Minneapolis: University of Minnesota Press, 1996.

Arax, Mark. "A Final Turf War." *Los Angeles Times*, June 14, 1992, A3.

———. "Nation's First Suburban Chinatown." *Los Angeles Times*, Apr. 6, 1987, p. 11.

Arenson, Jourdan. "Thai Immigrants Come Together in America." *Asian Week*, July 3, 1992.

Arreola, Daniel D. "Chinatown in Literature: A Novel Look at Landscape." *The China Geographer* 4 (Spring 1976): 49–68.

Ash, Robert F., amd Y. Y. Yueh. "Economic Integration Within Greater China: Trade and Investment Flows Between China, Hong Kong and Taiwan." *The China Quarterly* (1993): 711–45.

Ashford, Douglas E., ed. *Comparing Public Policies: New Concepts and Methods*. Beverly Hills: Sage, 1978.

"Asia's Flagging Alliance." *The Economist* (Apr. 13, 1996): 13–14.

Awanohara, Susumu. "Hit by a Backlash: A Grumpy Mainstream America Worries About Immigration." *Far Eastern Economic Review* (Mar. 26, 1992): 30–31.

Ayabe, Tsuneo, and Masaki Onozawa, eds. *Continuity and Change in Overseas Chinese Communities in the Pan Pacific Area*. Tsukuba, Japan: Research Group for Overseas Chinese Studies, University of Tsukuba, 1993.

Balibar, Etienne. "Class Racism." In Balibar and Wallerstein, 204–16.

———. "Paradoxes of Universality." In David Goldberg, ed., *Anatomy of Racism*, 41–49.

Balibar, Etienne, and Immanuel Wallerstein. *Race, Nation, Class: Ambiguous Identities*. Trans. Chris Turner. London and New York: Verso, 1991. First published as *Race, nation, classe: les identités ambigües*, Paris: Editions La Découverte, 1988.

Barth, Fredrik. "Introduction." In Barth, *Ethnic Groups*, 9–37.

Barth, Fredrik, ed. *Ethnic Groups and Boundaries*. Boston: Little, Brown, 1969.

Barthes, Roland. "The Photographic Message." In Barthes, *Image, Music, Text*. Trans. Stephen Heath. New York: Hill and Wang, 1977, 15–31.

———. *Mythologies*. Trans. Annette Laver. New York: Hill and Wang, 1972.

Bass, Thomas A. *Vietnamerica: The War Comes Home*. New York: Soho Press, 1996.

Bean, Robert Bennett. *The Races of Man*. New York: The University Society, 1935.

Becker, Ernest. *The Denial of Death*. New York: The Free Press, 1973.

Bell, David. "The Triumph of Asian Americans." *The New Republic* (July 1985): 24–31.

Bellah, Robert. "Evil and the American Ethos." In Sanford et al., 177–91.

Bello, Madge, and Vincent Reyes, "Filipino Americans and the Marcos Overthrow: The Transformation of Consciousness." *Amerasia Journal* 13, no. 1 (1986–87): 73–83.

Bello, Walden. "The End of the Asian Miracle." *The Nation* (Jan. 12, 1998): 16–21.

Bellour, Raymond. *L'Analyse du film*. Paris: Albatros, 1979.

———. *L'Entre Images*. Paris: La Difference, 1990.

———. *Eye for I*. New York: Independent Curators, 1989.

Bender, John, and David E. Wellbery, eds. *Chronotypes: The Construction of Time*. Stanford, Calif.: Stanford University Press, 1991.

Benson, Janet E. "Good Neighbors: Ethnic Relations in Garden City Trailer Courts." *Urban Anthropology* 19, no. 4 (1990): 361–86.

Berger, Mark T. "Yellow Mythologies: The East Asian Miracle and Post–Cold War Capitalism." *positions: east asia cultures critique* 4, no. 1 (1996): 90–126.

Berger, Peter. "East Asian Development Model?" In Berger and Hsiao.

———, and Hsin-huang Michael Hsiao, eds. *In Search of an East Asian Development Model*. New Brunswick, N.J.: Transaction Books, 1988.

Berlant, Lauren. "The Face of America and the State of Emergency." In Nelson and Gaonkar, 397–439.

Berman, Russell. *Modern Culture and Critical Theory*. Madison: University of Wisconsin Press, 1989.

Bernstein, Richard, and Ross H. Munro. "The Coming Conflict with China." *Foreign Affairs* (Mar. /Apr. 1997): 18–32.

———. *The Coming Conflict with China*. New York: Knopf, 1997.

Besher, Alexander. *RIM: A Novel of Virtual Reality*. New York: Harper, 1994.

Beyette, Beverly. "Old Ties in a New World." *Los Angeles Times* (Aug. 21, 1991).

Bhabha, Homi K. "DissemiNation—Time Narrative, and the Margins of the Modern Nation," in Bhabha, *Nation and Narration*, 291–322.

———. ed. *Nation and Narration*. London: Routledge, 1990.

Bhabha, Jacqueline. "Embodied Rights: Gender Persecution, State Sovereignty, and Refugees." *Public Culture* 9, no. 1 (1996): 3–32.

Binet, Alfred. "The Hysterical Eye." *Open Court* 3, no. 102 (Aug. 1889): 1763–65.

———. "The Relations Between the Two Consciousnesses of Hysterical Individuals." *Open Court* 3, no. 101 (Aug. 1, 1889): 1751–54.

Blanc, Cristina Szanton. "The Thoroughly Modern 'Asian': Capital, Culture, and Nation in Thailand and the Philippines." In Ong and Nonini, eds., *Ungrounded Empires*, 261–86.

Blanchard, Kendall. "Sport, Leisure, and Identity: Reinventing Lao Culture in Middle Tennessee." *Play and Culture* 4 (1991): 169–84.

Boelhower, William. *Through a Glass Darkly: Ethnic Semiosis in American Literature*. New York: Oxford University Press, 1987.

Bonacich, Edna, Lucie Cheng, Norma Chinchilla, Nora Hamilton, and Paul Ong, eds. *Global Production: The Apparel Industry in the Pacific Rim*. Philadelphia: Temple University Press, 1994.

Bond-Harrell, B. E., and E. Voutira. "Anthropology and the Study of Refugees." *Anthropology Today* 8, no. 4 (Aug. 1992): 6–10.

Born, Georgia. "Modern Music Culture: On Shock, Pop, and Synthesis." *New Formations* 1, no. 2 (1987): 51–78.

Borthwick, Mark. *Pacific Century: The Emergence of Modern Pacific Asia*. Boulder, Colo.: Westview Press, 1992.

Boyle, T. Coraghessan. *Road to Wellville*. New York: Viking, 1993.

Bratt, Rachel G., Chester Hartman, and Ann Meyerson, eds. *Critical Perspectives on Housing*. Philadelphia: Temple University Press, 1986.

Brauchli, Marcus W. "Asian Money Nourishes Politics in California." *The Wall Street Journal*, May 12, 1997.

Broder, John M. "Foreign Taint on National Elections? A Boomerang for U.S." *New York Times*, Mar. 31, 1997.

Browne, Nick. "Race: The Political Unconscious of American Film." *East/West Film Journal* 6 (Jan. 1992): 5–16.

Bruce, Dickson D. "W. E. B. DuBois and the Idea of Double Consciousness." *American Literature* 64, no. 2 (1992): 299–309.

Bruchac, Joseph, ed. *Breaking Silence: An Anthology of Contemporary Asian American Poets*. Greenfield Center, N.Y.: Greenfield Review Press, 1983.

Brzezinski, Zbigniew. "America's New Geostrategy." *Foreign Affairs* 66, no. 4 (1988): 680–99.

————. "A Geostrategy for Eurasia." *Foreign Affairs* 76, no. 5 (Sept./Oct. 1997): 50–64.

Buaken, Manuel. *I Have Lived with the American People.* Caldwell, Idaho: Caxton Printers, 1948.

Bukatman, Scott. "Gibson's Typewriter." In Dery, 71–89.

————. *Terminal Identity.* Durham: Duke University Press, 1993.

Buruma, Ian. *Wages of Guilt.* New York: Meridian, 1994.

Business Week. "The Immigrants: How They're Helping to Revitalize the U.S. Economy" (July 13, 1992): 114–22.

Butler, Judith. *The Psychic Life of Power: Theories in Subjection.* Stanford, Calif.: Stanford University Press, 1997.

Cabral, Amilcar. "National Liberation and Culture." In Williams and Crisman, 53–65.

Cacas, Samuel P. "Relative at Best: Asian American 'Success' and Its Social Impact on Filipino Americans." *Journal of Filipino American Historical Society* 1, no. 2 (1992): 35–40.

Calderon, José Zapata. "Latinos and Ethnic Conflict in Suburbia: The Case of Monterey Park." *Latino Studies Journal* (May 1990): 23–32.

Capra, Frank. *The Name Above the Title: An Autobiography.* New York: Macmillan, 1971.

Carlson, Lewis H., and George A. Colburn. *In Their Place: White America Defines Her Minorities, 1850–1950.* New York: Wiley and Sons, 1972.

Carney, Raymond. *American Vision: The Films of Frank Capra.* Cambridge: Cambridge University Press, 1986.

Carson, Clayborne. *Malcolm X: The FBI File.* New York: Carroll and Graf, 1991.

Carter, Stephen L. *Reflections of an Affirmative Action Baby.* New York: Basic Books, 1991.

Castells, Manuel. *The Urban Question: A Marxist Approach.* Cambridge, Mass.: MIT Press, 1977.

Castillo, Victor M., and Ramón de Jésus Ramírez Acosta. "Restructuring Manufacturing: Mexican *Maquiladoras* and East Asian EPZs in the Presence of the North American Free Trade Agreement." In Dirlik, 69–88.

Catapusan, Benicio T. "The Filipinos and the Labor Unions." *American Federationist* 47 (1940): 173–76.

Caudill, William, and George DeVos. "Achievement, Culture and Personality: The Case of the Japanese Americans." *American Anthropologist* 58 (1956): 1102–26.

Center for Contemporary Cultural Studies. *The Empire Strikes Back: Race and Racism in 70s Britain.* London: Hutchinson, 1982.

Chambers, Ross. "The Unexamined." In Hill, 187–203.

Chan, Jeffrey Paul, Frank Chin, Lawson Fusao Inada, and Shawn Wong, eds. *The Big AIIIEEEEE!: An Anthology of Chinese American and Japanese American Literature.* New York: Meridian, 1991.

Chan, Sucheng. *Asian Americans: An Interpretive History.* Boston: Twayne, 1991.

————. ed. *Hmong Means Free: Life in Laos and America.* Introduction by Sucheng Chan. Philadelphia: Temple University Press, 1994.

Chance, Paul. "Imported Apple Pie." *Psychology Today* (July 1986): 52.

Chang, Edward. "Korean Community Politics in Los Angeles: The Impact of the Kwangju Uprising." *Amerasia Journal* 14, no. 1 (1988): 51–67.

Chang, Jeff. "Local Knowledge(s): Notes on Race Relations, Panethnicity and History in Hawai'i." *Amerasia Journal* 22, no. 2 (1996): 1–30.

Chang, Gordon. *Morning Glory, Evening Shadow: Yamato Ichihashi and His Internment Writings, 1942–1945*. Stanford, Calif.: Stanford University Press, 1997.

Chang, Irene. "For Asians in U.S.: A New Focus on Eye Surgery." *Los Angeles Times*, Aug. 22, 1989: Part 5, page 1.

Charr, Easurk Emsen. *The Golden Mountain: The Autobiography of a Korean Immigrant 1895–1960*. Urbana and Chicago: University of Illinois Press, 1961; 1996.

Chen, Hsiang-shui. *Chinatown No More: Taiwan Immigrants in Contemporary New York*. Ithaca: Cornell University Press, 1992.

Chen, Xiangming. "China's Growing Integration with the Asia-Pacific Economy." In Dirlik, 89–119.

Chesneaux, Jean. *Brave Modern World: Prospects for Survival*. New York: Thames and Hudson, 1992.

Cheung, King-kok. *Articulate Silences*. Ithaca: Cornell University Press, 1993.

Chin, Frank. "Come All Ye Asian American Writers—the Real and the Fake." In Chan et al., 1–92.

———. "This Is Not an Autobiography." *Genre* 18, no. 2 (1985): 109–30.

Chin, Frank, and Jeffrey Paul Chan. "Racist Love." In Kostelanetz, 65–79.

Chin, Frank, Jeffrey Paul Chan, Lawson Fusao Inada, and Shawn Wong, eds. *AIIIEEEEE!: An Anthology of Asian-American Writers*. Washington, D.C.: Howard University Press, 1974; rpt. 1983.

Ching, Leo. "Imaginings in the Empires of the Sun: Japanese Mass Culture in Asia." *boundary 2* 21, no. 1 (Spring 1994): 198–219.

Cho, Namju. "Check Out, Not In: Koreana Wilshire/Hyatt Take-Over and the Los Angeles Korean Community." *Amerasia Journal* 18, no. 1 (1992): 131–40.

Chow Tse-tsung. *The May Fourth Movement: Intellectual Revolution in Modern China*. Cambridge, Mass.: Harvard University Press, 1960.

Choy, Curtis, dir. *The Fall of the I Hotel*. Distributed by NAATA/CrossCurrent Media, San Francisco, Calif., 1983.

Choy, Peggy. "Racial Order and Contestation: Asian-American Internees and Soldiers at Camp McCoy, Wisconsin, 1942–1943." In Hune et al., 87–102.

Christy, Arthur E. "More Comments on the Study of Intercultural Relations." *Amerasia* 1, no. 12 (Feb. 1938): 564–70.

———. "On the Study of Intercultural Relations." *Amerasia* 1, no. 11 (Jan. 1938): 521–22.

Chun, Allen. "Discourses of Identity in the Changing Spaces of Public Culture in Taiwan, Hong Kong and Singapore" *Theory, Culture & Society* 13, no. 1 (1996): 51–75.

Chung-hua Institution for Economic Resarch. *Conference on Confucianism and Economic Development in East Asia*. Taipei: Chung-hua Institution, 1989.

Citizens' Commission on Civil Rights. "The Federal Government and Equal Housing Opportunity: A Continuing Failure." In Bratt et al., 296–324.

Clark, David Scott Clark, "Hong Kong's Migrant Millionares." *World Monitor*, May 1989, 38–43.

Clancy, Tom. *Debt of Honor*. New York: HarperCollins, 1994.

Clines, Francis X. "Analysis: Few Hard Facts on 'Soft Money'" *New York Times*. July 31, 1997.

Cohen, Marc J. "Gangsters, Goons, and Guidance Systems: Taiwan Government Agents in the U.S." *CovertAction* 34 (Summer 1990): 55–58.

Colker, Ruth. *Hybrid: Bisexuals, Multiracials, and Other Misfits under American Law*. New York: New York University Press, 1996.

Collier, Peter, and Helga Geyer-Ryan, eds. *Literary Theory Today*. Ithaca: Cornell University Press, 1990.

Commager, Henry Steele. *Documents in American History*. New York: Appleton-Century-Crofts, 1963.

Connery, Christopher L. "The Oceanic Feeling and the Regional Imaginary." In Wilson and Dirlik, 284–311.

———. "Pacific Rim Discourse: The U.S. Global Imaginary in the Late Cold War Years." *boundary 2* 21, no. 1 (Spring 1994): 30–56.

Connor, John W. "Changing Trends in Japanese American Academic Achievement." *Journal of Ethnic Studies* 2 (1975): 95–98.

Corwin, Edward Samuel. *The Constitution and World Organization*. Princeton: Princeton University Press, 1944.

Cowley, Geoffrey. "The Biology of Beauty." *Newsweek* (June 3, 1996): 61–66.

Cros, Edmond. *Theory and Practice of Sociocriticism*. Trans. Jerome Schwartz. Foreword by Jürgen Link and Ursula Link-Heer. Minneapolis: University of Minnesota Press, 1988.

Crow, Carl. *Foreign Devils in the Flowery Kingdom*. London: Hamish Hamilton, 1941.

———. "When an American Travels." Crow Papers, n.d.

Crozier, Michel, ed. *The Crisis of Democracy: Report on the Governability of Democracies to the Trilateral Commission*. New York: New York University Press, 1975.

Cruso, Solomon. *The Last of the Japs and the Jews*. New York: Herman Lefkowitz, 1933.

Csicsery-Ronay, Istvan, Jr. "Cyberpunk and Neuromanticism." In McCaffrey, 182–93.

Cumings, Bruce. "Rimspeak; or, The Discourse of the 'Pacific Rim'." In Dirlik, 29–47.

Cunningham, Michael R., et al. "Their Ideas of Beauty on the Whole, the Same as Ours: Consistency and Variability in the Cross-Cultural Perception of Female Physical Attractiveness." *Journal of Personality and Social Psychology* 68, no. 2 (1995): 261–79.

Daniels, Roger. *Concentration Camps USA: Japanese Americans and World War II*. New York: Holt, Rinehart and Winston, 1972.

———. "U.S. Policy Towards Asian Immigrants: Contemporary Developments in Historical Perspective." *International Journal* 63, no. 2 (Spring 1993): 310–34.

Daniels, Roger, Sandra C. Taylor, and Harry H. L. Kitano. *Japanese Americans: From Relocation to Redress*. Seattle: University of Washington Press, 1986.

Davis, Mike. "*Chinatown*, Part Two?: The 'Internationalization' of Downtown Los Angeles." *New Left Review* 164 (July/Aug. 1987): 65–86.

———. *City of Quartz*. London: Verso, 1990.

———. "Kajima's Throne of Blood." *The Nation* (Feb. 12, 1996): 18–20.

———. "Monop-L.A." *L.A. Weekly* (Mar. 2–8, 1990): 20–24.

Dear, Michael, and Allen J. Scott, eds. *Urbanization and Urban Planning in Capitalist Society*. New York: Methuen, 1981.

DeBonis, Steven. *Children of the Enemy: Oral Histories of Vietnamese Amerasians and Their Mothers*. Jefferson, N.C.: McFarland, 1995.

Deleuze, Gilles, and Félix Guattari. *A Thousand Plateaus: Capitalism and Schizophrenia*. Trans. Brian Massumi. Minneapolis: University of Minnesota Press, 1987.

————. *Kafka: Toward a Minor Literature*. Trans. Dana Polan. Minneapolis: University of Minnesota Press, 1986.

DeMonaco, Mary Kim. "Disorderly Departure: Analysis of the United States Policy Toward Amerasian Immigration." *Brooklyn Journal of International Law* 15 (Dec. 1989): 641–709.

Densch, Geoff. *Minorities in the Open Society: Prisoners of Ambivalence*. New York: Routledge and Kegan Paul, 1986.

Dery, Mark, ed. *Flame Wars: The Discourse of Cyberculture*. Durham: Duke University Press, 1994.

Desmond, Edward W. "The Failed Miracle." *Time* (Apr. 22, 1996): 60–64.

DeWitt, Howard. *Violence in the Fields: California Filipino Farm Labor Unionization during the Great Depression*. Saratoga, Calif.: Century Twenty One Publishing, 1980.

Dick, Philip K. *Do Androids Dream of Electric Sheep?* New York: Ballantine, 1968; 1982.

————. *The Man in the High Castle*. New York: Vintage, 1962; 1992.

Dinnerstein, Leonard, and Frederic Cople Jaher. *The Aliens: A History of Ethnic Minorities in America*. New York: Appleton-Century-Crofts, 1970.

Dirlik, Arif. "The Asia-Pacific Idea: Reality and Representation in the Invention of a Regional Structure." *Journal of World History* 3, no. 1 (1992): 55–79.

————. "The Asia-Pacific in Asian-American Perspective." In Dirlik, 305–29.

————. "Asians on the Rim: Transnational Capital and Local Community in the Making of Contemporary Asian America." *Amerasia Journal* 22, no. 3 (1996): 1–24.

————. "Confucius in the Borderlands: Global Capitalism and the Reinvention of Confucianism." *boundary 2* 22, no. 3 (1995): 229–73.

————. "The Global in the Local." In Wilson and Dirlik, 21–45.

————. "Introducing the Pacific." In Dirlik, 3–12.

————. "Place-Based Imagination: Globalism and the Politics of Place." Unpublished ms., Durham, N.C., 1997.

————. ed. *What Is in a Rim? Critical Perspectives on the Pacific Region Idea*. Boulder, Colo.: Westview Press, 1993.

Dowie, Mark, and Joel Millman. "A Brazen Act of Terrorism: The Killing of Henry Liu." *Mother Jones Magazine* (May 1985): 16–49.

Drinnon, Richard. *Keeper of Concentration Camps: Dillon S. Myer and American Racism*. Berkeley: University of California Press, 1987.

Duara, Prasenjit. "Nationalists Among Transnationals: Overseas Chinese and the Idea of China, 1900–1911." In Ong and Nonini, 39–60.

DuBois, Thomas A. "Constructions Construed: The Representation of Southeast Asian Refugees in Academic, Popular, and Adolescent Discourse." *Amerasia Journal* 19, no. 3 (1993): 1–26.

DuBois, W. E. B. "Strivings of the Negro People." *Atlantic Monthly* 80 (Aug. 1897): 194–95.

——. *The Oxford W. E. B. DuBois Reader*. Ed. Eric Sundquist. New York and Oxford: Oxford University Press, 1996.

DuCille, Ann. *Skin Trade*. Cambridge, Mass.: Harvard University Press, 1996.

Duus, Peter. "Discussion of Cheng Chung-ying, 'Totality and Mutuality: Confucian Ethics and Economic Development'." In Chung-hua, 57–62.

——. "Imperialism Without Colonies [Shokuminchi naki teikokushgi]." *Shisō* 814 (1992).

Eagleton, Terry. *The Ideology of the Aesthetic*. Cambridge: Basil Blackwell, 1990.

Ebihara, May M., Carol A. Mortland, and Judy Ledgerwood, eds. *Cambodian Culture Since 1975: Homeland and Exile*. Ithaca: Cornell University Press, 1994.

Eisuke, Sakakibara. *Beyond Capitalism: The Japanese Model of Market Economics*. Lanham, Md.: University Press of America, 1993.

Espiritu, Yen Le. "Beyond the 'Boat People': Ethnicization of American Life." *Amerasia Journal* 15, no. 2 (1989): 49–67.

——. "Crossroads and Possibilities: Asian Americans on the Eve of the Twenty-First Century." *Amerasia Journal* 22, no. 2 (1996): vii–xii.

Fainstein, Norman I., and Susan S. Fainstein. "Regime Strategies, Communal Resistance, and Economic Forces." In Fainstein et al., 245–81.

Fainstein, Susan S., and Norman I. Fainstein. "Economic Change, National Policy, and the System of Cities." In Fainstein et al., 1–26.

Fainstein, Susan S., Norman I. Fainstein, and P. Jefferson Armistead. "San Francisco: Urban Transformation and the Local State." In Fainstein et al., 202–44.

Fainstein, Susan S., Norman I. Fainstein, Richard Child Hill, Dennis Judd, Michael Peter Smith, eds. *Restructuring the City: The Political Economy of Urban Redevelopment*. New York and London: Longman, 1983.

Fallows, James. *Looking at the Sun: The Rise of the New East Asian Economic and Political System*. New York: Pantheon, 1994.

——. *More Like Us: Making America Great Again*. Boston: Houghton Mifflin, 1989.

Fanon, Frantz. *Black Skin, White Masks*. New York: Grove Weidenfeld, 1967.

——. *The Wretched of the Earth*. New York: Weidenfeld, 1963.

Farquhar, Judith, and James Hevia. "Culture and Postwar American Historiography of China." *positions* 1, no. 2 (1993): 486–525.

Featherstone, Mike, Mike Hepworth, and Bryan S. Turner, eds. *The Body: Social Process and Cultural Theory*. London: Sage, 1991.

Fegan, Joe R. "Urban Real Estate Speculation in the United States: Implications for Social Science and Urban Planning." In Bratt et al., 99–118.

Fishkin, Shelly Fisher. "Interrogating 'Whiteness,' Complicating 'Blackness': Remapping American Culture." *American Quarterly* (Sept. 1995): 428–66.

Fong, Timothy P. *The First Suburban Chinatown: The Remaking of Monterey Park, California*. Philadelphia: Temple University Press, 1994.

Fortune 125. "Up From Inscrutable." (Apr. 6, 1992): 120.

Foucault, Michel. *The Order of Things*. New York: Random House, 1973.

————. *Technologies of the Self.* Ed. Luther H. Martin, H. Gutman, P. H. Hutton. Amherst: University of Massachusetts Press, 1988.

Frankenberg, Ruth. *The Social Construction of Whiteness: White Woman, Race Matters.* Minneapolis: University of Minnesota Press, 1993.

Freeman, James M. *Hearts of Sorrow: Vietnamese-American Lives.* Stanford, Calif.: Stanford University Press, 1989.

Friedland, Roger, Francis Fox Piven, Robert R. Alford. "Political Conflict, Urban Structure, and the Fiscal Crisis." In Ashford, 197–226.

Friedman, Lester, ed. *Unspeakable Images: Ethnicity and the American Cinema.* Urbana and Chicago: University of Illinois Press, 1995.

Fuchs, Miriam. "Reading Toward the Indigenous Pacific: Patricia Grace's *Poltiki,* A Case Study." *boundary 2* 21, no. 1 (Spring 1994): 165–84.

Fujioka, Gen, and Jo Ann C. Gong. "The Challenges of Asian American Suburbanization." *Asian American Policy Review* (Spring 1991): 81–89.

Fukuyama, Francis. *The End of History and the Last Man.* New York: Free Press, 1992.

Gaines, Jane. "White Privilege and Looking Relations: Race and Gender in Feminist Film Theory." *Cultural Critique* 4 (1986): 59–79.

Gans, Herbert J. "The Balanced Community: Homogeneity or Heterogeneity in Residential Areas?" In Pynoos et al., 141–52.

Gao Fang. *Ping disanci langchao* (Criticizing the Third Wave). Beijing: Guangming ribao chubanshe, 1986.

Gardiner, C. Harvey. "The Latin-American Japanese and World War II." In Daniels et al., eds., 142–47.

Garth, Thomas R. *Race Psychology.* New York: McGraw-Hill, 1931.

Gates, Henry Louis, Jr. *Figures in Black: Words, Signs, and the "Racial" Self.* New York: Oxford University Press, 1987.

Gee, Emma, ed. *Counterpoint: Perspectives on Asian America.* Los Angeles: Asian American Studies Center, University of California, Los Angeles, 1976.

Gelderman, Carol. *Henry Ford: The Wayward Capitalist.* New York: Dial Press, 1981.

Gereffi, Gary. "Global Sourcing and Regional Divisions of Labor in the Pacific Rim." In Dirlik, 51–68.

Gesensway, Deborah, and Mindy Roseman, eds. *Beyond Words: Images from America's Concentration Camps.* Ithaca: Cornell University Press, 1987.

Gibney, Frank. *The Pacific Century: America and Asia in a Changing World.* New York: Charles Scribner's Sons, 1992.

Gibson, Arrell Morgan. *Yankees in Paradise: The Pacific Basin Frontier.* Albuquerque: University of New Mexico Press. 1993.

Gibson, William. *Idoru.* New York: Berkley Books, 1997.

————. *Neuromancer.* New York: Ace Books, 1984.

Gillin, Donald G. *Warlord: Yen Hsi-shan in Shansi Province, 1911–1949.* Princeton: Princeton University Press, 1967.

Gillis, John, ed. *Commemorations: The Politics of National Identity.* Princeton, Princeton University Press, 1994.

Gilman, Sander. *On Blackness Without Blacks: Essays on the Image of the Black in Germany*. Boston: G. K. Hall, 1982.

Glazer, Nathan. "Is Assimilation Dead?" *The Annals of the American Academy* 530 (Nov. 1993): 22–136.

Goethe, C. M. "Filipino Immigration Viewed as Peril." *Current History* 34 (June 1931): 354.

Goffman, Erving. *The Presentation of Self in Everyday Life*. New York: Anchor Doubleday, 1959.

Gold, Steve, and Nazli Kibria. "Vietnamese Refugees and Blocked Mobility." *Asian and Pacific Migration Journal* 2, no. 1 (1993): 27–56.

Goldberg, David Theo, ed. *The Anatomy of Racism*. Minneapolis: University of Minnesota Press, 1990.

Goldman, Peter. *The Death and Life of Malcolm X*. New York: Harper and Row, 1973.

Goldstein, Jonathan, Jerry Israel, and Hilary Conroy, eds. *America Views China: American Images of China Then and Now*. Bethlehem: Lehigh University Press; London and Toronto: Associated University Presses, 1991.

Gooding-Williams, Robert, ed. *Reading Rodney King, Reading Urban Uprising*. New York: Routledge, 1993.

Gordon, Milton. *Assimilation in American Life: The Role of Race, Religion, and National Origins*. New York: Oxford University Press, 1964.

Gossett, Thomas F. *Race: The History of an Idea in America*. Dallas: Southern Methodist University Press, 1963.

Gottdiener, M. *The Social Production of Urban Space*. Austin: University of Texas Press, 1985.

Gourevitch, Peter A. "The Pacific Rim: Current Debates." *Annals of the Academy of Political and Social Science* 505 (1989): 8–23.

Gramsci, Antonio. *Selections from the Prison Notebooks*. Ed. and trans. G. Nowell Smith and Q. Hoare. New York: International Publications, 1971.

Grant, Bruce. *The Boat People*. New York: Penguin, 1979.

Grant, Madison. *The Passing of the Great Race*. New York: Charles Scribner's Sons, 1916.

Grewal, Inderpal. "Autobiographic Subjects and Diasporic Locations: *Meatless Days* and *Borderlands*." In Grewal and Kaplan, 231–54.

Grewal, Inderpal, and Caren Kaplan. "Introduction: Transnational Feminist Practices and Questions of Postmodernity." In Grewal and Kaplan, 1–36.

————, eds. *Scattered Hegemonies: Postmodernity and Transnational Feminist Practices*. Minneapolis: University of Minnesota Press, 1994.

Griswold, A. Whitney. *The Far Eastern Policy of the United States*. New York: Harcourt, Brace, 1938.

Grodzins, Morton. *Americans Betrayed: Politics and the Japanese Evacuation*. Chicago: University of Chicago Press, 1949.

Grossman, Steve. "Vietnamese Death Squads in America? A Casebook." *Asia Insights* 2 (Summer 1986): 1–8.

Grove, John, and Jiping Wu. "Who Benefitted from the Gains of Asian-Americans, 1940–1980?" In Shepherd and Penna, 99–111.

Gupta, Akhil. "The Song of the Non-Aligned World: Transnational Identities and the Reinscription of Space in Late Capitalism." In Gupta and Ferguson, 179–202.

Gupta, Akhil, and James Ferguson. "Beyond 'Culture': Space, Identity, and the Politics of Difference." In Gupta and Ferguson, 33–51.

————, eds. *Culture Power Place: Explorations in Critical Anthropology.* Durham, N.C.: Duke University Press, 1997.

Haines, David W. "Sentiment in Public Policy: The Southeast Asian Diaspora." In Hopkins, 42–52.

Halbwachs, Maurice. *On Collective Memory.* Trans. and ed. Lewis A. Coser. Chicago and London: University of Chicago Press, 1992.

Hall, Stuart. "Gramsci's Relevance for the Study of Race and Ethnicity." *Journal of Communication Inquiry* 10 (Summer 1986): 5–27.

Haller, Mark, H. *Eugenics: Hereditarian Attitudes in American Thought.* New Brunswick, N.J.: Rutgers University Press, 1963.

Hamamoto, Darrell Y. *Monitored Peril: Asian Americans and the Politics of T.V. Representation.* Minneapolis: University of Minnesota Press, 1994.

Handlin, Oscar. *Race and Nationality in American Life.* Garden City, N.J.: Doubleday, 1957.

Hannah, Norman B. "The Open Book Memorial." *The National Review* 33 (Dec. 11, 1981): 1476.

Hardayal, Lala. *Hints for Self Culture.* Dehra Dun: Current Events, 1934.

Harris, Scott. "Little India." *Los Angeles Times*, Sept. 1, 1992: B1.

Harrison, Laird. "No One Dares to Disagree: Vietnamese Enforce Consensus on Anti-Communism." *Asian Week* 21 (Aug. 1987): 5, 22.

Harrison, Lawrence E. "America and Its Immigrants." *The National Interest* (Summer 1992): 37–46.

Hartman, Chester. "San Francisco's International Hotel: Case Study of a Turf Struggle." *Radical America* (May/June 1978): 47–58.

————. *The Transformation of San Francisco.* Totowa, N.J.: Rowman and Allen, 1984.

————. *Yerba Buena: Land Grab and Community Resistance in San Francisco.* San Francisco: Glide Publications, 1974.

Harvey, David. *Justice, Nature, and the Geography of Difference.* Oxford: Blackwell, 1996.

————. *The Urban Experience.* Baltimore: Johns Hopkins University Press, 1989.

Hatamiya, Leslie. *Righting a Wrong: Japanese Americans and the Passage of the Civil Liberties Act of 1988.* Stanford, Calif.: Stanford University Press, 1993.

Hawley, Sandra. "The Importance of Being Charlie Chan." In Goldstein, Israel, Conroy, 132–47.

Hayashi, Haruo, and Paul R. Abramson. "Self Identity of Japanese Americans Interned During World War 2: An Archival Study." *Psychologia* 30 (1987): 127–36.

Hazlett, T. W. "Mything the Point." *Reason* (Oct. 1992): 66.

Hegel, G. W. F. *The Philosophy of History.* New York: Dover, 1956.

Hein, Jeremy. "Do 'New Immigrants' Become 'New Minorities'? The Meaning of Ethnic Minority for Indochinese Refugees in the United States." *Sociological Perspectives* 34, no. 1 (Spring 1991): 61–77.

————. *From Vietnam, Laos, and Cambodia: A Refugee Experience in the United States.* Boston: Twayne, 1995.

————. "Indochinese Refugees' Responses to Resettlement Via the Social Welfare System." In Hune et al., 153–67.

Heng, Geraldine, and Janadas Devan. "State Fatherhood: The Politics of Nationalism, Sexuality and Race in Singapore." In Parker et al., 343–64.

Henry, Charles. "Understanding the Underclass: The Role of Culture and Economic Progress." In Jennings, 67–86.

Higashi, Sumiko. "Ethnicity, Class, and Gender in Film: DeMille's *The Cheat*." In Friedman, 112–40.

Hill, Mike. *Whiteness: A Critical Reader.* New York: New York University Press, 1997.

Hing, Bill Ong. *Making and Remaking Asian America Through Immigration Policy, 1850–1990.* Stanford, Calif.: Stanford University Press, 1993.

Hirabayashi, Gordon K. "The Japanese Canadians and World War II." In Daniels et al., eds., 139–41.

Hobsbawm, Eric. *Nations and Nationalisms Since 1780.* Cambridge: Cambridge University Press, 1990.

Holston, James, and Arjun Appadurai. "Cities and Citizenship." *Public Culture* 8, no. 2 (Winter 1996): 187–204.

Hom, Marlon K. "A Case of Mutual Exclusion: Portrayals by Immigrant and American-Born Chinese of Each Other in Literature." *Amerasia Journal* 11, no. 2 (1984): 29–45.

————. "Chinatown Literature During the Last Ten Years (1939–1949), by Wenquan." *Amerasia Journal* 9, no. 1 (1982): 75–100.

hooks, bell. *Sisters of the Yam: Black Women and Self-Recovery.* Boston: South End Press, 1992.

————. "Straightening Our Hair." *Zeta Magazine* (Sept. 1988): 33–37.

Hopkins, MaryCarol, ed. *Selected Papers on Refugee Issues II.* American Anthropological Association publication, 1993.

Horton, John. "The Politics of Ethnic Change: Grass-Roots Responses to Economic and Demographic Restructuring in Monterey Park, California." *Urban Geography* 10, no. 6 (1989): 578–92.

————. *The Politics of Diversity: Immigration, Resistance, and Change in Monterey Park, California.* Philadelphia: Temple University Press, 1995.

Howell, David R. "Refugee Resettlement and Public Policy." *Anthropological Quarterly* 55 (July 1982): 119–25.

Hu-Dehart, Evelyn, ed. *TransPacific Articulations: Asian Americans in the Age of Globalization.* Philadelphia: Temple University Press, forthcoming.

Hune, Shirley, Hyung-chan Kim, Stephen S. Fugita, and Amy Ling, eds. *Asian Americans: Comparative and Global Perspectives.* Pullman: Washington State University Press, 1991.

Hunt, Michael H. *The Making of a Special Relationship: The United States and China to 1914.* New York: Columbia University Press, 1983.

Hunter, Ian. *Culture and Government.* Houndmills, Hampshire: Macmillan, 1988.

Huntington, Samuel P. "The Erosion of American Interests." *Foreign Affairs* 76, no. 5 (Sept. /Oct. 1997): 28–49.

———. "The United States." In Crozier.

———. *American Politics: The Promise of Disharmony*. Cambridge, Mass.: Harvard University Press, 1981.

———. *The Clash of Civilizations and the Remaking of World Order*. New York: Simon and Schuster, 1996.

Hurh, Wom Moo, and Kwang Chung Kim. "The 'Success' Image of Asian Americans: Its Validity and Its Practical and Theoretical Implications." *Ethnic and Racial Studies* 12, no. 4 (Oct. 1989): 512–38.

Huyssen, Andreas. *Twilight Memories: Marking Time in a Culture of Amnesia*. New York: Routledge, 1995.

Ichioka, Yuji. "A Study in Dualism: James Yoshinori Sakamoto and the *Japanese American Courier*, 1928–1942." *Amerasia Journal* 13, no. 2 (1986–87): 49–81.

"Indochinese-Americans: From the Boats to the Suburbs." *Economist* 323 (Apr. 4, 1992): 28–29.

Isaacs, Harold R. *Scratches on Our Minds: American Images of China and India*. New York: John Day, 1958.

Ishi, Tomoji. "Adjusting to the Rim: Japanese Corporate Social Responsibility in the United States." In Dirlik, 121–34.

Israel, Jerry. "Carl Crow, Edgar Snow, and Shifting American Journalistic Perceptions of China." In Goldstein, Israel, and Conroy, 148–70.

Iwai, Yumi, and Kimberly J. Simi. "Conflicts and Concerns in Servicing Minority Communities: A Case Study of Yaohan, a Japanese Multinational Supermarket." Berkeley: Japan Pacific Resource Network, JPRN Working Paper Series, Feb. 25, 1990.

Iwata, Ed. "Race Without Face." *San Francisco Focus* (May 1991): 50–53, 128–132.

James, C. L. R. *American Civilization*. Ed. and intro. by Anna Grimshaw and Keith Hart. Oxford: Blackwell, 1993.

Jameson, Fredric. "'Art Naif' and the Admixture of Worlds." In Jameson, *Geopolitical Aesthetic*, 186–213.

———. "Remapping Taipei." In Jameson, *Geopolitical Aesthetic*, 114–57.

———. *The Geopolitical Aesthetic*. Bloomington: Indiana University Press, 1992.

———. *The Political Unconscious: Narrative as a Socially Symbolic Act*. Ithaca: Cornell University Press, 1981.

———. *Postmodernism: Or the Cultural Logic of Late Capitalism*. Durham, N.C.: Duke University Press, 1991.

Jay, Gregory S. *America the Scrivener: Deconstruction and the Subject of Literary History*. Ithaca: Cornell University Press, 1980.

Jennings, James. *Race, Politics, and Economic Development: Community Perspectives*. London and New York: Verso, 1992.

Jensen, Joan M. *Passage from India: Asian Indian Immigrants in North America*. New Haven and London: Yale University Press, 1988.

Jespersen, T. Christopher. *American Images of China, 1931–1949*. Stanford, Calif.: Stanford University Press, 1996.

Jones, Dorothy B. *The Portrayal of China and India on the American Screen, 1896–1955.* Cambridge, Mass.: MIT Center for International Studies, 1955.

Kahn, Herman. *World Economic Development: 1979 and Beyond.* New York: Morrow Quill Paperbacks, 1979.

Kang, K. Connie. "A Village Cries Out for Help." *Los Angeles Times*, Aug. 12, 1993: Section A, page 11.

Kang, Younghill. *East Goes West.* New York: Charles Scribner's Sons, 1937.

Kaplan, Robert D. "The Coming Anarchy." *The Atlantic Monthly* (Feb. 1994): 44–76.

Kaw, Eugenia. "Medicalization of Racial Features." *Medical Anthropology Quarterly* 7, no. 1 (1993): 74–89.

Kawakami, Kiyoshi K. *Asia at the Door: A Study of the Japanese Question in Continental United States, Hawaii, and Canada.* London and Edinburgh: Fleming H. Revell, 1914.

Keating, W. Dennis. *The Suburban Racial Dilemma.* Philadelphia: Temple University Press, 1994.

Kelley, Gail P. "Coping With America: Refugees from Vietnam, Cambodia, and Laos in the 1970s and 1980s." *Annals of the American Academy of Political and Social Science* 487 (Sept. 1986): 138–49.

Kelley, Robin D. G. *Yo' Mama's Disfunktional!* Boston: Beacon Press, 1997.

Kessner, Thomas, and Betty Boyd Caroli. *Today's Immigrants, Their Stories: A New Look at the Newest Americans.* New York and Oxford: Oxford University Press, 1981.

Kevles, Daniel J. *In the Name of Eugenics: Genetics and the Uses of Human Heredity.* Berkeley: University of California Press, 1985.

Kim, Bok-Lim C. "Asian Americans: No Model Minority." *Social Work* 18 (May 1973): 44–53.

——. "Asian Wives of U.S. Servicemen: Women in Shadows." *Amerasia Journal* 4, no. 1 (1977): 91–115.

Kim, Elaine H. "Home Is Where the *Han* Is: A Korean-American Perspective on the Los Angeles Upheavals." In Gooding-Williams, 215–35.

——. *Asian American Literature: An Introduction to the Writings and Their Social Context.* Philadelphia: Temple University Press, 1982.

Kim, Ronyoung. *Clay Walls.* Seattle: University of Washington Press, 1990.

King, Anthony, ed. *Re-Presenting the City: Ethnicity, Capital and Culture in the 21st Century Metropolis.* New York: New York University Press, 1995.

Kingston, Maxine Hong. *China Men.* New York: Vintage, 1977.

——. *Tripmaster Monkey: His Fake Book.* New York: Knopf, 1987.

——. *The Woman Warrior: Memoirs of a Girlhood Among Ghosts.* New York: Vintage, 1975; 1989 ed.

Kitano, Harry H. L., et al. "Asian-American Interracial Marriage." *Journal of Marriage and the Family* (Feb. 1984): 179–90.

Kitano, Harry H. L., and Roger Daniels. *Asian Americans: Emerging Minorities.* Englewood Cliffs, N.J.: Prentice Hall, 1988.

Kling, Rob, Spencer Olin, and Mark Poster. "The Emergence of Postsuburbia: An Introduction." In *PostSuburban California*, 1–24.

———. *Postsuburban California: The Transformation of Orange County Since World War Two*. Berkeley: University of California Press, 1991.

Kogawa, Joy. *Obasan*. Boston: Godine, 1984.

Konvitz, Milton R. *The Alien and the Asiatic in American Law*. Ithaca: Cornell University Press, 1946.

Koptiuch, Kristin. "Third-Worlding at Home." In Gupta and Ferguson, 234–48.

Kostelanetz, Richard, ed. *Seeing Through Shuck*. New York: Ballantine Books, 1972.

Kotkin, Joel. *Tribes: How Race, Religion, and Identity Determine Success in the New Global Economy*. New York: Random House, 1993.

Kotkin, Joel, and Vincent Diau. "Red Star Over Silicon Valley." *California Magazine* (Sept. 1990): 24–27.

Kotkin, Joel, and Paul Grabowicz. *California, Inc.* New York: Rawson, Wade, 1982.

Krauthammer, Charles. "Memorials." *The New Republic* 182 (May 23, 1981): 7f.

Kwong, Peter. "New York Is Not Hong Kong: The Little Hong Kong That Never Was." In Skelton, 256–68.

———. *The New Chinatown*. New York: Hill and Wang, 1987.

Laclau, Ernesto. "Universalism, Particularism, and the Question of Identity." *October* 61 (Summer 1992): 83–90.

———, ed. *The Making of Political Identities*. London and New York: Verso, 1994.

Lai, Him Mark. "The Chinese Press in the United States and Canada Since World War II: A Diversity of Voices." *Chinese America: History and Perspectives* (1990): 107–55.

———. "To Bring Forth a New China, To Build a Better America: The Chinese Marxist Left in America to the 1960s." *Chinese America: History and Perspectives* (1992): 1–82.

Lal, Barbara Ballis. *The Romance of Culture in an Urban Civilization: Robert E. Park on Race and Ethnic Relations in Cities*. New York: Routledge, 1990.

Lam, Andrew. "Love, Money, Prison, Sin, Revenge." *Los Angeles Times Magazine* (Mar. 13, 1994): 24–30, 56–58.

Lando, Gail, and Grace Sandness, eds. *Pearls of Great Price: Southeast Asian Writings*. Maple Grove, Minn.: Mini-World Publications, 1986.

Lash, Scott. "Genealogy of the Body: Foucault/Deleuze/Nietzsche." In Featherstone et al., 256–80.

Latkiewicz, John, and Colette Anderson. "Industries' Reactions to the Indochinese Refugees as Employees." *Migration Today* 11, nos. 2/3 (1983): 14–20.

Law-Yone, Wendy. *The Coffin Tree*. New York: Knopf, 1983.

Lawrence, Errol. "In the Abundance of Water the Fool Is Thirsty: Sociology and Black 'Pathology'." In Center for Contemporary Cultural Studies, *The Empire Strikes Back*, 47–94.

Lawyers Committee for Human Rights. *The Implementation of the Refugee Act of 1980: A Decade of Experience*. New York: Lawyers' Committee for Human Rights, 1990.

Layoun, Mary. "A Capital Idea: Producers, Consumers, and Re-producers in 'the merchandising of our type of democracy'." In Palumbo-Liu and Gumbrecht, 97–110.

Lazarovici, Laureen. "Foreign Capital, Local Lockouts." *L.A. Weekly* (Jan. 26–Feb. 1, 1990): 14–16.

Lee, C. Y. *The Flower Drum Song*. New York: Farrar, Straus and Cudahy, 1957.

Lee, Chang-rae. *Native Speaker*. New York: Riverhead, 1995.

Lee, Dong Ok. "The Commodification of Ethnicity: The Sociospatial Reproduction of Immigrant Enrepreneurs." *Urban Affairs Quarterly* 28, no. 2 (Dec. 1992): 258–75.

Lee, Douglas W. "The Overseas Chinese Affairs Commission and the Politics of Patriotism in Chinese America in the Nanking Era, 1928–1945." *Annals of the Chinese Historical Society of the Pacific Northwest*. Bellingham, Wash. (1984): 198–231.

Lee, Gregory B. *Troubadours, Trumpeters, Troubled Makers: Lyricism, Nationalism, and Hybridity in China and Its Others*. London: Hurst, 1996.

Lee, Gus. *China Boy*. New York: Signet, 1992.

Lee, Leo Ou-fan. "On the Margins of the Chinese Discourse: Some Personal Thoughts on the Cultural Meaning of the Periphery." In Tu, 221–38.

Lefebvre, Henri. *The Production of Space*. Trans. Donald Nicholson Smith. Oxford: Blackwell, 1991.

Leff, Leonard J., and Jerold L. Simmons. *The Dame in the Kimono: Hollywood, Censorship, and the Production Code from the 1920s to the 1960s*. New York: Grove Weidenfeld, 1990.

Lefort, Claude. "The Image of the Body and Totalitarianism." In J. Thompson, *The Political Forms of Modern Society*, 292–306.

LeGoff, Jacques. *History and Memory*. New York: Columbia University Press, 1992.

Leland, John, and Gregory Beals. "In Living Color." *Newsweek* (May 5, 1997): 58–60.

Lemann, Nicholas. "Growing Pains." *The Atlantic* 261, no. 1 (Jan. 1988): 57–63.

Leonard, Karen. "Finding One's Own Place: Asian Landscapes Re-visioned in Rural California." In Gupta and Ferguson, 118–36.

———. *Making Ethnic Choices: California's Punjabi Mexican Americans*. Philadelphia: Temple University Press, 1992.

Leong, Russell. *Country of Dreams and Dust*. Albuquerque: West End Press, 1993.

Leung, James. "California Tries to Lure Rich Asian Immigrants." *San Francisco Chronicle*, Feb. 11, 1991: Section A, page 1.

Levine, Marc V. "The Politics of Partnership: Urban Redevelopment Since 1945." In Squires, 12–34.

Lidbetter, Ernest J. *Heredity and the Social Problem Group*. Vol. 1. New York: Edward A. Arnold, 1933.

Lim, Shirley Geok-lin, and Amy Ling, eds. *Reading the Literatures of Asian American*. Philadelphia: Temple University Press, 1992.

Lin, Yutang. *Chinatown Family*. New York: John Day, 1948.

Little Tokyo Anti-Eviction Task Force. "Redevelopment in Los Angeles' Little Tokyo." In Gee, 327–33.

Liu, John M., and Lucie Cheng. "Pacific Rim Development and the Duality of Post-1965 Asian Immigration to the United States." In P. Ong et al., 74–99.

Liu, William T. *Transition to Nowhere: Vietnamese Refugees in America*. Nashville: Charter House Publishers, 1979.

Lo, Karl K. "The Chinese Vernacular Presses in North America 1900–1950: Their Role in Social Cohesion." *Annals of the Chinese Historical Society of the Pacific Northwest* (1984): 170–78.

Lo, Steven C. *The Incorporation of Eric Chung.* Chapel Hill, N.C.: Algonquin Books, 1989.

Loewen, James W. *The Mississippi Chinese.* Cambridge, Mass.: 1971.

Loo, Chalsa M. *Chinatown: Most Time, Hard Time.* New York: Praeger, 1991.

Loomba, Ania. "Overworlding the 'Third World'." In Williams and Crisman, 305–23.

Lopez, Ian Haney. *White By Law.* New York: New York University Press, 1996.

Lott, Eric. *Love and Theft: Blackface Minstrelsy and the American Working Class.* New York and Oxford: Oxford University Press, 1993.

Lowe, Donald. *The Body in Late-Capitalist U.S.A.* Durham, N.C.: Duke University Press, 1995.

Lowe, Lisa. *Immigrant Acts: On Asian American Cultural Politics.* Durham, N.C.: Duke University Press, 1996.

Lowenthal, David. "Identity, Heritage, and History." In Gillis, 41–57.

Luckmann, Thomas. "The Construction of Human Life in Time." In Bender and Wellbery, 151–67.

Lung, Chieng Fu. "A Chinese Student and Western Culture." *Sociology and Social Research* 66, no. 1 (Sept–Oct. 1931): 23–38.

Luttwak, Edward. *The Endangered Dream of America.* New York: Simon and Schuster, 1993.

Lye, Colleen. "*M. Butterfly* and the Rhetoric of Antiessentialism: Minority Discourse in an International Frame." In Palumbo-Liu, 260–89.

Lyman, Stanford M. *The Chinese Americans.* New York: Random House, 1974.

———. "Marginalizing the Self: A Study of Citizenship, Color, and Ethnoracial Identity in American Society." *Symbolic Interaction* 16, no. 4 (1993): 379–93.

———. "The Race Relations Cycle of Robert E. Park." *Pacific Sociological Review* 11, no. 1 (1968): 16–22.

Lyu, Kingsley K. "Korean Nationalist Activities in Hawaii and the Continental United States, 1900–1945." *Amerasia Journal* 4, no. 1 (1977): 23–89.

M. Consuelo León W. "Foundations of the American Image of the Pacific." *boundary 2* 21, no. 1 (Spring 1994): 17–29.

MacKerras, Colin. *Western Images of China.* Oxford: Oxford University Press, 1989.

McCaffrey, Larry. "An Interview with William Gibson." In McCaffrey, 263–85.

———, ed. *Storming the Reality Studio: A Casebook of Cyberpunk and Postmodern Science Fiction.* Durham, N.C.: Duke University Press, 1991.

MacFarquhar, Roderick. "The Post-Confucian Challenge." *The Economist* (Feb. 9, 1980): 67–72.

Mackerras, Colin. *Western Images of China.* Oxford and New York: Oxford University Press, 1989.

Mahbubani, Kishore. "An Asia-Pacific Consensus." *Foreign Affairs* 76, no. 5 (Sept./Oct. 1997): 149–58.

Malkki, Liisa H. "National Geographic: The Rooting of Peoples and the Territorialization of National Identity among Scholars and Refugees." In Gupta and Ferguson, 52–74.

Mankekar, Purnima. "Reflections on Diasporic Identities: A Prolegomenon to an Analysis of Political Bifocality." *Diaspora* 3, no. 3 (1994): 349–71.

Marchetti, Gina. "Ethnicity, the Cinema and Cultural Studies." In Friedman, 277–307.

———. *Romance and the "Yellow Peril": Race, Sex, and Discursive Strategies in Hollywood Fiction*. Berkeley: University of California Press, 1993.

Marcuse, Peter. "Housing Policy and the Myth of the Benevolent State." In Bratt et al., 248–57.

Martin, Emily. "Toward an Anthropology of Immunology." *Medical Anthropology Quarterly* 4, no. 4 (1990): 410–26.

———. *Flexible Bodies: Tracking Immunity in American Culture—From the Days of Polio to the Age of AIDS*. Boston: Beacon Press, 1994.

Marzio, Peter. *A Nation of Nations*. New York: Harper and Row, 1976.

Matsunaga, Ronald S. "Westernization of the Asian Eyelid." *Archives Otolaryngology* 111 (1985): 149–53.

Matthews, Fred H. "White Community and 'Yellow Peril'." In Dinnerstein and Jaher, 268–84.

Mayne, Judith. *Cinema and Spectatorship*. New York: Routledge, 1993.

McBride, Joseph. *Frank Capra: The Catastrophe of Success*. New York: Simon and Schuster, 1992.

McCurdy, John R. *Cosmetic Surgery of the Asian Face*. New York: Thieme Medical Publishers, 1990.

McDougall, William. *Is America Safe for Democracy?* New York: Charles Scribner's Sons, 1921.

McLeod, Beverly. "The Oriental Express." *Psychology Today* (July 1986): 48–52.

McNulty, Sheila. "Asians Bear the Knife for Western Look." *San Jose Mercury News*, Feb. 21, 1995.

Melendy, H. Brett. *Asians in America: Filipinos, Koreans, and East Indians*. Boston: Twayne, 1977.

Millard, D. Ralph, Jr. "Oriental Pereginations." *Plastic and Reconstructive Surgery* 16 (1955): 319–36.

———. *Principalization of Plastic Surgery*. Boston: Little, Brown, 1986.

Mitchell, Katharyne. "Transnational Subjects: Constituting the Cultural Citizen in the Era of Pacific Rim Capital." In Ong and Nonini, 228–58.

Modell, John, ed. *The Kikuchi Diary: Chronicle from an American Concentration Camp—the Tanforan Journals of Charles Kikuchi*. Urbana: University of Illinois Press, 1973.

Mohanty, Chandra Talpade. "On Race and Voice: Challenges for Liberal Education in the 1990s." *Cultural Critique* 14 (Winter 1989–90): 179–208.

Mori, Toshio. *The Chauvinist*. Los Angeles: Asian American Studies Center UCLA, 1979.

———. *Yokohama, California*. Caldwell, Idaho: Caxton Printers, 1949.

Morishima, Michio. *Why Has Japan "Succeeded"? Western Technology and the Japanese Ethos*. Cambridge: Cambridge University Press, 1989.

Mortland, Carol A. "Transforming Refugees in Refugee Camps." *Urban Anthropology* 16, nos. 3–4 (1987): 375–404.

Mouffe, Chantal. "Citizenship and Political Identity." *October* 61 (Summer 1992): 28–32.

Moy, James. *Marginal Sight: Staging the Chinese in America.* Iowa City: University of Iowa Press, 1993.

Mulvey, Laura. "Afterthoughts on 'Visual Pleasure and Narrative Cinema'." In Penley, 69–79.

————. "Visual Pleasure and Narrative Cinema." In Penley, 57–68.

Murayama, Milton. *All I Asking For Is My Body.* San Francisco: Supa Press, 1975.

Nachman, Elizabeth. "The Lure of Interracial Romance." *AsiAm* (Aug. 1987): 19–25.

Naisbitt, John, and Patricia Aburdene. *Megatrends 2000: Ten New Directions for the 1990s.* New York: Avon, 1990.

Nakagawa, Gordon. "'No Japs Allowed': Negation and Naming as Subject-Constituting Strategies Reflected in Contemporary Stories of Japanese American Internment." *Communication Reports* 3, no. 1 (Winter 1990): 22–27.

Nakajima, Mineo. "Economic Development in East Asia and Confucian Ethics." *Social Compass* 41, no. 1 (1994): 113–19.

Nakayama, Thomas K. "'Model Minority' and the Media: Discourse of Asian America." *Journal of Communication Inquiry* 12, no. 1 (1988): 65–73.

Nelson, Cary, and Dilip Parameshwar Gaonkar, eds. *Disciplinarity and Dissent in Cultural Studies.* New York: Routledge, 1996.

Nelson, Cary, and Lawrence Grossberg, eds. *Marxism and the Interpretation of Culture.* Urbana: University of Illinois Press, 1988.

Newsweek, Aug. 9, 1993. "America: Still the Melting Pot?" (Cover story). Lexis-Nexis.

Ng, Fay Mynne. *Bone.* New York: Hyperion, 1993.

Ng, Franklin. "Maya Lin and the Vietnam Veterans Memorial." In *Chinese America: History and Perspectives.* Chinese Historical Society, 1994: 201–21.

————. "Towards a Second Generation Hmong History." *Amerasia Journal* 19, no. 3 (1993): 51–70.

Ng, Roxanna. "Immigrant Women: The Construction of a Labour Market Category." *Canadian Journal of Women and Law* 4 (1990): 96–112.

Nixon, Richard. "Asia After Vietnam." *Foreign Affairs* 46, no. 1 (1967): 111–25.

Nonini, Donald M. "On the Outs on the Rim: An Ethnographic Grounding of the 'Asia-Pacific' Imaginary." In Dirlik, 161–82.

Nonini, Donald M., and Aihwa Ong. "Chinese Transnationalism as an Alternative Modernity." In Ong and Nonini, 3–37.

Ogawa, Dennis M., and Evarts C. Fox, Jr. "Japanese Internment and Relocation: The Hawaii Experience." In Daniels, Taylor, and Kitano, 135–38.

Ohmae, Kenichi. *The Borderless World.* New York: Harper Business, 1990.

Okamura, Raymond, Robert Takasugi, Hiroshi Kanno, and Edison Uno. "Campaign to Repeal the Emergency Detention Act." *Amerasia Journal* 2 (Fall 1974): 71–80.

Okihiro, Gary Y. *Margins and Mainstreams: Asians in American History and Culture.* Seattle: University of Washington Press, 1994.

————, ed. *Reflections on Shattered Windows: Promises and Prospects for Asian American Studies*. Pullman: Washington State University Press, 1988.

Okihiro, Gary Y., and David Drummond. "The Concentration Camps and Japanese Economic Loss: Questions and Perspectives." In Daniels et al., 168–75.

Okimoto, Daniel I. *American in Disguise*. New York and Tokyo: Weatherhill, 1971.

Omatsu, Glenn. "The 'Four Prisons' and the Movements of Liberation: Asian American Activism from the 1960s to the 1990s." In Aguilar-San Juan, 19–70.

Ong, Aihwa. "Chinese Modernities: Narratives of Nation and of Capitalism." In Ong and Nonini, 171–202.

————. "Making the Biopolitical Subject: Khmer Immigrants, Refugee Medicine, and Cultural Citizenship in California." *Social Science and Medicine* 40, no. 9 (1995): 1243–57.

————. "On the Edges of Empires: Flexible Citizenship Among Chinese in Diaspora." *positions: east asia cultures critique* 1, no. 3 (Winter 1993): 745–78.

Ong, Aihwa, and Donald Nonini. "Toward a Cultural Politics of Diaspora and Transnationalism." In Ong and Nonini, 323–32.

————, eds. *Ungrounded Empires: The Cultural Politics of Modern Chinese Transnationalism*. New York: Routledge, 1997.

Ong, Kenneth R., M.D. "New York Chinatown: A Community Fights Gentrification." *East Wind* (Fall/Winter 1982): 10–12.

Ong, Paul, Edna Bonachich, and Lucie Cheng. "The Political Economy of Capitalist Restructuring and the New Asian Immigration." In Paul Ong et al., 3–38.

————, eds. *The New Asian Immigration in Los Angeles and Global Restructuring*. Philadelphia: Temple University Press, 1994.

Orfield, Gary. "Minorities and Suburbanization." In Bratt et al., 221–29.

————. "Race and the Liberal Agenda: The Loss of the Integrationist Dream, 1965–1974." In Weir, 313–55.

Osajima, Keith. "Asian Americans as the Model Minority: An Analysis of the Popular Press Image in the 1960s and 1980s." In Okihiro, ed., *Reflections on Shattered Windows*, 165–74.

Ostrow, Ronald J. "China Spies in U.S. Increase, Sessions Says." *Los Angeles Times*, Apr. 6, 1990: Section A, page 21.

Osumi, Megumi Dick. "Asians and California's Anti-Miscegenation Laws." In Tsuchida, 38–55.

Ouchi, William. *Theory Z: How American Business Can Meet the Japanese Challenge*. New York: Avon Books, 1981.

Oxnam, Robert B. "Why Asians Succeed Here." *New York Times Magazine* (Nov. 30, 1986): 74–75.

Palmer, Albert W. *Orientals in American Life*. New York: Friendship Press, 1934.

Palumbo-Liu, David. "The Politics of Memory: Remembering History in Alice Walker and Joy Kogawa." In Singh et al., 211–26.

————. "Toshio Mori and the Attachments of Spirit." *Amerasia Journal* 17, no. 3 (1991): 41–49.

————. "Universalisms and Minority Culture." *differences: A Journal of Feminist Cultural Studies* 7 (Spring 1995): 188–208.

————, ed. *The Ethnic Canon: Histories, Institutions, Interventions*. Minneapolis: University of Minnesota Press, 1995.

Palumbo-Liu, David, and Hans Ulrich Gumbrecht, eds. *Streams of Cultural Capital: Transnational Cultural Studies*. Stanford, Calif.: Stanford University Press, 1997.

Pan, Erica Y. Z. *The Impact of the 1906 Earthquake on San Francisco's Chinatown*. New York: Peter Lang, 1995.

Pan, Lynn. *Sons of the Yellow Emperor: A History of the Chinese Diaspora*. New York, Tokyo, London: Kodansha International, 1994.

Park, Robert E. "Assimilation, Social." In *Encyclopedia of the Social Sciences*, ed. Edwin R. A. Seligman and Alvin Johnson. New York: Macmillan, 1930. Vol. 2, p. 281.

————. "Human Ecology." *American Journal of Sociology* 42 (1936): 1–15.

————. *Race and Culture: Essays in the Sociology of Contemporary Man*. New York: The Free Press, 1950.

Park, Robert E., and Ernest W. Burgess. *Introduction to the Science of Sociology*. Chicago: University of Chicago Press, 1921.

Parker, Andrew, Mary Russo, Doris Sommer, and Patricia Yaeger, eds. *Nationalities and Sexualities*. New York: Routledge, 1992.

Paul, Rodman W. "The Origin of the Chinese Issue in California." In Dinnerstein and Jaher, 161–72.

Penley, Constance, ed. *Feminism and Film Theory*. New York: Routledge, Chapman and Hall, 1988.

Petersen, William. *Japanese Americans: Oppression and Success*. New York: Random House, 1971.

Peterson, Jonathan. "The Southland Emerges as a Global Village." *Los Angeles Times*, Dec. 24, 1989: Section D, page 1.

Pincus, Walter. "Republicans Intensify Security Focus on Beijing." *Washington Post*, July 13, 1997: Section A, page 8.

Piven, Francis Fox, and Richard A. Cloward. "The Case Against Urban Desegregation." In Pynoos et al., 100–110.

Porte, Joel. *In Respect to Egotism*. Cambridge: Cambridge University Press, 1991.

Posadas, Barbara M. "Crossed Boundaries in Interracial Chicago: Pilipino American Families since 1925." *Amerasia Journal* 8, no. 2 (1981): 31–52.

————. "The Hierarchy of Color and Psychological Adjustment in an Industrial Environment: Filipinos, the Pullman Company, and the Brotherhood of Sleeping Car Porters." *Labor History* 23, no. 3 (1982): 349–73.

Puette, William J. *The Hilo Massacre: Hawaii's Bloody Monday, August 1, 1938*. Honolulu: University of Hawaii, Center for Labor Education and Research, 1988.

Pynoos, Jon, Robert Schafer, and Chester W. Hartman, eds. *Housing Urban America*. 2d ed. New York: Aldine, 1980.

Quan, Robert S. *Lotus Among the Magnolias: The Mississippi Chinese*. Jackson: University Press of Mississippi, 1982.

Radhakrishnan, Rajagapolan. *Diasporic Mediations: Between Home and Location*. Minneapolis: University of Minnesota Press, 1996.

Rafael, Vincente L. "'Your Grief Is Our Gossip': Overseas Filipinos and Other Spectral Presences." *Public Culture* 9 (1997): 267–91.

―――, ed. *Discrepant Histories: Translocal Essays on Filipino Cultures.* Philadelphia: Temple University Press, 1995.

Rainwater, Lee. "The Lessons of Pruitt-Igoe." In Pynoos et al., 597–604.

Ramirez, Anthony. "America's Super Minority." *Fortune* (Nov. 24, 1986): 148–61.

Rasbridge, Lance A. "Beyond Catharsis: Reciprocity and Interaction Through Cambodian Life Histories." In Hopkins, 53–63.

Redfield, Robert, Ralph Linton, and Melville J. Herskovits. "Memorandum for the Study of Acculturation." *American Anthropologist* 38, no. 1 (Jan.–Mar. 1936): 149–52.

Reed, Adolph Jr. "The Scholarship of Backlash." *The Nation* (Oct. 30, 1995): 506–10.

Reimers, David. *Still the Golden Door: The Third World Comes to America.* 2d ed. New York: Columbia University Press, 1992.

Robear, Ernest C. "The Dust of Life: The Legal and Political Ramifications of the Continuing Vietnamese Amerasian Problem." *Dickinson Journal of International Law* 8, no. 1 (Fall 1989): 125–46.

Robertson, Roland. *Globalization: Social Theory and Global Culture.* London: Sage, 1992.

Rogin, Michael. *Blackface, White Noise: Jewish Immigrants in the Hollywood Melting Pot.* Berkeley: University of California Press, 1996.

Rohmer, Sax. *President Fu Manchu.* New York: P. F. Collier and Son, 1936.

Root, Maria P. P. "Multiracial Asians: Models of Ethnic Identity." *Amerasia Journal* 23, no. 1 (1997): 29–42.

Rose, Peter I. "Asian Americans: From Pariahs to Paragons." In Nathan Glazer, ed. *Clamor at the Gates: The New American Immigration.* San Francisco: ICS Press, 1985, 181–212.

―――. "From Southeast Asia to America." *Migration Today* 9, no. 4 (1981): 22–28.

―――. "Links in a Chain." *Migration Today* 9, no. 3 (1981): 7–23.

Rosenbaum, David E. "Trie Offered Gifts to Clinton Legal Trust." *New York Times*, July 31, 1997.

Rothkopf, David J. "Perspective on Asia." *Los Angeles Times*, July 21, 1997.

Rouse, Roger. "Thinking Through Transnationalism: Notes on the Cultural Politics of Class Relations in the Contemporary United States." *Public Culture* 7, no. 2 (1995): 353–402.

Rowe, John Carlos, and Rick Berg, eds. *The Vietnam War and American Culture.* New York: Columbia University Press, 1991.

Rupert, Paul. "Corporate Feast in the Pacific." *Pacific Research and World Empire Telegram* 1, no. 4 (Jan.–Mar. 1970): 3.

Rushton, J. Philippe. *Race, Evolution and Behavior: A Life History Perspective.* New Brunswick, N.J.: Transaction Publishers, 1995.

Rutten, Mario. *Asian Capitalists in the European Mirror.* Amsterdam: VU University Press, 1994.

San Juan, E., Jr. *The Philippine Temptation: Dialectics of Philippine-U.S. Literary Relations.* Philadelphia: Temple University Press, 1996.

Sanders, Joel. "The Mien of Alabama: A Hill Tribe Clusters in the South." *Journal of Refugee Resettlement* 1, no. 3 (May 1981): 27–30.

Sanford, Nivett, Craig Comstock, and associates, eds. *Sanctions for Evil*. San Francisco: Jossey-Bass, 1971.

Santos, Bienvenido. *What the Hell For You Left Your Heart in San Francisco?* Quezon City, Philippines: New Day Publishers, 1987.

Saroyan, William. "An Informal Introduction to the Short Stories of the New American Writer from California, Toshio Mori." In Toshio Mori, *Yokohama, California*. Caldwell, Idaho: Caxton Printers, 1949, 7–10.

Sassen, Saskia. "Analytic Borderlands: Race, Gender and Representation in the New City." In King, 183–202.

————. "Whose City Is It? Globalization and the Formation of New Claims." *Public Culture* 8, no. 2 (1996): 205–24.

————. *Global City: New York, London, Tokyo*. Princeton: Princeton University Press, 1991.

————. *Losing Control*. New York: Columbia University Press, 1996.

Sautman, Barry. "Theories of East Asian Intellectual and Behavioral Superiority and Discourses on 'Race Differences'." *positions: east asia cultures critique* 4, no. 3 (1996): 519–68.

Schlesinger, Arthur, Jr. "Has Democracy a Future?" *Foreign Affairs* 76, no. 5 (Sept./Oct. 1997): 2–12.

Schoch, Jim, ed. *Where Has All the Housing Gone? Readings on the Housing Crisis and What's Being Done About It*. San Francisco: New American Movement, 1979.

Schwendinger, Herman, and Julia R. Schwendinger. *The Sociologists of the Chair: A Radical Analysis of the Formative Years of North American Sociology (1883–1922)*. New York: Basic Books, 1974.

Scott, David Clark. "Hong Kong's Migrant Millionaires." *World Monitor* (May 1989): 38–43.

Scott, George M. "The Hmong Refugee Community in San Diego." *Anthropological Quarterly* 55 (July 1982): 146–60.

Scott, Joan W. "The Evidence of Experience." *Critical Inquiry* 17 (Summer 1991): 773–97.

Scruggs, Jan C., and Joel L. Swerdlow. *To Heal a Nation: The Vietnam Veterans Memorial*. New York: Harper and Row, 1985.

Seagrave, Sterling. *Lords of the Rim*. New York: Putnam, 1995.

Shafer, Michael D., ed. *The Legacy: The Vietnam War in the American Imagination*. Boston: Beacon Press, 1990.

Shephard, George W., Jr., and David Penna. *Racism and the Underclass: State Policy and Discrimination Against Minorities*. New York: Greenwood Press, 1991.

Shenon, Philip. "Saipan Sweatshops Are No American Dream." *New York Times International*, July 18, 1993: Section A, page 1.

Shinagawa, Larry Hajime, and Gin Young Pang. "Intraethnic and Interracial Marriages Among Asian Americans in California, 1980." *Berkeley Journal of Sociology* (1988): 95–114.

Silverman, Edwin B. "Indochina Legacy: The Refugee Act of 1980." *Publius* (Winter 1980): 27–41.

Silverstein, Ken. "The New China Hands: How the Fortune 500 Is China's Strongest Lobby." *The Nation* (Feb. 17, 1997): 11–16.

Singh, Amrijit, Joseph Skerret, Jr., and Robert E. Hogan, eds. *Memory and Cultural Politics*. Boston: Northeastern University Press, 1996.

Skelton, Ronald, ed. *Reluctant Exiles? Migration from Hong Kong and the New Overseas Chinese*. Armonk, N.Y.: M. E. Sharpe, 1994.

Skerry, Peter. "Individualist America and Today's Immigrants." *Public Interest* 102 (Winter 1991): 104–18.

Skinner, Kenneth A., and Glenn L. Hendricks. "The Shaping of Ethnic Self-Identity Among Indochinese Refugees." *Journal of Ethnic Studies* 7, no. 3 (1979): 25–41.

Smith, Frank. "Cultural Consumption: Cambodian Peasant Refugees and Television in the 'First World'." In Ebihara, Mortland, and Ledgerwood, 141–68.

Smith, George H. *Who Is Ronald Reagan?* New York: Pyramid Books, 1968.

Smith, William Carlson. *Americans in Process: Our American Citizens of Oriental Ancestry*. Ann Arbor: Edwards Brothers, 1937. Reprint, New York: Arno Press, 1970.

Smither, Robert. "American Ambivalence Toward Refugees." *Migration Today* 8, no. 4 (1980): 20–24.

Snyder, C. R., and Donelson R. Forsyth. *Handbook of Social and Clinical Psychology*. New York: Pergamon Press, 1991.

Soja, Edward. *Postmodern Geographies*. London: Verso, 1989.

Sommers, Vita S. "The Impact of Dual-Cultural Membership on Identity." *Psychiatry* 27, no. 4 (1964): 332–44.

Song, John Huey-Long, and John Dombrink. "'Good Guys' and Bad Guys: Media, Asians, and the Framing of a Criminal Event." *Amerasia Journal* 22, no. 3 (1996): 25–46.

Spence, Jonathan. *The Search for Modern China*. New York: Norton, 1990.

Spickard, Paul. "What Must I Be? Asian Americans and the Question of Multiethnic Identity." *Amerasia Journal* 23, no. 1 (1997): 43–60.

————. *Mixed Blood: Intermarriage and Ethnic Identity in Twentieth-Century America*. Madison: University of Wisconsin Press, 1989.

Spivak, Gayatri Chakravorty. "Can the Subaltern Speak?" In Nelson and Grossberg, 271–313.

Squires, Gregory D. "Public-Private Partnerships: Who Gets What and Why." In Squires, 1–11.

————, ed. *Unequal Partnerships: The Political Economy of Urban Redevelopment in Postwar America*. New Brunswick: Rutgers University Press, 1989.

Staiger, Janet. "'The Handmaiden of Villany': Methods and Problems in Studying the Historical Reception of a Film." *Wide Angle* 8, no. 1 (1986): 19–27.

Starr, Paul D., and Alden E. Roberts. "Attitudes Toward New Americans: Perceptions of Indo-Chinese in Nine Cities." *Research in Race and Ethnic Relations* 3 (1982): 165–86.

Steele, Shelby. *The Content of Our Character*. New York: St. Martin's Press, 1990.

Stern, Lewis S. "Response to Vietnamese Refugees: Surveys of Public Opinion." *Social Work* (July 1981): 306–11.

Stone, Grace Zarling. *The Bitter Tea of General Yen*. Indianapolis: Bobbs-Merrill, 1930.

Stone, Michael E. "Housing and the Dynamics of U.S. Capitalism." In Bratt et al., 41–67.

Stonequist, Everett V. *The Marginal Man: A Study in Personality and Culture Conflict*. New York: Charles Scribner's Sons, 1937.

Strand, Paul J., and Woodrow Jones, Jr. *Indochinese Refugees in America: Problems of Adaptation and Assimilation*. Durham, N.C.: Duke University Press, 1985.

Strobel, Leny Mendoza. "'Born-Again Filipino': Filipino American Identity and Asian Panethnicity." *Amerasia Journal* 22, no. 2 (1996): 31–53.

Sue, Stanley, and Derald W. Sue. "Chinese-American Personality and Mental Health." *Amerasia Journal* 1, no. 2 (July 1971): 36–49.

——— . "Chinese-American Personality and Mental Health: A Reply to Tong's Criticisms." *Amerasia Journal* 1, no. 4 (Feb. 1972): 60–65.

Sue, Stanley, and Sumie Okazaki. "Explanations for Asian American Achievements: A Reply." *American Psychologist* 46, no. 8 (Aug. 1991): 878–80.

Suleri, Sara. "Feminism Skin Deep." *Critical Inquiry* 18, no. 4 (Summer 1992): 756–69.

Sumida, Stephen H. *And the View from the Shore: Literary Traditions of Hawai'i*. Seattle: University of Washington Press, 1991.

Sun, Lena H. "Fund-Raising Probe Goes Public This Week: Senate Panel Stymied on Some Basic Questions." *Washington Post*, July 6, 1997: Section A, page 14.

Surh, Jerry. "Asian American Identity and Politics." *Amerasia Journal* 2 (Fall 1974): 158–72.

Suvin, Darko. "On Gibson and Cyberpunk." In McCaffrey, 349–65.

Suzuki, Bob H. "Education and Socialization of Asian Americans: A Revisionist Analysis of the 'Model Minority' Thesis." *Amerasia Journal* 4, no. 2 (1977): 23–51.

Szwed, John. "Race and the Embodiment of Culture." *Ethnicity* 2 (1975): 19–33.

Tadiar, Neferti Xina. "Manila's New Metropolitan Form." In Rafael, 285–313.

Tai, Hung-chao. "The Oriental Alternative: An Hypothesis on Culture and Economy." In Tai, 6–37.

——— , ed. *Confucianism and Economic Development: An Oriental Alternative?* Washington, D.C.: Washington Institute Press, 1989.

Takagi, Dana Y. *The Retreat from Race: Asian-American Admissions and Racial Politics*. New Brunswick, N.J.: Rutgers University Press, 1992.

Takagi, Paul. "The Myth of 'Assimilation in American Life'." *Amerasia Journal* 2 (1973): 149–58.

Takaki, Ronald T. *Iron Cages: Race and Culture in Nineteenth-Century America*. New York: Alfred A. Knopf, 1979.

Tapp, Nicholas. "The Reformation of Culture: Hmong Refugees from Laos." *Journal of Refugee Studies* 1, no. 1 (1988): 20–37.

Tatsumi, Takayuki. "The Japanese Reflection of Mirrorshades." In McCaffrey, 366–73.

Tatsuno, Sheridan. "The Political and Economic Effects of Urban Renewal on Ethnic Communities: A Case Study of San Francisco's Japantown." *Amerasia Journal* 1, no. 1 (Mar. 1971): 33–51.

Tei-Yamashita, Karen. *Brazil Maru*. Minneapolis: Coffee House Press, 1992.

tenBroek, Jacobus, Edward N. Barnhart, and Floyd W. Matson. *Prejudice, War and the Constitution*. Berkeley: University of California Press, 1968.

Terkel, Studs. *Race: How Blacks and Whites Think and Feel About the American Obsession.* New York: Anchor Doubleday, 1993.

Thompson, John B. *The Political Forms of Modern Society: Bureaucracy, Democracy, Totalitarianism.* Cambridge, Mass.: MIT Press, 1986.

Thompson, Richard Austin. *The Yellow Peril.* New York: Arno, 1978.

Thompson, Richard H. *Toronto's Chinatown: The Changing Social Organization of an Ethnic Community.* New York: AMS Press, 1989.

Time, July 8, 1985. "Immigrants: The Changing Face of America." Lexis-Nexis.

Toffler, Alvin. *The Third Wave.* New York: William Morrow, 1980.

Tollefson, James W. "Indochinese Refugees: A Challenge to America's Memory of Vietnam." In Shafer, 262–79.

———. *Alien Winds: The Reeducation of America's Indochinese Refugees.* New York: Praeger, 1989.

Tomiyama Ichirō. "Colonialism and the Sciences of the Tropical Zone: The Academic Analysis of Difference in 'the Island Peoples'." *positions* 3, no. 2 (1995): 367–91.

Tong, Ben R. "The Ghetto of the Mind: Notes on the Historical Psychology of Chinese America." *Amerasia Journal* 1, no. 3 (Nov. 1971): 1–31.

———. "A Living Death Defended as the Legacy of a Superior Culture." *Amerasia Journal* 2 (Fall 1974): 178–202.

———. "Reply to the Sues." *Amerasia Journal* 1, no. 4 (Feb. 1972): 65–67.

Tran, Hieu. "The Day I Left for the USA." In Lando and Sandness, 71f.

Truong, Monique Thuy-Dung. "The Emergence of Voices: Vietnamese American Literature 1975–1990." *Amerasia Journal* 19, no. 3 (1993): 27–50.

Tsai, Shih-shan Henry. "The Chinese in Arkansas." *Amerasia Journal* 8, no. 1 (1981): 1–18.

Tseng, Yen-Fen. "Beyond 'Little Taipei': The Development of Taiwanese Immigrant Businesses in Los Angeles." *International Migration Review* 29, no. 1 (1995): 33–58.

Tsiang, H. T. *And China Has Hands.* New York: Robert Speller, 1937.

Tsuchida, Nobuya, ed. *Asian and Pacific American Experiences: Women's Perspectives.* Minneapolis: Asian/Pacific American Learning Center and General College, University of Minnesota, 1982.

Tu, Wei-ming. "A Confucian Perspective on the Rise of Industrial East Asia." In Silke Krieger, ed., *Confucianism and the Modernization of China.* Mainz, Germany: V. Hase and Koehler, 1991.

———. "Cultural China: The Periphery as the Center." In Tu, 1–34.

———. Preface to *The Living Tree,* v–x.

———, ed. *The Living Tree: The Changing Meaning of Being Chinese Today.* Stanford, Calif.: Stanford University Press, 1994.

Tu, Wei-ming, Milan Hejtmanek, and Alan Wachman, eds. *The Confucian World Observed: A Contemporary Discussion of Confucian Humanism in East Asia.* Honolulu: The East-West Center, 1992.

Turner, Bryan. *The Body and Society: Explorations in Social Theory.* Oxford: Basil Blackwell, 1984.

Turner, Victor. *The Forest of Symbols.* Ithaca: Cornell University Press, 1967.

Uhalley, Stephen, Jr. "'Greater China': The Contest of a Term." *positions: east asia cultures critique* 2, no. 2 (1994): 274–93.

Uhl, Michael. "Travels with Charlie." *The Nation* (Feb. 27, 1995): 281–84.

United States Department of War. *Final Report: Japanese Evacuation from the West Coast.* 1943; rpt. New York: Arno, 1978.

Van Kemenade, Willem. *China, Hong Kong, Taiwan, Inc.* Trans. Diane Webb. New York: Knopf, 1997.

Vasconcelos, Jose. *The Cosmic Race.* Baltimore: Johns Hopkins University Press, 1997.

Vidal, Gore. "The Empire Lovers Strike Back." *The Nation* (Mar. 1986): 350–53.

———. "Exchange." *The Nation* (Apr. 26, 1986): 570, 602.

———. "Requiem for the American Empire." *The Nation* (Jan. 11, 1986): 1, 15–19.

Virilio, Paul. *Cybermonde, la politique du pire.* Paris: Les éditions Textuel, 1996.

Viviano, Frank, and Alton Chinn. "The Hong Kong Connection." *San Francisco Magazine* (Feb. 1982): 54–60.

Vogel, Ezra. *Japan as Number One: Lessons for America.* Cambridge, Mass.: Harvard University Press, 1979.

Waldinger, Roger, and Yenfen Tseng. "Divergent Diasporas: The Chinese Communities of New York and Los Angeles Compared." *Revue Européene des Migrations Internationales* 8, no. 3 (1992): 91–114.

Waldman, Tom. "Monterey Park—The Rise and Fall of an All-American City." *California Journal* 20 (May 1989): 203–8.

Walker, Richard A. "A Theory of Suburbanization: Capitalism and the Construction of Urban Space in the United States." In Dear and Scott, 383–429.

Wallerstein, Immanuel. "Culture as the Ideological Battleground of the Modern World-System." *Theory, Culture & Society* 7 (1990): 31–55.

Walsh, Joan. "Asian Women, Caucasian Men." *Image Magazine* (Dec. 2, 1990): 11–16.

Wang, Gungwu. "Among Non-Chinese." In Tu, 127–47.

———. "Greater China and the Chinese Overseas." *The China Quarterly* (1993): 926–48.

Wang, John. "Behind the Boom: Power and Economics in Chinatown." *New York Affairs* (Spring 1979): 77–81.

Wang, L. Ling-chi. "Put Focus on Reform, Not Race." *San Francisco Chronicle*, Mar. 28, 1997.

———. "Roots and the Changing Identity of the Chinese in the United States." In Tu, 185–212.

Wattenberg, Ben, and Karl Zinsmeister. "The Case for More Immigration." *Commentary* 89, no. 4 (Apr. 1990): 19–25.

Weber, Max. *The Religion of China.* New York: Macmillan, 1951.

Wee, C. J. W.-L. "Staging the New Asia: Singapore's Dick Lee, Pop Music, and a Counter-Modernity." *Public Culture* 8, no. 3 (1996): 489–510.

Weglyn, Michi Nishiura. *Years of Infamy: The Untold Story of America's Concentration Camps.* Seattle: University of Washington Press, 1976; updated ed., 1996.

Weidenbaum, Murray, and Samuel Hughes. *The Bamboo Network: How Expatriate Chinese Entrepreneurs Are Creating a New Economic Superpower in Asia.* New York, London: Martin Kessler Books, 1996.

Weimann, Robert. "Text, Author-Function, and Society: Towards a Sociology of Representation and Appropriation in Modern Narrative." In Collier and Ryan, pp. 91–106.

Weir, Margaret, Ann Shola Orloff, and Theda Skocpol, eds. *The Politics of Social Policy in the United States*. Princeton: Princeton University Press, 1988.

Weiss, Melford. "Chinese American Beauty Pagent." In Stanley Sue, ed., *Asian-Americans: Psychological Perspectives*, Ben Lomond, Calif.: Science and Behavioral Books, 1973, 75–78.

Welaratna, Usha. *Beyond the Killing Fields: Voices of Nine Cambodian Survivors in America*. Stanford, Calif.: Stanford University Press, 1993.

White, Hayden. *Tropics of Discourse: Essays in Cultural Criticism*. Baltimore: Johns Hopkins University Press, 1978.

White, Jack E. "I'm Just Who I Am." *Time* (May 5, 1997): 33–36.

Whitman, David. "Trouble for America's 'Model Minority'." *U.S. News and World Report* (Feb. 23, 1987): 18f.

Williams, Brackette F. "The Impact of the Precepts of Nationalism on the Concept of Culture." *Cultural Critique* (Spring 1993): 143–91.

Williams, Bruce. "Asian Refugees: An Invisible Market." *Advertising Age* (Dec. 5, 1983): M-58.

Williams, Patricia. *The Alchemy of Race and Rights*. Cambridge, Mass.: Harvard University Press, 1991.

Williams, Patrick, and Laura Crisman, eds. *Colonial Discourse and Post-Colonial Theory*. New York: Columbia University Press, 1994.

Willis, Donald C. *The Films of Frank Capra*. Metuchen, N.J.: Scarecrow Press, 1974.

Wilson, Rob. *American Sublime*. Madison: University of Wisconsin Press, 1991.

———. "Blue Hawaii: *Bamboo Ridge* as 'Critical Regionalism'." In Dirlik, 281–304.

———. "*Goodbye Paradise*: Global Localism in the American Pacific." In Wilson and Dissanayake, 312–36.

———. "Imagining Asia-Pacific: Forgetting Colonialism in the Magical Waters of the Pacific." Unpublished ms.

———. "Producing American Selves." *boundary 2* 18, no. 2 (Summer 1991): 104–29.

———. "Towards an 'Asia/Pacific Cultural Studies'." *Studies in Language and Literature* 7 (Aug. 1996): 1–18.

Wilson, Rob, and Arif Dirlik. "Introduction: Asia/Pacific as Space of Cultural Production." *boundary 2* 21, no. 1 (Spring 1994): 1–16.

Wilson, Rob, and Wimal Dissanayake, eds. *Global/Local: Cultural Production in the Transnational Imaginary*. Durham, N.C.: Duke University Press, 1996.

Winks, Robin W., and James R. Rush, eds. *Asia in Western Fiction*. Honolulu: University of Hawaii Press, 1990.

Winnick, Louis. "America's 'Model Minority'." *Commentary* 90, no. 2 (Aug. 1990): 22–29.

Wong, Bernard. "China and the Chinese Americans: Impacts of Political Changes in the Mother Country on the Chinese Americans." In Ayabe and Onozawa, 54–67.

Wong, Cindy H. "Chinese Outside Chinatown: A Chinese Community in South Florida." *Chinese America: History and Perspectives* (1991): 49–65.

Wong, Eugene Franklin. *On Visual Media Racism: Asians in the American Motion Pictures.* New York: Arno Press, 1978.

Wong, Jade Snow. *Fifth Chinese Daughter.* 1945. Reprint, Seattle: University of Washington Press, 1989.

Wong, Sau-ling Cynthia. "'Astronaut Wives' and 'Little Dragons': Identity Negotiations by Diasporic Chinese Women in Two Popular Novels of the 1980s." In L. Ling-chi Wang and Wang Gungwu, eds., *Proceedings of the 1992 Luodi-Shenggen International Conference on Overseas Chinese.* Singapore: Times Academic Press, forthcoming.

———. "Ethnicizing Gender: An Exploration of Sexuality as Sign in Chinese Immigrant Literature." In Lim and Ling, 111–30.

———. "Is There a *Mulberry and Peach* in This Field? The Protean Character of a Border-Crossing Text." In Kandice Chuh and Karen Shimakawa, eds., *Disciplining Asia: Theorizing Studies in the Asian Diaspora* (forthcoming, Duke University Press).

———. "Subverting Desire: Reading the Body in the 1991 Asian Pacific Islander Men's Calendar." *Critical Mass: A Journal of Asian American Cultural Criticism* 1, no. 1 (Fall 1993): 63–74.

———. "Sugar Sisterhood: Reading the Amy Tan Phenomenon." In Palumbo-Liu, ed., *The Ethnic Canon,* 174–212.

———. *Reading Asian American Literature: From Necessity to Extravagance.* Princeton: Princeton University Press, 1993.

Woodside, Alexander. "The Asia-Pacific Idea as a Mobilization Myth." In Dirlik, 13–28.

Woodward, Bob. "FBI Cleared China Funds Revelation." *Washington Post,* July 13, 1997: Section A, page 1.

———. "Top Chinese Linked to Plan to Buy Favor." *Washington Post,* Apr. 25, 1997: Section A, page 1.

World Health Organization. *Lexicon of Psychiatric and Mental Health Terms.* 2d ed. Geneva: World Health Organization, 1994.

Wriston, Walter B. "Bits, Bytes, and Diplomacy." *Foreign Affairs* 76, no. 5 (Sept./Oct. 1997): 172–82.

Wu, David Yen-ho. "The Construction of Chinese and Non-Chinese Identities." In Tu, 148–67.

Wu, William F. *The Yellow Peril: Chinese Americans in American Fiction, 1850–1940.* Hamden, Conn.: Archon Books, 1982.

X, Malcolm. "The Ballot or the Bullet." In George Breitman, ed., *Malcolm X Speaks: Selected Speeches and Statements.* New York: Merit Publishers, 1965.

Young, James E. *The Texture of Memory: Holocaust Memorials and Meaning.* New Haven and London: Yale University Press, 1983.

Young, Robert J. C. *Colonial Desire: Hybridity in Theory, Culture and Race.* New York: Routledge, 1995.

Yu, Chung-hsun. "Economic Development of the Overseas Ethnic Chinese in the Age of Asia-Pacific." In Ayabe and Onozawa, 21–31.

Yu, Renqiu. *To Save China, To Save Ourselves: The Chinese Hand Laundry Alliance of New York.* Philadelphia: Temple University Press, 1992.

Yun, Grace, ed. *A Look Beyond the Model Minority Image: Critical Issues in Asian America.* New York: Minority Rights Group, 1989.

Zinn, Howard. *A People's History of the United States.* New York: Harper Perennial, 1980. Rev. ed. 1995.

Žižek, Slavoj. "Identity and Its Vicissitudes: Hegel's 'Logic of Essence' as a Theory of Ideology." In Laclau, 40–75.

———. *The Sublime Object of Ideology.* New York and London: Verso, 1989.

Zuckerman, Laurence. "Taiwan Keeps a Step Ahead of China in U.S. Lobbying." *New York Times*, Mar. 14, 1997.

Index

In this index an "f" after a number indicates a separate reference on the next page, and an "ff" indicates separate references on the next two pages. A continuous discussion over two or more pages is indicated by a span of page numbers, e.g., "57–59." *Passim* is used for a cluster of references in close but not consecutive sequence.

Library of Congress Cataloging-in-Publication Data

Palumbo-Liu, David.
   Asian/American : historical crossings of a racial frontier /
David Palumbo-Liu.
       p.   cm.
   Includes bibliographical references and index.
   ISBN 0-8047-3444-5 (cloth : alk. paper) —
   ISBN 0-8047-3445-3 (pbk. : alk paper)
    1. Asian Americans—History.   2. Asian Americans—
Cultural assimilation.   3. Asian Americans—Race identity.
4. United States—Race relations.   I. Title.
E184.06P26   1999
973'.0495073—dc21   98-48250
                                           Revised